THE LEGAL GUIDE TO
AFFORDABLE HOUSING
DEVELOPMENT

Third Edition

Tim Iglesias,
Rochelle E. Lento
& Rigel C. Oliveri
—EDITORS

AMERICANBARASSOCIATION

Forum on Affordable
Housing and Community
Development

Cover design by Amanda Fry/ABA Design

Printed in the United States of America.

26 25 24 23 22   5 4 3 2 1

A catalog record for this book is available from the Library of Congress.

Discounts are available for books ordered in bulk. Special consideration is given to state bars, CLE programs, and other bar-related organizations. Inquire at Book Publishing, ABA Publishing, American Bar Association, 321 N. Clark Street, Chicago, Illinois 60654-7598.

www.shopABA.org

Summary Contents

Contents

Chapter 2
Planning for Housing Requirements
Ngai Pindell

Chapter 3
Exclusionary Zoning: Constitutional and Federal Statutory Responses
Ken Zimmerman and Noah Kazis

Chapter 6
Federal, State, and Local Building and Housing Codes
Affecting Affordable Housing   183
Ronald S. Javor and Michael Allen

Part II
Regulation and Provision of Affordable Housing Finance   219

Chapter 7
Using the Qualified Opportunity Zone Incentive with Affordable Housing   221
Glenn A. Graff, Megan Murphy, and John Sciarretti

Chapter 9
Federal Sources of Financing 291
Rochelle E. Lento

Chapter 10
State Sources of Housing Finance
Carlie J. Boos with Peter Salsich

Chapter 11
Local Government Financing Powers and Sources of Funding
Barbara E. Kautz with Roy J. Koegen

Chapter 12
Mixed-Finance Development of Public Housing 399
A.M. McClain

Chapter 13
Structuring Mixed-Use Developments: Financing and Real Estate Issues   427
Angela M. Christy

Chapter 16
Federal Relocation and Replacement Housing Law 487
Karen Tiedemann

Chapter 17
The Future of Affordable Housing and Community Reinvestment
George L. Weidenfeller

Acknowledgments

The editors wish to thank the ABA Forum on Affordable Housing and Community Development Law and, in particular, Kelly Rushin (past chair) and Daniel Rosen (current chair); Dina Schlossberg, co-chair of the Publications Commission, and the rest of the Governing Board of the ABA Forum for making this third edition possible. Special gratitude goes to the chapter authors, who have donated many hours of hard work to share their knowledge and experience within the field. Finally, the editors offer thanks to Lorraine Murray of the ABA Book Publishing staff and Courtney Coffman of Lachina for their editorial assistance, and to Dawn Holiday, ABA Forum staff.

About the Editors

Tim Iglesias is a professor at the University of San Francisco School of Law. Before teaching, he spent six years assisting nonprofit affordable housing developers to obtain local government approvals in the face of community opposition. Tim teaches property, housing discrimination, eviction law and litigation, community property, and contemplative lawyering. He writes in the areas of affordable housing law, fair housing law, and housing theory. He is a member of the California Fair Employment and Housing Council (https://www.dfeh.ca.gov/fehcouncil/).

Rochelle E. Lento is a member at Dykema Gossett PLLC in Detroit, spearheading the firm's affordable housing practice in the Real Estate Group. She has worked in the area of affordable housing in Michigan and the Midwest for the past 30 years; representing primarily nonprofit developers, public housing commissions, and lenders. Rochelle has concentrated her practice on the development of real estate with the Low-Income Housing Tax Credit, the Historic Rehabilitation Tax Credit, CDBG and HOME, the Rental Assistance Demonstration (RAD) Program ,and various HUD financing tools. She is a former chair of the ABA Forum on Affordable Housing and Community Development Law, chair of the Publications Committee, and co-editor of prior editions of this book.

Rigel Oliveri is the Isabelle Wade and Paul C. Lyda Professor of Law at the University of Missouri. She is a nationally recognized expert on housing discrimination law. Her scholarship focuses on housing discrimination, residential segregation, zoning and property rights, and sexual harassment. Prior to teaching she served as a trial attorney for the U.S. Department of Justice Civil Rights Division in the Housing and Civil Enforcement Section. She currently serves as a commissioner for the Columbia Housing Authority in Columbia, Missouri.

About the Contributors

Jessie Alfaro-Cassella, Esq. is a deputy city attorney at the City and County of San Francisco, where she focuses on affordable housing and real estate matters. Prior to working at the City and County of San Francisco, she was an associate attorney at Klein Hornig LLP and a staff attorney at the National Housing Law Project, where she focused on the preservation of federally assisted housing properties.

Michael Allen is a partner in the civil rights firm Relman Colfax, PLLC. His practice focuses on plaintiff-side litigation under the Fair Housing Act. He frequently speaks and writes on topics ranging from accessibility to the obligation to "affirmatively further fair housing."

Carlie J. Boos, Esq. is the executive director of the Affordable Housing Alliance of Central Ohio. In her role, she provides leadership and strategic direction to members, stakeholders, and the local community to expand affordable housing resources.

Maeve Elise Brown is executive director of Housing and Economic Rights Advocates (HERA), a California statewide nonprofit dedicated to asset preservation, with a special focus on helping low- and moderate-income homeowners keep their homes and on protecting all Californians against fair housing and economic abuses. She has been a public interest attorney for 32 years.

Angela Christy is the head of Faegre Drinker Biddle & Reith LLP's Housing and Community Development Practice and works in the Minneapolis office. She has 40 years' experience representing developers, lenders, investors, and governmental entities in affordable housing and economic development transactions. Angela is a former chair of the ABA Forum on Affordable Housing and Community Development Law, former chair of the Minnesota State Bar Association Real Property Section, and a fellow in the American College of Real Estate Lawyers.

Nathaniel S. Cushman (Nate) is a partner in the Washington, D.C., office of Nixon Peabody, LLP. He represents owners and developers of affordable housing across the country on regulatory and transactional matters involving acquisition, ownership, development, financing, rehabilitation, and preservation.

Charles "Chuck" L. Edson is senior counsel at Nixon Peabody LLP, co-editor in chief of the *Housing and Development Reporter*, and an adjunct professor of affordable housing law at the Georgetown University Law Center. He practiced affordable housing law exclusively from 1968 to his retirement in 2002, representing housing organizations before Congress and the administrative agencies concerned with affordable housing, as well as representing private clients in affordable housing transactions and litigation. He is the founding chair of the ABA Forum on Affordable Housing and Community Development Law and the recipient of its Michael S. Scher Award.

Glenn A. Graff is a partner at the law firm of Applegate & Thorne-Thomsen where he is the chair of the firm's tax group. Mr. Graff is also a member of the governing committee of the American Bar Association's Forum on Affordable Housing and Community Development Law. Applegate & Thorne-Thomsen is a boutique law firm with more than 40 attorneys specializing in all aspects of affordable housing and community development. For the last 20 years Mr. Graff has concentrated his practice on the development of real estate with the Low-Income Housing Tax Credit, Qualified Opportunity Zones, the Historic Rehabilitation Tax Credit, the Investment Tax Credit for Renewable Energy Property, and state tax credits.

Navneet K. Grewal has practiced housing throughout her career, and specializes in tenants' rights, antidiscrimination, land use, and subsidized housing.

Priya S. Gupta is professor of law at Southwestern Law School and is currently Wainwright Senior Fellow at McGill University Faculty of Law. She specializes in property rights and law and economic development.

Ronald S. Javor is the former assistant deputy director, Housing Standards, for the California Department of Housing and Community Development, Division of Codes and Standards, and is the former department chief counsel. Housing law has been his primary area of practice for more than 40 years, including transactional, regulatory, legislative, and litigation activity.

Barbara E. Kautz is a partner with Goldfarb & Lipman LLP in Oakland, California. She practices in the area of land-use law, with an emphasis on new California housing laws, affordable housing, and inclusionary zoning, and she has more than 30 years of land-use and local government experience. Barbara is also a fellow of the American Institute of Certified Planners, former editor of the Land Use chapter in the *Municipal Law Handbook*, and a former member of the board of directors for the League of California Cities.

Noah Kazis is a legal fellow at the New York University Furman Center for Real Estate and Urban Policy, where his research focuses on land use and local government law. His scholarship on fair housing has been published in the *Harvard Law Review*. Prior to joining NYU, he served as a Corporation Counsel Honors Fellow at the New York City Law Department and a law clerk for the Honorable Douglas P. Woodlock of the U.S. District Court for the District of Massachusetts and the Honorable Joseph A. Greenaway, Jr. of the U.S. Court of Appeals for the Third Circuit.

Roy J. Koegen is a partner with Kutak Rock LLP and has more than four decades' experience serving as bond counsel to states, municipalities, schools and universities, special purpose districts, underwriters, and many of the world's largest banks. In addition, he advises clients with respect to tax, investment, finance, and regulatory issues. Mr. Koegen currently chairs the ABA's State and Local Government Law Section's Public Finance Committee, is the immediate past chair of the National Association of Bond Lawyers' Professional Responsibility Committee, and currently serves as liaison to the ABA for the Association of State Treasurers and the National Association of Bond Lawyers. He also serves as an out-of-state delegate for the Oregon State Bar Association. Mr. Koegen's civic contributions include serving as current chair of the Downtown Spokane Partnership, and he has held leadership positions with the Nature Conservancy of Washington and the National Park Foundation.

Amy M. McClain is a partner and the chair of the Ballard Spahr LLP's nationally recognized Real Estate Department. She primarily represents public housing authorities and affordable housing developers throughout the country in the context of mixed-finance transactions involving a variety of private and public debt and equity resources. Ms. McClain's practice increasingly focuses on sustainable housing and transit-oriented development through creative public–private partnerships. She is also a member of the Governing Committee of the ABA Forum on Affordable Housing and Community Development Law, serving on multiple committees and as co-chair of the Forum's 20th Annual Conference.

Megan Murphy is a principal with Novogradac & Company, a national professional services organization. Novogradac maintains clients in a broad range of industries with a major emphasis in the real estate sector, providing clients a full spectrum of audit, tax, valuation, trust, and litigation support and general consulting services. Ms. Murphy has an extensive tax background spanning nearly 15 years between her work at Novogradac, Big Four firms, and in the legal and finance functions as a multinational asset manager. At Novogradac, Ms. Murphy has been active in the Novogradac Opportunity Zones Working Group and has served as a subject matter expert for the firm with respect to private letter rulings and in areas of developing guidance, such as COVID-19-response legislation and the Centralized Partnership Audit Regime. Ms. Murphy earned her bachelor's degree in economics and in business administration from Transylvania University in 2002 and her juris doctorate from the University of Michigan in 2005.

Ngai Pindell is a professor of law at the William S. Boyd School of Law at the University of Nevada, Las Vegas. He teaches and writes in the areas of property, land use, and community economic development.

Peter Salsich is a professor emeritus, formerly McDonnell Chair of Justice in the American Society at Saint Louis University School of Law, with a secondary appointment in the Department of Public Policy. He is a fellow of the American College of Real Estate Lawyers. His former positions include chair of the ABA Commission on Homelessness and Poverty, editor of the *ABA Journal of Affordable Housing and Community Development Law,* and member of the Council of the ABA Section of Real Property, Probate and Trust Law. He taught and wrote in the areas of housing, land use, local government, and property law.

John Sciarretti is a partner with Novogradac, where he specializes in the real estate finance, community development, and renewable energy industries. John has extensive financial experience working with businesses, including more than 25 years in public accounting and four years as an executive financial manager. Mr. Sciarretti provides a broad range of advisory services to qualified opportunity funds and businesses, including transaction structuring; development and implementation of internal compliance policies and procedures; compliance review and reporting; and advising on accounting, tax, and regulatory matters. John leads and coordinates the Novogradac Opportunity Zones Working Group and has published numerous articles; he also contributes content to the Novogradac *Journal of Tax Credits* and is a frequent speaker at industry events. John earned a bachelor's degree in finance and accounting from the University of Dayton and a master's degree in taxation from the University of Akron. He is licensed as a certified public accountant in Ohio.

Rebecca Simon is an associate in Nixon Peabody's Affordable Housing and Real Estate practice group. She works with developers, public housing authorities, management agents, and other clients across the country on regulatory and transactional matters involving multifamily affordable housing ownership, development, financing, enforcement, rehabilitation, and preservation. Rebecca represents clients on affordable housing matters and applications before the U.S. Department of HUD, the U.S. Department of Agriculture–Rural Development, as well as many state and local agencies. She also assists clients facing enforcement actions from the federal government related to affordable housing. She previously worked as an attorney in HUD's Office of General Counsel.

Karen Tiedemann is a partner in the firm of Goldfarb & Lipman, LLP, located in Oakland, California, with an emphasis on practice in affordable housing, environmental law, and redevelopment. She is co-author of both the National and California editions of *Between the Lines: A Question & Answer Guide on Legal Issues in Supportive Housing,* a legal guide for supportive housing providers.

George Weidenfeller is executive vice president and general counsel at Telesis Corp since 2019, working on developing, financing, preserving, and managing affordable housing. Prior to Telesis, George was special counsel at the AFL-CIO Housing Investment Trust (HIT) focusing on investments in the finance, development, construction, and/or rehabilitation of multifamily housing, especially involving transactions associated with HUD and FHA, as well as projects involving the Low-Income Housing Tax Credits. Prior to joining HIT, George was a partner in the law firm of Reno & Cavanaugh, PLLC and earlier was at Goulston and Stores. George served for more than 16 years as deputy general counsel and acting general counsel in the HUD Office of General Counsel in Washington D.C., under six HUD secretaries.

Ken Zimmerman is a noted policy maker, fair housing expert, and civil rights attorney. He has devoted his career to justice and equality issues, having served in leadership positions in government, philanthropy, and the nonprofit sector. He is currently a distinguished fellow at NYU's Furman Center and teaches at the NYU Wagner Graduate School for Public Service. Drawing on his experience at the U.S. Department of Housing and Urban Development during the Obama and Clinton administrations and extensive litigation experience in the U.S. Department of Justice, Zimmerman has focused on the intersection of equity and housing, with a particular interest in how the new forms of social advocacy can advance transformative change. Previously, he served as the director of U.S. Programs for the Open Society Foundations, where he oversaw the annual dissemination of more than $100 million in grants to organizations focused on equality, fairness, and justice; chief counsel for New Jersey Governor Jon Corzine; and as the founding executive director of the New Jersey Institute of Social Justice.

Introduction

In 1949, Congress declared that the nation should realize:

> as soon as feasible . . . the goal of a decent home and a suitable living environment for every American family, thus contributing to the development and redevelopment of communities and to the advancement of the growth, wealth, and security of the nation.[1]

In the last century, the United States has made great advances in improving housing standards and reducing housing discrimination. Since at least the 1970s, however, the United States has suffered from a chronic shortage of affordable housing. Despite fluctuations in the economy, there has never been sufficient affordable housing to meet the need. The most vulnerable persons in our communities have always been the victims of this shortage, and now the harm is spreading to those in the middle class.

Beginning in the early 1980s, federal affordable housing development programs were severely cut. Yet, during the same period, state and local governments became more deeply engaged in responding to the problem. Overpromotion of homeownership, financial deregulation, and other factors led to a boom and bust of historic dimensions in the entire national economy, including profound disruptions in the lending and housing markets. The proliferation of subprime and predatory mortgage loans in the early 2000s caused an unprecedented foreclosure crisis, which in turn fueled an increase in homelessness and low- and middle-income renters in need of affordable housing.

Even as the economy recovered from the financial crisis of 2008, the need for affordable housing continued to outpace demand. In 2016, nearly half of renters were cost burdened (defined as spending 30 percent or more of their income on rent). The National Low-Income Housing Coalition found in 2018 that there was no county in the United States in which a renter working 40 hours a week and earning minimum wage could afford a typical two-bedroom apartment without being cost burdened.

And then, in March of 2020, the COVID-19 pandemic spread across the nation and world. The disease and the public health response to it led to widespread business and school closures. Millions of people lost jobs or were unable to work, and unable to make rent or mortgage payments. The federal government responded with financial rescue payments and an unprecedented eviction moratorium. Some state and local governments revised their policies and created special COVID-19 programs. But these were temporary fixes for a problem that only continues to grow in scale and severity.

---

1. Housing Act of 1949, Pub. L. No. 81-171.

We are now in a period of deep uncertainty and long-term adjustment. Legislative and regulatory responses to the foreclosure and COVID-19 crises could lead to a fundamental reworking of federal housing policy. Fannie Mae and Freddie Mac were placed in conservatorship under the Federal Housing Finance Agency after the 2008 foreclosure crisis, where they remain as of this writing. Improvements to the Low-Income Housing Tax Credit Program and a significant push for greater funding as part of the economic recovery offer transformative potential. At the same time, state and local governments have faced unique challenges. In some cities, skyrocketing rents have led to an increase in homelessness and the pricing out of the middle class. In response, cities are experimenting with new approaches, including the elimination of single-family zoning altogether.

Thus, the challenge of serving the housing needs of the lowest-income households and those in greatest need will be more difficult than ever. However, because of the ongoing needs and the crucial importance of housing, there will always also be new opportunities. The message is: Fasten your seatbelts, affordable housing development will continue to be a wild ride. The good news is that, historically, the affordable housing development community has proven to be creative, committed, and successful in managing a seemingly endless series of changes and crises.

Housing has never been recognized as a constitutional right, and affordable housing proposals are often opposed, but both for-profit and nonprofit housing developers all over the nation have demonstrated that contemporary affordable housing can be safe, attractive, energy-efficient, professionally managed, and a community asset. Many religious and community-based organizations have been committed to affordable housing development for dozens of years. More recently, as the housing crisis has affected a broader range of income levels, business groups have joined in the search for solutions. Thus, the goal established by Congress in 1949 is still a shared, albeit elusive, ideal.

Producing and maintaining quality affordable housing is not an intractable social problem, but one that requires putting together the essential pieces of the puzzle—a development concept responsive to community needs, suitable land, permissive land-use regulations, climate and energy concerns, adequate government funding programs, and creative public–private partnerships—all of which require sustained political will. Key considerations for affordable housing development include determining what population(s) and income levels to serve, the legal form of ownership and affordability restrictions, and design. Developers must identify and gain site control over an appropriate location with adequate infrastructure (or the potential for it) and obtain relevant federal, state, and local government zoning and environmental approvals and permits. Seeking public approval often requires dealing with local opposition and sometimes resorting to fair housing or other antidiscrimination laws designed to blunt exclusionary zoning and NIMBY ("not in my backyard") attitudes. Because of the wide variety of affordable housing developments, the process of gathering and assembling the puzzle pieces does not occur in the same temporal sequence, much less in a rigid predictable manner.

This third edition represents the American Bar Association's continuing contribution to support the development of affordable housing in the United States. It covers the most important areas of law that apply to affordable housing development. All of the chapters from the second edition have been completely updated and revised to cover continuing legal challenges, additional financing opportunities, the "greening" of affordable housing development, and other new dimensions. The book should be useful for a broad range of attorneys, including those representing local governments (municipalities, counties, housing authorities, and redevelopment agencies), housing developers (both for-profit and non-profit), investors, financial institutions, and populations eligible for the housing.

For most parts of this book, "affordable housing" is defined as housing that is legally restricted by household income level. Affordable housing development combines a development concept with financing, land, and regulatory approvals. Affordable housing development provides housing that is affordable to a targeted population. It is made affordable by financing subsidies that specify periods of affordability during which the housing is restricted for use by that population. Developers must secure a combination of public and private sources sufficient to acquire the property, to obtain necessary discretionary approvals, and to build the structures, as well as to manage and maintain the property.

Part I begins with a history of affordable housing in the United States intended to offer perspective and a lay of the land. The rest of this part covers the regulatory framework of developing affordable housing. It includes chapters on planning requirements and zoning issues, a wide variety of constitutional and statutory provisions promoting affordable housing, and a consideration of building and housing codes affecting affordable housing. Each chapter has been revised and updated to address current issues, such as continuing legal challenges to inclusionary zoning and the emergence of "greening" requirements.

In Part II, the provision of affordable housing finance is covered, including local, state, and federal regulation of private, local, state, and federal sources of finance. In addition, two chapters survey important contemporary types of developments that involve creative and legally complex partnerships: one on mixed-finance housing development (the book's only coverage of public housing) and another on mixed-use developments.

Part III surveys critical legal obligations that affect affordable housing after it has been built, including regulatory compliance and enforcement at the state and federal levels. This part also includes chapters on preservation of subsidized housing as well as federal relocation and replacement law that concerns housing acquired for the purpose of making it affordable.

Finally, the Appendix is an updated Affordable Housing Development Resource List, which offers a list of websites and other citations to general reference works and technical materials concerning affordable housing development as well as compilations and evaluations of affordable housing strategies.

Topics not covered in the book include public housing (except for Chapter 12), landlord–tenant law, and housing for persons with disabilities (except briefly in Chapters 5, 6, and 9). Private financing tools and the civil rights dimension of subsidized housing receive brief coverage.

This book attempts to provide as comprehensive an overview of affordable housing laws as possible given the limitations of cost and space. The information is also frozen in time, and as politics and governments change, some programs or laws will become outdated. When topics could reasonably be covered in more than one place (e.g., housing impact fees as a regulatory device or as a local funding mechanism), we placed them in what we thought was the most logical location. We hope that our substantial cross-referencing to other chapters and the extensive index will be helpful to those whose minds work differently.

We hope you find this publication useful. Please send any feedback or comments to:

Tim Iglesias
Professor of Law
University of San Francisco School of Law
2130 Fulton Street
San Francisco, California 94117-1080
(415) 422-5870
iglesias@usfca.edu

Rochelle E. Lento
Dykema
400 Renaissance Center
Detroit, Michigan 48243
(313) 568-5322
rlento@dykema.com

Rigel C. Oliveri
Isabelle Wade and Paul C. Lyda Professor of Law
University of Missouri School of Law
317 Hulston Hall
Columbia, MO 65211
(573) 882-5068
oliverir@missouri.edu

History and Regulatory Foundation of Affordable Housing Development

I

Affordable Housing: An Intimate History

1

Nathaniel S. Cushman*

I. INTRODUCTION

The United States Ship-Building Corporation? Yes, Congress made it the first federal entity in the affordable housing field by authorizing $100 million in 1918 to build 25 war worker projects, providing more than 5,000 homes. Previously, in 1892, Congress authorized $20,000 for a federal investigation of slum conditions; in 1908, President Theodore Roosevelt appointed the President's Housing Commission to look into the needs for decent housing for low-income Americans and recommended federal aid. Nothing came of either effort.[1]

This bit of history reveals a pattern of housing programs and funding that continues to this day: Affordable housing is not deemed to be an end in itself but a way to serve another purpose, whether it be to house defense workers during the world wars, to create jobs during the Depression, to provide an antidote to civil unrest in the 1960s, or to stimulate the economy during the Great Recession. We may soon see this history repeat again: As of this publication, the Biden administration's infrastructure proposal, designed to help the economy recover from the coronavirus pandemic, includes affordable housing funding as about 10 percent of that stimulus effort.[2]

This will not be a chronological history. Rather it primarily addresses key areas: public housing, nonprofit and private sector programs, tax incentives for housing, housing preservation, and low income homeownership. Fair

---

*Initially authored by Charles L. Edson.

1. BARRY G. JACOBS, KENNETH R. HARNEY, CHARLES L. EDSON & BRUCE S. LANE, GUIDE TO FEDERAL HOUSING PROGRAMS 3–4 (The Bureau of National Affairs, Inc. 1986) (1982).

2. *See, e.g.*, Press Release, FACT SHEET: The American Jobs Plan, The White House Briefing Room (Mar. 31, 2021), https://www.whitehouse.gov/briefing-room/statements-releases/2021/03/31/fact-sheet-the-american-jobs-plan/.

housing, a subject of crucial importance, presents a long, separate, and important story that cannot readily be summarized in this chapter.

I participated in the legislative struggles that produced each of the housing programs of the 20th century, except for the 1937 enactment of public housing when I was only two years old. Although this history will be accurate and factual, as is the case for all histories, the interpretations and perspectives included are those of the author. If any are controversial, and serve to keep the reader awake, so much the better.

II. THE PUBLIC HOUSING PROGRAM

A. The Beginning

As World War I produced the United States Ship-Building Corporation, the Great Depression produced public housing. Significantly, Congress did not address decent housing for low-income Americans as its first priority in the New Deal era. The primary concern was to stabilize the housing market for middle income Americans by creating a mechanism to encourage banks to lend money for home purchases. The first seminal piece of housing legislation, the National Housing Act of 1934,[3] created the Federal Housing Administration (FHA), now an integral part of the Department of Housing and Urban Development (HUD), to insure single family housing loans. Congress amended this act through the years to insure multifamily projects and, as will be later discussed, added some subsidy programs to the mix. But basically FHA should be viewed as an insurance company with middle-class housing its prime concern.

After a two-year struggle, Congress enacted the United States Housing Act[4] in 1937, creating the statutory structure for public housing—for many years the nation's prime affordable housing effort. Its structure remains intact until this day. Catherine Bauer, a regional planner turned lobbyist, led the legislative effort through the Labor Housing Conference.[5] Her efforts led to Senate passage by a 64–16 margin with equal success in the House. Very significantly, the statutory preamble lists job creation as the act's first purpose, followed by providing decent housing.[6] Again, this is an apt example of affordable housing being a means to the more popular end of job creation.

The act created the United States Housing Authority (USHA) to administer the program and placed it in the Interior Department under the crusty New Dealer Harold Ickes.[7] The USHA soon gave way to the United States Public Housing Administration (USPHA) as the program administrator. USPHA became a constituent of the Housing and Home Finance Agency (HHFA) and, along with FHA, the Urban Renewal Administration, and the Community Facilities Administration, morphed into the Department of Housing and

---

3. National Housing Act of 1934, Pub. L. No. 84-345, 69 Stat. 646, 12 U.S.C. § 1701.

4. United States Housing Act of 1937 (Wagner-Steagall Act), Pub. L. No. 93-383, 88 Stat. 653, 42 U.S.C. § 1437.

5. H. Peter Oberlander & Eva Newbrun, Houser: The Life and Work of Catherine Bauer 118 (UBC Press 1999) (*Houser* is perhaps the raciest housing book ever written. In addition to describing Bauer's titanic efforts to get the bill passed, it also details her affair with Lewis Mumford, one of the most renowned urbanists of the early 20th century.).

6. United States Housing Act of 1937, Pub. L. No. 93-383, 88 Stat. 653, 42 U.S.C. § 1437.

7. Oberlander & Newbrun, *supra* note 5, at 155.

Urban Development in 1965.[8] Because the Sixth Circuit ruled that federal government housing ownership under the Public Works Administration was unconstitutional,[9] the act directed that the program be administered by local public housing authorities, 3,095 in number as of 2012, and owning more than 1,100,000 units of public housing.[10]

Congress authorized the USPHA to make loans, capital grants, and annual contributions to the local authorities. A hybrid financing mechanism evolved. The local public housing authority (PHA) would issue tax-exempt bonds to finance the project's construction. The federal government would make annual contributions in amounts sufficient to amortize the principal and interest on the bonds. A New York City bond lawyer named John Mitchell (who later became the Attorney General under President Nixon) created this structure. Project tenants would pay rent in an amount necessary to cover operating expenses.

This arrangement worked well in the early days of the program. Tenants were mainly nuclear families who had fallen on hard times during the Depression. Then came World War II and a requirement under the Lanham Act[11] that PHAs house defense workers in their projects. After the war, returning veterans populated the projects at a time of severe housing shortage. In virtually the only time that housing was at the top of the political agenda, Congress, in the Housing Act of 1949,[12] expanded the program dramatically, authorizing up to 810,000 units, and set the goal of "a decent home and a suitable living environment for all Americans."[13] Thus, there was a tenancy that could pay rent equal to operating expenses.

Things changed dramatically by the mid-1960s. Relatively easy homeownership terms sucked middle-class families out of the projects to be replaced by single-parent households, many on welfare. PHAs had to charge rents to cover operating expenses, and these rents jumped to 60–70 percent of a tenant's income in many cases. In response, Congress capped tenant rent at 25 percent of income (increased to 30 percent in 1981), but this necessitated federal payment of operating subsidies to the PHAs, accomplished by an amendment to the act by Senator Edward Brooke of Massachusetts, popularly known as the Brooke Amendment.[14] As the federal operating subsidy amount began to spiral steeply upward, pundits claimed that there was one too many letter "o"s in Brooke.

As public housing tenancy has evolved, so have income limits. Up until 1981, PHAs had leeway in setting eligible tenants' income generally below 80 percent of the area median. In that year, Congress limited public housing occupancy to families designated as "very low-income," in other words, families with household income less than 50 percent of area median. Congress, reacting to the desperate need of even poorer families, required that 40

---

8. Housing and Urban Development Act of 1965, Pub. L. No. 89–117, 79 Stat. 451, 12 U.S.C. § 1701, Sec. 101 (2010).

9. United States v. Certain Lands in Louisville, 78 F.2d 684 (6th Cir. 1935).

10. Alex F. Schwartz, Housing Policy of the United States 164–65 (Routledge 3d ed. 2015).

11. Lanham Public War Housing Act, ch. 862, 54 Stat. 1125 (1940), 42 U.S.C. § 1521.

12. Housing Act of 1949, ch. 338, 63 Stat. 413, 42 U.S.C. § 1441.

13. *Id.* § 2.

14. Housing and Urban Development Act of 1969 (Brooke Amendments), Pub. L. No. 91-152, 83 Stat. 379, 12 U.S.C. § 1701.

percent of public housing units be reserved for families below 30 percent of area median, that is, those under HUD's "extremely low-income" limit.[15]

B. Public Housing Evolves

Through the late 1960s, public housing was administered in a conservative fashion, both by the U.S. Public Housing Administration and, after 1965, by HUD. Public housing was always on shaky political ground, as exemplified by a successful 1970 California initiative that required voters to approve new public housing in their jurisdiction. The U.S. Supreme Court upheld this requirement against a constitutional challenge in *James v. Valtierra*.[16] Also, PHAs were very wary of the emerging tenant rights movement. It was not until the late 1960s that HUD promulgated elaborate Lease and Grievance Procedures assuring tenants a modicum of due process in both admissions and evictions.[17] It took a U.S. Supreme Court decision[18] to get a recalcitrant PHA to follow a HUD directive to inform a tenant of the reasons for her eviction from a public housing project.

In the late 1960s, things began to change. For example, PHAs traditionally built new housing projects through the conventional means of competitive bids, rigorous PHA supervision, and overall bureaucratic controls—a very time-consuming process. Through the creative efforts of Joseph Burstein, a longtime HUD Assistant General Counsel for Public Housing, HUD created the Turnkey Program. Under this far more expeditious program, a private developer would build the project on its own land, and then turn the key over to the PHA.

Beginning in the 1980s, PHAs started to become more entrepreneurial. The major impetus was the advent of the Low-Income Housing Tax Credit (LIHTC) in 1986, discussed in Section IV. Several PHAs created limited partnerships as subsidiaries or affiliates and became general partners in tax credit projects. Proceeds from the resulting equity syndication achieved the twin goals of building affordable housing and producing revenue for the Authority. These public–private ventures were the prelude of large-scale ventures under the HOPE VI program, Choice Neighborhoods program, and Rental Assistance Demonstration.

The National Commission on Severely Distressed Public Housing suggested, and in 1993 Congress adopted, the HOPE VI program to demolish distressed housing and to support its replacement with new developments.[19] Generally, a limited partnership, with a PHA and developer general partner and a syndication entity as the limited partner, developed the project. Attractive design is the hallmark of these projects, with low-rise, less dense units replacing the obsolete multistory development of the 1950s and 1960s. Many of the projects were mixed income and resulted in a reduction in the overall number of affordable units on-site, which means that not all former tenants could return. These displaced tenants

---

15. Housing and Community Development Amendments of 1981, Pub. L. No. 97-35, 95 Stat. 384, 42 U.S.C. § 8107.

16. James v. Valtierra, 402 U.S. 137 (1971).

17. 24 C.F.R. § 966.

18. Thorpe v. Hous. Auth. of Durham, 393 U.S. 268 (1969).

19. Departments of Veterans Affairs and Housing and Urban Development, and Independent Agencies Appropriations Act of 1993, Pub. L. No. 102-389, 106 Stat. 1571.

received housing vouchers, not always a perfect solution, but on balance HOPE VI was a very successful program.[20]

The last HOPE VI Revitalization Grant funding was in 2010, which was also the first year of the Choice Neighborhoods program. A product of the Obama administration, Choice Neighborhoods started with the HOPE VI template and pumped up the ambition, providing grants for both planning and implementation while also expanding the scope of the implementation grant from solely housing to the neighborhood scale. Choice Neighborhoods also addressed criticism of the HOPE VI reduction in assisted units by incorporating a requirement for 1-for-1 replacement of all public housing with new publicly or privately owned, HUD-assisted units.

In addition to HOPE VI and Choice Neighborhood funding, Congress appropriates funds annually for capital improvements in PHA projects. Between 2005 and 2009, regular appropriations to the capital fund stood at approximately $2.5 billion per year. As part of the 2010 stimulus package following the Great Recession, Congress funded $4 billion on top of its annual appropriations.[21] By the fiscal year 2020 appropriations act, Congress was appropriating more than $3 billion for such purposes between the public housing capital fund and Choice Neighborhoods. As generous as these billions may seem, the need was substantially greater. Congress mandated a study of capital needs in the fiscal year 2008 appropriations act. The final study, released by HUD in 2011, found an extensive capital need of more than $25 billion and also estimated that new needs of about $90 billion would arise by 2030.[22] Congressional appropriations were not sufficient to keep pace with new needs, nor to solve the significant backlog.

Reacting to this reality, Congress created the Rental Assistance Demonstration (RAD) program in the 2012 appropriations act, initially limiting the demonstration to 60,000 public housing units. Congress has reauthorized, revised, and expanded RAD in subsequent appropriations acts, and has increased the unit cap to 455,000 units—almost one-half of all public housing. Under RAD, public housing units are converted from public housing into Section 8: The traditional annual contributions contract is replaced by a long-term Section 8 contract, either project based rental assistance or project-based vouchers (discussed *infra* Sections II and VI, respectively) and the property is restricted for use as affordable housing by a use agreement. This approach is consistent with a LIHTC financing structure in which the housing authority can own the project in a private–public partnership, syndicate the project using the LIHTC, and bring in needed revenue for project modernization and revitalization. And RAD is more than just a path to LIHTC: PHAs can access many more financing, transactional, and ownership structures under a long-term Section 8 contract than under the traditional public housing requirements.[23] As of October 2018, more than

---

20. Barry G. Jacobs, Handbook of Housing and Development Law 108–09, § 2:101 (West 2009–2010) (2009).

21. American Recovery and Reinvestment Act of 2009, Pub. L. No. 111-5, 123 Stat. 115, 26 U.S.C. § 1.

22. Meryl Finkel et al., *prepared for* U.S. Dep't of Hous. & Urban Dev. *by* Abt Associates Inc., Capital Needs in the Public Housing Program (Nov. 24, 2010).

23. Dennis Stout et al., *prepared for* U.S. Dep't of Hous. & Urban Dev. *by* Econometrica Inc. *in partnership with* Urban Institute (June 2019). Roughly 40 percent of units converted through RAD to date have accessed equity investment, including through LIHTC. This represents

100,000 units of public housing had converted through RAD,[24] and many more have converted since. Through these RAD conversions, PHAs are accessing capital to meet current rehab needs in participating public housing properties, and in many cases to make significant physical improvements.[25] The trend toward private–public partnerships owning PHA projects seems unstoppable, because proceeds of equity syndication are a much needed source of revenue to cash-strapped public bodies.

III. THE NONPROFIT AND PRIVATE-SECTOR PROGRAMS

A. Section 202 and Section 221(d)(3) BMIR

Until 1959, public housing authorities had a monopoly in providing affordable housing. Congress broke this pattern by creating the Section 202 program in the Housing Act of 1959. Under the 202 program, as it is popularly known, HUD made direct loans to nonprofit developers of elderly housing.[26] The statute originally permitted limited dividend developers, but every year the appropriations act limited participation to nonprofits at the behest of the powerful elderly lobby. Originally, the interest rate was 3 percent, but Congress soon set the rate based on the cost of federal funds.

In the Cranston-Gonzalez National Affordable Housing Act of 1990 (Cranston-Gonzalez), Congress restructured the program, creating a separate program for the handicapped (Section 811) and replacing the federal loans with capital advance grants and project rental assistance payments, also known as PRACs.[27] In 2000, Congress[28] removed the restriction on limited dividend sponsorship as long as the general partner is a nonprofit, thus permitting tax credit syndication.

The program has been exceedingly popular and oversubscribed for its 50-plus years of life, with more than 360,000 units under occupancy.[29] Funding for new construction of Section 202 properties was on hiatus from 2010 until a small congressional appropriation in fiscal year 2017 and increasing appropriations thereafter. HUD published a Notice of Funding Availability (NOFA) in 2019, and further NOFAs are expected so long as further funds are appropriated.

In 1961, when the Kennedy administration proposed, and Congress adopted, the Section 221(d)(3) Below Market Interest Rate (BMIR) program, few were aware of this revolutionary development.[30] From then on, the nation would look to the private sector to provide the vast bulk of the nation's affordable housing. Under the program, Fannie Mae, then a governmental agency, purchased loans at a 3 percent rate that were made to mainly limited

---

the largest RAD conversion source by amount (nearly $5 billion at the time of this study) but was not used in even a majority of RAD conversions. *Id.* at 5, 6.

24. *Id.* at vi, 38.

25. *Id.* at 8–10.

26. Housing Act of 1959, Pub. L. No. 86-372, 73 Stat. 654, 12 U.S.C. § 1701, Sec. 202.

27. Cranston-Gonzalez National Affordable Housing Act, Pub. L. No. 101-625, 104 Stat. 4079 (1990), 42 U.S.C. § 12701, Sec. 811.

28. American Homeownership and Economic Opportunity Act of 2000, Pub. L. No. 106-569, 114 Stat. 2944, 12 U.S.C. § 1701.

29. Schwartz, *supra* note 10, at 313.

30. Housing Act of 1961, Pub. L. No. 87-70, 87 Stat. 149, 12 U.S.C. § 1701.

dividend sponsors. The developer would in effect pass the subsidy through to the tenants in the form of reduced rents.

Under newly adopted budget procedures, the total loan amount was charged against the federal budget for the year the loan was made. Congress reacted by terminating the 221 program in 1968. In the same year, Congress created the Section 236 program, which utilizes an annual subsidy mechanism with a lesser budgetary impact. The Section 221(d)(3) program created 184,000 units in its seven years.[31]

B. Section 236 and Section 515

The mid-1960s were a period of great urban unrest; large-scale urban civil disturbances prevailed during that period, culminating in the severe rioting triggered by the assassination of Martin Luther King Jr. in April 1968. Deplorable housing conditions for low-income Americans, especially minorities, were one cause of the unrest. In response, President Johnson appointed two commissions to suggest new efforts to remedy this situation: the President's Commission on Urban Housing, chaired by famed industrialist Henry Kaiser, and the National Commission on Urban Problems, chaired by venerated Illinois Senator Paul Douglas. Again, this is yet another example of external events shaping federal government's involvement in affordable housing. Following the general recommendations of the Kaiser Commission, in 1968 Congress created the Section 236 program, which, in conjunction with favorable tax provisions enacted the next year, harnessed a full-scale private effort to provide affordable housing.

Under the Section 236 program, a private lender would make an FHA insured loan[32] at the then prevailing interest rate—about 7 percent—to limited dividend and nonprofit developers. HUD would then make interest assistance payments to the lender, subsidizing the rate actually paid by the developer down to 1 percent. This enabled the owner to charge lower rents than available under the 3 percent loans of the 221(d)(3) program. Not to neglect our rural areas, in the same act, Congress provided the same interest subsidy to multifamily direct loans made by the Farmers Home Administration (now the Rural Housing Service) under its Section 515 program. About 450,000 units are currently subsidized under that program.[33]

Section 236 proved very popular, producing about 544,000 units. However, the subsidy mechanism proved too inflexible during inflationary times. Analogous to the situation in public housing, the tenant had to pay rent sufficient to amortize a 1 percent loan, cover operating expenses, and provide a return to the owner. This discipline caused many tenants to pay an inordinate portion of their income for rent. Congress alleviated this situation somewhat by permitting rent supplement payments under Rent Supplement and Rental Assistance Payments (RAP) contracts, and later Section 8, to be used in Section 236 projects.[34]

---

31. Schwartz, *supra* note 10, at 204.
32. Except in the case of state housing finance agencies who could make uninsured loans pursuant to Section 236(b).
33. Schwartz, *supra* note 10, at 206.
34. Jacobs et al., *supra* note 1, at 125.

On January 8, 1973, President Nixon declared a moratorium on all federally assisted housing programs. For rental programs, the brunt of this decision fell on Section 236, then the most active program by far. The president impounded funds for these programs, triggering a rash of constitutional court challenges.[35] However, President Nixon did not intend to end assisted housing altogether. Instead, he appointed a task force to develop a replacement program leading to the birth of the Section 8 program.[36]

C. Section 8

As January 8, 1973, was a day of anguish to the affordable housing community, September 19, 1973, was a day of great joy. On that date, President Nixon announced the results of his task force stating that the Section 23 Leased Housing Program, with significant modifications, could be the basis of the country's new housing effort.[37]

Section 23 was a curious predecessor. Congress added the section in the Housing and Urban Development Act of 1965[38] under the sponsorship of Republican Representative William Widnall of New Jersey to utilize existing housing instead of building new structures under the Rent Supplement program favored by the Democratic majority in the same legislation. Under Section 23, a housing authority would lease private existing units in the community and then sublease the same units to low-income tenants. Thus, it was a precursor to the certificate and voucher programs discussed in Section VI, *infra*. Although the statute specifically required that the assisted units be "existing," and that the contract have a maximum term of five years, HUD's creative Assistant General Counsel Joseph Burstein turned the program into a significant new construction effort. Burstein construed "existing" to mean "new," as once a project is built it exists. He also permitted the five-year contract to be renewed up to seven times at the start of the first term; the 40-year lease term resulted. These interpretations enabled private developers to enter into a handshake deal with the housing authority whereby the PHA agreed to lease the unit once it was built, that is, became existing. The private development community liked the program very much and was thrilled that President Nixon announced it as the program of the future. However, the Nixon administration had other things in mind.

In the early 1970s, HUD commissioned widespread demonstrations of a housing allowance program in which the government would provide funding to low-income people to rent individual units in the private market. The administration was pleased with the results of this experiment. It envisioned that the revised Section 23 program (soon to be renumbered as Section 8) would mainly be a certificate program. New housing projects could only be eligible for assistance if they were not FHA insured, not financed by tax-exempt bonds, and did not house more than 20 percent low-income families.[39] No production program could exist under these circumstances; the terms were a far cry from the PHA rental

---

35. *Brief Claims That Section 236 and Rent Supplement Contract Authority Will Be Virtually Exhausted by HUD*, 1 HOUS. & DEV. REP., CURRENT DEVS. A-15-16 (1973).

36. LAWRENCE L. THOMPSON, A HISTORY OF HUD 9–11 (Thompson 2006).

37. *Nixon Housing Proposals Stress Easing Credit Crunch, and New Subsidized Production*, 1 HOUS. & DEV. REP., CURRENT DEVS. AA-1-4 (1973).

38. Housing and Urban Development Act of 1965.

39. *House Subcommittee Completes Mark-up*, 2 HOUS. & DEV. REP., CURRENT DEVS. AA-1 (1974).

of all project units under the Section 23 construction-for-leasing program or the guaranteed subsidy stream under Section 236.

During the spring and summer of 1974, the affordable housing community brought its concerns to Congress through furious lobbying by such groups as the National Association of Homebuilders, the Section 23 Leased Housing Association (now the National Leased Housing Association), the National Council of State Housing Agencies, and the National Low Income Housing Coalition. As a result, in the Housing and Community Development Act of 1974, Congress passed a workable program to fund new construction or substantial rehabilitation with the administration's restrictions removed. However, the administration succeeded in obtaining a significant housing certificate program (discussed in Section VI, *infra*).

Under the Section 8 program, HUD, either directly or acting through a state finance agency[40] or local housing finance agency, would subsidize the difference between a HUD-approved contract rent (based on the Fair Market Rent published for the area), and 25 percent (raised to 30 percent in 1981) of the tenant's income. To keep up with inflation, rents would be raised annually by published Annual Adjustment Factors. Thus Section 8 avoided the pitfalls of the original public housing program and Section 236 because it did not raise the subsidy with inflation.

The Section 8 program prospered. During the later years of the Ford administration and early years of President Carter's administration, Congress funded the program at the 200,000-unit level. Overall, the program contributed about 850,000 units to the affordable housing stock until 1983, when Congress, at the request of the Reagan administration, terminated the new construction–substantial rehabilitation part of the program.[41]

The Section 8 program is now expanding again through the RAD demonstration, primarily via conversion of public housing (as discussed in Section I, *supra*) to both the project based rental assistance discussed here and the project-based vouchers discussed in Section VI, *infra*. More than 100,000 units have converted from public housing to Section 8 through RAD, and HUD expects future conversions of hundreds of thousands more units.[42] In addition to public housing, RAD's Second Component allowed for the preservation of projects assisted by other operating subsidies, with attendant administrative simplification: Rent Supplement and RAP with great success,[43] Moderate Rehabilitation with more measured success to date, and now expanding into conversion of Section 202 PRACs.

---

40. This provision gave significant impetus to the creation of state housing finance agencies. During the Section 236 era only about seven of such agencies existed, but as a result of the ability to administer the Section 8 contract, such agencies now prevail in all states.

41. Housing and Urban-Rural Recovery Act of 1983, Pub. L. No. 98-181, 97 Stat. 1159-1240, 12 U.S.C. § 1701.

42. HUD Office of Multifamily Housing Programs, *100,000 Homes Preserved* (Oct. 13, 2018), https://www.hud.gov/sites/dfiles/Housing/documents/RAD_100000_Homes_20180813.pdf.

43. As of December 31, 2019, all remaining Rent Supplement and RAP projects had been converted under the Second Component of RAD, converting more than 28,000 units to project-based rental assistance or project-based vouchers under Section 8. *RADBlast!* Electronic Communication, HUD Office of Multifamily Housing, *RAD Successfully Winds Down RAP Legacy Program, Preserving 14,462 Affordable Homes, Saving Residents from Displacement* (Jan. 23, 2020), https://www.hud.gov/sites/dfiles/Housing/documents/RADBlast_2020_0123.pdf.

IV. CAPITAL GRANT PROGRAMS

The Section 8 and Section 236 programs imposed costly ongoing budget burdens on the federal government for up to 40 years. The housing community began looking for a one-time grant mechanism to finance housing construction to obviate the reliance on annual appropriations. The first effort in this regard was the short-lived Housing Development Action Grant Program (HoDAG), which started in 1983 and ended in 1988.[44] It was patterned after the successful Urban Development Action Grant Program (UDAG), an initiative of the Carter administration in 1977, which funded local urban and economic development projects. Likewise, under HoDAG, HUD made grants to developers to construct affordable housing.

A. The HOME Program

In 1989, a blue-ribbon task force headed by James Rouse, a visionary developer, and David Maxwell, a former president of Fannie Mae, recommended a block grant program for housing patterned after the popular Community Development Block Grant (CDBG) program in effect since 1974. States and localities could only use CDBG funds for housing on a very limited basis, for example, to purchase land for housing, for infrastructure improvements, and so on. The Rouse Maxwell task force fashioned a block grant program exclusively for housing. Congress, in the Cranston-Gonzales National Affordable Housing Act in 1990 established the housing block grant in the HOME (fortunately not an acronym for anything) program.[45]

Under HOME, HUD funds local participating jurisdictions (60 percent of funding) and states (40 percent) for housing development purposes. Fifteen percent of the grant amount must go to nonprofits known as Community Housing Development Organizations, or CHDOs. For rental projects, HOME alone is not sufficient; generally, it is combined with the LIHTC to make the project feasible.

HOME funds can be used for development costs, land costs, soft costs, and reserves. For rental housing, the assistance is generally in the form of long-term, non-interest-bearing loans. Through 2012, about $24 billion in funding had been used to fund completed projects, assisting about 1.3 million families with incomes under 80 percent of median (for homeownership uses) and 50–60 percent of median (for rental housing use).[46] In recent years, the HOME appropriation has been between $1 billion and $1.5 billion annually. In 1993, Congress amended the HOME statute to make it consistent with the LIHTC rules; this change accounts for much of its success.[47]

---

44. *Id.*

45. Cranston-Gonzales National Affordable Housing Act of 1990, P.L. 101-625, 104 Stat. 4085, 42 U.S.C. 12701.

46. Schwartz, *supra* note 10, at 272–73.

47. Joseph A. Haas & Robert S. Swierczek, *Clinton Signs Budget with Permanent Tax Credit, Mortgage Bond Extensions, Enterprise Zones*, 21 Hous. & Dev. Rep., Current Devs. 193, 222–23 (1993).

B. Other Grant Programs

1. McKinney–Vento Homeless Assistance Act

In the mid-1980s, homelessness reached the national housing agenda, in part because of the shortage of housing for low-income families, and in significant part because of an emerging practice of mainstreaming persons into society who had been institutionalized for mental disabilities.

Congress, in the Homeless Housing Act of 1986,[48] appropriated $15 million for a shelter demonstration program. The following year Congress made $500 million available for homeless assistance and renamed the legislation the "Stewart B. McKinney Homeless Assistance Act of 1987" to honor the memory of Stu McKinney, a moderate Republican congressman from Connecticut and a tireless housing advocate. In 2000, after the death of Bruce Vento, a Democrat from Minnesota who was equally zealous on housing issues, Congress renamed the legislation the McKinney–Vento Act.

A principal thrust of the legislation is to fund emergency shelter grants to bring buildings into suitable conditions to become homeless shelters. Funds are also available for tenant services, rental assistance, and funding for permanent housing for homeless people.

2. Federal Housing Finance Board Affordable Housing Program

In 1989, Congress passed the Financial Institutions Reform, Recovery and Enforcement Act[49] to bail out and restructure the savings and loan industry. Representative Henry Gonzales, chair of the Banking, Housing, and Urban Affairs Committee and a staunch friend of affordable housing, insisted that the legislation include a program to assist affordable housing. Congress required the 12 Federal Home Loan Banks to establish an Affordable Housing Program (AHP) by making subsidized cash advances to member institutions, generally savings and loans, so they could make below-market rate loans for affordable housing. The legislation also required each Federal Home Loan Bank to contribute the greater of 10 percent of earnings or $100,000,000 to its affordable housing fund. Member banks utilize the funds to finance the purchase, construction, or rehabilitation of single and multifamily housing for low- and moderate-income families. Such funds are often used to aid the feasibility of LIHTC projects.

3. Housing Trust Fund

In the early years of the 21st century, housing advocates, led by the National Low Income Housing Coalition, actively lobbied for a federally funded housing trust fund. Due to this activity, and strong support of such traditional housing supporters as Senators John Kerry (D-MA), Bernie Sanders (I-VT), and Jack Reed (D-RI), and Representative Barney Frank (D-MA), Congress authorized the Housing Trust Fund in the Housing and Economic Recovery Act of 2008. The program is funded outside of appropriations by a fee on Freddie Mac and Fannie Mae activity. This funding was initially delayed due to concerns about Freddie Mac and Fannie Mae following the financial crisis. The first funding was allocated

---

48. Homeless Housing Act of 1986, Pub. L. No. 99-500, § 101(g), 100 Stat. 1783-242, and Pub. L. No. 99-591, § 101(g), 100 Stat. 3341-242, 42 U.S.C. § 11361.

49. Financial Institutions Reform, Recovery, and Enforcement Act of 1989, Pub. L. No. 101-73, 103 Stat. 183, 12 U.S.C. § 1811.

in 2016, and in subsequent years the program has generated roughly $200 million annually. The fund follows the block grant mechanism pioneered by HOME. However, fund-assisted projects have stricter income limits, usually 30 percent of median.

V. TAX INCENTIVES FOR AFFORDABLE HOUSING

A. The Early Incentives

As previously discussed, in the late 1960s, the nation faced unprecedented urban unrest, poor housing being a significant cause. Congress launched a two-pronged attack on the problem. First, it created the Section 236 program in 1968. Next, the Tax Reform Act of 1969 created favored tax treatment for affordable housing projects. The groundwork for the latter change was the aforementioned report of the President's Commission on Urban Housing chaired by industrialist Henry Kaiser. The Commission recommended favorable tax incentives for low-income housing and recommended the creation of a federally chartered private sector entity—the National Housing Partnerships.[50]

Congress adopted both recommendations, favoring affordable housing development by such tax devices as rapid depreciation, the ability to deduct construction interest during the construction period, a five-year write off for rehabilitation expenses, liberalized recapture rules, and a rollover of gain if a Section 236 project is sold for low-income homeownership.[51] Congress also created the National Corporation for Housing Partnerships to encourage business investments in affordable housing.[52] The well-intentioned Congress need not have bothered to create such an entity, as private syndication firms quickly jumped into the business of attracting private investors needing tax shelters.

Indeed, proceeds from equity syndication were the engine that made Section 236 and Section 8 successful. Housing programs and the Internal Revenue Code were as intertwined as bagels and lox.

B. The Low-Income Housing Tax Credit (LIHTC)

All this came to a crashing end when Congress enacted the Tax Reform Act of 1986. Congress's overriding intent was to eliminate tax shelters that permitted wealthy individuals to escape paying taxes altogether while lowering the basic tax rate to 28 percent. However, in so doing, it created a new and better shelter for affordable housing: the Low-Income Housing Tax Credit (LIHTC). Although skeptics at first doubted that it would work, LIHTC has proven successful beyond its sponsors' wildest dreams.

In the legislative process, the House passed a bill that would keep the traditional incentives for low-income housing. The Senate Finance Committee took an entirely different approach by creating a tax credit, worth a dollar on the dollar, instead of income tax deductions whose value varied depending on the taxpayer's bracket. The Committee bill would not permit use of the credit with subsidy programs such as Section 8 or Section 515, but

---

50. THE PRESIDENT'S COMMITTEE ON URBAN HOUSING, A DECENT HOME 85–86 (1968).

51. Jacobs et al., *supra* note 1, at ch. 10.

52. Housing and Urban Development Act of 1968, Pub. L. No. 90-448, 82 Stat. 476, 12 U.S.C. § 106.

Senator George Mitchell (D-ME) sponsored a successful amendment on the Senate floor to remove such restrictions.[53]

Congress outlined its rationale for the credit in the "General Explanation" of the bill prepared by the Joint Committee on Taxation. The report criticized prior tax subsidies because they were scattered throughout the Internal Revenue Code in incoherent fashion, were not sufficiently targeted to low-income people, and the subsidy was not linked to the number of low-income units in the project.[54]

The LIHTC program addresses these problems by limiting occupancy to 50 or 60 percent of area median, limiting the credit to qualified low-income units, and recapturing the credit if units are not occupied by low income persons. (Chapter 9, Federal Sources of Financing, provides a full discussion of the program.)

The credit got off to a slow start in 1987 and 1988, but by the end of the decade was going full blast. By 2018, it had produced more than 2.3 million units of affordable housing in more than 37,000 properties.[55] However, legislative and policy struggles persist up to the present day. First, Congress provided that the LIHTC would sunset at the end of 1989. Congress did extend the program on a yearly basis until the end of 1992. For the first half of 1993, there was no authorization for the credit. However, in August of that year, Congress voted to make the credit permanent.[56]

Permanent, however, did not mean permanent if some in Congress had their way. After the Republicans took Congress in 2004, William Archer (R-TX) became chair of the Ways and Means Committee and proposed to sunset the credit on December 31, 2007. Archer was displeased that the preceding Congress made the housing tax credit permanent but not some of his favorites, such as research and development. In 1996, Congress actually passed a tax act that, among other things, did sunset the LIHTC, but President Clinton's veto ended that effort.[57]

In 2003, President George W. Bush's proposal to exempt corporate dividends from taxation presented the credit's next challenge. Under the proposal, such exemption would not apply if the corporation's income was sheltered through the use of LIHTC. If adopted, this provision would have choked off corporate demand for the credit. After substantial lobbying from a unified affordable housing and tax credit community, the proposal was dropped.[58]

The Great Recession beginning in 2007 proved another challenge. Corporations no longer needed to purchase the credit to shelter nonexistent income. This was especially true in the case of Fannie Mae, Freddie Mac, and large banks. Congress adopted two measures to mitigate the problem. First, it passed the Tax Credit Assistance Program (TCAP) in the

---

53. *Senate Passes Tax Reform Bill after Modifying Low-Income Housing Tax Credit*, 14 Hous. & Dev. Rep., Current Devs. 95, 98–99 (1986).

54. General Explanation of the Tax Reform Act of 1986, H.R. 3838, 99th Cong. P. 152 (1986).

55. Corianne Payton Scally et al., Urban Institute, The Low-Income Housing Tax Credit: Past Achievements, Future Challenges 15 (July 2018).

56. Revenue Reconciliation Act of 1993, Pub. L. No. 103-66, Aug. 10, 1993, 107 Stat. 416, 26 U.S.C. 1.

57. Seven-Year Balanced Budget Reconciliation Act of 1995, H.R. 2491, 104th Cong. (as vetoed by the president, Dec. 6, 1995).

58. Barry G. Jacobs, *Dividend Cut in Final Tax Bill Doesn't Threaten Housing Tax Credit*, 31 Hous. & Dev. Rep., Current Devs. 321, 351 (2003).

American Recovery and Reinvestment Act of 2009, which provided $2.25 billion additional HOME funding for tax credit projects.[59] Second, in the same bill, Congress created a credit exchange program whereby the state agency administering the credit could exchange tax credits for cash grants to the developers.[60] (See Chapter 7 for a detailed discussion of TCAP and the Tax Credit Exchange Program.)

In an echo of 2003, the results of the 2016 election created significant turbulence in LIHTC transactions. Many observers had expected Hillary Clinton to win the presidency and Republicans to retain control of the House and Senate, a recipe for no significant legislative action. When Donald Trump emerged as the president-elect in early November, the upcoming unified Republican control of the legislature and the presidency meant certain action on Republicans' legislative priorities. Corporate tax reform was near the top of this list,[61] with a reduction in the top corporate tax rate of 35 percent as a major priority. Uncertainty surrounding the future corporate tax rate—Trump was said to be seeking a reduction to 15 percent[62]—meant similar uncertainty about the future value of LIHTCs to corporate investors.

After months of turmoil, prognostication, and negotiation, LIHTC markets found a path forward: By the end of the first quarter of 2017, transactions were proceeding with the assumption that the reformed corporate tax rate would be 25 percent and with agreements to adjust the final LIHTC investment amounts based on the outcome of tax reform. The finale came with the law's passage in December 2017, setting a top corporate tax rate of 21 percent.

The consequences of this outcome were incorporated into transactions, and legislative attention turned to addressing the reduced value of the LIHTC. As one step, the March 2018 appropriations law increased the amount of LIHTC by 12.5 percent annually for four years. As another, the December 2020 appropriations law set a minimum 4 percent rate for LIHTC received in connection with projects financed with tax-exempt bonds, a significant increase in tax credits for those projects.[63] Related proposals remain under active consideration, even as the coronavirus pandemic and associated economic crisis continue to create headwinds for LIHTC properties.

To sum up previous significant housing production programs—Section 221(d)(3), Section 236, and Section 8 each had seven-year lives. However, the LIHTC, which started slowly, has lived to be bar mitzvahed in 2000, to vote in 2005, to take a legal drink in 2008, and to celebrate the 30th anniversary of its enactment in 2016, and still keeps going today.

---

59. American Recovery and Reinvestment Act, Pub. L. No. 111-5, tit. XII (2009).

60. *Id.*

61. Tax reform legislation was introduced in the 115th Congress as H.R.1, a designation usually reserved for priority legislation and used to convey a message about the incoming Congress's priorities.

62. Julie Hirschfield Davis & Alan Rappeport, *Trump Is Said to Seek Cutting Corporate Tax Rate to 15 Percent*, N.Y. TIMES (Apr. 24, 2017), https://www.nytimes.com/2017/04/24/us/politics/trump-corporate-tax-rate-15-percent.html.

63. Consolidate Appropriations Act, 2021, Division EE—Taxpayer Certainty and Disaster Tax Relief Act of 2020, Section 201.

VI. AFFORDABLE HOUSING PRESERVATION

A. Sections 515, 221(d)(3), and 236

The preservation battle began in the countryside; the Section 515 rural rental housing program was the battlefield. In the late 1970s, a handful of owners prepaid their 50-year loans from the FHA and converted the projects to market rate, resulting in the displacement of low-income tenants. Owners enjoyed this prepayment right under their loan agreement with Farmers Home, and indeed were required to prepay if they could obtain credit elsewhere. In the Housing and Community Development Act of 1979, Congress, at the behest of tenant advocates, retroactively restricted this prepayment right and, in so doing, abrogated the owners' contractual right. In 1980, Congress, shocked at what it had done, repealed the retroactive prepayment restriction.[64]

Congress's shock did not last very long. More rural prepayments occurred in the mid-1980s, and in appropriations acts in 1985 and 1986, Congress again restricted the prepayment right. When prepayment started to occur in HUD 221(d)(3) projects, the stage was set for the Emergency Low-Income Housing Preservation Act of 1987 (ELIHPA).

ELIHPA treated the HUD programs and Section 515 differently. For Section 515, Congress adopted permanent legislation that effectively barred loan prepayment. Incentives were provided such as increased return, refinancing of the original loan, and fair market sale to a nonprofit buyer. However, these provisions were convoluted and not adequately funded, thus giving rise to the successful litigation discussed later. For HUD projects, Congress effectively barred the prepayment right, but again provided incentives, specifically Section 8 assistance, thus enhancing their income stream. The restrictions on HUD prepayment expired in two years (extended for another year in 1990), necessitating permanent legislation.[65]

In 1987, the private owner community was somewhat taken by surprise by the enactment of ELIHPA. By 1990, it prepared well for the legislative struggle that ensued over enacting permanent legislation for the HUD programs. Owners maintained that prepayment restrictions abrogated their contractual right to prepay their mortgage after 20 years. Tenant and nonprofit housing advocates cited the dire need that the relatively small stock of affordable housing continue to be available to low-income persons. The question really boiled down to who should bear the burden of preserving affordable housing—the owners or the public at large? After much back and forth, Congress adopted the Low-Income Housing Preservation and Resident Homeownership Act (LIHPRHA) of 1990 that attempted to provide fair compensation to the owners for extending the use restriction.[66] Again, subsequent litigation demonstrated that the compensation was not as full as it should have been.

LIHPRHA provided that in exchange for maintaining the low-income restriction for the project's remaining useful life, the owner would receive an 8 percent return on the

---

64. Housing and Community Development Act of 1980, Pub. L. No. 95-128, Oct. 8, 1980, 94 Stat. 1614, 42 U.S.C. 5301.

65. Housing and Community Development Act of 1987, Pub. L. No. 100-242, tit. II, Feb. 5, 1988, 101 Stat. 1815, 42 U.S.C. 5301.

66. Low-Income Housing Preservation and Resident Homeownership Act of 1990, Pub. L. No. 100-242, tit. II, Feb. 5, 1988, 101 Stat. 1877, 12 U.S.C. 4101.

project's appraised value.[67] Using an insured equity take out loan under Section 241 of the National Housing Act, the owner could convert the enhanced income stream to a lump sum of cash. The incentives, although not fully compensating owners, still proved very expensive, and in 1996, Congress deemed them too expensive. Congress repealed the incentives and the prepayment restrictions.

The enactment of LIHPRHA launched a wave of litigation that continues to this day, with owners contending that application of LIHPRHA constituted either a breach by the United States of their contractual right to prepay or an uncompensated taking of that right in violation of the Fifth Amendment. In a controversial 2–1 decision, the Court of Appeals for the Federal Circuit reversed the Court of Federal Claims and held for HUD on the contract claim, deciding that there was no privity of contract between the owner and HUD since the loan was from a third-party lender.[68] However, HUD owners have started to have some success on the takings theory. In fact, LIHPRHA has been described by the Federal Circuit as having the character of a taking by the federal government because it was similar to a "physical invasion," akin to "a holdover tenant—HUD effectively rented apartment buildings from the Owners beyond the term of the agreed leasehold and then sublet apartments to low-income tenants."[69] Some settlements have been reached, but other cases must be tried on their individual facts. Concerning the Section 515 litigation, owners have succeeded on the contract theory since under that program the owner's loan is directly with the Rural Services Administration—a direct loan. The government has paid many millions in settlement payments.

Preservation efforts by no means ended with LIHPRHA's demise in 1996. Creative developers and their lawyers soon devised an innovative way to obtain capital for preservation of Section 236 projects known as IRP Decoupling. Under this method, HUD permits the owner to cancel the FHA insurance on the loan, to decouple the subsidy from supporting the first loan, and to utilize the subsidy to support a bond issuance to raise funds for project rehabilitation. Section 8 Certificates and LIHTC syndication proceeds provided the necessary financing.[70] In the years following 2010, HUD worked with developers and their lawyers to allow for "re-decoupling" of previously decoupled transactions to allow for further capital improvement and longer-term preservation, a practice that was formalized in 2013.[71] Although many Section 236 projects were preserved through these methods, for most Section 236 projects, the schedule of IRP payments has now run its course or is in its final years. Tax credit syndications and Section 8 vouchers have also been used in other preservation efforts.

---

67. High by today's standards, 8 percent was a normal return at the time.

68. Cienega Gardens v. United States, 162 F.3d 1123 (Fed. Cir. 1998). *See also* CCA Associates v. United States, 91 Fed. Cl. 580, 598 (2010) (for a critical analysis of this decision by a claims court judge who felt bound to follow the decision even though he disagreed with its failure to recognize HUD as the real party of interest on the loan).

69. Cienega Gardens v. United States, 331 F.3d 1319, 1338 (Fed. Cir. 2003) (*Cienega VIII*).

70. EMILY P. ACHTENBERG, STEMMING THE TIDE: A HANDBOOK ON PRESERVING SUBSIDIZED MULTIFAMILY HOUSING 2 (Local Initiatives Support Corporation 2002).

71. U.S. DEP'T OF HOUS. & URBAN DEV., NOTICE H 2013-25 (2013).

B. Section 8 Projects

About 850,000 Section 8 New Construction and Substantial Rehabilitation projects were built in the late 1970s and early 1980s. Projects not utilizing tax exempt financing had 20-year Section 8 Housing Assistance Payment (HAP) contracts. Accordingly, in the late 1990s, Section 8 preservation became the cardinal housing issue. Congress addressed this issue in the Multifamily Assisted Housing Reform and Affordability Act of 1997 (MAHRAA).[72]

During the legislative process leading up to MAHRAA, Congress focused on renewing the Section 8 contracts for up to 20 years. However, there was great concern that Section 8 rents became too high due to HUD's faulty administration of the Housing Assistance Payment (HAP) contract provision limiting Section 8 project rent increases to those of comparable unassisted projects. The issue spawned multiple litigations, including *Cisneros v. Alpine Ridge Group*,[73] which upheld HUD's right to conduct project-based comparability studies. Thus, on renewals Congress instructed HUD to mark the rents down to then current market rents—"mark to market" as it was popularly called. This created problems for HUD in the case of an FHA insured mortgage if the reduced rents were not sufficient to permit mortgage amortization. To solve this problem, Congress also authorized HUD to reduce the size of the FHA insured mortgage under the Mark-to-Market restructuring program.[74]

An unexpected consequence occurred shortly after this legislation was enacted, due to significantly increasing market rents: It turned out that in many cases, Section 8 contract rents were not above market but below it. Naturally, owners with expiring contracts indicated that given the alternative of below-market rents under a HUD contract or market rents without it, the choice was obvious. For that reason, in 1999, Congress directed a reluctant HUD to mark rents up to market to encourage owners to stay with the program.[75] Mark Up to Market has been quite successful in getting owners to stay in the program.

As of September 2013, more than 3,600 projects had entered the Mark-to-Market restructuring program and HUD had completed more than 2,700 restructurings.[76]

VII. CERTIFICATES AND VOUCHERS

Generally, affordable housing has been a very bipartisan or nonpartisan issue. Beginning with the United States Housing Act of 1937, Congress usually enacts housing legislation with large majorities from both sides. If there has been any difference between the parties, it is on the issue of whether to construct new units or to utilize the existing stock.

Although there is no clear-cut line, generally Republicans emphasize existing housing units and Democrats favor new construction. For example, as mentioned earlier, the Section 23 Leased Housing Program, championed by Representative William Widnall,

72. Multifamily Assisted Housing Reform and Affordability Act of 1997 (MAHRAA), Pub. L. No. 105-65, tit. V, Oct. 27, 1997, 111 Stat. 1384, 12 U.S.C. 1701.
73. Cisneros v. Alpine Ridge Group, 508 U.S. 10 (1993).
74. MAHRAA, *supra* note 72.
75. *House Hearing Shows Bipartisan Support for Legislation to Address Section 8 Opt-Out Problem*, 62 Hous. & Dev. Rep., Current Devs. 1 (1999).
76. Schwartz, *supra* note 10, at 215–16.

ranking Republican on the House Banking and Urban Affairs Committee, was designed to house public housing tenants in units leased from private owners. Likewise, the Nixon administration in the early 1970s conducted housing allowance demonstrations to examine the feasibility of voucher-type programs. And President Nixon, in his 1973 announcement ending the housing moratorium, proposed Section 8 as mainly an existing housing program because of his favored restraints on new construction.

There is now general consensus in the housing field that if there is an adequate supply of existing housing in an area, vouchers should be utilized to make the units affordable for low-income families.[77] In the absence of such supply, new units should be built.

The landmark Housing and Community Development Act of 1974 authorized the Section 8 existing program. Similar to the Section 8 new construction–substantial rehabilitation provisions, an owner would enter into a HAP contract with the government agency administering the program, usually the local public housing authority. The owner agrees to receive a contract rent based on the Fair Market Rent (FMR) set by HUD for the area. The owner enters into a lease with a tenant who has obtained a Section 8 Certificate from the PHA and agrees to pay a portion of the rent equal to 30 percent (25 percent before 1981) of family income. The PHA pays the owner a housing assistance payment (HAP) equal to the contract rent minus the tenant's share.

In 1983, in the Housing Urban and Rural Recovery Act, Congress created a demonstration voucher program, and the program became permanent in 1987. In contrast to certificates, voucher tenants could pay more than 30 percent of their income for rent, and the owner could receive rent greater than the HUD-designated payment standard.

From 1983 to 1998, HUD administered both the certificate and voucher programs. However, in 1998, Congress enacted the Quality Housing and Work Responsibility Act (QHWRA) that merged the two programs, with vouchers the clear winner.[78] Under the revised voucher program, tenants could pay up to 40 percent of their income for rent; rents would not be subject to the Fair Market Rent limitation, but the PHA must find the rent "reasonable"—the so-called rent reasonableness test.

Although the voucher program emphasizes the use of existing housing, it does not do so exclusively. In a 2000 revision to the United States Housing Act, a PHA can utilize 20 percent of its funding for project-based units, meaning that a departing tenant cannot take the voucher with him or her, and the Section 8 subsidy remains with the project. In such cases the owner can obtain financing backed by this guaranteed income stream. Generally, in a project no more than the greater of 25 percent of the units or 25 total units can be assisted with project-based vouchers.[79]

---

77. *See, e.g., Hearing on Evaluating Efforts to Help Families Support Their Children and Escape Poverty before the Subcomm. on Human Resources of the H. Comm. on Ways and Means*, 113th Cong. 1 (July 17, 2013) (public submission for the record of Margery Austin Turner, The Urban Institute) (describing the experimental demonstration programs of the 1970s, the precursors of today's tenant-based voucher programs, in which "cash allowances [were] made to families according to need," and summarizing the research on one of these experimental programs as "show[ing] that participants enjoyed improved quality of housing, that the program did not cause rent inflation, and that vouchers were actually cheaper than production programs").

78. Quality Housing and Work Responsibility Act of 1998, Pub. L. No. 105-276, tit. V, Oct. 21, 1998, 112 Stat. 2518, 42 U.S.C. 1437.

79. *See* U.S. Dep't of Hous. & Urban Dev., Notice PIH 2017-21 (2017).

By 2009, HUD was assisting more than 2,200,000 units under the voucher program, more than any other program.[80] Vouchers are an extremely flexible form of assistance. They can be utilized in LIHTC developments, including new construction. Many RAD conversions have created new PBV contracts (see Sections I and II, *supra*, for discussion of RAD). HUD and Congress have also used the voucher platform to provide "tenant protection" vouchers to residents in certain circumstances in which their unit might otherwise become unaffordable, such as prepayment of a Section 236 mortgage or Section 202 mortgage, expiration of use restrictions in low vacancy areas, or termination of a project-based Section 8 HAP contract. In certain cases, these vouchers can be provided as project-based vouchers, and thereby continue to render units affordable even after the original tenant has moved on. In other specified cases, the provided voucher is "enhanced" and affords the tenant the right to remain in the unit and to receive a market rent subsidy, even if that market rent is above the PHA's payment standard.[81]

In 2016, Congress passed the Housing Opportunity Through Modernization Act (HOTMA),[82] which revised the voucher program rules in an effort to refine the program and facilitate greater use of project-based voucher assistance. HUD has made some of the flexibilities authorized in HOTMA available to PHAs and owners, while others are on hold pending further implementation guidance from HUD.[83]

VIII. LOW-INCOME HOMEOWNERSHIP

Homeownership is the American dream long extolled by both political parties and society at large. It seems only right that lower-income Americans should share in that dream. However, the history of governmental programs to make low-income families homeowners tells a very mixed story. HUD's efforts in this regard have generally not worked, and federal homeownership policy was swept up in political debate over the cause of the Great Recession.

A. HUD Programs

During the legislative process leading up to the enactment of the Housing and Urban Development Act of 1968, Senators Robert Kennedy (D-NY) and Charles Percy (R-IL) led the effort to include subsidized homeownership in the act. Their efforts resulted in adding Section 235 to the National Housing Act. Analogous to its multifamily counterpart, HUD would subsidize the difference between the loan's market rate and 1 percent for income-eligible borrowers. Initially, the program spurred significant new construction during slow economic times in the early 1970s. "Stay alive through 235" became a popular slogan among single-family developers. HUD assisted 500,000 units between 1969 and 1973, significant activity during the credit crunch of that era.[84]

---

80. Schwartz, *supra* note 10, at 231.
81. *See, e.g.*, Hayes v. Harvey, 874 F.3d 98, 106 n.3 (3d Cir. 2018) *reh'g en banc granted, judgment vacated.*
82. Housing Opportunity through Modernization Act of 2016, Pub. L. No. 114-201, 130 Stat. 782 (2016).
83. *See* U.S. Dep't of Hous. & Urban Dev., Notice PIH 2017–21 (2017).
84. Jacobs et al., *supra* note 1, at 101.

It did not take long for the program to become troubled. Default rates soared to an unacceptable 10 percent level. A major scandal developed, resulting from developers making cosmetic repairs to existing homes and then reselling them at exorbitant profits. In cities such as Detroit, the combination of Section 235 with Section 223(e) (which directed HUD to insure loans in declining areas) led to large-scale defaults that decimated some neighborhoods.[85]

President Nixon's 1973 moratorium halted Section 235 activity. Although HUD revised the program, it limped along until Congress ceased funding for it as of October 1, 1989.[86]

Also in the late 1960s, HUD administratively created a homeownership program utilizing the public housing program. Another innovation of HUD's creative assistant general counsel Joseph Burstein, the program in effect diverted HUD's annual contributions from building up equity for the PHA owning the project to the tenants in the project. Thus, when the bonds financing the project were paid off, the project tenants, instead of the housing authority, would own the units.[87] The tenants were required to perform routine maintenance; the amount budgeted for this work by the PHA was credited to the tenant, providing additional funding to pay off the bonded indebtedness.

Although several PHAs initiated Turnkey IIIs in their jurisdictions, the program really never got off the ground. It was very complicated to administer and to explain to potential tenant participants. The program is no longer active.

HUD Secretary Jack Kemp was a strong believer in homeownership. At his urging in 1990, Congress enacted several homeownership initiatives, namely the HOPE programs (Homeownership and Opportunity for People Everywhere). Under this program, HUD would provide financial assistance to purchase units in public housing and other HUD held, assisted, or insured properties. Congress did not fund the program, and subsequent administrations were less than enthusiastic.[88]

Another Kemp homeownership initiative in the 1990 legislation proved equally unsuccessful. As discussed in Section V, *supra*, to address the prepayment problem, Congress adopted LIHPRHA. At Secretary Kemp's urging, Congress enacted provisions providing for purchase by the tenant resident council of properties where the owners sought to prepay. No known tenant purchases were made under this provision.

The HUD record of assisting homeownership is bleak. However, the section 502 rural housing program has proven more successful.[89] Under that program the Rural Housing Service (formerly Farmers Home Administration) makes direct loans to low- and very low-income families at a 1 percent rate. The statute permits 60 percent of the funds to be used for low-income families at 80 percent of area median with only 40 percent of the funds available for very low-income families at 50 percent of median.[90] Thus, it is not a homeownership program for the really poor. Likewise, the single-family mortgage bond

---

85. *Id.*
86. Sec. 401(d) of the Housing and Community Development Act of 1987.
87. Jacobs et al., *supra* note 1, at ch. 8.
88. Jacobs, *supra* note 58, at 423, § 5:34.
89. National Housing Act of 1949, Pub. L. No. 81-171, 63 Stat. 413, 42 U.S.C. 1490.
90. Jacobs, *supra* note 58, at 524, § 6.2.

program, in which state housing finance agencies utilize their tax-exempt financing to make below-market loans, is directed to moderate income families.

B. Subprime Loan Confusion

The specific causes of the Great Recession are the subject of some debate, and multiple narratives have been advanced to explain the cause of the economic contraction. The casual observer will know that home prices and subprime loans were involved, a reality that implicates homeownership and related government policy.

Core causes of the recession likely include unregulated banking activity by investment banks and other nondepository financial entities and widespread failure to regulate this activity; a "bubble" in housing prices, fueled by a sense that housing prices had never declined in the past and therefore would not decline in the future; ballooning household debt at all homeowner income levels, including via loans secured by home equity; subprime loans and similar predatory lending schemes; failures in corporate governance and risk management at systemically important ("too big to fail") financial institutions; and "a systemic breakdown of accountability and ethics."[91]

Despite these complex causes, some say the recession was caused by government policies to encourage homeownership even for those who could not afford it. This was probably at most a marginal contributing factor and far less central than other causes.[92] Nonetheless, this argument has been perpetuated, debated, and politicized. Affordable housing advocates have had to respond. Even allowing that this argument has some marginal validity, some see the subtext as scapegoating low-income homeowners—who were relatively unsophisticated and chasing the American Dream—while ignoring the culpability of many highly sophisticated and financially motivated actors, including mortgage originators, mortgage lenders, appraisers, packagers, Wall Street investment bankers, bond rating firms, guarantors, insurance agencies, and investors.

Affordable housing advocates have also had to point out to an understandably confused public that, whatever the role of homeownership might be, this entire process had nothing to do with the HUD and LIHTC programs for affordable rental housing.

IX. CONCLUDING THOUGHTS

All Americans recognize that they share a vital interest in such domestic issues as health care, energy, transportation, environment, and education. As demonstrated by the ongoing debate over climate change (long after climate scientists have reached consensus on the issue) and the ongoing debate over the Affordable Care Act (more than a decade after its enactment), these issues captivate the public. However, except for a few years after World War II, there has never been such public concern on housing issues, especially affordable housing. The reason is simple—the vast majority of Americans are well-housed, so the

---

91. THE FINANCIAL CRISIS INQUIRY COMMISSION, FINANCIAL CRISIS INQUIRY REPORT: FINAL REPORT OF THE NATIONAL COMMISSION ON THE CAUSES OF THE FINANCIAL AND ECONOMIC CRISIS IN THE UNITED STATES, xvii–xxii (Jan. 2011), http://fcic-static.law.stanford.edu/cdn_media/fcic-reports/fcic_final_report_conclusions.pdf.

92. *See id.* at xxvi–xxvii.

issue is of no real concern to them. This explains why providing housing has generally been a secondary goal to some other purpose for enacting affordable housing legislation.

This by no means minimizes the need for affordable housing for the people that it serves. Nor does it minimize the efforts of the often lonely advocates in the housing community who for nearly a century have fought, in the face of general public apathy, for the enactment and funding of the housing programs described in these pages.

Today's programs are the product of past struggles undertaken by participants in all sectors of the housing community. The future will be no different.

Planning for Housing Requirements | 2

Ngai Pindell*

I. INTRODUCTION

This chapter primarily considers state and federal legally mandated planning and planning-related activities conducted by public agencies and their relationships to affordable housing development.[1] Section I offers a brief introduction emphasizing the importance of planning for affordable housing development. Section II discusses two leading models of planning requirements. Section III considers the risks and opportunities that current growth management, "smart growth," and similar proposals pose for affordable housing. Section IV briefly discusses the relationship between environmental planning and review requirements and affordable housing development. Finally, Section V provides an overview of federal housing planning requirements that affect affordable housing development, including the Consolidated Plan, certifications to "affirmatively further fair housing," and the analysis of impediments to fair housing choice.

---

*The author would like to thank UNLV William S. Boyd School of Law student Victoria Nguyen for her excellent research and editing assistance.

1. While many housing proposals require federal, state, and local government approvals, this chapter will focus on local government approvals. See Chapters 3–5 for additional discussion of zoning. This chapter assumes familiarity with the general land-use development approval process. For an introduction to planning and zoning law, *see* JULIAN CONRAD JUERGENSMEYER & THOMAS E. ROBERTS, LAND USE PLANNING AND DEVELOPMENT REGULATION LAW (4th ed. 2018); PETER W. SALSICH, JR. & TIMOTHY J. TRYNIECKI, LAND USE REGULATION: A LEGAL ANALYSIS AND PRACTICAL APPLICATION OF LAND USE LAW (2d ed. 2003); and DANIEL R. MANDELKER, LAND USE LAW (5th ed. LEXIS 2003). For a detailed reference book on affordable housing development, *see* BENNETT L. HECHT, DEVELOPING AFFORDABLE HOUSING: A PRACTICAL GUIDE FOR NONPROFIT ORGANIZATIONS (3d ed. 2006). And *see* BARRY JACOBS, HANDBOOK OF HOUSING AND DEVELOPMENT LAW (2010–11).

States that are committed to promoting affordable housing development by their local governments through the imposition of planning requirements are still experimenting with the most effective combination of "sticks" and "carrots" to achieve affordable housing goals while respecting specific local conditions and authority.

Planning is significant for affordable housing development in numerous ways. Planning that does not anticipate affordable housing needs will make this housing more difficult to develop because zoning ordinances and planning standards will not accommodate it. For example, "multifamily housing" might not be a permitted use in a district, or maximum densities might be too low.[2] If such planning is legally mandated, affordable housing advocates might be able to push local governments to adopt pro-affordable housing zoning ordinances and planning standards, as well as other policies and programs.[3] Later, affordable housing developers can use those local laws and standards to obtain necessary discretionary land-use approvals and funding for their particular proposals. Finally, proper planning can prevent or reduce the opportunities for opponents of affordable housing to block, delay, and impose additional costs on development proposals because fewer discretionary land-use approvals are needed and zoning/planning standards are likely to be more accommodating to affordable housing.[4]

The subprime lending and foreclosure crisis between 2007 and 2010 put housing into the national conversation, but *affordable* housing did not get a similar level of attention.[5] In 2020, the worldwide COVID-19 pandemic and the Black Lives Matter movement again put housing into the national conversation. COVID-19 made access to affordable housing a public health issue and forced communities to confront what it means to quarantine or "shelter in place" when families lack access to suitable housing. Emergency declarations at the local, state, and national levels temporarily banned residential evictions under most circumstances.[6] The Black Lives Matter movement drew attention to structural racism and inequality in law enforcement, the workplace, and housing opportunity.[7]

---

2. Of course, when land-use decisions are made without any reference to planning, affordable housing development is even less likely.

3. See Chapters 4 and 5.

4. *See, e.g.*, Roderick M. Hills, Jr. & David Schleicher, *Planning an Affordable City*, 101 Iowa L. Rev. 91, 94 (2015) ("The solution to this housing crisis is [that] local governments should deregulate their housing markets to allow an increased housing supply to meet a rising demand for housing. As a political matter, however, incumbent residents who already own housing vociferously and effectively protest against the reduction of zoning restrictions. . . . [Thus] the solution to excessive zoning is centralized, comprehensive, and binding land-use policies.").

5. Nonetheless, there are several important connections between the housing crisis generally and affordable housing. In some regions with lots of foreclosures, the supply of market-rate, "affordable" housing units for sale should have increased; former homeowners forced to rent because of foreclosure put upward pressure on rents and increased the affordability challenge for low-income renters; and some renters were evicted from foreclosed multiunit buildings, adding even more pressure in those markets.

6. The federal Centers for Disease Control (CDC) issued an order halting residential evictions effective Sept. 4, 2020, until Dec. 31, 2020. 85 Fed. Reg. 55292 (Sept. 4, 2020).

7. *See, e.g.*, Anna Orso & Oona Goodin-Smith, *How Philly's Summer of Protests Revitalized the Affordable Housing Movement*, Philadelphia Inquirer, Sept. 15, 2020 (describing the links between policing, mass incarceration, and homelessness).

Planning does not take place in a vacuum. Four essential contexts for contemporary planning activities affecting affordable housing are (1) legal requirements for planning; (2) the growth management, "smart growth," and "New Urbanism" movements; (3) the effects of environmental planning and review on affordable housing development; and (4) exclusionary zoning and other forms of local opposition to affordable housing development. The first three topics will be discussed in this chapter after a discussion of state statutory planning requirements. Exclusionary zoning, local opposition issues, and inclusionary responses are discussed in Chapters 3 through 5.

II. STATE AND REGIONAL PLANNING REQUIREMENTS THAT AFFECT AFFORDABLE HOUSING

A. Varying State Involvement in Local Government Planning

Generally, states delegate land-use authority to their local governments.[8] State involvement in the planning process and local governments' land-use decision making vary.[9] Many states do not require any planning but authorize local jurisdictions to engage in a planning process if they wish.[10] (Even if states do not require planning for affordable housing, local governments that receive certain federal funds are required to perform some planning activities, as discussed *infra*.) While most state zoning-enabling acts include language requiring that zoning be adopted "in accordance with a comprehensive plan," many courts have not interpreted that provision to require the development of a separate planning document and have located the "comprehensive plan" within the zoning ordinance itself.[11] The national trend, however, is toward the creation of a separate plan, and the legal conversation increasingly involves how much weight it should be given rather than whether it is required or not.[12]

---

8. Each state has enacted zoning enabling legislation for local governments, primarily municipalities. Home rule powers under state constitutions may also confer authority over land use issues to local governments. *See* Juergensmeyer & Roberts, Land Use Planning and Development Regulation Law, *supra* note 1, at 46–47.

9. Some states delegate virtually all authority over local land use decisions to local government, while other states have maintained more statewide controls. The increasing role of some states in planning efforts is detailed in Fred Bosselman & David Callies, The Quiet Revolution (1971). *See also* John Infranca, *The New State Zoning: Land Use Preemption Amid a Housing Crisis*, 60 B.C. L. Rev. 823, 825 (2019); David Callies, *The Quiet Revolution Revisited: A Quarter Century of Progress*, 26 Urb. Law. 197 (1994).

10. *See, e.g.,* Tex. Local gov't Code Ann. § 213.002 (2019).

11. *See, e.g.,* Timber Trails Assocs. v. Planning & Zoning Comm'n, 916 A.2d 99, 111 (2007) ("In the absence of a formally adopted comprehensive plan, a town's comprehensive plan is to be found in the scheme of the zoning regulations themselves."); Dutko v. Planning & Zoning Bd., 954 A.2d 866 (Conn. App. Ct. 2008). *See also* Charles Haar, *In Accordance with a Comprehensive Plan*, 68 Harv. L. Rev. 1154 (1955).

12. Edward J. Sullivan, *Recent Developments in Comprehensive Planning Law*, 40 Urb. Law. 549, 549–50 (2008). *See also* Edward J. Sullivan, *Recent Developments in Comprehensive Planning Law*, 41 Urb. Law. 547, 561 (2009) ("[T]he trend continues to shift away from the conflation of planning and zoning to a greater judicial respect for the plan in evaluating zone changes and permits in the land-use area, especially in the manner of adjudication of plan amendment and plan interpretation."); Jillian M. Nobis, *To Apply or Not to Apply? That Is the Question of Intergovernmental*

States that require local jurisdictions to develop comprehensive plans vary in the degree to which they mandate the goals these plans must achieve or the specific content they must include.[13] Some states condition the requirement to prepare a comprehensive plan on the establishment of a planning commission or on a local jurisdiction's size.[14] Some states create detailed mandates that jurisdictions must include in their local plans.[15] Still others delve deeper into the planning process to become directly involved in local planning decisions.[16] States engaged in requiring local governments to plan for housing, including affordable housing, utilize a combination of approaches, each reflecting some degree of political and economic compromise.[17] Not all states require local governments to act "consistently" with their plans. Some local governments are not required to conform their zoning ordinances, specific plans, or zoning decisions to their plans.[18] However, a few states

---

Zoning, 23 ROGER WILLIAMS U. L. REV. 580, 592 (2018) ("A comprehensive plan is different than a zoning ordinance and the two are governed by separate statutes.").

13. One study found that about 25 states require local governments to adopt comprehensive plans, and in about 12 of these states, the comprehensive plan must also meet state growth management requirements. ROLF PENDALL, FROM HURDLES TO BRIDGES: LOCAL LAND-USE REGULATIONS AND THE PURSUIT OF AFFORDABLE RENTAL HOUSING, HARVARD UNIVERSITY JOINT CENTER FOR HOUSING STUDIES 7 (2007). *See, e.g.*, FLA. STAT. ANN. § 163.3177 (2019) (requiring numerous mandatory elements and allowing optional elements). *See also* N.H. REV. STAT. ANN. § 36:47 II (2019) (requiring regional housing plans) and N.H. REV. STAT. ANN. § 674:2 III (2019). *And see* STUART MECK ET AL., REGIONAL APPROACHES TO AFFORDABLE HOUSING 76–87 (2003).

14. ARIZ. REV. STAT. ANN. §§ 9-461.01–.05 (2019) (conditioning development of general plan on creation of planning department).

15. *See* discussion of California and Florida, *infra* Sections II and III.

16. *See* discussion of Oregon, *infra* Section III.

17. Ideally, a municipality preparing a detailed housing element will be required to consider a range of local and regional issues affecting the availability of affordable housing. Some states require that municipalities prepare housing elements. *See, e.g.*, ARIZ. REV. STAT. § 9-461.05 (2019); CAL. GOV'T CODE § 65300 (West 2019); FLA. STAT. §§ 163.3161 to .3215 (2019); FLA. STAT. §§ 186.001–187.201 (2019); GA. CODE ANN. §§ 36-70-1 to -5 (2019); ME. REV. STAT. ANN. tit. 30A §§ 4312–4347-A (2019); OR. REV. STAT. §§ 197.005 to .860 (2019); R.I. GEN. LAWS §§ 45-22.2-1 to -14 (2019); VT. STAT. ANN. tit. 24 §§ 4301–4387 (2019); WASH. REV. CODE ANN. §§ 36.70.010 to .980 & 36.70A.010 to .904 (2019). Some states' administrative codes provide more detail for local jurisdictions on how to prepare the housing element, e.g., GA. COMP. R. & REGS. 110-3-2-.04(5)(e) (1992); OR. ADMIN. R. 660-008-0000 to -0040 (Interpretation of Goal 10 Housing); WASH. ADMIN. CODE § 365-196-410 (2019).

18. *See, e.g.*, consistency requirements in the statutes of Arizona (ARIZ. REV. STAT. § 9-462.01(F) (2019)), California (CAL. GOV'T CODE § 65350 (West 2019)), and Florida (FLA. STAT. ANN. § 163.3194 (2019)). These states' statutes also provide standards for how courts and administrative bodies should evaluate consistency. (ARIZ. REV. STAT. § 9-462.01(F) (2019); CAL. GOV'T CODE § 65860(a) (West 2019); FLA. STAT. ANN. § 163.3194(4)(a) (2019)). *See also* Durant v. D.C. Zoning Comm'n, 65 A.3d 1161, 1167 (D.C. 2013) (ruling the Commission may not approve a project or rezone an area in a manner inconsistent with the Comprehensive Plan); Pinecrest Lakes, Inc. v. Shidel, 795 So. 2d 191 (Fla. App. 4 Dist. 2001) (affirming trial court's order to demolish or remove buildings that were not consistent with comprehensive plan); Dunlap v. Orange County, 971 So. 2d 171 (Fla. Dist. Ct. App. 2007) (granting standing to homeowners who challenged a development order's consistency with the comprehensive plan). *See also* Daniel Mandelker, *The Role of the Local Comprehensive Plan in Land Use Regulation*, 74 MICH. L. REV. 299 (1976); Stuart Meck, *The Legislative Requirement That Zoning and Land Use Controls Be Consistent with an Independently Adopted Local Comprehensive Plan: A Model Statute*, 3 WASH. U. J.L. & POL'Y 295, 306–15 (2000).

require consistency of plans among neighboring jurisdictions as an additional element of comprehensive planning.[19]

Statutes containing additional planning requirements for affordable housing production and location strive in part to increase affordable housing opportunities by forcing a local government to integrate affordable housing considerations into its aggregate land-use decision-making process.[20] For states that require them, the comprehensive plan (also called the general plan, master plan, or long-range plan in some states) serves as a local jurisdiction's guide for future land-use development and investment. Comprehensive plans contain reports on current patterns of demographics, land uses, transportation, housing, and similar issues. Considering present conditions, these plans assess future needs in each subject area and identify priority investments, uses, and growth patterns, and then adopt policies to achieve their goals. In theory, the results of a thoughtful, comprehensive planning process should be incorporated into and enforced by a jurisdiction's zoning ordinance and planning code. Many planning and zoning departments, however, are more reactive than proactive in regard to a jurisdiction's growth. Consequently, individual developments often incrementally direct a community's growth through discrete amendments to underlying plans or existing zoning.

There is currently no national consensus on what state planning requirement regime best promotes the development of affordable housing. This section will discuss and present some preliminary evaluation of distinct regimes from two states.[21]

B. California: Legislative Mandatory Fair Share Requirements with Limited Enforcement

The California statute requires jurisdictions to prepare a comprehensive plan. The statute details a local government's obligation to fulfill the housing element requirement of the comprehensive plan. This housing element must address the housing needs of all economic segments of the community.[22] Regional councils of government (COGs), in consultation with the State Department of Housing and Community Development (HCD), determine

---

19. *See, e.g.*, WASH. REV. CODE § 36.70A.100 (2019).

20. Ideally, statutes require jurisdictions to adopt written procedures for public participation to ensure the effective participation of those populations most likely to be affected by affordable housing planning and production. However, statutes include a wide variety of requirements for public participation. *See, e.g.*, ARIZ. REV. STAT. § 9-461.06 (Supp. 2019); FLA STAT. ANN. § 163.3181 (West 2019); R.I. STAT. § 45-22.2-8 (2019); WASH. REV. CODE § 36.70A.140 (2019); WIS. STAT. ANN. § 66.1001 (Supp. 2019).

21. In addition, Oregon, Washington, and Florida will be discussed in the following section. Other regimes, some largely similar, will be mentioned in footnotes.

22. CAL. GOV'T CODE §§ 65580 *et seq.* (West 2019). The procedural detail in the statute provides strong guidance for local jurisdictions' planning efforts. *See, e.g.*, PUBLIC INTEREST LAW PROJECT, CALIFORNIA HOUSING ELEMENT MANUAL 14 (4th ed. 2019) ("Although the housing element obligation does not mandate that local governments build affordable housing, it requires communities to limit other development until they plan for affordable housing—and that often provides sufficient incentive for them to do a lot more than plan, including making commitments in their housing elements to provide land and financial resources.") *But see* PAUL G. LEWIS, CALIFORNIA'S HOUSING LAW ELEMENT: THE ISSUE OF LOCAL NONCOMPLIANCE xii (2003) ("Highly detailed statutes are often evidence of widespread disagreement on a given policy, as waves of 'reform' occur in which opposing interests seek to have their specific concerns addressed and preserved in law.").

and allocate each local jurisdiction's "fair share" of regional housing needs for all income levels to be included in their local housing plans.[23] The process for allocating regional housing targets was amended in 2018. Housing targets remain connected to population projections, but housing targets must account for the number of cost-burdened households in the region relative to the number of cost-burdened households in a comparable "healthy housing market."[24] The planning statute sets the schedule for housing element revision,[25] and each jurisdiction must adopt a housing element that includes four primary parts: (1) an assessment of housing needs and inventory of resources and constraints;[26] (2) a statement of community affordable housing goals, objectives, and policies; (3) a five-year schedule of actions to achieve these goals, objectives, and policies; and (4) an evaluation of a jurisdiction's previous element and progress toward goals.[27]

As part of its housing needs analysis, the element must contain an analysis of each of the following: (1) population and employment trends, and the need for housing for all income levels; (2) conditions of the housing stock, including rates of overcrowding and an inventory of land suitable for residential housing; (3) governmental and other barriers to affordable housing development; (4) housing opportunities for populations with special needs, such as the elderly, people with disabilities, farmworkers, large families, female-headed families, and families in need of emergency shelter; (5) the needs concerning the preservation of existing low-income housing; and (6) opportunities for energy conservation.[28]

Amendments to the statute enacted in 2005 require jurisdictions to identify affordable housing sites with greater precision, and in turn give local jurisdictions greater guidance about the level of detail necessary for a housing element to comply with state law.[29] The amendments require the inventory of land suitable for residential housing to be site-specific;[30] to describe the zoning, environmental constraints, and water and sewer

---

23. CAL. GOV'T CODE § 65584 (West 2019). Local governments must plan for existing and projected need for new housing. Jurisdiction may not review an allocation determination in court but may challenge the determination through HCD administrative processes. City of Irvine v. S. Cal. Ass'n of Gov'ts, 175 Cal. App. 4th 506, 96 Cal. Rptr. 3d 78 (June 30, 2009), *order modified and rehearing denied*, 2009 WL 2157127 (Cal. App. 4, July 21, 2009)). *See also* Matt Cody, *Coordinated Land Use Planning Not Enough to Improve Housing Supply*, 39 McGEORGE L. REV. 503, 506–11 (2008) (describing interaction between COGs and HCD in review process and alternative process in Southern California).

24. CAL. GOV'T CODE § 65584.01.

25. Local governments must plan and revise housing element generally every eight years. CAL. GOV'T CODE §§ 65580–65589.8 (West 2019).

26. *See, e.g.*, Urban Habitat Program v. City of Pleasanton, 164 Cal. App. 4th 1561 (2008) (Pleasanton's growth cap, adopted by initiative, was inconsistent with the Housing Element Law.).

27. CAL. GOV'T CODE §§ 65583(a)–65588(a) (West 2019).

28. *Id.* § 65583(a)(1)–(9).

29. Before the amendments, "an aggregate listing or summary of vacant sites and sites having potential for redevelopment with general analysis of zoning and facilities was all that was required." Fonseca v. City of Gilroy, 56 Cal. Rptr. 3d 374, 390 (2007).

30. The inventory or land suitable for residential development includes: "(1) Vacant sites zoned for residential use. (2) Vacant sites zoned for nonresidential use that allows residential development. (3) Residentially zoned sites that are capable of being developed at a higher density. [and] (4) Sites zoned for nonresidential use that can be redeveloped for residential use, and for which the housing element includes a program to rezone the site, as necessary, rezoned for, to permit residential use[.]" CAL. GOV'T CODE § 65583.2(a) (West 2019).

availability;[31] and to include a determination of the number of housing units that can be accommodated on each site based on an analysis of applicable density requirements and their ability to accommodate a jurisdiction's share of the regional housing need.[32]

Each local jurisdiction must submit a draft of its housing element to HCD for review to determine whether it complies with state planning requirements.[33] HCD makes a written determination regarding the draft housing element's compliance, provides comments to local jurisdictions, and may suggest changes to make the housing element compliant.[34] Local jurisdictions may revise the draft housing element according to HCD's recommendations and adopt the revised version.[35] Alternatively, if a local jurisdiction disagrees with HCD's determination that the housing element is not compliant, the jurisdiction may still adopt that element if it includes written findings explaining the reasons why it believes the element does substantially comply with state law.[36] While HCD's determinations of compliance are important, the exact standard courts apply to reviewing a housing element for compliance appears to be unsettled. While one court noted that courts give "great weight" to HCD's determination,[37] another took a less deferential position, noting the court "still must exercise [its] independent duty to state the meaning of the statutes at issue here, giving consideration to [HCD's] views."[38]

The California regime relies on judicial enforcement of local affordable housing planning and the statute provides for a private right of action to challenge compliance.[39] Amendments to the statute in 2019 broaden enforcement of planning requirements by adding the

---

31. *Id.* § 65583.2(b).

32. *Id.* § 65583.2(c). Where the inventory analysis falls short of identifying sufficient sites to satisfy a jurisdiction's share of regional housing needs, the jurisdiction's schedule of actions must provide sufficient sites developable "by right" to make up the shortfall in low- and very low-income sites demonstrated in the inventory. "By right" means the site does not require any discretionary government review or approval (other than design review) that would subject the development to review under the state's environmental law. *Id.* § 65583.2(h). *See* discussion of California environmental law, CEQA, *infra*. *See also* RICHARD A. MARCANTONIO, ZONING FOR AFFORDABLE AND SUSTAINABLE COMMUNITIES: A CASE STUDY IN THE IMPLEMENTATION OF HOUSING ELEMENTS IN MARIN COUNTY 11 (Public Advocates, Inc., 2009). The statute also includes a range of applicable density bonuses for developments that include affordable housing. CAL. GOV'T CODE § 65583(c)(6) (West 2019).

33. CAL. GOV'T CODE § 65585(b)–(d) (West 2019).

34. *Id.*

35. *Id.* § 65585(f)(1).

36. *Id.* § 65585(f)(2).

37. Hoffmaster v. City of San Diego, 64 Cal. Rptr. 2d 684, 693 n.13 (1997).

38. Fonseca v. City of Gilroy, 56 Cal. Rptr. 3d 374, 389 (2007).

39. CAL. GOV'T CODE § 65587(b)–(c) (West 2010). Challenges to housing element compliance with statutory public participation requirements may be difficult. Leading cases applying the statute include Camp v. Mendocino Cnty. Bd. of Supervisors, 176 Cal. Rptr. 620 (1981) (finding a violation and ordering a remedy); Buena Vista Gardens Apts. Ass'n v. City of San Diego Planning Dep't, 175 Cal. App. 3d 289 (1985) (reviewing housing element for substantial compliance with statutory requirements and enjoining demolition of apartment homes until defect in plan corrected); Hernandez v. City of Encinitas, 28 Cal. App. 4th 1048 (1994) (finding city's housing element substantially complied with requirement to quantify assessment of housing needs, make inventory of land suitable for residential development, and analyze and remove constraints to affordable housing); Bldg. Indus. Ass'n v. City of Oceanside, 27 Cal. App. 4th 744 (1994) (reviewing impact of growth initiative on construction of affordable housing); and Hoffmaster v. City of San Diego, 55 Cal. App. 4th 1098

attorney general can also bring suit alleging noncompliance with planning requirements if notified by HCD of local noncompliance.[40] A court can issue an order or judgment directing a local government to come into compliance, and continued noncompliance can result in substantial fines that multiply over time.[41] The statute provides for a wide range of other remedies, including ordering the locality to halt development until an adequate element is adopted or ordering approval of specific affordable housing developments.[42] Local governments are also required to submit yearly reports to HCD detailing their progress in meeting the deadlines outlined in their housing elements.[43] California requires local governments to make land-use decisions that are consistent with their general plans, including their housing elements.[44] This provides another ground for legal challenge.

Regional bodies supplement the efforts of local governments to plan for and develop affordable housing. For example, CASA (the Committee to House the Bay Area) was convened by the Association of Bay Area Governments and the Metropolitan Transportation Commission.[45] The Compact is a 15-year policy plan to address the San Francisco Bay region's housing crisis. It contains ten policy elements, including elements addressing minimum zoning near transit, reforming the process of approving affordable housing, expediting approvals and financial incentives for select housing, unlocking public land for affordable housing, and establishing a regional housing enterprise to implement the CASA Compact.

The strength of the California statute is its focus on procedure. California's housing element statute has been revised frequently, in part to make its procedural requirements clearer and more exacting. This focus on procedure forces jurisdictions to carefully study their affordable housing needs while giving them the freedom to adopt individualized approaches to address those needs.[46] This focus on procedure also forces jurisdictions to develop a professional planning staff (or hire a consultant) to satisfy statutory planning

---

(1997) (finding city's inventory of housing opportunities for the homeless does not substantially comply with requirements of statute).

40. CAL. GOV'T CODE § 65585(j) (West 2019).

41. *Id.* § 65585(j)–(n). In addition to bringing suit, "the Attorney General may seek all remedies available under law." *Id.* § 65585(n).

42. CAL. GOV'T CODE §§ 65754–65755 (West 2010). *See, e.g.*, Urban Habitat Program v. City of Pleasanton, Mar. 12, 2010, at 9 ("[city] must cease issuing non-residential building permits and all related building permits for any construction or development . . . until the City brings its General Plan into compliance with the requirements of State Law."). *See also* Camp v. Mendocino Cnty. Bd. of Supervisors, 176 Cal. Rptr. 620 (1981) *and* Buena Vista Gardens v. City of San Diego, 220 Cal. Rptr. 732 (1985). For other evaluations of California's Housing Element law, see Ben Field, *Why Our Fair Share Housing Laws Fail*, 34 SANTA CLARA L. REV. 35 (1993) (criticizing judicial enforcement of housing element standards); Brian Augusta, Comment, *Building Housing from the Ground Up: Strengthening California Law to Ensure Adequate Locations for Affordable Housing*, 39 SANTA CLARA L. REV. 503 (1999).

43. CAL. GOV'T CODE § 65400 (West 2010).

44. *Id.* § 65589(d). If an affordable housing development project is consistent with the provision of the housing element, jurisdictions may not disapprove it even if it is inconsistent with the jurisdiction's zoning laws and general land use plan unless the jurisdiction can make at least one other specific finding. *Id.* § 65589.5(d)(5).

45. CASA Compact: A 15-Year Emergency Policy Package to Confront the Housing Crisis in the San Francisco Bay Area, January 2019.

46. PENDALL, *supra* note 13, at 36, 37.

requirements and fosters the development of sophisticated nonprofit agencies to monitor and enforce compliance with affordable housing standards.[47]

Critics argue the statute focuses more on determining whether housing elements comply with state law than whether affordable housing is actually being built.[48] They suggest that a focus on planning for an equitable distribution of affordable housing may be insufficient to advance the goal of producing more housing units generally, and affordable housing in particular.[49] The relatively lower numbers of affordable housing units actually produced compared to actual needs indicates a stronger commitment is needed to enforce the implementation of housing goals, and additional strategies may be required,[50] including the development of bottom-up political incentives for local officials to respond to prospective residents' demands for additional housing production.[51] The gap may also derive from other causes, such as fiscal zoning, the lack of sufficient subsidies for affordable housing, local opposition to the siting of affordable housing, and other reasons.

---

47. *Id.*

48. *See, e.g.*, Liam Dillon, *California Lawmakers Have Tried for 50 Years to Fix the State's Housing Crisis. Here's Why They've Failed*, L.A. TIMES (June 29, 2017, 3:00 AM), https://www .latimes.com/projects/la-pol-ca-housing-supply/ (A Bay Area councilman called the housing element law a "failure," pointing to the 87-page housing plan that Foster City spent more than a year and $50,000 to develop, with "no intention of actually building the units."); Nico Calavita et al., *Inclusionary Housing in California and New Jersey: A Comparative Analysis*, 8 HOUSING POL'Y DEBATE 109, 118 (1997). The authors later note that the fear of litigation over the housing element can be an important tool in forcing jurisdictions to adopt compliant housing elements and, in turn, develop inclusionary housing programs to achieve their stated housing goals. *Id.* at 136.

49. *See, e.g.*, Christopher S. Elmendorf et al., *Making It Work: Legal Foundations for Administrative Reform of California's Housing Framework*, 46 ECOLOGY L.Q. 5 (2020) (arguing that housing elements plan for far more affordable housing than is actually developed and such housing is largely not in high-demand coastal areas), Paul G. Lewis, *Can State Review of Local Planning Increase Housing Production?*, 16 HOUSING POL'Y DEBATE 173, 190–91 (2005) (finding that housing element noncompliance was not a factor in housing production in the 1990s because other factors, such as the size of the city, the city's previous rate of growth, and the size of the employment sector predominate.). *See also* Paul G. Lewis, *California's Housing Law Element: The Issue of Local Noncompliance*, PUB. POL'Y INST. CAL. (2003). For an additional evaluation of California's housing element, *see* Little Hoover Commission, *Rebuilding the Dream: Solving California's Affordable Housing Crisis*, May 2002.

50. *See* Dep't of Hous. & Cmty. Dev., *California's Housing Future: Challenges and Opportunities* 5 (Feb. 2018), https://www.hcd.ca.gov/policy-research/plans-reports/docs/sha_final_combined. pdf. The Department of Housing and Community Development estimates approximately 180,000 new homes are needed annually to meet projected population and household growth from 2015–2025. *See also* Dep't of Hous. & Cmty. Dev., *Raising the Roof: California Development Projections and Constraints 1997–2020, Statewide Housing Plan* 9 (May 2000). The previous estimate was 200,000 housing units per year. By comparison, the state has averaged about 100,000 units per year since 1990. Currently, the bulk of enforcement actions are brought by legal service attorneys and other public interest law firms with the assistance of the California Affordable Housing Law Project. *See also* Paul G. Lewis, *Can State Review of Local Planning Increase Housing Production?*, 16 HOUS. POL'Y DEBATE 173, 195 (2005) (noting state preemption of some local land use powers might be a more direct way to shape housing plans than the California approach).

51. Christopher S. Elmendorf, *Beyond the Double Veto: Housing Plans as Preemptive Intergovernmental Compacts*, 71 HASTINGS L.J. 79, 85 (2019).

C. New Jersey: Constitutional and Legislative Fair Share Approach Struggling with "Growth Share"

Affordable housing planning requirements that incorporate "fair share" elements require a local jurisdiction to consider the housing needs of a larger geographical area in addition to its own housing needs. Planning for affordable housing in New Jersey centers around the fair share statutory provisions adopted in response to the well-known *Mount Laurel* litigation, which challenged the exclusionary zoning practices of New Jersey's suburban areas.[52] At the heart of the fair share obligation is a requirement that local municipalities adopt zoning ordinances, planning standards, and other policies to provide a "realistic opportunity" for their regional "fair share" of affordable housing.[53]

In the first implementation of Mount Laurel requirements, a state agency, the Council on Affordable Housing (COAH), calculated and allocated to each municipality its proportional obligation of low- and moderate-income housing.[54] A municipality could voluntarily

---

52. The Mount Laurel litigation comprised a series of cases: S. Burlington Cnty. NAACP v. Twp. of Mount Laurel, 67 N.J. 151 (1975) (*Mount Laurel I*), S. Burlington Cnty. NAACP v. Twp. of Mount Laurel, 92 N.J. 158 (1983) (*Mount Laurel II*). Following the *Mount Laurel* litigation, the New Jersey Fair Housing Act of 1985 created the Council on Affordable Housing. New Jersey Fair Housing Act, N.J. Stat. Rev. Ann. §§ 52:27D-301 to -329 (West 2019). *See* Hills Dev. Co. v. Bernards Twp. 103 N.J. 1 (1986) (upholding constitutionality of the act). *See also* Roderick M. Hills, Jr., *Saving Mount Laurel?*, 40 Fordham Urb. L.J. 1611, 1612 (2013) ("The Mount Laurel doctrine seems perennially hovering on the brink of extinction. It was surrounded by controversy when it was finally made effective with a 'builder's remedy' in 1983, and it barely survived its transition to statutory implementation in the form of the New Jersey Fair Housing Act in 1985."). *See also* discussion of the *Mount Laurel* doctrine and N.J. Fair Housing Act in Chapter 3, *infra*.

53. *Mount Laurel I* at 713. The *Mount Laurel* regime is also tied to the State Development Guide Plan. *See* John M. Payne, *General Welfare and Regional Planning: How the Law of Unintended Consequences and the Mount Laurel Doctrine Gave New Jersey a Modern State Plan*, 73 St. John's L. Rev. 1103 (1999).

This section discusses fair share in the context of regional allocations of affordable housing need and comprehensive planning. Fair share considerations applied to housing appeal boards in Massachusetts, Rhode Island, Connecticut, New Jersey, New Hampshire, California, and Illinois are discussed in Chapter 4, *infra*.

Connecticut experimented with voluntary fair share allocations through the Connecticut Fair Share Compact Pilot Program in 1988, discussed in Charles E. Connerly & Marc Smith, *Developing a Fair Share Housing Policy for Florida*, 12 J. Land Use & Envtl. L. 63, 89 (1996), and Thomas A. Brown, Note, *Democratizing the American Dream: The Role of a Regional Housing Legislature in the Production of Affordable Housing*, 37 U. Mich. J.L. Reform 599, 641 (2004).

The Illinois General Assembly passed the Affordable Housing Planning and Appeal Act to require Illinois communities to address affordable housing needs and the link between housing and jobs in suburban Chicago regions. 310 Ill. Comp. Stat. 67/1 (2019). Local governments not exempt under the statute's criteria must adopt an affordable housing plan that consists of (1) a report of the number of affordable housing units necessary to achieve exempt status; (2) identification of land appropriate for new affordable housing construction or rehabilitation; (3) identification of incentives; and (4) one of three goals of increased affordable housing production: (a) at least 15 percent of new development must consist of affordable housing, (b) overall affordable housing stock must increase by three percentage points, or (c) a jurisdiction must meet the overall 10 percent affordable housing as part of a total stock test. 310 Ill. Comp. Stat 67/25(b) (2019). See Chapter 4, *infra*, for a discussion of the zoning appeals part of the legislation.

54. N.J. Rev. Stat. § 52:27D-307c(1) (2019). This complicated fair share allocation formula is clearly explained in Meck et al., *supra* note 13, at 35–37.

complete a housing element and fair share plan[55] and petition COAH for substantive certi-fication of the fair share plan.[56]

If a jurisdiction prepares a housing element, it must (1) consider current and future projections of housing stock, including low- and moderate-income housing; (2) analyze demographic and employment characteristics; and (3) determine its capacity to accommo-date a fair share of the region's low- and moderate-income housing needs.[57]

If COAH certified that the housing element complied with state law, this certifica-tion conferred a presumption of validity on the jurisdiction's housing element against any claims made under an exclusionary zoning suit. Only "clear and convincing evidence" would overcome this presumption of validity, and this certification immunized munici-palities from a "builder's remedy."[58] To qualify for a builder's remedy, a developer must successfully challenge the local government's denial of a particular housing proposal in exclusionary zoning litigation and demonstrate that at least 20 percent of the units proposed are designated as affordable units.[59] While compliance with COAH regulations immunized local jurisdictions from the builder's remedy, "[a] COAH certification does not mean that a municipality has reached a limit for affordable housing."[60] Other affordable housing obliga-tions still remain in effect.[61]

---

55. N.J. Rev. Stat. § 52:27D-320 (2019).

56. *Id.* § 52:27D-314.

57. *Id.* § 52:27D-310 (2019). *See also* N.J. Rev. Stat. § 52:27D-311 (2019). Municipalities used to be able to trade up to one-half of their fair share requirement to another receiving municipality under a controversial Regional Contribution Agreement (RCA), but the RCA was ended by legisla-tion in 2008. RCAs had been criticized on the grounds they allowed relatively wealthy suburban municipalities to achieve COAH certification without having to actually construct lower-income housing within the municipality by sending cash payments to more urban municipalities. *See, e.g.,* Richard G. Lorenz, *Good Fences Make Bad Neighbors,* 33 Urb. L. 45, 92 (2001); John M. Payne, *Fairly Sharing Affordable Housing Obligations: The Mount Laurel Matrix,* 22 W. New Eng. L. Rev. 365, 367–68 (2001). Multiple bills aimed at re-authorizing the use of RCAs to meet affordable housing needs have been introduced, but none have succeeded. *See, e.g.,* S.B. 465, 128th Leg., Reg. Sess. (N.J. 2018).

58. N.J. Rev. Stat. § 52:27D-317 (2019). COAH can grant "substantive certification" if it finds the plan "make[s] the achievement of the municipality's fair share of low- and moderate-income housing realistically possible." *Id.* at §§ 52:27D-313, -314. *See also In re* Fair Lawn Borough, Ber-gen Cnty., Motion of Landmark at Radburn, 968 A.2d 180 (2009) (supporting COAH's denial of a municipality's certification). "The Fair Housing Act . . . contemplates the provision of actual afford-able housing, not endless promises of future compliance. . . . The FHA grants a municipality sig-nificant discretion in structuring its housing element. . . . But the statute does not require COAH to sanction the playing of 'shell games,' in which towns include properties in their fair share plans for decades, only to seek their removal from the plans when the developers are close to building the affordable housing." *Id.* at 185.

59. *Mount Laurel II* describes the general parameters of the builder's remedy, and notes a builder's remedy is appropriate unless the "municipality establishes that because of environmental or other substantial planning concerns, the plaintiff's proposed project is clearly contrary to sound land use planning." 92 N.J. at 279–80. *See also* Toll Brothers, Inc. v. Twp. of W. Windsor, 173 N.J. 502 (2002) (clarifying the circumstances in which a builder's remedy is appropriately granted).

60. Homes of Hope v. Easthampton Twp. Land Use Planning Bd., 976 A.2d 1128, 1134 (2009) (*Homes of Hope*).

61. In *Homes of Hope,* a developer sought to develop an eight-unit affordable housing building and needed a variance for a multifamily building in a residential district. "To obtain a use vari-ance . . . an applicant must satisfy both . . . positive and negative criteria. The positive criteria require

Criticism of the COAH fair share methodology led to the development of a growth share process, which aimed to create a more direct connection between affordable housing obligations and the actual growth of local jurisdictions.[62] COAH and the judiciary, however, were not able to agree on an approach to growth share. Much of the disagreement centered on the precise formula for calculating projected growth share and whether jurisdictions that decide not to grow should be able to avoid their share of affordable housing obligations. COAH's first attempts to adopt growth share allocations (so-called Third Round Rules allocating affordable housing obligations to municipalities)[63] were invalidated by the state courts.[64] In 2014, the COAH board deadlocked at 3–3 in its attempt to approve Third Round Rules and did not schedule any future meetings to consider the issue further. COAH failed to adopt municipal housing obligations despite orders from the New Jersey Supreme Court to do so. As a result, the court declared the agency defunct and held housing advocates and municipalities could appeal directly to the state court system to determine whether municipalities have complied with constitutional fair share housing obligations.[65] Under the judicial approval system, a municipality files a declaratory judgment to obtain court approval of its affordable housing plan. The court later held municipalities have a constitutional obligation to address the affordable housing needs that arose between 1999 and 2015—the period when COAH failed to adopt viable Third Round Rules.[66]

---

the applicant to demonstrate special reasons for the grant of the variance. . . . An inherently beneficial use presumptively satisfies the positive criteria, while other uses must demonstrate that they are particularly suited for the location." *Id.* at 1131. The court ruled that affordable housing still qualifies as an inherently beneficial use after a jurisdiction's compliance with its COAH fair share obligation. "Affordable housing continues to foster the general welfare and constitutes a special reason to support a use variance." *Id.* at 1130. The approval of the variance still depends on site-specific conditions, including the development's compliance with the "negative criteria," which examines whether the development will result in substantial detriment to the public good or substantially impair the intent and the purpose of the zone plan and zoning ordinance.

62. For early discussions of growth share in general and New Jersey's growth-share plan, *see* John M. Payne, *Rethinking Fair Share: The Judicial Enforcement of Affordable Housing Policies*, 16 REAL ESTATE L.J. 20 (1984); John M. Payne, *The Growth Share Approach to Ending Exclusionary Zoning*, 49 LAND USE LAW & ZONING DIGEST 3 (1997); TIM EVANS, "REALISTIC OPPORTUNITY?" THE DISTRIBUTION OF AFFORDABLE HOUSING AND JOBS IN NEW JERSEY (2003), https://www.njfuture.org/wp-content/uploads/2011/06/Housing-and-Jobs-07-03.pdf (supporting growth share in theory to link affordable housing to wherever growth is occurring).

63. The First Round of affordable housing obligations addressed 1987–1983, and the Second Round addressed 1993–1999.

64. *In re* Adoption of N.J.A.C. 5:94 & 5:95, 914 A.2d 348 (App. Div.), *cert. denied*, 926 A.2d 856 (2007). The appellate division and the state supreme court rejected a revised methodology in 2010 and in 2013. *See In re* Adoption of N.J.A.C. 5:96 & 5.97, 416 N.J. Super. 462 (App. Div. 2010) and *In re* Adoption of N.J.A.C. 5:96 & 5:97, 215 N.J. 578 (2013).

65. "The FHA's exhaustion-of-administrative-remedies requirement, which staves off civil actions, is premised on the existence of a functioning agency, not a moribund one." *In re* Adoption of N.J.A.C. 5:96 a& 5:97 *ex rel.* New Jersey, 221 N.J. 1 (2015) at 5.

66. *In re* Declaratory Judgment Actions Filed by Various Municipalities, Cty. of Ocean, 227 N.J. 508 (2017) ("We now hold that a form of present-need analysis under the Fair Housing Act, *N.J.S.A.* 52:27D-301 to -329 (FHA)—redefined to include a component premised on a calculation of those low- and moderate-income New Jersey households, newly formed since 1999, that presently exist and are entitled to their opportunity of access to affordable housing—provides the appropriate approach to addressing statewide and regional need.").

Since 2015, at least two municipalities have lost their immunity from builder's remedy lawsuits because they were found constitutionally noncompliant with Mount Laurel affordable housing requirements—Englewood Cliffs and South Brunswick. In 2020, a Superior Court judge approved a builder's remedy lawsuit forcing Englewood Cliffs to approve 120 affordable housing units within a new 600-unit development and to amend its zoning ordinances to provide for 147 additional affordable units.[67]

A Superior Court judge revoked immunity for the Township of South Brunswick, determined its fair share of the region's prospective need for affordable housing was 1,533 units, and created an "interactive process" to prioritize site-specific builder's remedy suits guided by

> (1) an assessment of whether any project was clearly more likely to result in actual construction than other projects; (2) the availability of infrastructure; (3) the project's proximity to goods and services; (4) its regional accessibility; and (5) the property's environmental suitability and compatibility with neighboring land uses.[68]

The threat or actual implementation of a builder's remedy lies at the heart of New Jersey's approach to generating effective planning for affordable housing.[69] Evaluation of New Jersey's approach to producing affordable housing presents a mixed picture of the effectiveness of the implementation of the Mount Laurel decision.

More affordable housing units have been built under COAH than there likely would have been without it.[70] However, far fewer units were constructed than were actually needed, few low-income people moved from the cities to the suburbs under COAH,[71] racial integration goals were not met,[72] and the growth share approach has been controversial.[73] Moreover, the program is weakened because local jurisdictions are not required to create housing elements. While the threat of litigation induces some municipalities to include

---

67. *See In re* Borough of Englewood Cliffs, No. L-6119-15 (Law Div. Jan. 17, 2020).

68. In the Matter of the Application of the Township of South Brunswick for a Judgment of Compliance and Repose and Temporary Immunity from Mount Laurel Lawsuits, 448 N.J. Super. 441 (July 21, 2016).

69. The determination and administration of affordable housing needs are designed to be administrative processes. Objections to a submitted plan can be resolved through a "mediation and review process" provided in the statute. N.J. Rev. Stat. § 52:27D-315 (West 2019). However, the court has weighed in on important occasions. *See, e.g.*, Holmdel Builder's Ass'n v. Holmdel Twp., 121 N.J. 550 (1990) (upholding development fees), and *In re* Twp. of Warren, 132 N.J. 1 (1993) (invalidating COAH regulation authorizing an occupancy preference).

70. John M. Payne, *Norman Williams, Exclusionary Zoning, and the Mount Laurel Doctrine: Making the Theory Fit the Facts*, 20 Vt. L. Rev. 665, 681 (1996). *See also* Henry A. Span, *How the Courts Should Fight Exclusionary Zoning*, 32 Seton Hall L. Rev. 1, 48–72 (2001).

71. *See generally* Peter H. Schuck, *Judging Remedies: Judicial Approaches to Housing Segregation*, 37 Harv. C.R.-C.L. L. Rev. 289, 315 (2002); Naomi Bailin Wish & Stephen Eisendorfer, *The Impact of Mount Laurel Initiatives: An Analysis of the Characteristics of Applicants and Occupants*, 27 Seton Hall L. Rev. 1268 (1997).

72. *See* Joel Norwood, *Trading Affordable Housing Obligations: Selling A Civic Duty or Buying Efficient Development?*, 39 Conn. L. Rev. 347, 349 (2006); Florence Wagman Roisman, *The Role of the State, the Necessity of Race-Conscious Remedies, and Other Lessons from the Mount Laurel Study*, 27 Seton Hall L. Rev. 1386 (1997).

73. *See* discussion *infra*.

affordable housing in some instances, the builder's remedy does not necessarily lead to better planning in advance. Indeed, new construction under the builder's remedy containing a relatively small set-aside of affordable housing can lead to sprawl and increasing mismatches between where housing is available and where low-income people live and work.[74] An additional criticism is that local governments may chafe at being subject to the stick of the builder's remedy and the oversight of a state agency or state courts rather than participating in a more collaborative, incentive-based process to plan for and create affordable housing.[75]

In conclusion, the challenge for affordable housing planning regimes is to properly connect planning for affordable housing *opportunities* with enforcement of their *implementation* so that actual and sufficient affordable housing is produced. The actual or threatened use of strong enforcement measures combined with effective planning through fair share or detailed requirements can be an effective strategy to increase affordable housing. A requirement that local jurisdictions consider regional housing needs in the development of their own local plans or be consistent with regional housing plans is helpful as well. But affordable housing considerations must also be balanced with fiscal needs and other planning considerations, such as environmental, transportation, and growth concerns. The achievements of affordable housing planning requirements will always be limited unless sufficient resources (including housing subsidies) are available, and effective responses to various forms of exclusionary zoning and local opposition to affordable housing development are in place.[76]

III. GROWTH MANAGEMENT AND AFFORDABLE HOUSING: RISKS AND OPPORTUNITIES

Affordable housing development proposals are inevitably caught up in the current maelstrom about development and/or growth. There are many varieties of "growth control,"[77] "growth

---

74. Daniel R. Mandelker, *The Affordable Housing Element in Comprehensive Plans*, 30 B.C. ENVTL L. REV. 555, 562–63 (2003). *See also* Edward J. Sullivan & Jessica Yeh, *Smart Growth: State Strategies in Managing Sprawl*, 45 URB. LAW. 349, 350–51 (2013); HOUSING OPPORTUNITY TASK FORCE FINDINGS & RECOMMENDATIONS 20 (New Jersey, Mar. 2010) (noting sprawl concerns). For more information on the *Mount Laurel* litigation, *see* John M. Payne, *Fairly Sharing Affordable Housing Obligations: The Mount Laurel Matrix*, 22 W. NEW ENG. L. REV. 365 (2001); Payne, *supra* note 70; Schuck, *supra* note 71; and a 1997 symposium on *Mount Laurel* published in Vol. 27 of the *Seton Hall Law Review*; DAVID KIRP ET AL., OUR TOWN: RACE, HOUSING AND THE SOUL OF SUBURBIA (1995); CHARLES M. HAAR, SUBURBS UNDER SIEGE: RACE, SPACE, AND AUDACIOUS JUDGES (1996).

75. "One may criticize the towns for resisting their constitutional obligations in bad faith, but perhaps criticism is more properly directed at COAH, whose responsibility it is to properly motivate and negotiate with municipalities to build some affordable housing. A less combative approach, with more discretion afforded to COAH to reward good behavior, would be more effective than the current carrot-less (and stick-less) method." Daniel Meyler, Note, *Is Growth Share Working for New Jersey?*, 13 N.Y.U. J. LEGIS. & PUB. POL'Y 219, 245 (2010).

76. Part II of the book surveys federal, state, and local resources to support affordable housing development. Chapter 3 considers various forms of exclusionary zoning and local opposition to affordable housing as well as federal, state, and local responses to them.

77. "Whereas growth management accommodates projected development in a manner that achieves broad public goals, growth control limits or rations development. Typical growth control

management,"[78] "smart growth,"[79] "New Urbanism,"[80] and "sustainable development."[81] (This section employs the phrase "growth management" to refer to any of these.) While any particular version of growth management can, in principle, be compatible with the development of affordable housing, each can have the intentional or unintentional effect of excluding it. Similarly, while no version of growth management is necessarily consistent with or supportive of the development of affordable housing, each response to potential growth will affect the potential for affordable housing development. The effects of growth management include the availability of developable land, the price of land, allowed

---

tools are building moratoriums, permitting caps, development quotas, and the like." Arthur C. Nelson et al., *The Link between Growth Management and Housing Affordability: The Academic Evidence, in* GROWTH MANAGEMENT AND AFFORDABLE HOUSING: DO THEY CONFLICT? 117, 119 (Anthony Downs ed. 2004). Growth control policies are explicitly aimed at limiting housing growth, either directly or indirectly, and have proven to be effective at limiting growth and consequently increasing housing costs. Edward Sullivan & A. Dan Tarlock, *The Western Urban Landscape & Climate Change*, 49 ENVTL. L. 931, 948 (2019) (noting a study of growth controls in California cities revealed that each additional growth control policy a community added was linked to an increase in home prices by 3 to 5 percent).

78. "'[U]rban growth management' [is] the deliberate and integrated use of the planning, regulatory, and fiscal authority of state and local governments to influence the pattern of growth and development in order to meet projected needs. Included in this definition are such tools as comprehensive planning, zoning, subdivision regulations, property taxes and development fees, infrastructure investments, and other policy instruments that significantly influence the development of land and the construction of housing." Nelson et al., *supra* note 77, at 119. *See also* Julian C. Juergensmeyer, *Infrastructure and the Law: Florida's Past, Present, and Future*, 23 J. LAND USE & ENVTL. L. 441 (2008) (discussing Florida's infrastructure-funding techniques).

79. "*Smart growth* is a particular kind of growth management tool that focuses specifically on policies intended to preserve open space, encourage higher densities, reduce reliance on automobiles, and allow more mixing of residential and commercial development." Samuel R. Staley, Comment, *Does Growth Management Aid Affordable Housing?, in* GROWTH MANAGEMENT AND AFFORDABLE HOUSING 69, 71 (Anthony Downs ed. 2004). Smart Growth "encourages local governments to break free of the Euclidean focus on land use compatibility and nuisance abatement." Patricia Salkin, *Planning and Smart Growth*, 4 AM. L. ZONING § 36:8 (5th ed.) (2020).

80. New urbanism is based on "the principles of restoring the walkability of the urban landscape, revitalizing communities through the diversification of land uses and social interactions, and preserving the natural and national legacy of America." Timothy Polmateer, *How Localism's Rationales Limit New Urbanism's Success & What New Regionalism Can Do About It*, 41 FORDHAM URB. L.J. 1085, 1089–90 (2014). *See generally* Congress for the New Urbanism and the Charter of the New Urbanism, http://www.cnu.org/who-we-are/charter-new-urbanism.

81. "For more than a decade the term 'sustainable development' has denoted an effort to meld concerns for environmental protection, economic well-being, and social justice." J. William Futrell, *Defining Sustainable Development Law*, 19 NAT. RESOURCES & ENV'T 9, 9 (2004). *See also* Robert H. Freilich & Neil M. Popowitz, *The Umbrella of Sustainability: Smart Growth, New Urbanism, Renewable Energy and Green Development in the 21st Century*, 42 URB. LAW. 1, 4 (2010) ("[T]he umbrella term 'sustainability' consists of four fundamental and unifying sub-systems: . . . 'smart growth'. . . 'new urbanism' . . . 'renewable energy' . . . and 'green development.'"). John R. Nolon, *An Environmental Understanding of the Local Land Use System*, 45 ENVTL. L. REP. 10215, 10234 (2015) ("Sustainable development is the key to creating buildings, neighborhoods, and communities that will help mitigate climate change. . . . Sustainable development uses less material, avoids consuming wetlands or eroding watersheds, consumes less energy, emits less CO_2, lessens stormwater runoff, reduces ground and surface water pollution, and creates healthier places for living, working, and recreating.").

and preferred uses, required minimum or maximum densities, and the degree to which it accommodates or promotes affordable housing development. This section will focus on the risks and opportunities that growth management regimes (whether adopted by states or by localities) pose to affordable housing development.[82]

A. The Need for Planning to Guide Growth Management

Growth management schemes that ignore or fail to specifically provide for affordable housing harm the prospects for affordable housing development. Growth management schemes that aim to control the timing of development or limit the supply of developable land can create upward pressure on land and housing prices. And when smart growth strategies such as infill development and brownfield redevelopment are paired with urban revitalization efforts, these policies can displace existing residents and cause gentrification when previously distressed neighborhoods become more attractive to upper-income buyers. These risks have been widely recognized by commentators.[83]

Even when affordable housing is incorporated into the growth management scheme, it is important that specific standards and strong enforcement measures are included.[84] The urban growth area scheme in Washington is "guided" by state planning goals, including an affordable housing goal,[85] and municipalities must plan for the housing needs of "all economic segments of the community," including an "inventory and analysis of existing and

---

82. See Chapters 3, 5, and 6 for potential legal challenges to growth management programs. Early leading cases include *Constr. Indus. Ass'n of Sonoma County v. The City of Petaluma*, 522 F.2d 897 (9th Cir. 1975) and *Golden v. Planning Board of the Town of Ramapo*, 30 N.Y.2d 359 (1972). *See also* Michael Soules, *Constitutional Limitations of State Growth Management Programs*, 18 J. LAND USE & ENVTL. LAW 145 (2002).

83. *See, e.g.*, Sarah Fox, *Environmental Gentrification*, 90 U. COLO. L. REV. 803 (2019); Diane K. Levy et al., *In the Face of Gentrification: Case Studies of Local Efforts to Mitigate Displacement*, 16 J. AFFORDABLE HOUS. & CMTY. DEV. L. 238 (2007); Douglas R. Porter, *The Promise and the Practice of Inclusionary Zoning*, in GROWTH MANAGEMENT AND AFFORDABLE HOUSING 212 (Anthony Downs ed. 2004); Rolf Pendall, *Local Land Use Regulation and the Chain of Exclusion*, 66 J. AM. PLANNING ASS'N 125 (2000); Florence Wagman Roisman, *Sustainable Development in the Suburbs and Their Cities: The Environmental and Financial Imperatives of Racial, Ethnic, and Economic Inclusion*, 3 WIDENER L. SYMP. J. 87 (1998).

84. "[S]mart growth programs that lack an affordable housing element have been associated with increases in housing cost burdens, especially for owners." GREGORY K. INGRAM & YU-HUNG HONG, EVALUATING SMART GROWTH: STATE AND LOCAL POLICY OUTCOMES 28 (Lincoln Inst. of Land Policy, May 2009). *See also* Jennifer Steffel Johnson & Emily Talen, *Affordable Housing in New Urbanist Communities: A Survey of Developers*, HOUS. POL'Y DEBATE 583, 601 (2008) (noting the results of a survey of New Urbanist developers demonstrate that state and local affordable housing requirements were important determinants of affordable housing construction in New Urbanism communities).

85. WASH. REV. CODE § 36.70A.020(4) (2019). The Growth Management Act (GMA) establishes a comprehensive land use planning system that requires more rapidly growing and populous counties, cities, and towns to establish land use plans that are consistent with GMA goals and requirements. Tim Butler & Matthew King, *The Growth Management Act*, 24 WASH. PRAC., ENVTL. L. & PRAC. § 17.32 (2d ed., July 2017 Supp.).

projected housing needs that identifies the number of housing units necessary to manage projected growth."[86] Counties must review their plans every eight years.[87]

The statute contains penalties for continued noncompliance, including the loss of certain revenue.[88] But one study notes "the existing legislative predicate for affordable housing remains a destination without the barest directions to achieve its objective[,]" leading to "paralysis," NIMBY-ism, and entrenching the power of vested interests favoring the status quo.[89] Housing advocates may petition a growth management board to review local comprehensive plans for compliance with the state planning goals,[90] but this board, rather than the state legislature, must incrementally define and interpret the content of the state's affordable housing goal.[91] Without a mandatory state approval process, it is up to public interest groups to effectively enforce the Growth Management Act by bringing petitions to the hearing board.[92] But this "citizen enforcement" quality of the program may have had the advantage of deflecting political opposition to a growth management scheme that, in another state with more state enforcement, would be focused on the actions of a centralized

---

86. WASH. REV. CODE § 36.70A.070(2) (2019). The statute requires that each housing element: "(a) Includes an inventory and analysis of existing and projected housing needs that identifies the number of housing units necessary to manage projected growth; (b) includes a statement of goals, policies, objectives, and mandatory provisions for the preservation, improvement, and development of housing, including single-family residences; (c) identifies sufficient land for housing, including, but not limited to, government-assisted housing, housing for low-income families, manufactured housing, multifamily housing, and group homes and foster care facilities; and (d) makes adequate provisions for existing and projected needs of all economic segments of the community." To determine its inventory, analysis, and adequate provision of projected housing needs, a city may "rely upon reasonable assumptions derived from available data of a statewide or regional nature or representative of jurisdictions of comparable size and growth rates." Stickney v. Cent. Puget Sound Growth Mgmt. Hearings Bd., 453 P.3d 25, 32 (Wash. App. Div. 2, 2019). WASH. REV. CODE § 36.70A.130(5) (2019). *See also State Resources for the Growth Management Act Update of Comprehensive Plans and Development Regulations*, WASHINGTON STATE DEP'T OF COMMERCE (2016), https://deptofcommerce.box.com/s/1shb0hcimnxxdlvfw1xh08r0kbr0g5l5.

87. WASH. REV. CODE § 36.70A.130(5) (2019). *See also State Resources for the Growth Management Act Update of Comprehensive Plans and Development Regulations, supra* note 86.

88. *See* WASH. REV. CODE § 36.70A.330–.345 (2019).

89. Henry W. McGee, Jr., *Equity and Efficacy in Washington State's GMA Affordable Housing Goal*, 3 WASH. U. J.L. & POL'Y 539, 546 (2000).

90. WASH. REV. CODE § 36.70A.250–.320 (2019). The board must find a comprehensive plan compliant unless the government's action is "clearly erroneous." *Id.* § 36.70A.320. To find an action "clearly erroneous," the Board has to be "left with the firm and definite conviction that a mistake has been committed." Whatcom Cty. v. W. Wash. Growth Mgmt. Hr'gs Bd., 381 P.3d 1, 8 (Wash. App. Div. 2, 2016) (citations omitted).

91. McGee, *supra* note 89, at 544; *Whatcom Cty.*, 381 P.3d at 22 (finding plan inadequate). *See also* Seattle Coalition for Affordability, Livability, and Equity (SCALE) et al. v. City of Seattle, 2019 WL 7598711, at *51–52 (finding plan adequate).

92. WASH. REV. CODE § 36.70A.280 (2019). The board hears petitions to determine housing element compliance with the state growth management goals. The board must presume a plan is valid and can invalidate it if a challenger can demonstrate noncompliance. *Stickney*, 453 P.3d at 36. Henry W. McGee, Jr., *Washington's Way: Dispersed Enforcement of Growth Management Controls and the Crucial Role of NGOs*, 31 SEATTLE U.L. REV. 1, 33 (2007) (discussing the enforcement success of Futurewise [formerly the 1000 Friends of Washington]).

state government bureaucracy.[93] The regional hearing boards were consolidated into one statewide board in 2010, but many of the regional characteristics of the previous scheme remain, including board membership by regional affiliation and hearings held in the region of the dispute.[94] In 2020, the board implemented changes aimed at increasing efficiency, including lowering membership to five board members and addressing workload disparities between specific regions as well as between attorney and non-attorney members.[95]

B. The Benefits of Recognizing Common Interests

Some growth control efforts are simply slow- or no-growth movements and they can be superseded by state planning mandates.[96] However, environmentalists concerned about "sprawl" (typically referred to as "smart growth" or "sustainable development" advocates) drive many of the most popular current efforts to manage growth.[97] Some of these efforts recognize, at least in principle, the importance of affordable housing and the need to provide for it in planning and zoning schemes designed to reduce sprawl.[98]

Affordable housing developers and advocates have some important *potential* common interests with this subgroup of growth management advocates and environmentalists. These common interests may include, for example, increasing residential density, promotion of greater variety of housing choice (especially multifamily and mixed-use developments), a focus on the revitalization of existing neighborhoods, creation of pedestrian-friendly communities and transit-oriented development, promotion of mixed-income communities, provisions of incentives for infill and brownfields redevelopment, development encouraging neighbor interaction and creation of social capital, and the opportunity to connect neighborhood development to regional development decisions.[99]

Affordable housing advocates can advance these potential common interests by ensuring that growth management laws provide adequate sites for affordable housing development (with appropriate zoning, planning standards, and access to infrastructure) and financing to make affordable housing development feasible. Advocates can encourage affordable housing by incorporating zoning strategies typically associated with New

---

93. McGee, *supra* note 92, at 33. The perception of an overreaching state agency led to dramatic changes to Florida's growth management scheme. *See* discussion of Florida, *infra*.

94. Substitute S.B. 6214, Ch. 211, Laws of 2010, pp. 10–15 *amending* WASH. REV. CODE §§ 36.70A.250 *et seq.*

95. S. B. REP., 66-6574, at 4 (Wash. 2020).

96. Urban Habitat Program v. City of Pleasanton, Cal. Super. Ct., Mar. 12, 2010, 6 (preempting local housing cap law by state affordable housing planning law).

97. *See, e.g.*, 1000 Friends of Florida (www.1000friendsofflorida.org) and 1000 Friends of Oregon (www.friends.org) (last visited Oct. 24, 2020).

98. See discussion of Washington, *supra*, and Oregon, *infra*. Many of the examples, analyses, and model legislation developed under the American Planning Association's Growing Smart project include the connection between smart growth and affordable housing. *See* http://www.planning.org /growingsmart/ (last visited Oct. 24, 2020).

99. Angela Glover Blackwell & Sarah Treuhaft, *Regional Equity and the Quest for Full Inclusion* (2008) archived at http://perma.cc/V3LE-U9L2; Danielle Arigoni, National Neighborhood Coalition, *Affordable Housing and Smart Growth: Making the Connection* 20–21 (2001), https:// www.novoco.com/sites/default/files/atoms/files/affordablehousing_and_smartgrowth.pdf. For more information on the links between housing and other neighborhood infrastructure resources, see the resources at www.policylink.org.

Urbanism principles to allow for increased densities and for housing types and patterns traditionally resisted by conventional zoning.[100] Concentrating development along transportation corridors using transit-oriented development zoning[101] (such as mixed-use, high-density zoning near subway centers and parking credits) is one approach that has been used successfully in many cities around the nation,[102] and is a key feature of California's planning statute limiting greenhouse gas emissions.[103]

C. Statewide and Comprehensive Planning

To minimize potential displacement and gentrification from infill redevelopment policies, advocates can enforce statutory redevelopment plan requirements.[104] In some states, redevelopment plans can only be adopted after the adoption of a comprehensive plan,[105] and the redevelopment plan must be consistent with the comprehensive plan.[106] Other state statutes authorize municipalities to condition development in redevelopment areas on the set-aside of affordable housing units or contributions to a housing trust fund.[107] Finally, the state may require the redevelopment plan to assess affordable housing availability for temporary or permanent relocation.[108]

---

100. Besides raising minimum densities for residential development, enacting a well-designed "inclusionary zoning ordinance" is a primary tool to balance environmental and affordable housing goals. *See* Brian W. Ohm & Robert J. Sitkowski, *Integrating New Urbanism and Affordable Housing Tools*, 36 URB. LAW. 857 (2004) (proposing inclusionary zoning and housing appeal statute policies). *See also* Cydnee V. Bence, *A House Is Not a Home: Learning from Our Mistakes to Prevent Unequitable Gentrification on A Local Level*, 44 VT. L. REV. 429, 459 (2019) (An inclusionary zoning ordinance generally requires developers of new residential or commercial projects above a certain size to either include a scaling number of low-income housing options or contribute to a low-income housing fund.). *See also* Chapters 3 and 4.

101. *See* CAL. GOV'T CODE § 65460–.11 (2019) (providing guidelines for transit-oriented planning). *See also* AMERICAN PLANNING ASSOCIATION, GROWING SMART LEGISLATIVE GUIDEBOOK: MODEL STATUTES FOR PLANNING AND MANAGEMENT OF CHANGE 7–184 (Stuart Meck ed., 2002) (describing a Model Transit-Oriented Development Plan).

102. *See, e.g.*, Sara C. Bronin, *Comprehensive Rezonings*, 2019 BYU L. REV. 725 (2020) (detailing the reasons for the success of transit-oriented development in Hartford, Conn.); *Transit-Oriented Development: Models and Best Practices*, DEMOCRACY COLLABORATIVE, https://community-wealth. org/strategies/panel/tod/models.html (last visited Oct. 24, 2020) (listing Portland, Oregon, and Washington, D.C. among the national leaders in transit-oriented development)).

103. *See* discussion of California's S.B. 375, *infra*.

104. Revitalizing and reusing vacant land within the city limits curbs sprawl on the city outskirts. If properly designed, nuisance abatement and vacant house rehabilitation programs can revitalize neighborhoods as well as provide new affordable housing units. *See, e.g.*, Julie Gilgoff, *Local Responses to Today's Housing Crisis: Permanently Affordable Housing Models*, 20 CUNY L. REV. 587, 595 (2017); Sarah Treuhaft et al., *When Investors Buy Up the Neighborhood: Preventing Investor Ownership from Causing Neighborhood Decline*, POLICYLINK (2010).

105. *See, e.g.*, CAL. GOV'T CODE § 65450 (2019).

106. *Id.* § 65454.

107. *See, e.g.*, N.J. REV. STAT. § 40A:12A-4.1 (2019).

108. *Id.* § 40A:12A-7a.(3). Affordable housing supporters can also prevent gentrification and displacement by promoting replacement housing ordinances, condominium conversion regulations, laws increasing affordability periods for housing in exchange for the public subsidies commonly granted to market-rate developments, and a variety of anti-displacement measures, including land assembly, land trusts, land banking measures, and counseling and asset-building opportunities for

Statewide planning allows for state authorities to make trade-offs between affordable housing and environmental concerns, such as open space, rather than making these determinations on an isolated, case-by-case basis at the local level, where affordable housing interests are more likely to be slighted.[109] Oregon uses a state agency and specific statutory mandates to incorporate affordable housing planning into its urban growth boundary (UGB) scheme.[110]

In 1973, Oregon created the Land Conservation and Development Commission (LCDC).[111] LCDC has established 19 planning goals, among them a housing goal (Goal 10) and a well-known urban growth boundary goal (Goal 14). The housing goal requires local governments to maintain land necessary for the housing needs of all income segments and to include housing elements in their local plans.[112] The LCDC reviews local plans for consistency with state planning goals and guidelines[113] and has strong enforcement powers, including the power to obtain judicial enforcement of its determinations.[114] The Land Use Board of Appeals (LUBA), established in 1979 and independent from LCDC, is a specialized, three-member panel replacing the jurisdiction of Oregon circuit courts to review challenges to local government land-use decisions.[115] Appeals of LUBA decisions are heard by an intermediate appellate court, the Oregon Court of Appeals.[116]

---

affected residents. See Chapters 3, 4, 5, 11, 15, and 16 for more information on many of these techniques.

109. *See also* Arthur C. Nelson & Susan M. Wachter, *Growth Management and Affordable Housing Policy*, 12 J. AFFORDABLE HOUS. & CMTY. DEV. L. 173, 181 (2003) (noting Oregon's statewide integrated planning approach may facilitate inclusionary zoning and other affordable housing planning by local governments).

110. Ballot Measure 37, passed in Oregon in 2004, had the potential to chill efforts in Oregon and elsewhere to effectively implement smart growth policies. Measure 37 required jurisdictions to pay compensation to owners whose property value is reduced as a result of a land use restriction, subject to limited exceptions. Ballot Measure 37, OR. REV. STAT. ch. 197 (2004). In 2007, Oregon voters passed Measure 49, substantially limiting the effect of Measure 37. As of 2019, most of the farm and forest properties made available for development in Oregon under Measure 49 had not yet been subdivided. Mateusz Perkowski, *Most Oregon Measure 49 Properties Remain Undeveloped*, CAPITAL PRESS, Nov. 25, 2019, https://www.capitalpress.com/state/oregon/most-oregon-measure-49-properties-remain-undeveloped/article_1bdbac8c-0d5e-11ea-b472-4b90514ac7a4.html.

111. OR. REV. STAT. § 197.030 (2019).

112. LAND CONSERV. AND DEV. COMM'N, OREGON'S STATEWIDE PLANNING GOALS 10. *See also* OR. REV. STAT. § 197.295–.314 (2019). The fair share approach in Oregon emphasizes the obligation of local governments to consider regional affordable housing needs. *See* Terry D. Morgan, *Exclusionary Zoning: Remedies under Oregon's Land Use Planning Program*, 14 ENVTL L. 779, 783 (1984).

113. OR. REV. STAT. § 197.250–.251 (2019).

114. *Id.* § 197.319–.350. Oregon can invalidate a land use permit when a local jurisdiction has a noncompliant housing element, and local jurisdictions can deny permits only on the basis of objective criteria. *Id.* 197.307(4). *See also* Christopher S. Elmendorf, *Beyond the Double Veto: Housing Plans as Preemptive Intergovernmental Compacts*, 71 HASTINGS L.J. 79, 103–04 (2019) (noting the LCDC can enjoin non-compliant local governments from issuing land use permits and invalidate permits do not conform to the state's land use goals).

115. OR. REV. STAT. § 197.825 (2019).

116. *Id.* § 197.825(2)(b). Oregon allows state governments to plan for local governments if local governments do not plan consistent with state interests, but this stick has never been used. Similarly, Oregon can withhold money under a revenue-sharing plan but has never done so. A more effective tool has been a building permit moratorium, which has been used twice. Arthur C. Nelson, *Comment*

Oregon's scheme tempers limits on developable land outside UGBs with increases in density, requiring jurisdictions to provide and zone sufficient land to accommodate identified affordable housing needs.[117] This scheme also prohibits cities from engaging in certain zoning practices that effectively exclude affordable housing.[118] At least within the Portland area, zoning for higher-density uses, including multifamily use, has increased.[119] Since affordable housing is often multifamily housing, one result of increases in density in Portland is to maintain opportunities for affordable housing construction. Under the Metropolitan Housing Rule, all but the smallest jurisdictions in the Portland area must zone at minimum densities and must make allowance for at least 50 percent of new housing to be either multifamily or attached single-family units.[120] The effects of growth management policies on housing prices in Oregon have been much studied, with several studies finding an insignificant or only a slight connection between the UGB and decreased housing affordability.[121]

Metro, an elected regional government comprising 25 cities and three counties in the Portland (Oregon) area, manages the Portland-area Urban Growth Boundary (UGB) and is subject to LCDC review for compliance with statewide planning goals.[122] Metro's Regional Framework Plan (RFP) contains the regional government's land-use planning polices and requirements. Under the RFP, local jurisdictions are encouraged to meet voluntary affordable housing production goals, and are also encouraged to adopt a number of specific tools and strategies to promote affordable housing.[123] Metro tracks the development of new

---

on Paul G. Lewis's "Can State Review of Local Planning Increase Housing Production?" 16 Hous. Pol'y Debate 201, 207 (2005).

117. Or. Stat. Ann. § 197.303, .307, .480 (2019).

118. *Id.* § 197.312.

119. *See* Michael Andersen, *Portland Just Passed the Best Low-Density Zoning Reform in US History*, Sightline Institute (Aug. 11, 2020, 3:01 PM), https://www.sightline.org/2020/08/11/on-wednesday-portland-will-pass-the-best-low-density-zoning-reform-in-us-history/ (reporting Portland's new rules to allow four homes on most lots or up to six homes for price-regulated projects).

120. Or. Admin. Rule § 660-007-0000 to -0060.

121. A study of urban growth boundaries found negative effects with regard to race and class gentrification. Jesse Simpson et al., Gentrification as Urban Strategy: Evaluating Inequity & Portland's Urban Growth Boundary 20 (Apr. 2016), https://jimproctor.us/archive/envsalums/jessesimpson/wp-content/uploads/sites/97/2016/04/GentrificationUGB-2.pdf ("This gentrification has amounted to massive, continual displacement with racial and class implications . . . minorities, such as many residents of Northeast Portland communities, are likely to pay the steepest costs for its existence."). *But see* Shishir Mathir, *Impact of Urban Growth Boundary on Housing and Land Prices: Evidence from King County, Washington*, 29 House. Studs. 128, 130 (2014) (finding that although a UGB very likely increases land prices, its impact on housing prices varies, e.g., government policies that enable greater housing supply can offset those land supply constraints. A UGB that is part of a comprehensive growth management program may not increase housing prices.).

122. Or. Rev. Stat. § 197.274 (2019).

123. Jurisdictions should consider such strategies as density bonuses, replacement housing, voluntary inclusionary zoning, and transfers of development rights. Jurisdictions should also adopt affordable housing policies that address the needs of the elderly and disabled, eliminate local regulatory constraints to providing affordable housing, and ensure parking requirements do not interfere with the provision of affordable housing. Metro Regional Framework Plan, Land Use, ch. 1.3.4 (Mar. 2015). *See also* Urban Growth Management Functional Plan, 3.07.710-760 (Apr. 2018) (implementing the Regional Framework Plan). For more information on several of those techniques, see Chapters 4, 5, 6, and 11.

affordable housing and maintains a Regional Inventory of Regulated Affordable Rental Housing.[124] Metro also has a Transit-Oriented Development Program that incentivizes affordable housing near transit opportunities.[125] Additionally, Oregon largely eliminated single-family zoning, allowing duplexes and similar accessory units to be built in areas traditionally zoned for single-family use only.[126]

A 2006 study found few jurisdictions had adopted the voluntary affordable housing production goals due to barriers such as lack of funding and a perception that compliance with other extensive Metro planning goals creates sufficient opportunities for affordable housing production.[127] In 2016, Oregon lawmakers addressed the state's "increasingly urgent need for affordable housing"[128] by enacting a bill that lifted the 17-year ban on mandatory inclusionary zoning and requires a certain number of affordable housing units in larger new developments in exchange for incentives.[129]

Metro's experience with voluntary goals shares *some* similarity with that of the Metropolitan Council, an appointed regional planning authority in the Minneapolis–St. Paul region in Minnesota. Local governments may voluntarily participate in an incentives-based program for the production of affordable housing through the Livable Communities Act (LCA),[130] which allows local governments to negotiate affordable housing goals with the Metropolitan Council to become eligible for certain loans and grants.[131] Critics argue that under the LCA, affordable housing production falls far below actual regional

---

124. *Regional Inventory of Regulated Affordable Housing*, METRO (Jan. 2019), https://www .oregonmetro.gov/regional-inventory-regulated-affordable-housing.

125. *2019 Annual Report: Transit-Oriented Development Program*, METRO (May 2019), https:// www.oregonmetro.gov/sites/default/files/2020/05/05/Annual%20report%202019_1.9.2020.pdf.

126. Laurel Wamsley, *Oregon Legislature Votes to Essentially Ban Single-Family Zoning*, NPR (July 1, 2019, 7:03 PM), https://www.npr.org/2019/07/01/737798440/oregon-legislature-votes-to -essentially-ban-single-family-zoning.

127. REGIONAL HOUSING CHOICE IMPLEMENTATION STRATEGY, RECOMMENDATION OF THE HOUSING CHOICE TASK FORCE ACCEPTED BY THE METRO COUNCIL 26 (Mar. 2006). The Housing Choice Task Force made several recommendations to Metro to improve planning for affordable housing, including integrating affordable housing into all Metro housing and policy decisions, creating a Housing Choice Advisory Committee, developing a permanent source of regional affordable housing financing, removing regulatory barriers, and providing technical assistance to local governments. REGIONAL HOUSING CHOICE IMPLEMENTATION STRATEGY, RECOMMENDATION OF THE HOUSING CHOICE TASK FORCE ACCEPTED BY THE METRO COUNCIL 7–8 (Mar. 2006). *See also* Tej Kumar Karki, *Mandatory versus Incentive-Based State Zoning Reform Policies for Affordable Housing in the United States: A Comparative Assessment*, HOUSING POLICY DEBATE (2015) ("Lack of incentives play an important role in the prevalence of noncompliance with state mandates, public resentment toward the mandates, and minimal achievements in housing production.").

128. Staff Measure Summary, Feb. 10, 2016, 2016 Legis. Bill Hist. OR S.B. 1533.

129. S.B. 1533, 78th Leg. Assemb., Reg. Sess. (Or. 2016).

130. MINN. STAT. ANN. § 473.25–.255 (2019).

131. Critics argue incentives to local governments to plan and develop affordable housing should be increased. On the stick side, local governments should "punish localities that fail to adopt policies that aid the development of affordable housing (e.g., setting housing densities below minimum standards)." MYRON ORFIELD & THOMAS F. LUCE, JR., REGION: PLANNING THE FUTURE OF THE TWIN CITIES 82 (2010). *See, e.g.,* Laura Bliss, *California's New Governor Would Punish Cities over Affordable Housing*, BLOOMBERG CITYLAB (Jan. 11, 2019, 3:36 PM), https://www.bloomberg.com /news/articles/2019-01-11/california-s-new-plan-to-enforce-affordable-housing (Governor Gavin Newsom sought to encourage local governments to produce more housing by offering increased

needs because local participation is merely voluntary.[132] The Metropolitan Council experience suggests that when local governments are not required to consider the full amount of regional fair share affordable housing needs, they will not do so on their own.

Florida offers a cautionary lesson for advocates of affordable housing in a growth management regime. In 2011, the legislature substantially rewrote the state planning laws to significantly reduce state involvement in the approval of local comprehensive plans. Prior to 2011, a state agency, the Department of Community Affairs, reviewed local comprehensive plans for compliance with the state plan and provided affordable housing data to local jurisdictions. In response to a perception that the DCA overreached in its review of local plans, limiting development and making it more expensive, the DCA was reduced and reorganized under another state agency.[133] The state agency no longer reviews local plans, except in limited circumstances.[134] Individuals may challenge a local plan's compliance with the statute, but the standard of review is a "fairly debatable standard and the state agency is not permitted to intervene.[135]

Rare among the states, Florida has a large, dedicated revenue source in the State Housing Initiatives Partnership (SHIP) program to promote the fulfillment of affordable housing needs.[136] Planning requirements under Florida's statute and the concomitant identification of affordable housing needs helped to support the creation of the SHIP program.[137] The SHIP program complements and strengthens the statutory housing element requirements because it requires local governments seeking funding under the program to provide a

---

funding to municipalities that complied with housing requirements and withholding state tax dollars from those that fell short.).

132. *See* Myron Orfield & Will Stancil, *Why Are the Twin Cities So Segregated?*, 43 MITCHELL HAMLINE L. REV. 1, 39 (2017) (arguing the LCA "created little additional pressure for cities to integrate" because it conditioned no preexisting funding on their compliance); ORFIELD & LUCE, JR., *supra* note 131, at 58 (arguing the LCA suffers from too many political concessions, local government voluntary participation, and affordable housing benchmarks that are not based on regional need); Edward G. Goetz, *Fair Share or Status Quo? The Twin Cities' Livable Communities Act*, 20 J. PLAN. EDUC. & RES. 37 (2000); Edward G. Goetz et al., *The Minnesota Land Use Planning Act and the Promotion of Low- and Moderate-Income Housing in Suburbia*, 22 LAW & INEQ. 31 (2004); Alliance for Metro. Stability v. Metro. Council, 671 N.W.2d 905 (2003) (rejecting a challenge to LCA's negotiated planning goals).

133. Nancy Stroud, *A History and New Turns in Florida's New Growth*, 45 J. MARSHALL L. REV. 397, 409–15 (2012).

134. FLA. STAT. § 163.3184 (2019).

135. *Id.*

136. *Id.* § 420.907–.9089. SHIP comprises the local portion of the William E. Sadowski Affordable Housing Act, which splits revenue generated from a real estate transfer tax between a state and local housing trust fund. Between 1992 and 2007, Florida appropriated more than $1.7 billion to the SHIP program, assisting more than 145,000 households. THE AFFORDABLE HOUSING STUDY COMMISSION FINAL REPORT 2007 FLORIDA, at 5. SHIP provides money for affordable housing production and planning "to further the housing element of the local government comprehensive plan specific to affordable housing." FLA. STAT. § 420.9072 (2019). Funding levels are based on population size and are not competitive. For more information about Florida affordable housing planning, *see* 1000 FRIENDS OF FLORIDA, *Creating Inclusive Communities in Florida* (2005), https://1000fof.org/wp-content/themes/Divi-child/formpop/form-pop.php?q=creating_inclusive_communities_in_florida.

137. THE AFFORDABLE HOUSING STUDY COMMISSION FINAL REPORT 2007 FLORIDA, at 11 (describing a coalition of housing stakeholders supporting the creation of a dedicated funding source for affordable housing).

more detailed Local Housing Assistance Plan to receive SHIP funding,[138] and because it requires local governments to review the effectiveness of their affordable housing incentives annually.[139] However, SHIP funds have been vulnerable to raiding by the legislature to cover other state budget shortfalls.

Reviews of Florida's affordable housing scheme are mixed. A 2014 study found the housing element mandate[140] "put the issue of affordable housing in front of local officials, forced public discussion, and educated stakeholders on the tools available to encourage affordable housing."[141] But public subsidies are still required to build affordable housing and planning does not guarantee the housing will be built.[142] Calls for greater state involvement in the creation and enforcement of local affordable housing provisions were largely thwarted by the 2011 statutory amendments.[143]

Growth management does not have to limit affordable housing. The challenge for affordable housing supporters is to ensure growth management laws incorporate sufficient and appropriate measures to provide for needed affordable housing development. The devil is truly in the details.

IV. ENVIRONMENTAL PLANNING AND REVIEW OF AFFORDABLE HOUSING DEVELOPMENT

This section will address how environmental planning and review affects affordable housing development.[144] Since the early 1970s, federal, state, and local governments have adopted a wide variety of environmental regulations affecting housing development, many of which interrelate and sometimes overlap. At the federal level, primary examples

---

138. FLA. STAT. § 420.9072(2)(a) (2019) (specifying that eligibility for funding requires the submission of a Local Housing Assistance Plan) and *id.* § 420.9075(1)(a) (specifying contents of the Local Housing Assistance Plan). The SHIP program also requires recipients to engage in regulatory reform by adopting "local housing incentive strategies," e.g., permit streamlining procedures. *Id.* § 420.9072(2)(a)(2).

139. Local governments must create an Affordable Housing Advisory Committee, which reviews local policies and laws annually. *Id.* § 420.9076.

140. A local government must prepare a housing element that includes "principles, guidelines, standards, and strategies to be followed in . . . [t]he provision of housing for all current and anticipated future residents of the jurisdiction." The housing element must also include "adequate sites for future housing, including affordable workforce housing." *Id.* § 163.3177.

141. Andrew Aurand, *Florida's Planning Requirements and Affordability for Low-Income Households,* 29 HOUSING STUDIES 677, 694 (2014).

142. *Id.* at 695.

143. *See, e.g.,* Jerry Anthony, *The Effects of Florida's Growth Management Act on Housing Affordability,* 69 J. AM. PLANNING ASS'N 282, 288–91 (2003) (finding the statute's housing element requirements lack specificity, the DCA has not strongly enforced housing element provisions concerning affordable housing, and housing affordability has decreased); Marc T. Smith & Ruth L. Steiner, *Affordable Housing as an Adequate Public Facility,* 36 VAL. U. L. REV. 443 (2002) (discussing enforcement of affordable housing provisions in states' housing elements and proposing that affordable housing be required under concurrency standard in Florida's growth management statute); Charles E. Connerly & Marc Smith, *Developing a Fair Share Housing Policy for Florida,* 12 J. LAND USE & ENVTL. L. 63 (1996) (calling for Florida to adopt a "fair share" regime).

144. *See also* JUERGENSMEYER & ROBERTS, *supra* note 1, at 590–646; DANIEL R. MANDELKER, NEPA LAW AND LITIGATION (2d. ed. 2020); LINDA A. MALONE, ENVIRONMENTAL REGULATION OF LAND USE (Oct. 20 Update).

include the National Environmental Policy Act (NEPA),[145] the Clean Air Act,[146] the Clean Water Act,[147] laws regulating hazardous waste,[148] the Endangered Species Act,[149] and laws protecting wetlands.[150]

States have enacted their own versions of NEPA,[151] coastal management acts,[152] laws protecting wetlands,[153] laws regulating floodplains,[154] and laws protecting agricultural lands.[155] States have increasingly incorporated environmental elements into statutory planning requirements for local jurisdictions.[156] Some of these laws mandate planning to protect the natural environment. Others provide for reviews and discretionary approvals of land development proposals that might affect the natural environment.[157] In addition, global warming concerns have prompted new regulatory responses at the state and local level that also impact housing.[158] States and local governments have been assertive in pursuing regulatory efforts to combat climate change, with more than 30 states setting renewable energy goals.[159]

---

145. 42 U.S.C. §§ 4321–4370(f).

146. 42 U.S.C.A. §§ 7401–7431.

147. 33 U.S.C.A. §§ 1251–1275. Among other requirements, developers must typically comply with storm water permitting requirements under the National Pollutant Discharge Elimination System (NPDES) to control runoff from construction activities. 40 C.F.R. § 122.26.

148. Resource Conservation and Recovery Act (RCRA) (42 U.S.C.A. §§ 6901–6908(a)) and the Comprehensive Environmental Response, Compensation, and Liability Act of 1980 (CERCLA) (42 U.S.C.A. §§ 9601–9628).

149. 33 U.S.C. §§ 1251–1378. *See* Brian J. Perron, *Just Another Goldfish Down the Toilet? The Fate of Pacific Salmon after Alsea Valley and the De Facto Rescission of the 4(D) Rule*, 33 Envtl. L. 547 (2003) (considering possible effects of salmon protection measures on affordable housing).

150. *See, e.g.*, section 404 of the Clean Water Act, 33 U.S.C. § 1344.

151. *See, e.g.*, the State Environmental Quality Review Act in New York, N.Y. Comp. Codes R. & Regs. tit. 6 § 617.1(c).

152. *See, e.g.*, Fla. Stat. § 373.403–.463 (2019), La. Rev. Stat. § 49:214.21–.42 (2019), Md. Envir. Code § 5-901 to -911 (2018), N.J. Rev. Stat. § 13:9B-1 to -30 (2019).

153. *See, e.g.*, Del. Code Ann. tit. 7, §§ 6601–6620 (2019); Md. Envir. Code § 16-101 to -107 (2018); N.J. Rev. Stat. § 13:13A-1 to -15 (2019).

154. *See, e.g.*, Ala. Code § 11-19-1 to -24 (2019); Minn. Stat. Ann. § 103F.101–.151 (2019); Pa. Stat. Ann. tit. 32, § 679.101–.601 (West 2018).

155. *See, e.g.*, Ill. Comp. Stat. Ann. § 5/5-12001 (2019).

156. *See, e.g.*, Cal. Gov't Code § 65302(d) (2019) and Fla. Stat. Ann. § 163.3177(6)(d) (2019) (conservation elements). *See also* Md. Nat. Res. Code § 8-1801 (West 2019) and Fla. Stat. § 380.05 (West 2019) (areas of critical state concern).

157. In addition, some funding programs link environmental protection or improvement with new development, e.g., HUD's Brownfield Economic Development Initiative discussed in Chapter 8.

158. *See generally* Robert H. Freilich & Neil M. Popowitz, *The Umbrella of Sustainability: Smart Growth, New Urbanism, Renewable Energy and Green Development in the 21st Century*, 42 Urb. Law. 1 (2010); Matthew J. Parlow, *Healthy Zoning*, 44 Fordham Urb. L.J. 33, 46–47 (2017).

159. *State Renewable Portfolio Standards and Goals*, National Conference of State Legislatures, Apr. 17, 2020 (https://www.ncsl.org/research/energy/renewable-portfolio-standards. aspx). *See also* Dan Farber, *Continuity and Transformation in Environmental Regulation*, 10 Ariz. J. Envtl. L. & Pol'y 1, 2 (2019); Elise Hansen, *Policy Trends for Construction Attys to Watch in 2020*, Law360 (Jan. 1, 2020) ("The fight [against] climate change is really starting at the municipal level as far as incorporating energy efficiency and sustainable practices into local construction codes and ordinances.").

Environmental laws can have five primary effects on affordable housing development.[160] First, such laws will inevitably increase the costs and complexity of affordable housing development in the same ways they do for any type of residential development. An environmental impact statement under NEPA requires a detailed statement on the environmental impact of an action, consideration of alternatives, and possible mitigation measures.[161] NEPA reviews are triggered by federal actions that have a significant impact on the environment, which include not only actions taken by the federal government itself but also projects for which the federal government provides funding or a permit.[162] The environmental impact statement process is designed to encourage agencies to consider the environmental effects of their actions and reach more informed decisions through the consideration of alternatives and mitigation measures.[163]

The average EIS is more than 600 pages long and takes four and a half years to complete.[164] This preparation can be costly, with delays in starting construction on public projects costing the nation an estimated $3.9 trillion.[165] To address these inefficiencies, the Council on Environmental Quality issued new NEPA regulations, which came into effect on September 14, 2020, and marked the first significant changes to the regulations since they were promulgated in 1978.[166] The new rules limit each EIS to 150 pages (or 300 pages for proposals of unusual scope or complexity) and give federal agencies two years to complete them from the date the notice of intent is issued.[167]

Affordable housing developers may encounter state environmental protection statutes (sometimes called SEPAs) that create similar requirements as those under NEPA.[168] SEPAs generally require an initial preliminary assessment of the environmental impact of a project, and state statutes impose this environmental review on state and local government projects, the approval of comprehensive plans, and, in some states, private developments.[169]

---

160. Other environmental laws, for example, lead abatement laws, may have a significant financial impact on preserving affordable housing. Chapter 9 discusses a lead abatement program. Chapter 15 covers preservation of affordable housing.

161. 42 U.S.C. § 4332 (2018). In most cases, developers seek a "negative declaration," which ends the process without the necessity of preparing a full environmental impact statement.

162. MANDELKER, NEPA LAW, *supra* note 144, at § 1:1. The new NEPA regulations include a list of exclusions to "major Federal actions," thus narrowing the scope of required environmental review. 40 C.F.R. § 1508.1.

163. NEPA does not provide substantive standards, unlike other federal environmental statutes. Instead, NEPA's strength is in its procedural requirements. *See, e.g.*, Strycker's Bay Neighborhood Council Inc. v. Karlen, 444 U.S. 223 (1980).

164. 85 Fed. Reg. 43304 (July 16, 2020).

165. *Id.*

166. *Id.*

167. 40 C.F.R. §§ 1502.7, 1501.10.

168. In interpreting state environmental statutes, some state courts look to NEPA cases for persuasive authority. *See, e.g.*, Washoe Meadows Cmty. v. Dep't of Parks & Recreation, 225 Cal. Rptr. 3d 238, 248 (2017).

169. Washington requires a SEPA review of comprehensive plans. *See* WASH. ADMIN. CODE § 365-196-620 (2019). *See also* Matter of Adirondack Wild: Friends of the Forest Pres. v. N.Y. State Dep't of Envtl. Conservation, 116 N.Y.S.3d 535, 538 (Sup. Ct. 2019) (applying New York environmental law, SEQRA, to the implementation of a unit management plan); Small Prop. Owners of S.F. Inst. v. City & Cty. of S.F., 231 Cal. Rptr. 3d 225, 229 (2018) (applying CEQA to an ordinance); Friends of Mammoth v. Board of Supervisors of Mono County, 502 P.2d 1049 (Cal. 1974) (applying

State and local governments have also begun to enact green building requirements.[170] The benefits of green building—sustainability, energy conservation, pollution reduction, and health benefits—can be, of course, beneficial to affordable housing communities and residents.[171] At the same time, these green building requirements may impact affordable housing production. While some jurisdictions employ a carrot approach to combine incentives for affordable housing and green building,[172] other green requirements condition development approvals or financing on complying with green building requirements.[173] While compliance with these standards necessarily leads to higher development costs,[174] there is some evidence that affordable housing developments can accrue energy cost savings that

---

California Environmental Quality Act (CEQA) to a conditional use permit for a private development project); Save a Neighborhood Env't (SANE) v. City of Seattle, 676 P.2d 1006 (1984) (applying Washington's law to the approval of a low-income elderly apartment complex).

170. Washington state requires state Housing Trust Fund projects to satisfy an Evergreen Sustainable Development Standard. Wash. Rev. Code § 39.35D.080 (2019). The U.S. Green Building Council estimates 45 states, including 442 localities, have green building initiatives, including legislation, executive orders, resolutions, ordinances, policies and incentives. *See* USGBC Northern California Information, USGBC (last visited Oct. 29, 2020), https://www.usgbc.org/resources/usgbc-northern-california-information; Sarah Stanley, *LEED Reaches New Milestone, Surpasses 100,000 Commercial Green Building Projects*, USGBC (Nov. 7, 2019), https://www.usgbc.org/articles/leed-reaches-new-milestone-surpasses-100000-commercial-green-building-projects. For example, San Francisco requires new construction to meet green building requirements. City and County of San Francisco, Dep't of Bldg. Inspection, Admin. Bull. No. AB-093, Implementation of Green Building Regulations (2020), https://sfdbi.org/sites/default/files/AB-093.pdf. For further discussion of local-level green building requirements, *see* Katrina M. Wyman & Danielle Spiegel-Feld, *The Urban Environmental Renaissance*, 108 Calif. L. Rev. 305 (2020); Sarah B. Schindler, *Following Industry's LEED®: Municipal Adoption of Private Green Building Standards*, 62 U. Fla. L. Rev. 285 (2010); Sara C. Bronin, *The Quiet Revolution Revived: Sustainable Design, Land Use Regulation, and the States*, 93 Minn. L. Rev. 231 (2008).

171. *See, e.g.*, Alex Trachtenberg et al., *The Impact of Green Affordable Housing*, Southface & the Virginia Center for Housing Research (Jan. 2016), https://4553qr1wvuj43kndml31ma60-wpengine.netdna-ssl.com/wp-content/uploads/2016/07/impact-of-green-affordable-housing-report-1.pdf.

172. *See, e.g.*, Seattle, Wash., Land Use Code § 23.49.011 (2020) (granting a floor-area ratio exemption to any addition of a parking floor area if it is developed to LEED Gold standards).

173. *See, e.g.*, San Francisco, Cal., Building Code ch. 3 (2019) (requiring LEED or other green building practices).

174. By one estimate, the most basic green requirements add two percent to development costs. Carmen Hertas-Noble et al., *The Greening of Community Economic Development: Dispatches from New York City*, 31 W. New. Eng. L. Rev. 645, 661 (2009). The LEED application process is costly and time-consuming, and developers must employ LEED-accredited design professionals, which adds to the cost. *Id.* at 663.

Compliance with green requirements can also be challenging for affordable housing developers in other ways. The Local Initiatives Support Coalition (LISC) identified barriers to implementing energy efficiency in affordable housing: (1) scarce financial resources; (2) staffing challenges (overburdened, untrained, and frequent turnover); (3) layered bureaucratic processes; (4) split incentives caused by tenants paying utilities and owners paying for capital cost of energy upgrades; (5) time lines of budget cycles that are long and subject to multiple regulatory review; (6) distrust of utility and third-part programs; (7) lack of reliable contractors; and (8) challenges in obtaining tenant information and access to tenant's units to check efficacy of installed measures. LISC Bay Area, Energy & Affordable Housing in California: Lessons Learned from the Field 21–22 (2006).

exceed the initial cost of compliance.[175] The federal government offers tax credits, grants, and loans to help offset the costs of implementing renewable energy technologies.[176]

Second, opponents of affordable housing motivated by non-environmental concerns can use these laws to block, delay, change, and increase the costs of affordable housing developments by claiming such proposals will cause environmental harms. Established communities sometimes raise environmental issues to oppose affordable housing as infill development.[177] Emphasis on historic preservation and other aesthetic factors have also been used to impede affordable housing goals.[178] Additionally, opponents of affordable housing have used these laws to promote other agendas. For example, there is evidence that enforcement of CEQA is often "aimed at promoting the economic agendas of competitors and labor union leaders, or the discriminatory 'Not In My Backyard' (NIMBY) agendas of those seeking to exclude housing, park, and school projects that would diversify communities by serving members of other races and economic classes."[179]

Third, some environmental planning laws and funding programs, such as the promotion of infill development on brownfields, may advance affordable housing because they make more land available for affordable housing development, facilitate the location of jobs near urban housing areas providing wage opportunities,[180] or assist in the mitigation of potential environmental harms so developments can be approved.[181] The possibility of building affordable housing on infill sites formerly occupied by uses like gas stations and dry cleaners has led to states enacting brownfields legislation. State statutes specify standards for remediation of the contamination and immunize developers from future

---

175. DANA L. BOURLAND, INCREMENTAL COST, MEASURABLE SAVINGS: ENTERPRISE GREEN COMMUNITIES CRITERIA 4 (2010). ("In summary, estimated lifetime savings exceed the initial costs of incorporating the Enterprise Green Communities Criteria into affordable housing."). *See also* Kevin Kampschroer, *Benefits of Green Buildings on Costs, the Environment and Jobs*, U.S. GENERAL SERVICES ADMINISTRATION (July 16, 2009), https://www.gsa.gov/about-us/newsroom /congressional-testimony/benefits-of-green-buildings-on-costs-the-environment-and-jobs.

176. *Renewable Energy Explained*, U.S. ENERGY INFORMATION ADMINISTRATION (last updated June 22, 2020), https://www.eia.gov/energyexplained/renewable-sources/.

177. *See, e.g.*, Bowman v. City of Berkeley, 18 Cal. Rptr. 3d 814 (2004) (rejecting opponents' CEQA challenges to approval of a prototypical example of mixed-use, infill affordable housing development).

178. Sarah Fox, *Environmental Gentrification*, 90 U. COLO. L. REV. 803, 844 (2019).

179. Jennifer Hernandez, *California Environmental Quality Act Lawsuits and California's Housing Crisis*, 24 HASTINGS ENVTL. L.J. 21, 22 (2018).

180. Luis Inaraja Vera, *Assessing the Performance of Voluntary Environmental Programs*, 2020 UTAH L. REV. 795, 836 (2020) (citing New York City programs aimed at providing an alternative for brownfields that bring in new businesses, jobs, affordable housing, and open space). *See also* Richard P. Voith & David L. Crawford, *Smart Growth and Affordable Housing, in* GROWTH MANAGEMENT AND AFFORDABLE HOUSING 82, 97–98, (2004) (citing examples of successful brownfields redevelopment). *See also* Ira Whitman, *Overcoming Environmental Constraints to Redevelopment, in* REDEVELOPMENT: PLANNING, LAW, AND PROJECT IMPLEMENTATION 175 (Brian Blaesser & Thomas Cody eds., 2008) (explaining the process of redeveloping property with environmental issues).

181. *See, e.g.*, Reed D. Rubinstein, *Developing Affordable Housing on Brownfields: Implementing the "Joseph Paradigm,"* 13 J. AFFORDABLE HOUS. & CMTY. DEV. L. 364 (2004) (noting brownfield redevelopment for affordable housing use poses risks and potential inefficiencies, and providing a checklist to mitigate risks).

environmental action under state law.[182] Some state statutes also assist in the development of affordable housing by providing financial incentives to developers building on land burdened by contamination.

Some states have included provisions in their environmental laws that favor affordable housing, or at least blunt the law's effects on affordable housing development. For example, California's law governing the state's coastal zone regulates the conversion or demolition of low- and moderate-income housing in the state's coastal zone by providing for replacement housing to be constructed in most instances and requiring the inclusion of affordable housing in new developments in that area.[183] In Washington, "minor new construction," including multifamily residential properties with up to 60 units in fully planning GMA counties, is exempt from the State Environmental Policy Act's threshold determinations and the EIS requirement.[184]

The fourth primary effect of environmental law on affordable housing development is that where environmental planning and review requirements apply, the presence of certain environmental problems will discourage funders—particularly private lenders—from funding a development or may result in onerous environmental representations and warranties for a developer.

A fifth issue, and a more recent regulatory concern, involves regulations addressing climate change concerns. In 2008, California became one of the first states to pass global-warming legislation affecting transportation and land-use planning with the passage of the Sustainable Communities and Climate Protection Act.[185] In addition to amending the housing element statute,[186] this legislation directs a state agency (the Air Board) to set regional greenhouse gas emissions targets and requires each metropolitan planning region to prepare a "sustainable community strategy" based on these targets.[187] Establishing these regional targets is complicated, and a Regional Targets Advisory Committee comprising

182. *See, e.g.*, U.S. ENVIRONMENTAL PROTECTION AGENCY, STATE BROWNFIELDS AND VOLUNTARY RESPONSE PROGRAMS: AN UPDATE FROM THE STATES (2017) (providing a state-by-state reference guide), https://www.epa.gov/sites/production/files/2017-12/documents/state_brownfields_voluntary_response_program_report_508_11-2017_web.pdf (last visited Oct. 30, 2020).

183. CAL. GOV. CODE § 65590–.1 (West 2019). *See also* CAL. PUB. RES. CODE §§ 30000–30013 (West 2019). Density bonuses, modifications of zoning and subdivision restrictions, expedited permit reviews, and waivers of fees are also available.

184. WASH. ADMIN. CODE § 197-11-800(1)(d) (2019). *See also* Josh Cohen, *State Environmental Law Slowed Housing Construction in Seattle. Lawmakers Want to Pick Up the Pace*, CROSSCUT (Jan. 7, 2020), https://crosscut.com/2020/01/state-environmental-law-slowed-housing-construction-seattle-lawmakers-want-pick-pace (reporting that Seattle City Council raised the threshold for mandatory environmental review for buildings in Seattle's urban centers to 200 units).

185. S.B. 375 is codified in scattered sections of the CAL. GOV'T CODE and the CAL. PUB. RES. CODE. This legislation comes on the heels of the California Global Warming Solutions Act of 2006 (A.B. 32), CAL. HEALTH & SAFETY CODE §§ 38500–38599 (2019).

186. These amendments are discussed *supra* Section II.B, § 65588(b).

187. CAL. GOV'T CODE § 65080(b)(2) (West 2010). S.B. 375 itself does not require communities to comply with these plans. State housing element laws remain the stick to get localities to comply with planning requirements.

stakeholders, including affordable housing advocates, will offer advice that the Air Board must consider.[188]

The Sustainable Communities and Climate Protection Act affects housing planning and policy in California in three main ways: (1) it requires the metropolitan planning agencies to develop a Sustainable Communities Strategy (SCS) for accommodating projected growth while reducing vehicle miles traveled and greenhouse gas emissions; (2) it encourages local jurisdictions to plan for housing development consistent with the SCS; and (3) it streamlines the CEQA review process for development projects consistent with SCS.[189] So far, the act has generally resulted in a greater Regional Housing Needs Assessment toward urban jurisdictions with good job accessibility, but local jurisdictions remain resistant to approving projects in compliance with the housing planning process.[190] This resistance can be attributed to such factors as NIMBY[191] and a lack of incentives and enforcement mechanisms to effect plans.[192]

Incorporating housing development with transportation and air quality goals has the potential to benefit affordable housing goals by encouraging affordable housing development near transportation and employment nodes. This form of development also lowers transportation costs for affected households. The challenge for affordable housing supporters is to effectively include affordable housing considerations within the methodology for setting emissions and other environmental targets. Done correctly, affordable housing supporters can lower transportation costs for affected households, minimize the effects of rising housing prices associated with potentially smaller development footprints, and minimize the displacement of lower-income families due to gentrification.[193]

V. FEDERAL HOUSING PLANNING REQUIREMENTS THAT AFFECT AFFORDABLE HOUSING

States and many local jurisdictions rely on certain federal funding programs, such as Community Development Block Grants (CDBG), HOME Investment Partnership funds, Emergency Shelter Grants (ESG), Housing Opportunities for Persons with AIDS (HOPWA), and the national Housing Trust Fund (HTF), to bridge the funding gap for making affordable housing development economically feasible.[194] The Consolidated Plan (ConPlan),

---

188. *Id.* § 65080(b)(2)(A)(i). Projects consistent with the sustainable community strategy (SCS) will be exempted from some CEQA reviews. *See also* Adam Livingston, *Sustainable Communities Strategies & Conservation*, THE NATURE CONSERVANCY (2016), http://www.southernsierrapartnership.org/uploads/2/3/7/6/23766303/sustainable_communities_strategies_and_conservation__2016__-_final.pdf.

189. SARAH MAWHORTER ET AL., TERNER CENTER, CALIFORNIA'S SB 375 AND THE PURSUIT OF SUSTAINABLE AND AFFORDABLE DEVELOPMENT 5 (2018).

190. *Id.* at 11.

191. Symposium, *Promises Still to Keep: The Fair Housing Act Fifty Years Later*, 40 CARDOZO L. REV. 1207, 1229–30 (2019).

192. Andrea J. Boyack, *Responsible Devolution of Affordable Housing*, 46 FORDHAM URB. L.J. 1183 (2019).

193. If gentrification occurs, the displacement of lower-income families would lead to an increase in vehicle miles traveled (VMTs), which would negatively affect emissions. Here, environmental and housing planning interests converge.

194. See Chapter 9 for a discussion of these programs.

first authorized under the Cranston–Gonzalez National Affordable Housing Act of 1990, mandates certain planning activities and related certifications by recipients of federal funding under these and other programs.[195]

A. Consolidated Plan

In 1995, HUD centralized into one document, the ConPlan, the planning, application, and reporting requirements of several federal planning and funding programs mentioned *supra*.[196] The centralization of this process into one document reflects the hope that states, large cities, and urban counties will engage in better planning efforts if they are required to integrate their comprehensive planning with the more specific priorities of federal funding.[197]

In this five-year planning document, jurisdictions must assess their affordable housing needs (including homelessness) by analyzing the local housing market, identifying general barriers to affordable housing development, developing strategies for creating more affordable housing, and proposing means to monitor short- and long-term compliance in achieving affordable housing goals.[198] The ConPlan also requires local governments to

---

195. Cranston-Gonzalez Act, 42 U.S.C. § 12701.

196. 24 C.F.R. § 91.2(a). The Consolidated Plan continues the planning process required under the Comprehensive Housing Affordability Strategy, or CHAS. The Consolidated Plan regulations list another seventeen federal programs that require either that a recipient jurisdiction has an approved Consolidated Plan or the application for funding under those programs contain a certification of consistency with the Consolidated Plan. 24 C.F.R. § 91.2(b)(1)–(17). The requirement of consistency with a Consolidated Plan may help housing advocates in lawsuits alleging the implementation of a particular funding program is inconsistent with the goals and strategies articulated in the Consolidated Plan.

197. States, local governments, or consortia of local governments can apply for funding under the Consolidated Plan. For more information on effectively using the Consolidated Plan for the benefit of low-income communities, *see* National Low Income Advocacy Coalition, 2020 Advocates' Guide to Housing & Community Development Policy 376–82 (2020) on the National Low-Income Housing Coalition website at https://nlihc.org/explore-issues/publications-research/advocates-guide (last visited Sept. 5, 2020); Ed Gramlich, HUD's Consolidated Plan: An Action Guide for Involving Low-Income Communities 1998; Ed Gramlich, *Consolidated Plan and Community Development Block Grant Advocacy*, 32 Clearinghouse Rev. 173 (1998); Piecing It All Together in Your Community: Playing the Housing Game: Learning to Use HUD's Consolidated Plan to Expand Housing Opportunities for People with Disabilities, Technical Assistance Collaborative, Inc., Boston, Mass., Dec. 1999. For general information on the Consolidated Plan, including suggestions for improvement, *see* Margery Austin Turner, et al., Planning to Meet Local Housing Needs: The Role of HUD's Consolidated Planning Requirements in the 1990s (2002).

198. 24 C.F.R. § 91.205, .210 (local governments); 24 C.F.R. § 91.305, 24 C.F.R. § 91.310 (states). In assessing barriers to affordable housing, jurisdictions "must explain whether the cost of housing or the incentives to develop, maintain, or improve affordable housing in the jurisdiction are affected by public policies, particularly by policies of the jurisdiction, including tax policies affecting land and other property, land use controls, zoning ordinances, building codes, fees and charges, growth limits, and policies that affect the return on residential investment." 24 C.F.R. § 91.210(e) (local governments). States have a similar requirement under 24 C.F.R. § 91.310(d).

develop a strategic plan and an action plan to implement affordable housing assessments and analyses.[199]

The ConPlan process directs local jurisdictions to assess their local affordable housing needs and to participate in directing housing development toward the needs of low-income communities.[200] This opportunity may be particularly useful for housing advocates in communities where state statutes do not require the inclusion of a detailed housing element as part of the local community's planning process.[201] The ConPlan requires communities to develop a written plan to encourage effective citizen participation in its preparation.[202] HUD regulations specifically encourage the participation of a broad range of people most affected by the application of the ConPlan, including traditionally excluded minority populations, such as non-English-speaking persons and persons with disabilities.[203]

The Cranston–Gonzalez National Affordable Housing Act,[204] the Housing and Community Development Act of 1974 (CDBG),[205] and accompanying regulations[206] provide the bases for enforcement of the Consolidated Plan requirements by HUD and private parties. HUD reviews each ConPlan for compliance with statutory and regulatory requirements.[207] HUD has a duty to withhold funds if the ConPlan or housing strategy is inconsistent with the law or incomplete.[208] Once a plan is approved, a jurisdiction must submit an annual performance report to HUD for evaluation.[209]

Housing advocates can encourage HUD review of local ConPlans by filing written complaints of the plan with the local jurisdiction.[210] Advocates can seek judicial review

---

199. 24 C.F.R. §91.215 (strategic plan); 24 C.F.R. §91.220 (action plan). States have a similar requirement under 24 C.F.R. §91.315, .320. The action plan must also include affordable housing one-year goals by household characteristics and by housing characteristics. 24 C.F.R. §91.220(g), .320(g).

200. *See* Ed Gramlich, *Consolidated Plan and Community Development Block Grant Advocacy*, 32 CLEARINGHOUSE REV. 173 (1998). A "fair share" approach can be used to examine whether the group of people with the most severe needs are being served with a proportionate share of resources. *Id.* at 182.

201. See discussion of the variety of state planning mandates, *supra.*

202. 24 C.F.R. §91.105.

203. *Id.* The regulations require jurisdictions to publish the plan in order to allow time for public comment, hold at least two public hearings per year, consider public comments, and explain why any public comments were not incorporated into the ConPlan. States have similar requirements under 24 C.F.R. §91.115.

204. Cranston-Gonzalez National Affordable Housing Act, 42 U.S.C. §§12701–12713.

205. Housing and Community Development Act of 1974, 42 U.S.C. §§5301–5321.

206. 24 C.F.R. §91.1–.600; 24 C.F.R. §570.1–.913.

207. 24 C.F.R. §91.500 (2009) (Plans must be consistent with the purposes of the Cranston-Gonzalez National Affordable Housing Act under 42 U.S.C. §12703 (2018)).

208. 42 U.S.C. §12705(a) (2018). A ConPlan is incomplete if: it is developed without required citizen participation, it does not contain all required elements, or a required certification is inaccurate. 24 C.F.R. §91.500(b) (2020). A jurisdiction must amend its plan if it makes changes to its allocation priorities, carries out new activities, or changes the "purpose, scope, location, or beneficiaries of an activity." 24 C.F.R. §91.505 (2020).

209. 24 C.F.R. §91.525 (2020). *See* 24 C.F.R. §91.520 (2016) (describing requirements of the performance report) & §91.520(b) (describing the requirements of the affordable housing component of this report).

210. The jurisdiction must respond to these complaints in writing. 42 U.S.C. §12707(d) (2018), 24 C.F.R. §§ 91.105(j), 91.115(h) (2020). HUD reviews these written complaints to determine if a

of the consolidated plan housing strategy,[211] challenge a violation of the ConPlan statutes pursuant to Section 1983,[212] pursue a private right of action under the Administrative Procedures Act,[213] or allege unlawful discrimination under the Fair Housing Act.[214]

B. Certifications "Affirmatively to Further Fair Housing" and the Analysis of Impediments to Fair Housing Choice

The Fair Housing Act requires HUD and other federal agencies to administer their housing programs "in a manner affirmatively to further" fair housing.[215] This requirement is imposed on recipients of federal funds through the ConPlan.[216] States are required under CDBG regulations to ensure that units of local government funded by the state comply with their certifications to affirmatively further fair housing.[217] The requirement is also imposed on federally assisted public housing agencies[218] and recipients of low-income housing tax credits.[219]

The ConPlan requires each jurisdiction to certify it will affirmatively further fair housing, meaning a jurisdiction must (1) conduct an analysis to identify impediments to fair housing choice; (2) take appropriate actions to overcome the effects of any impediments

---

plan is "substantially complete." 42 U.S.C. § 12705(c)(1) (2018). Advocates may also file a complaint directly with HUD.

211. 42 U.S.C. § 12708(c) (2018).

212. 42 U.S.C. §§ 1981–87 (2018). *See* Ave. 6E Invs., Ltd. Liab. Co. v. City of Yuma, 818 F.3d 493 (9th Cir. 2016).

213. 5 U.S.C. §§ 551–559 (2018).

214. Title VIII of the Civil Rights Act of 1968, 42 U.S.C. §§ 3601–19 (2018). For more information on enforcement of the Consolidated Plan, *see* Michael Rawson, *Administrative and Judicial Enforcement of the Department of Housing and Urban Development's Consolidated Plan Obligations*, 32 CLEARINGHOUSE REV. 192 (1998).

215. 42 U.S.C. § 3608(e)(5) (2018) (for HUD). 42 U.S.C. § 3608(d) mandates that "[a]ll executive departments and agencies shall administer their programs and activities relating to housing and urban development (including any Federal agency having regulatory or supervisory authority over financial institutions) in a manner affirmatively to further the purposes of [the Fair Housing Act]." *See also* Exec. Order 11063, 27 Fed. Reg. 11527 (Nov. 20, 1962); Exec. Order 12259, 46 Fed. Reg. 1253 (Dec. 31, 1980), revoked and replaced by Exec. Order 12.892, 59 Fed. Reg. 2939 (Jan. 17, 1994). For additional discussion of this requirement, see Chapters 3 and 8. For a thorough discussion of the duty to affirmatively further fair housing in the disability context, *see* HENRY KORMAN, MEETING LOCAL HOUSING NEEDS: A PRACTICE GUIDE FOR IMPLEMENTING SELECTION PREFERENCES AND CIVIL RIGHTS REQUIREMENTS IN AFFORDABLE HOUSING PROGRAMS 82 (2004).

216. 24 C.F.R. § 91.225 (2009) (local governments); 24 C.F.R. § 91.325 (2009) (states).

217. 24 C.F.R. § 570.487(b)(4) (2009). *See also* 42 U.S.C. § 5306(d)(7)(B) (2006) (statutory requirement for community development block grant program to affirmatively further fair housing).

218. 24 C.F.R. § 903.7(o)(3) (2009).

219. *See also* Florence Wagman Roisman, *Mandates Unsatisfied: The Low Income Housing Tax Credit Program and the Civil Rights Laws*, 52 U. MIAMI L. REV. 1011, 1039–40 (1998). For additional agencies required to affirmatively further fair housing, s*ee generally* ROBERT G. SCHWEMM, HOUSING DISCRIMINATION LAW AND LITIGATION (West Group 2004) and Florence Wagman Roisman, *Housing, Poverty, and Racial Justice: How Civil Rights Laws Can Redress the Housing Problems of Poor People*, 36 CLEARINGHOUSE REV. 21, 27 (2002).

identified through that analysis; and (3) maintain records reflecting the analysis and actions.[220]

While the Fair Housing Act has included the obligation to affirmatively further fair housing since 1968, there was no effective framework or accountability system for HUD grantees until recently. In 2015, the Obama administration issued a regulation that required communities receiving federal subsidies to analyze patterns of discrimination, racial segregation, and disparities in housing and to create an actionable plan to promote greater integration and equity.[221] The rule provided a detailed definition of AFFH and introduced a process called an assessment of fair housing (AFH) to replace the analysis of impediments.[222] However, in 2018, the Trump administration halted enforcement of the rule, and HUD withdrew the AFH assessment tool after reviewing early submissions and finding the assessment tool "unduly burdensome and unworkable."[223]

In January 2020, HUD proposed a revised rule aimed at reducing both federal control of local housing decisions and the burden of data requirements imposed on local governments.[224] HUD published the Preserving Community and Neighborhood Choice rule, which came into effect on September 8, 2020, repealing both the 2015 AFFH rule and 1994 analysis of impediments requirements.[225] The rule returns to the pre-1994 understanding of the FHA's obligation to AFFH, which is characterized by a general commitment to take active steps to promote fair housing.[226] Now *any* action that is rationally related to promoting fair housing will be deemed sufficient to AFFH.[227] This interpretation marks a significant departure from the 2015 rule, and related court opinions, that impose on HUD and

---

220. 24 C.F.R. §91.225(a)(1) (2009) (local governments); 24 C.F.R. §91.325(a)(1) (states) (2009). Adequate recordkeeping includes: (1) a description of the governing body's commitment to fair housing planning; (2) a description of financial and in-kind support for fair housing planning; (3) a list of groups participating in the formulation of fair housing planning; (4) transcripts of public meetings and citizen comments; and, (5) progress reports. DEP'T OF HOUSING AND URBAN DEV., FAIR HOUSING PLANNING GUIDE 2–26 (1996).

221. 80 Fed. Reg. 42271 (July 16, 2015).

222. Affirmatively Furthering Fair Housing, 80 Fed. Reg. 42272-01 (July 16, 2015).

223. Affirmatively Furthering Fair Housing: Withdrawal of the Assessment Tool for Local Governments, 83 Fed. Reg. 23923 (May 23, 2018).

224. 85 Fed. Reg. 2041–42 (Jan. 14, 2020). HUD's amended AFFH rule is intended to give local communities maximum flexibility in designing and implementing policies tailored to their unique local needs. It is also meant to eliminate reporting and monitoring requirements deemed "overly burdensome."

225. Preserving Community and Neighborhood Choice, 85 Fed. Reg. 47899 (Aug. 7, 2020) (to be codified at 24 C.F.R. pts. 5, 91, 92, 570, 574, 576, 903).

226. *Id.* "Fair housing" is defined as "housing that, among other attributes, is affordable, safe, decent, free of unlawful discrimination, and accessible as required under civil rights laws." 24 C.F.R. §5.150.

227. *Id.* "Affirmatively further" refers to "any action rationally related to promoting any attribute or attributes of fair housing as defined in the preceding subsection." *See also* Churches United for Fair Hous., Inc. v. De Blasio, 180 A.D.3d 549, 550 (2020) (finding New York City's facially race-neutral measures to promote affordable housing sufficient and not requiring the city to consider any impact on racial and ethnic concentration).

its grantees a substantive obligation to promote racial and economic integration in order to rectify decades of racist housing policies.[228]

When President Donald Trump announced in July that his administration was rescinding the AFFH rule, he tweeted: "I am happy to inform all of the people living their Suburban Lifestyle Dream that you will no longer be bothered or financially hurt by having low income housing built in your neighborhood."[229] President Trump took to social media again two weeks later to brag about ending "the long running program where low income housing would invade" suburban neighborhoods.[230]

Prior to the repeal of the federal requirements, the California legislature adopted its own affirmatively furthering fair housing obligations.[231] All housing elements approved after January 1, 2021, must include a program to affirmatively further fair housing, and jurisdictions should use the federal Affirmatively Fair Housing Rule as adopted on July 16, 2015, for guidance. Under the California rule, programs that affirmatively further fair housing must analyze and assess contributing factors to "segregation patterns and trends, racially or ethnically concentrated areas of poverty, disparities in access to opportunity, and disproportionate housing needs within the jurisdiction, including displacement risk," and then implement strategies to address these issues.[232]

Common obstacles include limited funding, regulatory barriers, labor shortages, land scarcity, rising construction costs, and local resistance to high-density development.[233] States try to overcome these barriers by encouraging development of new affordable housing in areas of opportunity, preserving existing affordable housing, and protecting existing residents from displacement.[234] Some states are analyzing the effectiveness of these strategies in a systematic way to inform future policy.[235]

---

228. *See* 2015 Rule definition of AFFH (24 C.F.R. § 5.152) (AFFH means "taking meaningful actions, in addition to combating discrimination, that overcome patterns of segregation and foster inclusive communities free from barriers that restrict access to opportunity based on protected characteristics" and "replacing segregated living patterns with truly integrated and balanced living patterns."). *See also* Texas Dep't of Hous. & Cmty. Affairs v. Inclusive Communities Project, Inc., 135 S. Ct. 2507, 2525–26 (2015) (interpreting AFFH to mean housing policies that inadvertently hurt minorities—i.e.. those that create a disparate impact—were as harmful as those that were explicitly discriminatory).

229. Donald J. Trump (@realDonaldTrump), Twitter (July 29, 2020, 9:19 AM), https://twitter.com/realDonaldTrump/status/1288509568578777088.

230. Donald J. Trump (@realDonaldTrump), Twitter (Aug. 12, 2020, 4:59 AM), https://twitter.com/realDonaldTrump/status/1293517514798960640.

231. Cal. Gov't Code § 8899.50 (2019).

232. *California Housing Element Manual*, Public Interest Law Project at 81 (4th ed. 2019); Cal. Gov't Code §§ 65583(c)(10)(A)(i)–(iv).

233. *See generally* Joint Center of Housing Studies of Harvard University, *America's Rental Housing 2020, available at* https://www.jchs.harvard.edu/sites/default/files/reports/files/Harvard_JCHS_Americas_Rental_Housing_2020.pdf. *See also 2019 Housing Impact Report*, Public & Affordable Housing Research Corp. (last visited Oct. 30, 2020), http://www.pahrc.org/wp-content/uploads/2020/02/Housing-Impact-Report-2019.pdf.

234. *California Housing Element Manual*, *supra* note 22, at 81; Cal. Gov't Code § 65583(c)(10)(A)(v).

235. *See, e.g.*, the FairHousingMattersNY strategy in New York, https://hcr.ny.gov/fairhousingmattersny.

HUD, under President Joseph Biden, appears poised to take a different approach than under the Trump administration. On January 26, 2021, President Biden issued an Executive Order acknowledging the nation's history of structural racial discrimination in providing equal housing opportunities for all Americans, instructing the HUD Secretary to examine the effects of the Trump administration's actions with respect to AFFH, and to "take any necessary steps . . . to implement the Fair Housing Act's requirements that HUD administer its programs in a manner that affirmatively furthers fair housing and HUD's overall duty to administer the Act . . . including by preventing practices with an unjustified discriminatory effect."[236]

---

236. Exec. Order 13985, 86 Fed. Reg. 7009 (Jan. 26, 2021).

Exclusionary Zoning: Constitutional and Federal Statutory Responses

3

Ken Zimmerman and Noah Kazis

I. INTRODUCTION

Many local governments use their land use powers to exclude, effectively wielding zoning to keep out low-income households and people of color, as well as people with disabilities. In response, civil rights groups, housing developers, nonprofit organizations, and others have framed constitutional and statutory legal challenges. Courts have largely deferred to local governments' authority to enact local zoning codes, especially as a federal constitutional matter. But both state constitutions and federal civil rights law have provided critical mechanisms for constraining exclusionary practices in some circumstances. Exclusionary zoning continues to pose a significant challenge to housing production generally, and especially to affordable housing development. However, there is new attention being paid to the immense social costs that exclusionary zoning creates: not only entrenching segregation but also decreasing housing affordability, reducing economic mobility, and even exacerbating climate change.

This chapter provides an introduction to the potential for challenging exclusionary zoning through federal litigation, and under state constitutions (the important, and arguably more direct, interventions made by state statutes are addressed in the following chapter). Section II of this chapter provides a brief background on exclusionary zoning. Section III first discusses the largely limited application of federal constitutional law, after which Section IV provides a discussion of several state constitutions that have been applied to more actively restrict exclusionary zoning practices. Finally, Section V discusses the federal Fair Housing Act, which has served as the most important federal statutory tool for addressing exclusionary zoning.

II. EXCLUSIONARY ZONING: BACKGROUND

Comprehensive zoning laws limiting the type of activity (commercial, industrial, and residential) and the type, size, and design of buildings on privately owned land were introduced in the early 20th century in response to urban growth. Beginning in the 19th century, state and local governments began to regulate buildings' size and use—including for racially discriminatory purposes.[1] And, in 1916, New York City became the first municipality to pass a comprehensive zoning ordinance. Once again, the push for regulation came from both legitimate land use needs, such as decreasing congestion and increasing tax revenues generated by particular land uses, and discriminatory desires to keep lower-income (largely immigrant) workers away from high-end shopping districts.[2] From the start, zoning has always featured a strong undercurrent of exclusion, by race and class.[3] Indeed, exclusionary zoning spread and became stricter precisely when express racial discrimination in housing was outlawed by the Fair Housing Act, as many communities sought a new tool for maintaining residential segregation.

At the same time, courts—including, most importantly, the U.S. Supreme Court in its 1926 landmark decision, *Village of Euclid v. Ambler Realty* in 1926[4]—have granted local governments extremely broad latitude in regulating land use through the zoning power. This deference, when combined with the discriminatory ends for which zoning has often been used, has allowed for the creation of additional zoning techniques that can effectively bar access to certain communities for certain types of people. The term *exclusionary zoning* has been defined in various ways, but broadly refers to zoning practices that have the intent and/or effect of excluding disadvantaged groups, particularly low- and moderate-income people of color, from a locality.[5] Techniques and targets have varied over time. While explicit racial restrictions are no longer permitted, other zoning mechanisms—whether so intended or not—have had the similar effect of excluding many households of color, in large part due to the widespread correlation between income and race (or ethnicity).

In a now-classic 1971 study of the zoning practices of four New Jersey counties on the outskirts of New York City, Norman Williams and Thomas Norman identified six popular land-use regulatory techniques that had particular impact on housing opportunities for low- and moderate-income persons: (1) minimum building size (floor space); (2) exclusion of multiple dwellings; (3) restrictions on the number of bedrooms; (4) prohibition of mobile homes; (5) frontage (lot width) requirements; and (6) minimum lot size requirements.[6]

---

1. *See, e.g.*, Welch v. Swasey, 214 U.S. 91 (1909), Attorney General v. Williams, 174 Mass. 476 (1899) (each dealing with Boston height limits); Yick Wo v. Hopkins, 118 U.S. 356 (1886) (restrictions on location and operation of laundries used as device to discriminate against Chinese Americans).

2. *See* Robert A.M. Stern, *One Hundred Years of Zoning*, Zoning@100, AIA New York (2016), https://www.aiany.org/membership/special-projects/article/zoning-100/one-hundred-years-of-zoning/.

3. Jessica Trounstine, Segregation by Design (2018).

4. 272 U.S. 365, 395 (1926).

5. For various definitions of exclusionary zoning, *see* Kenneth H. Young, Anderson's Am. Law of Zoning, § 8:2 (Clark Boardman Callaghan 2004); Davidoff & Davidoff, *Opening the Suburbs: Toward Inclusionary Land Use Controls*, 22 Syracuse L. Rev. 511 (1971).

6. Norman Williams, Jr. & Thomas Norman, *Exclusionary Land Use Controls: The Case of NorthEastern New Jersey*, 22 Syracuse L. Rev. 475, 481–84 (1971). The siting and regulation of

They singled out minimum floor space requirements and prohibition of multiple dwellings as the most significant.[7] In the half-century since, the variety of tools that have been used to exclusionary ends has only multiplied: Today, a similar list could include discretionary review processes (as opposed to as-of-right development), impact fees and other exactions, lengthy approval processes and project delays, building moratoria, excessive and prescriptive design standards, permitting only age-restricted housing, and even land use tools from outside the zoning toolkit, like historic preservation laws. And other zoning practices more specifically exclude people with disabilities, such as special permitting requirements for group homes and certain occupancy restrictions.[8]

In understanding the dynamics that give rise to exclusionary zoning practices, it is important to note the fiscal implications and motivations of land-use provisions. Many ordinances are justified as forms of "fiscal zoning"—zoning to attract activities such as commercial and light industrial uses or high-end single-family housing that would increase the tax base, rather than multifamily housing that some fear draws on the tax base by requiring increased expenditures, especially for public schools.[9] While such motivations may be understandable, they can also be used to justify increases in the required standard of housing quality beyond those necessary for health and safety, and thereby "interfere seriously with the availability of low and moderate-cost housing where it is needed."[10] It is in this context that exclusionary zoning arises. It should be noted that exclusionary zoning is

---

mobile homes (or manufactured housing) and other specific types of affordable housing are discussed in Chapter 5.

7. The impact of restrictions on multifamily housing can be illustrated as follows. According to one recent analysis of an affluent Boston suburb, a new single-family house on a typical lot would cost $1.9 million. Townhouses built on the same lot, in contrast, would cost around $800,000 per unit, and apartments would come in at under $500,000 per unit. Sarah Crump, et al., *Zoned Out: Why Massachusetts Needs to Legalize Apartments Near Transit*, BOSTON INDICATORS (2020), https://www.bostonindicators.org/reports/report-website-pages/zoned-out.

8. *See* City of Cleburne v. Cleburne Living Center, Inc., 473 U.S. 432 (1985); City of Edmonds v. Oxford House, Inc., 514 U.S. 725 (1995). See Chapter 5 for a discussion of state and local regulation affecting the siting of many forms of affordable housing that are not traditional single-family or multifamily dwellings.

9. Accordingly, fiscal devices that decrease the importance of local property taxes, including programs that promote revenue-sharing across municipalities or help fund public schools regionally or at the state level, can help address some legitimate concerns while exposing those that are only exclusionary.

10. Williams & Norman, *supra* note 6, at 478. *See generally* MICHAEL N. DANIELSON, THE POLITICS OF EXCLUSION (1976); LEONARD S. RUBINOWITZ, LOW INCOME HOUSING: SUBURBAN STRATEGIES (1974); Eric J. Branfman et al., *Measuring the Invisible Wall: Land Use Controls and the Residential Patterns of the Poor*, 82 YALE L. J. 483 (1973); Lawrence G. Sager, *Tight Little Islands: Exclusionary Zoning, Equal Protection and the Indigent*, 21 STANFORD L. REV. 767 (1969). An amicus curiae brief of the American Planning Association argued that Exclusionary zoning is particularly pernicious because lower-income individuals are unable to find affordable housing near suburban places of work, necessitating lengthy commuting trips. As these areas typically have limited, if any, mass transit, the journey to work must be by automobile, creating additional economic hardship for lower-income individuals. RICHARD F. BABCOCK & FRED P. BOSSELMAN, EXCLUSIONARY ZONING: LAND USE REGULATION AND HOUSING IN THE 1970s, 114–15 (Am. Planning Ass'n, 1973).

thus a significant, but not the exclusive, means by which "not-in-my-backyard" (NIMBY) sentiments are manifested.[11]

Though exclusionary zoning has existed since zoning's inception, and has long been a topic of concern for civil rights activists and scholars alike, recent years have seen new attention being paid to the many harms caused by the practice. Research has uncovered the depth of the historical connections between zoning and racial discrimination and exclusion,[12] while new economic analysis has measured how seriously exclusionary zoning impedes upward social mobility and slows economic growth nationwide.[13] As cities have revitalized, exclusionary zoning has taken on new, more urban forms in addition to its traditionally suburban cast.[14] And politicians from across the political spectrum are showing new interest in the issue.[15] The extent, and harms, of exclusionary zoning, and the ways in which it is emerging in the context of new dynamics in urban revitalization and economic growth strategies, are increasingly well-understood—and understood to be substantial.

III. FEDERAL CONSTITUTIONAL AND STATUTORY LAW

A. The Zoning Power

Over the past century, courts have recognized and broadened the general authority of local governments under their police power to enact zoning schemes of their choosing. Courts presume that local zoning and other land-use mechanisms are valid unless a landowner or other party can demonstrate a conflict with an essential constitutional interest or statutory right. It is worth noting that the presumption of validity granted local zoning provisions applies both to regulations that hinder affordable housing development (such as density

---

11. Transportation planning and school districting are two other prominent policy areas in which NIMBY sentiments arise, as are private land use controls enacted through deed restrictions.

12. JESSICA TROUNSTINE, SEGREGATION BY DESIGN (2018), RICHARD ROTHSTEIN, THE COLOR OF LAW (2017).

13. Raj Chetty, Nathaniel Hendren & Lawrence F. Katz, *The Effects of Exposure to Better Neighborhoods on Children: New Evidence from the Moving to Opportunity Experiment*, 106 AM. ECON. REV. 855 (2016); Peter Ganong & Daniel Shoag, *Why Has Regional Income Convergence in the U.S. Declined?* 102 J. URB. ECON. 76 (2017); Chang-Tai Hsieh & Enrico Moretti, *Housing Constraints and Spatial Misallocation*, Nat'l Bureau of Econ. Res., Working Paper No. 21154 (2017).

14. Traditionally, urban areas were thought to favor new development, and renters in particular were thought less likely to demand exclusionary land use policies. Today, however, some entire regions, including center cities, have so restricted housing supply as to be exclusionary. John Mangin, *The New Exclusionary Zoning*, 25 STAN. L. & POL'Y REV. 91 (2014); Vicki Been, Ingrid Gould Ellen & Katherine O'Regan, *Supply Skepticism: Housing Supply and Affordability*, 29 HOUS. POL'Y DEBATE 25 (2019).

15. In the 2020 primaries, Democrats from center to left proposed new federal strategies that would help combat exclusionary zoning, including Joe Biden, Amy Klobuchar, Cory Booker, Elizabeth Warren, and Bernie Sanders. Megan Haberle & LeGrand Northcutt, The 2020 Democratic Candidates' Positions on Fair and Affordable Housing, Poverty & Race Research Action Council (July 2019), https://prrac.org/pdf/2020-democratic-candidates-housing-platforms.pdf. Meanwhile, the Trump administration endorsed a renewed focus on regulatory barriers to affordable housing production, before subsequently reversing that focus in the heat of the 2020 election, and congressional legislation on the subject has received bipartisan support in both chambers. White House Council on Eliminating Regulatory Barriers to Affordable Housing, Request for Information, 84 Fed. Reg. 64549 (Nov. 22, 2019); YIMBY Act, S.1919 (116th Cong.).

limitations and minimum lot sizes) and to those that promote or even mandate the creation of affordable housing (zoning overrides or fair-share requirements).

Federal courts' treatment of local zoning power was largely established by the U.S. Supreme Court's seminal 1926 decision in *Euclid v. Ambler Realty*, which declared that restrictions on land use would stand unless "clearly arbitrary and unreasonable, having no substantial relation to the public health, safety, morals or general welfare."[16] The Court emphasized in a well-known passage: "If the validity of the legislative classification for zoning purposes be fairly debatable, the legislative judgment must be allowed to control."[17] The Court clarified that the range of "fairly debatable" government interests was quite broad, including not just health and safety concerns but also aesthetic and other subjective considerations.[18]

The Supreme Court has reinforced and expanded this basic premise since *Euclid*.[19] In its 1954 decision in *Berman v. Parker*, for example, the Court addressed a constitutional challenge by a property owner whose viable commercial property was being taken pursuant to a legislatively authorized redevelopment plan.[20] In rejecting that takings claim, the Court also clarified more broadly the scope of the police power in land use, declaring that "[p]ublic safety, public health, morality, peace and quiet, law and order . . . [m]erely illustrate the scope of the power and do not delimit it. It is within the power of the legislature to determine that the community should be beautiful as well as healthy, spacious as well as clean, well-balanced as well as carefully patrolled."[21] As the Supreme Court subsequently stated in *Village of Belle Terre v. Boraas*, "[t]he police power is not confined to elimination of filth, stench and unhealthy places. It is ample to lay out zones where family values, youth values, and the blessings of quiet seclusion and clean air make the area a sanctuary for people."[22]

In sum, the federal courts will view zoning as permissible economic or social legislation absent a specified constitutional or statutory basis for challenge. In these circumstances,

---

16. Vill. of Euclid v. Ambler Realty, 272 U.S. 365, 395 (1926). This precise formulation, which reflected the substantive due process jurisprudence of the day, has been clarified in the modern era to require only rational basis review. *See* Greater Chicago Combine & Ctr., Inc. v. City of Chicago, 431 F.3d 1065, 1071 (7th Cir. 2005).

17. 272 U.S. 365 at 388.

18. In reaching this conclusion, the *Euclid* Court departed from the older doctrine that allowed land use regulations based upon controlling nuisances (such as factories and industrial uses) and emphasized the value of creating residential districts. *Id.* at 394. In passing, the Court noted ambivalence about multifamily housing in areas zoned for single-family housing, noting that "apartment houses, which in a different environment would be not only entirely unobjectionable but highly desirable, come very near to being nuisances." *Id.* at 395.

19. The Court's decision in Nectow v. Cambridge, 277 U.S. 183 (1928), which clarified that (at least under the more exacting due process scrutiny of that era) at least some zoning decisions could be ruled unconstitutional, was essentially a minor speed bump on this path.

20. 348 U.S. 26 (1954).

21. *Id.* at 32–33. The "public use" requirement of the Takings Clause, at issue in Berman, is coterminous with the scope of the police power. Hawaii Hous. Auth. v. Midkiff, 467 U.S. 229, 240 (1984); *but see* Kelo v. City of New London, Conn., 545 U.S. 469, 501 (2005) (O'Connor, J., dissenting) (arguing that "coterminous" language was dicta and that two concepts may, at times, diverge).

22. 416 U.S. 1, 9 (1974).

the ordinance will be upheld if the law is "reasonable, not arbitrary" and "bears a rational relationship to a (permissible) state objective."[23]

B. Federal Constitutional Claims

Despite the strong presumption of validity for local land-use provisions, courts have struck down zoning ordinances for violating the U.S. Constitution. While federal legislation, most notably the Fair Housing Act, has largely superseded the use of constitutional arguments to invalidate zoning ordinances alleging discrimination against protected groups, constitutional claims are frequently included in exclusionary zoning cases and remain an important starting point in the legal framework. Moreover, as new constitutional doctrines become increasingly salient in the land-use context, they may become relevant to exclusionary zoning as well.[24]

1. Equal Protection

In contrast to the typical rational basis review applied to local zoning regulations, strict judicial scrutiny is triggered when the regulation implicates a suspect classification or limits a fundamental right under the Fourteenth Amendment.[25] Thus, a racially motivated zoning ordinance is impermissible, as is one that undermines a family's structure or association.

Historically, prohibition against racially explicit zoning laws have been determined to violate the Equal Protection Clause since long before the Supreme Court determined that "separate but equal" was unconstitutional in *Brown v. Board of Education*.[26] In 1917, the Supreme Court, in *Buchanan v. Warley*,[27] struck down a city ordinance that barred an African American family from acquiring real property in a white residential area. While this decision preceded *Euclid* and its increased deference to local zoning decisions, the Supreme Court reiterated in *Harmon v. Tyler* and other post-*Euclid* cases that racially explicit land-use measures remained in violation of the Fourteenth Amendment.[28]

In response, landowners began to use restrictive covenants to maintain racially segregated living areas and received strong institutional support from government entities. These included the Federal Housing Administration, which in the 1930s drafted a model

---

23. *Village of Belle Torre,* 416 U.S. at 8.

24. For example, the First Amendment limits local zoning powers with respect to adult and religious uses. *See* City of Los Angeles v. Alameda Books, Inc., 535 U.S. 425, 434 (2002) (adult uses); Redemption Cmty. Church v. City of Laurel, Maryland, 333 F. Supp. 3d 521, 537 (D. Md. 2018) (Free Exercise); Vision Church v. Vill. of Long Grove, 468 F.3d 975, 991 (7th Cir. 2006) (Establishment Clause). The First Amendment has not been a significant issue in residential zoning, to date.

25. *See* Eide v. Sarasota County, 908 F.2d 716, 722 (Fla. Dist. Ct. App. 1990) ("[I]f the claim is simply that the regulation treats the plaintiff different from someone else and neither a suspect class nor a fundamental right is involved, the regulation (and its classification) must only be rationally related to a legitimate government purpose.").

26. 347 U.S. 483 (1954).

27. 245 U.S. 60 (1917); *see* ROBERT G. SCHWEMM, HOUSING DISCRIMINATION: LAW AND LITIGATION § 3:2 (West Group 2004) (hereinafter SCHWEMM).

28. *See, e.g.,* Harmon v. Tyler, 273 U.S. 668 (1927) (finding unconstitutional a law that prohibited blacks from living in white areas unless written consent obtained); City of Richmond v. Deans, 281 U.S. 704 (1930).

restrictive covenant for use in home sales that it financed.[29] Over the succeeding decades, the Supreme Court also struck these down, notably in its 1948 decision in *Shelley v. Kramer*,[30] where it held that enforcement of such covenants by state courts ran afoul of the Equal Protection Clause. These decisions acknowledged, however, that "voluntary adherence" to restrictive covenants fell outside the reach of the Fourteenth Amendment, which applied only to governmental action. It was not until 1968, when the Fair Housing Act and *Jones v. Alfred Mayer Co.*[31] provided statutory prohibitions against private as well as governmental discrimination, that racial covenants were entirely proscribed.

Beginning in the 1970s, the Equal Protection Clause has been interpreted in ways that limit its use in challenging exclusionary zoning. As an initial matter, the Supreme Court's determinations that housing is not a fundamental right[32] and that wealth is not a suspect class[33] mean that the direct consequences of exclusionary zoning are insufficient to trigger strict scrutiny. Similarly, the restrictive standing requirements for exclusionary zoning claims brought under the Fourteenth Amendment, especially when contrasted to the broad reach of the Fair Housing Act discussed later, also circumscribe its utility. In the leading case of *Warth v. Seldin*,[34] for example, the court addressed who had standing to challenge an exclusionary zoning ordinance and rebuffed a range of individuals and groups. Groups denied standing included "low-income . . . black and/or Puerto Rican/Spanish" home seekers in the area who expressed generalized concern about the exclusionary practices and taxpayers in a neighboring town who contended that their municipality was overburdened as a result.[35]

Perhaps more significantly, a violation of the Equal Protection Clause may only be proved by showing intentional discrimination, as the Supreme Court determined in *Washington v. Davis*.[36] In other words, and again in contrast to the Fair Housing Act, "official action will not be held unconstitutional solely because it results in a racially disproportionate impact."[37] This can be determinative, as illustrated by the Supreme Court's decision in *Village of Arlington Heights v. Metropolitan Housing Development Corp.*[38] There, the

---

29. *See* Bradley v. School Board of the City of Richmond, 338 F. Supp. 67, 215–20 (E.D. Va.), *rev'd on other grounds*, 462 F.2d 1058 (4th Cir. 1972), *aff'd*, 412 U.S. 92 (1973); Schwemm, *supra* note 27, § 3.3.

30. 334 U.S. 1 (1948).

31. 392 U.S. 409 (1968) (holding that § 1982 of the Civil Rights Act of 1866 bars all racial discrimination in the sale or rental of property, including discrimination by private actors). Title VIII of the Fair Housing Act forbids any notice or statement that indicates discriminatory preference in housing sales or rentals. 42 U.S.C. § 3604(c).

32. Lindsey v. Normet, 405 U.S. 56 (1972).

33. San Antonio Ind. School Dist. v. Rodriguez, 411 U.S. 1, 20 (1973); *see also* James A. Kushner, Government Discrimination: Equal Protection Law and Litigation § 5:17 (Thomson West 2004).

34. 422 U.S. 490 (1975).

35. *Id.* at 499, 503 and n.1. The restrictive standing requirements of *Warth* for constitutional claims were explicitly confirmed by *Vill. of Arlington Heights v. Metro. Housing Dev. Corp.*, a decision that clarified many of the differences between claims arising under the Fourteenth Amendment and the Federal Fair Housing Act. 429 U.S. 252, 260–64 (1977).

36. 426 U.S. 229 (1976).

37. *Id.* at 265.

38. 429 U.S. 252 (1977).

Supreme Court dismissed an Equal Protection challenge to an allegedly discriminatory land-use decision because of insufficient evidence that it was motivated by a discriminatory purpose, but permitted a federal Fair Housing Act statutory claim to proceed based on evidence of discriminatory impact.[39]

While proof of discriminatory intent may be a significant undertaking, it is important to emphasize that the courts are directed to undertake a searching inquiry into this question. As the Supreme Court stated in *Arlington Heights*, "determining whether invidious discriminatory purpose was a motivating factor demands a sensitive inquiry into such circumstantial and direct evidence of intent as may be available."[40] The Court emphasized a number of factors that might be relevant, including (1) the impact of the zoning ordinance, which "may provide an important starting point," although it is not determinative; (2) historical background (e.g., whether the municipality was involved in other discriminatory practices); (3) the sequence of events, especially if it involved a departure from normal procedural sequence; (4) substantive factors in the land-use decision; and (5) legislative or administrative history.[41]

While Equal Protection jurisprudence demands a significant showing to trigger heightened scrutiny of a municipal zoning provision, the Supreme Court has suggested that "rational basis" review is not always an empty one and, in at least one well-known case, has struck down a local land-use provision under this test. In *City of Cleburne v. Cleburne Living Center, Inc.*, the Supreme Court examined a local ordinance that required a group home for the mentally retarded to obtain a special use permit, although this was not required of other multifamily housing units, such as apartment buildings, fraternity houses, or homes for the elderly.[42] The Court concluded that "mental retardation" was not a suspect class and thus did not trigger heightened scrutiny of the ordinance at issue, but nonetheless found the reasons advanced by the city for requiring and denying the permit to be insufficient under the Equal Protection Clause.[43] *Cleburne*'s analysis, however, should not be assumed to extend broadly to ordinary rational basis review; rather, it reflects a "more searching form of rational basis review" that applies to laws based on a bare desire to harm a politically unpopular group, a category that courts have applied only in rare circumstances.[44]

---

39. *Id.* at 271.

40. *Id.* at 266.

41. *Id.* at 564–67.

42. 473 U.S. 432 (1985).

43. *Id.* at 446, 450. Courts have continued to strike down land-use or housing ordinances affecting persons with disabilities as insufficient under the rational basis standard of the Equal Protection Clause. *See* Sullivan v. City of Pittsburgh, 811 F.2d 171 (3d Cir. 1987) (relying on *Cleburne* to use rational basis test in striking down city ordinance that discriminated against an alcohol rehabilitation center); *see* Open Homes Fellowship, Inc. v. Orange Cnty., 325 F. Supp. 2d 1349 (M.D. Fla. 2004) (applying rational basis test and *Cleburne* to hold that county's requirement that drug and rehabilitation center get special permit when other dwellings of a similar nature are not so required served no rational relationship to a legitimate state interest).

44. Lawrence v. Texas, 539 U.S. 558, 580 (2003) (O'Connor, J., concurring in the judgment); U.S. Dep't of Agriculture v. Moreno, 413 U.S. 528, 534 (1973).

2. Due Process

The Due Process Clause of the Fourteenth Amendment has also been the basis for successful challenges to local zoning ordinances.[45] In *Moore v. City of East Cleveland*,[46] the Court invalidated a local zoning ordinance that limited occupancy in a single-family home to only a few categories of related individuals, essentially those in the nuclear family.[47] Upholding the challenge of a woman who sought to live with her grandson, the Court recognized that the freedom of personal choice in matters of family life was a fundamental interest protected by the Fourteenth Amendment, thus triggering a higher level of scrutiny. The Court invalidated the ordinance because the municipality's limitation of family composition bore "but a tenuous relation" to its stated objectives of reducing traffic and financial burden on the school system.[48]

The limited scope of *Moore* is revealed by a comparison to the Supreme Court's earlier decision in *Belle Terre v. Boraas*, where the Court upheld an ordinance that did not restrict related persons from living together as a family, but did limit occupancy to only two unrelated persons in a single-person home.[49] Due process protected the special associational interests involved when the state regulates the family, but not the associational interests of unrelated housemates.[50]

Similarly, the courts have upheld procedural due process claims against municipalities when there is a marked irregularity in zoning procedures or other arbitrary aspects of local land-use rules. A classic example is *Seattle Title Trust Co. v. Roberge*,[51] where the Supreme Court struck down a zoning ordinance that permitted a "philanthropic home for children or old people" only when written consent from two-thirds of neighboring property owners was obtained. The Court held the provision unconstitutionally arbitrary, since those owners could "withhold consent for selfish reasons or arbitrarily and may subject the owner to their will or caprice."[52] Similarly, in *Scott v. Greenville County*,[53] a developer prevailed when the local governmental entity interrupted the routine permitting process and, without any authorization under local law, attempted to rezone the area to exclude his proposed development.[54]

---

45. *See* Griswold v. Conn., 381 U.S. 479 (1965); Roe v. Wade, 410 U.S. 113 (1973).

46. 431 U.S. 494 (1977).

47. *Id.* at 495.

48. *Id.* at 499–500. Because the number of persons per family (and the number of occupants per dwelling) was not limited, the court determined that the ordinance would not reduce the potential of overcrowding. *Id.*

49. 416 U.S. 1, 2 (1974). The text of the ordinance defined a family as "one or more persons related by blood, adoption, or marriage, living and cooking together as a single housekeeping unit . . . [or a] number of persons but not exceeding two (2) living and cooking together as a single housekeeping unit though not related by blood, adoption or marriage."

50. Other specifically identified due process interests can give rise to similar claims. Note, for example, that the infringement of the right to travel has been used to challenge local zoning ordinances. *See* Constr. Indus. Ass'n v. City of Petaluma, 375 F. Supp. 574 (N.D. Cal. 1974), *rev'd on other grounds*, 522 F.2d 897 (9th Cir. 1975), *cert. denied*, 422 U.S. 934 (1976).

51. 278 U.S. 116 (1928).

52. *Id.* at 122.

53. 716 F.2d 1409 (4th Cir. 1983).

54. *Id.* at 1418–19. For an example of an unsuccessful due process claim (by far the more common variety), *see* Constr. Indus. Ass'n v. City of Petaluma, 522 F.2d 897 (9th Cir. 1975), *cert. denied*, 422 U.S. 934 (1976).

3. Takings

The Takings Clause also imposes limits on the power of state and local governments to zone and otherwise regulate land use. As a general rule, ordinary zoning ordinances do not constitute regulatory takings, even if they diminish a property's value or even destroy certain real property interests.[55] But when a zoning code goes "too far," it can constitute an unconstitutional "regulatory taking."[56] This has always been an "ad hoc, factual" inquiry, which looks at factors including the economic impact of the regulation, its interference with investment-backed expectations, and the character of the government action.[57] Where a regulation effects a permanent, physical occupation of property, or where it deprives a landowner of all economically beneficial use of its land, that regulation is categorically considered a taking.[58] The boundaries of what constitutes a regulatory taking are, by design, open-ended and difficult to succinctly summarize.[59] They are also likely to continue evolving faster, as the Supreme Court's recent decision in *Knick v. Township of Scott* moves more of these cases into federal court.[60]

One subset of takings cases bears special mention: limitations on exactions. When a government conditions a zoning approval on a landowner giving over a piece of its property to the public, those conditions must meet additional standards.[61] There must be both a "nexus" and "rough proportionality" between the property exacted and the social harms of the proposed land use.[62] This test applies to "monetary exactions" as well as physical exactions.[63] It is not clear, however, whether this test applies to generally applicable legislative rules or only to individually negotiated exactions.[64] Because both certain land-use regulations meant to serve exclusionary ends and certain land-use regulations meant to

---

55. Murr v. Wisconsin, 137 S. Ct. 1933, 1947 (2017) ("reasonable land-use regulations do not work a taking"); Penn Central Transp. Co. v. City of New York, 438 U.S. 104, 125 (1978) (stating "in instances in which a state tribunal reasonably concluded that 'the health, safety, morals, or general welfare' would be promoted by prohibiting particular contemplated uses of land, this Court has upheld land-use regulations that destroyed or adversely affected recognized real property interests. . . . Zoning laws are, of course, the classic example.").

56. *Murr*, 137 S. Ct. at 1942 (quoting Pennsylvania Coal Co. v. Mahon, 260 U.S. 393, 415 (1922)).

57. *Id.* at 1942–43.

58. Loretto v. Teleprompter Manhattan CATV Corp., 458 U.S. 419 (1982); Lucas v. South Carolina Coastal Comm'n, 505 U.S. 1003 (1992) (finding a regulatory taking with regard to regulations protecting South Carolina's barrier islands, which prevented any development of permanent habitations on petitioner's two lots). A so-called "total taking" may still be permissible if based on preexisting background principles of state property law, like nuisance. *Id.* at 1029.

59. For some additional leading cases, in addition to those cited above, *see* Lingle v. Chevron U.S.A. Inc., 544 U.S. 528 (2005); Tahoe-Sierra Pres. Council, Inc. v. Tahoe Reg'l Planning Agency, 535 U.S. 302 (2002); Palazzolo v. Rhode Island, 533 U.S. 606 (2001). For a general overview of regulatory takings, *see* AMERICAN JURISPRUDENCE: EMINENT DOMAIN §§ 10–12, 43 & 44.

60. 139 S. Ct. 2162 (2019).

61. Koontz v. St. Johns River Water Mgmt. Dist., 570 U.S. 595, 599 (2013) (citing Nollan v. California Coastal Comm'n, 483 U.S. 825 (1987), and Dolan v. City of Tigard, 512 U.S. 374 (1994)).

62. *Id.*

63. *Id.* at 612.

64. *See* California Bldg. Indus. Ass'n v. City of San Jose, 136 S. Ct. 928, 928 (2016) (Thomas, J., concurring in denial of certiorari).

serve inclusionary ends, as well as some that could be seen in either light, can be categorized as exactions, this area of law bears close attention in understanding limits on local zoning powers.[65]

IV. STATE CONSTITUTIONAL RESPONSES

While the federal constitutional provisions just discussed have had only a limited effect on exclusionary zoning, state constitutions and statutes have proven much more significant. In some respects, state law provides a more natural starting point for addressing exclusionary zoning because land-use provisions are historically creatures of state and local law. One might say that federal law provides mechanisms that address discriminatory zoning and other specific abuses of land use power, but state law forms the framework in which all local land-use provisions, exclusionary and otherwise, will operate. In some instances, such as New Jersey's *Mount Laurel* doctrine or Massachusetts' anti-snob zoning law (discussed in the following chapter), this has led to broad policies to promote affordable housing development throughout a jurisdiction. In other settings, state constitutional and statutory provisions have largely reinforced the deferential standards to local land-use reflected in *Euclid*.[66]

The following section discusses state constitutions and how they have been used to address affordable housing opportunities and constraints, using the experience of three states—New Jersey, Pennsylvania, and New York—as examples.[67] As these three cases illustrate, there are substantial differences in how state constitutional provisions apply, if they limit exclusionary zoning at all. These differences can be attributed to variation in the relevant constitutional provisions, differing common-law and other preexisting state land-use doctrines, and, probably most important, the willingness of particular state courts to address these issues. State legislative responses to exclusionary zoning are addressed in the next section.[68]

A. New Jersey

In the most famous and wide-reaching state constitutional response to exclusionary zoning, New Jersey's Supreme Court, in a series of landmark decisions commonly referred to as the *Mount Laurel* cases,[69] has found that the New Jersey Constitution prohibits exclusionary

---

65. See Cherk v. Marin Cnty., California, 140 S. Ct. 652 (2019) (denying certiorari in case concerning Marin County's inclusionary housing program).

66. *See, e.g.*, Blank v. Town of Lake Clarke Shores, 161 So. 2d 683, 686 (Fla. Dist. Ct. App. 1964).

67. This section is not exhaustive in covering state court responses to exclusionary zoning. For example, New Hampshire's supreme court has issued a decision that draws heavily on New Jersey's *Mount Laurel* line of cases, although it relied on the state's zoning enabling act rather than the constitution. Britton v. Town of Chester, 595 A.2d 492 (N.H. 1991).

68. In California, another state where the courts found state constitutional law to require heightened scrutiny of exclusionary zoning, see Associated Home Builders etc., Inc. v. City of Livermore, 18 Cal. 3d 582, 557 P.2d 473 (1976), state legislation has left judicial enforcement largely irrelevant as a source of law. However, California has, especially in recent years, been a hotbed of legislative energy on this topic, including the ways in which exclusionary zoning connects with climate issues.

69. S. Burlington Cnty. NAACP v. Mount Laurel Twp., 336 A.2d 713 (N.J. 1975) (*Mount Laurel I*) and S. Burlington NAACP v. Mount Laurel Twp., 456 A.2d 390 (N.J. 1983) (*Mount Laurel II*).

zoning and imposes an affirmative obligation on each municipality to provide its fair share of the regional need for affordable housing. The doctrine represents a significant reversal of the traditional deference to local land-use provisions, emphasizing instead a constitutionally derived commitment to the development of affordable housing in all 566 of New Jersey's municipalities. New Jersey has taken many different approaches to implementing that constitutional obligation—with complexity and controversy along the way—but the fundamental constitutional duty has provided the foundation for a thorough remaking of land-use law in the state.

Stemming from a series of cases brought by a local chapter of the NAACP and decided by the New Jersey Supreme Court beginning in 1975, the heart of the doctrine is the court's determination that, to satisfy the state constitutional obligation to exercise the police power in furtherance of the general welfare, the zoning authority granted by the state to municipalities carries with it an obligation to provide housing opportunity for all households, including low-income households. Furthermore, consideration of the general welfare does not stop at municipal boundaries; the *regional* need for low- and moderate-income housing must be considered. As the court stated in the inaugural *Mount Laurel* case, a municipality "cannot foreclose the opportunity of the classes of people mentioned for low- and moderate-income housing and in its regulations [it] must affirmatively afford that opportunity, at least to the extent of the municipality's fair share of the present and prospective regional need therefor."[70]

The consequences for local zoning and land-use provisions are significant. Rather than the deferential *Euclid* standard that presumes the appropriateness of a local zoning ordinance,[71] the *Mount Laurel* doctrine imposes an affirmative duty that anticipates that the general welfare can only be achieved by the creation of broad housing opportunity. The court has emphasized that providing a "realistic opportunity . . . may require more than the elimination of unnecessary cost-producing requirements and restrictions. Affirmative governmental devices should be used to make that opportunity realistic, including lower-income density bonuses and mandatory set-asides."[72] Thus, upon a showing that a municipality has adopted restrictive zoning or other land-use regulations, or even that it has failed

---

These cases initially involved the township of Mount Laurel's extremely restrictive zoning ordinance, which allowed only single-family homes on large lots. The court rejected the municipality's fiscal argument, based on alleged very high tax burdens, and other rationales, such as concerns about provision of water and sewer services. The initial history of the case produced substantial litigation but, in the eight years between *Mount Laurel I* and *II*, nothing in the way of affordable housing. In fact, the first low-income housing development in Mount Laurel was only opened more than 25 years after the first *Mount Laurel* decision and is named for the lead plaintiff, Ethel Lawrence. For a history of Mount Laurel, *see* Douglas Massey et al., Climbing Mount Laurel: The Struggle for Affordable Housing and Social Mobility in an American Suburb (2013); David Kirp et al., Our Town: Race, Housing and the Soul of Suburbia (1995); and John M. Payne, *Lawyers, Judges and the Public Interest*, 96 Mich. L. Rev. 1685 (1998) (reviewing Charles M. Haar, Suburbs Under Siege: Race, Space and Audacious Judges (1996)).

70. *Mount Laurel I*, 336 A.2d at 724–25.

71. Village of Euclid v. Ambler Realty, 272 U.S. 365, 395 (1926).

72. *Mount Laurel II*, 92 N.J. at 217.

to take affirmative advantage of housing subsidies or other resources potentially available, it may have the "heavy" burden of establishing a valid basis for its actions.[73]

Over the past 30 years, the practical dimensions of the doctrine have been significantly shaped by legislative and regulatory implementation measures, most notably the state's Fair Housing Act[74] enacted in 1985 at the court's urging.[75] While the administrative details were complex, they essentially provided that the state, through the Council on Affordable Housing (COAH), was to provide a specific number to reflect how many units of lower-income housing each municipality is obligated to provide. This number was intended to reflect both the municipality's own affordable housing needs and its fair share of the present and prospective regional need for such housing. Through a process known as substantive certification, municipalities could become substantially insulated against legal challenge under the *Mount Laurel* doctrine by submitting an acceptable plan to COAH regarding how the particular jurisdiction will meet its fair-share obligation based on specific plans for identified properties.[76] If municipalities chose not to go through this process (or were unable to develop an acceptable plan), builders or others proposing a development that includes a substantial amount of lower-income housing units (usually at least 20 percent) who were refused discretionary permits could proceed through litigation. If such litigation was successful, the court would issue an order overriding local zoning and enabling the developer to proceed. This "builder's remedy," which the Supreme Court authorized and explicitly understood would be "controversial," was intended as a substantial incentive for municipalities to comply with the constitutional mandate.[77]

More recently, however, executive branch resistance to the *Mount Laurel* doctrine led to gridlock at COAH and a failure to update the COAH rules after 1999. In response, the state Supreme Court declared COAH "nonfunctioning" and "moribund" and returned primary control of many aspects of the *Mount Laurel* process to the judiciary.[78] Upon doing so, the courts also recognized that the lengthy period of COAH's inaction had

---

73. *Mount Laurel I*, 336 A.2d at 717 (stating, "[W]hen it is shown that a developing municipality in its land use regulations has not made realistically possible a variety and choice of housing, including adequate provision to afford the opportunity for low and moderate income housing, or has expressly prescribed requirements or restrictions which preclude or substantially hinder it, a facial showing of violation of substantive due process or equal protection under the state constitution has been made out and the burden, and it is a heavy one, shifts to the municipality to establish a valid basis for its action or non-action.").

74. N.J. STAT. ANN. § 52:27D-301.

75. For additional discussion of New Jersey's fair housing act, see Chapter 2.

76. These plans are supposed to provide "a realistic, not just a theoretical, opportunity for the construction of lower-income housing." Holmdel Builders v. Twp. of Holmdel, 121 N.J. 550, 562 (1990). "Whether the opportunity is realistic will depend on whether there is in fact a likelihood—to the extent economic conditions allow—that the lower income housing will actually be constructed." *Mount Laurel II*, 92 N.J. at 222.

77. *Mount Laurel II*, 92 N.J. at 279. While there have been very few fully litigated builder's remedy lawsuits since the original *Mount Laurel* cases, the practical effect has been to force negotiation between municipalities and developers in those communities without substantive certification. For cases granting builder's remedies, *see* Rosenshein Assocs. v. Borough of Palisades Park, 701 A.2d 448 (N.J. Super. 1997); Toll Bros. Inc. v. Twp. of W. Windsor, 756 A.2d 1074 (N.J. Super. 2000); Sod Farm Assocs. v. Twp. of Springfield, 840 A.2d 885 (N.J. Super. 2004).

78. *In re* Adoption of N.J.A.C. 5:96 & 5:97 *ex rel.* New Jersey Council on Affordable Hous., 221 N.J. 1, 5 (2015).

generated an immense "pent-up need" for housing, which also had to be addressed as part of municipalities' constitutional obligations.[79] Taking that pent-up need into account, the courts' current methodology is calculated based on a determination that the state has an affordable housing need of 155,000 affordable housing units by 2025.[80] In many ways, this marks a return to the origins of the *Mount Laurel* process and underscores the importance of the constitutional foundation of the doctrine.

Rather than be subject to builders' remedy suits, since 2015 most New Jersey municipalities—representing the bulk of the developable, suburban land in the state—have instead reached voluntary, judicially approved settlements. These settlements have, among other things, led to substantially different and more inclusive zoning rules across the state. Already, observers have noticed a significant increase in multifamily development. And even before these settlements took effect, *Mount Laurel* had achieved significant results. As of 2011, the doctrine had led to the construction of more than 60,000 new affordable housing units, the rehabilitation of more than 15,000 units, and the collection of hundreds of millions of dollars in development fees.[81]

Over the years, the program has been criticized on a number of grounds, including that (1) the doctrine became unduly bureaucratic and incomprehensible to the public; (2) COAH's fair-share calculations resulted in substantially less housing than the overall affordable housing need in the state; (3) the use of the builder's remedy as the primary enforcement mechanism had unintended consequences, such as the exclusion of nonprofit developers from significant roles in development intended to meet *Mt. Laurel* obligations and development inconsistent with sound planning principles; and (4) in earlier rounds of *Mt. Laurel* compliance, wealthy jurisdictions were allowed to buy their way out of their fair share obligations.[82] Many of these critiques have been addressed as the doctrine and implementation of *Mt. Laurel* continues to evolve.

While much more could be said about the development of New Jersey's land-use system, the broader point is the *Mount Laurel* doctrine brings a fundamentally different perspective to local zoning and land-use ordinances. Rather than the broad deference granted under *Euclid* and related cases, the *Mount Laurel* doctrine holds local zoning and land use to a higher standard, animated by broad, constitutionally derived general welfare principles. And in contrast to the Equal Protection or the FHA framework, which scrutinize exclusionary zoning only through a narrower antidiscrimination framework, the New Jersey constitution requires the state and its municipalities to exercise their zoning authority to proactively further the fulfillment of the state's responsibilities regarding housing to all of its residents.

---

79. *In re* Declaratory Judgment Actions Filed by Various Municipalities, 227 N.J. 508, 513 (2017).

80. Maddie Hanna, *Judge's Order for More Affordable Housing in Princeton Could Ripple across New Jersey*, PHILA. INQUIRER (Mar. 8, 2018), https://www.inquirer.com/philly/news/new _jersey/nj-affordable-housing-ruling-princeton-west-windsor-20180308.html.

81. *New Jersey Council on Affordable Housing, Proposed and Completed Affordable Units* (Mar. 1, 2011), https://www.nj.gov/dca/divisions/lps/hss/transinfo/reports/units.pdf.

82. *See, e.g.,* John M. Payne, *Rethinking Fair Share: The Judicial Enforcement of Affordable Housing Policies*, 16 REAL ESTATE L. J. 20 (Summer 1987); John M. Payne, *Fairly Sharing Affordable Housing Obligations: The Mount Laurel Matrix*, 22 WN. NEW ENGLAND L. REV. 365 (2001).

B. Pennsylvania

While New Jersey's approach under the *Mount Laurel* doctrine remains the most substantial state constitutional mandate regarding affordable housing, Pennsylvania doctrine shows an alternative path to a constitutionally derived judicial skepticism of exclusionary zoning. Pennsylvania's jurisprudence originated from a very different ideological and legal angle, stemming more from a property rights perspective.[83] It has not generated the same elaborate judicial and administrative apparatuses for implementing the doctrine. And the Pennsylvania cases emphasize the need for diverse housing *types* (e.g., multifamily, townhouse, mobile home) rather than focusing on unit affordability.[84] All told, the approach differs substantially from that of *Mount Laurel*.

Pennsylvania's willingness to more carefully scrutinize exclusionary zoning is reflected in the seminal case of *National Land & Investment Co. v. Kohn*, decided by the Supreme Court of Pennsylvania in 1965.[85] In response to a challenge from the owner of a large plot of undeveloped land, the court determined that the town's use of four-acre-minimum lot zoning was constitutionally invalid. Review of a zoning ordinance under the traditional standard focused upon whether it was reasonably enacted for health, safety, morals, or the general welfare.[86] Here, the court used a fact-specific and detailed approach, indicating a higher standard than deferential scrutiny of any "fairly debatable" legislative purpose. The court carefully evaluated each purpose presented by the town and found all of them inadequate.[87] The court concluded that the purpose of the zoning ordinance was exclusionary and declared that the township could not stand in the way of the "natural forces" sending growing populations in search of comfortable places to live.[88]

Today, Pennsylvania doctrine forbids any local jurisdiction from enacting an outright, de jure ban on all population growth or all multifamily housing.[89] Nor may a jurisdiction evade this prohibition on exclusionary zoning through "tokenism" or "selective admission";

---

83. *See* BAC, Inc. v. Bd. of Sup'rs of Millcreek Twp., 633 A.2d 144, 146 (1993).

84. *See* Willistown Twp. v. Chesterdale Farms, Inc., 341 A.2d 466 (Pa. 1975) (while the court states that localities must meet the needs of "all categories of people" desirous of living in the community, and quotes *Mount Laurel I* language framing the fair-share obligation in terms of low- and moderate-income housing, the apartment development involved was not explicitly affordable). *See also* Surrick v. Zoning Hearing Bd. of Twp. of Upper Providence, 382 A.2d 105, 109 (Pa. 1977) (applying *Willistown*, and also involving a proposed apartment development with no explicit affordability provisions).

85. 215 A.2d 597 (Pa. 1965).

86. *Id.* at 607.

87. *Id.* at 611. For example, against the argument that four-acre zoning was required to ensure adequate sewage disposal, the court pointed out the existence of sanitary regulations and subdivision requirements for larger lots where percolation tests indicated inadequate drainage: "[t]hese legislatively sanctioned methods for dealing with the sewage problem compel the conclusion that a four-acre minimum is neither a necessary nor a reasonable method by which Easttown can protect itself from the menace of pollution." Similarly, in response to the claimed purpose of creating a greenbelt, the court pointed out that "appellants betray their argument that there is a ready market for four-acre plots. Only if there is no market for four-acre lots will the land continue to be open and undeveloped and greenbelt created." *Id.*

88. *Id.* at 612.

89. *Appeal of Girsh*, 263 A.2d 395 (Pa. 1970).

zoning must allow for a true, meaningful chance to build the housing needed for growth.[90] In determining how much multifamily housing is enough, the Pennsylvania courts examine three factors: whether the jurisdiction is in the path of regional growth, whether it is already highly developed, and whether it has provided its fair share of the type of housing under consideration.[91] In addition to multiple dwellings generally, this doctrine has also been successfully used in Pennsylvania to challenge the exclusion of mobile home parks.[92]

Pennsylvania courts tie this analysis to an assessment of regional need. "If [a town] is located so that it is a place where apartment living is in demand, it must provide for apartments in its plan for future growth; it cannot be allowed to close its doors to others seeking a 'comfortable place to live.'"[93] While regional need can be used affirmatively by challengers of ordinances that limit certain types of development, the location of a municipality *outside* a growing or developing area cannot be used by the township as a defense, at least where the total prohibition of multifamily dwellings is at issue.[94]

As recently as 2011, the Commonwealth Court of Pennsylvania found a local zoning ordinance unconstitutionally exclusionary. In *Main St. Dev. Grp., Inc. v. Tinicum Twp. Bd. of Supervisors*,[95] the court considered local zoning that, in effect, required 95 percent of land in the township to be used for agricultural purposes. In response to a challenge from a developer looking to build 192 garden apartments, the court struck down the zoning, finding that the ordinance failed to "balance the need for development and agricultural uses."[96]

Overall, the Pennsylvania courts appear to have determined that the state constitution represents a constraint on exclusionary zoning and some commitment to fair share analysis, but in a manner that must be resolved based on the specifics of the situation at hand and that is tied to the types of housing allowed rather than affordability levels.

C. New York

New York represents a further step on the continuum, imposing some state constitutional constraints on broad exclusionary zoning provisions but providing greater deference to local jurisdictions compared to New Jersey or Pennsylvania.

New York's leading exclusionary zoning case is *Berenson v. Town of New Castle*.[97] At issue was the constitutionality of an ordinance completely excluding multifamily housing from the town. Although the Court of Appeals (New York's highest court) began by restating the *Euclid* presumption that zoning ordinances are presumptively valid unless they bear no substantial relation to public health, safety, morals, or the general welfare, it quickly moved on to establish a higher standard of scrutiny for potentially exclusionary zoning ordinances. The court established a two-tiered test for evaluating the validity

---

90. Township of Willistown v. Chesterdale Farms, Inc., 462 Pa. 445, 341 A.2d 466 (1975).

91. Surrick v. Zoning Hearing Bd. of Twp. of Upper Providence, 382 A.2d 105 (Pa. 1977).

92. *See, e.g.,* Envtl. Communities of Pa., Inc. v. North Coventry Twp., 412 A.2d 650 (Pa. Commw. Ct. 1980); Zajac v. Zoning Hearing Bd. of Mifflin Twp., 398 A.2d 244 (Pa. Commw. Ct. 1979); *see also* 2 ANDERSON'S AM. LAW. ZONING § 14:1 (4th ed. 2004). For additional discussion of exclusionary zoning and mobile homes/manufactured housing, see Chapter 5.

93. *Appeal of Girsh*, 263 A.2d at 399.

94. Fernley v. Bd. of Supervisors of Schuylkill Twp., 502 A.2d 585 (Pa. 1985).

95. 19 A.3d 21 (Pa. Commw. Ct. 2011).

96. *Id.* at 28.

97. 38 N.Y.2d 102 (N.Y. 1975).

of restrictive ordinances. The first tier requires the existence of "a properly balanced and well-ordered plan for the community" addressing the present and future needs of community residents.[98] The exact form and content of the plan is unspecified. It may be a formal planning document or it may be implied by the zoning actions of the town.[99] *Berenson* uses a case-by-case approach in which specific facts, such as the town's size, are relevant in assessing the balance of the plan, as a very small town might legitimately be only one "use" district.[100]

The second tier of *Berenson* requires that local zoning consider regional needs. The town must consider the needs of the neighboring communities because "it must be recognized that zoning often has a substantial impact beyond the boundaries of the municipality."[101] This language led to some speculation that New York would adopt a fair-share doctrine similar to the one established by New Jersey's *Mt. Laurel* cases. Indeed, on remand, the trial court found an unmet regional need and mandated a number of affirmative measures, including incentives for developers to construct low-cost housing. But the New York courts limited the remedies available under *Berenson*, leaving the doctrine far weaker than *Mount Laurel*. On a second appeal of the original *Berenson* case, relief was limited to the rezoning of the plaintiff's plot to multifamily use and the direction that the town make a "good faith effort" to amend its ordinance to address the unmet need.[102]

The limited direct application of New York's exclusionary zoning doctrine to affordability issues was further illustrated in *Suffolk Housing Services v. Town of Brookhaven*,[103] where the Appellate Division declined to read the *Berenson* balance and regional needs tests as requiring consideration of the affordability of different types of housing. "Berenson does not address the question of . . . who, if anyone, will be able to afford the kinds of housing which are ultimately built, nor does it purport to mandate that a zoning ordinance make it possible for people of all classes to live in a given community."[104] And although Brookhaven's zoning imposed a special use permit requirement on multifamily housing (but not single-family housing), the court considered this to satisfy the *Berenson* standard since multiple dwelling types were permitted and had actually been approved and built.[105]

The New York courts continued to limit the reach of the *Berenson* doctrine in the case of *Kurzius v. Vill. of Upper Brookville*.[106] There, the Court of Appeals upheld the constitutionality of zoning that required five-acre lots, repeatedly endorsing the virtues of

---

98. *Id.* at 110.

99. *See, e.g.,* Udell v. Haas, 21 N.Y.2d 463, 469–71 (N.Y. 1968).

100. 38 N.Y.2d 102, 110 (N.Y. 1975).

101. *Id.*

102. Berenson v. New Castle, 67 A.D.2d 506, 524 (N.Y. App. Div. 1979). The New Jersey Supreme Court rejected a similar "good faith effort" test in its 1983 decision, discussed *supra*.

103. 109 A.D.2d 323 (N.Y. App. Div. 1985). The *Brookhaven* litigation began in the seventies and is also notable for its relaxation of New York's traditionally restrictive standing requirements for challenges to zoning provisions. *See* Suffolk Housing Servs. v. Town of Brookhaven, 397 N.Y.S.2d 302 (N.Y. Super. Ct. 1977) (rejecting restrictive standing requirements of prior New York case law and rejecting *Warth* as applicable only to the federal courts), *aff'd as modified*, 63 A.D.2d 731 (N.Y. App. Div. 1978).

104. *Id.* at 331.

105. *Id.* at 329.

106. 51 N.Y.2d 338 (N.Y. 1980).

large-lot zoning for avoiding what it called "the ill-effects of urbanization" and promoting a low-density style of living.[107] And the court held that the unconstitutionality of a zoning ordinance must be proved "beyond a reasonable doubt."[108] Periodically, plaintiffs are able to successfully bring litigation against exclusionary zoning under the *Berenson* doctrine.[109] But between the weak remedies available, the heavy burden of proof placed on plaintiffs, and the acceptance of exclusionary techniques like large-lot zoning, New York's approach is essentially deferential to local zoning and planning decisions, unless they completely restrict housing other than single-family detached homes or are enacted for an illegitimate motive.[110] Partly a result, New York builds less housing in its suburban areas than states like New Jersey or Pennsylvania.[111] The New York courts have suggested that legislative intervention is warranted, but have generally failed to adopt standards that would address problematic zoning practices in the absence of such action.[112]

V. THE FEDERAL FAIR HOUSING ACT

With the enactment of the Fair Housing Act (FHA) in 1968, the legal basis to challenge exclusionary zoning was significantly enhanced. Especially as the courts constrained the use of the Equal Protection Clause,[113] the FHA has become the central federal vehicle for such cases. Unlike the Equal Protection Clause, the FHA allows for disparate impact liability and covers non-state action; it also allows for broad standing to bring claims and offers a wide array of relief once a claim is proven. The significance of the FHA has been enlarged due to the passage of the Fair Housing Amendments Act of 1988 (hereinafter FHAA), which both expanded the groups protected under the act and added a strengthened governmental enforcement structure. The following section begins with a brief overview of the structure and context for the FHA, then addresses key issues such as disparate impact liability, and concludes with some pragmatic considerations.[114] It should be noted that almost every state has its own version of a fair housing act,[115] and some states offer considerably broader protections against discrimination than the federal act.

---

107. *Id.* at 344.

108. *Id.*

109. *See, e.g.*, Land Master Montg I, LLC v. Town of Montgomery, 13 Misc. 3d 870, 880, 821 N.Y.S.2d 432, 440 (Sup. Ct. 2006), *aff'd*, 54 A.D.3d 408, 863 N.Y.S.2d 692 (2008).

110. Plaintiffs may also establish proof of discriminatory motives. *See, e.g.*, Continental Bldg. Co., Inc. v. Town of North Salem, 625 N.Y.S.2d 700 (N.Y. App. Div. 1995).

111. Nicholas Marantz & Huixin Zheng, *Exclusionary Zoning and the Limits of Judicial Impact*, J. Planning Education & Research (2018).

112. *See* Nolan & Bacher, Affordable Housing in the New York Courts: A Case for Legislative Action (2006) (Pace Law School), https://digitalcommons.pace.edu/cgi/viewcontent .cgi?article=1639&context=lawfaculty.

113. *See* discussion, *supra*, regarding the Equal Protection Clause.

114. For those interested in more detail than the overview provided here, the authors highly recommend the leading treatise on housing discrimination, *see* Schwemm, *supra* note 27.

115. This is incentivized by the FHA itself, through the Fair Housing Assistance Program (FHAP). *See* 42 U.S.C. § 3616; 24 C.F.R. §§ 115.201, 115.307.

A. Overview

Enacted in April 1968 in the immediate aftermath of the assassination of Dr. Martin Luther King Jr., and in response to the race riots of 1967 and the Kerner Commission Report, the FHA seeks "to provide, within constitutional limitations, for fair housing throughout the United States."[116] As the Supreme Court noted in its unanimous decision in *Trafficante v. Metropolitan Life Insurance Co.*,[117] the FHA's language is "broad and inclusive," and the act carries out a "policy that Congress considered to be of the highest priority." As a result, the courts early on recognized this policy by giving a "generous construction" to the statute, noting that "Congress was aware that the measure would have a very broad reach, and indeed the legislation was seen as an attempt to alter the whole character of the housing market."[118]

This is reflected in both the breadth of its reach and the means of its enforcement. The FHA prohibits discrimination in the rental, sale, advertising, and development of housing, reinforcing its scope by the inclusion of a catchall prohibition on practices that "otherwise make unavailable or deny" a dwelling based on any of the protected classes.[119] While part of the FHA's original significance was its application to the private housing market, it has been equally clear since its passage that it applies to municipal governments and other public actors in a wide range of activities that implicate housing.[120] These include not only the passage or implementation of zoning ordinances but also the funding and siting of publicly assisted housing,[121] the operation of occupancy restrictions,[122] the targeting of code enforcement operations,[123] the granting or denial of variances or special use permits,[124] decisions to abandon construction of or demolish housing,[125] the application of residency

---

116. 42 U.S.C. § 3601.

117. 409 U.S. 205 (1972).

118. Mayers v. Ridley, 465 F.2d 630, 652 (D.C. Cir. 1972) (en banc) (Wilkey, J. concurring). *See* discussion in SCHWEMM, *supra* note 27, § 7 for legislative history and construction.

119. *See* 42 U.S.C. § 3604(a) (for the general prohibition), 42 U.S.C. § 3604(e) (for specific prohibitions on blockbusting), and 42 U.S.C. § 3605 (for prohibition on real estate–related financial transactions).

120. *See, e.g.*, United States v. City of Parma, Ohio, 661 F.2d 562 (6th Cir. 1981), *cert. denied*, City of Parma, Ohio v. United States, 456 U.S. 926 (1982) (city is a person under the act); Casa Marie, Inc. v. Sup. Ct. of Puerto Rico, 988 F.2d 252, 257 n.6 (1st Cir. 1993) (stating that "[t]he phrase 'otherwise make unavailable or deny' encompasses a wide array of housing practices . . . and specifically targets the discriminatory use of zoning laws and restrictive covenants."). The Supreme Court has identified exclusionary zoning cases as the "heartland" of disparate impact liability under the FHA. Texas Dep't of Hous. & Cmty. Affairs v. Inclusive Communities Project, Inc., 576 U.S. 519, 539 (2015).

121. United States v. Yonkers Bd. of Educ., 837 F.2d 1181, 1218–22 (2d Cir. 1987), *cert. denied*, 486 U.S. 1055 (1988) (finding that the practice of construction of subsidized housing projects in areas of high minority concentration violated § 3604).

122. *See, e.g.*, Fair Housing Advocates Ass'n, Inc. v. City of Richmond Heights, Ohio, 209 F.3d 626 (6th Cir. 2000); City of Edmonds v. Oxford House, Inc., 514 U.S. 725 (1995).

123. *See, e.g.*, *City of Parma*, 661 F.2d at 562.

124. *See, e.g.*, United States v. City of Philadelphia, Pa., 838 F. Supp. 223 (E.D. Pa. 1993), *aff'd*, 30 F.3d 1488 (3d Cir. 1994) (No. 93-2095, 93-2096).

125. *See Yonkers Bd. of Educ.*, 837 F.2d at 1218 (stating that "the absence of a general obligation to construct does not give the municipality license to proceed discriminatorily once it has started down the road to construction"). *See also* Acevedo v. Nassau County, 500 F.2d 1078, 1082 (2d Cir.

or "citizenship" preferences,[126] and voter referendums related to the provision of housing.[127] Some of these types of claims may face greater challenges when based on disparate impact theories rather than discriminatory intent, however.[128]

In addition to this prohibition against discrimination, the FHA imposes an affirmative duty on all executive departments and agencies in the federal government to further the act's purposes through the administration of its programs and activities.[129] This obligation involves not only preventing discrimination against individuals but also promoting racially integrated housing.[130] The courts have found that this obligation extends to state and local governments that utilize federal funds.[131]

The FHA initially protected individuals from discrimination based on their race, color, religion, and national origin. Subsequent amendments to the act added sex, family status, and disability to the protected classes.[132] While claims based on the original protected classes are usually straightforward, it is worth noting that "national origin" has been interpreted to include claims from Latinos or other groups who believe they have been discriminated against due to their country of origin. It is also likely that the prohibition on

---

1974); Smith v. Town of Clarkton, 682 F.2d 1055 (4th Cir. 1982) (termination of a planned housing project had a discriminatory effect on African American residents).

126. *See* United States v. Housing Authority of the City of Chickasaw, 504 F. Supp. 716 (S.D. Ala. 1980) (limitation of eligibility to existing residents violated the Fair Housing Act); *see also* Langlois v. Abington Housing Auth., 207 F.3d 43 (1st Cir. 2000) (trial court's finding of disparate racial impact of residency preference should not be disturbed, but rejection of government's justification using a balancing test was incorrect. Remanded for consideration of alternate legal theories based on FHA's "affirmatively further" language.).

127. *See, e.g., City of Parma*, 661 F.2d at 562; *but see* Arthur v. City of Toledo, Ohio, 782 F.2d 565, 574–75 (6th Cir. 1986) (stating "[a]bsent highly unusual circumstances, the discriminatory effect of a referendum cannot establish a violation of the Fair Housing Act"). However, the court notes that a referendum could be challenged on equal protection and FHA grounds if it had a discriminatory intent, as indicated by facial discrimination or the absence of any non-racial rationale. *Id. See also* City of Cuyahoga Falls, Ohio v. Buckeye Cmty. Hope Found., 538 U.S. 188 (2003) (Finding no discriminatory intent under the Equal Protection Clause, despite evidence of racially discriminatory motivations on the part of private citizens supporting a referendum).

128. Ellis v. City of Minneapolis, 860 F.3d 1106, 1114 (8th Cir. 2017) (rejecting challenge to code enforcement, holding that "Governmental entities therefore must have the leeway to apply reasonable housing-code provisions without fear of inviting a costly lawsuit."); *City of Joliet v. New West, L.P.* 825 F.3d 827, 830 (7th Cir. 2016) (rejecting challenge to the demolition of dilapidated housing). *See generally* Texas Dep't of Hous. & Cmty. Affairs v. Inclusive Communities Project, Inc., 576 U.S. 519, 540–42 (2015) (expressing doubt that decisions such as where to allocate low-income housing tax credits could give rise to disparate impact liability).

129. 42 U.S.C. § 3608(d) & (e)(5). For more discussion of the FHAA's application to federal government affordable housing funding programs, see Chapters 2, 6, and 8.

130. N.A.A.C.P. v. Secretary of Hous. & Urban Dev., 817 F.2d 149 (1st Cir. 1987).

131. *See, e.g.,* Otero v. N.Y. City Hous. Auth., 484 F.2d 1122, 1133–34 (2d Cir.1973) (finding that the affirmative duty to further fair housing also applies to "other agencies administering federally-assisted housing programs"); Shannon v. U.S. Dep't of Hous. & Urban Dev., 305 F. Supp. 205 (D.C. Pa. 1969); *see also In re* Adoption of the 2003 LIHTC Qualified Allocation Plan, 848 A.2d 1 (N.J. Super. App. Div. 2004).

132. While the Fair Housing Amendment Act of 1988 uses the term "handicap," the term "disability" is used here.

sex discrimination also prohibits discrimination against gay or transgender people.[133] The two most recently added classes, familial status and disability, raise less traditional issues. Under the act, "familial status" focuses upon families (biological or adoptive) with a child under 18.[134] Familial status issues are raised when, among other things, a municipality adopts or enforces occupancy standards that might restrict the number of family members in an apartment of a certain size, or when a zoning ordinance singles out for special treatment group homes for children or those in foster care.[135] As discussed in the following section, the inclusion of disability has even greater implications for municipal land-use ordinances, as it means that land-use restrictions of group homes for the disabled may raise issues under the FHA. A broad array of persons is covered by the definition of disability under the FHA, including recovering substance abusers.[136]

The FHA can be enforced through traditional court proceedings by both private parties and the government. Notably, the act provides that the attorney general of the United States may bring affirmative actions when a "pattern or practice of discrimination" is at issue, and may obtain not only injunctive relief but monetary damages for aggrieved persons and civil penalties.[137] Moreover, as expanded by the 1988 amendments to the FHA, the act authorizes any individual who believes he or she has been discriminated against to file a complaint with the U.S. Department of Housing and Urban Development (HUD).[138] HUD is obligated to investigate the complaint and, if reasonable cause exists, to issue a charge of discrimination. Subsequently, either HUD or the U.S. Department of Justice (DOJ) will represent the individual in an administrative proceeding or in federal court.

---

133. Bostock v. Clayton County, Georgia, 590 U.S. __ (2020) (holding same under analogous provisions of Title VII). *See also* Quid Pro Quo and Hostile Environment Harassment and Liability for Discriminatory Housing Practices under the Fair Housing Act, 81 Fed. Reg. 63,054, 63,058-59 (Sept. 14, 2016) (HUD reaffirming position that the FHA "prohibits discrimination because of gender identity" based on reasoning similar to *Bostock*). *See* Rigel C. Oliveri, *Sexual Orientation and Gender Identity Discrimination under the Fair Housing Act after* Bostock v. Clayton County, 69 U. Kan. Law Rev. (forthcoming 2021).

134. 42 U.S.C. § 3602(k).

135. While a full discussion of occupancy standards and the circumstances under which they may violate the FHA exceeds the scope of this chapter, the central issue turns on whether they simply govern the number of individuals in a dwelling unit and, if so, their "reasonableness" given the FHA's exemption of such provisions. *See* 42 U.S.C. § 3607(b)(1); Pfaff v. HUD, 88 F.3d 739 (9th Cir. 1996) (concerning occupancy standards). There are multiple other issues involving the familial status provisions, including when the exemption related to housing for seniors applies. *See* 42 U.S.C. § 3607(b)(2). *See also* Doe v. City of Butler, 892 F.2d 315 (3d Cir. 1989) (rejecting FHA challenge from group of abused women whose desired housing violated local zoning laws). For a treatment of the interaction of the occupancy standard exception with racial discrimination in housing, *see* Tim Iglesias, *Clarifying the Federal Fair Housing Act's Exemption for Reasonable Occupancy Restrictions*, 31 Fordham Urb. L.J. 1211 (2004).

136. *See* United States v. Southern Mgmt. Corp., 955 F.2d 914, 919–23 (4th Cir. 1992).

137. 42 U.S.C. § 3614.

138. *Id.* § 3613. The FHAA increased the statute of limitations for private lawsuits from 180 days to two years. *Id.* § 3613(a)(1)(A). *See also* H.R. Rep. No. 711, 100th Cong., 2d Sess. 1988 (noting that private enforcement prior to 1988 was hampered by a short statute of limitations of 180 days).

While an individual is permitted to file a complaint with HUD regarding an alleged exclusionary zoning or other land-use matter, these complaints are referred directly to the DOJ for investigation.[139]

B. Theories of Discrimination

There are three principal theories by which a local land-use ordinance can be found to have violated the FHA: (1) intentional discrimination; (2) discriminatory effects; or, (3) in cases involving disability, failure to provide reasonable accommodation. Such theories are not mutually exclusive and are frequently pled as alternatives. Each is discussed in turn.

As noted in the prior discussion of the Equal Protection Clause, a municipality will be found to have violated both the Fourteenth Amendment and the FHA if its zoning ordinance or other land-use provision is enacted or utilized for a discriminatory purpose. A court will engage in a searching inquiry to determine whether such a purpose exists, as exemplified by the factors set out in *Arlington Heights*.[140]

Two additional points are worth noting. First, although the most common conception of illegal discrimination is that which is motivated by animus against a protected group, this is not necessary. The touchstone is whether race or other protected characteristic formed a motivating factor in the municipality's decision, which means an entity can violate the FHA even if it is motivated by paternalistic or beneficial rationales.[141] Thus, the courts have struck down ordinances that required group homes for the disabled to be separated by minimum distances even though the proffered rationale, to avoid the creation of a disability "ghetto," was not necessarily motivated by animus.[142] Second, a municipality can be found to have violated the FHA when it responds to improperly motivated pressure from private citizens. In circumstances, for example, where concerns about the racial makeup of an affordable housing development prompt widespread public opposition, a municipality that accedes to such pressures can be found to have violated the FHA.[143]

---

139. *Id.* § 3610(g)(C).

140. *Arlington Heights*, 99 S. Ct. at 564–67.

141. It is unclear whether the "motivating factor" standard means that *any* consideration of protected characteristics constitutes a violation, or whether the impermissible consideration must be the "but-for" cause of the action taken. *See* SCHWEMM, *supra* note 27, at 10:3 n.37. Complicating matters further is the fact that government entities may consider race to some extent in their efforts to affirmatively further fair housing. *See* Texas Dep't of Hous. & Cmty. Affairs v. Inclusive Communities Project, Inc., 576 U.S. 519, 545 (2015) ("When setting their larger goals, local housing authorities may choose to foster diversity and combat racial isolation with race-neutral tools, and mere awareness of race in attempting to solve the problems facing inner cities does not doom that endeavor at the outset.").

142. Horizon House Dev. Servs., Inc. v. Twp. of Upper Southampton, 804 F. Supp. 683 (E.D. Pa. 1992) (benign motive is irrelevant when an ordinance is facially discriminatory). Courts are not always clear on which standard to apply, however, and the nature of the analysis may depend on the facts of the case. *Compare* Community House, Inc. v. City of Boise, 490 F.3d 1041, 1050 (9th Cir. 2007) (discussing circuit split over how to treat facially discriminatory restrictions which benefit people with a protected characteristic).

143. *See, e.g.*, United States v. City of Birmingham, Mich., 727 F.2d 560, 562–63 (6th Cir.), *cert denied*, 469 U.S. 821 (1984):

> [I]n order to demonstrate a city's racially discriminatory intent, it is sufficient to show that the decision-making body acted for the sole purpose of effectuating the desires of private

The second category of FHA violation is generally referred to as discriminatory effects and encompasses two types of claims: disparate impact liability and perpetuation of segregation claims, each of which courts have recognized for decades. Liability under these theories does not require a showing of intentional discrimination. Recognizing that "the FHA must play an important part in avoiding the Kerner Commission's grim prophecy that '[o]ur Nation is moving toward two societies, one black, one white—separate and unequal,'" the Supreme Court affirmed the availability of discriminatory effects liability under the FHA in its landmark 2015 decision in *Texas Department of Housing and Community Affairs v. Inclusive Communities Project, Inc.*[144] For its part, HUD developed regulations in 2013 to recognize the availability of discriminatory effects liability and clarify the applicable standards for such claims in the face of various splits among the circuits.[145]

Inclusive Communities and the HUD regulations apply the same framework for disparate impact claims. First, the plaintiff must show that the challenged practice caused or will cause a discriminatory effect. Second, if the plaintiff makes that showing, the burden shifts to the defendant to show that it has a valid justification for the challenged practice: HUD defines this as being "necessary to achieve one or more substantial, legitimate, nondiscriminatory interests." Finally, the plaintiff may still prevail if it shows that those interests could be furthered by a less discriminatory practice.[146] There remain some open questions about precisely how to apply this framework. The lower courts are currently working through the questions whether the Supreme Court in *Inclusive Communities* in fact adopted HUD's framework and, if not, which standard governs.[147] Additionally, *Inclusive Communities* appeared to either impose new or reinforce existing "safeguards" on the scope of disparate impact liability, including by reiterating that defendants should not be forced to choose between two valid approaches to housing policy and suggesting that showings of causation must be "robust."[148] The lower courts have divided in their interpretations of what these safeguards demand.[149]

Additionally, both the courts and HUD have recognized liability where a practice perpetuates segregation.[150] The framework for perpetuation-of-segregation claims is essentially the same as for disparate impact liability, using the same three-part burden-shifting approach, with a different harm at issue.[151] To understand fully the nature of the

---

citizens, that racial considerations were a motivating factor behind those desires, and that members of the decision-making body were aware of the motivations of the private citizens.

144. 576 U.S. 519.

145. 24 C.F.R. § 100.500.

146. *Id.*

147. See Mhany Mgmt., Inc. v. Cty. of Nassau, 819 F.3d 581, 618 (2d Cir. 2016); *Reyes v. Waples Mobile Home Park Ltd. P'ship*, 903 F.3d 415, 424 n.4 (4th Cir. 2018); Inclusive Communities Project, Inc. v. Lincoln Prop. Co., 920 F.3d 890, 902 (5th Cir. 2019).

148. 576 U.S. at 542.

149. *See Inclusive Communities Project, Inc.*, 920 F.3d at 903–06 (comparing judicial treatments of causation standard).

150. For a thorough analysis of perpetuation of segregation claims, *see* Robert G. Schwemm, Segregative-Effect Claims under the Fair Housing Act, 20 N.Y.U. J. Leg. & Pub. Pol'y 709 (2017).

151. 24 C.F.R. § 100.500; *see also* 576 U.S. at 540 ("the FHA aims to ensure that those priorities can be achieved without arbitrarily creating discriminatory effects *or perpetuating segregation*" (emphasis added)).

perpetuation-of-segregation claim, it is important to recognize that the purpose of the FHA, as made clear in the Supreme Court's *Trafficante* decision, was not just to advance the rights of people of color and other protected groups but to create "truly integrated and balanced living patterns."[152] While tensions have occasionally emerged between the anti-discrimination and pro-integration interests of the FHA in other contexts,[153] this type of claim typically arises when a developer seeks to build an affordable housing complex that would add a significant non-white population to an all-white or virtually all-white neighborhood or municipality. In such circumstances, the proof would focus upon the extent of segregation in the area and the integrative effect of the proposed housing complex.[154]

It should be noted that under the Trump administration, HUD unsuccessfully attempted to rewrite and substantially weaken the standards for discriminatory effects liability.[155] Among other changes, these new regulations would have imposed an onerous five-part pleading standard for plaintiffs in disparate impact cases and removed any mention of perpetuation-of-segregation liability.[156] However, courts enjoined the implementation and enforcement of the Trump administration's rule,[157] and the Biden administration has proposed restoring the preexisting framework.[158]

The third means of proving that a municipality's land-use activity violates the FHA arises exclusively in disability cases, pursuant to the section of the act that requires a "reasonable accommodation in rules, practices, policies, or services, when such accommodations may be necessary to afford such person equal opportunity to use and enjoy a dwelling."[159] This provision applies to zoning and other land-use activities. For example, in *Oxford House, Inc. v. Township of Cherry Hill*, the plaintiffs were a group of recovering substance abusers who sought to live together as part of a therapeutic national program.[160] They were thwarted by the municipality, which allowed an unlimited number of *related* persons to live together but required a variance for more than a specific number of *unrelated* persons to live together. In this case, when the group of individuals in recovery sought the variance, the municipality denied their request. Under the reasonable accommodation provision, the court determined that the municipality would not suffer a substantial impairment to a fundamental activity by granting them a variance from its rules, and that this

---

152. 409 U.S. at 211 (quoting legislative sponsor Senator Mondale).

153. The most prominent example of this tension occurred in *United States v. Starrett City*, 840 F.2d 1096 (2d Cir.), *cert. denied,* 488 U.S. 946 (1988) (concluding that maintenance of an integrated apartment complex was an insufficient rationale to justify the maintenance of two separate waiting lists designed to maintain a racial balance so as to avoid white flight).

154. *See, e.g.*, Huntington Branch, NAACP v. Town of Huntington, 844 F.2d 926, 937–38 (2d Cir.), *aff'd per curiam*, 488 U.S. 15 (1988).

155. HUD's Implementation of the Fair Housing Act's Disparate Treatment Standard, 85 Fed. Reg. 60,288 (Sept. 24, 2020).

156. *Id.*

157. Massachusetts Fair Hous. Ctr. v. United States Dep't of Hous. & Urban Dev., No. CV 20-11765-MGM, 2020 WL 6390143, at *8 (D. Mass. Oct. 25, 2020).

158. Reinstatement of HUD's Discriminatory Effects Standard, 86 Fed. Reg. 33,590 (June 25, 2021).

159. 42 U.S.C. § 3604(f)(3)(B).

160. Oxford House, Inc. v. Twp. of Cherry Hill, 799 F. Supp. 450 (1992).

variance was necessary for the plaintiffs to have an equal opportunity to use and enjoy housing.[161]

Since its addition to the FHA in 1988, the reasonable accommodation provision, imported from cases interpreting Section 504 of the Rehabilitation Act,[162] has become increasingly significant in land-use matters and has now been applied in a broad array of circumstances. While the particulars differ, the central thrust is that a municipality must grant an exception or waiver to its rules, policies, or decision if (1) the plaintiff has requested it, (2) the plaintiff has established its necessity, and (3) the municipality cannot show that it will cause undue financial or administrative burdens or require fundamental alterations in its operation.[163] Although the evidence used in establishing a reasonable accommodation claim may be similar to that in a disparate impact case, it is important to note that a reasonable accommodation claim involves only the plaintiff at issue and does not invalidate the provision or rule as it affects any other entity.

C. Standing

In 1972, the Court determined in *Trafficante v. Metropolitan Life Insurance Company*[164] that Congress's intent in the FHA was to define standing as broadly as was consistent with Article III of the Constitution.[165] In *Trafficante*, standing was recognized for white residents of an apartment complex that discriminated against people of color. The alleged injury was the loss of personal and business advantages to be gained from living in an integrated environment. As noted earlier, this contrasts with the limited standing for exclusionary zoning claims under the Fourteenth Amendment, as exemplified by the Supreme Court's decision in *Warth* rejecting the contention that white residents of a town had standing to bring a similar claim under the Fourteenth Amendment.[166] The Supreme Court recently reiterated in *Bank of America Corp. v. City of Miami* that standing under the FHA stretches as broadly as Article III allows.[167] *Bank of America* did, however, highlight that proximate cause requirements under the FHA may, under a different doctrinal framework, limit how the FHA applies to more remotely caused claims.[168]

The Fair Housing Act expands standing far beyond individuals deprived of specific housing opportunities. In addition to white residents denied the benefits of integration, the federal courts have granted standing under the FHA in cases brought by developers

---

161. *Id.* at 461–63.

162. *See* Se. Cmty. Coll. v. Davis, 442 U.S. 397, 410–12 (1979). Accommodations are unreasonable only if they create undue financial and administrative burdens or alter the fundamental nature of a program.

163. *See, e.g.,* Oconomowoc Residential Programs v. City of Milwaukee, 300 F.3d 775 (7th Cir. 2002); Hovsons, Inc. v. Twp. of Brick, 89 F.3d 1096 (3d Cir. 1996); Smith & Lee Assocs., Inc. v. City of Taylor, Mich., 102 F.3d 781 (6th Cir. 1996).

164. 409 U.S. 205 (1972).

165. *Id.* at 209. *See also* Havens Realty Corp. v. Coleman, 455 U.S. 363, 372 (1982) (stating that "the courts . . . lack the authority to create prudential barriers to standing in suits brought under that section [§ 3612, allowing complaints to be brought as civil suits]").

166. Warth v. Seldin, 422 U.S. 490, 514 (1975).

167. 137 S. Ct. 1296 (2017).

168. *Id.* The Supreme Court declined at the time to draw the precise bounds of proximate cause under the FHA.

when they can allege an injury in fact, such as the denial of a permit application or variance request.[169] Civil rights and fair housing advocacy organizations are entitled to sue on their own behalf if the discriminatory act impairs their activities and drains their resources (for example, by requiring them to expend funds on testers).[170] The testers themselves have standing if they received false information.[171]

D. Affirmatively Furthering Fair Housing and Other FHA Provisions

There are three other mechanisms by which the FHA applies beyond its direct, statutory antidiscrimination protections that are worth mentioning. First, under the FHA, HUD is authorized to promulgate regulations and provide guidance regarding the scope and nature of obligations under the act.[172] These provisions include extensive regulations and guidance concerning such issues as occupancy standards for federally subsidized housing, accessibility standards for housing development, and procedures related to the processing of complaints.[173] HUD has not issued regulations directly related to exclusionary zoning.[174]

Second, the obligation to affirmatively further fair housing (AFFH) set forth in the FHA, as discussed earlier, has been elaborated by HUD in a sequence of rulemakings. Under the Obama administration, HUD effectuated the AFFH requirement for state and local governments by creating a planning process, in which they were required to use data and solicit public feedback to identify obstacles to fair housing in their jurisdiction and develop a plan for how to overcome those obstacles.[175] The Trump administration halted enforcement of that process, instead proposing two alternatives. The first, which was not ultimately finalized, would have focused on regulatory barriers to the production of housing—as opposed to a focus on disparities among protected classes—but aimed to maintain a federally enforced AFFH process.[176] The second, in contrast, would leave state and local governments with only the most minimal AFFH obligations.[177] In the Biden administration, HUD has partially restored the Obama-era regulation while rethinking how best to implement the AFFH mandate of the FHA.[178]

While the regulatory actions will provide the most detailed guidance and legally binding standards and processes for AFFH, it is notable that the AFFH obligation has been

---

169. *See, e.g.,* Baytree of Inverrary Realty Partners v. City of Lauderhill, 873 F.2d 1407 (11th Cir. 1989).

170. *See, e.g.,* Havens Realty Corp. v. Coleman, 455 U.S. 363 (1982).

171. *Id.*

172. The Department of Justice, through its enforcement criteria, can also play an important role in providing guidance as to how the FHA is interpreted and implemented.

173. *See* Fair Housing Enforcement—Occupancy Standards Notice of Statement of Policy, 63 Fed. Reg. 70,256–301 (Dec. 18, 1998); 24 C.F.R. § 100.205 (involving design and construction requirements); 24 C.F.R. § 103 (involving complaint processing).

174. HUD has issued informal guidance over the years, including several handbooks regarding how to promote fair housing principles in land-use and other activities. *See* Dep't of Housing & Urban Dev., Office of Fair Housing and Equal Opportunity, Fair Housing Planning Guide (1996).

175. Affirmatively Furthering Fair Housing, 80 Fed. Reg. 42271 (July 16, 2015).

176. Affirmatively Furthering Fair Housing, 85 Fed. Reg. 2041 (Jan. 14, 2020).

177. Preserving Community and Neighborhood Choice, 85 Fed. Reg. 47,899 (Aug. 7, 2020).

178. Restoring Affirmatively Furthering Fair Housing Definitions and Certifications, 86 Fed. Reg. 30,779 (June 10, 2021).

reinforced by three executive orders. These were issued by Presidents Kennedy, Carter, and Clinton, respectively.[179] They all reemphasize the broad scope of the FHA and its application not only to HUD but to all federal governmental entities with housing-related responsibilities or duties. For example, President Kennedy's 1962 order, titled Equal Opportunity in Housing, directed all executive branch agencies "insofar as their functions relate to the provision, rehabilitation, or operation of housing and related facilities, to take all action necessary and appropriate to prevent discrimination because of race, color, creed, or national origin."[180] Executive orders have been cited as additional support for requiring public agencies to take steps to promote racially integrated housing and communities.[181]

Finally, AFFH obligations[182] and the False Claims Act[183] (FCA) have been used together in a new approach to address exclusionary zoning. In a 2008 decision from the Southern District of New York,[184] the court found that a jurisdiction that receives HUD funds may be liable under the FCA if it submits an AFFH certification required by HUD but fails to undertake the requisite analysis, planning, and action required under federal standards. More specifically, in *United States ex rel. Anti-Discrimination Center v. Westchester County*, U.S. District Judge Denise Cote held that Westchester County (New York) had submitted over a period of years the required AFFH certification to HUD but had failed to consider the existence and impact of racial discrimination and segregation on housing choices and opportunities.[185] As a result, the court concluded that the county was potentially subject to treble damages, which could have equaled three times the amount of the HUD funds it had received over the period of time involved.

It is premature to assess the long-term viability of this approach. It could be quite significant, as more than 1,100 state and local jurisdictions receive HUD funds and must submit AFFH certifications. And the importance of the FCA as an enforcement option may wax and wane, depending on how HUD rulemakings address the AFFH requirement. Even so, the settlement of the *Westchester* case, which set out a framework for AFFH compliance that addresses exclusionary zoning practices, shows the relevance of this approach to land-use issues. The settlement evidenced an interest in promoting greater distribution of affordable housing and a more robust array of measures to address potentially exclusionary zoning and land-use measures. Among other terms, it requires that the county (1) expend

---

179. Exec. Order No. 11063, 27 Fed. Reg. 11,527 (Nov. 20, 1962); Exec. Order No. 12259, 46 Fed. Reg. 1253 (Dec. 31, 1980), *revoked and replaced by* Exec. Order No. 12.892, 59 Fed. Reg. 2939 (Jan. 17, 1994). For more discussion of the FHA's duty to affirmatively further fair housing, see Chapters 2 and 8.

180. Exec. Order 11063, 3 C.F.R. 1959-1963 Comp., p. 652.

181. *See, e.g.*, Langlois v. Abington Housing Auth., 234 F. Supp. 2d 33 (D. Mass 2002).

182. 31 U.S.C. §§ 3729, *et seq.*

183. *Id.*

184. United States *ex rel.* Anti-Discrimination Center of Metro New York, Inc. v. Westchester Cnty., 495 F. Supp. 2d 375 (S.D.N.Y. 2007).

185. Under HUD regulations, grantees who receive funds from the Community Development Block Grant program (CDBG), the HOME program, and two other programs are required to "assume the responsibility for fair housing planning by conducting an analysis to identify impediments to fair housing choice within its jurisdiction, taking appropriate actions to overcome the effects of any impediments identified through that analysis, and maintaining records reflecting the analysis and actions in this regard." 24 C.F.R. § 570.601(a)(2). *See Westchester*, 495 F. Supp. 2d at 386.

$51 million of its own funds to develop 750 units of affordable housing in mostly white areas of the county; (2) acknowledge that it has the authority to take legal action against municipalities if they hinder or impede the county's efforts to facilitate the development of such housing; (3) develop a comprehensive plan to address barriers to housing choice and integrated living patterns, including the development of a model ordinance featuring inclusionary zoning and affirmative marketing provisions; and (4) agree to and pay for a monitor with wide-ranging powers to facilitate and implement the settlement.[186]

HUD has taken other actions, most notably withholding CDBG funds from the state of Texas partially on grounds related to its AFFH compliance, which further show the potential importance of the agency ensuring that grantees take these obligations seriously, even in the absence of a regulatory framework like that established under the Obama administration.[187]

While there are other federal statutes that provide supplemental bases for claims involving municipal land-use provisions and decisions, they generally do not expand upon what is available under the FHA. For example, the Civil Rights Act of 1866, although providing a small amount of supplemental coverage in other contexts, does not meaningfully expand upon the FHA as it applies to land-use matters.[188]

E. Emerging Topics in Fair Housing Law

In addition to the core questions of exclusionary zoning, such as restrictions on multifamily housing or large lot sizes, which remain important issues of fair housing litigation,[189] fair housing advocacy has also expanded to identify other ways that housing law works to exclude certain people from certain places. Though not strictly about exclusionary zoning, a brief discussion of some of these topics is useful to understanding both the many ways that housing regulation can entrench segregation and the various protections of the Fair Housing Act.

A first category of recent activity involves scrutinizing the legacy of the War on Crime, as it applies to housing. Thus, HUD has issued guidance suggesting that when housing providers discriminate on the basis of arrest history, or have blanket prohibitions on renting to

---

186. WestchesterGov.Com, Stipulation and Order of Settlement and Dismissal. *See also* Joshua Brustein, *Westchester Board Approves a Housing-Integration Pact*, N.Y. Times, Sept. 23, 2009, www.nytimes.com/2009/09/23/nyregion/23housing.html.

187. This matter stemmed from complaints by local advocates that the state of Texas had violated fair housing laws, including its obligation to affirmatively further fair housing, regarding the distribution of $1.7 billion in Community Block Grant disaster relief funds. HUD initially held up the state of Texas's ability to distribute the funds and ultimately resolved the matter through a conciliation agreement, see http://portal.hud.gov/hudportal/documents/huddoc?id=DOC_4305.pdf, that required Texas to reallocate its funds and develop a new Analysis of Impediments. See https://archives.hud.gov/news/2010/pr10-106.cfm.

188. While prior to the passage of the Fair Housing Act the 1866 Civil Rights Act played an important part in addressing discriminatory practices (see discussion of restrictive covenants and *Jones v. Mayer, supra*), its central significance today is prohibiting discriminatory housing practices involving private parties that may not be covered by the Fair Housing Act due to one of the FHA's exemptions. For example, the FHA exempts from its coverage owner-occupied dwellings of four units or less. Such practices fall within the 1866 Civil Rights Act's coverage, however.

189. *See, e.g.*, Ave. 6E Investments, LLC v. City of Yuma, Ariz., 818 F.3d 493, 496 (9th Cir. 2016); Mhany Mgmt., Inc. v. Cty. of Nassau, 819 F.3d 581, 587 (2d Cir. 2016).

people with a criminal conviction (outside certain drug crimes), this will constitute racial discrimination.[190] Instead, a person's criminal history should be based on an individualized assessment that focuses on convictions rather than arrests.[191] Similarly, in *Fortune Society v. Sandcastle Towers Housing Development Fund Corp.*, a court recent denied summary judgment against claims that a housing provider's criminal history policy illegally imposed disparate impact on the basis of race.[192] There has also been extensive activity surrounding crime-free housing ordinances and chronic nuisance ordinances, which seek to enlist landlords in the policing of criminal or disruptive behavior. As HUD has recognized in guidance, these policies are disproportionately enforced against domestic violence victims, and thereby have a disparate impact on women.[193] Litigation has resulted in the removal of many of these ordinances[194] (which also disproportionately affect people of color and people with disabilities[195]).

There has also been renewed interest in the legality of community preference policies that favor a jurisdiction's existing residents in the allocation of subsidized housing. Community preferences can be a legitimate tool of cities and public housing authorities and are, under certain circumstances, authorized and regulated by HUD.[196] But historically, community preference policies have often been used by predominantly white communities as a tool for preserving racial segregation, even while providing affordable housing. Courts have found such policies to violate the FHA both as intentional discrimination and for having a disparate impact.[197] More recently, controversies have emerged in urban areas, when cities are using community preferences to fight gentrification and displacement or to win more public support for affordable housing development. In a suit challenging New York City's

---

190. U.S. Dep't of Hous. & Urban Dev., Office of General Counsel Guidance on Application of Fair Housing Act Standards to the Use of Criminal Records by Providers of Housing and Real Estate-Related Transactions (Apr. 4, 2016), https://www.hud.gov/sites/documents/HUD_OGCGUIDAPPFHASTANDCR.PDF.

191. *Id.*

192. 388 F. Supp. 3d 145 (E.D.N.Y. 2019).

193. U.S. Dep't of Hous. & Urban Dev., Office of General Counsel Guidance on Application of Fair Housing Act Standards to the Enforcement of Local Nuisance and Crime-Free Housing Ordinances Against Victims of Domestic Violence, Other Crime Victims, and Others Who Require Police or Emergency Services (Sept. 13, 2016), https://www.hud.gov/sites/documents/FINALNUISANCEORDGDNCE.PDF.

194. *See, e.g.,* Conciliation Agreement, U.S. Dep't of Hous. & Urban Dev. v. Municipality of Norristown, Secretary Initiated Complaint No. 03-13-0277-8 & 03-13-0277-9 (2014), http://nhlp.org/files/Briggs-HUD-Conciliation-Agreement.pdf, Conciliation Agreement, U.S. Dep't of Hous. & Urban Dev. v. City of Berlin, N.H., Secretary Initiated Complaint No. 01-15-0017-8 (2015), http://nhlp.org/files/City-of-Berlin.pdf; Release and Settlement Agreement, Watson v. Maplewood, No. 4:17CV1268 (E.D. Mo.), https://www.aclu.org/legal-document/watson-v-maplewood-settlement.

195. *See* Matthew Desmond and Nicol Valdez, *Unpolicing the Urban Poor: Consequences of Third-Party Policing for Inner-City Women,* 78 Am. Soc. Rev. 117 (2012); Alisha Jarwala & Sejal Singh, *When Disability Is a "Nuisance": How Chronic Nuisance Ordinances Push Residents with Disabilities Out of Their Homes,* 54 Harv. C.R.-C.L. L. Rev. 875 (2019)

196. *See, e.g.,* 24 C.F.R. §§ 5.655(c)(1) (project-based section 8); 982.207 (Housing Choice Vouchers).

197. *See* Comer v. Cisneros, 37 F.3d 775, 793 (2d Cir. 1994); United States v. Hous. Auth. of Chickasaw, 504 F. Supp. 716 (S.D. Ala. 1980); Langlois v. Abington Hous. Auth., 234 F. Supp. 2d 33 (D. Mass. 2002).

community preference policy, a court recently denied a motion to dismiss, finding that plaintiffs stated a claim that the policy was intended to, or had the effect of, perpetuating segregation.[198] HUD also rejected San Francisco's community preference policy, although it allowed a substitute policy giving preference to households at risk of displacement.[199]

Finally, as immigration remains a high-profile issue nationally it has become an important front in fair housing law. Many state laws, local ordinances, and private landlord behaviors discriminate, directly or indirectly, on the basis of immigration status. Immigration status, per se, is not a protected characteristic under the FHA, but it can violate the FHA where discrimination on the basis of immigration status has the "purpose or effect of discriminating on the basis of national origin."[200] Today, it is a particularly live issue when classifications based on immigration status constitute illegal discrimination against Latinos.[201] Other important areas of litigation concerning immigrants' rights and national origin discrimination include language access issues[202] and the discriminatory enactment or over-enforcement of building and occupancy codes.[203] Other anti-immigrant housing laws have been successfully challenged on preemption grounds (rather than fair housing), as impermissible attempts by local governments to regulate the federal realm of immigration policy.[204]

---

198. Winfield v. City of New York, No. 15CV5236-LTS-DCF, 2016 WL 6208564 (S.D.N.Y. Oct. 24, 2016).

199. Richard Gonzales, *Feds to Allow Preferences for Low-Income Applicants in S.F. Housing Complex*, NPR (Sept. 23, 2016), https://www.npr.org/2016/09/23/495237494/feds-to-allow-preferences-for-low-income-applicants-in-s-f-housing-complex.

200. Espinoza v. Farah Mfg. Co., 414 U.S. 86 (1973).

201. *See* Cent. Alabama Fair Hous. Ctr. v. Magee, 835 F. Supp. 2d 1165, 1172 (M.D. Ala. 2011) (Alabama statutes requiring proof of legal status to live in manufactured homes enjoined and then repealed); Reyes v. Waples Mobile Home Park Ltd. P'ship, 903 F.3d 415, 419 (4th Cir. 2018) (affirming decision striking down landlord policy requiring legal status to live in mobile home park); Keller v. City of Fremont, 719 F.3d 931 (8th Cir. 2013) (rejecting FHA challenge to anti-immigrant rental housing ordinance).

202. *Compare* Cabrera v. Alvarez, 977 F. Supp. 2d 969 (N.D. Cal. 2013) *with* Vialez v. N.Y.C. Hous. Auth., 783 F. Supp. 109 (S.D.N.Y. 1991). *See also* HUD, Final Guidance to Federal Financial Assistance Recipients Regarding Title VI Prohibition against National Origin Discrimination Affecting Limited English Proficient Persons, 72 Fed. Reg. 2731 (Jan. 22, 2007) (describing language access obligations of federally funded housing providers under Title VI of the Civil Rights Act).

203. *See, e.g.*, Consent Order, United States v. Town of Cicero, No. 93C-1805 (N.D. Ill.), https://www.justice.gov/crt/housing-and-civil-enforcement-cases-documents-522; Stefan H. Krieger, *A Clash of Cultures: Immigration and Housing Code Enforcement on Long Island*, 36 Hofstra L. Rev. 1227 (2008).

204. *E.g.*, Lozano v. City of Hazleton, 724 F.3d 297 (3d Cir. 2013).

State and Local Regulation Promoting Affordable Housing* | 4

Priya S. Gupta and Navneet K. Grewal

I. INTRODUCTION: THE WIDE RANGE OF "INCLUSIONARY" RESPONSES TO EXCLUSIONARY ZONING

A major impediment to the development of housing that is affordable for low- and moderate-income households has been the tendency of local governments, particularly in the suburbs, to use the local zoning power to block or severely restrict high-density and multifamily housing developments through "exclusionary zoning."[1] This chapter will discuss the wide variety of state and local statutory responses to exclusionary zoning.[2]

Since the 1970s, hundreds of local governments have adopted some version of inclusionary zoning that requires private developers to include some affordable housing units in their proposals. A team of researchers for the National Association of Home Builders has defined "inclusionary zoning" as "any municipal or county ordinance that requires or allows a property owner, builder, or developer to restrict the sale or resale price or rent of a specified percentage of residential units in a development as a condition of receiving permission to construct that development."[3] Applying this definition, the

---

*Portions of this chapter originally appeared in Chapter 9 of P. SALSICH & T. TRYNIECKI, LAND USE REGULATION 377–420 (2d ed. 2003), © American Bar Association, and are used with permission.

1. See Chapter 3 for an explanation of "exclusionary zoning."

2. See also state and local housing funding programs discussed in Chapters 10 and 11. For a review of local housing programs, *see* BRUCE KATZ, ET AL., RETHINKING LOCAL AFFORDABLE HOUSING STRATEGIES: LESSONS FROM 70 YEARS OF POLICY AND PRACTICE (Brookings Inst. 2003).

3. TIMOTHY S. HOLLISTER, ET AL., NATIONAL SURVEY OF STATUTORY AUTHORITY AND PRACTICAL CONSIDERATIONS FOR THE IMPLEMENTATION OF INCLUSIONARY ZONING ORDINANCES 1 (2007), https://inclusionaryhousing.org/wp-content

researchers concluded that 13 states "expressly authorize inclusionary zoning or clearly imply such authority by granting broad powers to promote affordable housing."[4]

To that list, we can now add California and Oregon as well.[5] In a variation of the inclusionary zoning technique, states have increasingly enacted statutes modifying local zoning procedures for reviewing housing development applications and establishing procedures to override or limit local governments' zoning decisions when development proposals include affordable housing. As John Infranca has argued, there has recently been an increase in the willingness of states to respond to exclusionary zoning by mandating the permitting of (and by providing incentives for) certain inclusive housing structures.[6] As Infranca notes, there has been increased "national attention amid broader recognition of the effects of zoning regulations not only on housing supply and affordability but also on regional and national economic growth, social mobility, economic equality, racial integration, and the environment."[7]

State responses have included the adoption of planning statutes that require local governments to include affordable housing needs analyses in their local comprehensive plans and that make exercise of the zoning power, as well as authority to create redevelopment

---

/uploads/2016/08/Hollister-et-al.-2007-National-Survey-of-Statutory-Authority-and-Practic.pdf (last visited Jan. 30, 2021).

4. *Id.* at 2. The states are:

> Connecticut, CONN. GEN. STAT. §§ 8-2i & 8-30g (2017)
> Florida, FLA. STAT. ANN. § 163.3202 (2020)
> Illinois, 55 ILL. COMP. STAT. 5/5-12001 (2015) (counties), 65 ILL. COMP. STAT. 5/11-13-1(11) (2015) (municipalities), 310 ILL. COMP. STAT. 67/1 (2015) (Affordable Housing Planning and Appeal Act)
> Louisiana, LA. REV. STAT. ANN. § 33:5002 (2009)
> Maryland, MD. CODE ANN., 66B, § 7-401 (West 2012)
> Massachusetts, MASS. GEN. LAWS ANN. ch. 40R §§ 6, 9 (West 2004 & Supp. 2021) (smart growth zoning districts)
> Minnesota, MINN. STAT. §§ 473.254, 473.255 (2014)
> Nevada, NEV. REV. STAT. § 278.250 (2013)
> New Hampshire, N.H. REV. STAT. ANN. § 674:21 (2017)
> New Jersey, N.J. STAT. ANN. §§ 52:27D-301-:27D-329.19 (West 2019) (N.J Fair Housing Act), N.J. ADMIN. CODE § 5:94-4.4 (2010) (Council on Affordable Housing Regulations)
> Rhode Island, R.I. GEN. LAWS § 45-24-46.1 (2016)
> Vermont, VT. STAT. ANN. tit. 24 § 4414(7) (2019 & Supp. 2020)
> Virginia, VA. CODE ANN. § 15.2-735.1(2) (2020)

The researchers also note that Texas has enacted legislation prohibiting local governments from enacting mandatory inclusionary zoning ordinances, but permitting voluntary measures, NAT'L SURVEY, *supra* note 3, at 2, 42–43; TEX. LOC. GOV'T CODE ANN. § 214.905(a) (Vernon 2009) (mandatory provisions prohibited), TEX. LOC. GOV'T CODE ANN. § 214.905(b)(1) (Vernon 2009) (voluntary measures permitted).

5. CAL. GOV'T. CODE § 65850.01 (2017); ORE. REV. STAT. § 197.309 (2016).

6. For a comprehensive account and argument in favor of such interventions, see John Infranca, *The New State Zoning: Land Use Preemption amid a Housing Crisis*, 60 B.C.L. REV. 823 (2019). For a spirited account of homeowner opposition to inclusionary zoning, see Kenneth A. Stahl, *The Challenge of Inclusion*, 89 TEMPLE L. REV. 487 (2017).

7. Infranca, *supra* note 6, at 825–26.

agencies,[8] conditional upon adoption of such plans.[9] They have also modified rent regulations and mandated the permitting of accessory dwelling units (ADUs) and other forms of inclusionary structures. Other states supplement federal fair housing law with their own antidiscrimination statutes, including state-level fair housing acts.[10] In addition, some states require localities to provide certain regulatory exemptions to facilitate affordable housing development.[11] While earlier state interventions were aimed at "channeling local decisions and in some instances allowed appeals to a state entity from adverse local decisions," more recent measures "tend to expressly preempt and displace specific elements of local zoning."[12]

Many local governments, in states with inclusionary zoning legislation and in those without, have adopted other programs to promote affordable housing development and/or to maintain the affordability of housing, such as density bonuses and other forms of developer incentives, land banking, community benefit agreements, community land trusts, and rent control. These approaches are discussed *infra*.[13]

II. STATE STATUTORY RESPONSES

A. Zoning Override ("Antisnob") Legislation

Some states have responded legislatively to affordable housing issues by modifying the local zoning procedures for reviewing affordable housing development applications. These modifications may include changes in the zoning appeals procedures and standards of review.

Four states (Illinois, Massachusetts, New Jersey,[14] and Rhode Island) have established *administrative* procedures for reviewing local land-use decisions rejecting or restricting affordable housing development proposals. California, Connecticut, and New Hampshire,

---

8. See discussion of these in Chapter 9.

9. These planning requirements are discussed in Chapter 2. They sometimes interact with the laws discussed in this chapter. For example, the zoning override laws might promote planning for affordable housing. Other state statutory means for promoting affordable housing, not discussed in this chapter, include Florida's Development of Regional Impact review. FLA. STAT. ANN. § 380.06 (West 2009). Under this statute, a regional planning agency conducts a review of certain large-scale development projects to determine, inter alia, how the development affects housing availability in the region. *See* Southlake Cmty. Found., Inc. v. Havill, 707 So. 2d 361 (Fla. Ct. App. 1998) (requiring one-half of rental units to be set aside for very low-, low-, and moderate income families).

10. For example, some of California's antidiscrimination laws are discussed in Section II.A.2 *infra* and state Fair Housing Acts in Section II.B. *infra*. See Chapter 3 for an overview of federal fair housing laws.

11. *See* Section II.B. *infra*.

12. Infranca, *supra* note 6, at 828–29.

13. For an overview of tools for inclusive development, see *Grounded Solutions Network, What About Housing?: A Policy Toolkit For Inclusive Growth*, https://groundedsolutions.org/sites/default/files/2018-11/17%20What%20About%20Housing%20-%20A%20Policy%20Toolkit%20for%20Inclusive%20Growth.pdf (last visited Sept. 16, 2021).

14. New Jersey's Council on Affordable Housing (COAH), established by the New Jersey Fair Housing Act of 1985, N.J. STAT. §§ 52:27D-301 *et seq.*, has "primary jurisdiction for the administration of housing obligations in accordance with sound regional planning considerations." *Id.* § 304. COAH is discussed in Chapter 2 in conjunction with the discussion of state and regional planning affecting affordable housing.

on the other hand, provide for *judicial* review of such decisions. All seven states include a shift in the burden of proof requiring local governments to establish valid reasons for rejecting or restricting such proposals.

1. Administrative Review Procedures

a. Massachusetts

One of the first states to respond legislatively to the exclusionary zoning phenomenon was Massachusetts, when it enacted its celebrated "antisnob" law in 1969.[15] Rather than mandate affordable housing set-asides or authorize density bonuses, the antisnob law established a housing appeals committee in the state Department of Community Affairs, now the Department of Housing and Community Development (DHCD). The committee holds the authority to override local zoning decisions blocking low or moderate-income housing developments, defined as housing subsidized by any federal or state housing production program.[16]

(i) Chapter 40B

Under the Massachusetts statute, dubbed "40B" after its statutory cite, public agencies and private organizations proposing to build low- and moderate-income housing may bypass local regulatory agencies by submitting a single application to the local zoning board of appeals, which is responsible for coordinating an analysis of the application by interested regulatory agencies, conducting a public hearing, and making a decision regarding the application. Comprehensive permits or approvals may be issued by the board of appeals, which must act within 40 days after termination of the public hearing.[17]

If the application is denied or approved with conditions that make the project "uneconomic," the developer may appeal to the state Housing Appeals Committee (HAC) to determine whether the decision is "reasonable and consistent with local needs."[18] The statute provides that requirements or regulations are "consistent with local needs" (1) if they are "reasonable in view of the regional need for low and moderate income housing" and the need "to protect the health or safety" of the occupants or the residents of the community, or "to promote better site and building design," or to "preserve open spaces"; and (2) if the regulations "are applied as equally as possible to both subsidized and unsubsidized housing."[19]

---

15. Mass. Gen. Laws Ann. ch. 40B, §§ 20–23 (West 2018). For a review of the Massachusetts statute and recent case law construing the statute, *see* Theodore C. Regnante & Paul J. Haverty, *Compelling Reasons Why the Legislature Should Resist the Call to Repeal Chapter 40B*, 88 Mass. L. Rev. 77 (2003). For an analysis of the mediation feature of the statute, *see* Lauren J. Resnick, *Mediating Affordable Housing Disputes in Massachusetts: Optimal Intervention Points*, 45(2) Arb. J. 15 (June 1990). The *Western New England Law Review* published a symposium reviewing the Massachusetts and other New England statutes which it inspired, *Symposium: Increasing Affordable Housing and Regional Housing Opportunity in Three New England States and New Jersey*, 23 W. New Eng. L. Rev. 1 (2001).

16. Mass. Gen. Laws Ann. ch. 40B, § 20 (West 2018).

17. *Id.* § 21. Local boards subject to the comprehensive permit provision include local historic committees operating within local historic districts. Dennis Housing Corp. v. Zoning Bd. of Appeals, 785 N.E.2d 682 (Mass. 2003).

18. Mass. Gen. Laws Ann. ch. 40B, § 23 (West 2018).

19. *Id.* § 20.

In addition, the statute provides that regulations are consistent with local needs when they are imposed after a comprehensive hearing in one of the following two situations:

> (1) more than 10 percent of the housing units, or at least 1.5 percent of the total land area zoned for residential, commercial, or industrial use in the municipality, is low- or moderate-income housing; or (2) the proposal would result in low- or moderate-income housing construction starts on more than three tenths of 1 percent of the land area, or ten acres, whichever is larger, in a calendar year.[20]

When a decision is appealed to the state HAC, the "central question . . . is whether the decision . . . is consistent with local needs. Under the Committee's regulations, a developer 'may establish a *prima facie* case by proving . . . that its proposal complies with federal or state statutes or regulations, or with generally recognized standards as to matters of health, safety, the environment, design, open space, or other matters of Local Concern.'"[21] Once a developer establishes a prima facie case, the burden shifts to the local zoning board to establish the presence of a valid concern enumerated above that "outweighs the regional need for low or moderate income housing."[22] A municipality's "failure to meet statutory minimum housing obligations 'will provide compelling evidence that the regional need for housing does in fact outweigh the objections to the proposal.'"[23] Traffic congestion objections that did not rise to the level of "significant public safety concerns" have been held "insufficient to outweigh the regional need for affordable housing."[24]

If a municipality approves a development proposal but adds conditions to address local concerns, a developer challenging those conditions must first prove that the conditions "make the building of the project uneconomic."[25] The term, "uneconomic" is defined as "impossible to proceed . . . and still realize a reasonable return."[26] If the developer establishes that the conditions do make the development uneconomic, the burden then shifts to

---

20. *Id. See also* Bd. of Appeals v. Hous. Appeals Comm. in Dep't of Cmty. Affairs, 363 Mass. 339, 294 N.E.2d 393 (1973) (upholding statute against illegal spot zoning, violation of home rule, and vagueness challenges). A community with numbers of affordable housing units exceeding 10 percent of total housing can most effectively demonstrate that its denial of the project was consistent with local needs and therefore permissible under Housing Appeals Committee procedures. Communities making steady progress toward the 10 percent threshold may also survive a challenge to the Housing Appeals Committee.

21. Herring Brook Meadow, LLC v. Scituate Zoning Bd. of Appeals, No. 07-15, slip op. at 6 (Mass. Housing Appeals Comm. May 26, 2010), quoting 760 C.M.R. 56.07(2)(a)(2).

22. *Id.* at 9.

23. *Id.* at 9–10, quoting Bd. of Appeals of Hanover v. Housing Appeals Comm., 294 N.E.2d 393, 413 (Mass. 1973) and citing Woburn Bd. of Appeals v. Housing Appeals Comm., 847 N.E.2d 1140 (Mass. App. 2006), *further appellate review denied*, Bd. of Appeals of Woburn v. Housing Appeals Comm., 853 N.E.2d 1059 (Mass. 2006).

24. Zoning Bd. of Appeals of Canton v. Housing Appeals Comm., 923 N.E.2d 114, 120 (Mass. App. 2010).

25. Autumnwood, LLC v. Sandwich Zoning Bd. of Appeals, No. 05-06, slip op. at 14 (Mass. Housing Appeals Comm., Mar. 8, 2010).

26. *Id.* at 2, quoting 760 C.M.R. 56.02. A "reasonable return" is "a minimum 15%," calculated by a "Return on Total Cost (ROTC) analysis." Autumnwood, *supra* note 25, at 3, n.3, citing Massachusetts Housing Partnership & Edith M. Netter, Local 40B Review and Decision Guidelines: A Practical Guide for Zoning Boards of Appeal Reviewing Applications for Comprehensive Permits Pursuant to M.G.L. Chapter 40B (2005). "[U]pper 'limitations on

the municipality to prove that the local concerns that caused conditions to be attached to its approval outweigh the regional need for affordable housing.[27] If the developer fails to establish that conditions imposed by the municipality make the project uneconomic, the housing appeals committee does not have the authority to alter or set aside the municipality's conditions.[28]

If the HAC concludes that the local zoning decision is not consistent with local needs, it vacates the decision and orders a comprehensive permit or approval to be issued, provided that the proposed housing would not violate safety standards contained in federal or state building and site plan requirements.[29] The statute is silent on the question of how long a development approved under the 40B procedures must remain affordable. In *Zoning Board of Appeals of Wellesley v. Ardemore Apartments Limited Partnership*, the Supreme Judicial Court of Massachusetts held that "where a comprehensive permit itself does not specify for how long housing units must remain below market, the Act requires an owner to maintain the units as affordable for as long as the housing is not in compliance with local zoning requirements, regardless of the terms of any attendant construction subsidy agreement."[30]

Comprehensive regulations for Chapter 40B were adopted by DHCD in 2008 in order to provide "comprehensive standards and procedures to govern the course of project review, from an initial determination of eligibility by the federal or state agency that is providing a subsidy (the 'Subsidizing Agency'), through local permitting review by the Board, to issuance or denial of a Comprehensive Permit, potential appeals to the HAC, and post-permitting procedures."[31] The new regulations also include the Subsidized Housing Inventory maintained by DHCD, and "codify issues that have been decided by judicial or administrative decisions or are general practice as reflected in policy documents of the Department."[32]

---

profits' are set at "20 percent of total development costs," Autumnwood, *supra* note 25, at 3, n.2, citing DEP'T OF HOUSING AND CMTY. DEV., COMPREHENSIVE PERMIT GUIDELINES § IV-C(1) (2008).

27. Autumnwood, *supra* note 25, at 14.

28. Bd. of Appeals of Woburn v. Housing Appeals Comm., 887 N.E.2d 1051, 1061 (Mass. 2008). *But see* Zoning Bd. of Appeals of Amesbury v. Housing Appeals Comm., 99 N.E.2d 74 (Mass. 9/3/2010) (holding that the Housing Appeals Committee has authority under section 23 of the act to review and strike, where appropriate, conditions imposed by zoning boards of appeals).

29. MASS. GEN. LAWS ANN. ch. 40B, § 23 (West 2004). *See also* Herring Brook Meadow, LLC v. Scituate Zoning Bd. of Appeals, No. 07-15, slip op. at 6 (Mass. Housing Appeals Comm. May 26, 2010).

30. 767 N.E.2d 584, 586 (Mass. 2002). The project in question had been funded by the Massachusetts Housing Finance Agency (MHFA), which required a specified percent of the units to remain affordable to low- and moderate-income persons for at least 15 years, until July 2000. *Id.* In refusing to permit the owner to convert the units to market rate rentals, the court stated that its decision was consistent with the legislature's intent "to create a long-term solution to the shortage of affordable housing. . . . We see nothing in the Act to suggest that the Legislature intended to override local zoning autonomy only to create a fleeting increase in affordable housing stock, leaving cities and towns vulnerable to successive zoning overrides, and the issuance of a never-ending series of comprehensive permits." *Id.* at 587.

31. 760 MASS. CODE. REGS. 56.00–56.08 (2008). For a summary, *see* Mass. Citizens' Housing and Planning Ass'n, *Chapter 40(B): The State's Affordable Housing Law, available at* https://www.chapa.org/sites/default/files/40%20B%20fact%20sheet_0.pdf (last visited June 5, 2021).

32. The Subsidized Housing Inventory is *available at* https://www.mass.gov/service-details/subsidized-housing-inventory-shi (last visited Feb. 6, 2021).

Housing advocates report that the state HAC has been aggressive in enforcing the spirit as well as the text of the law. In 1999, the HAC ruled that a limited partnership proposing to develop a condominium with shallow subsidies from the New England Fund (NEF) of the Federal Home Loan Bank of Boston (FHLBB) met the jurisdictional standards to qualify for a comprehensive permit.[33] The Committee's willingness to read the statutory and regulatory provisions liberally has been credited with increasing the popularity of the program with affordable housing developers. A fact sheet updated in October 2011 by the Citizens' Housing and Planning Association, "a non-profit umbrella organization for affordable housing and community development activities in Massachusetts," states that more than 60,000 affordable housing units had been built or were under construction in almost 1,200 developments throughout the state.[34] Approximately 70 percent of the units are rental apartments and the balance are homeownership units; the units are divided almost equally between market rate units serving middle-income households (between 100 percent and 150 percent of area median income) and affordable units serving households making less than 80 percent of area median income.[35]

Most of the residents in the affordable apartments and homes earn less than $50,000 per year. Typical occupations include health care (nurses, medical assistants, therapists, dental assistants), educators (teachers, counselors), retail employees, construction trades (carpenters, plumbers, electricians), office management and administrative staff, financial services (bookkeepers, payroll managers, accounting), human services, and other occupations.[36]

While DHCD's Subsidized Housing Inventory shows that as of December 21, 2020, what might be called Chapter 40B's statewide goal of 10 percent affordable housing units was met (10.1 percent), only 77 of 351 municipalities (22.9 percent) had met the statutory quota. Another 36 were in striking range (8 percent or more affordable units).[37] However, planners and land-use attorneys have expressed concerns that without more effective statutory requirements for planning at the local, regional, and state level to incorporate environmental and open space concerns as well as affordable housing needs, Section 40B can be

---

33. Stuborn Ltd. P'ship v. Barnstable Bd. of Appeals, No. 98-01 (Mass. Housing Appeals Comm., Mar. 5, 1999). In a subsequent decision, the court of appeals held that it was "within the competence of the [Housing Appeals Committee] to determine that [the shallow subsidy provided by] NEF funding meets the jurisdictional requirements" of the statute. Bd. of Appeals of Wayland v. Housing Appeals Comm., 03-P-806 (Aug. 25, 2004), unreported, *aff'd*, 814 N.E.2d 36 (2004).

34. Citizens' Housing and Planning Ass'n, *Fact Sheet on Chapter 40B: The State's Affordable Housing Zoning Law* 1, https://www.chapa.org/sites/default/files/Fact%20Sheet%20on%20Chap ter%2040B%202011%20update.pdf (last visited Feb. 6, 2021). Mediation services offered by the Massachusetts Mediation Service, a state agency, have been instrumental in resolving many of the cases appealed to the state Housing Appeals Committee. Resnick, *supra* note 15, at 15, 20.

35. Citizens' Housing, *supra* note 34.

36. *Id.* at 2.

37. *Subsidized Housing Inventory*, *supra* note 32. Despite the low percentage of municipalities meeting the 10 percent quota, a task force appointed by Governor Mitt Romney to study Chapter 40B reported that it "is effectively the only tool to create multifamily housing in many cities and towns in the Commonwealth." Chapter 40B Task Force, *Findings and Recommendations: Report to Governor Mitt Romney* 2 (2003), *available at* http://archives.lib.state.ma.us/handle/2452/38695 (last visited June 5, 2021). The task force's recommendations are reviewed by Regnante & Haverty, *supra* note 15, at 85–88.

used by developers and speculators to "cram down" high-density housing developments on "historically undevelopable lands."[38]

Following a series of reports by the Massachusetts Inspector General critical of the 40B program,[39] a coalition of planners, lawyers, and other representatives from cities and towns across the state sought to repeal Chapter 40B on the grounds that it is too costly and open to developer abuse.[40] Supporters of a repeal initiative on the ballot in November 2010 argued that inclusionary zoning of the type implemented by Montgomery County, Maryland,[41] would be a better alternative.[42] The Campaign to Protect the Affordable Housing Law, a self-described "diverse coalition" of academics, activists, community leaders, municipal officials, and residents organized to oppose the initiative, argued that the statute has played an important role in encouraging cities and towns outside the state's largest cities to be receptive to affordable housing.[43] A study of controversies during the permitting process of four developments prepared by researchers at Tufts University for the Citizens' Housing and Planning Association concluded that the controversies "were not realized to the extent feared." While the concerns varied from project to project, "the underlying roots of these controversies are the loss of local control over zoning and fear of the unknown

---

38. Jonathan D. Witten, *The Cost of Developing Affordable Housing: At What Price?* 30 B.C. ENVTL. AFF. L. REV. 509 (2004). "Providing affordable housing is a good thing, but being forced to approve density bonuses for a paltry number of affordable units on land that is environmentally sensitive and unable to support a grid subdivision is a bad thing, period, asserts Tom Broadrick, planning director of the Town of Duxbury, Massachusetts." Broadrick, *My Two Cents,* 54 LAND USE L. & ZONING DIGEST 6 (Jan. 2002). "He advocates a so-called 'friendly 40B' (the statutory cite for the Anti-Snob Zoning Act is Chapter 40B), in which a developer and a community can create an affordable housing development partnership on 'good land' (not marginal or environmentally sensitive land) [about which] both the community and the developer can feel comfortable." The "streamlining" permitted by Chapter 40B can work, he believes, "if a comprehensive plan is in place with a housing inventory, housing strategy, affordable housing committee, and an appropriate permitting process." *Id.* at 8.

39. *See, e.g.*, Office of the Inspector General of Massachusetts, Letter to Tina Brooks, Undersecretary, Department of Housing and Community Development, Regarding Proposed Changes to Chapter 40B Regulations, Dec. 21, 2009, https://www.mass.gov/doc/letter-to-tina-brooks-undersecretary-department-of-housing-community-development-regarding/download; Office of the Inspector General, Letter to Senator Marc R. Pacheco, Chair, Senate Committee on Post Audit and Oversight, Regarding Chapter 40B, Sept. 11, 2008, https://www.mass.gov/doc/letter-to-senator-marc-r-pacheco-chair-senate-committee-on-post-audit-oversight-regarding/download.

40. The Coalition to Repeal 40B Materials, http://www.newtonvillagesalliance.org/uploads/2/6/2/6/26263417/the_coalition_to_repeal_40b_materials.pdf (last visited Feb. 6, 2021).

41. *See infra* notes 165 to 181 and accompanying text.

42. *See* Kara L. Dardeno, Note, *Chapter 40B Should Buy the Farm,* 42 SUFFOLK U. L. REV. 129 (2008) (arguing that 40B is too inefficient and should be repealed in favor of mandatory inclusionary zoning, citing Jonathan Douglas Witten, *The Cost of Developing Affordable Housing: At What Price?* 30 B.C. ENVTL. AFF. L. REV. 509, 548 (2003), and Brian R. Lerman, Note, *Mandatory Inclusionary Zoning—the Answer to the Affordable Housing Problem,* 33 B.C. ENVTL. AFF. L. REV. 383, 409–10 (2006)).

43. Campaign to Protect the Affordable Housing Law. Coalition members argue that Chapter 40B is responsible for 80 percent of new affordable housing outside the state's largest cities in the past decade; that 51 communities (of 316) had exceeded the 10 percent threshold as of April, 2010, and that another 40 communities were in the 8–9 percent range. *Id.*

impacts of the developments." Two years after the developments were built and occupied, "most of the controversies [had] evaporated," the researchers noted.[44]

Ultimately, voters decisively defeated the ballot initiative that would have repealed the law.

(ii) Chapter 40R

Chapter 40R, the Massachusetts Smart Growth Zoning and Housing Production Act, was enacted by the Massachusetts legislature in 2004 "to encourage smart growth and increased housing production."[45] Smart growth is defined as:

> a principle of land development that emphasizes mixing land uses, increases the availability of affordable housing by creating a range of housing opportunities in neighborhoods, takes advantage of compact design, fosters distinctive and attractive communities, preserves open space, farmland, natural beauty and critical environmental areas, strengthens existing communities, provides a variety of transportation choices, makes development decisions predictable, fair and cost-effective and encourages community and stakeholder collaboration in development decisions.[46]

The statute authorizes cities and towns to adopt smart growth overlay zoning districts,[47] which, when approved by the state Department of Housing and Community Development, become eligible for financial incentives and priorities of state expenditures,[48] including "zoning incentive payment[s]" based on "projected units of new construction" to be developed in the district and "one-time density bonus payment[s]" based on the number of new units actually constructed in the district.[49] Cities and towns with approved smart-growth zoning districts also receive favorable consideration when discretionary state environmental, housing, and transportation funds are awarded.[50] The statute requires minimum residential densities of 8 units per acre for single-family homes, 12 units per acre for two- and three-family buildings, and 20 units per acre for multifamily housing, and requires at least 20 percent of the units constructed in the district to be affordable to persons making less than 80 percent of the area median income.[51]

Chapter 40R has been touted as an alternative to Chapter 40B, which permits cities and towns to retain more control over their land-use planning and development policies.[52] Using the Chapter 40R Smart Growth District mechanism, municipalities can "plan [their] own growth rather than leave the planning to capital-driven developers."[53]

---

44. Alexandra DeGenova, Brendan Goodwin, Shannon Moriarty & Jeremy Robitaille, On the Ground: 40B Developments Before and After 60–63 (2009).

45. Mass. Gen. Laws pt. 1, tit. VII, ch. 40R, § 1.

46. *Id.*

47. *Id.* § 3.

48. *Id.* § 9.

49. *Id.* § 4.

50. *Id.*

51. *Id.* § 6.

52. Kara L. Dardeno, *Chapter 40B Should Buy the Farm*, 42 Suffolk U. L. Rev. 129, 150–51 (2008).

53. *Id.* at 156.

b. Rhode Island

The Rhode Island Low- and Moderate-Income Housing Act, enacted in 1991,[54] tracks the Massachusetts statute in that a "one-stop" review procedure for low- and moderate-income housing proposals is established, and a state administrative agency is given authority to override local land-use regulatory decisions unfavorable to such affordable housing development proposals.[55] The act authorizes public agencies, nonprofit organizations, and limited equity housing cooperatives to submit to a zoning board of review "a single application for a comprehensive permit to build [low- and moderate-income] housing in lieu of separate applications to the applicable local boards [planning commissions, city councils, etc.]."[56] The board must notify all agencies being bypassed that the application has been filed, must hold a public hearing within 30 days of receipt of the application, and must make a decision within 40 days after the public hearing ends. Under the act, the board has the same decision-making authority as any local board or official has with respect to the application, including the power to add conditions to an approval.[57] Communities in which at least 10 percent of the housing in the community is affordable are accorded greater deference in rejecting affordable housing applications.[58]

Decisions of a zoning board of review regarding low- and moderate-income housing special exception applications may be appealed to a state housing appeals board (SHAB). In considering a denial of an application, the act requires SHAB to determine whether the denial was "reasonable and consistent with local needs."[59] In considering approvals to which conditions and requirements have been attached, a SHAB must determine whether "those conditions and requirements make the construction or operation of the housing infeasible and whether those conditions and requirements are consistent with an approved affordable housing plan, or if the town does not have an approved affordable housing plan, are consistent with local needs."[60]

Zoning decisions are consistent with local needs if (1) they are made by a city or town council following a public hearing; (2) the community has met or exceeded its statutory minimum for low- and moderate-income housing units, which is generally more than 10 percent of the total housing units in the community;[61] and (3) the municipality has "adopted a comprehensive plan that includes a housing element that addresses the need for

---

54. R.I. Gen. Laws §§ 45-53-1 to 45-53-9 (2009 & Supp. 2020).

55. *Id.* at § 45-53-4(a)(1)(iv). Under the act as amended in 2002, private developers seeking to use the expedited proceedings must retain the low- and moderate-income status for at least 30 years after initial occupancy. *Id.*

56. *Id.* § 45-53-4(a)(1)(ii).

57. *Id.* § 45-53-6(a)–(b).

58. *See id.* § 45-53-4(a)(4)(vii)(D). In communities with more than 5,000 rental units, it is possible to satisfy this statutory requirement by a formula different from the 10 percent threshold. *Id.* § 45-53-3(2)(ii).

59. *Id.* § 45-53-6(b)(i).

60. *Id.* § 45-53-6(b)(ii).

61. *Id.* § 45-53-3(4)(i)(B). *See* Coventry Zoning Bd. of Rev. v. Omni Dev. Corp., 814 A.2d 889, 898–99 (R.I. 2003). The standard for urban cities with more than 5,000 occupied rental units constituting 25 percent or more of the total housing units is 15 percent of the total occupied rental units. R.I. Gen. Laws § 45-53-3(4)(i)(A).

low and moderate income housing for that community."[62] For communities that have not met the statutory quota, a finding that a decision is "consistent with local needs" requires a determination that the local land-use ordinance is:

(1) reasonable in view of the state need for low- and moderate-income housing, taking into account:
a) the number of low-income persons in the city or town affected,
b) the need to protect the health and safety of the occupants of the proposed housing and the residence [*sic*] of the city or town,
c) the need to promote better site and building design in relation to the surroundings,
d) or to preserve open spaces, and
(2) is applied as equally as possible to both subsidized and unsubsidized housing.[63]

In cases where such communities have attached conditions and requirements to approvals, parties appealing those conditions and requirements must establish that they "make it impossible for the developer to proceed without financial loss and there are no alternative measures or modifications that can be accomplished to render construction of the project viable and capable of success."[64]

The statute as originally enacted was broad enough to include land development proposals for single-family housing that required subdivision review, even though the focus of the act was on difficulties multifamily housing developers faced in obtaining approval under local zoning ordinances.[65] An amendment in 2002 restricted zoning board review to zoning ordinance questions regarding multifamily development proposals and provided that planning boards would be the designated body to review applications involving land development projects or subdivisions under regulations promulgated by SHAB.[66]

In a case of first impression, the Supreme Court of Rhode Island conducted a major review of the act and its relationship to local subdivision regulations. In remanding a SHAB decision overriding conditions attached to local approval of a 43-lot cluster subdivision containing 20 affordable single-family houses and 23 market-rate houses, the court stressed that the standard for evaluating conditions or requirements (such as vertical face concrete street curbs, minimum lot sizes, secondary access roads, and impact fees attached to subdivision approval) is whether such conditions or requirements "make it impossible" for the developer to proceed, not whether they create "an unnecessary restriction on affordability."[67] Also, the SHAB cannot dismiss requirements, such as vertical face curbs or appropriate secondary access roads, as "planning preferences" without making written

---

62. *Coventry*, 814 A.2d at 889. In such cases, SHAB has no authority to override their decisions. *Id.*

63. R.H. GEN. LAWS § 45-53-3(4). *See Coventry*, 814 A.2d at 899–900 (applying the statute).

64. *Coventry*, 814 A.2d at 900. The Supreme Court of Rhode Island noted that the burden of proof "necessarily entails full disclosure of the financial plans that underlay the project, including accurate cost projections and the anticipated price of the homes." *Id.*

65. *Id.* at 901.

66. *Id.* at 901 n.6 (discussing the amended statute Pub. L. 2002, ch. 416, § 1, amending § 45-53-4).

67. *Id.* at 904–06.

findings evaluating evidence submitted concerning the impact of such requirements on health and safety.[68]

c. Illinois

Illinois enacted an affordable housing appeals statute with passage of its Affordable Housing Planning and Appeal Act, effective January 1, 2004.[69] The act, said to be inspired by the Massachusetts statute just described, expresses a twofold legislative purpose: (1) to encourage local governments to "incorporate affordable housing within their housing stock sufficient to meet the needs" of their communities, and (2) to enable developers "who believe they have been unfairly treated" because their development proposals contain affordable housing to "seek relief from local ordinances and regulations that may inhibit" development of affordable housing.[70]

Based on the most recent decennial census, local governments whose total year-round housing units include at least 10 percent that are affordable to low- or moderate-income households, or who have less than 1,000 residents, are exempt from the appeals process.[71] All nonexempt local governments were required to approve an affordable housing plan by April 1, 2005, and submit it to the Illinois Housing Development Authority (IHDA) within 60 days after approval.[72] Exempt local governments that became nonexempt after the 2010 Census had 18 months from the date of notification of nonexempt status to approve an affordable housing plan.[73] Beginning January 1, 2009, affordable housing developers whose applications are denied (or approved with conditions which make them infeasible) by nonexempt local governments may submit to the State Housing Appeals Board information regarding why the developer believes the denial or conditional approval was unfair.[74] The board is required to maintain the information and publish an annual report summarizing the developers' reports.[75]

Appeals challenging local denials or conditional approvals may be taken to the board. The developer has the burden of "demonstrating that he or she has been unfairly denied or unreasonable conditions have been placed on tentative approval" of an application.[76] Appeals will be dismissed if the challenged local government has approved, filed, and implemented an affordable housing plan and has met its affordable housing goal as established in its plan.[77] In addition, the appeal will be dismissed if the local government has based its decision on non-appealable requirements that protect the public health and safety.[78] Board decisions that may affirm, reverse, modify, or add conditions to local government

---

68. *Id.*

69. 310 ILL. COMP. STAT. ANN. 67/1 to 67/60 (West 2018).

70. 310 ILL. COMP. STAT. 67/10.

71. *Id.* at 67/15; *see also id.* at 67/20 (demonstrating how the Illinois Housing Development Authority makes its determinations).

72. *Id.* at 67/25(a).

73. *Id.*

74. 310 ILL. COMP. STAT. ANN. 67/30(b) (West 2018).

75. *Id.* at 67/30(c).

76. 310 ILL. COMP. STAT. 67/30(b).

77. *Id.* at 67/30(d).

78. *Id.* at 67/30(e) (referencing other relevant sections).

actions being appealed are binding on the local government.[79] The state appellate court has exclusive jurisdiction to review board decisions.[80]

2. Judicial Review/Burden of Proof Shift

a. California

California has enacted a series of provisions designed to improve the procedural posture of affordable housing development proposals, including limitations on the imposition of adverse design criteria, requiring specific public health or safety reasons for disapproving or reducing densities of housing developments that are consistent with local zoning and general plans, and imposing the burden of proof on local governments when a developer or other person appeals a permit denial or density reduction.[81] Municipalities must designate and zone "sufficient vacant land for residential use . . . to meet housing needs for all income categories as identified in the housing element of the general plan."[82] Certain restrictive local practices "are presumed to have an impact on the supply of residential units available" including ordinances that limit the number of residential building permits that may be issued, limit buildable lots that may be residentially developed, or change the standards of residential development so that insufficient vacant land is available to meet housing needs.[83] If the validity of such ordinances is challenged, the burden shifts to the enacting municipality to establish that the ordinance is "necessary for the protection" of public health, safety, or welfare.[84]

Housing development proposals for very low-, low-, or moderate-income households may not be disapproved or made infeasible by conditions, including design review standards, attached to approval unless "written findings, based upon a preponderance of the evidence in the record," establish one of the following: (1) "the jurisdiction has met or exceeded its share of the regional housing need allocation"; (2) the proposed development would have a "significant, quantifiable, direct, and unavoidable impact" on public health

---

79. *Id.* at 67/30(f).

80. *Id.* at 67/30(g).

81. *See, e.g.*, CAL. EVID. CODE § 669.5 (West 2019); CAL. GOV'T CODE § 65913.2(a) (West 2009), CAL. GOV'T. CODE § 65589.5(d)–(f) (West 2010 & Supp. 2021), CAL. GOV'T. CODE § 65589.6 (West 2010), discussed in Katherine E. Stone & Philip A. Seymour, *California Land Use Planning Law: State Pre-emption and Local Control, in* STATE AND REGIONAL COMPREHENSIVE PLANNING 203 (Peter C. Buchsbaum & Larry J. Smith eds., 1993). *See also* Chapter 2 (California's comprehensive mandatory planning).

82. CAL. GOV'T CODE §§ 65913–65914 (West 2009 & Supp. 2021). For the primary cases discussing the application of these statutes, *see* Bldg. Indus. Ass'n v. City of Oceanside, 27 Cal. App. 4th 744 (Cal. Ct. App. 1994) (invalidating an ordinance adopted by initiative in part because of its conflict with § 65913.1); Hernandez v. City of Encinitas, 28 Cal. App. 4th 1048 (Cal. Ct. App. 1994) (finding no violation in variety of general plan and zoning policies); Shea Homes Ltd. P'ship v. Cnty. of Alameda, 110 Cal. App. 4th 1246 (Cal. Ct. App. 2003) (finding no conflict between restrictive zoning initiative and least-cost zoning requirement).

83. CAL. EVID. CODE § 669.5 (a) (West 2019).

84. *Id.* § 669.5 (b). An excellent source of information regarding California's affordable housing law is the *California Housing Element Manual*, 4th ed. (2019), produced by the California Affordable Housing Law Project of the Public Interest Law Project, http://www.pilpca.org/wp-content/uploads/2019/04/PILP-California-Housing-Element-Manual-Law-Advocacy-and-Litigation-4th-Edition-January-2019.pdf (last visited June 5, 2021).

or safety; (3) denial or conditioning approval is required under state or federal law, and there is "no feasible method to comply without rendering the development unaffordable"; (4) the development is proposed for an agricultural or resource preservation area; or (5) the development is "inconsistent" with both the zoning ordinance and the general plan of a municipality that has adopted a housing element that complies with state law.[85] Municipalities that disapprove a project or condition approval on reducing its density (or other specified conditions) bear the burden of proof to show that their decisions are consistent with the statutorily mandated findings and that the findings are supported by substantial evidence in the record.[86]

Another California law prohibits discrimination against affordable housing (including emergency shelters) by local agencies exercising their planning and land-use powers.[87] Prohibited discrimination includes denial or conditioning of such developments based on an extensive set of reasons. In addition to protecting classes included in fair housing laws (e.g., color, race, national origin, religion, familial status, and disability), this law extends protection on the basis of age, occupation, the "method of financing of the development," and "the intended occupancy of the development by persons or families of low, moderate or middle income."[88] The statute specifically excludes "preferential treatment" for affordable housing developments from its definition of discrimination.[89] Violation of the statute renders the local law void.[90]

California has also adopted laws that, in some cases, require plaintiffs seeking to halt affordable housing developments to post bonds,[91] and also offer the award of attorneys' fees to prevailing public entities.[92] Finally, other statutes promote affordable housing development by requiring localities to give them preferences in water and sewer services[93] and to adopt ordinances that provide substantial density bonuses and other incentives to developers who propose to build qualifying affordable housing developments.[94]

---

85. CAL. GOV'T CODE §§ 65589.5(d)(1)–(5). This subdivision cannot be utilized to disapprove the development project if it is proposed on a site that is identified for very low-, low-, or moderate-income households in the jurisdiction's housing element, and the project is consistent with the density specified in the jurisdiction's housing element, even if it is inconsistent with both the jurisdiction's zoning ordinance and general plan land-use designation. The statutory burden shifting does not apply to moratoria of limited duration, ordinances protecting agricultural land, or certain ordinances adopted by referendum or initiative. *Id.* § 65589.5(d)(A).

86. *Id.* § 65589.5(i).

87. CAL. GOV'T CODE § 65008. For the leading cases applying this statute, *see* Bldg. Indus. Ass'n v. City of Oceanside, 27 Cal. App. 4th 744 (Cal. Ct. App. 1994) (invalidating ordinance adopted by initiative in part because of its conflict with § 65008); Bruce v. City of Alameda, 212 Cal. Rptr. 304 (Cal. Ct. App. 1985) (voiding initiative ordinance because of conflict); Keith v. Volpe, 858 F.2d 467 (9th Cir. 1988), *cert denied*, 493 U.S. 813 (granting standing to project developer and state housing department and holding that a showing of discriminatory impact is sufficient to establish a violation); and Shea Homes Ltd. P'ship v. Cnty. of Alameda, 110 Cal. App. 4th 1246 (Cal. Ct. App. 2003) (finding no violation by ordinance adopted by initiative that protected open space and agricultural lands).

88. CAL. GOV'T CODE § 65008 (West 2010 & Supp. 2021).

89. *Id.* § 65008(e)(2).

90. *Id.* § 65008(a).

91. CAL. CIV. PROC. CODE § 529.2 (West 2011).

92. CAL. GOV'T CODE § 65914 (West 2009).

93. *Id.* § 65589.7.

94. *Id.* §§ 65915–65918.

b. Connecticut

Twenty years after the Massachusetts statute was enacted, Connecticut followed suit with a similar zoning-override procedure, the Connecticut Affordable Housing Appeals Act (Appeals Act), although the override power was delegated to the judiciary rather than to a state administrative agency.[95] Developers of affordable housing may appeal adverse land-use regulatory decisions to the Superior Court of Hartford–New Britain. Affordable housing is defined as assisted housing, or housing in which at least 30 percent of the dwelling units will be conveyed by deeds containing 40-year covenants or restrictions limiting sale prices or rents to levels that enable persons and families with median income or less to pay no more than 30 percent of their annual income for housing.[96]

Upon appeal, the burden shifts to the local agency to prove, based on the evidence in the record, that its decision being appealed is supported by sufficient evidence; that the decision is necessary to protect substantial public interests in health, safety, or other matters that the commission may legally consider; and that these interests "clearly outweigh" the need for affordable housing and "cannot be protected by reasonable changes" to the development. Alternative grounds for denial include (1) the proposal would locate affordable housing in an industrial zone that does not permit residential uses or (2) the development does not meet the statutory definition of affordable housing.[97]

If the burden is not met, the court is directed to "revise, modify, remand, or reverse" the decision consistent with the evidence presented.[98] Communities are exempt from the affordable housing override provisions if at least 10 percent of the existing housing units are affordable or they have received a certificate of affordable housing project completion from the Connecticut Commissioner of Economic and Community Development, which carries with it a one-year exemption.[99]

The Appeals Act has been controversial. Municipalities have objected that the statute abrogates their home rule authority. Planners have feared that builders could blackmail communities into accepting development proposals despite planning objections by threatening to file an affordable housing proposal if their first proposal was rejected. Amendments in 2000 increased the percentage of required affordable housing units to 30 percent and the required length of affordability to 40 years.[100] Developers seeking affordable housing approval must file two new documents: an Affordability Plan and a Conceptual Site Plan. The Affordability Plan must include "draft zoning regulations, conditions of

---

95. CONN. GEN. STAT. ANN. § 8-30g (West 2010 & Supp. 2021).

96. *Id.* § 8-30g(a)(1), (6) (defining "set-aside development"). The original statute required only 20 percent of the units to be set aside. *See generally* Kaufman v. Zoning Comm'n of City of Danbury, 653 A.2d 798, 803 (Conn. 1995) (original statute discussed). The 30 percent figure was added in 2000. Act of June 29, 1999, § 1, 1999 Conn. Acts 261 (Reg. Sess.) (codified as amended at CONN. GEN. STAT. § 8-30g (2010 & Supp. 2021)).

97. CONN. GEN. STAT. ANN. § 8-30g(g).

98. *Id. See, e.g.*, CMB Capital Appreciation v. Planning and Zoning Comm'n of the Town of North Haven, 124 Conn. App. 379 (Conn. App. Ct. 10/12/2010) (affirming trial court's decision that reversed town's denial of site plan approval application).

99. *Id.* § 8-30g(k), (l).

100. Terry J. Tondro, *Connecticut's Affordable Housing Appeals Statute: After Ten Years of Hope, Why Only Middling Results?* 23 W. NEW ENG. L. REV. 115, 152 (2001) (discussing amendments enacted in 2000).

approvals, deeds, restrictive covenants or lease provisions that will govern affordable dwelling units."[101]

c. New Hampshire

New Hampshire has recognized a fair-share requirement for local governments since the *Britton v. Chester* decision in 1991.[102] In 2008, the legislature amended the state's voluntary inclusionary zoning statute to require municipalities, as a condition of exercising their zoning power, to "provide reasonable and realistic opportunities for the development of workforce housing, including rental multi-family housing . . . in a majority . . . of the land area" zoned for residential use.[103] A legislative statement of purpose asserts that the amendments were enacted "to clarify the [fair share] requirements of *Britton v. Chester*[104] . . . and to provide additional guidance . . . to local officials and the public."[105] Municipalities can meet their obligations by adopting inclusionary zoning[106] ordinances, so long as those ordinances do not "rely on inducements that render workforce housing developments economically unviable."[107] "Workforce housing" is defined as for-sale housing for families whose income does not exceed 100 percent of area median income for a four-person household and rental housing for families with incomes that do not exceed 60 percent of area median for a three-person household.[108] A municipality is providing "reasonable and realistic opportunities" for workforce housing if its "existing housing stock is sufficient to accommodate its fair share of the current and reasonably foreseeable regional need for such housing."[109] Municipalities are not required to allow workforce housing that fails to meet "reasonable standards or conditions of approval related to environmental protection, water supply, sanitary disposal, traffic safety, and fire and life safety protection."[110]

An expedited appeals procedure is provided, with a hearing on the merits within six months of filing, to a developer of workforce housing whose application is rejected or

---

101. *Id.* at 138–52 (discussing Christian Activities Council, Congregational v. Town Council (Glastonbury), 735 A.2d 231 (Conn. 1999)). Connecticut law professor Terry Tondro, a co-chair of the Blue Ribbon Commission on Housing that proposed the Appeals Act, gives mixed reviews to the first ten years of experience with the Act. On the one hand, local planning and zoning bodies now must state the reasons for their decisions regarding affordable housing proposals. On the other hand, the Connecticut Supreme Court has accepted the use of "unsupported assertions" as reasons and has limited the area of need determinations to the municipality in which the site in question is located. *Id.* at 164. In addition, the 2000 amendments have, in Tondro's opinion, "increased the complexity of the reviews required for affordable housing projects, so that instead of simplifying these applications we have burdened them even more than before." *Id.* at 164.

102. 595 A.2d 492 (N.H. 1991).

103. N.H. Rev. Stat. Ann. § 674:59 (2016). In an important qualification, the statute expressly provides that *multifamily* housing does not have to be allowed in a majority of the residential land area. *Id.* (emphasis added).

104. 595 A.2d 492, 496 (N.H.1991).

105. 2008 N.H. Laws, SB 342, (codified as amended at N.H. Rev. Stat. Ann. §§ 674:58–674:61) (2016).

106. Inclusionary zoning is defined in N.H. Rev Stat. Ann. § 674:21(IV)(a) (2016 & Supp. 2020).

107. *Id.* § 674:59 (II).

108. N.H. Rev. Stat. Ann. § 674:58(IV) (2016).

109. *Id.* § 674:59 (III).

110. *Id.* § 674:59 (IV).

approved with conditions "which have a substantial adverse effect on the viability" of the development as long as the developer filed a written statement of intent that the development qualify as workforce housing when the application for approval was submitted to the local land-use board.[111] The burden of proof remains on the applicant, and the municipality may assert as an affirmative defense its belief that it has provided its fair share of workforce housing.[112] If a court or referee awards a "builder's remedy" (permission to build the proposed development), the parties must "negotiate in good faith over assurances that the project will be maintained for the long term as workforce housing." Should the parties deadlock, an additional hearing will be held to determine an "appropriate term and form of use restrictions to be applied to the project."[113]

B. State Fair Housing Acts

To complement the federal Fair Housing Act, a majority of states have their own fair housing laws that provide at least the same level of protections.[114] While the FHA prohibits discrimination on the basis of race, color, religion, national origin, sex, familial status, and disability, many state or local laws provide stronger, broader, or more specific protections.

For example, California's Fair Employment and Housing Act includes several protected classes more than the FHA: gender, gender identity, gender expression, sexual orientation, marital status, ancestry, source of income, veteran or military status, or genetic information of that person.[115] Indeed, the statute was amended in 2019 to prohibit discrimination against people using government housing subsidies to pay some or all of their rent.[116] These protected classes are further complemented by other state laws that prohibit discrimination, such as the Unruh Act, which applies to all business establishments and additionally includes citizenship, primary language, or immigration status as protected classes.[117]

Additionally, California's Fair Employment and Housing Act makes certain types of discrimination explicitly illegal. For example, the law makes it illegal to "discriminate through public or private land use practices, decisions, and authorizations" based on protected classes, including through practices such as "restrictive covenants, zoning laws, denials of use permits, and other actions authorized under the Planning and Zoning Law (Title 7 (commencing with Section 65000)), that make housing opportunities unavailable."[118] This provision can complement and strengthen challenges to zoning discrimination or denials of affordable housing production. And, the statute explicitly endorses a disparate effect

---

111. *Id.* § 674:61 (I). A referee is to be appointed if the superior court determines that it cannot meet the six-month hearing deadline. *Id.* § 674.61(II).

112. *Id.*; N.H. Workforce Housing Council, https://www.nhhfa.org/wp-content/uploads/2019/06/Workforce_Housing_Guidebook.pdf (last accessed June 7, 2021).

113. N.H. Rev. Stat. Ann. 674:61 (III). *See also* Britton v. Town of Chester, 595 A.2d 492, 496 (N.H. 1991) (awarded builder's remedy).

114. The Policy Surveillance Project of the Center for Public Health Law Research (CPHLR) at Temple University's Beasley School of Law provides information regarding state and local fair housing laws, http://lawatlas.org/datasets/state-fair-housing-protections-1498143743.

115. Cal. Gov't. Code § 12955(a).

116. *Id.* § 12927(i) as amended by Stats. 2019, c. 600 (S.B.329).

117. Cal. Civ. Code § 51.

118. Cal. Gov't. Code § 12955(l).

theory of liability.[119] In contrast, the FHA faced several challenges to this theory of liability, though it was ultimately upheld by the Supreme Court.[120] Critically, these statutes are fleshed out by an extensive regulatory scheme, which elaborates on the types of practices prohibited (e.g., denying housing based on arrest that did not lead to conviction).[121] Reviewing state or local fair housing laws can provide a wealth of additional protections beyond those found in federal antidiscrimination law.

C. State Reforms to Single-Family Zoning

According to the *New York Times*, in 2019, "the effect of single-family zoning is far-reaching: It is illegal on 75 percent of the residential land in many American cities to build anything other than a detached single-family home."[122] The exclusivity of zoning for single-family houses has perpetuated segregation and widespread racial inequality in housing and, consequently, access to education, public infrastructure, health care, food, and employment opportunities.[123]

There has recently been a variety of reforms and reform efforts to move away from exclusive single-family house zoning at both the local and state levels.

- In 2019, the Oregon legislature passed HB 2001, which revises zoning laws statewide.[124] It requires cities of a population between 10,000 and 25,000 to allow duplexes on every lot previously zoned for single-family houses. It also requires that cities of over 25,000, as well as unincorporated areas around Portland, to allow duplexes, triplexes, quadplexes, cottage clusters, and townhouses on such lots. The reform is meant to provide for "middle housing," which faces shortages in many places, not just in Oregon. If cities do not meet their respective deadlines to implement the reform, a model zoning code will automatically go into effect.

- Minneapolis, Minnesota, passed a comprehensive city plan in 2018 that included a commitment to revising single-family zoning. The Minneapolis 2040 Plan envisioned: "In neighborhood interiors farthest from downtown that today contain primarily single-family homes, increase housing choice and supply by allowing up to

---

119. *Id.* § 12955.8(b).

120. Texas Dep't of Hous. & Community Affairs v. Inclusive Communities Project, Inc., 576 U.S. 519 (2015).

121. 2 Cal. Code Reg. §§ 12005 *et seq.*

122. Emily Badger & Quotrung Bui, *Cities Start to Question an American Ideal: A House with a Yard on Every Lot*, N.Y. Times (June 18, 2019).

123. Priya S. Gupta, *Governing the Single-Family House: A (Brief) Legal History*, 37 U. Haw. L. Rev. 187–243 (2015). For a masterful account of segregationist law and its effects, see James A. Kushner, *Apartheid in America: An Historical and Legal Analysis of Contemporary Racial Residential Segregation in the United States,* 22 Howard L.J. 547 (1979). For a recent review of mixed-incoming housing efforts and the tensions between a market economy and the public idea of inclusion, see Audrey G. McFarlane, *The Properties of Integration: Mixed-Income Housing as Discrimination Management* 66 UCLA L. Rev. 1140 (2019). On segregation and wealth disparity, see Douglas S. Massey & Jonathan Tannen, *Segregation, Race, and the Social Worlds of Rich and Poor, in* The Dynamics of Opportunity in America (Irwin Kirsch & Henry Braun eds., 2016) 13–33.

124. Or. HB 2001 (2019); Or. Stat. §§ 197.296, 197.303, 197.312 and 455.610; Section 1, Chapter 47 (Oregon Laws 2018).

three dwelling units on an individual lot."[125] In the interim to the implementation of the plan, an ordinance was passed that allows for temporary measures.[126]

- California has come close to passing a similar reform to single-family zoning, but as of the time of writing, various efforts have failed. The most recent efforts in 2020, SB 1120, would have required local governments to approve duplexes on plots within areas zoned for single-family residences.[127] Owners would have been able to convert existing single-family houses into duplexes or demolish single-family houses and build a duplex or two single-family houses. SB 1120 failed on account of procedural issues.[128] In the meantime, there have been a number of piecemeal efforts to enable additional affordable housing units to be built, notably a collection of 15 measures in 2017, including bonds and additional fundraising meant to be invested in affordable housing, and incentives for development with mandatory affordable housing targets.[129] California did, however, pass a number of measures to allow for accessory dwelling units (ADUs).[130]

- Washington state considered similar reforms to single-family zoning in early 2020, but the bill did not make it to a floor vote in its State Senate or House.[131] Newton, Massachusetts, passed a rezoning measure in 2020.[132] Similar re-zoning measures are being considered in Maryland,[133] Nebraska,[134] and Virginia.[135]

---

125. *Minneapolis 2040: The City's Comprehensive Plan* (2018) 106.

126. Minneapolis Ord. 2018-082 (12/7/2018).

127. Ca. SB 1120 (2020).

128. Andrew Khouri, *Duplex Bill, SB 1120, Dies: Assembly Approval Comes too Late*, L.A. TIMES (Sept. 1, 2020), https://www.latimes.com/homeless-housing/story/2020-09-01/california-assembly-sb-1120-duplexes.

129. The measures include CA SB 2, CA SB 3, CA SB 35, CA AB 73, and CA SB 540. Liam Dillon, *Gov. Brown Just Signed 15 Housing Bills. Here's How They're Supposed to Help the Affordability Crisis*, L.A. TIMES (Sept. 29, 2017), https://www.latimes.com/politics/la-pol-ca-housing-legislation-signed-20170929-htmlstory.html.

130. For a discussion of these and other housing measures in 2020, see (Chelsea Maclean, et al., *California's 2020 Housing Laws: What You Need to Know* HOLLAND & KNIGHT (Oct. 18, 2019), https://www.hklaw.com/en/insights/publications/2019/10/californias-2020-housing-laws-what-you-need-to-know.

131. Dan Bertolet, *Washington to Consider Re-legalizing Duplexes and Rowhouses Statewide*, SIGHTLINE INST. (Jan. 21, 2020), https://www.sightline.org/2020/01/21/washington-to-consider-re-legalizing-duplexes-and-rowhouses-statewide/.

132. John Hilliard, *Newton Takes Aim at Its History of Single-Family Zoning*, BOSTON GLOBE (Oct. 22, 2020), https://www.bostonglobe.com/2020/10/22/metro/should-single-family-housing-become-relic-newtons-past/.

133. Md. HB 1406 (Planning for Modest Homes Act of 2020); *Newton Rezoning and Newton's Non-Condo Single-Family and Two-Family Homes*, NEWTON REZONING (SEPT. 16, 2021), https://newtonrezoning.org/newton-single-two-family-homesb/.

134. Adam Weinberg, *Bill Seeks Increased Housing Options in Nebraska Cities*, PLATTE INST. (Aug. 4, 2020), https://platteinstitute.org/bill-seeks-increased-housing-options-in-nebraska-cities/.

135. VA HB151 and VA HB152 (2020). These bills were tabled during 2020, but may be returned to in the future.

D. Regulatory Exemptions for Affordable Housing

Another regulatory incentive some states offer affordable housing developers is an exemption from certain land-use regulations, including open space regulations, development impact fees, and environmental review. Connecticut exempts affordable housing developments from open space requirements that municipalities may impose through local subdivision regulations.[136] To qualify for the exemption, at least 20 percent or more of the units in a proposed development must be affordable to households making area median income or less and paying no more than 30 percent of their income for the housing.[137]

Several states exempt affordable housing from various impact fees.[138] For example, Georgia's statute imposing minimum standards for local development impact fee ordinances authorizes local governments to exempt "all or part of" affordable housing development projects from development impact fees if the local comprehensive plan contains the public policy supporting the exemption, and if an alternate revenue source will fund the development's "proportionate share of the system improvement."[139] Hawaii's definition of "public facility capital improvement costs," which are eligible to be funded through impact fees, excludes "expenditures for required affordable housing."[140] The Texas statute authorizing local governments to impose impact fees and regulating their use permits allows local governments to reduce or waive such fees for residential units that qualify as affordable housing under the federal HOME program.[141] The reduction or waiver may begin once the unit is constructed. If affordable housing is not constructed, the reduction/waiver decision may be reversed and an impact fee may be assessed.[142]

California mandates that local governments provide a density bonus and other regulatory relief for certain affordable housing developments, discussed *infra*. In addition, affordable housing developments with fewer than 100 units on less than four acres and meeting certain other criteria are exempt from the provisions of the California Environmental Quality Act (CEQA).[143]

---

136. CONN. GEN. STAT. § 8-25(a).

137. *Id.* § 8-39a; § 8-25(a).

138. See Chapter 11 for discussion of fee waivers by local governments and for a discussion of commercial linkage fees (impact fees that local governments impose on certain developments to help fund affordable housing development).

139. GA. CODE ANN. § 36-71-4(l). The Georgia statute also makes the same exemption available to projects expected "to create extraordinary economic development and employment growth." *Id.*

140. HAW. REV. STAT. § 46-141.

141. TEX. LOC. GOV. CODE ANN. § 395.016 (g). (Vernon 2009). For the HOME program, *see* 42 U.S.C. § 12745 (requiring the following for qualification of affordable rental housing: rents not to exceed 30 percent of income for households making 65 percent of area median income, at least 20 percent of the units occupied by very low-income families (30 percent of area median income), open to Section 8 voucher or certificate holders, and will remain affordable under binding commitments for the remaining useful life of the property or other period of time as determined by HUD). See Chapter 9 for a description of the HOME program.

142. TEX. LOC. GOV. CODE ANN. § 395.016(g) (Vernon 2009).

143. CAL. PUB. RES. CODE § 21159.24. California also created a CEQA exemption for residential projects consistent with the greenhouse gas reduction strategy from the requirements of its Sustainable Communities and Climate Protection Act (S.B. 375) enacted in 2008 and discussed in Chapter 2, *supra*.

III. LOCAL GOVERNMENT RESPONSES

A. Local Inclusionary Zoning[144]

1. Introduction

Local governments' contributions to inclusionary zoning for affordable housing began in the Washington, D.C., metropolitan area a few years before the first *Mount Laurel* decision—in Fairfax County, Virginia, in 1971 and in Montgomery County, Maryland, in 1973.[145]

While Fairfax County's program was stalled by the Virginia Supreme Court,[146] Montgomery County's ordinance has become a national model.[147] Since that time, California has become the state with the most active inclusionary programs, with 170 cities and counties adopting inclusionary zoning ordinances.[148]

2. Two Techniques

Two techniques have most commonly been utilized: (1) the set-aside program, in which a specified percentage of units in a residential development are required to be offered at prices affordable to low- and moderate-income families,[149] and (2) the density bonus program, in which awards are made granting increases in allowable densities when affordable housing is included in residential developments. Local inclusionary ordinances generally specify the following: (1) the threshold size of a development (number of units) that triggers the inclusionary requirement; (2) the percentage of units that must be made affordable; (3) the target population for the affordable units; and (4) the length of the affordability term.

a. Set-Asides (and In-Lieu Fees)

Set-aside programs may be either voluntary or mandatory. Voluntary set-aside programs provide a number of concessions to developers. For example, density levels above those approved by the local zoning ordinance are permitted in return for inclusion of a specified

---

144. See Chapter 11 for a discussion of inclusionary zoning "in lieu" fees.

145. Burchell & Galley, *Inclusionary Zoning: Pros and Cons*, 1(2) New Century Housing 3–4 (2000).

146. Bd. of Supervisors v. De Groff Enters., 198 S.E.2d 600 (Va. 1973).

147. *See., e.g.*, Robert Burchell et al., *Inclusionary Zoning: A Viable Solution to the Affordable Housing Crisis?*, 1(2) New Century Housing 25–26 (2000). *See* Montgomery County Moderately Priced Dwelling Unit (MPDU) Program, https://www.montgomerycountymd.gov/DHCA/housing/singlefamily/mpdu/index.html (last visited June 5, 2021).

148. For reviews of inclusionary zoning practices, *see Inclusionary Housing in the United States: Prevalence, practices, and Production in Local Jurisdictions as of 2019*, https://groundedsolutions.org/tools-for-success/resource-library/inclusionary-housing-united-states (last visited June 5, 2021); California Coalition for Rural Housing, Inclusionary Zoning in California: 30 Years of Innovation (2003), https://docs.wixstatic.com/ugd/8d7a46_878c00a513674a548da628 48197c944b.pdf (last visited June 5, 2021). *See also* Calivita & Grimes, *Inclusionary Housing in California: The Experience of Two Decades,* 64 J. Am. Plan. Ass'n 159 (1998); Calivita et al., *Inclusionary Housing in California and New Jersey: A Comparative Analysis,* 8 Hous. Pol. Debate 109 (1997); Padilla, *Reflections on Inclusionary Zoning and a Renewed Look at Its Viability,* 23 Hofstra L. Rev. 539 (1995).

149. *See* Andrew G. Dietderich, *An Egalitarian's Market: The Economics of Inclusionary Zoning Reclaimed*, 24 Fordham Urb. L.J. 23, 45–47 (1996).

percentage of affordable housing units in a larger residential development.[150] Alternatively, a specified amount of money can be paid into a municipal affordable housing trust fund.[151] Such programs can work in areas where the housing market is strong enough to encourage local builders to "fund the sale of a number of low-income units at prices below the costs of such units' construction."[152] Voluntary set-aside programs in essence provide developers with variances "to construct whatever sort of housing is the most profitable, including dense, luxury housing, as long as some portion of the resulting profits are used to build affordable units below cost."[153]

Early studies found that developers generally were reluctant to participate in voluntary set-aside programs, leading advocates to press for mandatory programs.[154] Mandatory set-aside programs typically require a relatively small percentage (usually 5 percent to 25 percent) of developments in certain zones or in certain configurations, such as planned-unit developments (PUDs), to be composed of low- or moderate-cost housing.[155] They are typically imposed as conditions to rezoning or site-plan approval[156] and are subject to a variety of constitutional challenges.[157]

New Jersey's experience in the late 1980s, the first five years after *Mount Laurel II*,[158] illuminates two profit-related problems with mandatory set-asides: (1) the difficulty in producing a profitable multifamily development when a percentage of the rents must be set at a below-market rate, and (2) the clear preference of developers for ownership units, single-family or condominium, over apartments. As a result, analysts concluded that, while set-aside programs might be effective in producing affordable housing for low- and moderate-income households (income above 80 percent of area median incomes), they were not likely to produce affordable housing for households with incomes below that range without substantial federal or state housing subsidies.[159] In recent years, however,

---

150. *Id.* at 47–50.

151. *See, e.g.*, Montgomery County, Md. Moderately Priced Development Unit (MPDU) ordinance, *infra* note 167 and accompanying text. *See also* Chapter 11 *infra*.

152. Dietderich, *supra* note 149, at 49.

153. *Id.* at 50.

154. *See, e.g.*, S. Burlington County NAACP v. Mount Laurel (*Mount Laurel II*), 456 A.2d 390, 445–46 (N.J. 1983).

155. *Id.*

156. *See, e.g.*, Va. Code Ann. § 15.22201 (2010) (authorizing "reasonable conditions"); Va. Code Ann. §§ 15.22304–15.22305 (2010) (authorizing affordable housing ordinances that include density bonuses of up to 20 percent together with set-asides of at least 17 percent of the units as affordable housing).

157. *See* Lucas v. S.C. Coastal Council, 505 U.S. 1003 (1992); Nollan v. Cal. Coastal Comm'n, 483 U.S. 825 (1987); Dolan v. City of Tigard, 512 U.S. 374 (1994).

158. 456 A.2d 390 (N.J. 1983).

159. For a detailed analysis concluding that the Mount Laurel approach can produce affordable housing but that more than judicially mandated set-asides is required for a complete housing policy, *see* Martha Lamar et al., *Mount Laurel at Work: Affordable Housing in New Jersey, 1983–88,* 41 Rutgers L. Rev. 1197 (1989). *See also* John M. Payne, *Fairly Sharing Affordable Housing Obligations: The Mount Laurel Matrix*, 22 W. New Eng. L. Rev. 365, 368 (2000) (stating that 15,000–20,000 low- and moderate-income housing units and a "substantial amount of middle-income housing in suburban areas, consisting of market-rate units in inclusionary developments," have been produced under *Mount Laurel* influence).

California has had greater success in reaching households with incomes below 80 percent of area median incomes.[160]

b. Density Bonuses

Density bonus programs (sometimes called incentive zoning) are voluntary programs that offer developers an increase in the permitted density of residential projects. The density increases are calculated either by a sliding scale that increases the permitted density as the number of low- or moderate-cost units increases or by a fixed amount for participation in an affordable housing program.[161] For example, in Virginia, projects may be increased by 30 percent of the applicable density range for single-family housing, detached or attached, and for multiple-family housing, in return for allocations of at least 17 percent of the total number of units to affordable single-family housing and at least 6.25 percent to affordable multiple-family housing.[162]

Set-aside and density bonus programs may be operated separately from each other and may be voluntary or mandatory. The *Mount Laurel* court noted that many observers believe their potential is most likely to be realized when they are combined in a mandatory set-aside program that grants density bonuses as a form of compensation to participating developers.[163]

Mandatory set-asides must overcome several problems, including constitutional questions, political objections, and the possibility of developer evasion of set-aside requirements by building conventional units first and then not completing the project.[164] They must also state both the initial period of required affordability of set-aside units and how to preserve affordability after this initial period expires.

3. Current Variations

a. Montgomery County, Maryland's Ordinance

Montgomery County, Maryland, provides a good example of the different ways that inclusionary zoning ordinances can effectively be utilized.[165] In 1974, Montgomery County enacted its Moderately Priced Development Unit (MPDU) ordinance,[166] which requires all subdivisions of 35 or more dwelling units to include a minimum number (between

160. Non-Profit Housing Ass'n, et al., *Affordable by Choice*: *Trends in California Inclusionary Housing Programs* at 14, Fig. 3 (2007) ("More than three-quarters of the inclusionary-development units serve households earning low-, very low- or extremely low incomes."), https://inclusionary housing.org/wp-content/uploads/2016/08/NPH-IHinCA2006.pdf.

161. *Mount Laurel II*, 456 A.2d at 445 (citing Gregory Mellon Fox & Barbara Rosenfeld Davis, *Density Bonus Zoning to Provide Low and Moderate Cost Housing*, 3 HASTINGS CONST. L. Q. 1015, 1060–62 (1976)).

162. VA. CODE ANN. § 15.2-2305(B) (2012). *See* Theodore Taub, *The Future of Affordable Housing*, 22 URB. LAW. 659, 666 (1990) (noting the statute).

163. *Mount Laurel II*, 456 A.2d at 445–50.

164. For an argument grounded in economic theory that voluntary set-aside programs offer more potential than mandatory ones because of voluntary programs' reliance on market forces, *see* Dietderich, *supra* note 149, at 49–65.

165. For an earlier version of this discussion of the Montgomery County ordinance, *see* Peter Salsich, *Affordable Housing: Can NIMBYism Be Transformed into OKIMBYism?*, 19 ST. LOUIS U. PUB. L. REV. 453, 462–64 (2000).

166. MONTGOMERY COUNTY, MD. CODE § 25A, https://codelibrary.amlegal.com/codes/mont gomerycounty/latest/montgomeryco_md_comcor/0-0-0-13342 (last visited June 5, 2021).

12.5 percent and 15 percent) of moderately priced units of varying sizes to accommodate different family sizes.[167] Developers are allowed to increase the number of dwelling units to be constructed on a particular site by up to 22 percent over the allowable zoning density in return for including MPDUs in the development.[168] Single-family MPDUs must have two or more bedrooms, and multifamily MPDUs must not be predominantly efficiency or one-bedroom units.[169]

The ordinance is implemented through written agreements, called MPDU agreements, approved by the director of the County Department of Housing and Community Affairs and the county attorney.[170] County officials may not issue building permits unless applicable MPDU agreements have been signed,[171] and covenants "running with the land for the entire period of control" have been recorded that have priority over all permanent financing instruments.[172]

The MPDU ordinance provides some alternative approaches for developers "in exceptional cases."[173] In lieu of the standard MPDU approach, developers may offer to (1) build "significantly more" MPDUs at one or more adjoining sites within the same or adjoining planning area; (2) convey land suitable "in size, location and physical condition for significantly more MPDUs"; (3) contribute to the County Housing Initiative Fund monies to "produce significantly more" MPDUs; or (4) any combination of the above.[174] An offer to follow one of the alternative approaches must be accepted if the director finds that (1) the original proposal included an "indivisible package of resident services and facilities" for all households that would make the MPDU units "effectively unaffordable," (2) the alternative proposal by the developer "will achieve significantly more" affordable MPDUs, and (3) the public benefits of the alternative proposal "outweigh the benefits of constructing MPDUs in each subdivision throughout the county."[175]

The land transfer provision may be implemented by transferring land to the county. The agreement may be for either (1) finished lots, with the developer being reimbursed for the costs of finishing the lots but not for the cost of acquisition or value of the transferred lots, or (2) unfinished lots, or finished lots with the developer waiving reimbursement when no county funds are available.[176]

One significant feature that sets the Montgomery County MPDU program apart from most of the other inclusionary ordinances across the country is the authorization for the County Housing Authority (also referred to as the County Housing Opportunity Commission) to purchase up to 40 percent of the affordable housing units.[177] Approximately 1,500 have been purchased by the County's Housing Opportunities Commission for rent to

167. *Id.* §§ 25A-2(5), 25A-5(b)(3).
168. *Id.* § 25A-5(c)(3).
169. *Id.* § 25A-5(b)(2)–(3).
170. *Id.* § 25A-5(a).
171. *Id.* § 25A-5(g)–(h).
172. *Id.* § 25A-5(k)(3).
173. *Id.* § 25A-5A.
174. *Id.* § 25A-5A(a).
175. *Id.* § 25A-5A(a)(1)–(2).
176. *Id.* § 25A-5(f)(1).
177. *Id.* § 25A-8(b).

persons who are eligible for public housing or Section 8 subsidies, enabling this program to serve more households of lower incomes than many other inclusionary programs.[178]

Because of the success of the Montgomery County program, the state legislature in 1991 specifically authorized all Maryland counties and municipalities to enact such ordinances.[179] The Montgomery County MPDU program is cited frequently as an example of what courageous and imaginative people can accomplish.[180] A series of ordinances adopted in November 2004, effective April 1, 2005, made several modifications to the MPDU program, including permitting MPDU developers to include up to 100 percent of single-family units as attached or semi-detached units in a single-family residential zone when necessary to achieve MPDU goals on-site, as long as the units are compatible with adjacent existing housing.[181]

b. California Inclusionary Ordinances

Despite originating on the East Coast, inclusionary zoning has become most popular in California. California statutes require inclusionary housing policies coastal communities,[182] and require local governments to adopt ordinances providing density bonuses or other incentives to housing developers.[183] In addition, many local governments have adopted their own inclusionary zoning ordinances. The complex relationship between these state and local laws has become important.

The California density bonus statute is a blend of mandatory and voluntary provisions. Developers may request, and local governments are required to grant, density bonuses, or acceptance of land donations for housing, and related concessions (such as waiver or modification of development and zoning standards, including minimum lot size, side-yard setbacks, and public works placement requirements) when proposing to construct, for example, (1) 10 percent of the units in a development for lower-income households; (2) 5 percent of the units for very low-income households; (3) a senior citizen housing development or mobile home park; or (4) 10 percent of the units in a condominium project

---

178. Richard Tustian, former planning director for Montgomery County, believes this provision, and a similar one in Fairfax County, Va.'s voluntary program, is particularly noteworthy "because it gives protection to the Housing Commission to use public funding to subsidize units in scattered sites without the 'not-in-my-backyard' location battle." Richard Tustian, *Inclusionary Zoning and Affordable Housing*, 1(2) NEW CENTURY HOUSING 25 (October 2000) (citing DAVID RUSK, INSIDE GAME OUTSIDE GAME 184 (1999).

179. MD. ANN. CODE LAND USE § 7-401 (West 2012). Frederick County adopted an MPDU program in 2002, Ordinance No. 02-25-321, effective Nov. 22, 2002, adding §§ 1-6A-1 and –ff. The Frederick County program focuses only on residents with moderate income and "moderately priced housing." *Id.* § 1-6A-2 (2)–(3).

180. *See, e.g.*, RUSK, *supra* note 178, at 178–200.

181. Ord. Nos. 15-34, 15-35, 15-36, 15-37, effective Apr. 1, 2005, https://www.montgomery countymd.gov/council/Resources/Files/zta/2004/04-11.pdf;https://www.montgomerycountymd.gov /council/Resources/Files/zta/2004/04-12.pdf; https://www.montgomerycountymd.gov/council/Reso urces/Files/zta/2004/04-13.pdf;https://www.montgomerycountymd.gov/council/Resources/Files/zta /2004/04-14.pdf (last visited June 9, 2021).

182. CAL. PUB. RES. CODE §§ 30604 *et seq.*

183. CAL. GOV'T. CODE §§ 65915 *et seq.*

or planned development for moderate income households.[184] The law has been amended to include additional categories in recent years. Importantly, the law also includes a "no net loss" provision, prohibiting the granting of density bonuses where the property has become vacant/demolished in the previous five years, is rent-restricted, "or occupied by lower or very low income households" unless those units are replaced and the project either meets the density bonus requirements or is entirely affordable.[185]

How many incentives and concessions are granted depends on the percentage of affordable housing units by income level that will be available in the development.[186] So, for example, a greater amount of units restricted to the lowest income levels will result in a higher percentage of allowable density. Developments that include approved child-care facilities receive either an additional density bonus of residential space equal to or greater than the child-care facility space or "an additional concession or incentive that contributes significantly to the economic feasibility of the construction of the child-care facility."[187] Municipalities may exceed the statutory density bonus percentages "if permitted by local ordinance."[188]

A local government may not refuse to grant the incentives or concessions sought unless it makes a written finding, based on substantial evidence, of one of the following: (1) the concession or incentive is not required to provide affordable housing; (2) the concession or incentive would have a "specific adverse impact" on public health and safety, the physical environment, or property listed as historic, and there is "no feasible method to satisfactorily mitigate or avoid" the adverse effect without making the development unaffordable to low- and moderate-income households; or (3) the concession or incentive would violate state or federal law.[189] Waivers or modifications of development standards "that will have the effect of physically precluding the construction" of developments qualifying for density bonuses may be requested and must be granted, unless doing so would trigger the "specific adverse impacts" just noted or would violate state or federal law.[190]

Surveys completed in 2003 and 2006 by the California Coalition for Rural Housing (CCRH) and the Non-Profit Housing Association of Northern California (NPH) reported significant growth in the number of California jurisdictions employing inclusionary zoning or other regulatory practices to encourage production of affordable housing. That data shows that in 1994 only 64 cities and counties (12 percent of the total) employed these practices, while in 2006, 170 cities and counties (32 percent of the total) had employed some form of inclusionary zoning.[191]

Illustrative of the growth is the fact that while approximately 34,000 affordable units were reported produced in the 30 years since Palo Alto adopted the first inclusionary

---

184. *Id.* § 65915(a), (b) & (k) (West 2009 & Supp. 2020). Density bonus units must remain affordable to lower- and/or very low-income households for at least 55 years. *Id.* § 65915(c)(1).

185. *Id.* § 65915(c)(3)(A).

186. *Id.* § 65915(f).

187. *Id.* § 65915(h).

188. *Id.* § 65915(n).

189. *Id.* § 65915(d)(1)(A), (B), (C).

190. *Id.* § 65915(e).

191. CALIFORNIA COALITION FOR RURAL HOUSING, *supra* note 148, at 7; Non-Profit Housing Ass'n, et al., *supra* note 160, at 9.

zoning ordinance in 1973, more than 29,000 additional units were created in six and a half years (January 1999–June 2006).[192] The 2003 study reported that inclusionary requirements ranged from 4 percent to 30 percent. The most common percentage was 10 percent, but approximately half of the jurisdictions require at least 15 percent. Required required"terms of affordability ranged from ten years to perpetuity. All but 6 percent of the reporting programs were mandatory, and mandatory programs had produced the most very low- and low-income-affordable units compared to units produced under voluntary programs. Eighty percent of respondents were reported to "believe that their inclusionary program has stimulated the production of affordable housing that would not have been built otherwise."[193]

The 2006 study examined trends in the implementation of inclusionary programs. Most inclusionary housing is rental.[194] Seventy-six percent serves persons with incomes of no more than 80 percent of area median income (AMI): 47 percent low-income (50 percent to 80 percent AMI); 25 percent very low-income (30 percent to 50 percent AMI); and 4 percent extremely low-income (less than 30 percent AMI). Ownership units tend to be marketed to moderate-income persons (80 percent to 120 percent AMI). A growing number of units are offered through "development partnerships . . . between market-rate and affordable builders."[195]

The California Institute for Local Self Government has prepared best practices for communities considering inclusionary housing programs.[196] The best practices include seven broad categories: making a clear statement of need,[197] identifying the affordability, type of housing, location, and length of the inclusionary requirements,[198] coupling the requirement with incentives and concessions to offset the cost of the units;[199] having clear development standards;[200] establishing alternative methods of compliance that maximize on-site production of units;[201] including procedures for waivers or reductions,[202] monitoring implementation, and compliance.[203] Each policy within these categories should be designed to "increase housing affordability and develop diverse, inclusive neighborhoods."[204]

---

192. Non-Profit Housing Ass'n, et al., *supra* note 160, at 10.

193. *Id.* at 7–10, 19–20.

194. *Id.* at 14. A 2008 study done for the National Association of Home Builders concluded that inclusioning zoning requirements "cause[d] a measurable shift from single-family to multifamily housing production." Nat'l Ctr. for Smart Growth Research and Educ., Housing Market Impacts of Inclusionary Zoning 14 (2008), https://drum.lib.umd.edu/handle/1903/21499 (last visited Sept. 16, 2021).

195. Non-Profit Housing Ass'n, et al., *supra* note 160, at 8–9, 14–16.

196. Inst. for Local Self Government, *Meeting California's Housing Needs: Best Practices for Inclusionary Housing* (2018), https://www.lgc.org/wordpress/wp-content/uploads/2018/11/inclusionary-factsheet_v2.pdf.

197. *Id.* at 2.

198. *Id.* at 3–4.

199. *Id.* at 5.

200. *Id.*

201. *Id.* at 6.

202. *Id.* at 7.

203. *Id.* at 8.

204. *Id.* at 1.

The California Court of Appeals, in *Palmer/Sixth Street Properties L.P. v. City of Los Angeles*,[205] delivered a reminder that inclusionary zoning ordinances enacted by local governments are subject to relevant state law. In a challenge to the city's conditional approval of a mixed-use development in the Central City West area of Los Angeles, the court held that local regulations imposing inclusionary requirements on rental housing, such as "forcing [developers of new rental housing] to provide affordable housing units at regulated rents in order to obtain project approval," conflicted with, and were preempted by, the state rent-control statute that permits landlords "to establish the initial rental rate for a dwelling or unit."[206] The court refused to accept the city's argument that its inclusionary housing ordinance was not a rent-control statute but simply a requirement that the developer replace 60 affordable units that had been demolished or pay an in-lieu fee. The court said that "not only does [the ordinance] clearly restrict the initial rents for those units, but it imposes deed restrictions to control the rents 'for the life of the dwelling units or for 30 years, whichever is greater.'"[207] Affordable housing advocates expressed concern over the decision's impact on new rental housing developments and were pressing for "clarifying amendments" from the state legislature.[208] And ultimately, the legislature essentially reversed the Palmer decision through AB 1505, enacted in 2017, which once again allows local governments to enact their own mandatory inclusionary ordinances.[209]

Implementation of an inclusionary housing policy can produce controversies with neighbors, as *Wollmer v. City of Berkeley*[210] illustrates. In *Wollmer*, a nearby resident and an unincorporated association of Berkeley residents and businesspeople challenged the calculation of a density bonus and the granting of zoning variances for a mixed-use residential and commercial development. While the parties differed on the mandatory density bonus calculation by only one unit (31 versus 32),[211] the controversy centered on the city's granting of a discretionary bonus of an additional 25 units and the granting of variances deemed necessary to make the project economically feasible.[212] In upholding the city's findings that variances in the number of stories, floor-area ratio, and height regulations, along with that discretionary density bonus of 25 additional units, were necessary to make the project economically feasible, the court concluded that "[i]f the Project as a whole was not economically feasible, then the below-market-rate housing units would not be built, and the purpose of the density bonus law to encourage the development of low- and moderate-income housing would not be achieved."[213]

---

205. 96 Cal. Rptr. 3d 875 (Cal. App. 2009).

206. *Id.* at 887; CAL. CIV. CODE §§ 1954.50 *et seq.*, popularly known as the Costa Hawkins Act. The quoted language is known as the act's "vacancy decontrol" provision.

207. *Palmer, supra* note 205, at 879.

208. The Public Interest Law Project and California Affordable Housing Law Project, Inclusionary Zoning After *Palmer & Patterson* 2 (April 2010); Goldfarb Lipman Attorneys, Law Alert: Cities and Counties Need to Amend Local Inclusionary Ordinances to Address *Palmer v. City of Los Angeles* (2010).

209. GOV'T. CODE § 65850.01.

210. 102 Cal. Rptr. 3d 19 (Cal. App. 2009).

211. *Id.* at 27.

212. *Id.* at 28–29.

213. *Id.* at 30.

c. Louisiana's Model Inclusionary Zoning Ordinance

In partial response to the 2005 hurricanes, the Louisiana legislature enacted legislation in 2006 authorizing parishes and municipalities to enact inclusionary zoning ordinances.[214] One year later, the legislature adopted a concurrent resolution recommending a model inclusionary zoning ordinance.[215] The model ordinance contains a statement of purpose, findings, definitions, inclusionary zoning standards, affordable housing standards, authorization for in-lieu fees, and other alternatives to inclusionary housing development, such as off-site construction; land dedication and preservation of existing units; compliance procedures, including establishment of inclusionary housing plans and implementation of inclusionary housing agreements; eligibility for inclusionary units; standards for owner-occupied units and rental units; provisions for adjustments, waivers, and a development review process; and administration of "affordability in perpetuity" through deed restrictions, resale restrictions, rent regulations, and agency option to purchase affordable units when offered for sale.[216] The model ordinance makes "[A]pproval of any subdivision plat or issuance of any building permit for a covered residential unit" conditional upon allocation of a minimum percentage (to be determined by the municipality or parish) of inclusionary units restricted to "moderate-, low-, or very low-income households."[217] A range of options is provided for "developer compensation," including density bonuses, a variety of fee reductions and refunds, eligibility for expedited processing, and financial assistance, "to the extent budgeted . . . and otherwise available," for the inclusionary housing component.[218]

d. Washington's Affordable Housing Incentive Program

Washington's Affordable Housing Incentive Program, first enacted in 2006 and amended in 2009,[219] authorizes cities and counties planning under Washington's Growth Management Act[220] to provide incentives to developers of affordable housing, including density bonuses within the urban growth area, height and bulk bonuses, fee waivers or exemptions, parking reductions, and expedited permitting.[221] Adopting an approach similar to the New Hampshire statute discussed *supra*,[222] the Washington statute directs jurisdictions adopting affordable housing incentive programs to adopt standards for serving low-income households and defines low-income households differently for rental and owner-occupancy housing: Rental housing units must be affordable to households with incomes of 50 percent or less of the county median family income, while owner-occupancy units must be affordable to households with incomes of 80 percent of the county median family income.[223] Low-income units must generally be distributed throughout the development and have the

---

214. La. Rev. Stat. Ann. §§ 33:5001–33:5003 (2017).
215. H.R. Con. Res. 123, 2007 Reg. Leg. Sess. (La. 2007).
216. *Id.*
217. *Id.* § 4.A.
218. *Id.* § 4.A(3).
219. Wash. Rev. Code Ann. § 36.70A.540 (2021).
220. *Id.* § 36.70A.040.
221. *Id.* § 36.70A.540(1)(a).
222. Notes 103 to 114 and accompanying text.
223. Wash. Rev. Code Ann. § 36.70A.540(2)(b) (2021).

"same functionality" as other units, and must be "committed to continuing affordability for at least fifty years."[224]

4. Constitutional Issues

As might be expected, the use of mandatory set-asides as part of an affirmative effort to provide affordable housing can cause intense political problems. Neighboring residents often oppose development proposals with increased allowable density, and developers fear loss of profit potential if mandatory set-asides are implemented.[225] In addition to the threshold issue of a local government's authority to enact an inclusionary zoning ordinance, the basic constitutional questions for inclusionary zoning programs are the familiar ones of taking, substantive due process, and equal protection.

Virginia's Supreme Court voided an early inclusionary zoning ordinance in *Board of Supervisors of Fairfax County v. DeGroff Enterprises* as both ultra vires and as an unconstitutional taking.[226] The *DeGroff* court found that while "providing low and moderate income housing serves a legitimate public purpose," it "exceeds the authority granted by the enabling act to the local governing body because it is socio-economic zoning. . . ."[227] And, in *Town of Telluride v. Lot Thirty-Four Venture, L.L.C.*, the Colorado Supreme Court found that a Colorado ski community's inclusionary ordinance was void because it conflicted with the state's anti-rent control statute.[228]

---

224. *Id.* § 36.70A.540(2)(d)–(e).

225. For an excellent analysis of the constitutional and political issues raised when courts become actively involved in seeking to resolve basic zoning problems through judicial remedies, *see* John M. Payne, *Delegation Doctrine in the Reform of Local Government Law: The Case of Exclusionary Zoning*, 29 RUTGERS L. REV. 803 (1976).

226. 198 S.E.2d 600, 601 (Va. 1973). Fairfax County now has a voluntary inclusionary zoning program (Affordable Dwelling Unit (ADU) Ordinance). Fairfax County has an Affordable Dwelling Unit (ADU) Ordinance. Fairfax County, Va., Zoning Ord., §§ 5101–5101.12, https://online.encodeplus .com/regs/fairfaxcounty-va/doc-viewer.aspx?secid=229#secid-247 (last accessed Sept. 16, 2021).

227. 198 S.E.2d at 601–02. The *DeGroff* court referred to a previous decision in which it had invalidated an exclusionary zoning ordinance because it was "socio-economic," and based its decision on the idea that the zoning enabling act authorized only "traditional zoning ordinances directed to physical characteristics and having the purpose neither to include nor exclude any particular socio-economic group." *Id.* at 602. This case prompted a sharp rejoinder from the *Mount Laurel II* court:

> It is nonsense to single out inclusionary zoning (providing a realistic opportunity for the construction of lower-income housing) and label it "socio-economic" if that is meant to imply that other aspects of zoning are not. It would be ironic if inclusionary zoning to encourage the construction of lower-income housing were ruled beyond the power of a municipality because it is "socio-economic" when its need has arisen from the socio-economic zoning of the past that excluded it.

Mount Laurel II, 456 A.2d at 449.

228. 3 P.3d 30, 32 (Colo. 2000) (containing mandatory set-aside for 40 percent of employees in new development and establishing a base rental). *See* Daniel J. Curtin, Jr., Cecily T. Talbert & Nadia L. Costa, *Inclusionary Housing Ordinance Survives Constitutional Challenge in Post-*Nollan-Dolan *Era:* Homebuilders Ass'n of N. Cal. v. City of Napa, 54(8) LAND USE L. & ZONING DIGEST 3, n.4 (Aug. 2002). For information about the inclusionary housing movement nationally, visit the Innovative Housing Institute, https://ihiusa.org/ (last visited June 9, 2021).

However, the New Jersey Supreme Court in *Mount Laurel II*, and more recently a California court of appeal, upheld an inclusionary zoning ordinance against a multipronged facial attack in *Homebuilders Ass'n of Northern California v. City of Napa*.[229]

In *Mount Laurel II*, the Supreme Court of New Jersey confronted the substantive due process question, posed in the guise of an attack on inclusionary zoning techniques, as "impermissible socioeconomic use[s] of the zoning power, . . . not substantially related to the use of land."[230] The court upheld the use of density bonuses and mandatory set-asides for construction of affordable housing when a showing was made that the *Mount Laurel* obligation to provide "a realistic opportunity for the construction of [a] fair share of the lower income housing allocation" cannot be satisfied "simply by removal of restrictive barriers."[231] Because the *Mount Laurel* court's holding is based in the court's expansive interpretation of New Jersey's Constitution, it is unclear whether or not other state courts would agree.[232]

The *Mount Laurel II* court did not directly respond to a takings challenge against inclusionary zoning,[233] and the *DeGroff* court's treatment of the takings claim was brief and conclusory, not applying any of the U.S. Supreme Court's takings tests.[234] In an important

---

229. 108 Cal. Rptr. 2d 60 (Cal. App. 2001), *cert. denied*, 535 U.S. 954 (2002).

230. *Mount Laurel II*, 456 A.2d at 448.

231. Citing its earlier decision rejecting due process and equal protection challenges to a zoning ordinance that permitted mobile homes in a zone restricted to elderly persons or families, the Court declared that "[T]he . . . special need of lower-income families for housing, and its impact on the general welfare, could justify a district limited to such use and certainly one of lesser restriction that requires only that multifamily housing within a district include such use (the equivalent of a mandatory set-aside)." *Mount Laurel II*, 456 A.2d 390, 443–48 (1983).

232. *Id.* at 448. For additional discussion of the Mount Laurel doctrine, *see* Peter H. Schuck, *Fudging Remedies: Judicial Approaches to Housing Segregation*, 37 Harv. C.R.-C.L. L. Rev. 289, 309–19 (2002); Richard G. Lorenz, *Good Fences Make Bad Neighbors*, 33 Urb. Law. 45 (2001); John M. Payne, *Fairly Sharing Affordable Housing Obligations: The Mount Laurel Matrix*, 22 W. New Eng. L. Rev. 365 (2001); Naomi Bailin Wish & Stephen Eisdorfer, *The Impact of Mount Laurel Initiatives: An Analysis of the Characteristics of Applicants and Occupants*, 27 Seton Hall L. Rev. 1268 (1997).

233. The Court appeared to reject such a challenge in an important footnote, the premise of which is supported by Supreme Court takings jurisprudence:

> The explicit requirement of lower-income units in a zoning provision may be necessary if the municipality's social goals are to prevail over neutral market forces. Zoning does not require that land be used for maximum profitability, and on occasion the goals of zoning may require something less.

Mount Laurel II, 456 A.2d at 450, n.34.

234. In *Board of Supvrs. v. DeGroff Enterprises*, the Virginia Supreme Court simply described the 15 percent set-aside requirement of the ordinance and immediately concluded that it was a taking. 198 S.E.2d at 602. Except when permanent physical occupation, *Loretto v. Teleprompter Manhattan CATV Corp.*, 458 U.S. 419 (1982), or loss of all economic use of property occurs, *Lucas v. South Carolina Coastal Council*, 505 U.S. 1003 (1992), the Supreme Court applies a three-prong analysis to regulatory takings challenges, examining (1) the character of the government action, (2) the economic impact of the regulation on the landowner, and (3) the "extent to which the regulation has interfered with distinct investment-backed expectations." Penn Central Transp. Co. v. New York City, 438 U.S. 104, 124 (1978), *applied in* Tahoe-Sierra Preservation Council, Inc. v. Tahoe Regional Planning Agency, 535 U.S. 302 (2002). Most takings cases are scrutinized on a rational basis standard, but a heightened level of scrutiny featuring an "individualized determination" of

test case, *Homebuilders Association of Northern California v. City of Napa*, a California court upheld a 10 percent mandatory set-aside requirement against due process and takings challenges.[235]

The challenged Napa ordinance imposed a "primary mandate" requiring that 10 percent of all new housing be "affordable," as that term is defined in the ordinance. The ordinance provides a number of benefits for affordable housing developments, including density bonuses, expedited processing, and fee deferrals.[236] The ordinance also provided developers with two alternatives: (1) land dedication or affordable housing construction on another site, or (2) payment of an in-lieu fee to the local housing trust fund.[237] The ordinance also permits developers to seek a reduction, adjustment, or complete waiver of the affordable housing requirements if there is an "absence of any reasonable relationship or nexus between the impact of the development and . . . the inclusionary requirement."[238]

The California court rejected the Homebuilders' facial challenge on several grounds. The Homebuilders Association of Northern California (plaintiffs) argued unsuccessfully that there was no "essential nexus" or "rough proportionality" between the impact of property development and the required set-aside.[239] In refusing to apply the "intermediate scrutiny" standard of *Nollan/Dolan*,[240] the court applied the California Supreme Court's determination in *Ehrlich v. City of Culver City*[241] and *Santa Monica Beach, Ltd. v. Superior Court*[242] that intermediate scrutiny is required only when approvals of specific land development proposals are conditioned by exactions of property interests in land. The court noted that it was faced with a "facial challenge to economic legislation that is generally applicable to *all* development" in the city (emphasis in original).[243] The court noted that while the ordinance imposes "significant burdens" on developers, it also provides "significant benefits to those who comply with its terms" and authorizes a "complete waiver" of the inclusionary requirements.[244] *Dolan*'s burden-shifting standard does not apply because

ends-means relationships is given to exactions of property interests such as easements in return for development permission. Nollan v. Cal. Coastal Comm'n, 483 U.S. 825 (1987); Dolan v. City of Tigard, 512 U.S. 374 (1994).

235. 108 Cal. Rptr. 2d 60 (2001), *cert. denied*, 535 U.S. 954 (2002).

236. *Id.* at 62.

237. Housing trust funds are discussed in Chapters 10 and 11.

238. *Id.* at 63. The quoted language responds to the Supreme Court's *Nollan/Dolan* heightened scrutiny constitutional takings test for land-use exactions. Nollan v. California Coastal Comm'n, 483 U.S. 825 (1987); Dolan v. City of Tigard, 512 U.S. 374 (1994).

239. *Homebuilders Ass'n of N. Cal.*, 108 Cal. Rptr. 2d at 60. *See* Curtin et al., *supra* note 228, at 5–6; *Constitutional Law—Fifth Amendment Takings Clause—California Court of Appeal Finds Nollan's and Dolan's Heightened Scrutiny Inapplicable to Inclusionary Zoning Ordinance*, 115 Harv. L. Rev. 2058 (2002): Barbara Kautz, *In Defense of Exclusionary Zoning: Successfully Creating Affordable Housing*, 36 U.S.F. L. Rev. 971 (2002).

240. Nollan v. Cal. Coastal Comm'n, 483 U.S. 825 (1987); Dolan v. City of Tigard, 512 U.S. 374 (1994).

241. 911 P.2d 429 (Cal. 1996).

242. 968 P.2d 993 (Cal. 1999).

243. *Homebuilders Ass'n of N. Cal.*, 108 Cal. Rptr. 2d at 65–66.

244. *Id.* at 64.

the ordinance is a "generally applicable legislative enactment rather than an individualized assessment imposed as a condition of development."[245]

The Homebuilders also challenged the inclusionary zoning ordinance under the *Agins v. Tiburon* requirement that a regulation must "substantially advance legitimate state interests" to avoid a constitutional taking finding.[246] The court stated that it was "unpersuaded" by the argument that the inclusionary zoning ordinance did not meet that standard: "[W]e have no doubt that creating affordable housing for low and moderate families is a legitimate state interest . . . by requiring developers . . . to create a modest amount of affordable housing (or to comply with one of the alternatives) the ordinance will necessarily increase the supply of affordable housing."[247]

A similar facial challenge was dismissed under *Nollan/Dolan* in *Action Apartments Association v. City of Santa Monica*.[248] Reiterating that the two-part *Nollan/Dolan* test "applies only in the case of individual adjudicative permit approval decisions," the California Court of Appeals refused to consider a facial challenge to the city's ordinance modifying existing density bonus regulations and low- and moderate-income housing construction requirements on multifamily housing construction.[249] The court also refused to accept the argument that the Supreme Court's decision in *Lingle v. Chevron U.S.A., Inc.*[250] permitted a facial challenge to the ordinance. Noting that *Lingle* abrogated the stand-alone "substantially advances" takings test of *Agins v. City of Tiburon*,[251] the court held that "*Lingle* does [not] abrogate the rule that the *Nollan/Dolan* nexus and rough proportionality test applies only in the context of judicial review of individual adjudicative land use decisions."[252]

A California Supreme Court case, *CBIA. v. City of San Jose*, affirmed that inclusionary ordinances are not exactions and also held such ordinances need not demonstrate that they be "reasonably related to the impact of a particular development to which the ordinance applies."[253] The court determined that an inclusionary ordinance is not an exaction, but is like any other land use regulation impacting property, like rent control or density rules, and only subject to the same level of review.[254] Additionally, because inclusionary ordinances fall within a municipality's police powers, it need only show that they are reasonably related to the general welfare purposes for which they are enacted, explicitly overturning a state Court of Appeal case that had held otherwise.[255]

---

245. *Id.*
246. 447 U.S. 255, 260 (1980).
247. *Homebuilders Ass'n of N. Cal.*, 108 Cal. Rptr. 2d at 64–65. The Supreme Court subsequently determined that the *Agins* "substantially advances" test is applicable only to Due Process Clause challenges and is not a proper part of a takings analysis. Lingle v. Chevron U.S.A., Inc., 544 U.S. 528 (2005).
248. 82 Cal. Rptr. 3d 722 (Cal. App. 2008).
249. *Id.* at 728, 732.
250. *See Lingle*, 544 U.S. at 545–47.
251. 447 U.S. 255, 260 (1980).
252. Action Apts. Ass'n v. City of Santa Monica, 82 Cal. Rptr. 3d at 733.
253. CBIA. v. City of San Jose, 61 Cal. 4th 435 (2015).
254. *Id.* at 461–64.
255. *Id.* at 469–79, rejecting decision in Bldg. Indus. Ass'n. of Central Cal. v. City of Patterson, 90 Cal. Rptr. 3d 63, 72 (Cal. App. 2009).

State and local governments facing the growth pressures and spatial mismatches between jobs and affordable housing have developed increasingly sophisticated responses, as noted in this section. Courts have upheld these techniques when they are demonstrated to be authorized, expressly or by implication, by state and local land-use laws, and they are implemented through a planning process that considers affordable housing needs as well as other important community concerns and respects the legitimate property interests of affected landowners.

IV. OTHER METHODS OF REGULATING FOR INCLUSION

A. Land Banking

States and local governments increasingly are using the land-assemblage technique called "land banking" to assist developers of affordable housing. Land banking involves the acquisition of land parcels, or the development rights to the land, to accomplish a public purpose.[256] The technique has been used for the preservation of farmland, wetlands, and other environmentally sensitive land,[257] as well as the assemblage of land for major industrial development projects.[258] However, the technique has fallen out of favor for city redevelopment because of displacement controversies arising out of the old urban renewal program[259] and still raises concerns among neighborhood advocates.[260]

Michigan's Land Bank Fast Track Act, enacted in 2003, establishes the Michigan Fast Track Land Bank Authority within the Department of Labor and Economic Growth (Authority).[261] The statute gives the Authority power to assemble parcels in a coordinated fashion and clear title to land that is owned by state or local government entities, or private land that has been abandoned or that has reverted to the state because of nonpayment of taxes.[262] The Authority does not have the power to tax or impose special assessments; nor does it have the power to condemn land or acquire it through exercise of the power of

---

256. *See, e.g.*, MICH. COMP. LAWS ANN. §§ 124.751–124.774 (West 2006).

257. *See, e.g.*, MONT. CODE ANN. §§ 77-2-361 to 77-2-367 (West 2009) (state lands). The Montana Department of Natural Resources and Conservation maintains a website in the state's land banking program, http://dnrc.mt.gov/divisions/trust/real-estate/land-banking.

258. *See, e.g.*, Claire Taylor, *Officials Consider I-49 Land Bank,* LA. DAILY ADVERTISER (Lafayette), May 7, 2003, at 2B.

259. 42 U.S.C §§ 1450–1451 (omitted). Authority to make grants and loans under the urban renewal program was terminated after January 1, 1975, when the program was folded into the community development block grant (CDBG) program. 42 U.S.C. § 5316 (1983). For discussion of the displacement issue, *see* HUD, Displacement Report (1979); LAWRENCE M. FRIEDMAN, GOVERNMENT AND SLUM HOUSING: A CENTURY OF FRUSTRATION (1968); Sandra Newman & Michael S. Owens, *Residential Displacement: Extent, Nature and Effects*, 38 J. SOC. ISSUES 135 (1982).

260. *See, e.g.*, Mike Snyder, *Demand Hurts Housing Plan; Redevelopment Agency Shut Out of Bidding on Properties,* HOUS. CHRON., June 28, 2004, at A4 ("My fear is that cities will go marching through African-American neighborhoods, gobbling up property.") (quoting John Henneberger, co-director of the Texas Low-Income Housing Information Service (Austin)).

261. MICH. COMP. LAWS §§ 124.751–124.774 (West 2006).

262. *Id.* § 124.754–124.

eminent domain.[263] The land the Authority does assemble can be sold or leased to public or private developers, including not-for-profit entities, for redevelopment purposes.[264]

The statute provides an expedited quiet title and foreclosure action for property held by the Authority as well as interests in tax-reverted property that includes recorded public notice, the filing of a single petition in circuit court for all the property interests being quieted, mailing by the Authority of notices of the hearing to owners of record, a posting of notice on the property, a hearing within 90 days of the filing of the petition, judgment by the court within ten days of the hearing, and an expedited appeals process.[265] Title acquired by the Authority following a successful action is in fee simple absolute, subject to natural resources and environmental protection special assessments and liens, as well as visible or recorded easements or right-of-ways, private deed restrictions, plat restrictions, and any other natural resources or environmental protection restrictions.[266]

The statute authorizes the Authority to enter into intergovernmental agreements with the Michigan Economic Development Corporation and the Michigan State Housing Development Authority (MSHDA) for the "joint exercise" of the respective agencies' powers and duties, and the provision of economic development and/or redevelopment services "related to the activities of the authority."[267] Intergovernmental agreements may provide for the transfer of tax-reverted property by the local governments to the Authority for several purposes, including title clearance and return of the property to the particular local government.[268] In addition, the statute authorizes counties and "qualified cities" (ones containing first-class school districts)[269] to enter into intergovernmental agreements with the Authority to create local land bank authorities, which would be delegated the powers granted the state authority.[270]

Texas has also enacted a statute authorizing its major cities to adopt an urban land bank demonstration program.[271] Vacant property that is scheduled to be sold at a public sale because of foreclosure of a tax lien, whose market value is less than the taxes due, or property for which taxes have been delinquent for at least five years, may be sold in a private sale to a land bank established under the statute, as long as the municipality operating the land bank has executed interlocal agreements with other taxing units to participate in the program.[272]

A key element in the program is that local community housing development organizations[273] must be given a right of first refusal before land in the land bank can be resold.

---

263. *Id.* § 124.754 (7)–(8).

264. *Id.* § 124.755 (2)(b). However, authority powers or funds may not be used to assist in the development of casinos. *Id.* § 124.754(6).

265. *Id.* § 124.759.

266. *Id.*

267. *Id.* § 124.773(1) & (2).

268. *Id.* § 124.773(3).

269. *Id.* § 124.753(n).

270. *Id.* § 124.773(4) & (5).

271. Tex. Loc. Gov't. Code Ann. § 379C.001-379C.013 (2009).

272. *Id.* § 379C.008. The interlocal agreement must enable the other taxing units to "withhold consent to the sale of specific properties to the land bank." *Id.* § 379C.008(a)(4).

273. Such organizations must operate in an area that contains at least a portion of the property being offered for sale by the land bank, must have built at least three single-family houses or

Participation in the program requires the city to adopt annually an urban land bank demonstration plan that must include (1) a list of qualified community housing development organizations, (2) a list of parcels of real estate that may become eligible for land banking within the coming year, (3) the municipality's plan for affordable housing development on those sites, and (4) sources and amounts of funds expected to be available from the municipality for housing development subsidies.[274] Before adopting the plan, a public hearing must be held, with notice being sent to all community housing development organizations and neighborhood associations operating within the area in which properties that are candidates for the land bank that year are located.[275]

Property may be sold to the land bank for less than its market value if taxing jurisdictions that are parties to the delinquent tax judgment do not object to the sale price and if the owner of record has not submitted a written request that the property not be sold to the land bank.[276] The land bank must give qualified nonprofit organizations six months from the date the property was conveyed to the land bank to exercise their right of first refusal.[277] If the right of first refusal is not exercised with the time allotted, the land bank may sell to a "qualified participating developer," defined as an developer that has built three or more housing units within the preceding three-year period, has a development plan for the land bank property approved by the municipality, and has complied with any other requirements adopted by the municipality.[278] The statute also requires deed restrictions to be placed on property sold by the land bank that mandate that at least 25 percent of all property developed for sale be restricted to households with gross household incomes not exceeding 60 percent of the area median income, and that rental property be deed-restricted for at least 15 years as follows: 100 percent of the units restricted to households with incomes not greater than 60 percent of area median and 40 percent of the units restricted to households with incomes not exceeding 50 percent of the area median, or 20 percent of the units restricted to households with incomes not exceeding 30 percent of area median income.[279]

B. Community Benefits Agreements

A relatively new form of collaboration between and among developers and local community-based organizations is the community benefits agreement. Community benefits agreements (CBAs) have been defined as:

---

duplexes or one four- or more-unit multifamily residential dwelling within the previous two years that complies with all applicable codes and is within the organization's designated area of operation, and have built housing units in the past two years that are within a one-half mile radius of property being offered by the land bank. *Id.* § 379C.011.

274. *Id.* § 379C.006.
275. *Id.* § 379C.007.
276. *Id.* § 379C.008 (d)–(h).
277. *Id.* § 379C.011(d).
278. *Id.* § 379C.005.
279. *Id.* § 379C.010. For a discussion of land-banking strategies used by five cities—St. Louis, Cleveland, Louisville, Atlanta, and Flint—to "break barriers to renewal of inner-city properties" that are vacant, abandoned, and tax-delinquent, *see* Frank S. Alexander, *Land Bank Strategies for Renewal Urban Land*, 14 J. Aff. Housing & Comm. Dev. L. 140, 140 (2005).

legally binding, private contract[s] between a developer and community-based organizations, under which the developer commits to providing specified community benefits through a proposed development project, and participating community groups agree to support the project in the governmental approval process.[280]

Advocates of CBAs stress the "core values of inclusiveness and accountability," believing that CBAs offer a mechanism for community concerns to be "heard and addressed" and for promises to be made "specific, legally binding and enforceable by the community."[281]

CBAs were first used in Los Angeles in 1998 in conjunction with the development of the Hollywood and Highland Center and in 2001 with the Staples Center.[282] Over the next decade, CBAs were included in numerous large, multi-use urban development projects across the country.[283] CBAs resemble, but are different from, development agreements negotiated by developers and local governments in which zoning is frozen for a period of time in return for developer promises to restrict land uses or provide specific public benefits.[284] While local governments typically have no formal part in CBAs, as the agreements are between developers and private, community-based organizations,[285] CBAs may be incorporated into development agreements, as was the case in the Los Angeles Sports and Entertainment District project around the Staples Center.[286] Early CBAs focused on mitigating "physical disruption caused by the projects themselves," while later CBAs added

---

280. Julian Gross, Community Benefits Agreements, Building Healthy Communities: A Guide to Community Economic Development for Advocates, Lawyers, and Policymakers 189, 190 (Roger A. Clay & Susan R. Jones eds., 2009); Julian Gross, *Community Benefits Agreements: Definitions, Values, and Legal Enforceability,* 17 A.B.A. J. Affordable Housing & Cmty. Dev. L. 35, 37 (2008).

281. Gross, *supra* note 280, at 37–39; Community Benefits Law Center, *Community Benefits Agreements*, https://www.forworkingfamilies.org/cblc/cba (last visited Sept. 16, 2021). The Partnership for Working Families, sponsor of the Community Benefits Law Center, maintains on its website summaries and excerpts from CBAs negotiated by developers and community-based organizations in Denver, Los Angeles, New Haven, Oakland, Pittsburgh, San Diego, San Francisco, and Seattle, https://www.forworkingfamilies.org/resources/community-benefits-agreements-framework-success (last visited Sept. 16, 2021).

282. Patricia E. Salkin & Amy Lavine, *Negotiating for Social Justice and the Promise of Community Benefits Agreements: Case Studies of Current and Developing Agreements,* 17 ABA J. Affordable Housing & Cmty. Dev. L. 113, 116 (2008).

283. *Id.* at 117–30 (summarizing additional CBAs in Los Angeles, Oakland, San Diego, and San Jose, California; New York, New Haven, Denver, Milwaukee, Minneapolis, Pittsburgh, Cramer Hill (N.J.), New Orleans, and Washington, D.C.).

284. *Id.* at 131 n.5 (identifying statutory authorization for development agreements in 13 states: Arizona, California, Colorado, Florida, Hawaii, Idaho, Louisiana, Nevada, New Jersey, Oregon, South Carolina, Virginia, and Washington).

285. One view of CBAs has them filling a gap in the decision-making process concerning major development projects:

> For example, who gets to decide whether a proposed residential project in downtown includes affordable housing units? Whether a proposed grocery store in Koreatown [Los Angeles] pays a living wage? Whether a vacant lot in South Central [Los Angeles] becomes a liquor store or a health clinic?

Benjamin S. Beach, *Strategies and Lessons from the Los Angeles Community Benefits Experience,* 17 A.B.A. J. Affordable Housing & Cmty. Dev. L. 77, 79 (2008).

286. *Id.* at 98.

provisions addressing "wage standards for construction workers and permanent employees, employment opportunities, job training, and affordable housing in low income neighborhoods surrounding project sites."[287]

CBAs raise a number of legal and political issues, including the identity and membership of the community for whose benefit the CBA is being negotiated,[288] the role that local officials may play in the CBA negotiation and implementation processes,[289] the relationship of the CBA process to local comprehensive planning,[290] the necessity for effective monitoring and enforcement of CBAs,[291] and the possibility of developer manipulation of the CBA process to limit, rather than expand, community participation in decision making regarding development.[292]

CBAs offer "promise . . . to change the way cities, developers, and communities approach development projects,"[293] but they also "have the potential for misuse and have substantial limitations as a long-term strategy in community economic development."[294] Patricia Salkin and Amy Lavine highlight the potential and the pitfalls of CBAs with the following comment:

> [A]ssuming there is equal bargaining power among the parties to a CBA negotiation, that there is full support of the community coalition from community members, and that the developer's assumptions about government approvals and project design are accurate enough to enable full compliance with the agreed to terms, CBAs can be an empowering social justice tool.[295]

Julian Gross, director of the Community Benefits Law Center, the legal program of the Partnership for Working Families, emphasizes that for CBAs to realize their potential, they must be crafted from a "truly inclusive process" and must contain "legally enforceable commitments."[296]

C. Community Land Trusts

Another technique that is becoming increasingly popular is the community land trust (CLT). Since the 1970s, CLTs have been used in more than 240 communities in 45 states

---

287. Laura Wolf-Powers, *Community Benefits Agreements and Local Government: A Review of Recent Evidence*, 76(2) J. AM. PLAN. ASS'N 1, 6 (Spring 2010). Wolf-Powers cites a website and blog maintained by the Government Law Center of Albany Law School that identifies 27 CBAs: Amy Lavine, *Community Benefits Agreements*, www.communitybenefits.blogspot.com, last visited July 20, 2010.

288. Beach, *supra* note 285, at 100.

289. Salkin & Lavine, *supra* note 282, at 130–31, note 4.

290. Patricia Salkin & Amy Lavine, *Community Benefits Agreements and Comprehensive Planning: Balancing Community Empowerment and the Police Power*, 18 J.L. & POL'Y 157 (2009).

291. Gross, *supra* note 280, at 47.

292. *Id.* at 52 ("The New York experience suggests that supporters of controversial projects see a different type of potential in the term and concept: the potential to control and limit community involvement and dampen opposition to controversial projects.").

293. ANNIE E. CASEY FOUND., COMMUNITY BENEFITS AGREEMENTS 5 (2007).

294. GROSS, *supra* note 280, at 189.

295. Salkin & Lavine, *supra* note 282, at 113.

296. Gross, *supra* note 280, at 52.

and the District of Columbia[297] as a device for encouraging affordable housing by regulating the price and use of land. The Institute for Community Economics, an organization that provided technical assistance to CLTs for many years, defines a CLT as:

> an organization created to hold land for the benefit of a community and of individuals within the community. It is a democratically structured nonprofit corporation, with an open membership and a board of trustees elected by its membership. . . . The CLT acquires land through purchase or donation with an intention to retain title in perpetuity, thus removing the land from the speculative market.[298]

Two key elements of the CLT approach are (1) the separation of the ownership interest in land from the ownership interest in a house, apartment, or condominium unit on that land, and (2) a preemptive option retained by the CLT to purchase the housing unit at a predetermined price designed to keep the housing permanently affordable to households of low and moderate income.[299] The separation of ownership interests and the preemptive

---

297. National Community Land Trust Network, U.S. Directory of CLTs, www.cltnetwork.org (last visited June 24, 2010). For a collection of essays concerning the history of the community land trust movement and reflections on its present condition, *see* THE COMMUNITY LAND TRUST READER (John Emmeus Davis ed., 2010).

298. INST. FOR COMMUNITY ECONOMICS, THE COMMUNITY LAND TRUST HANDBOOK (1982), *reprinted in* THE COMMUNITY LAND TRUST READER, *supra* note 306, at 241. Another popular definition describes a CLT as a "democratically controlled nonprofit organization that owns real estate in order to provide benefits to its local community—and in particular to make land and housing available to residents who cannot otherwise afford them." *See, e.g.*, https://abclt.org/glossary-of-terms/ and https://www.prosper.org.au/2008/05/community-land-trusts-explained/. David Abromowitz, a Boston attorney and advisor to a number of CLTs, observes that

> [t]he CLT model is designed to address two central issues: (1) How can affordable housing programs accommodate the interests of the community as a whole in land use and development with the desires of individuals for housing ownership and control over property? (2) How do we insure that housing which is initially affordable to low- and moderate-income persons remains affordable well into the future?

David M. Abromowitz, *Community Land Trusts and Ground Leases,* 1 J. AFFORDABLE HOUSING & COMM. DEV. L. 5 (Spring 1992).

299. COMMUNITY LAND TRUST READER, *supra* note 306, at 242. The most recent version of the Cranston-Gonzales National Affordable Housing Act authorizing federal support for CLTs defines a CLT as a "community housing development organization":

> **(1)** that is not sponsored by a for-profit organization;
> **(2)** that is established to carry out the activities under paragraph (3);
> **(3)** that—
>   **(A)** acquires parcels of land, held in perpetuity, primarily for conveyance under long-term ground leases;
>   **(B)** transfers ownership of any structural improvements located on such leased parcels to the lessees; and
>   **(C)** retains a preemptive option to purchase any such structural improvement at a price determined by formula that is designed to ensure that the improvement remains affordable to low- and moderate-income families in perpetuity; . . . .

42 U.S.C. § 12773 (b)(6) & (f)(3).

option to purchase are designed to "build wealth for both the community and the individual homeowners," while at the same time retaining affordability.[300]

While the CLT concept has become quite popular in affordable housing circles, organizers and supporters report that the communal ownership and limited equity features impose "a psychological and cultural challenge" for prospective participants in a CLT to whom this legal regime may appear unfamiliar.[301] They also can impose legal challenges under familiar property law doctrines, such as the rule against perpetuities and the rule against unreasonable restraints on alienation.[302]

To clarify the legal relationships in a CLT, a number of states have enacted legislation recognizing the CLT entity. For example, a Connecticut statute defines community land trusts as nonprofit organizations incorporated under the Connecticut non-stock corporation statute[303] and provides that one of their purposes shall be "the holding of land and leasing of such land for the purpose of preserving the long-term eligibility and accessibility of housing predominantly for very low income, low income and moderate income persons and families."[304] In addition to the powers of a non-stock corporation, the statute grants CLTs the power to "buy and sell land, to mortgage and otherwise encumber land and to enter into renewable or self-extending ground leases with an initial term of up to ninety-nine years."[305]

Under Connecticut law, CLT membership must be open to the public, but no more than 30 percent of the members may reside outside the municipality or municipalities in which the land trust operates.[306] At least 51 percent of the governing board must be elected by the

---

300. Winton Pitcoff, *Affordable Forever: Land Trusts Keep Housing within Reach*, 121 SHELTERFORCE ONLINE 2 (Jan./Feb. 2002) (quoting Sarah Page, ICE Executive Director), http://www.nhi.org/online/issues/121/LandTrusts.html. For an analysis of the use of community land trusts in conjunction with affordable housing initiatives, *see* Julie Farrell Curtin & Lance Bocarsly, *CLTs: A Growing Trend in Affordable Home Ownership*, 17 J. AFFORDABLE HOUS. & CMTY. DEV. L. 367 (2008), *reprinted in* COMMUNITY LAND TRUST READER, *supra* note 299, at 289.

301. Pitcoff, *supra* note 309, at 3 (quoting Karen Seabury, a program officer at The John D. & Catherine T. MacArthur Foundation, one of ICE's main funding sources).

302. ICE published a *Community Land Trust Legal Manual*, drafted by a team of lawyers headed by David Abromowitz in 1991 and revised in 2002, which addressed these legal issues. DAVID ABROMOWITZ ET AL., THE COMMUNITY LAND TRUST LEGAL MANUAL: A HANDBOOK FOR COMMUNITY LAND TRUSTS AND THEIR ATTORNEYS (Institute for Community Economics 2002). The Manual was updated by Grounded Solutions Network in 2011 and renamed the 2011 Community Land Trust Technical Manual. When ICE merged with the National Housing Trust in 2008, the rights to the *Legal Manual*, along with other CLT-related publications, were transferred to Equity Trust, Inc., a self-described "small, national non-profit organization committed to changing the spirit and character of our material relationships." Equity Trust Home, http://www.equity trust.org/index.htm (last visited June 24, 2010). The *Manual* and companion pieces like *Managing the Money Side: Financial Management for Community-Based Housing Organizations*, are available at http://equitytrust.org/category/publications/clt-resources/ (last visited Sept. 16, 2021).

303. CONN. GEN. STAT. ANN. §47-300(6); §§33-1000 to 33-1290 (2010) (stating the nonstick corporation statute).

304. *Id.* §47-301 (a). The income ranges for the categories are: very low-income (at or below 25 percent of area median income), low-income (between 26 percent and 50 percent of area median income), and moderate-income (between 51 percent and 80 percent of area median income). *Id.* §47-300(2)–(4).

305. *Id.* §47-301(a).

306. *Id.* §47-301(b).

membership, and between 25 percent and 40 percent must be lessees, their representatives, or residents of eligible housing on CLT-owned land. The balance, if any, may be appointed by elected public officials.[307] The Connecticut statute provides that a CLT holds title to the land and can lease it to very low-income, low-income, and moderate-income persons as well as limited equity cooperatives or other corporations by means of ground leases as long as the leases give the CLT "first option to purchase" the housing and buildings on the land for a "limited equity price" included in the ground lease.[308] The "limited equity price" concept is a compromise that enables the CLT to retain the unit as an affordable one while permitting the unit owner to realize a percentage of any appreciation in value upon moving. A 25 percent/75 percent split in equity is common.[309] In addition to the CLT's first option to purchase, the ground lease may also include restrictions on resale, subletting, or assignment of lessees' interests. The statute specifically provides that such restrictions are not subject to "any general statute or rule of law limiting the duration, degree or nature of restraints on real property, including, but not limited to, the common law rule against perpetuities, the uniform statutory rule against perpetuities and the rule against unreasonable restraints on alienation."[310] Lessees' interests are in "real property," and loans made to lessees may be secured by those interests in the same manner as other real estate loans.[311] Connecticut also provides financial assistance to CLTs through the issuance of bonds, the proceeds of which are deposited in a "Community Housing Land Bank and Land Trust Fund."[312]

D. Rent Control

One of the earliest forms of land-use regulation to preserve housing affordability was rent control. Rent control was first enacted in the District of Columbia during World War I and was approved by the Supreme Court as a "temporary measure" because of the wartime emergency discussed in *Block v. Hirsh*.[313] New York City's complex, multitiered system of rent control and rent stabilization originally was imposed by the federal government during World War II and was continued by the state in 1946. New York City enacted its own

---

307. *Id.* § 47-301(b).

308. *Id.* § 47-301(c). "Limited equity price" is defined in the statute as a price "determined by means of a formula or similar calculation designed to maintain such building or improvement as eligible housing for the longest term possible, but not less than the term of the applicable ground lease." *Id.* § 47-300(9).

309. *See, e.g.*, Rondo Cmty. Land Trust, St. Paul, Minn., *How Rondo CLT Keeps Homeownership Affordable*, http://www.rondoclt.org (last visited Sept. 16, 2021);; Mike Ivey, *How Does Land Trust Project Work?*, Capital Times (Madison, Wis.), Sept. 9, 2004, at 2E (explaining Madison Area Community Land Trust house purchases and land rent agreement limiting resale price to original price plus 25 percent of market value increase).

310. Conn. Gen. Stat. Ann. § 47-303.

311. *Id.* § 47-302.

312. *Id.* § 8-214c. Financial assistance to affordable housing developments is discussed in § 8-214d. In Michigan, a special task force has been convened of local practitioners by the Community Legal Resources Program, a pro bono referral agency. The CLT Project intends to develop a Michigan manual on CLTs explaining the issues under Michigan law that impact the ground lease and other legal aspects of establishing a CLT.

313. 256 U.S. 135, 157 (1921).

regulations in 1962 (rent control) and in 1969 (rent stabilization) pursuant to state authorization.[314] During the 1970s, a tenants' movement in New Jersey succeeded in gaining passage of rent control ordinances in approximately 100 municipalities.[315] Massachusetts legislation enacted during that period authorized local rent control, but an initiative rejecting rent control was approved by the voters in 1994.[316] A number of California municipalities enacted rent control ordinances, and many remain in effect.[317]

Rent control laws typically restrict two aspects of the landlord–tenant relationship: the amount of rent the landlord can charge and the flexibility of the landlord to refuse to renew the lease of a rent-paying tenant or change the use of the property.[318] Modern rent control laws permit a "fair rate of return," as determined by an administrative or legislative process that provides for periodic reviews.[319] The land-use regulatory aspect of rent control is contained in the lease renewal control. In essence, a tenant who pays the rent in a timely fashion and abides by reasonable rules and regulations can stay as long as he or she desires.[320] This feature has survived regulatory takings challenges in the Supreme Court.[321] However, the New York Court of Appeals held that an ordinance requiring owners of single room occupancy (SRO) hotels who wished to convert them to condominiums, to restore them to SRO condition, and to offer them at controlled rents amounted to a taking of property without just compensation.[322]

Rent control remains extremely controversial and limited in use. Some states have enacted statutes prohibiting local rent control ordinances[323] or severely limiting them.[324] The Supreme Court of Colorado struck down an inclusionary housing ordinance as viola-

---

314. Resolution Trust Corp. v. Diamond, 18 F. 3d 111, 114 (2d Cir. 1994) (holding that the federal Financial Institutions Reform, Recovery, and Enforcement Act of 1989 (FIRREA) preempted contrary state and local rent-control laws). A case decided by the U.S. Supreme Court, Lingle v. Chevron, U.S.A., Inc., 544 U.S. 528 (2005), may affect residential rent-control laws. The Court reversed a takings finding against a Hawaii rent-control statute because the lower courts used the "substantially advances a legitimate state interest" test from *Agins*. The Court held that test to be applicable only for Due Process Clause challenges.

315. Kenneth K. Baar, *Rent Control in the 1970s: The Case of the New Jersey Tenants' Movement,* 28 HASTINGS L.J. 631 (1977) (cited in A. JAMES CASNER ET AL., CASES AND TEXT ON PROPERTY 484 n.13 (5th ed., Aspen 2004)).

316. CASNER ET AL., *supra* note 315, at n.14 (citing 1994 Mass. Adv. Legis. Serv. 282) (LexisNexis).

317. *Id.* at 484 n.15 (citing ANTHONY DOWNS, RESIDENTIAL RENT CONTROLS 3 (1988)); *id.* at 484 (citing ROBERT SCHOSHINSKI, AMERICAN LAW OF LANDLORD AND TENANT, §§ 7.1–7.10 (1980)).

318. These two restrictions can trigger intense legal controversies, as illustrated by the *Palmer* case, discussed *supra* note 214. The most recent case challenging rent control is *Guggenheim v. City of Goleta*, 582 F.3d 996 (9th Cir. 2009) (finding a rent-control ordinance in a mobile home park worked a facial taking under the *Penn Central* ad hoc balancing test), *rehearing en banc granted*, Mar. 12, 2010.

319. CASNER ET AL., *supra* note 315, at 484.

320. *Resolution Trust Corp.,* 18 F.3d at 114.

321. Yee v. City of Escondido, 503 U.S. 519 (1992).

322. Seawall Assocs. v. City of New York, 542 N.E.2d 1059 (N.Y. 1989), *cert. denied*, 493 U.S. 976 (1989).

323. *See, e.g.,* COLO. REV. STAT. § 38-12-301 (2007) (amended 2010); FLA. STAT. ANN. § 125.0103 (2009).

324. *See, e.g.,* CAL. CIV. CODE §§ 1954.50–1954.535 (2010) (Costa-Hawkins Rental Housing Act).

tive of the state's anti-rent control statute.[325] Law and economics theorists generally disfavor rent control as causing more problems than it solves,[326] or accept it only if a particular situation causes demand to "rise sharply at the same time that new construction of such units has been legally restricted in order to conserve resources—as during wartime."[327] Affordable housing advocates, on the other hand, are buttressed by theory and policy arguments such as "a tenant's expectation or desire to continue in her home is more important than the commercial landlord's expectation or desire to continue in the landlord business over some other business that will yield a better return,"[328] and claim that the evidence cited by economists is inconclusive.[329]

1. New York City's Sweeping Rent Control Reform

In 2019, New York state enacted widespread reform to its housing regulations in the Housing Stability and Tenant Protection Act of 2019 (HSTPA).[330] The regulations will have significant effects on housing affordability, in particular in relation to rent-controlled and rent-stabilized units in New York City. What follows is a brief overview of some of those changes.[331]

- One of those significant changes politically was the elimination of sunset provisions on rent control and rent-stabilization measures. As Lebovits, Lansden, and Howard describe, this revision changes the cyclic political struggle during the reviews of rent stabilization. In doing so, it provides a measure of stability for tenants who faced a "perpetual, existential threat to rent regulation" and a "long-lasting shortage of affordable housing."[332]
- Under the old law, a unit could be deregulated away from rent-control or rent-stabilization units if the income of the renter reached a legally specified level two years in a row or after the unit was vacated if the rent was above a certain legal threshold (most recently $200,000/year and $2,774/month, respectively). Both of these routes to deregulation were abolished in the new law.[333]
- The old law allowed for rent increases in rent-controlled/rent-stabilized units for building improvements to individual units (known as individual apartment

---

325. Town of Telluride v. Lot Thirty-four Venture, L.L.C., 3 P.3d 30, 38–40.

326. *See, e.g.*, Richard A. Epstein, *Rent Control and the Theory of Efficient Regulation,* 54 BROOK. L. REV. 741 (1988).

327. Anthony Downs, *Residential Rent Controls: An Evaluation* 1–2, cited in CASNER ET AL., *supra* note 315, at 486.

328. Margaret Jane Radin, *Residential Rent Control,* 15 PHIL. & PUB. AFF. 350, 359 (1986). *See also* Jeffrey James Minton, *Rent Control: Can and Should It Be Used to Combat Gentrification?,* 23 OHIO N.U. L. REV. 823 (1997).

329. Curtis J. Berger, *Home Is Where the Heart Is: A Brief Reply to Professor Epstein,* 54 BROOK. L. REV. 1239, 1246–47 (1989).

330. For a comprehensive overview of these changes, see Gerald Lebovits, John S. Lansden & Damon P. Howard, *New York's Housing Stability and Tenant Protection Act of 2019: What Lawyers Must Know,* 29 J. AFFORDABLE HOUS. & CMTY. DEV. L. 75 (2020).

331. The following discussion draws from Lebovits, Lansden, and Howard's detailed review of the HSTPA.

332. Lebovits, Lansden & Howard, *supra* note 330, at 93.

333. NYC ADMIN. CODE 26-504.2 and 26-504.3.

improvements (IAIs)) or to the building itself (known as major capital improvements (MCIs)). The new law continues this practice but tightens the conditions around which such rent increases can be implemented, including limits on the number of such improvements, sunset provisions on such increases, consent procedures, a cap on aggregate costs, an annual cap for MCIs reduction from 6 percent to 2 percent, and a further specification of what kinds of building works qualify as MCIs.[334]

- The new law repeals the vacancy increase (and longevity bonus) allowances.[335]
- The geographic area of rent stabilization was expanded to other municipalities in the state.[336]
- The new law makes it easier to access remedies for over-charging of rents, including by the elimination of the statute of limitations.[337]
- The new law also puts additional conditions on the removal of preferential rents and the recovery of apartments for owner's use.[338] It also removes the nonprofit organization rent-stabilization exemption for homelessness-related nonprofits, it removes the fuel cost pass-along, and it decreases the annual increase limit.[339]
- The new law also enacts a constellation of tenant-friendly measures in respect to lease expiration, eviction, land-lord tenant substantive and procedural regulations, including with respect to legal proceedings.[340]

2. Other Rent Control Reforms

In early 2019, Oregon passed Senate Bill 608, making it the first state with statewide rent control.[341] The measures limit annual rent increases to 7 percent plus inflation, with exemptions for small and newer buildings. Later in 2019, California enacted the Tenant Protection Act of 2019, which caps annual rent increases to 5 percent plus inflation for the next ten years, with exemptions for newer buildings.[342] California also enacted SB 329 on Housing Discrimination, which prohibits discrimination of tenants who rely on housing assistance.

---

334. *Id.* 26-511(13), 26-511.1, 26-511(6), and 26-405.1.
335. *Id.* 26-510(j).
336. Lebovits, Lansden & Howard, *supra* note 330, at 79, 94.
337. NYC Admin. Code 26-516(a); N.Y. Civil Practice Law & Rules (CPLR) 213-a.
338. NYC Admin. Code 26-511(14); NYC Admin. Code 26-511(b), 26-408(1).
339. Lebovits, Lansden & Howard, *supra* note 330, at 80; NYC Admin. Code 26-405(a)(5); 26-407.1.
340. Lebovits, Lansden & Howard, *supra* note 330, at 81–92, 107–22.
341. OR SB 608 (2019).
342. CA Assembly Bill 1482 (2019).

State and Local Regulation of Particular Types of Affordable Housing

5

Tim Iglesias*

I. INTRODUCTION

This chapter will consider several types of affordable housing that are neither traditional single-family nor multifamily housing. In this chapter "affordable housing" is construed more broadly than in the rest of the book, that is housing that is often "affordable" to lower-income households without legal restrictions and without government subsidy in the private market. Specifically, the chapter discusses micro-housing (Section II), manufactured housing (Section III), farmworker housing (Section IV), accessory or secondary units (Section V), single-room occupancy hotels (SROs) (Section VI), condominium conversion regulation (Section VII), and emergency shelters and transitional housing, including domestic violence shelters (Section VIII).[1] For each type of housing, this chapter will discuss the following topics: (1) how

*The author thanks the following University of San Francisco School of Law students for their excellent research assistance for the original version of this chapter and for updates: Bartosz Rost, Julie Pollock, Melissa Owens, Elliot Millerd-Taylor, Anthony Carandang, Tracy Cook, Peter O'Hare, Zachary Toran, and Paloma Wu.

1. Funding for these types of affordable housing will be briefly mentioned and cross-references made to coverage in other parts of the book. This chapter will not discuss the application of the federal Fair Housing Act to these types of housing. Chapter 3 contains coverage of exclusionary zoning and fair housing law. *See also* Chapter 4 for state and local laws promoting affordable housing. This chapter does not cover most forms of congregate housing, shared living housing, licensed group homes, or treatment centers because these are not traditionally considered a form of "affordable housing," and they are generally supported by distinct funding streams. For these forms of housing, see Bazelon Center for Mental Health Law, *What "Fair Housing" Means for People with Disabilities*, https://secureservercdn .net/198.71.233.254/d25.2ac.myftpupload.com/wp-content/uploads/2018/05

is this type of housing defined and what are its variations; (2) how this type of housing responds to the affordability problem; (3) the current extent of the use of this type of housing and whether it is increasing or decreasing in any significant way; (4) the legal issues implicated in this type of housing, and how legislatures and courts deal with those issues. Three topics—SROs, condominium conversion, and emergency shelters and transitional housing—primarily concern regulatory authority employed to create and/or preserve the supply and affordability of these housing units.

II. MICRO-HOUSING

In the last decade a new type of housing development called "micro-housing" has been spreading nationwide.[2] As the name suggests, micro-housing refers to dwelling units that are below general standards in terms of space, usually in conflict with existing planning, zoning, or building codes. While they average around 300 square feet, micro-housing comes in a variety of names and forms, including micro-apartments, micro-units, efficiency units,

---

/Fair-Housing-Guide_2018-Update.pdf. And see the Corporation for Supportive Housing, https://www.csh.org/?s=permanent+supportive+housing.

　　Fair housing issues for senior housing are covered in Robert Schwemm & Michael Allen, *For the Rest of Their Lives: Seniors and the Fair Housing Act*, 90 Iowa L. Rev. 121 (2004).

　　2. The growing literature on micro-housing includes: Justin Fair, Tiny Houses and the Black Experience in Baltimore, a master's project submitted in partial fulfillment of the requirements for the degree Master of City and Regional Planning (May 2020) (on file with author); Lisa T. Alexander, *Community in Property: Lessons from Tiny Homes Villages*, 104 Minn. L. Rev. 385 (2019); Yashesh Panchal, Developing housing for a changing demography: Analyzing the implications of the regulations governing the development of small-housing units, a thesis presented to the faculty of Architecture, Planning, and Preservation in partial fulfillment of the requirements for the degree master of science in urban planning, Columbia University (May 3, 2018); David Morley, *Practice Micro Apartments* (hereafter Morley), Zoning Practice, Vol. 35, No. 3, American Planning Association (2018); Emily Keable, *Building on the Tiny House Movement: A Viable Solution to Meet Affordable Housing Needs*, 11 U. St. Thomas J. L. & Pub. Pol'y 111 (2017); John Infranca, *Sharing Economy, Sharing City: Urban Law and the New Economy*, 43 Fordham Urb. L.J. 1 (2016); Katherine M. Vail, *Saving the American Dream: The Legalization of the Tiny House Movement*, 54 U. Louisville L. Rev. 357 (2016); John Infranca, *Housing Changing Households: Regulatory Challenges for Micro-Units and Accessory Dwelling Units* (hereafter "Infranca"), 25 Stanford Law & Policy Review 53 (2014) (reviewing micro-units in Austin (TX), Denver (CO), New York (NY), Seattle (WA), and Washington, D.C.); Dawn Withers, *Looking for a Home: How Micro-Housing Can Help California* (hereafter "Withers"), 6 Golden Gate U. Envtl L.J. 125 (2012). Micro-housing has become the subject of several websites, blogs, and even a cable television series called "Tiny House Nation." *See, e.g.*, www.TinyHouseTalk.com and www.TinyHouseNewsletter.com created and moderated by Alex Pino; Penelope Green, *So Small but Already a TV Star* (hereafter "Green"), N.Y. Times, July 3, 2014, D2 (commenting on the TV show). Micro-housing is also found outside of North America, e.g., *Tiny and Small Houses Can Be Found All Around Europe* (hereafter "Europe"), www.Affordable Housing Designs.com, http://affordable housingdesigns.com/the-latest/tiny-houses/tiny-houses-europe/.

studio apartments,[3] single-room occupancy units,[4] accessory dwelling units (aka secondary units),[5] rooming or boarding houses,[6] mobile homes/manufactured housing,[7] aPodments, "tiny houses," micro-loft[8] and "dormstyle" apartments.[9] Other sections of this chapter discuss accessory dwelling units, single-room occupancy units, and mobile homes/manufactured housing. This section will focus on the other variations of micro-housing, especially micro-apartments (including micro-units, efficiency units or studio apartments, micro-loft and "hostel-style" apartments) and detached "tiny houses." This section will first describe micro-housing is more detail, articulate the proponents' and opponents' views, explain how it could be a partial solution to the affordable housing problem for several segments of the population, and then discuss regulatory challenges to its expansion.

Micro-housing is usually defined by smaller relative square footage per unit compared to historical standards. The dimensions of micro-apartments vary from state to state.[10] Generally micro-homes are comprised of fewer than 300 square feet;[11] but they can range as small as 84 square feet[12] and as large as 500 square feet.[13] As this housing form is still

---

3. Efficiency units are most like micro-apartments because they have undivided interior space and full kitchens, except that micro-apartments are usually smaller than traditional efficiency units. Historically, micro-housing could be contrasted with lofts, an unconventional urban housing option with undivided interior space that has been popular since the 1980s. Lofts are also geared to draw people to cities and are sometimes affordable, but in contrast to micro-apartments are usually larger than conventional dwellings.

4. John McIlwain, *Is Small Beautiful Again? The Sudden Interest in Micro-Apartments*, Urban-land (Oct. 25, 2012), http://urbanland.uli.org/infrastructure-transit/is-small-beautiful-again-the-sudden-interest-in-micro-apartments/. SROs are most like micro-apartments, particularly those with kitchenettes.

5. Infranca, *supra* note 2; Withers, *supra* note 2 (arguing for reform of California's Building Code to promote micro-units as secondary units). Accessory Dwelling Units are most like the ownership version of micro-units, single units built by owners, in contrast to micro-apartments, which are multi-unit developments built by developers.

6. Mark Hinshaw & Brianna Holan, *Rooming House Redux*, Planning, November 2011; Kathy Stack, *Is It Time to Revive Boarding Houses?* (hereafter "Stack"), www.Governing Magazine .com (Feb. 14, 2013), http://www.governing.com/columns/Is-It-Time-to-Revive-Boarding-Houses .html. Boarding houses are most like micro-apartments, particularly those with shared kitchens.

7. One article compared micro-housing communities to trailer parks, noting the possible negative connotation this may give to micro-housing. Eve Andrews, *How Tiny House Communities Can Work for Both Haves and Have Nots*, www.Grist.org (Mar. 21, 2014), http://grist.org/living /how-tiny-house-communities-can-work-for-both-the-haves-and-the-have-nots/.

8. *See* Infranca, *supra* note 2, at note 76.

9. Nellie Bowles, *Dorm Living for Professionals Comes to San Francisco*, N.Y. Times, Mar. 4, 2018, https://www.nytimes.com/2018/03/04/technology/dorm-living-grown-ups-san-francisco .html.

10. *What Is a Micro Apartment?*, www.LifeEdited.com, http://www.lifeedited.com/what-the -heck-is-a-micro-apartment/.

11. Withers, *supra* note 2, at 126; Les Christie, *Micro-apartments: The anti-McMansions* (hereafter "Christie") www.CNN.com (June 21, 2013) http://money.cnn.com/2013/06/21/real_estate /micro-apartments/index.html.

12. Steve Kurutz, *Square Feet: 84. Possessions: 305* (hereafter "Kurutz"), N.Y. Times, April, 17, 2014, at D1, http://www.nytimes.com/2014/04/17/garden/square-feet-84-possessions-305.html.

13. *See* Wisegeek, *What Is a MicroHouse?* (hereafter "Wisegeek"), www.wisegeek.com, http:// www.wisegeek.com/what-is-a-micro-house.htm.

emerging, it is not clear where the range begins and ends.[14] Ultimately, this issue will be resolved by state and local regulation.

Micro-housing comes in for-sale versions and rental versions. Single-family owned detached dwellings—sometimes called "tiny houses"—are often custom-designed by buyers.[15] Some are equipped for traveling, sometimes to avoid regulatory limits.[16] Mobile versions blend into more traditional mobile homes, but they are typically not mass-produced. Micro-homes are often located in suburban spaces, sometimes in lots authorized by owners or even in the backyards of others.[17] There are also communities of micro-homes that are located outside city limits or in vacant lots in suburban areas.[18] And some promote tiny homes for rural communities.[19] In cities such as Austin, Texas, and Olympia, Washington, micro-homes have been used to serve as stable homes and communities for formerly homeless people.[20]

The rental form of micro-housing ("micro-apartment") is most prevalent in large cities with dense populations. Micro-apartments are rented like normal apartments, sometimes below market value and sometimes above.[21] They can also be developed as a condominium and then rented by the owner.[22]

---

14. *See, e.g.*, E. 118th St. in University Circle, Cleveland, OH by WXZ Development. This development offers rental apartments in the 600- to 800-square foot range to attract young professionals that some consider micro-housing. (Source on file with author.) Perhaps at the limit would be "capsule hotels," small plastic pods that measure about 6.5 feet by 5 feet and provide a space to sleep and store personal possessions along with communal bathing and eating facilities. Hiroko Tabuchi, *For Some in Japan, Home Is a Tiny Plastic Bunk*, N.Y. TIMES, Jan. 2, 2010, at A1.

15. Michael Tortorello, *Small World; Big Idea* (hereafter "Tortorello"), N.Y. TIMES, Feb. 20, 2014, at D1, http://www.nytimes.com/2014/02/20/garden/small-world-big-idea.html; Sandy Keenan, *The Anti-McMansion*, N.Y. TIMES, Feb. 13, 2014, at D4, http://www.nytimes.com/2014/02/13/greathome sanddestinations/the-anti-mcmansion.html; Sandy Keenan, *Freedom in 704 Square Feet*, N.Y. TIMES, Jan. 23, 2014, at D5, http://www.nytimes.com/2014/01/23/garden/freedom-in-704-square-feet.html; *Tiny Houses* (hereafter "DesignBoom"), WWW.DESIGNBOOM.COM, http://www.designboom.com /contemporary/tiny_houses2.html; Green, *supra* note 2.

16. Tortorello, *supra* note 15; Green, *supra* note 2.

17. Kurutz, *supra* note 12.

18. *Can Tiny Houses Help Solve the Problem of Homelessness?* (hereafter "Problem of Homelessness"), www.Apartment Therapy.com, http://www.apartmenttherapy.com/in-austin-and -olympia-small-spaces-make-a-big-difference-200592.

19. Caitlyn Greene, *Food, Shelter, Hope: Examining the Possibilities of Agricultural Tiny Home Communities for the Homeless*, 27 GEO. J. ON POVERTY L. & POL'Y 3, 4 (2019) ("Tiny home communities centered around agriculture offer an opportunity to combat [homelessness and food insecurity] while also providing a host of additional benefits for community residents and the surrounding areas.").

20. Tortorello, *supra* note 15; Linda Federico-O'Murcu, *Tiny Houses: A Big Idea to End Homelessness*, www.NBCNEWS.COM (Feb. 26, 2014), http://www.nbcnews.com/business/real-estate/tiny -houses-big-idea-end-homelessness-n39316; Problem of Homelessness, *supra* note 18.

21. Christie, *supra* note 11; David Noriega, *Micro-Apartments: More Trouble Than Their Worth?* (hereafter "Noriega") WWW.REMAPPING DEBATE.ORG, http://www.remappingdebate.org/article /micro-apartments-more-trouble-they%E2%80%99re-worth?page=0,2.

22. *See, e.g.*, Sas Ansari & Sujoy Chatterjee, *November 8, 2013: Comments and Feedback on "Growing Up: Ontario's Condominium Communities Enter a New Era"* at 4 (hereafter "Ansari and Chatterjee"), http://www.scribd.com/doc/186725874/Comments-Re-Condominium -Act-Review-Urban-Law-Centre-Osgoode-Hall-Law-School.

Micro-apartments tend to be located in urban centers where there is a rise in the tech community.[23] The leading innovators of micro-apartments in the United States are Seattle, San Francisco, New York City, and Boston.[24] There is some skepticism about whether micro-apartments will become popular in smaller cities and suburban areas where rents are not growing as rapidly, there is no mass transit, or there is a lack of cultural facilities and amenities to lure people.[25] However, some cities such as Cincinnati, Ohio; Providence, Rhode Island; and Worcester, Massachusetts, have been experimenting with micro-apartments to develop their downtowns by increasing single-person households.[26]

Micro-housing serves young singles, low-income people, seniors, and others.[27] Micro-apartments are marketed to singles in their 20s and 30s who comprise the most likely renter population in general.[28] Many micro-units serve young professionals, especially "techies."[29] The project in New York also targeted low-income people, allotting 40 percent of their units to people making 80 percent to 115 percent of the median income.[30] The elderly and their adult children or in-home caretakers are also possible residents of micro-units.[31]

Some micro-housing utilizes traditional construction, but much of it employs diverse building forms. Micro-homes come in a great variety of shapes and sizes, including tall,

23. Abigail Mooney & Sarah J. Kilpatrick, *New Urban Housing Trend—Micro-Apartments* (hereafter "Mooney & Kilpatrick"), www.GreenfieldAdvisors.com (Jan. 31, 2013), https://www.greenfieldadvisors.com/2013/01/new-urban-housing-trend-micro-apartments/.

24. *More Detail on New York's Stunning Micro-Unit Competition Winner*, www.Treehugger.com (Jan. 22, 2013), http://www.treehugger.com/modular-design/more-detail-new-yorks-stunning-micro-unit-competition-winner.html.

25. Kris Hudson, *Cities Try to Lure Young Professionals with Cheap 'Micro' Units* (hereafter "Hudson"), Wall St. J., Dec. 20, 2013, http://online.wsj.com/news/articles/SB10001424052702304173704579262173337853070.

26. Irvin Dawid, *Developers Bet that Micro Apartments Will Work in Smaller Cities*, www.Planetizen.com (Dec. 26, 2013), http://planetizen.com/node/66631.

27. For some examples of marketing of micro-units, see http://www.ulive.com/video/300-square-feet-2-stylish-tiny-nyc-apartments and http://www.frontdoor.com/photos/tiny-san-francisco-apartment.

28. Christie, *supra* note 11; Elaine Porterfield, *Now Americans Are Going Crazy About Tiny 'Micro" Apartments* (hereafter "Porterfield"), www.BusinessInsider.com (June 3, 2013), http://www.businessinsider.com/micro-apartments-2013-6).

29. Leslie Braunstein, *Micro-Units Fill an Affordability Niche for Young and Older Residents*, Urbanland (Apr. 26, 2014), http://urbanland.uli.org/development-business/micro-units-fill-affordability-niche-young-older-residents/; *Panoramic Interests in San Francisco, CA Markets*, Smart-Space Soma to techies. (Source on file with author.)

30. July 17, 2013, Recommendation on ULURP Application Nos.: C 130235 ZMM and C 130236 HAM by the New York City Department of Housing Preservation and Development (hereafter Recommendation), at 3, chrome-extension://efaidnbmnnnibpcajpcglclefindmkaj/viewer.html?pdfurl=http%3A%2F%2Farchive.citylaw.org%2Fbpm%2F2013%2FULURPNYCHousingPresDevpt.pdf&clen=143427&chunk=true.

31. Withers, *supra* note 2, at 143; Braunstein, *supra* note 29.

multilevel homes, shipping containers,[32] modular and prefabricated apartments,[33] and pods (serving the homeless community).[34]

There are also wide variations in micro-housing interior design. What is included in the unit versus what is shared with others or separately purchased varies considerably. Standard features include a bed, a living area, a bathroom, and small storage space,[35] but "pods" may consist merely of a sleeping space or possibly a sleeping space with a bathroom.[36] Micro-units often take advantage of multipurpose features, for example, a table becomes a bed or a bed folds over to create more living space. One distinguishing feature is whether each unit includes a kitchen, a kitchenette, or no kitchen. Some include only a small refrigerator and microwave (or hotplate) like a hotel suite. Other micro-apartments share a full kitchen and other common areas with other tenants.[37] Another distinguishing feature is what amenities are included in the building that micro-unit dwellers can access. Some have extensive, even luxurious, amenities.[38] Many include more common spaces to make up for the reduction in private space.[39]

Proponents present micro-housing in several perspectives. It's a rational developer response to the demographic trend of smaller households, resolving a mismatch between existing housing supply and current demand.[40] It's a solution to the affordability crisis.[41] It offers a market-proven infill alternative to sprawl and a promising strategy to revitalize cities with attractive workforce housing.[42] And, it's a solution to our environmental crisis—a new truly efficient and sustainable form of residential living that will help us adapt to climate change, including by reducing carbon emissions from vehicles.[43]

---

32. DesignBoom, *supra* note 15; Ryan Mitchell, *Hausman Style Tiny House* (hereafter "Mitchell"), www.THETINYLIFE.COM (May 29, 2012), http://thetinylife.com/tag/micro-house/.

33. For example, SmartSpace Soma in San Francisco, CA, are constructed from prefabricated materials (Source on file with author.); Brett Widness, *Next Evolution in Micro-Housing: Smarter, Shared, and Modular* (hereafter "Widness"), URBAN LAND (Nov. 18, 2013).

34. Waltnekrosius, *Gary Pickering Builds "Tiny House" Survival Pods for the Homeless* (hereafter "Pickering"), www.INSTEADING.COM, http://insteading.com/2013/08/12/survival-pods-for-tough-times/; Johnny Diaz, *Portable Homes for the Homeless? Food Truck Builder Designs Micro Pod* (hereafter "Diaz").

35. Mitchell, *supra* note 32; DesignBoom, *supra* note 15.

36. Green, *supra* note 2 (no toilet; backup shower); Pickering, *supra* note 34; Diaz, *supra* note 34.

37. Infranca, *supra* note 2 at 78–79; Porterfield, *supra* note 28.

38. Carl Malcolm, *Micro Units: The Essential Ingredients*, www.MultifamilyExecutive.com (May 28, 2014), http://www.multifamilyexecutive.com/low-rise-projects/micro-units-the-essential-ingredients_o.aspx; Braunstein, *supra* note 31.

39. What's In? Micro-Units, Connection (Young Architects Forum, American Institute of Architects) Jan. 2013, http://www.aia.org/practicing/AIAB098185; Braunstein, *supra* note 31.

40. Infranca, *supra* note 2, at 54–55.

41. *Id.* at 61–63; Withers, *supra* note 2, at 134–37; Braunstein, *supra* note 31; What's In? Micro-Units, *supra* note 39.

42. For enthusiastic support for micro-housing, see Withers, *supra* note 2, at 139–43.

43. *Id.* at 139–46. *See also* Wisegeek, *supra* note 13 ("A small house that is energy efficient and designed strategically to maximize usable space while minimizing ecological footprint.").

But micro-housing is controversial.[44] Some fear micro-housing is merely a profit-maximizing scheme by developers[45] that will solve none of these problems, but rather strain infrastructure, discriminate against families, undermine urban quality of life, exploit new workers, and threaten long-standing habitability standards by promoting "overcrowding." Moreover, the feasibility of micro-housing in an age of the coronavirus is questionable.[46]

In principle, even without subsidy or legal restrictions, micro-apartments can be more affordable than other traditional market-rate apartments because their smaller size enables efficiencies in land use, that is, more units per acre, reducing development costs that can be transferred to renters as lower rents.[47] In addition, there can be lower construction costs—both labor and materials—because of their size and the reduced level of expected amenities. And construction costs per unit can be reduced by the use of prefabricated materials. Detached tiny houses can be more affordable for similar reasons.

However, there's no guarantee that a micro-apartment will be affordable. Indeed, some are concerned that micro-housing will not actually serve affordable housing needs but merely serve developers' bottom lines. They argue that micro-housing is not inherently more affordable and note that the prices of some micro-apartments cost more per square foot than regular apartments. "For example, one micro-unit project in San Francisco would rent for $5.91 to $6.82 per square foot, compared to $4.21 per square foot for the average sized studio in the city."[48] So, developers profit more on the lower development costs, while renters pay more money for less space. And high rents for small units could increase rents overall.[49] Finally, in some cities, micro-apartments are replacing what had been affordable housing (e.g., SROs) that affordable housing developers would like to rehabilitate and preserve.[50]

The counter argument is that—all other things being equal—economic theory would predict that "if micro-units increase housing supply in a city they should reduce, or at the very least not increase, rents. . . . In addition, micro-units may reduce the demand among singles for shared two-to-four bedroom housing units, which could render those units more affordable to families."[51] On this view, "[h]igher average rents for micro-units may simply reflect demand for new construction, particular locations within a city, or the attractiveness of the new housing options."[52] And, without the availability of micro-units, high demand

---

44. Donald Elliott & Peter Sullivan, *Tiny Houses, and the Not-So-Tiny Questions They Raise*, 32(11) Zoning Practice (2015).

45. Randyl Drummer, *Investors Bet Tiny Micro Apts. Can Yield Outsized Returns* (hereafter "Drummer"), www.CoStarNews.com (May 29, 2103), https://www.multibriefs.com/briefs /CAAORG/CAAORG060413.php#micro (last accessed Aug. 16, 2014).

46. Joseph Pimentel, *Is Micro-Housing Viable in the Age of Coronavirus? One Developer Is Betting on It in Los Angeles*, Spectrum News (Oct. 11, 2020), https://spectrumnews1.com/ca/la-west /business/2020/10/09/is-micro-housing-viable-in-the-age-of-coronavirus--one-developer-is-betting -on-it.

47. Emily Keable, *Building on the Tiny House Movement: A Viable Solution to Meet Affordable Housing Needs*, 11 U. St. Thomas J. L. & Pub. Pol'y 111 (2017).

48. Infranca, *supra* note 2, at 61.

49. *Id.* at 61–62.

50. *Id.* at 64.

51. *Id.* at 62.

52. *Id.*

for smaller (and more affordable) units fuels the creation of illegal units.[53] Of course, the important determinants are regional and local housing market conditions.

Developers see an emerging and growing market for micro-apartments, particularly among young professionals, especially "techies" who have distinct lifestyles.[54] Research points to a high demand for micro-housing based on the increased demand for studios and city living.[55] Many millennials are currently living at home as "boomerang" children, but many of them will be entering the market soon as renters. They are potential renters of micro-apartments because some will be starting at lower salaries.[56] Despite some uncertainty about financing,[57] developers want municipalities to allow these units to be built and let consumers decide.[58] Some even seek tax exemptions for micro-apartment development.[59]

Most local governments that approve micro-housing do so for two sets of policy reasons. First, they believe micro-housing will meet existing and unmet housing needs as well as emerging housing needs.[60] Consistent with the demographic trend of smaller household size, single-person households continue to grow, especially in urban centers.[61] Some governments in high cost areas fear that if they do not provide micro-housing, the influx of young professional renters will increase rents further.[62] Some localities see micro-housing as an "urban necessity" similar to SROs and boarding houses.[63]

Some localities in high-cost housing areas support micro-apartments as a source of affordable housing, especially for low-wage workers.[64] Some micro-units are being proposed or built by nonprofit developers specifically as legally restricted, affordable housing or are required to be affordable by the jurisdiction.[65] Some versions of micro-housing serve as special needs housing, including for homeless people.[66]

---

53. *Id.* at 64.

54. Lew Sichelman, *"Micro-Unit" Developers See Big Future*, www.ULI.COM (May 20, 2013), http://urbanland.uli.org/industry-sectors/residential/micro-unit-developers-see-big-future/; Hudson, *supra* note 25.

55. Drummer, *supra* note 45; Miller Hamrick, *Prefabricated Micro-Apartments—Pretty Fabulous,* www.AXIOMETRICS.COM (Apr. 23, 2014), https://www.panoramic.com/wp-content/uploads /2014/05/PreFabricated-Micro-Apartments-Pretty-Fabulous-5_1_2014.pdf.

56. Josh Miller, *Living at Home as an Investment*, www.EYEONHOUSING.ORG (Aug. 21, 2013), http://eyeonhousing.org/2013/08/21/living-at-home-as-an-investment/.

57. "Micro-unit [. . .] developers may face difficulties obtaining financing for a project or constructing units in a cost-effective manner." Infranca, *supra* note 2, at 84–85.

58. *CHPC Testifies in Favor of HPD adAPT Application*, www.CHPCNY.ORG (Oct. 3, 2013), http://chpcny.org/2013/10/chpc-testifies-in-favor-of-hpd-adapt-application/.

59. *Microhousing*, http://www.smartgrowthseattle.org/micro-housing/.

60. The host of the tiny housing TV series articulates four attractions: (1) a "young, adventurous lifestyle" avoiding being tied down by rent or a mortgage; (2) minimalist lifestyle that puts relationships and other passions above possessions; (3) economical; and (4) environmentally friendly. Green, *supra* note 2.

61. Drummer, *supra* note 45.

62. Mooney & Kilpatrick, *supra* note 23; Porterfield, *supra* note 28.

63. Stack, *supra* note 6.

64. Mooney & Kilpatrick, *supra* note 23.

65. Infranca, *supra* note 2, at 70; Forty percent of the units in the first NYC micro-apartment (My Micro NY, Monadnock Development LLC) are dedicated for affordable housing.

66. Tom Fisher, *The Ethics of Housing the Poor*, https://arch3711.files.wordpress.com/2015/11 /fisher-the-ethics-of-housing-the-poor.pdf (last visited Dec. 6, 2021).

Second, many local governments envision micro-housing as part of a broader city planning strategy. For these, micro-housing promises city revitalization by attracting people, especially young professionals, to come live and stay downtown.[67] They hope that micro-housing will also "attract larger employers concerned about residential opportunities for employees."[68]

Other localities view micro-housing as promoting an environmentally friendly housing strategy.[69] In general, micro-apartments will make more efficient use of land because they are higher-density housing. And, smaller units are more likely to be energy efficient than traditional dwellings, because they will use less resources to heat or cool, and there will be fewer unused rooms that are unnecessarily heated or cooled.[70] If they are built near public transit or in walkable neighborhoods, their occupants will be likely to produce less greenhouse gases by reduced auto use.[71]

Disputes and controversies about micro-housing generally fall into three categories: Will micro-housing be good for the city as a whole, good for tenants, and good for neighbors?

Some doubt that micro-housing will be quality development for the city. Some early micro-apartments in Seattle caused controversy because they were developed without design and environmental reviews while developers received tax breaks.[72] Seattle has apparently abandoned its experiment with micro-housing as a solution to its affordable housing crisis.[73] Micro-apartments increase density, but without appropriate planning, they will burden (perhaps already overburdened) infrastructure.[74] And depending upon the location of micro-units in relation to other land uses, some fear these units could create a new version of "ghetto" with concentrations of low-wage workers.

The other housing need concern is that typically micro-housing does not serve families.[75] Markets, such as San Francisco, need affordable family housing, but micro-apartments do not usually serve families due to their size.

---

67. Infranca, *supra* note 2, at 55.

68. *Id.* at 62.

69. A. Robin Donnelly, *Smart Growth through Tiny Homes: Incentivizing Freedom of Housing*, 4 Tex. A&M J. Prop. L. 327 (2018) (a proposal to expand the EPA's Smart Growth program to include pre-planned Tiny Home Eco communities); Wisegeek, *supra* note 13.

70. Thanks to Sas Ansari for these insights. Withers, *supra* note 2, at 139–46. Sandy Keenan, *A House That Sips Energy*, N.Y. Times, July 3, 2014, at D3 (describing a 800-square foot model prototype house entered into the 2014 Solar Decathlon Europe competition engineered to use 65 percent less heating and cooling energy than traditional homes).

71. Infranca, *supra* note 2, at 62; Withers, *supra* note 2, at 139–46.

72. Dominic Holden, *The Fight against Small Apartments: Why Neighborhood Groups Are Uniting to Stop Developers from Building Tiny, Affordable Units* (hereafter "Holden"), www.thestranger.com (May 8, 2013), http://www.thestranger.com/seattle/the-fight-against-small-apartments/Content?oid=16701155.

73. "By the end of 2014, Seattle recognized these issues and implemented code changes that effectively quashed any continued micro-unit development." Taylor Haines, *Micro-Housing in Seattle Update: Combating "Seattle-ization*," 43 Seattle U.L. Rev. 11, 12 (2020).

74. Ansari & Chatterjee, *supra* note 22.

75. Noriega, *supra* note 21; Malia Wollan, *San Franciscans Divide over Pint-Sized Apartments* (hereafter "Wollan"), N.Y. Times, Sept. 27, 2012, at A20, http://www.nytimes.com/2012/09/27/us/micro-unit-apartment-proposal-divides-san-francisco.html?_r=1&.

Some micro-housing skeptics express concerns for tenants. They argue that the small spaces that micro-apartments provide will undermine tenants' quality of life.[76] However, other studies report contrary findings and raise other questions.[77] While residential occupancy standards and housing code standards for habitability provide some parameters, our housing law and policy has never resolved the issue of how much space people need to live a healthy life.[78] And fundamental issues remain unresolved, for example, are minimum healthy standards objective or subjective and culturally dependent?[79] And who should decide: government, developers/the market, or housing dwellers?

While certain people may have no trouble acclimating to a limited space, some housing proponents see micro-apartment development as a slippery slope, and an unwinding of the zoning laws that sought to uphold a decent quality of life.[80] If we reduce required minimum standards for housing for purely economic reasons, this could increase supply and, on certain additional assumptions, increase affordability, but it also sets up a precedent to push farther below the new floor in the future. Perceptions about micro-housing among different demographic groups may affect its viability.[81]

Housing advocates also raise equity issues: Do we have different housing standards for different classes of people, for example, lower standards for (formerly) homeless people?[82] To the degree micro-units are marketed to young professionals, this concern may be misplaced, because with large disposable incomes, they can supplement their lifestyles outside

---

76. Jacoba Urist, *The Health Risks of Small Apartments: Living in Tiny Spaces Can Cause Psychological Problems*, WWW.THEATLANTIC.COM (Dec. 19, 2013), http://www.theatlantic.com/health /archive/2013/12/the-health-risks-of-small-apartments/282150/.

77. Residential occupancy standards have a history steeped in controversy regarding the mixed motives behind their promotion. *See, e.g.*, Frank S. Alexander, *The Housing of America's Families: Control, Exclusion, and Privilege*, 54 EMORY L.J. 1231, 1251–52 (2005) (describing cultural and racial bias); Ellen Pader, *Housing Occupancy Standards: Inscribing Ethnicity and Family Relations on the Land*, 19 J. ARCHITECTURAL & PLAN. RES. 300, 305 (2002).

78. *See* Tim Iglesias, *Clarifying the Federal Fair Housing Act's Exemption for Reasonable Occupancy Standards*, 21 FORDHAM URB. L.J. 1211, 1211–19 (substantial discussion of these issues with numerous citations to other sources); Wollan, *supra* note 75; Emilie Raguso, *Zoning Board Asks Micro-Unit Developer to Shrink Proposal* (hereafter "Raguso"), WWW.BERKELEYSIDE.COM (Sept. 27, 2013), http://www.berkeleyside.com/2013/09/27/zoning-board-asks-micro-unit-developer-to -shrink-proposal/; Lee Anne Fennell, *Property in Housing*, ACADEMIA SINICA L.J. 31, 56 (2013) ("[H]ow much space a given household finds necessary for its well-being depends upon the cultural context and on which activities are contained within the household, as opposed to being socialized within a larger community or procured privately outside the home.").

79. Some might query what's the problem if micro-apartments are more or less same dimensions as a hotel room? Hotel rooms generally intended only for temporary lodging. But some hotels do much longer residencies in the same rooms. *See, e.g.*, Extended Stay America, http://www.extended stayamerica.com/suites/hotel-rooms-and-amenities.html, which includes links to floor plans and to discounts on more than 30 day consecutive stays.

80. Infranca, *supra* note 2, at 63–64. Adele Peters, *Why I Hate Living in My Tiny House*, FAST COMPANY (Oct. 2, 2019), https://www.fastcompany.com/90407740/why-i-hate-living-in-my-tiny-house.

81. *See, e.g.*, JUSTIN FAIR, TINY HOUSES AND THE BLACK EXPERIENCE IN BALTIMORE, A master's project submitted in partial fulfillment of the requirements for the degree Master of City and Regional Planning (May 2020) (on file with author).

82. Micro-housing could be compared to IKEA's "refugee housing units" intended for temporary shelter for people in dire straits. See http://www.ikea.com/ms/en_US/img/ad_content/IKEA_Foun dation_USA_September_2013.pdf.

of their home. However, when micro-apartments are intended for low-wage workers or homeless people, the concern is more salient, especially if these units have few amenities.

Would-be neighbors of micro-units, especially single family neighborhoods and neighboring business communities, have voiced traditional concerns about density and property values.[83] If micro-apartments are sited in already dense districts, increased traffic and parking problems that will accompany an influx of new residents are likely to be a particularly strong concern,[84] and even more intense if the locality reduces parking standards for micro-apartments located downtown.[85] Owners of neighboring buildings may protest the height of infill micro-apartments that might block light.[86] Some homeowners and property owners claim that micro-units lower their property values.[87]

Other concerns of neighbors focus on the prospective tenants themselves. To the extent the units will be affordable housing, neighbors express the fears typical of all local opposition to affordable housing[88]—they will attract "itinerant" and "sketchy" people, homeless people, criminals, or those with drug problems.[89]

Because micro-housing is a relatively new form of housing, there is not yet much empirical evidence of its actual effects. Data on historical parallels (e.g., tenements in New York City) may only be suggestive because so many other factors are distinct. In his review of micro-housing, Professor Infranca recognizes some policy concerns but suggests "[a]pplying reasonable regulations to the development of micro-units . . . can provide a safe and affordable alternative that reduces demand for illegal units."[90]

Most localities have the legal authority to zone and plan for residential uses that meet their communities' housing needs. However, many existing zoning ordinances and planning codes do not anticipate micro-housing. Therefore, usually localities need to revise their planning codes and zoning ordinances to allow micro-units[91] or to bring them under review

---

83. Raguso, *supra* note 78; Holden, *supra* note 72.

84. Zak Burns, *Micro-housing Trend in Seattle Ruining Property Values, Warns Real Estate Agent* (hereafter "Burns"), www.mynorthwest.com (Mar. 20, 2014), https://mynorthwest .com/7965/microhousing-trend-in-seattle-ruining-property-values-warns-real-estate-agent/; Raguso, *supra* note 78.

85. Infranca, *supra* note 2, at 80. Interestingly, sometimes investors may require developers to include parking even if the city does not. *Id.* at 84.

86. Emilie Raguso, *Zoning Board Denies Berkeley Micro-unit Proposal*, www.berkeleyside .com (Nov. 21, 2013), http://www.berkeleyside.com/2013/11/21/zoning-board-denies-berkeley-micro -unit-proposal/; Raguso, *supra* note 78.

87. Burns, *supra* note 84.

88. *See* Tim Iglesias, *Managing Local Opposition to Affordable Housing: A New Approach to NIMBY*, 12 J. Affordable Hous. & Cmty. Dev. L. 78, 81–83, 89–92 (Fall 2002).

89. Holden, *supra* note 72; Infranca, *supra* note 2, at 62–63.

90. Infranca, *supra* note 2, at 64.

91. Seattle, Washington's micro-housing developments required amendments to its Land Use Code. In particular, the city amended and added to the original code in order to define micro-housing in terms of its purpose and standards (see http://www.seattle.gov/documents/Departments /SDCI/Vault/MicroHousing/MicroHousingSEPADNS.pdf (last accessed Dec. 6, 2021)). New York City (NY) amended its zoning ordinance, including Section 28-21 (requiring a minimum of 400 square feet of living quarters); Section 23-22 (regarding the number of dwelling units); Section 35-22(b) (regarding bulk); Section 35-24(b)(2)(i) (regarding height); Sections 28-33 (regarding planting); and Sections 23-145 (regarding lot coverage), available at https://www1.nyc.gov

where they would otherwise escape review under current definitions and standards.[92] In some cases, approving micro-housing may require revising state law, particularly a state's building code, or getting waivers or exceptions to it.[93]

In some cases, micro-units have been developed under special circumstances. After conducting a design competition for micro-housing, New York City waived certain requirements because the development would be constructed on city-owned property.[94] San Francisco amended its zoning laws to create a limited pilot program to allow a limited number of micro-apartments to be built.[95] The feasibility of micro-housing in some locales may depend on nongovernmental partners, such as churches.[96]

If a locality wants to enable a substantial number of micro-units to be built, it will need to review and revise its planning code and zoning ordinance carefully, both to ensure that these developments will serve its planning and development goals and to anticipate potential lawsuits by developers, property owners, neighbors, and other interested groups.[97]

The potential scope and effects of micro-housing are unknown, but they appear somewhat promising. Localities would do well to consider their value to their communities while attending to the policy controversies. And, if they choose to proceed, they should

---

/assets/planning/download/pdf/plans-studies/zqa/adoption-overview.pdf?r=1 (last accessed Dec. 6, 2021). San Francisco (CA) amended Sections 318, 135, and 140 of its Planning Code defining and adding efficiency dwelling units to its Code, as well as regulating common areas in cases where units are 220 square feet. San Francisco Planning Department, New Planning Code Summary: Efficiency Dwelling Units: Numerical Cap and Open & Common Space Requirements, Case Number: Board File No. 12-0996, Ordinance No. 242-12 (Jan. 7, 2013), https://sfplanning.org/sites/default/files /documents/legis/code-summaries/120996_Cap_on_Efficiency_Dwelling_Units.pdf.

92. Seattle's early micro-apartments were controversial in part because under existing regulations they were not required to undergo design review. *Mapping Capitol Hill Microhousing—15 Buildings, 500+ Units, 2 Reviews*, WWW.CAPITOLHILLSEATTLE.COM (Sept. 27, 2012), http://www.capitolhillseattle.com/2012/09/mapping-capitol-hill-microhousing-14-buildings -500-units-2-reviews/. Micro-units (AKA tiny houses) sometimes try to escape traditional residential use regulation by putting on wheels to become recreational vehicle/manufactured housing which is subject to different (and less) regulation. *How to Get around Building Codes and Zoning for Tiny House Living*, WWW.TINYHOUSETALK.COM (Jan. 20, 2012), http://tinyhousetalk.com /building-codes-and-zoning-for-tiny-house-living/.

93. Withers, *supra* note 2, at 125–26, 150–51; *see* Ciara Turner, *It Takes a Village: Designating "Tiny House" Villages As Transitional Housing Campgrounds*, 50 U. MICH. J.L. REFORM 931 (2017) (proposing the creation of a new state-level zoning classification of "transitional campgrounds" for getting around these zoning and building code challenges, without drastic overhauls to health and safety codes). For several years, Hawaii has considered bills to promote micro-housing for Native Hawaiians: https://www.capitol.hawaii.gov/session2018/bills/HB2473_.HTM.

94. Recommendation, *supra* note 30.

95. S.F. Planning Commission, Planning Commission Motion No. 18788, Section 309 (Jan. 10, 2013), http://commissions.sfplanning.org/cpcmotions/2013/18788.pdf.

96. Scott Greenstone, *Seattle Looks to Churches for Help with Tiny House Villages—but Continued Tensions Could Complicate Efforts*, SEATTLE TIMES (Sept. 18, 2019), https://www.seattletimes .com/seattle-news/homeless/seattle-looks-to-churches-for-help-with-tiny-house-villages-but-contin ued-tensions-could-complicate-efforts/.

97. Andrew Lane, *Is Your Community Ready for Micro-Housing?*, Planning Advisor, Municipal Research and Services Center (Nov. 2014), http://mrsc.org/Home/Stay-Informed/MRSC-Insight /November-2014/Is-Your-Community-Ready-for-Micro-Housing.aspx.

carefully revise their planning codes and zoning ordinances to ensure that the promises will be realized and the potential perils avoided.

III. MOBILE HOMES AND MANUFACTURED HOUSING

"Mobile homes,"[98] "manufactured housing,"[99] and "modular rooms, units or housing"[100] provide an important source of affordable housing for seniors, farmworkers,[101] Native Americans,[102] and low-income households, especially in rural communities, such as Appalachia.[103] According to a 2017 study, manufactured housing is the single largest source of unsubsidized affordable housing in the United States.[104] "There are approximately

---

98. "Mobile Homes" have two basic variations which refer to the size of the home itself: single-wide and double-wide. The "wide" in either single- or double-wide refers to the dimensions of the home itself. A single-wide is roughly 15 feet by 72 feet and ranges from 900 to 1,400 square feet of living space. A double-wide is roughly 26 feet by 56 feet and ranges from 1,110 to 2,500 square feet. Generally speaking, a mobile home was constructed prior to 1976 and a manufactured home was constructed after 1976 and is a prefabricated structure that may or may not be permanently placed on the land to which it is shipped. pre-1976 homes are generally considered some of the worst housing stock in America. Mel Jones, et al., *Mobile and Manufactured Homes in Central Appalachia and Alabama: Age, Condition , and Need for Replacement*, VIRGINIA CENTER FOR HOUSING RESEARCH (VHCR) AT VIRGINIA TECH (2016), https://prosperitynow.org/sites/default/files/resources/VCHR _Study_Final.pdf at 4 (hereafter Jones).

99. A "manufactured home" is defined in federal law as "a structure, transportable in one or more sections . . . which is built on a permanent chassis and designed to be used as a dwelling with or without a permanent foundation when connected to the required utilities, and includes the plumbing, heating, air-conditioning, and electrical systems contained in the structure." 24 C.F.R. § 3280.2. The federal definition of a manufactured home excludes "any self-propelled *recreational* vehicle." *Id.*

100. "Modular homes" are factory-built housing "designed only for erection or installation on a site-built permanent foundation." 24 C.F.R. § 3282.12(b)(1). "Factory-built homes" and "pre-fab homes" are generally synonyms for modular homes. They are often constructed to comply with the state or local building codes where they will be installed. "Panelized homes" are constructed using factory-built panels and are generally constructed to comply with state building codes.

101. See discussion *infra* in Section IV regarding "Farmworker Housing."

102. See https://prosperitynow.org/resources/native-american-experience-manufactured-hous ing-plenary.

103. See special issue dedicated to manufactured housing of Land Lines, Lincoln Institute (Jan. 2018): https://www.lincolninst.edu/publications/issues/land-lines-january-2018. *See also* Amy J. Schmitz, *Promoting the Promise Manufactured Homes Provide for Affordable Housing*, 13 AFFORD-ABLE HOUS. & CMTY. ECON. DEV. L. 384 (2004); LAWRENCE A. FROLIK, RESIDENCE OPTIONS FOR OLDER OR DISABLED CLIENTS §§ 7-2 to 7-4 (1997 & Supp. 2002); HOUSING ASSISTANCE COUN-CIL, RENTAL HOUSING IN RURAL AMERICA 1 (2003). *Also see* a recent study, *Affordable Manufac-tured Housing Best Practices: Opportunities for California Affordable Housing Developers*, https:// aeae507d-e90c-449b-9332-a6e33d13c0ca.filesusr.com/ugd/8d7a46_19981fe480194efbb2842061 90cadc9f.pdf, published by the California Coalition for Rural Housing in 2010, which provides in-depth and valuable case studies demonstrating the cost-effectiveness, quality, and versatility of manufactured housing as an affordable housing option. A study of the Appalachians found that man-ufactured housing in these states constitutes roughly 13 percent to 19 percent of the housing stock. In some counties this is as high as 37 percent of the housing stock. See Jones, *supra* note 98, at 14.

104. Esther Sullivan, *Moving Out: Mapping Mobile Home Park Closures to Analyze Spatial Pat-terns of Low-Income Residential Displacement*, 16(3) CITY AND COMMUNITY 304 (Sept. 2017). And see generally, issue dedicated to Factory-Built Housing, Evidence Matters, Winter/Spring 2020, U.S. HUD ("Factory-Built Housing").

6.7 million occupied manufactured homes in the U.S., comprising about 6 percent of the nation's housing stock."[105] There is voluminous literature advocating manufactured housing as one part of the solution to our ongoing affordability crisis.[106] Over the past 20 years its role has grown and is expected to continue to increase, moving from rural areas to suburban and urban contexts[107] and from mobile home parks to privately owned land.[108]

The popular use of the term "mobile home" encompasses a wide variety of dwellings, including "house trailers," manufactured housing built prior to and after the National Manufactured Housing Construction and Safety Standards Act of 1980, and trailers and vans designed primarily for temporary recreational use. The terminology is complex and is complicated by federal regulation, industry changes over the last three decades, and proponents' attempts to win community acceptance for this form of housing.[109]

---

105. Manufactured Housing in Rural America, Rural Research Brief, Housing Assistance Council 2 (July 2020); http://www.ruralhome.org/storage/documents/rrbriefs/Manufactured_Housing _RRB.pdf.

106. See publications cited throughout this section. And see Robert Solomon, *How to Increase Our Affordable Housing Stock*, in Legal Scholarship for the Urban Core: From the Ground Up 127–34 (eds. Peter Enrich & Rashmi Dyal-Chand 2019). Aaron Shroyer, *How Manufactured Housing Can Fill Affordable Housing Gaps*, Housing Matters (July 8, 2020), https://housing matters.urban.org/articles/how-manufactured-housing-can-fill-affordable-housing-gaps/; Ann M. Burkhart, Bringing Manufactured Housing into the Real Estate Finance System (arguing that manufactured housing should be recharacterized as real property), http://ssrn.com /abstract=1548441.

107. "Rural and suburban markets have traditionally been the stronghold of the industry. While this remains true even today, manufactured homes are increasingly being used in urban areas. Two converging factors virtually ensure manufactured housing will play an ever-growing role in providing housing in urban neighborhoods—the escalating cost of new housing, and the rising use of technological and design innovations in homes." *See, e.g.*, affordable housing infill manufactured housing development in Escondido, California, called Brotherton Square, described in *Manufactured Housing Best Practices: Opportunities for California Affordable Housing Developers*, *supra* note 103; *Understanding Today's Manufactured Housing*, p. 1, https://www.manufacturedhousing.org/wp-content/uploads/2017/10/Understanding-Manuactured-Housing.pdf. This publication presents the Manufactured Housing Institute's (MHI) perspective on the future of manufactured housing generally. *See also* a report on the MHI's Urban Design Demonstration Project at http://www.manufacturedhousing.org.php56-9.dfw3-2.websitetestlink.com/wp-content/uploads/2016/09/UDP_Booklet.pdf.

108. "According to the U.S. Census in 2008, over 75 percent of manufactured homes were placed on private property, while the remaining 25 percent were sited in residential land-lease communities. The percentage of manufactured homes placed on private property has been growing over the last decade, and this trend is expected to continue as more and more residential land is zoned appropriately to allow for manufactured housing." [citation omitted]. *Understanding Today's Manufactured Housing, supra* note 107, at 8. The availability of two-story, HUD-approved manufactured housing may increase demand.

109. In an attempt to engender broader public support, a 1980 federal statute officially substituted "manufactured housing" for all references to "mobile home" in federal statutes and regulations. *See* Housing and Community Development Act of 1980, Pub. L. No. 96-399, § 308(c)(4), 94 Stat. 1614, 1641 (1980). Some states and some courts have adopted the language. *See, e.g.*, Cal. Health & Safety Code §§ 18007–18008 (West 2010); W. Va. Code § 21-9-2(J) (West 2010); Carr v. Michael Motors, Inc., 557 S.E.2d 294 (2001). This language is confusing to the general public because the federal definition of "manufactured housing" includes reference to "permanent chassis,"

There is a second component in the definition of a manufactured/mobile home: the relationship between the land itself and the home. Some mobile homes are situated within land-lease communities in which the owner of the mobile home rents the land the home sits on from an entity in what is basically a landlord-tenant situation. Other homes are placed on private property owned by the owner of the manufactured home. Though the name implies mobility, because of the socio-economic situation of the people who own these types of property, the structure is often permanently affixed because of the relatively expensive costs of moving.[110]

While some mobile home parks are protected by rent control,[111] most mobile homes are "affordable" in market terms because they are less expensive to build than site-built housing.[112] Manufactured housing and modular housing can be affordable due to reduced construction costs, because the production process can be more efficient than on-site

---

which is associated with the phrase "mobile home" by the general public. *See, e.g.,* Bourgeois v. Parish of St. Tammany, 628 F. Supp. 159, 160 n.2 (1986) ("parties disagree over the application of the term 'manufactured home' or 'mobile home' to the structure in question") (invalidating ordinance provisions that provide that mobile homes" are not classifiable as a dwelling because the structure as assembled is mobile). Some people live in recreational vehicles (commonly called RVs) parked on city streets (not in RV parks) and have been subject to localities' regulations to limit their "residence" in a city by limiting parking hours. Although some farmworkers rely on RVs as homes, this book does not address them as forms of affordable housing.

110. In 2017, the average cost of relocating a mobile home was roughly $5,000 to $15,000. Esther Sullivan, *Displaced in Place: Manufactured Housing, Mass Eviction, and the Paradox of State Intervention*, 82(2) AM. SOCIO. REV. 309 (2017).

111. See Chapter 4 for a discussion of rent control. *See also* Yee v. City of Escondido, 503 U.S. 519 (1992) (finding no taking). *And see* Cashman v. City of Cotati, 374 F.3d 887 (9th Cir. 2004) (invalidating mobile home rent control without vacancy decontrol in California as a regulatory taking). However, the *Cashman* court's takings claim, which alleged that the rent control ordinance is an unconstitutional regulatory taking by failing to substantially advance a legitimate government interest, was foreclosed by the U.S. Supreme Court's unanimous decision in *Lingle v. Chevron U.S.A. Inc.*, 544 U.S. 528 (2005). Cashman v. City of Cotati, 415 F.3d 1027, 1028 (9th Cir. 2005). The most recent takings challenge to mobile home rent control is *Guggenheim v. City of Goleta* (9th Cir. 2009) (finding facial taking under Penn Central ad hoc balancing test), *rehearing en banc granted*, Mar. 12, 2010; MHC Financing Ltd. Partnership v. City of San Rafael, 714 F.3d 1118 (finding no taking per *Penn Central*).

112. In 2008, the cost per square foot of a new manufactured home (excluding land costs) was about half of the cost of a new single-family site-built house. See *infra* note 109. The average sales price of a manufactured home was $78,500 in 2020, https://www.manufacturedhousing.org/wp-con tent/uploads/2020/07/2020-MHI-Quick-Facts-updated-05-2020.pdf.

According to the Manufactured Housing Institute (MHI), the affordability of manufactured housing is "due to the efficiencies of the factory-building process" and "the economies of scale resulting from purchasing large quantities of materials, products and appliances." *Id.* at 6.

construction.[113] Manufactured housing can also be more affordable because it can be erected quickly, saving labor costs.[114]

The potential for mobile homes and manufactured/modular housing to provide a larger stock of affordable housing, including as accessory dwelling units,[115] is limited by five factors: (1) financing limitations; (2) the aging and inefficiency of existing mobile homes; (3) preservation of existing mobile home parks; (4) vulnerability to natural disasters increased by climate change; (5) siting restrictions imposed by local governments.

Prior to 2008, Freddie Mac and Fannie Mae did not back manufactured housing loans. The Housing and Economic Recovery Act of 2008 required Fannie Mae and Freddie Mac to better assist manufactured housing as one of three "underserved markets."[116] The development and preservation of manufactured housing may be subsidized by federal programs, such as the HOME Investment Partnership Program and the Community Development Block Grant Program, or by mortgage revenue bonds issued by state or local governments.[117]

Older mobile homes and manufactured housing (i.e., pre-1980) are energy inefficient and/or have severe habitability problems.[118] Because of the relative inefficiency of these properties, roughly 14 percent to 21 percent of manufactured homeowners are cost burdened.[119] More than 70,000 households in Appalachia who live in manufactured housing pay more than 30 percent of their income on utilities *alone*.[120] A USDA program called the Rural Energy Savings Program that used to help rural homeowners implement "durable cost-effective energy efficiency measures" with low or no interest loans is, unfortunately,

---

113. *See Factory-Built Housing*, Evidence Matters, espec. 14–22 (Winter/Spring 2020), U.S. HUD ("Factory-Built Housing") which proposes to address "removing barriers to factory-built housing in rural and Tribal communities." ("Cityscape") https://www.huduser.gov/portal/periodicals/cityscpe/call-for-papers-regulatory-barriers.html (last accessed Feb. 28, 2020). Manufactured or modular homes are not necessarily affordable. In California for example, the manufacturer Blu Homes produces a range of models that range in price from $195,000 to $545,000, not including land costs. *See* https://www.bluhomes.com/ (last accessed Feb. 28, 2020).

114. *See, e.g.*, Rob Roth, *Housing Development Erected in West Oakland in 10 Days*, KTVU (Aug. 26, 2019), www.ktvu.com/news/ktvu-local-news/housing-development-erected-in-west-oakland-in-10-days.

115. *See, e.g.*, Factory Built Housing, *supra* note 104, at 8–13. And see "Accessory Dwelling Units" section of this chapter, *infra*.

116. This act is discussed extensively in Chapter 8, *infra*, http://www.manufacturedhousing .org/lib/showtemp_detail.asp?id=844&cat=Regulatory (on file with author). See Federal Housing Finance Agency's final rule on Fannie Mae's and Freddie Mac's duty to serve underserved areas at 81 Federal Register 96242 (12/29/2016).

117. See Chapter 9, *infra*, for discussion of the HOME and CDBG programs. See Chapters 10 and 11, *infra*, for discussions of state and local bond financing of affordable housing. Qualifying manufactured housing units are also eligible for mortgage insurance available under 12 U.S.C. § 1709 (2010). Lending programs and requirements for manufactured housing may differ depending upon the type of support system used (e.g., perimeter wall block, "piers and blocks," or wooden pilings). For an analysis of the problems in financing manufactured housing development, see L.A. "Tony" Kovach, *Doug Ryan, CFED, Manufactured Housing and Financing—What's Wrong, What's Right*, INDUSTRY IN FOCUS REPORTS (Oct. 9, 2015), https://www.manufacturedhomepronews.com /doug-ryan-cfed-manufactured-housing-and-financing-whats-wrong-whats-right/.

118. Jones, *supra* note 98, at 23.

119. *Id.* at 31. HUD defines "cost-burdened" as families who pay more than 30 percent of their income for housing.

120. *Id.* at 4.

closed.[121] A bill named the Manufactured Housing Modernization Act of 2019, with bipartisan co-sponsors, would have modernized manufactured housing regulation, but was not enacted.[122]

According to the U.S. Commerce Department, roughly one-third of the people who are in mobile homes own their homes but rent their land.[123] In growing or gentrifying communities, owners of mobile home parks have strong economic incentives to sell the park to a developer, which leads to the eviction of the households renting spaces in the park. New spaces are likely hard to find in these situations, leading to the net loss of this housing stock. For example, a larger portion of mobile home residents live in Harris County, Texas, than any other metro area in the United States. In 2012–2013, Harris County oversaw the largest population growth of any county in the United States, and the loss of manufactured housing directly correlated to the outgrowth of the urban core.[124] Government programs to assist mobile homeowners to purchase their parks can help preserve them, but usually require government funding and some right of first refusal.[125] A 2015 study by the National Consumer Law Center found that as of 2014, only 19 states provided some form of right of first refusal requirement as to the sale of a mobile home park.[126] Some states, for example, Texas, which has one of the largest trailer park populations in the United States, provide no protections whatsoever.[127] While the eviction notice in some states is 60 days (six as of 2020), the majority require just 30 days. With low vacancy rates in other parks, and, in some instances, restrictions that prohibit used homes or restrict them based on age, brand, or size of the home, mobile homeowners facing eviction from their land often face extremely limited options and a lack of legal protections. As a result, the abandonment of manufactured homes is a significant problem.[128] Some federal aid may be available. Proposed legislation in the House of Representatives H.R. 5547, known as the Manufactured Housing Community Preservation Act, would have represented a massive (and the first) meaningful investment in helping to maintain manufactured housing communities but was not enacted.[129] A new HUD funding vehicle would grant up to one million per park with a caveat that the park/community remain operational for 20 years. This funding would also help to overcome burdens/bans that some communities have placed on building manufactured housing in residentially zoned communities, discussed *infra*.

---

121. *See* https://www.rd.usda.gov/programs-services/rural-energy-savings-program (last accessed Feb. 28, 2020).

122. Manufactured Housing Modernization Act of 2019, S.1804, 116th Cong. (2019).

123. *Displaced in Place, supra* note 112.

124. *Id.*

125. *See generally* National Consumer Law Center, *Manufactured Housing Resource Guide: Promoting Resident Ownership of Communities* (Feb. 2015), https://www.nclc.org/images/pdf/man ufactured_housing/cfed-purchase_guide.pdf. *And see* Chelsea Catto, *Manufactured Housing Cooperatives: Innovations in Wealth-Building and Permanent Affordability*, 26 J. AFFORDABLE HOUS. & CMTY. DEV. L. 13 (2017).

126. *Id.*

127. *Id.* at 7–8.

128. *See, e.g.*, a bill in Arizona, introduced in January of 2019, aims to amend AZ ST 33-1476.02 and would provide new remedies for abandonment.

129. Manufactured Housing Community Preservation Act, H.R. 554, 116th Cong. (2020).

Mobile homes and some manufactured housing are uniquely vulnerable to certain natural disasters, including hurricanes. Because climate change increases the strength and frequency of hurricanes, it stands to wreak havoc in portions of the country where people occupy mobile/manufactured homes. One possible solution would be to institute new building and code standards in order to help limit the damage to housing stock as a result of hurricanes.

The primary legal issue concerning the expanded use of manufactured housing is siting.[130] Local opposition, based in concerns about safety, aesthetics (including compatibility with neighborhood character), crime, property values, tax revenue generation, and their potential for transience, has plagued the expansion of this market by restricting siting opportunities.[131] Localities employ various strategies to limit or block siting (discussed *infra*). In response, some states have enacted statutes to protect or promote mobile homes and manufactured housing (discussed *infra*). The 2020 Federal Appropriations Bill includes requirements that HUD issue guidance for how recipients of federal housing funds can and should include manufactured housing in their planning.

Manufacturers of mobile homes and manufactured housing have attempted to address many of opponents' concerns, including by upgrading production standards[132] and designs and by highlighting their compliance with federal regulation of manufactured housing.[133] A federal statute and implementing regulations mandate minimum building standards for "manufactured homes."[134] HUD administers a program to enforce the standards primar-

---

130. Daniel Mandelker, *Zoning Barriers to Manufactured Housing*, 48(2) THE URBAN LAWYER (Spring 2016). *See generally* issue dedicated to Factory-Built Housing, Evidence Matters, Winter/Spring 2020, U.S. HUD ("Factory-Built Housing"), which proposes to address "removing barriers to factory-built housing in rural and Tribal communities." ("Cityscape") https://www.huduser.gov/portal/periodicals/cityscpe/call-for-papers-regulatory-barriers.html (last accessed Feb. 28, 2020). Mobile home park closure due to redevelopment and discriminatory code enforcement are also important issues but are not addressed in this chapter.

131. For a review of the issues, see *Factory-Built Construction and the American Homebuyer: Perceptions and Opportunities* (HUD's Office of Policy Development and Research, 2007), https://www.huduser.gov/Publications/pdf/Perceptions_of_factory_construction.pdf. *See, e.g., In re* Tadlock, 134 S.E.2d 177, 179 (N.C. 1964). Underlying class (and possibly racial) concerns may also fuel resistance.

132. *See, e.g., More About Panelized Construction*, RESEARCH WORKS 4–5 (HUD User, October 2007) (discussing research regarding the first comprehensive treatment of the connection systems used for the wall panels in panelized construction). *And see* Technology Roadmap: Advanced Panelized Construction, Year One Progress Report, *available at* https://www.huduser.gov/portal/Publications/PDF/panelized.pdf.

133. Understanding Today's Manufactured Housing, *supra* note 107. *And see Quick Facts: Trends and Information About the Manufactured Housing Industry*, MANUFACTURED HOUSING INSTITUTE (2016), http://www.manufacturedhousing.org.php56-9.dfw3-2.websitetestlink.com/wp-content/uploads/2016/09/1836temp.pdf. *See also* Yee v. City of Escondido, 503 U.S. 519, 532 (1992) (few mobile homes are actually moved after installation).

134. National Mobile Home Construction and Safety Standards Act of 1974, 42 U.S.C. §§ 5401 *et seq.* (2010); 24 C.F.R. pts. 3280 & 3282 (2010). The 1974 act was minimally amended in 1980, in 2000 by the Manufactured Housing Improvement Act of 2000, Pub. L. No. 106-569, 114 Stat. 2944 (2000), and in 2008 by the addition of the Manufactured Home Dispute Resolution Program found at 72 Fed. Reg. 27,222 (West 2010). Manufacturers may exclude "modular homes" from coverage by the federal standards by making a certification. 24 C.F.R. § 3282.12 (West 2010). Building standards for manufactured housing were subjected to federal regulation in part to establish "practical,

ily through approved states and private third parties.[135] When HUD standards apply, they preempt additional state or local building code standards governing the same components or standards.[136] Some states and localities impose additional requirements, particularly on mobile home parks, and especially where government subsidies are involved.[137]

There has been a general trend toward greater public acceptance, but suspicions about safety and the neighborhood effects of manufactured housing persist.[138] And, in the wake of the Katrina disaster, two safety issues have received media attention: (1) the safety of manufactured housing in hurricanes and (2) unhealthy mobile homes provided by the Federal Emergency Management Agency (FEMA) to hurricane survivors.

Explicit total exclusion of all manufactured housing from a jurisdiction is rare today because most courts will invalidate such zoning ordinances as arbitrary and capricious, and thus beyond a municipality's legitimate exercise of police power.[139] But localities may still severely limit the siting of manufactured housing. Specifically, localities may seek to and actually achieve total exclusion indirectly by formally allowing manufactured housing but excluding it de facto.[140] In addition, courts will sometimes enforce private restrictive covenants that exclude mobile homes or manufactured housing from neighborhoods.[141]

Many local jurisdictions ordinances explicitly exclude mobile homes from single-family residential zones and restrict them to designated zones, sometimes called "mobile

---

uniform, and, to the extent possible, performance-based Federal construction standards for manufactured homes." 42 U.S.C. § 5401(b)(3) (West 2010). See Chapter 6, *infra*, for a discussion of building codes regulation of manufactured housing.

135. *See* 42 U.S.C. § 5422 (West 2010).

136. See Chapter 6, *infra*, for a discussion of building codes regulation of manufactured housing.

137. *Id. And see* AB 338, a 2019 California law providing for certain point of sale requirements for used mobile homes and manufactured housing.

138. *See generally* Molly A. Sellman, *Equal Treatment of Housing: A Proposed Model State Code for Manufactured Housing*, 20 URB. L. 73 (1988). Interestingly, modular construction is now being applied to build mansions. Lisa Rein, *Mansions Go Modular as Costs, Timeline Lure High-end Buyers*, WASH. POST (Mar. 4, 2010), http://onebuildinc.com/sites/default/files/OneBuild%20Article%20Washington%20Post%20Mansions%20go%20modular%20as%20costs1.pdf.

139. *Compare* Koston v. Town of Newburgh, 256 N.Y.S.2d 837 (1965) *and* Barre Mobile Home Park, Inc. v. Petersham, 592 F. Supp. 633 (D. Mass. 1984) *with* Luczynski v. Temple, 497 A.2d 211, 213 (N.J. Super. Ct. Ch. Div.1985).

140. *See, e.g.*, English v. Augusta Twp., 514 N.W.2d 172 (Mich. Ct. App. 1994); Rottman v. Waterford, 164 N.W.2d 409 (Mich. Ct. App. 1968); Tocco v. Atlas Twp., 222 N.W.2d 264 (Mich. Ct. App. 1974).

141. Courts typically apply the specific language in the restrictive covenant. Where covenants have not been updated to include the newer nomenclature, the result turns on the court's interpretation and application of the terms "mobile home" or "manufactured home." *Compare* Tucker v. Wolfe, 968 P.2d 179 (Colo. Ct. App. 1998); Frander & Frander, Inc. v. Griffen, 457 So. 2d 375 (Ala. 1984); *and* Kinchen v. Layton, 457 So. 2d 343 (Miss. 1984); *with* Aragon v. Brown, 78 P.3d 913 (N.M. App. 2003) *and* Wilcox v. Timberon Protective Ass'n, 806 P.2d 1068 (N.M. App. 1990). *See also* CAL. CIV. CODE § 714.5 (West 2010) (preventing enforcement of covenants excluding manufactured housing after 1988).

home parks,"[142] and require a rezoning or conditional use permit to establish such a park.[143] Others have adopted planning standards, for example, establishing minimum width or a specified pitched roof, that have the effect of excluding older "mobile homes" as well as some contemporary manufactured housing.[144]

Many state courts allow these types of partial exclusions when they are challenged as violations of substantive due process or equal protection or as ultra vires acts.[145] But state constitutional challenges to these restrictions sometimes succeed. Some courts have rejected these forms of explicit partial exclusion, especially since the adoption of federal construction standards and other changes in the manufactured housing industry.[146] The leading case, *Robinson Township v. Knoll*,[147] held that "the per se exclusion of mobile homes from all areas not designated as mobile home parks has no reasonable basis under the police power, and is therefore unconstitutional."[148] And in state courts that interpret their state constitutions to require localities to provide their "fair share" of affordable housing opportunities, exclusion of manufactured housing can be successfully challenged.[149]

---

142. *See* Landon Holdings, Inc. v. Grattan Twp., 667 N.W.2d 93 (Mich. Ct. App. 2003); Mack T. Anderson Ins. Agency v. Belgrade, 803 P.2d 648 (Mont. 1990). Manufactured housing can also be excluded from commercial and industrial zones. *See, e.g.*, Hohl v. Readington, 181 A.2d 150 (N.J. 1962). Another way localities achieve the same effect is to define "single-family dwelling" or "detached dwelling" in one way and "mobile home" in another. EDWARD H. ZIEGLER ET AL., RATHKOPF'S THE LAW OF ZONING AND PLANNING § 28:17 (4th ed. 2010). Where an ordinance does not expressly define "manufactured housing" or "mobile home," courts will generally find that exclusion is not contemplated. *See, e.g.*, Reed v. Zoning Hearing Bd. of West Deer Twp., 377 A.2d 1020 (Pa. Commw. Ct. 1977).

143. Clark v. City of Asheboro, 524 S.E.2d 46 (N.C. Ct. App. 1999); Jensen's Inc. v. City of Dover, 547 A.2d 277, 282 (N.H. 1988).

144. *See, e.g.*, Georgia Manufactured Hous. Ass'n v. Spalding Cnty., 148 F.3d 1304 (11th Cir. 1998); Lex, Inc. v. Bd. of Trustees of Town of Paragon, 808 N.E.2d 104 (Ind. Ct. App. 2004); Bunker Hill Twp. v. Goodnoe, 337 N.W.2d 27 (Mich. Ct. App. 1983); Mobile Home City of Chattanooga v. Hamilton Cnty., 552 S.W.2d 86 (Tenn. Ct. App. 1976).

145. **Florida:** Grant v. County of Seminole, 817 F.2d 731, 736 (11th Cir. 1987); **Georgia:** King v. City of Bainbridge, 577 S.E.2d 772, 775 (Ga. 2003); **Idaho:** City of Lewiston v. Knieriem, 685 P.2d 821, 825 (Idaho 1984); **Illinois:** Clark v. County of Winnebago, 817 F.2d 407, 409 (7th Cir. 1987); **Kentucky:** McCollum v. City of Berea, 53 S.W.3d 106, 112 (Ct. App. Ky. 2000); **Michigan:** Gackler Land Co. v. Yankee Springs Twp., 359 N.W.2d 226, 228–29 (Ct. App. Mich. 1984), *aff'd*, 427 Mich. 562, 398 N.W.2d 393 (1986); **Montana:** Mack T. Anderson Ins. Agency v. City of Belgrade, 803 P.2d 648, 652 (S.C. Mt. 1990); **North Carolina:** Duggins v. Town of Walnut Cove, 306 S.E.2d 186 (N.C. Ct. App. 1983); **South Carolina:** Bibco Corp. v. City of Sumter, 504 S.E.2d 112, 117 (S.C. Ct. App. 1998); **Tennessee:** Mobile Home City of Chattanooga v. Hamilton County, 552 S.W.2d 86, 89 (Tenn. Ct. App. 1976); **Texas:** City of Brookside Village v. Comeau, 633 S.W.2d 790, 793–94 (Tex. 1982); **West Virginia:** Town of Stonewood v. Bell, 270 S.E.2d 787, 791 (Sup. Ct. App. W. Va.1980).

146. *See, e.g.*, Geiger v. Zoning Hearing Bd. of Twp. of Whitehall, 507 A.2d 361, 365 (Pa. 1986); Brown v. Dougherty Cnty., 300 S.E.2d 509 (Ga. 1983). *See also In re* Appeal of Shore, 573 A.2d 1011 (Pa. 1990); Petition of Carpenter v. City of Petal, 699 So. 2d 928, 934 (Miss. 1997).

147. 302 N.W.2d 146 (Mich. 1981).

148. *Id.* at 149.

149. *See, e.g.*, S. Burlington Cnty. NAACP v. Twp. of Mount Laurel, 456 A.2d 390, 450 (1983); Berenson v. New Castle, 341 N.E.2d 236 (N.Y. 1975); Surrick v. Zoning Hearing Bd. of Upper Providence Twp., 382 A.2d 105 (Pa. 1977); *In re* Appeal of Shore, 496 A.2d 876. *But see* Town of Pompey v. Parker, 385 N.Y.S.2d 959 (N.Y. App. Div. 1976).

However, without a separate statutory basis, generally courts will not require localities to afford manufactured housing "equal" treatment with traditional site-built housing.[150]

Some local jurisdictions allow manufactured housing on single lots in some residential districts outside of designated mobile home parks but require a rezoning or a special use or conditional use permit.[151] Most state courts uphold such permit requirements against prima facie constitutional challenges because they are typically based upon permissible objectives, such as promoting compatibility with traditional site-built housing or protecting property values.[152] Courts have upheld the application of conditional use permit requirements and accompanying regulations to deny permits to developers,[153] but they have also rejected unreasonable conditions[154] and mandated approvals.[155]

At least 20 states have adopted statutes attempting to promote the development of manufactured housing (or to protect it from discrimination) outside of mobile home parks.[156] Some mandate localities to include consideration of manufactured housing in

---

150. As the *Robinson Township* court stated, "[A] municipality need not permit all mobile homes, regardless of size, appearance, quality of manufacture or manner of on-site installation, to be placed in all residential neighborhoods." *Robinson Twp.*, 302 N.W.2d at 149. Zoning boards may exclude a home "if it fails to satisfy reasonable standards designed to assure favorable comparison of mobile homes with site-built housing which would be permitted on the site, and not merely because it is a mobile home." *Id.*

151. *See, e.g.*, Bach v. County of St. Clair, 576 N.E.2d 1236 (Ill. App. 1991).

152. *But see* Gackler Land Co. v. Yankee Springs Twp., 359 N.W.2d 226, 228–29 (Mich. Ct. App. 1984), *aff'd*, 398 N.W.2d 393 (1986); Chesterfield v. Brooks, 489 A.2d 600 (N.H. 1985); Bach v. County of St. Clair, 576 N.E.2d 1236 (Ill. App. 1991).

153. *See* Windy Point Partners, L.L.C. v. Boone Cnty., 100 S.W.3d 821 (Mo. Ct. App. 2003); Rolling Pines Ltd. P'ship v. City of Little Rock, 40 S.W.3d 828 (Ark. Ct. App. 2001); Crystal Forest Assocs., LP v. Buckingham Twp. Supervisors, 872 A.2d 206 (Pa. Commw. 2005); Town of Iva *ex rel.* Zoning Adm'r v. Holley, 649 S.E.2d 108 (S.C. App. 2007).

154. *See* Duggan v. Cook Cnty., 324 N.E.2d 406 (Ill. 1975) in conjunction with Bd. of Educ. v. Surety Developers, Inc., 347 N.E.2d 149 (Ill. 1975); Bach v. Cnty. of St. Clair, 576 N.E.2d 1236 (Ill. App. 1991).

155. Zajac v. Zoning Hearing Bd., 398 A.2d 244 (Pa. Commw. Ct. 1979).

156. *See* S. Mark White, *State and Federal Planning Legislation and Manufactured Housing: New Opportunities for Affordable, Single-Family Shelter*, 28 URB. LAW. 263, 266 n.17 (1996). White notes four types of state anti-discrimination legislation in decreasing order of protection: (1) accommodation, (2) equal treatment, (3) residential districting, and (4) prohibitions against complete exclusion. *Id.* at 270–71. The Manufactured Housing Institute website lists over 30 states with statutes governing mobile homes, ranging from very inclusive and expansive language to a brief sentence on a specific component of zoning. *See* http://www.manufacturedhousing.org/lib/showtemp_detail01 .asp?id=231&cat=3 (last accessed Feb. 28, 2020). *See also* Five C's, Inc. v. Cnty. of Pasquotank, 672 S.E.2d 737 (N.C. App. 2009) (held that N.C. GEN. STAT. § 160A-383.1 preempts municipalities from enacting regulations regarding the siting of manufactured and mobile homes in a manner inconsistent with state law). Note that these statutes do not necessarily promote the establishment of traditional "mobile home parks." New Jersey's Affordable Housing Act of 1983 had "the avowed purpose of promoting the use of manufactured homes." Luczynski v. Temple, 497 A.2d 211, 214 (N.J. Super. Ct. 1985).

comprehensive planning.[157] Courts have applied these provisions to provide some protection.[158] A leading case is *In re Lunde*,[159] in which Vermont's Supreme Court held that a regulation restricting mobile homes to mobile home parks violated 24 Vt. Stat. Ann. § 4406(4)(A), which called for equal treatment of housing.[160] Several other state courts have followed *Lunde*.[161] As applied, these statutes do not always enable the siting of manufactured housing, in part because they often allow localities to apply planning standards that are easily met by typical site-built single-family housing but not by manufactured homes, as long as they do so consistently.[162]

In contemporary urban and suburban installations of manufactured homes, the homeowner typically also owns the lot.[163] In contrast, previous installations, especially of mobile homes, involved the homeowner adding a single manufactured unit to a parcel with an existing conventional unit or placing the manufactured home in a land-lease community. These latter "homeowners" are vulnerable to the landowner's decision to sell the land for redevelopment or make other decisions forcing difficult (or impossible) relocation. In response, some states have adopted statutes providing these mobile homeowners protection akin to landlord-tenant laws[164] or adopted funding programs and other measures to assist them in relocating to another park.[165] However, these protections have received mixed receptions from courts.[166]

---

157. New Jersey, Oregon, California, and Florida are the leaders. White, *supra* note 156, at 286–88. For example, California's housing element law requires localities to identify adequate development sites for factory-built housing and mobile homes. Cal. Gov. Code § 65583(c)(1)(A) (West 2020). *See also* Or. Rev. Stat. § 197.307(5) (West 2020) and Wash. Rev. Code § 36.70A.070(2)(c) (West 2020).

158. *See, e.g.*, City of Freeport v. Vandergrifft, 26 S.W.3d 680 (Tex. Ct. App. 2000).

159. 688 A.2d 1312 (Vt. 1997).

160. *Id.* at 1313. The provision of the statute interpreted by the court was 24 Vt. Stat. Ann. § 4406(4)(A). *Note:* 2003, Adj. Sess., No. 115, § 119, repealed former § 4406(4)(A), which prior thereto provided in pertinent part: "no zoning regulation shall have the effect of excluding mobile homes, modular housing, or other forms of prefabricated housing from the municipality, except on the same terms and conditions as conventional housing is excluded."

161. *See, e.g.*, Bangs v. Wells, 760 A.2d 632, 638 (Me. 2000); Bahl v. City of Asbury, 656 N.W.2d 336, 345 (Iowa 2002); Cnty. of Wright v. Kennedy, 415 N.W.2d 728 (Minn. Ct. App. 1987).

162. *See, e.g.*, Colo. Rev. Stat. § 31-23-301(5)(b) (West 2010); Jensen's Inc. v. City of Dover, 547 A.2d 277, 282 (N.H. 1988).

163. *See* note 112, *supra*. But the proportions vary widely by state.

164. *See* Manufactured Housing Cmtys. of Wash. v. State of Wash., 13 P.3d 183, 224–26 (Wash. 2000) (providing list of 36 states providing such protection) (abrogated by *Chong Yim v. City of Seattle*, 194 Wash.2d 651 (2019), but list still generally valid. Some statutes are no longer in force, e.g. Mont. Code. Ann. § 70-24-436(2), *repealed* Sec. 52, Ch. 267, L. 2007. For more on relocation and replacement requirements, see Chapter 16, *infra*.

165. *See, e.g.*, Cal. Gov. Code § 66427.4–66427.5 (West 2019); Minn. Stat. § 327C.095 (West 2019).

166. *Compare* Arcadia Dev. Corp. v. City of Bloomington, 552 N.W.2d 281 (1996) and Greenfield Country Estates Tenants Ass'n v. Deep, 666 N.E.2d 988 (Mass. 1996) *with* Guimont v. Clarke, 854 P.2d 1 (Wash. 1993); Manufactured Housing Cmtys. v. State, 13 P.3d 183 (Wash. 2000).

IV. FARMWORKER HOUSING

This section will consider the development of housing for "migrant workers" and "seasonal workers"[167] (hereinafter "farmworkers"). Historically, farmworkers have endured dreadful housing conditions in the United States and received very little legal protection, in part because so many farmworkers are racial minorities and/or undocumented.[168] In addition to discrimination, farmworkers face an inadequate supply of housing that is often unaffordable and plagued by substandard physical conditions, overcrowding, and unique environmental hazards. Recent research has documented the health hazards that farmworkers face.[169] Hurricanes and other natural disasters that affect agricultural areas also negatively impact migrant workers and their housing. More recently, farmworker housing in California is threatened by annual wildfires.[170]

---

167. According to the Migrant and Seasonal Agricultural Worker Protection Act (MSPA), a "migrant agricultural worker" is "an individual who is employed in agricultural employment of a seasonal or temporary nature, and who is required to be absent overnight from his permanent place of residence," 29 U.S.C. § 1802(8)(A), and a "seasonal agricultural worker" is "an individual who is employed in agricultural employment of a seasonal or temporary nature and is not required to be absent from his permanent place of residence," 29 U.S.C. § 1802(10)(A). In 2003, estimates of seasonal workers and their dependents alone ranged from 1.9 million to 4 million. Housing Assistance Council, Migrant and Seasonal Farmworker Housing 1 (Sept. 2003).

168. *See generally* Housing Assistance Council, Taking Stock: Rural People, Poverty, and Housing at the Turn of the 21st Century (2012), http://www.ruraldataportal.org /docs/HAC_Taking-Stock-Full.pdf (last accessed Dec. 6, 2021); Housing Assistance Council, No Refuge From the Fields: Findings From a Survey of Farmworker Housing Conditions in the United States (2001), https://ruralhome.org/wp-content/uploads/storage/documents /norefuge.pdf (last accessed Dec. 6, 2021); Don Villarejo, *The Challenge of Housing California's Hired Farm Laborers*, https://www.prrac.org/projects/fair_housing_commission/los_angeles /TheChallenge-HousingCAhiredFarmLaborers-DVillarejo.pdf. The Housing Assistance Council (www.ruralhome.org) is the leading national advocate for rural housing, including farmworker housing. Farmworkers are a subset of the rural population that share many housing problems. *See generally* Housing Assistance Council, Race, Place, and Housing: Housing Conditions in Rural Minority Counties (2004), https://ruralhome.org/reports/race-place-and-housing-housing-condi tions-in-rural-minority-counties/ (last accessed Dec. 6, 2021); Housing in Rural America: Building Affordable and Inclusive Communities (Joseph N. Belden & Robert J. Wiener eds., Sage Publ'ns 1999).

169. *See* Sara A. Quandt et al., *Farmworker Housing in the United States and Its Impact on Health* (Farmworker Housing Quality and Health: A Transdisciplinary Conference, August 2015) https://journals.sagepub.com/doi/pdf/10.1177/1048291115601053; *see also* Farmworker Justice, Unfinished Harvest: The Agricultural Worker Protection Act at 30 (2013), https://www .farmworkerjustice.org/sites/default/files/FarmworkerJusticeUnfinishedHarvest.pdf (documenting physical ailments, sleep problems, and mental health issues associated with farmworker housing due to exposure to chemicals, mold, pests, pesticides, allergens, and lack of proper air conditioning/ ventilation).

170. Anna Maria Barry-Jester, *California Wildfires Threaten Farmworkers' Health, Wages and Housing*, Kaiser Health News (Oct. 28, 2019), https://khn.org/news/farmworkers-face-daunting -health-risks-in-californias-wildfires/.

The private housing market has not served the full spectrum of farmworker housing needs because of their low incomes[171] and the itinerancy of some farmworkers.[172] Housing provided by employers or labor contractors, for example, in migrant labor camps, has often been substandard, accompanied by exploitative terms, a failure to recognize farmworkers as "tenants,"[173] and inadequate health and safety standards. "Mutual self-help" or "sweat equity" housing has been an important strategy for providing farmworkers with homeownership opportunities.[174] Some federal and state subsidies are available for state-provided housing[175] and private nonprofit housing for farmworkers,[176] but never in sufficient quanti-

---

171. For data on the high poverty rates of migrant workers, see *Housing in Rural America* (Housing Assistance Council, Oct. 2010), http://ruralhome.org/storage/documents/ts2010/ts-report/ts10 _rural_housing.pdf (on file with author).

172. *See* Sara A. Quandt, Carol Brooke, & Kathleen Fagan, *Farmworker Housing in the United States and Its Impact on Health*, 25(3) New Solutions 263–86 (2015); Don Villarejo, *The Status of Farm Labor Housing and the Health of Workers*, Cal. Inst. for Rural Studies (Mar. 6, 2015), https://latinocaucus.legislature.ca.gov/sites/latinocaucus.legislature.ca.gov/files/housing-statu s_health_us_hired-farm-workers_2015.pdf.

The wide variety of farmworkers' housing needs (single workers; large families; single-family and multifamily; short-term and permanent) also present a challenge to the private market. Many farmworkers live in manufactured housing, trailers, or recreational vehicles. *See supra*, Section III on manufactured housing. See generally publications of Rural Community Assistance Corporation, a nonprofit organization that provides training, technical and financial resources and advocacy to rural communities, https://www.rcac.org/.

173. State courts take different approaches on the issue of whether farmworkers living in employer-supplied housing are "tenants" for purposes of a state's landlord tenant laws. *See* Sherylle Gordon, Note, *Michigan Housing Law Should Apply to Migrant Farm Workers*, 41 Wayne L. Rev. 1849, 1850–53 (1995). Some courts have held farmworkers living on employer-supplied housing are eligible for protection under the federal Fair Housing Act and state equivalents. *See, e.g.*, Villegas v. Sandy Farms, Inc., 929 F. Supp. 1324 (D. Or. 1996); Rivcom Corp. v. Agric. Labor Relations Bd., 34 Cal. 3d 743 (1983); S.P. Growers Ass'n v. Rodriguez, 17 Cal. 3d 719 (1976). *See also* additional employee housing protections in Cal. Health & Safety Code §§ 17031.5 and 17031.7 (West 2010).

174. This form of housing is usually organized by a nonprofit organization and often utilizes federal or state subsidies. *See Creating the Village: How Mutual Self-Help Housing Builds Community* (Housing Assistance Council 2005), https://www.virtualcap.org/downloads/US/US_USDA_Self _Help_Housing_Creating_the_Village.pdf (last accessed Dec. 6, 2021); USDA's Mutual Self-Help Housing Technical Assistance Grants program, https://www.rd.usda.gov/programs-services/mutual -self-help-housing-technical-assistance-grants (providing information about the program including the purpose, eligibility, terms, and standards).

175. *See* U.S. Dep't of Agric.'s Rural Information Center at https://www.nal.usda.gov/ric. *See also* Housing Assistance Council (www.ruralhome.org).

176. For federal programs, *see* Housing Assistance Council, A Guide to Federal Housing and Community Development Programs for Small Towns and Rural Areas (2003), https://docplayer.net/9115710-Housing-assistance-council-a-guide-to-federal-housing-and-com munity-development-programs-for-small-towns-and-rural-areas.html (last accessed Dec. 6, 2021). California has been a leader in providing state programs. *See, e.g.*, CA Housing and Community Development website page on farmworker programs at https://www.hcd.ca.gov/policy-research /specific-policy-areas/farmworkers.shtml; Office of Migrant Services (OMS) Program, Cal. Health & Safety Code §§ 50712.5 *et seq.* (West 2010) (funding migrant farm labor centers); Cal. Gov. Code § 25213.2 (West 2010) (enabling formation of "county service area" in County of Napa with authority to levy assessment on vineyards to help fund the development and maintenance of farmworker housing). Minnesota allows for loans or grants for residential housing for migrant farmworkers through its housing trust fund account. Minn. Stat. Ann. § 462A.201 (West 2010).

ties to meet the needs. Cooperative housing appears to be a promising alternative.[177] And affordable construction models have been developed and tested.[178]

Recently, there have been efforts by some states to improve farmworker housing, including by tightening up regulations. And, there have been developments that have completely modernized farmworker housing. Washington, Oregon, and California have created modern buildings to house seasonal farmworkers that are akin to suburban housing.[179] California has even gone so far as to create affordable and energy efficient farmworker housing.[180] Yet, there still exist farms where farmworkers live out of their cars, in shacks that farmworkers have built, in tents, and even without any shelter at all in sleeping bags.[181]

There is also a troubling trend in which farmworker housing for predominantly H2A visa holders offers better living conditions than housing for those migrant farmworkers who have no legal status.[182] Furthermore, there is a discrepancy between those migrant

---

177. *See* CAL. COALITION FOR RURAL HOUSING, CALIFORNIA'S FARMWORKER HOUSING COOPERATIVES: LESSONS ON FARMWORKER OWNERSHIP AND MANAGEMENT 59 (2002). *And see* Vinit Mukhija & David R. Mason, Resident-Owned, Informal Mobile Home Communities in Rural California: The Case of Rancho Don Antonio, Coachella Valley, Housing Policy Debate 25(1):179–94 (August 2014) (describing small, resident-owned, informal mobile home communities, called "polancos" (after the name of the legislator who sponsored the bill creating a new program) and discussing whether a new housing model based on the collectively owned polancos is possible).

178. *See Prototype Home Addresses Migrant Housing Shortage*, RESEARCH WORKS 6–7 (HUD User, Apr. 2007).

179. *See* U.S. DEP'T OF HOUSING AND URBAN DEVELOPMENT, AFFORDABLE HOUSING AND SERVICES FOR FARMWORKERS FAMILIES IN OREGON (2013), https://www.huduser.gov/portal/pdredge /pdr_edge_inpractice_090913.html; *see also* U.S. DEP'T OF HOUSING AND URBAN DEVELOPMENT, AFFORDABLE HOUSING IN CENTRAL WASHINGTON STATE FOR SEASONAL AGRICULTURAL WORKERS (2013), https://www.huduser.gov/portal/pdredge/pdr-edge-inpractice-102416.html.

180. A development called Mutual Housing at Spring Lake in Woodland, California, is the first of its kind. The project has solar panels and other energy efficient utilities such that it uses as much electricity as it produces in a year. As a result, the project received the U.S. Department of Energy's Zero Energy Ready Home certification. *See* U.S. DEP'T OF HOUSING AND URBAN DEVELOPMENT, ZERO NET ENERGY AFFORDABLE HOUSING: HOME FOR AGRICULTURAL WORKERS IN WOODLAND, CALIFORNIA (2015), https://www.huduser.gov/portal/pdredge/pdr-edge-inpractice-012516.html.

181. *See* SARA A. QUANDT ET AL., *Farmworker Housing in the United States and Its Impact on Health* (Farmworker Housing Quality and Health: A Transdisciplinary Conference, Aug. 2015), https://journals.sagepub.com/doi/pdf/10.1177/1048291115601053; *see also* TERESA WILTZ, *States Struggle to Provide Housing for Migrant Farmworkers*, PEW (May 2016), https://www.pewtrusts .org/en/research-and-analysis/blogs/stateline/2016/05/02/struggle-to-provide-housing-for-migrant -farmworkers.

182. *See* QUIRINA M. VALLEJOS ET AL., *Migrant Farmworkers' Housing Conditions Across an Agricultural Season in North Carolina*, AM. J. INDUSTRIAL MED. (Feb. 2011), https://onlinelibrary .wiley.com/doi/epdf/10.1002/ajim.20945; *see also* HUMAN RIGHTS WATCH, FIELDS OF PERIL, CHILD LABOR IN US AGRICULTURE (2010), https://www.hrw.org/report/2010/05/05/fields-peril/child -labor-us-agriculture (finding those working without legal status on farms were found to have, "over two times greater odds of having inadequate facilities compared to camps with residents who have H2A visas. . . . A multivariate model shows that camps with no residents who had an H2A visa were over three times more likely to have inadequate facilities than camps that included residents with an H2A visa."). *See also* S.B. 5438, 66th Leg., 2019-2020 Reg. Sess. (Wa. 2019) (creating an office of oversight specifically to monitor farmworker housing conditions, as well as health and safety, and labor conditions, but only specifically aimed at monitoring farms that currently utilize the H-2A visa program to acquire farmworkers).

farmworkers who speak an indigenous language and those who do not.[183] And, camps with female and child residents were found to be "more likely to be severely substandard than those that did not have any female or child residents."[184] Overall, it appears migrant workers without legal status are subject to harsher conditions as employers take advantage of them by providing inadequate living quarters. Many of those migrant workers are fearful to speak up due to their legal status within the United States. Some states have taken on initiatives to avoid this exploitation, but other states have left migrant workers to the mercy of their employers and to the federal government. Immigration and Customs Enforcement (ICE) raids on farmworker housing have become common. This forces many undocumented migrant workers to seek housing off the farm within urban areas, which in turn impacts the affordability of housing there. In 2019, two bills were introduced in Congress that could remedy these discrepancies in treatment of farmworkers with H2A visas and those without, but neither bill has been enacted.[185]

In addition to meeting the critical housing needs of farmworkers, additional migrant farmworker housing would ease the burden on rural housing, as farmworkers wouldn't have to resort to finding housing in nearby cities or localities, competing with everyone else in the market. Yet, farmworker housing is challenging to develop and maintain. Developers of farmworker housing face funding limitations, a lack of adequate infrastructure, potentially expensive environmental remediation, exclusionary zoning,[186] and local opposition to land-use approvals.[187] Once built, farmworker housing is subject to particular code and maintenance requirements.[188]

---

183. *See* QUIRINA M. VALLEJOS ET AL., *supra* note 182 ("Camps with residents who spoke an indigenous language were more likely to be severely substandard than those that did not have any indigenous language speakers.").

184. *Id.*

185. S. 175, 116th Cong. (2019) This bill, named the "Agricultural Worker Program Act of 2019," would effectively give legal status to undocumented farmworkers who have worked 100 days in the past two years. This legal status would be known as a "blue card." Those who maintain blue card status for either three to five years would then be eligible to adjust status to lawful permanent resident otherwise known as a green card. H.R. 5038, 116th Cong. (2019) known as the "Farm Workforce Modernization Act of 2019." This bill would give temporary status to certified agricultural workers. In order to qualify for certified agricultural worker status workers must have worked 1,035 hours of agricultural labor in the two years prior to November 12, 2019, they need to not be inadmissible for any other reason, and they must have continuously resided in the United States since November 12, 2017. This bill would also create the Housing Preservation and Revitalization Program, which would provide financial assistance for off farm labor housing and provide for funding to the U.S. Department of Agriculture's Rural Housing program.

186. *See also* Chapter 3, *supra*, for discussion of exclusionary zoning.

187. *See* ENCYCLOPEDIA OF HOUSING, 2d edition, Andrew T. Carswell, ed., 2012. ("Farmworker Housing" entry by Susan Peck); HOUSING ASSISTANCE COUNCIL, FAIR HOUSING, THE ZONING PROCESS, AND LAND USE POLITICS IN RURAL AREAS (1988); HOUSING ASSISTANCE COUNCIL, OVERCOMING EXCLUSION IN RURAL COMMUNITIES: NIMBY CASE STUDIES (1994). This section will not address the unique issues regarding conflicts with code setting and enforcement raised by "colonias" in Texas and other border states. To learn more on that topic, see HOUSING ASSISTANCE COUNCIL, THE BORDER COLONIAS REGION: CHALLENGES AND INNOVATIVE APPROACHES TO EFFECTIVE COMMUNITY DEVELOPMENT (1998).

188. This section will discuss code and maintenance requirements only briefly and focus on the other challenges to development. See Chapter 6, *infra*, for a discussion of building and housing codes, including concerning farmworker housing.

The federal government, some state governments, and some localities have acted to address these challenges. For example, in 1983, Congress enacted the Migrant and Seasonal Agricultural Worker Protection Act (MSPA),[189] which regulates health and safety requirements of housing provided for migrant workers[190] and provides enforcement provisions, including a private right of action.[191] The act provides that "each person who owns or controls a facility or real property which is used as housing for migrant agricultural workers shall be responsible for ensuring that the facility or real property complies with substantive Federal and State safety and health standards applicable to that housing."[192] The MSPA has been interpreted broadly to apply to anyone supplying any form of housing to farmworkers. Courts have validated farmworker housing rights under the MSPA concerning the failure of responsible federal agencies to implement the statute,[193] legal standards of liability for farm owners,[194] the scope of liability of growers,[195] and liabilities of farm owners.[196] Some farm owners and labor contractors (who serve as intermediaries between farm owners and farmworkers) continue to try to evade the MSPA requirements by exploiting its exceptions.[197] Congress intended the MSPA to supplement state law, not to preempt it.[198] Most states have enacted statutes regulating health and safety standards for farmworker housing that offer varying degrees of protection.[199] California's law ranks among the strongest.[200]

In 2012, the U.S. Department of Labor Office of Foreign Labor Certification required that employers who utilize the H2A agricultural visa who have employees who cannot "reasonably return to their permanent residence" must provide free farmworker housing.[201]

---

189. 29 U.S.C. §§ 1801–1872.

190. *Id.* § 1823.

191. *Id.* §§ 1851–1856.

192. *Id.* § 1823(a); 29 C.F.R. §§ 500.130–500.134.

193. Roman v. Korson, 918 F. Supp. 1108, 1113 (W.D. Mich. 1995); Arce-Mendez v. Eagle Produce P'ship, 2008 WL 659812 (D. Ariz. Mar. 6, 2008) (unpublished decision).

194. Conlan v. U.S. Dep't of Labor, 76 F.3d 271 (9th Cir. 1996).

195. Howard v. Malcolm, 852 F.2d 101, 106 (4th Cir. 1988).

196. *See, e.g.*, Sanchez v. Overmyer, 845 F. Supp. 1183 (N.D. Ohio 1993) (liability); Sanchez v. Overmyer, 891 F. Supp. 1253, 1261 (N.D. Ohio 1995) (damages).

197. Parada v. MJ's Labor Services, Inc., 2019 WL 4145224 (D. Or. 2019) (buildings operated by farm labor contractors did not qualify for the "innkeeper exception," because they had no signs, no website, accepted only cash payments, and supplied no towels); Fanette v. Steven Davis Farms, LLC, 28 F. Supp. 3d 1243 (N.D. Fla. 2014) (farmers who use the services of farm labor contractors are "employers" subject to MSPA requirements).

198. 29 U.S.C. § 1871.

199. *See* Fla. Stat. Ann. § 381.0086 (West 2010); Md. Code Ann., Lab. & Empl. § 7-401 (West 2010); Mich. Comp. Laws §§ 333.12411–333.12412 (West 2010); N.J. Stat. Ann. § 34:9A-20 to 34:9A-36 (West 2010); N.C. Gen. Stat. §§ 95-222 to 95-229 (West 2010); Ohio Rev. Code Ann. § 3733.42 (West 2010); Ohio Admin. Code § 3701-33 (West 2010); 43 Pa. Const. Stat. Ann. §§ 1301.301–1301.308 (West 2010); V.T.C.A., Gov't Code §§ 2306.921–2306.933 (West 2010); Va. Code Ann. §§ 32.1-203 to 32.1-211 (West 2010); Wash. Rev. Code §§ 70.114A.010 to 70.114A.901 (West 2010).

200. Cal. Health & Safety Code §§ 17000, *et seq.* (West 2010) and implementing regulations in Cal. Admin. Code, tit. 25, §§ 600 *et seq.* (West 2010). *See also* Colon v. Tedesco, 311 A.2d 393 (N.J. Super. Ct. Law Div. 1973).

201. *See* U.S. Department of Labor, Employment and Training Administration, Office of Foreign Labor Certification, Employer Guide to Participation in the H-2A Temporary

Also, in 2012, the U.S. Department of Agriculture Office of Rural Development expanded the availability of grants and loans for the development of farmworker housing.[202] In 2014, the USDA Office of Rural Development announced $29 million in loans and grants to create more affordable farmworker housing.[203] And, in 2016, the U.S. Department of Agriculture, Office of Rural Development announced $26 million dollars in funding for the development of affordable housing.[204]

In 2019, in response to California's housing shortage that has now spread to rural communities, California enacted Assembly Bill 1783. This law increased the housing supply for farmworkers, notably migrant farmworkers, by streamlining and creating incentives for the production of new units to house farmworkers on farmland where they work.[205]

In the state of Washington, Yakima County got creative with its farmworker housing. The county recognized that because farm work is seasonal (typically beginning in March/April and ending in October/November), the housing dedicated for farmworkers sits dormant through the winter months. So, the county made use of the underutilized housing as temporary housing for homeless families or families at risk of homelessness through the coldest months of the year. On average it takes a homeless family six months to find new housing, thus the county, after allocating additional resources, is killing two birds with one stone.[206]

There has also been a recent push to not only modernize the quality of farmworker housing but to also create an enriching community experience. Rather than simply serving nomadic farmworkers who come and go with the season, programs have sprung up in these new affordable farmworker housing communities to provide services and to build a

---

AGRICULTURAL PROGRAM (2012), https://www.foreignlaborcert.doleta.gov/pdf/h-2a_employer _handbook.pdf.

202. *See* U.S. DEPARTMENT OF AGRICULTURE, AGRICULTURE SECRETARY VILSACK ANNOUNCES AVAILABILITY OF LOANS AND GRANTS TO IMPROVE HOUSING FOR FARMWORKERS (2012), https://www .usda.gov/media/press-releases/2012/07/18/agriculture-secretary-vilsack-announces-availability -loans-and. The program has two parts. The first part pertains to on-site farmworker housing and will provide grants and loans to eligible groups such as housing authorities, state and local governments, nonprofit organization, etc. The second part will provide rental assistance to entities that create off-farm housing. The rental assistance will come in the form of paying the difference between the farm workers income (30 percent) and the monthly rent. The program provides that the farmworker housing must be operated on a nonprofit basis, and also gives priority to projects that are energy efficient and will provide energy via geothermal, solar panels, and/or wind turbines.

203. *See* U.S. DEPARTMENT OF AGRICULTURE, USDA ANNOUNCES $29 MILLION TO PROVIDE HOUSING FOR FARMWORKERS (2014), https://www.rd.usda.gov/newsroom/news-release/usda -announces-29-million-provide-housing-farmworkers-1.

204. *See* U.S. DEPARTMENT OF AGRICULTURE, USDA AWARDS MORE THAN $26 MILLION FOR AFFORDABLE FARMWORKER HOUSING (2016), https://www.usda.gov/media/press -releases/2016/07/13/usda-awards-more-26-million-affordable-farmworker-housing. The majority of this money went to projects in California, Florida, Texas, and Kansas.

205. *See* Louis Hansen, *New California Law Sets Path for More Farmworker Housing*, MERCURY NEWS, (Oct. 14, 2019), https://www.mercurynews.com/2019/10/14/new-law-sets-path-for -more-farmworker-housing/. *See also* A. 8419, 2019-2020 Reg. Sess. (NY. 2019) (ensures sanitary codes for all farmworker housing regardless of the number of occupants).

206. *See* U.S. DEP'T OF HOUSING AND URBAN DEVELOPMENT, YAKIMA COUNTY, WASHINGTON: CREATIVE USE OF FARMWORKER HOUSING AIDS HOMELESS FAMILIES (2017), https://www.huduser .gov/portal/casestudies/study-052819.html.

community. For example, some communities are providing classes and events on topics such as English as a second language, computer literacy, legal workshops, financial planning, and first-time home-buyer workshops.[207] For example, the Corporation for Better Housing, a nonprofit in California, used grant money to create affordable, energy-efficient farmworker housing/communities that it manages off-farm.[208]

Farmworker housing has long been subject to local opposition and other attempts to exclude it through localities' exercise of their planning and zoning power.[209] In response, some states enacted statutes to promote and protect the development of farmworker housing. These measures have included requirements to include farmworkers' housing needs in mandatory land-use planning[210] and to promote farmworker housing development within rural areas[211] and on agriculturally zoned land.[212] Other laws provide farmworker developments some protection against local opposition, including by requiring localities to treat employee housing of six or fewer units as single-family residences,[213] by limiting localities' discretion to deny farmworker housing proposals,[214] and by exempting some farmworker housing from review under the state environmental quality act.[215]

Farmworker housing development has also been protected against discriminatory treatment by localities under the federal Fair Housing Act and state equivalents.[216] A California statute prohibiting housing discrimination based upon "occupation" and level of

---

207. *See* U.S. Dep't of Housing and Urban Development, Zero Net Energy Affordable Housing: Home for Agricultural Workers in Woodland, California (2015), https://www.huduser.gov/portal/pdredge/pdr-edge-inpractice-012516.html; *see also* U.S. Dep't of Housing and Urban Development, Affordable Housing Options for Farmers in Ventura County (2012), https://www.huduser.gov/portal/pdredge/pdr_edge_inpractice_050313.html.

208. Corp. For Better Housing, http://www.corpforbetterhousing.com/property-type/farmworker-communities/.

209. *See supra* note 187.

210. California's housing element law requires localities to include analysis of farmworker housing needs (Cal. Gov. Code § 65583(a)(7) (West 2010)) and to identify adequate development sites for "housing for agricultural workers" (Cal. Gov't Code § 65583(c)(1) (West 2010)), and, in some circumstances, provide zoning that permits farmworker housing use by right (Cal. Gov't Code § 65583(c)(1)(C) (West 2010)).

211. Oregon's farmworker housing law provides that "farmworker housing within the rural area of a county shall be permitted in a zone or zones in rural centers and areas committed to nonresource uses." Or. Rev. Stat. § 197.685(2) (West 2010). *See also* Or. Rev. Stat. § 197.307(1) and (3)(a) (West 2010). During v. Wash. Cnty., 34 P.3d 169 (Or. Ct. App. 2001).

212. *See, e.g.*, Cal. Gov't Code §§ 51220, *et seq.* (West 2010). The "Williamson Act" allows landowners of "agricultural preserves" to subdivide land for development of "agricultural laborer housing facilities" and directs that such use is "compatible use" within agricultural preserve. *Id.* at § 51230.2.

213. Cal. Health & Safety Code § 17021.5 (West 2010).

214. California's Housing Accountability Act, Cal. Gov't Code § 65589.5(4)(d) (West 2020), limiting localities' discretion to disapprove proposed affordable housing developments, specifically includes farmworker housing.

215. Cal. Pub. Res. Code § 21159.22 (West 2010) exempts "residential housing for agricultural employees" from California's state environmental review statute.

216. *See, e.g.*, Lauer Farms, Inc. v. Waushara Cnty. Bd. of Adjustment, 986 F. Supp. 544 (E.D. Wis. 1997); Villegas v. Sandy Farms, Inc., 929 F. Supp. 1324, 1327–28 (D. Or. 1996); Hernandez v. Ever Fresh Co., 923 F. Supp. 1305, 1307–08 (D. Or. 1996). See Chapter 3, *supra*, for more on the federal Fair Housing Act.

income has been used to protect farmworkers.[217] Finally, farm owners have successfully used pro-agricultural statutes to override local zoning in order to site farmworker housing on their own farmland.[218]

V. ACCESSORY UNITS

The term accessory dwelling unit (ADU) refers to a small, secondary housing unit on the lot of a single-family home. The accessory unit may be planned within the interior of a house, attached to the house, or detached from the house. The secondary unit can be part of the original design of the house or it may be added at a later date. The secondary unit is a complete living space that includes a full bathroom and an operable kitchen.[219] They are generally less than 1,000 square feet and are usually built in the rear of the primary dwelling, in an attic, or over a garage. They are called by many names, including accessory dwelling unit, granny flat or elder cottage, in-law unit, secondary unit, and "ohana" (Hawaiian for extended family/kin group). This form of housing is broadly supported as a form of housing by HUD, planners, smart growth advocates, affordable housing advocates, advocates for seniors, and disability rights advocates because it typically serves adult children, the elderly (including in-laws), and persons with disabilities, as well as low-income people and smaller households.[220]

Accessory units are widely viewed as having a broad potential to increase the stock of market-affordable housing. They can be "market-affordable" by virtue of their smaller size and lower building costs.[221] Some second units are income-restricted by deed restrictions.[222] They may also provide low-income households with a unique opportunity for

---

217. *See* CAL. GOV. CODE § 65008 (West 2010).

218. *See* Town of Lysander v. Hafner, 759 N.E.2d 356 (N.Y. Ct. App. 2001); Braden Trust v. Cnty. of Yuma, 69 P.3d 510 (Ariz. Ct. App. 2003). *But see* Frens Orchards, Inc. v. Dayton Township Bd., 654 N.W.2d 346 (Mich. Ct. App. 2002).

219. *See* ENCYCLOPEDIA OF HOUSING, *supra* note 187, Vol. 1 at 5 ("Accessory Dwelling Units" entry by Julia Beamish) (2d edition, Andrew T. Carswell, ed., 2012). *See also* MUN. RESEARCH & SERVS. CTR. OF WASH., ACCESSORY DWELLING UNITS IN PLAIN ENGLISH (June 2010), http://www.mrsc.org/subjects/planning/LU/accessory.aspx/.

220. *See, e.g.*, *Accessory Dwelling Units: Case Study* (U.S. Dep't of Housing & Urban Dev., June 2008), https://www.huduser.gov/portal/publications/adu.pdf; AM. PLANNING ASS'N, REGIONAL APPROACHES TO AFFORDABLE HOUSING (2003), https://www.huduser.gov/Publications/pdf/reg_aff_hsg_ch.pdf; FUNDERS' NETWORK FOR SMART GROWTH AND LIVEABLE COMMUNITIES, AGING AND SMART GROWTH: BUILDING AGE-SENSITIVE COMMUNITIES 9–11 (Dec. 2001), http://www.fundersnetwork.org/files/learn/aging_paper.pdf; Rodney L. Cobb & Scott Dvorak, Public Policy Inst., *Accessory Dwelling Units: Model State Act and Local Ordinance* (2000) (the Public Policy Institute is part of the Research Group at AARP), https://assets.aarp.org/rgcenter/consume/d17158_dwell.pdf.

221. Depending on whether they are attached or detached, accessory units "could be built for about one-third the cost of constructing a conventional rental unit." ENCYCLOPEDIA OF HOUSING, *supra* note 187, at 3.

222. *See, e.g.*, California Government Code Section 65852.26 providing that local agencies may use ordinances to allow accessory units to be sold or conveyed separately from the primary residences to a qualified buyer meets some standards. Specifically, Section 65852.26(a)(3)(D) provides: "Affordability restrictions on the sale and conveyance of the property that ensure the property will be preserved for low-income housing for 45 years for owner-occupied housing units and will be sold or resold to a qualified buyer."

homeownership because rental income from the accessory unit can subsidize the mortgage of the primary unit.[223] Some newer single-family subdivisions include second units.[224] Some public funding is available for the development of accessory units for low-income households.[225]

Studies suggest that where city zoning and planning codes are permissive, accessory units can become up to an average of 10 percent of the housing stock.[226] In addition to enabling the development of accessory units through their zoning and planning codes, cities can encourage them by providing regulatory relief,[227] technical help to property owners, loan assistance, and other assistance.[228] Making pre-approved designs available is another supportive policy that makes applying, building, and permitting accessory units easier.[229] Another strategy is to allow currently illegal accessory units to become legalized.[230] However, many cities oppose them. Typical opposition concerns include higher density, increased traffic and parking congestion, burdening of infrastructure, changing the "character" of single-family neighborhoods, purported negative effects on property values, school overcrowding, and sometimes aesthetic concerns.[231]

---

223. Alan C. Weinstein, *Essay: The Challenge of Providing Adequate Housing for the Elderly . . . Along with Everyone Else*, 11 J.L. & HEALTH 133,140–41 (1996–97).

224. Such subdivisions have been built in Livermore and Santa Rosa, California. Seattle (WA) allows for two accessory units on a single property: http://www.seattle.gov/sdci/permits/common-projects/accessory-dwelling-units.

225. For example, HAW. REV. STAT. § 201H-201 to 201H-204, 210 (West 2010) (Rental Housing Trust Fund) gives a preference to accessory units (among other forms) for funding. Some jurisdictions waive or defer various fees to encourage development of accessory units. *See, e.g.*, SANTA CRUZ, CAL. MUN. CODE § 26.16.180 (2010). Clovis (California) helps finance accessory units: https://www.calhfa.ca.gov/about/press/press-releases/2019/pr2019-04-15.htm. The California Housing Finance Agency partnered with a nonprofit called Self-Help Enterprises to help finance accessory units. Not only does this program help fund the units, it also simplifies the construction of accessory units by providing three accessory unit models.

226. Urban League of Essex Cnty. v. Twp. of Mahwah, 504 A.2d 66, 72–74 (N.J. Super. L. Div. 1984).

227. Santa Cruz, California, waives development fees if the accessory unit is made available to low-income households. Santa Cruz Municipal Code §§ 24.16.300 *et seq.*: https://www.codepublishing.com/CA/SantaCruz/#!/SantaCruz24/SantaCruz2416.html#24.16.310.

228. Infranca, *supra* note 2, at 69.

229. On July 19, 2019, Seattle Mayor Jenny A. Durkan issued an executive order to encourage the use and construction of accessory dwelling units in the city. (Executive Order 2019-04: "Actions to encourage more affordable accessory dwelling units throughout Seattle" (2019). The order included a directive for the Seattle Department of Construction and Inspections (SDCI) to facilitate detached accessory dwelling units (DADUs). SDCI planned to hire architects to create designs that are at low-cost and can be built quickly.).

230. Margaret F. Brinig & Nicole Stelle Garnett, *A Room of One's Own? Accessory Dwelling Unit Reforms and Local Parochialism*, 45 URB. LAW. 519, 547 (2013). Illegal ADUs lead to unsafe and deplorable living conditions due to the lack of regulation. *Id.* at 548.

231. Sarah H. Gottlieb, *Florida's Accessory Dwelling Unit Laws: Mitigating Florida's Housing Woes through State-Encouraged Expansion of ADU Permitting* 46 STETSON L. REV. 627, 644–45 (2017). PATRICK H. HARE PLANNING & DESIGN, ACCESSORY UNITS: THE STATE OF THE ART: REPORT 1, SUMMARY OF EXPERIENCE 17–25 (Dec. 1989).

Apart from the threshold issue of defining whether a dwelling space is "accessory" or not,[232] exclusionary zoning and exacting planning standards are the primary legal issues limiting the development of accessory units.

Many local jurisdictions adopt a very restrictive approach to accessory units in single-family zoned neighborhoods, which is the primary desired location.[233] Some jurisdictions exclude them from single-family zones altogether.[234] Possibly as a result, many accessory units are constructed illegally—without permits and sometimes in violation of building codes.[235]

If accessory units are allowed, localities typically require a conditional or special use permit (and its attendant public hearing), site plan review, or even a zoning amendment.[236] In addition, accessory apartments are often subject to restrictive planning and design requirements[237] and other conditions, for example, limiting or preferring use by a particular population.[238]

---

232. The issue is when is a dwelling "accessory" to a primary dwelling, typically meaning that the use is "customary and subordinate to primary use," in contrast to being a "separate dwelling" for which multifamily zoning would normally be required. Trent v. City of Pittsburg, 619 P.2d 1171 (Kan. Ct. App. 1980); Twp. of Randolph v. Lamprecht, 542 A.2d 36 (N.J. Super. App. Div. 1988).

233. Edward H. Ziegler, Jr., *The Twilight of Single-Family Zoning*, 3 J. Envtl. L. 161, 195 (1983).

234. "A zoning amendment is often needed to permit accessory units, and . . . the zoning process can be used to severely limit the installation of accessory units." Patrick Hare, *Accessory Apartments for Today's Communities*, *in* 1 Planning Comm'rs J. 14 (1991).

235. Some cities have adopted legalization or amnesty programs for illegally constructed units. *See, e.g.*, Sherman v. Frazier, 446 N.Y.S.2d 372 (N.Y. App. Div. 1982); Ilasi v. City of Long Beach, 342 N.E.2d 594 (N.Y. 1976); Marin County, California, adopted a "Second Unit Amnesty Program" for the calendar year of 2007, which was subsequently extended for an additional year, http://www .co.marin.ca.us/comdev/comdev/CURRENT/second_unit_amnesty.cfm.

236. *See* Patrick Hare, Accessory Apartments: Using Surplus Space in Single-Family Houses 10–23 (1981). "ADUs are typically regulated either as a permitted use, with an administrative review, or as a conditional use, subject to a public hearing requirement." Mun. Research & Servs. Ctr. of Wash., *supra* note 219, at 26. See approval process at http://www.archhousing.org /current-residents/adu-basic-steps.html.

237. *See, e.g.*, Wash. County, Or. Cmty. Dev. Code § 430-2 (2010), https://library.municode. com/or/washington_county/codes/community_development_code?nodeId=ARTIVDEST_430SPU SST_430-2ACDWUN. In an attempt to create more "flexibility" for secondary and accessory units, the ordinance allows such units in the county, with restrictions on size (no more than 50 percent of the main house or less than 600 square feet), setbacks, and "a minimum contiguous rear or side yard outdoor area of four-hundred and fifty (450) square feet."

238. *See, e.g.*, The town of Ithaca, New York, permits "elder cottages" in residential districts as accessory uses subject to certain restrictions, e.g., age, occupancy, and size. Patricia Salkin, New York Zoning Law and Practice § 23:07 (4th ed. 2003). *See also* Kasper v. Town of Brookhaven, 535 N.Y.S.2d 621 (N.Y. App. Div. 1988) (upholding owner-occupancy requirement of local ordinance promoting secondary units against due process and equal protection attack); Solar v. Zoning Bd. of Appeals of Lincoln, 600 N.E.2d 187 (Mass. Ct. App. 1992) (citing 1972 ordinance promoting secondary units as affordable housing for town employees and refusing to enforce Planning Board's owner occupancy condition). *But see* City of Wilmington v. Hill, 189 N.C. Ct. App. 173 (2008) (holding unconstitutional a city ordinance that required owner of a garage apartment to reside in either the main residence or garage apartment; finding city was entitled to regulate only the *use* of property owner's single-family residence with the accessory use of a garage apartment, not the ownership).

A few states (California, Florida, and Washington) have enacted statutes to promote the development of accessory units.[239] Florida's law is of limited value because it limits the areas in which it promotes them and focuses on seniors. It neither requires nor incentivizes local governments to build accessory units.[240]

Over the past nearly 40 years, California has revised its statutes to stimulate accessory housing development. One stated purpose of California's initial second-unit statute in 1982 was to "[p]rovid[e] relatively affordable housing for low- and moderate-income households without public subsidy."[241] The current version of the law forbids outright exclusion unless a locality makes specific findings, requires that localities only impose ministerial (i.e., nondiscretionary) review of accessory unit applications, and provides maximum planning standards that apply in the absence of a local ordinance in compliance with the statute.[242] The statute was revised in 2018 to provide a limited amnesty to owners of illegal units.[243] In 2019, a new statute, Senate Bill No. 13,[244] made several substantial changes: (1) authorizes the creation of accessory dwelling units in areas zoned to allow single- and multifamily dwelling residential use; (2) prohibits local agencies from requiring the replacement of parking spaces if a garage, carport, or covered parking is demolished to build an accessory unit; (3) prohibits local agencies from imposing parking standards that are located within a half-mile from public transit; (4) prohibits local agencies from establishing a minimum square footage requirement and setting a maximum square footage measurement less than

---

239. As of 2017, only California, Vermont, and Washington have laws that prohibit local governments from completely outlawing accessory units. Sarah H. Gottlieb, *Florida's Accessory Dwelling Unit Laws: Mitigating Florida's Housing Woes Through State-Encouraged Expansion of ADU Permitting* 46 STETSON L. REV. 627, 635 (2017) (hereafter Gottlieb). In 1993, the state of Washington enacted legislation requiring cities and counties with populations over 20,000 that are subject to Washington's Growth Management Act to develop ordinances accommodating accessory units. Localities are allowed to incorporate appropriate developmental standards and other restrictions. WASH. REV. CODE § 43.63A.215 (West 2020). In 2002, Connecticut made accessory dwelling units qualify as "affordable housing" for purposes of its affordable housing land-use appeals law provided that they are legally approved and subject to recorded deeds limiting occupancy for at least 10 years to lower-income households. *See* CONN. GEN. STAT. § 8-30g(k) (West 2010). Requiring such deed restrictions may deter some homeowners from building accessory dwelling units.

240. Gottlieb, *supra* note 239, at 649–50.

241. CAL. STAT. 1982, ch. 1440, § 1(d)(2). *See also* Sounhein v. City of San Dimas, 55 Cal. Rptr. 2d 290, 294 (Cal. Ct. App. 1996). The second-unit law is codified at CAL. GOV. CODE § 65852.2 (West 2017). Since 1982, the statute has been amended twelve times (1986, 1990, 1994, 2002, 2004, 2006, 2009, 2010, 2011, 2012, 2016, and 2017). The code is currently subject to proposed legislation but has not been amended yet. See the statute's intent at: the intent of the statute stated at § 65852.150 (West 2020). CAL. GOV'T CODE § 65583.1 (West 2010) clarifies the state housing element law's requirement regarding accessory units; CAL. GOV'T CODE § 65852.2(j)(4)(B) (West 2020) provides that accessory units include a "manufactured home" as defined by CAL. HEALTH & SAFETY CODE § 18007 (West 2010).

242. *See* CAL. GOV. CODE § 65852.2(c) (West 2020) (circumstances in which second units may be prohibited); *id.* § 65852.2(a)(3) (West 2020) (requiring ministerial review); *id.* § 65852.2(b) (West 2020) (specifying state standards).

243. Under revised Health and Safety Code Section 17958.12 accessory units that were constructed without permits can be inspected by local building officials under the building standards from the time the unit was constructed.

244. SB-13 can be found here: http://leginfo.legislature.ca.gov/faces/billTextClient.xhtml?bill _id=201920200SB13&search_keywords=accessory+unit

850 square feet, or 1,000 square feet for units with more than one bedroom; (5) prohibits local agencies from imposing owner-occupancy requirements until January 1, 2025; and, (6) extends the prior amnesty provisions by authorizing accessory unit owners built before January 1, 2020, to have a five-year grace period to correct violations and abate nuisances if the violation is not necessary to protect health and safety. Results of the prior laws have been mixed. Some cities have complied with the statute.[245] Others have resisted it because it partially overrides local land use control.[246] While its ministerial review requirement has not been tested in court, courts have upheld the basic elements of the previous versions of the statute against city resistance[247] while also upholding denials of proposed accessory units in specific cases.[248]

Accessory units have also received favorable treatment by local governments in Santa Cruz, California;[249] Boulder, Colorado;[250] Boston, Massachusetts;[251] Portland, Oregon;[252] and Seattle, Washington.[253]

---

245. The city of Santa Cruz, California, has established a progressive policy in its Accessory Unit Development Program. *See* ADU Zoning Regs., ch. 24.16.100, *et seq.* Zoning Ordinance of the City of Santa Cruz, http://www.cityofsantacruz.com/home/showdocument?id=75149; *see* City of Santa Cruz Financing Guide 2017, http://www.sccoplanning.com/Portals/2/County/adu/ADU%20 Financing%20Guide_080917.pdf.

246. Note that there are innumerable ways cities can undermine the statute's goal and still not be out of compliance. Pursuant to CAL. GOV'T CODE § 65852.2(a)(1)(A) and (B) (West 2020), with some limitations cities can restrict areas where second units can be located, restrict maximum allowable density, and impose restrictive parking, height, setback, and lot coverage standards subject to the limits defined by § 65852.2(d) and (e) (West 2020). *See also, e.g.*, Wilson v. City of Laguna Beach, 7 Cal. Rptr. 2d 848, 849 (Cal. Ct. App. 1992).

247. *Wilson*, 7 Cal. Rptr. 2d at 850; Coalition Advocating Legal Housing Options v. City of Santa Monica, 105 Cal. Rptr. 2d 802 (Cal. Ct. App. 2001).

248. Harris v. City of Costa Mesa, 31 Cal. Rptr. 2d 1 (Cal. Ct. App. 1994); Desmond v. Cnty. of Contra Costa, 25 Cal. Rptr. 2d 842 (Cal. Ct. App. 1993).

249. *See supra* note 227.

250. *See* Accessory Dwelling Units section of City of Boulder website: https://bouldercolorado .gov/services/accessory-dwelling-units (last accessed Sept. 13, 2021).

251. Boston created an accessory dwelling unit (ADU) pilot program that lasted 18 months starting in November 2017. The experiment allowed owner-occupied homes in East Boston, Mattapan, and Jamaica Plain to add a single ADU to the home without an application for a zoning variance. It only allowed for homeowners to use the space inside their homes to create an ADU and was limited by very specific design requirements, e.g., required to be a full unit (with bathroom and kitchen) and meet ceiling height regulations and fire alarm and sprinkler system regulations. Boston's takeaway from the experiment was to permanently expand its accessory unit program. The future prospect is to simplify the application process to expedite the permitting process and reduce repetitive steps. https://docs.google.com/document/d/14DTrBoW2CGSiCclLGGnwhRXujCzVHbVineBlIKP RvHE/edit.

252. See City of Portland Municipal Code, Section 33.205 on accessory dwelling units at: https:// www.portlandoregon.gov/bps/article/53301.

253. In July 2019, Seattle expanded its accessory dwelling unit regulations to allow for properties to have two ADUs. In the fall of 2019, Seattle asked for submissions from developers and designers for plans to achieve their ADU goals. The goal is to have an online database the city will publish with a gallery of plans for homeowners to view and select online, including a low-cost option. The detached accessory dwelling unit plans should be low cost, have green building and design, maintain privacy, have a culturally diverse design, and have a certain construction time frame. http://www .seattle.gov/Documents/Departments/OPCD/OngoingInitiatives/EncouragingBackyardCottages /OPCDPreApprovedDADUSubmissionGuide.pdf. Other localities continue to give accessory units a

HUD has been very supportive of accessory unit development. A recent HUD report concluded that successful accessory unit development programs "must be flexible, uncomplicated, include fiscal incentives, and be supported by public education campaigns so as to engender and maintain community support."[254]

VI. SINGLE-RESIDENCE OCCUPANCY HOTELS

Single-residence occupancy hotels (SROs) historically served low-wage single workers and some small households "permanently or for long periods of time" in downtown locations by offering "single, unfurnished rooms without private kitchens."[255] They were "market affordable" for a long time, but became a disfavored form of housing and were subject to widespread demolition or conversion as part of urban renewal and urban redevelopment.[256] Many were converted into tourist hotels, luxury apartments or condos, and mixed uses. SROs continue to be a potential affordable housing resource, but their development is hobbled by a bad reputation.[257]

Beginning in the late 1970s, SROs were rediscovered as a source of permanent affordable housing, in particular as "supportive housing" to provide independent living with social services for a variety of populations with special needs, including homeless persons and persons with disabilities.[258] Several states and some large cities have led efforts to develop new SROs and to rehabilitate and save existing SROs from continuing threats of demolition or conversion.[259] Some federal and state funding is available for such efforts.[260]

---

mixed reception. *See e.g.*, Tara A. Scully, *Legalizing Accessory Units*, NEWSDAY C9 (June 26, 1998) (listing 12 of 14 localities in Long Island that allow secondary units for various types of residents and with various restrictions).

254. The Affordable Housing Potential of Manufactured ADUs, HUD USER, https://www .huduser.gov/portal/pdredge/pdr-edge-featd-article-110220.html; *see also* HUD Office of Policy and Research report *Accessory Dwelling Units: Case Study*, https://www.huduser.gov/portal/pub lications/adu.pdf.

255. ENCYCLOPEDIA OF HOUSING, *supra* note 187, at 538 ("Single-Room Occupancy Housing" entry by Karen A. Franck).

256. *Id. See also* Ann M. Burkhart, *The Constitutional Underpinnings of Homelessness*, 40 HOUS. L. REV. 211, 269 & nn.536–37 (2003); Andy Merrifield, *Lepers at the City Gate: Single Room Occupancy and the Housing Crisis*, 48 DISSENT 78 (2001).

257. Anne Wyatt, *'SRO' Has Got to Go: Why San Diego and Other Cities Should Rebrand this Type of Affordable Housing*, PLANNING 33, American Planning Association (July 2013).

258. SROs are currently the dominant form of supportive housing. Another model employs cooperative apartments using master leasing, which avoids the need for land-use approvals and the risk of local opposition while providing for more integration with typical housing. For more about supportive housing, visit the Corporation for Supportive Housing website at www.csh.org.

259. CHARLES HOCH & ROBERT A. SLAYTON, NEW HOMELESS AND OLD: COMMUNITY AND THE SKID ROW HOTEL (1989) (describing the loss of skid row and SRO hotels). Karen A. Franck credits Portland, Oregon, as the early leader in the effort. *See* ENCYCLOPEDIA OF HOUSING, *supra* note 187, at 538. *See also* Mary Lou Gallagher, *A Small Room at the Inn: San Diego Leads the Nation in Building Single Room Occupancy Hotels*, 59 PLANNING 20–25 (June 1993); CAL. CIV. CODE §§ 1940.1,1940.6 (providing tenant protections).

260. See Part II for discussion of funding for affordable housing. Federal funding examples: Section 8 Moderate Rehabilitation Single Room Occupancy Program, 24 C.F.R. pt. 882: subpart H—Section 8 Moderate Rehabilitation Single Room Occupancy Program for Homeless Individuals. State funding examples: MINN. STAT. § 462A.222 (2019); MO. REV. STAT. § 215.038; N.Y. SOC.

Revived SROs appear to be a flexible and successful model for certain populations.[261] Yet landowners (claiming the regulations constitute regulatory takings) and neighbors (preferring demolition or different uses, especially where they fear a proposed site might affect a downtown redevelopment scheme) have resisted their revival. Existing SROs remain under pressure to be converted to other uses, and the prospects for a revitalization of SROs continues to be uncertain.[262]

The primary legal issues concern municipal attempts to regulate the demolition and conversion of existing SROs.[263] Cities often first adopt a moratorium on demolition and conversion, and then adopt more comprehensive conversion control ordinances.[264] These ordinances typically include tenant notification requirements and impose permit requirements for conversion, which trigger replacement requirements or in-lieu fees.

Enforcement of SRO conversion ordinances has been controversial.[265] Property owners and developers have sought to circumvent these requirements by avoiding the classification of "SRO."[266] In two cases, California courts found that a state statute preempted San Francisco's SRO regulation.[267]

Property owners have also challenged the ordinances, particularly the replacement requirements, as unconstitutional takings. Currently, these ordinances appear to have withstood regulatory takings challenges. After decades of encouraging SRO demolition, New York City adopted a series of ordinances between 1985 and 1987 establishing a moratorium on the demolition of SROs.[268] Local Law No. 9, enacted in 1987, "prohibit[ed] the demolition, alteration, or conversion of single-room occupancy (SRO) properties and obligate[d]

Serv. Law § 45-a (2018); Or. Rev. Stat. §§ 280.440 and 280.410(1)(b). *See also* D.C. Code Ann. § 42-3508.06 (2020).

261. The Corporation for Supportive Housing website (www.csh.org) contains numerous academic studies demonstrating the cost-effectiveness of supportive housing over other options.

262. Brian J. Sullivan & Jonathan Burke, *Single-Room Occupancy Housing in New York City: The Origins and Dimensions of a Crisis*, 17 CUNY L. Rev. 113, 114 (2013) ("This effort will require stemming the conversion of existing SROs to other (higher profit) uses and creating legal avenues for the construction or reconversion of additional units.").

263. Whether or not SRO residents qualify as "tenants" under state landlord-tenant law has also been an issue. *See, e.g.*, Ann Arbor Tenants Union v. Ann Arbor YMCA, 581 N.W.2d 794 (Mich. Ct. App. 1998).

264. For example, in San Diego, a 1985 moratorium on demolition and conversion of SROs was replaced in 1997 by an SRO ordinance regulating demolition and conversion. *See* San Diego Mun. Code § 143.0510–.0590.

265. Kelly Davis, *Portrait of an Eviction: The Story of the Maryland Hotel*, San Diego City Beat 1 (Feb. 5, 2003) 1 (explaining a situation where San Diego SRO ordinance was not enforced).

266. City of New York v. 17 Vista Assocs., 642 N.E.2d 606 (N.Y. 1994).

267. *See* Bullock v. City & County of San Francisco, 271 Cal. Rptr. 44 (Cal. Ct. App. 1990); Reidy v. City & County of San Francisco, 19 Cal. Rptr. 3d 894 (Cal. Ct. App. 2004); Pieri v. City & County of San Francisco, 137 Cal. App. 4th 886 (2006); reaffirmed in Coyne v. City & County of San Francisco, Cal. App. 1 Dist., Mar. 21, 2017. However, as of January 1, 2004, subsequent state legislation overruled *Bullock* at least for the City and County of San Francisco and other cities "with a population over 1,000,000" where certain other conditions are met. *See* Cal. Gov't Code § 7060(a) (West 2004); *accord, Reidy*, 19 Cal. Rptr. 3d at 902–03.

268. *See* Seawall Assocs. v. City of New York, 542 N.E.2d 1059, 1060–61 (N.Y. 1989), *cert. denied*, 493 U.S. 976 (1989). A previous version of New York City's ordinance required that no harassment of tenants occur during a three-year period before application for renovation or demolition approval. Sadowsky v. New York, 732 F.2d 312 (2d Cir. 1984).

the owners to restore all units to habitable condition and lease them at controlled rents for an indefinite period." The law also guaranteed SRO owners an 8.5 percent rate of return.[269] In 1989, New York's highest court found that the ordinance on its face was unconstitutional both as a physical taking,[270] under *Loretto v. Teleprompter Manhattan CATV Corp.*,[271] and as a regulatory taking,[272] applying the "heightened scrutiny" of *Nollan v. California Coastal Commission.*[273] However, both of *Seawall*'s holdings appear to have been undermined by later cases. *Seawall*'s physical taking holding was impliedly overruled in *Yee v. City of Escondido*,[274] in which the Supreme Court held that a regulation that did not compel property owners to suffer the physical occupation of their property did not effect a per se physical taking.[275] And in *Monterey v. Del Monte Dunes*,[276] the Supreme Court held that *Nollan*'s heightened scrutiny was limited to regulatory takings cases involving exactions, and "inapposite" to permit denials and other land-use restrictions.[277]

Beginning in 1979, San Francisco adopted a series of measures to control the demolition and conversion of SROs.[278] The current ordinance requires a permit for conversion, notification to tenants, relocation payments to former tenants, and fulfillment of one of a variety of options for one-for-one replacement of lost units.[279] Despite the ordinance's complex interaction with a state statute limiting local governments' authority to enact and maintain rent control and providing owners with a right to exit the rental-housing business, it has largely endured sustained attacks combining constitutional claims and state statutory claims.[280] In the *San Remo Hotel* case, applying a deferential standard of scrutiny, California's Supreme Court held that the one-for-one replacement of lost units or alternative

---

269. *Seawall Assocs.*, 542 N.E.2d at 1060–62.

270. *Id.* at 1065.

271. 458 U.S. 419 (1982).

272. *Seawall Assocs.*, 542 N.E.2d. at 1065.

273. 483 U.S. 825 (1987). There is now doubt that compensation is necessary. The chapter has two cases that undermine this holding. It is also further called into doubt by Rodehorst Brothers v. City of Norfolk Board of Adjustment, 287 Neb. 779 (Mar. 28, 2014).

274. 503 U.S. 519 (1992).

275. *Id.* at 527.

276. 526 U.S. 687 (1999).

277. *Id.* at 702–03. *See* San Remo Hotel v. City & County of San Francisco, 27 Cal. 4th 643, 673 (2002) (noting that "[t]he New York Court of Appeals acknowledged the overruling in Bonnie Briar Syndicate v. Mamaroneck (1999) 94 N.Y.2d 96"). For a review of New York City's policies, a critique of the *Seawall* decision, and a checklist for drafting affordable housing programs to survive takings challenges, *see* Suzanne K. Sleep, *Stonewalled by* Seawall: *New York Decision Impedes Legislative Solutions to Affordable Housing Shortage*, 45 Miami L. Rev. 467 (1991).

278. A moratorium enacted in 1979 was followed in 1981 by an SRO conversion ordinance, which has been substantially revised several times. San Remo Hotel v. City & County of San Francisco, 27 Cal. 4th 643, 650 (2002).

279. S.F. Cal. Admin. Code ch. 41 (2003) (Residential Hotel Unit Conversion and Demolition Ordinance).

280. *See, e.g.*, San Remo Hotel v. City & County of San Francisco, 27 Cal. 4th 643 (2002) (affirming the city's conditional use requirement and upholding the HCO's legislatively mandated replacement fee provision against a regulatory takings claim as bearing a reasonable relationship to the loss of affordable housing in the city). *But see* Reidy v. City & County of San Francisco, 123 Cal. App. 4th 580 (Cal. App. 1 Dist., 2004) (finding HCO preempted by state law). *See also* Action Apt. Ass'n v. City of Santa Monica, 166 Cal. App. 4th 456 (upholding a similar ordinance requiring that developers of multifamily ownership housing projects construct affordable housing).

in-lieu fees did not effect an unconstitutional regulatory taking. The court reasoned that the legislatively enacted replacement fees requirement, which was applicable to more than 500 residential hotels in San Francisco, was "a burden placed broadly and nondiscriminatorily on changes in property's use" and "not the equivalent of an arbitrary decision to hold an individual's property for ransom" and thus not a taking.[281] In upholding the San Francisco ordinance, the California Supreme Court explicitly rejected the *Seawall* court's takings holding.[282]

In addition, courts have applied the federal Fair Housing Act's "reasonable accommodation" requirement as applied to homeless people with disabilities to support permits or variances to establish SRO housing for homeless people.[283]

SROs could still play an important role in providing needed affordable housing, especially in large urban areas, but for this to happen requires state and local policies to become more supportive of this form of housing. And for this to occur, "A new attitude towards and understanding of SROs is necessary to ensure that such housing can once again serve its vital function."[284]

VII. CONDOMINIUM CONVERSION REGULATION

In areas where housing and land prices are high and appear to be increasing, owners of existing apartment houses may find it profitable to convert their apartments into condominiums.[285] In response to the shortage of adequate and affordable housing exacerbated by frequent conversion of apartments to condominiums in the 1970s, some local governments adopted condominium conversion controls.[286] These ordinances are common in the S.F. Bay Area.[287] The ordinances are diverse in how they operate, for example, prohibiting

---

281. *San Remo*, 27 Cal. 4th at 677.

282. The *San Remo* court specifically rejected the *Seawall* decision, stating that *Seawall* relied upon a "heightened scrutiny" test which the court deemed inappropriate for reviewing San Francisco's HCO. *Id.* at 673 n.15.

283. *See, e.g.*, Homeless Action Comm. v. City of Albany, 1997 U.S. Dist. LEXIS 23423 (N.D.N.Y. Oct. 23, 1997); United States v. City of Philadelphia, 838 F. Supp. 223 (E.D. Pa. 1993); Judy B. v. Borough of Tioga, 889 F. Supp. 792 (M.D. Pa. 1995). For more on the federal Fair Housing Act, see Chapter 3.

284. Sullivan & Burke, *supra* note 262, at 114. "New York Multiple Dwelling Law § 248 and subsections 22-2077 and 27-2078 of the New York Administrative Code make all new SROs illegal by definition." *Id.* at note 139.

285. *See, e.g.*, OFFICE OF POLICY DEV. & RESEARCH, U.S. DEP'T OF HOUSING & URBAN DEV., THE CONVERSION OF RENTAL HOUSING TO CONDOMINIUMS & COOPERATIVES: A NATIONAL STUDY OF SCOPE, CAUSES AND IMPACTS (1980).

286. In addition to condominium conversion ordinances, some city officials are legislating "to make it harder to convert some small apartment buildings into single-family homes, a process blamed for the loss of affordable housing in gentrifying areas." Alex Nitkin, *'Anti-deconversion Ordinance' Will 'Interrupt' Loss of Cheap Housing Stock in Pilsen, 606 Area*, THE DAILY LINE (Dec. 2, 2020), https://www.housingstudies.org/media/filer_public/ac/2f/ac2fb59f-0d59-4b04-bf77-9cd122d9ec4c/anti-deconversion_ordinance_will_interrupt_loss_of_cheap_housing_stock_in_pilsen_606_area_officials_say___daily_line.pdf (last accessed Sept. 13, 2021).

287. Karolina Gorska & Mitchell Crispell, *Condominium Conversion Policy Brief*, Urban Displacement Project, Univ. of California at Berkeley 1 (2016) ("Seventy-three cities in the nine-county Bay Area have condominium conversion policies in place (67% of all cities, as of 2014)"), https://

conversion unless the vacancy rate in the city is above a certain level, limiting conversions based on the proportion of the housing stock that is rental, setting an annual limit on the number of units that may convert to condominiums, requiring replacement by an equal number of rental units priced as they were before, or by prohibiting conversion of small buildings.[288] The effectiveness of condominium conversion ordinances is debated because developers exploit loopholes in them.[289]

And, some courts have found local jurisdictions' attempts to regulate condominium conversions to be ultra vires or preempted by state law.[290]

Conflicts between local governments and condominium developers led Congress to enact the Condominium and Cooperative Conversion Protection and Abuse Relief Act of 1980.[291] This statute expressed the "sense of Congress" that "when multifamily rental housing projects are converted to condominium or cooperative use, tenants in those projects are entitled to adequate notice of the pending conversion and to receive the first opportunity to purchase units in the converted projects. . . . "[292] Congress left it to the states and local governments to implement its suggestion.[293] At least 34 states currently have statutes regulating condominium and cooperative conversions, providing a range of measures balancing the interests of condominium developers and apartment renters.[294] The push for

---

www.urbandisplacement.org/sites/default/files/images/urbandisplacementproject_condoconversionbrief_feb2016_revised.pdf.

288. *Id.* at 2.

289. For example, existing tenants can be pressured to accept buyouts to move, apartment owners can close the apartment complex exiting the rental business and then then sell the emptied building as condominiums. *Id.*

290. *See, e.g.*, Zussman v. Rent Control Board, 326 N.E.2d 876 (Mass. 1975); Claridge House One, Inc. v. Borough of Verona, 490 F. Supp. 706 (D.N.J. 1980), *aff'd without op.*, 633 F.2d 209 (3d Cir. 1980). *But see San Francisco Apartment Ass'n v. City & County of San Francisco* (ND CA 2015) 142 F. Supp. 3d 910, 928, *aff'd* (9th Cir. 2018) 881 F.3d 1169 ("Under the Subdivision Map Act, local governments possess the powers necessary to set condominium conversion restrictions."). Sometimes courts found other state laws applicable: Aries Dev. Co. v Cal. Coastal Zone Conservation Comm'n, 122 Cal. Rptr. 315 (Cal. Ct. App. 1975).

291. 15 U.S.C. §§ 3601–3616 (2010).

292. *Id.* § 3605.

293. *Id.* §§ 3605, 3610.

294. *See* **Alabama**, ALA. CODE § 35-8A-412 (2006); **Alaska**, ALASKA STAT. § 34.08.620 (2006); **California**, CAL. GOV'T CODE §§ 66427.1-66452.13 (West 1997 & Supp. 2008); **Colorado**, COLO. REV. STAT. ANN. § 38-33-112 (West 2007); **Connecticut**, CONN. GEN. STAT. ANN. §§ 47-282-47-295 (West 2004 & Supp. 2007); **District of Columbia**, D.C. CODE ANN. §§ 42-3401.01-42-3405.12 (LexisNexis 2006 & Supp. 2007); **Florida**, FLA. STAT. ANN. §§ 718.604-718.622 (West 2005 & Supp. 2007); **Georgia**, GA. CODE ANN. § 44-3-87 (1991 & Supp. 2007); **Hawaii,** HAW. REV. STAT. ANN. § 514B-1, § 521-38 (LexisNexis 2006); **Illinois**, 765 ILL. COMP. STAT. 605/30; **Maine**, ME. REV. STAT. ANN. tit. 33 § 1604-111 (1964); **Maryland**, MD. CODE ANN., REAL PROP. § 11-102.1 (LexisNexis 2003 & Supp. 2007); **Massachusetts**, MASS. GEN. LAWS ANN. ch. 183A § 1 (St. 1983, c. 527) (emergency legislation 1983) (West 2003); **Michigan**, MICH. COMP. LAWS ANN. § 559.204 (West 2007); **Minnesota**, MINN. STAT. ANN. § 515A.4-110 (West 2002 & Supp. 2007); **Missouri,** MO. ANN. STAT. § 448.4-112 (West 2000); **Nebraska**, NEB. REV. STAT. ANN. § 76-886 (LexisNexis 2004); **Nevada**, NEV. REV. STAT. ANN. § 116.4112 (LexisNexis 2004); **New Hampshire**, N.H. REV. STAT. ANN. §§ 356-C:1-356-C:10 (1995); **New Jersey**, N.J. STAT. ANN. §§ 2A:18-61.8-2A:18-61.11 (West 2000); **New Mexico**, N.M. STAT. § 47-7D-12 (1978 & Supp. 2007); **New York**, N.Y. GEN. BUS. LAW § 352-eeee (McKinney 1996 & Supp. 2007); **North Carolina**, N.C. GEN. STAT. §§ 47A-34-47A-37 (2005); **Ohio**, OHIO REV. CODE ANN. § 5311.25 (G) (LexisNexis 2004 & Supp. 2007);

homeownership during the second George W. Bush administration created renewed concern among tenants that their protections under these state laws were ineffective or not being enforced.[295] These concerns fueled attempts in some states to revisit these statutes.[296]

Some states' statutes include provisions primarily protecting condominium developers from being subjected to local regulation beyond what would normally be covered in their subdivision ordinances and regulations.[297] For example, some states adopted the Uniform Condominium Act (UCA). Sections 4-106 through 4-112 of the 1980 version of the UCA regulate condominium conversions.[298] Section 4-106 provides that local regulation may not prohibit condominium conversion or place any requirement on condominiums that would not be imposed on an identical development under a different type of ownership.[299] Some courts have enforced these provisions voiding local condominium conversion ordinances as preempted by state legislation.[300]

Other states enacted statutes ensuring that current apartment tenants would receive a timely notification of the proposed conversion,[301] providing existing tenants with an exclusive right to contract for the purchase of their own unit, providing tenants a right to comparable housing or temporary waiver of rent,[302] and allowing local governments to further

---

Oregon, Or. Rev. Stat. § 100.305 (2005); **Pennsylvania,** 68 Pa. Cons. Stat. Ann. § 3410 (West 2004 & Supp. 2007); **Rhode Island**, R.I. Gen. Laws § 34-36.1-4.12 (1995 & Supp. 2006); **South Carolina**, S.C. Code Ann. § 27-31-420 (2007); **Tennessee**, Tenn. Code Ann. § 66-27-123 (2004); **Texas**, Tex. Prop. Code Ann. § 82.160 (Vernon 2007); **Vermont**, Vt. Stat. Ann. tit. 27, §§ 1331-1339 (2006); **Virginia**, Va. Code Ann. § 55-79.94 (2007); **Washington**, Wash. Rev. Code Ann § 64.34.440 (West 2005); **West Virginia**, W. Va. Code Ann. § 36B-4-112 (LexisNexis 2005); and **Wisconsin**, Wis. Stat. Ann. § 703.08 (West 2001 & Supp. 2006). This list is taken from note 108 in Kathryn B. Richards, *The Illinois Condominium Property Act: An Analysis of Legislative Efforts to Improve Tenants' Rights in the Condominium Conversion Process*, 57 DePaul L. Rev. 829, 871 (2008).

295. *Id.* at 830.

296. *See, e.g., id.* at 839 (explaining and analyzing amendments to Illinois law).

297. *See, e.g.*, Natrella v. Board of Zoning Appeals, 345 S.E.2d 295, 301–02 (Va. 1986). In effect, these prohibit discrimination against condominiums by virtue of their form of ownership. Generally, an apartment owner seeking to convert must abide by the requirement of the state's subdivision act and obtain the local government's approval of its subdivision map. Subdivision acts typically regulate design and subdivision land improvements, but do not authorize regulation of the type included in some local condominium conversion ordinances, e.g., relocation obligations.

298. *See, e.g.*, Minn. Stat. Ann. § 515A.1-101 to 1-116 (West 2004); Mo. Stat. Ann. § 448.4-112 (West 2004); Tex. Prop. Code Ann. § 82.160 (Vernon 2004); Va. Code Ann. §§ 55-79.74:3, 55-79.94 (Mich. 2004).

299. Uniform Condo. Act § 1-106 (amended 1980).

300. *See, e.g.*, Miami Beach v. Rocio Corp., 404 So. 2d 1066 (Fla. Ct. App. 1981); Rockville Grosvenor, Inc. v. Montgomery County, 422 A.2d 353 (Md. Ct. App. 1980).

301. A majority of states provide 120 days' notice. Some state statutes provide for a minimum of 30 days' notice (e.g., 765 Il. Comp. Stat. § 605/30 (2005), others for one year (e.g., 68 Pa. Cons. Stat. Ann. § 3410 (West 1965 & Supp. 2004). These provisions have been enforced. *See, e.g.*, Glenn Chaffer, Inc. v. Kennedy, 433 A.2d 1018 (Conn. Super. Ct. 1981); Sibig & Co. v. Santos, 582 A.2d 840 (N.J. Super. Ct. App. Div. 1990).

302. *See, e.g.*, Cal. Gov't Code § 66427.1 (2004); Daskel Investors, Inc. v. Rosenbloom, 582 A.2d 854 (N.J. Super. Ct. Law Div. 1990). *But see* Sargo II, Inc. v. Philadelphia, 488 F. Supp. 1045 (E.D. Pa. 1980).

regulate condominium conversion under their zoning authority.[303] Other tenant benefits in state statutes include reimbursement for moving and relocation expenses,[304] prohibitions of evictions of tenants except for good cause,[305] and provision of a private right of action to aggrieved tenants.[306] In these states, courts have allowed local governments to require apartments converting to condominiums to obtain a conditional use permit (including tenant relocation and unit replacement provisions),[307] and to restrict the number of condominium conversions permitted annually.[308] Judicial review of constitutional challenges (e.g., due process, equal protection, and takings claims) to such protective legislation has reached mixed results.[309]

VIII. EMERGENCY SHELTERS AND TRANSITIONAL HOUSING, INCLUDING DOMESTIC VIOLENCE SHELTERS

This section considers various forms of "temporary" housing, primarily emergency shelters and transitional housing in which the persons housed generally have either attenuated rights as renters or none at all.

Homelessness, substance abuse, and domestic violence continue to present substantial and growing housing problems.[310] Emergency shelters provide shelter for a night at

---

303. *See, e.g.,* Cal. Gov't Code § 66427.1(E) (2004); City of Urbana v. County of Champaign, 389 N.E.2d 1185, 1187–88 (Ill. 1979); Griffin Dev. Co. v. City of Oxnard, 39 Cal. 3d 256 (1985). *But see* Sequoia Park Assocs v. County of Sonoma, 176 Cal. App. 4th 1270 (1st Dist. 2009) (declining to extend Griffin Dev. Co.). For a lengthy article chronicling landlords' successful evasion of D.C.'s strict condominium conversion ordinance, *see* Debbie Cenziper & Sarah Cohen, *The Profit in Decay: Landlords Who Empty Buildings of Tenants Reap Extra Benefits Under Law*, Wash. Post, Mar. 9, 2008.

304. *See* Conn. Gen. Stat. Ann. § 47-88d (West 1985 & Supp. 2004); 2001 D.C. Stat. 6-333.01–.02; Vt. Stat. Ann. tit. 27, § 1336 (2003). See also Chapter 16 on Relocation Law.

305. *See* Conn. Gen. Stat. Ann. § 47a-23c (West 1985 & Supp. 2004).

306. *See id.* § 47-88g.

307. *See* Krater v. City of Los Angeles, 181 Cal. Rptr. 923 (Cal. Ct. App. 1982).

308. *See* San Clemente, Cal., Mun. Code § 16.40.010.

309. *Compare* Leavenworth Props. v. City of San Francisco, 234 Cal. Rptr. 598 (Cal. Ct. App. 1987); Griffin Dev. Co. v. City of Oxnard, 39 Cal. 3d 256 (1985); and Rockville Grosvenor, Inc. v. Montgomery County, 422 A.2d 353, 368 (Md. Ct. App. 1980) *with* 19th Street Assocs. v. State, 568 N.Y.S.2d 771 (N.Y. 1991).

310. Nationally, in 2015, there was a diminishing gap between number of available beds and people experiencing homelessness. Alfred M. Clark III, *Homelessness and the Crisis of Affordable Housing: The Abandonment of A Federal Affordable Housing Policy*, J. Affordable Hous. & Cmty. Dev. L., 2016, at 85. However, the need for emergency shelters and transitional housing may grow due to cities' increasing criminalization of camping, sleeping in vehicles. "In a July [2015] study examining 187 U.S. cities, the National Law Center on Homelessness and Poverty (NLCHP) found a 119 percent increase since 2011 in city bans on sleeping in vehicles, a 25 percent increase in citywide laws against panhandling, a 60 percent increase in citywide camping bans, and a 35 percent increase in citywide loitering or vagrancy laws." Joanna Laine, *From Criminalization to Humanization: Ending Discrimination Against the Homeless*, 39 Harbinger 1, 4 (2015). Yet, there has also been a growing number of constitutional challenges to ordinances banning sleeping in vehicles and camping, discussed *infra*.

See generally Nat'l Law Center on Homelessness and Poverty, Homelessness in America: Overview of Data and Causes (2015), https://nlchp.org/wp-content/uploads/2018/10/Homeless_Stats_Fact_Sheet.pdf (on file with author). U.S. Conference of Mayors, A Status Report on

a time (often with a maximum stay of 30 days) primarily to homeless people, including subgroups such as persons with substance abuse issues and domestic violence survivors.[311] While variously defined, "transitional housing" typically provides time-limited housing (less than two years), often intended as a "step" between emergency shelter and permanent housing.[312] Transitional housing usually includes a program of substantial services, such as substance abuse counseling, job counseling and training, and money management.[313] Funding for emergency shelters and transitional housing comes from private sources (including private individuals, churches, businesses, and foundations) as well as government funding programs.[314]

Nationally, transitional housing beds are on the decline, as federal resources shift toward funding more permanent housing models.[315] "Transitional housing . . . has been criticized as being more expensive than alternative solutions to assist homelessness, includ-

Homelessness and Hunger in America's Cities (Dec. 2016), https://endhomelessness.org/wp-con tent/uploads/2017/02/US-Conference-of-Mayors-Report-on-Homelessness-and-Hunger_Final.pdf (last accessed Dec. 6, 2021); HUD 2019 Annual Homeless Assessment Report: https://files.hudex change.info/resources/documents/2019-AHAR-Part-1.pdf. Elizabeth Halpern, *What's Wrong with America's Homeless?*, 9 Geo. J. on Poverty L. & Pol'y 279, 280–82 (2002).

311. For more information on homelessness, *see* the National Law Center on Homelessness and Poverty website, http://www.nlchp.org/ or National Alliance to End Homelessness at http://www .endhomelessness.org/. For more information on domestic violence, *see generally* Nat'l Resource Center on Domestic Violence, http://www.nrcdv.org/; ABA Commission on Domestic Violence, http://www.abanet.org/domviol/; and the National Law Center on Homelessness and Poverty web-site at http://www.nlchp.org/.

312. Since 1994, transitional housing was conceived as a critical component of the U.S. Depart-ment of Housing and Urban Development's "Continuum of Care" solution to homelessness. The three-step plan includes (1) outreach and assessment of homeless people in public places and place-ment in emergency shelters; (2) transitional housing combined with rehabilitative services; and (3) supportive permanent housing designed around the specific individual needs of homeless fami-lies and individuals. *See* Continuum of Care 101, https://www.hudexchange.info/resource/1187/con tinuum-of-care-101/. For definitions on HUD's Continuum of Care, see https://www.hudexchange .info/programs/coc/coc-program-eligibility-requirements/. Stanley S. Herr & Stephen M.B. Pincus, *A Way to Go Home: Supportive Housing and Housing Assistance Preferences for the Homeless*, 23 Stetson L. Rev. 345, 377 (1994).

313. The McKinney-Vento Homeless Assistance Act defines transitional housing as "housing, the purpose of which is to facilitate the movement of homeless individuals and families to permanent housing within 24 months or such longer period as the Secretary determines necessary." 42 U.S.C. § 11360 (2020). Transitional housing is often provided in congregate living setting with no individual leases. Transitional housing serves many of the same populations as emergency shelters, but specific programs are often targeted to particular groups, e.g., women domestic violence survivors. While transitional housing always includes some social services associated with the housing, emergency shelters may provide little or none. Transitional housing can be contrasted with "supportive hous-ing," which is *permanent* housing with support services. For more information about supportive housing, visit the Corporation for Supportive Housing website, http://www.csh.org/.

314. *See* Part II, *infra*, for overviews of funding sources for affordable housing, and particularly Chapter 9, *infra*, for discussion of some federal programs funding housing for homeless people. *See, e.g.*, McKinney-Vento Homeless Assistance Act of 1987, Pub. L. No. 100-77, 101 Stat. 482 (codified in scattered sections of titles 7, 28, and 42 U.S.C.) (enacted to increase emergency services, housing, medical services, educational aid, and job training).

315. For HUD funding changes, see HUD funding changes: U.S. Dep't of Housing & Urban Devel., Office of Cmty. Planning and Devel., Continuum of Care 101 (June 2009), https:// files.hudexchange.info/resources/documents/CoC101.pdf.

ing the 'housing first' model and permanent supportive housing."[316] Permanent housing for people experiencing homelessness has been recognized as a best practice, resulting in an increase in the number of permanent housing options as opposed to temporary beds. "In 2007, 31 percent of homeless assistance beds were dedicated to permanent housing options. By 2018, that number was 57 percent."[317] Since 2012, HUD has instituted a significant shift in funding away from transitional housing programs and toward permanent supportive housing and rapid re-housing models.[318] "Transitional housing is the only intervention on the decline—there are 52 percent fewer beds in that category [in 2018] than there were in 2007. This follows a national trend of states and communities shifting resources away from temporary transitional housing and towards permanent housing options (such as permanent supportive housing and rapid rehousing)."[319] "Nationally, the most prevalent homeless assistance intervention is permanent supportive housing. The number of beds in this category has grown by 92 percent since 2007. Emergency shelter beds, the second most common intervention, have increased 35 percent since 2007."[320] "Rapid rehousing, the newest type of permanent housing intervention, has quickly grown by 450 percent over the last five years."[321]

This section will focus on restrictive city zoning and local opposition to the development of emergency shelters and transitional housing.[322] Other important legal issues raised by homelessness and these types of housing[323] include the constitutionality of ordinances

---

316. Alfred M. Clark III, *Homelessness and the Crisis of Affordable Housing: The Abandonment of A Federal Affordable Housing Policy*, J. Affordable Hous. & Cmty. Dev. L. 85 (2016).

317. National Alliance to end Homelessness, *State of Homelessness in America 2018* https://end homelessness.org/homelessness-in-america/homelessness-statistics/state-of-homelessness-report/.

318. Urban Initiatives, *The Realignment of HUD Continuum of Care Program Homeless Assistance Funding,* 2017. https://homelessstrategy.com/the-realignment-of-hud-continuum-of-care -program-homeless-assistance-funding-what-are-the-outcomes/; https://www.wypr.org/post/hud -funding-cuts-leave-transitional-housing-programs-scrambling; https://www.latimes.com/local /lanow/la-me-ln-transitional-housing-cutbacks-20160815-snap-story.html; https://www.post-gazette .com/local/region/2016/06/02/Local-nonprofits-say-they-will-lose-out-with-changes-in-HUD-fund ing/stories/201606020052; https://www.mcall.com/news/watchdog/mc-nws-hud-transitional-hous ing-end-20180129-story.html.

319. National Alliance to end Homelessness, *supra* note 317.

320. *Id.* In at least one case in which a city closed an emergency shelter in effort to expand its Permanent Supportive Housing program, a court found no violation of FHA, the Americans with Disabilities Act, the Due Process Clause, and other laws. Boykin v. Fenty, 650 F. App'x 42, 43 (D.C. Cir. 2016).

321. National Alliance to end Homelessness, *supra* note 317.

322. *See generally* Nat'l Law Center on Homelessness and Poverty, Access Delayed, Access Denied: Local Opposition to Housing and Services for Homeless People Across the United States (1997), https://www.homelesshub.ca/resource/access-delayed-access-denied -local-opposition-housing-and-services-homeless-people-across; Robert A. Nasdor, *Legal Support for Affordable Housing Development*, 156 N.J. Law. 23, 24 (Oct. 1993).

323. Because of this book's focus on housing development law, this section will not consider the important issue of the criminalization of homelessness and attempts to secure a right for homeless persons to sleep in public places. *See* Jonathan L. Hafetz, *Homeless Legal Advocacy: New Challenges and Directions for the Future*, (hereafter Hafetz) 30 Fordham Urb. L.J. 1215, 1235–40 (2003); Hannah Kieschnick, *A Cruel and Unusual Way to Regulate the Homeless: Extending the Status Crimes Doctrine to Anti-Homeless Ordinances*, 70 Stan. L. Rev. 1569, 1571 (2018). *See also A Dream Denied: The Criminalization of Homelessness in U.S. Cities*, a report by The National

that criminalize homelessness,[324] whether a state recognizes any "right to shelter,"[325] state regulation of the habitability of shelters,[326] and limited tenancy rights of persons living in transitional housing.[327]

Most localities zone emergency shelters and transitional housing restrictively if they allow them at all.[328] Most jurisdictions limit the zones in which these uses are allowed, nearly universally excluding them from single-family zones. Some localities limit emergency shelters to traditionally nonresidential areas, for example, industrial or commercial zones, either as permitted uses or with a zoning variance or conditional use permit.[329] Other

---

Coalition for the Homeless and The National Law Center on Homelessness & Poverty, https://www.nationalhomeless.org/publications/crimreport/report.pdf (last accessed Dec. 6, 2021); Housing Not Handcuffs, a 2019 report by the National Law Center on Homelessness & Poverty, http://nlchp.org/wp-content/uploads/2019/12/HOUSING-NOT-HANDCUFFS-2019-FINAL.pdf.

324. Courts have approved constitutional challenges to ordinances banning sleeping in vehicles, camping, and panhandling. "In 2014, the Ninth Circuit struck down a citywide ordinance banning sleeping in vehicles in *Desertrain v. City of Los Angeles*, holding the ordinance 'unconstitutionally vague on its face because it provides insufficient notice of the conduct it penalizes and promotes arbitrary and discriminatory enforcement.'" Joanna Laine, *From Criminalization to Humanization: Ending Discrimination Against the Homeless*, 39 HARBINGER 1, 4 (2015). In *Martin v. City of* Boise, 920 F.3d 584 (9th Cir. 2019) the court ruled the Eighth Amendment prohibited the imposition of criminal penalties for sitting, sleeping, or lying outside on public property on homeless individuals who could not obtain shelter.

325. There is no right to shelter recognized in the federal constitution. Lindsey v. Normet, 405 U.S. 56 (1972). *See generally* Ann M. Burkhart, *The Constitutional Underpinnings of Homelessness*, 40 HOUS. L. REV. 211, 211 (2003). However, some state constitutions and statutes have recognized limited rights to shelter; R. George Wright, *Homelessness, Criminal Responsibility, and the Pathologies of Policy: Triangulating on A Constitutional Right to Housing*, 93 ST. JOHN'S L. REV. 427, 428 (2019). *See* Hafetz, *supra* note 323, at 1231–34; Dennis D. Hirsch, Note, *Making Shelter Work: Placing Conditions on an Employable Person's Right to Shelter*, 100 YALE L.J. 491, 491 nn.5–7 (1990). *See, e.g.*, Hodge v. Ginsberg, 303 S.E.2d 245 (W. Va. 1983); Wash. State Coalition for the Homeless v. Dep't of Soc. & Health Servs., 949 P.2d 1291 (Wash. 1997).

326. Many states regulate the habitability of shelters, often via funding. *See* Dave Furman & Mike McGurrin, *Hunger and Homelessness in America: A Survey of State Legislation*, 66 DENV. U. L. REV. 277, 284 & n.59 (1989). *But see* Wilkins v. Perales, 487 N.Y.S.2d 961 (N.Y. Sup. Ct. 1985). Brown v. City of New York, 786 F. App'x 289 (2d. Cir. 2019) (claims by homeless shelter residents against city seeking damages resulting from alleged dangerous conditions and negligent treatment was dismissed).

327. States are split on the status and tenancy rights of persons living in transitional housing. California's Transitional Housing Participant Misconduct Act, CAL. CIVIL CODE §§ 1954.10 *et seq.* (West 2020), provides persons living in transitional housing with limited rights. Iowa excludes from residential landlord and tenant laws "[o]ccupancy in housing owned by a nonprofit organization whose purpose is to provide transitional housing for persons released from drug or alcohol treatment facilities and in housing for homeless persons." IOWA CODE ANN. § 562A.5(8) (West 2010). Massachusetts extends tenancy rights to women in domestic violence transitional housing programs. *See* Serreze v. YWCA of W. Mass., 572 N.E.2d 581 (Mass. App. Ct. 1991).

328. For example, *In re* Society for Preservation of Historic Oakwood, 571 S.E.2d 588 (N.C. Ct. App. 2002) (reviewing Raleigh City Code ordinance which excludes transitional housing from Shopping Center and Office and Institution-II district, but allows multifamily housing in that district).

329. *See, e.g.*, Sullivan v. Kuehling, 777 S.W.2d 952 (Mo. Ct. App. 1989) (finding homeless shelter permitted use in industrial zone). *And see* Beck v. City of Tillamook, 313 Or. 148 (Or. 1992) (conditional use permit); Vitti v. Zoning Bd. of Adjustment, 710 A.2d 653 (Pa. Commw. 1998) (variances and special exception).

jurisdictions apply spacing requirements to control the concentration of these uses.[330] Typically, local zoning ordinances require a conditional or special use permit either directly or indirectly for the establishment of emergency shelters and transitional housing in areas where they are permitted.[331] Some jurisdictions explicitly define "homeless shelter," "emergency shelter," or "transitional housing" as uses in their planning codes, and require a conditional or special use permit directly.[332] Other jurisdictions do not include these specific definitions in their planning codes, and require a conditional or special use permit for whatever category it is found to fit, such as considering an emergency shelter as a "community service," "community use," or some other type of nonresidential use that requires a special permit.[333]

When conditional or special use permits are approved, they often contain burdensome and sometimes expensive conditions.[334] In addition, many jurisdictions apply demanding development standards for emergency shelters and transitional housing for which variances or other regulatory relief must be sought.[335]

Some localities have adopted less restrictive zoning.[336] Local government zoning restrictions may not apply if an emergency shelter is operated on public land[337] or run by a government entity (or a closely associated private entity).[338] Emergency shelters or

---

330. *See* Elk Grove (California) Municipal Code 23.80.040(A)(1)(b) providing: "All emergency shelter programs must be situated more than three hundred (300' 0") feet from any other emergency shelter or day program serving primarily homeless individuals or households." https://www.codepublishing.com/CA/ElkGrove/html/ElkGrove23/ElkGrove2380.html.
See also Hoffmaster v. City of San Diego, 64 Cal. Rptr. 2d 684 (Cal. Ct. App. 1997); *disagreed with in* Fonseca v. City of Gilroy, 148 Cal. App. 4th 1174, n.32 (Cal. App. 2007), *review denied* (July 18, 2007), and *declined to extend in* St. Vincent's School for Boys, Catholic Charities CYO v. City of San Rafael, 161 Cal. App. 4th 989 (Cal. App. 2008); Doe v. City of Butler, 892 F.2d 315 (3d Cir. 1989).
331. *But see* Franklinton Coalition v. Open Shelter, Inc., 469 N.E.2d 861 (Ohio Ct. App. 1983).
332. *See, e.g.*, Siesta Hills Neighborhood Ass'n v. City of Albuquerque, 954 P.2d 102 (N.M. Ct. App. 1998); FORT LAUDERDALE, FLA., CODE § 47-18.32 (1999) (describing review process and standards).
333. *See* Wagner v. City of Erie Zoning Hearing Bd., 675 A.2d 791, 795 (Pa. Commw. Ct. 1996); Brennan v. Bd. of Zoning Appeals, Evansville, 695 N.E.2d 983 (Ind. Ct. App. 1998); Turning Point, Inc. v. City of Caldwell, 74 F.3d 941, 944 (9th Cir. 1996); Vitti v. Zoning Bd. of Adjustment, 710 A.2d 653, 656 (Pa. Commw. Ct. 1998). *But see* Concerned Citizens of Downtown v. Bd. of Adjustment, 94 N.C. App. 364 (1989) (considering homeless shelter as "community service" and therefore permitted use in commercial service district).
334. *See Turning Point, Inc.*, 74 F.3d at 945. Limitations on permitted occupancy is a common conflict, sometimes resolved by a condition in a permit.
335. *See, e.g., Wagner*, 675 A.2d at 799.
336. In response to a fair housing lawsuit, the city of Portland, Oregon, revised its planning and zoning ordinances, including for emergency shelters and transitional housing. The American Planning Association gave a national planning award to Portland for its work. *See* PORTLAND, OR., PLANNING & ZONING CODE ch. 33.285 (2020) for Portland's regulations of "short-term housing and mass shelters," https://www.portlandoregon.gov/bps/article/53328. *See also* Smith v. City of Portland, 814 P.2d 179 (Or. Ct. App. 1991); Tournier v. City of Portland, 16 Or. LUBA 546 (1988), available on page 46 at https://www.oregon.gov/LUBA/docs/Headnotes/1.1.1.pdf.
337. *See, e.g.*, Pittsfield Charter Twp. v. Washtenaw Cnty., 664 N.W.2d 193 (Mich. 2002).
338. *See, e.g.*, 85 Op. Att'y Gen. No. 00-010 (Apr. 27, 2000) (Maryland opinion finding domestic violence center House of Ruth exempt from local zoning because operating on public property

transitional housing programs intending to serve survivors of domestic violence sometimes receive more favorable zoning treatment than those serving other populations.[339] In some cases, no public hearings are required in order to protect the confidentiality and security of the residents.[340]

HUD funding requirements, the federal Fair Housing Act (FHA and its state counterparts), and Religious Land Use and Institutionalized Persons Act of 2000 (RLUIPA) each offer federal statutory support for the development of emergency shelters and transitional housing. HUD's Consolidated Plan requires participating jurisdictions to plan for the housing needs of homeless persons as a condition of receiving certain federal funding.[341] Localities may be liable under the federal FHA for zoning and planning decisions that discriminate against the rights of homeless people who qualify for its protection. Courts often consider emergency shelters as covered "dwellings" for purposes of the FHA, and the populations of homeless people that shelter sponsors seek to serve often qualify as members of classes protected under the FHA.[342] Courts have increasingly ruled that emergency shelters and transitional housing units are considered "dwellings" for purposes of applica-

---

and performing "public purpose" use), http://www.marylandattorneygeneral.gov/Opinions%20 Documents/2000/85oag114.pdf.

339. *See* N.J. Stat. Ann. § 40:55D-66.1 (West 2017); Metro. King County, Wash. Zoning Code § 21A.08.030 (June 2020), https://www.kingcounty.gov/council/legislation/kc_code/24_30 _Title_21A.aspx; Portland, Ore., permits "short-term housing" that exclusively serves victims of sexual or domestic violence as of right in several zones. Portland, Or., Planning & Zoning Code § 33.285.040(A)(4) (2020), https://www.portlandoregon.gov/bps/article/53328. While restricting admission to a domestic violence shelter to women could conceivably be challenged as illegal sex discrimination under the federal Fair Housing Act and state equivalents, no published opinion has ever come to this conclusion. The issue was not raised in *Doe v. City of Butler*, 892 F.2d 315 (3d Cir. 1989). The issue was raised in *Blumhorst v. Jewish Family Servs. of Los Angeles*, 126 Cal. App. 4th 993 (2d Dist. 2005), in which a male plaintiff sued multiple domestic violence shelters that received state funding, all of which exclusively served women, for sex discrimination pursuant to Cal. Gov't Code section 11135, but the court found that the plaintiff lacked standing to sue. *See generally* Susan A. Lynch, *Real Property: Land Use and Zoning, in* The Impact of Domestic Violence on Your Legal Practice: A Lawyer's Handbook (ABA 2016), https://www.americanbar .org/products/inv/book/315624650/.

340. *See, e.g.*, Detroit, Mich., City Code §§ 50-11-204, 50-12-165, 50-8-134, 50-8-164, 50-9-44, and 50-9-104 (2020) (providing that, for confidentiality and security, shelter for victims of domestic violence are permitted as of right in certain zoning districts); California Health & Safety Code § 33334.3(f)(3)(B)(iii) and § 33418(c)(2) (West 2020).

341. See Chapter 2, *supra*, for a discussion of consolidated plan requirements. And see Chapter 3, *supra*, for general coverage of the federal Fair Housing Act. For substantial coverage of fair housing issues, see Robert G. Schwemm, Housing Discrimination: Law and Litigation (Thompson Reuters 2020).

342. Determining whether or not any particular emergency shelter is a "dwelling" for purposes of the FHA is a fact issue. *See* Turning Point, Inc. v. City of Caldwell, 74 F.3d 941, 945 (9th Cir. 1996) (applying the FHA to a homeless shelter); Community House, Inc. v. City of Boise, 468 F.3d 1118, 1123 (9th Cir. 2006) (same with additional discussion); Woods v. Foster, 884 F. Supp. 1169 (N.D. Ill. 1995) (finding homeless shelter was a "dwelling" for purposes of the FHA); Johnson v. Dixon, 786 F. Supp. 1, 4 (D.D.C. 1991) (assuming without deciding that homeless shelter is a "dwelling" under the FHA); Intermountain Fair Housing Council v. Boise Rescue Mission Ministries, 717 F. Supp. 2d 1101 (D. Idaho 2010) (finding a temporary shelter is not a "dwelling" pursuant to the FHA); Renda v. Iowa Civil Rights Comm'n, 2010 WL 2218611 (Iowa 2010) (finding a correctional facility is not a "dwelling" pursuant to the FHA). Community notification and permit approval requirements as well

tion of federal Fair Housing Act (FHA).[343] Additionally, current HUD regulations identify "sleeping accommodations in shelters intended for occupancy as a residence for homeless persons" as an example of a "dwelling unit."[344] Courts have applied the FHA's "reasonable accommodation" requirement to force localities to give regulatory relief for development proposals designed to serve homeless people who are disproportionately persons with disabilities.[345]

When churches or religious entities sponsor the development of shelters or transitional housing, they may encounter particular forms of opposition, but also may have special opportunities. The RLUIPA prohibits enforcement of land-use regulations "that impose[] a substantial burden on the religious exercise of a person, including a religious assembly or institution."[346] Courts have applied RLUIPA's predecessor statute to enable the establishment of a religiously affiliated homeless shelter as "accessory use" to a church, a temple, or a mosque.[347] Some courts have found such uses as permissible accessory uses to religious institutions without reference to the federal statute.[348]

Several states encourage or enable the creation of emergency shelters and transitional housing. For, example, California, which has experienced a growing homelessness crisis, has enacted extensive legislation (13 bills in 2019) incentivizing local governments to build emergency shelters and temporary housing.[349] New York City, with record numbers

---

as denying or conditioning funding may be illegal if discriminatorily applied to housing for persons protected by the FHA.

343. The inquiry is based on a factual finding related to nature of the housing, including length of stay and whether the facility is intended to be treated as a home. *See, e.g.*, Defiore v. City Rescue Mission of New Castle, 995 F. Supp. 2d 413 (W.D. Pa. 2013) (holding emergency shelter with stays ranging from 1 to 90 days, where residents receive mail, receive medication dispensed by staff, and return to sleeping areas in evening, is a "dwelling" under the FHA); Hunter on behalf of A.H. v. D.C., 64 F. Supp. 3d 158 (D.D.C. 2014) (holding temporary homeless shelters can be "dwellings" under the FHA).

344. 24 C.F.R. § 100.201.

345. *Turning Point, Inc.*, 74 F.3d at 945.

346. 42 U.S.C. § 2000cc(a)(1) (West 2009). The Religious Land Use and Institutionalized Persons Act of 2000, 42 U.S.C. §§ 2000cc to cc-5 (West 2009) is Congress' second attempt to limit local government zoning authority over religious land uses. The Religious Freedom Restoration Act (RFRA), 42 U.S.C. § 2000bb to bb-4, was the predecessor to RLUIPA. The Supreme Court found RFRA unconstitutional as applied to the states in *City of Boerne v. P.F. Flores*, 521 U.S. 507 (1997). The constitutionality of RLUIPA is also disputed. *See, e.g.*, Lighthouse Inst. for Evangelism, Inc. v. City of Long Branch, 510 F.3d 253, 254, 268–69 (3d Cir. 2007). *And see* 181 A.L.R., Fed. 247, Validity, Construction, and Operation of Religious Land Use and Institutionalized Persons Act of 2000 (42 U.S.C.A. §§ 2000cc, *et seq.*).

347. Successful uses under RFRA include: Daytona Rescue Mission v. City of Daytona Beach, 885 F. Supp. 1554 (M.D. Fla. 1995); Western Presb. Church v. Bd. of Zoning Adjustment of D.C., 862 F. Supp. 538, 547 (D.D.C. 1994); and Jesus Ctr. v. Farmington Hills Zoning Bd. of Appeals, 544 N.W.2d 698 (Mich. Ct. App. 1996).

348. *See, e.g.*, Greentree at Murray Hill Condo v. Good Shepherd Episcopal Church, 550 N.Y.S.2d 981 (N.Y. Sup. Ct. 1989).

349. https://www.gov.ca.gov/2019/09/26/building-off-historic-investment-action-to-help-cities-and-counties-tackle-homelessness-governor-newsom-signs-series-of-bills-addressing-homelessness/.

of homeless individuals, has enacted legislation requiring designated affordable-housing projects to set aside 15 percent of the units for the homeless.[350]

Most states promote these housing options by prohibiting housing discrimination based upon the income status of the intended occupants;[351] requiring localities to plan for the siting of such housing developments in their jurisdiction;[352] making state facilities, for example, state armories, or other public land available as emergency shelters;[353] facilitating their development by reducing localities' legal liability for establishing their own shelters;[354] and granting standing for housing organizations to challenge local government disapproval of housing developments for very low, low, or moderate income households (including emergency shelters).[355] In some cases, courts find that local laws that would exclude emergency housing are preempted by state laws.[356]

350. https://www.nytimes.com/2019/12/12/nyregion/homeless-housing-nyc.html.

351. CAL. GOV'T CODE § 65008(c) (West 2010). *See* Keith v. Volpe, 858 F.2d 467 (9th Cir. 1988); Shea Homes Ltd. P'ship v. County of Alameda, 2 Cal. Rptr. 3d 739 (Cal. Ct. App. 2002); Bldg. Indus. Ass'n v. City of Oceanside, 33 Cal. Rptr. 2d 137 (Cal. Ct. App. 1994).

352. California's housing element law requires localities to include analysis of the housing needs of "families and persons in need of emergency shelter," CAL. GOV'T CODE § 65583(a)(7) (West 2010), and to identify adequate development sites for "emergency shelters" and "transitional housing," CAL. GOV'T CODE § 65583(c)(1) (West 2010). *See* Hoffmaster v. City of San Diego, 64 Cal. Rptr. 2d 684 (Cal. Ct. App. 1997); *disagreed with in* Fonseca v. City of Gilroy, 148 Cal. App. 4th 1174 n.32 (Cal. App. 2007), *review denied* (July 18, 2007), and *declined to extend in* St. Vincent's School for Boys, Catholic Charities CYO v. City of San Rafael, 161 Cal. App. 4th 989 (Cal. App. 2008).

353. *See, e.g.*, CAL. GOV. CODE § 15301.3 (West 2010). See Chapter 2, *supra*, for a discussion of California's Housing Element law.

354. *See, e.g.*, CAL. GOV. CODE § 8698.1 (West 2010).

355. California law AB 2584 (2016), https://leginfo.legislature.ca.gov/faces/billNavClient.xhtml?bill_id=201520160AB2584.

356. *See, e.g.*, City of New York v. Town of Blooming Grove Zoning Bd., 761 N.Y.S.2d 241 (N.Y. App. Div. 2003).

Federal, State, and Local Building and Housing Codes Affecting Affordable Housing

6

Ronald S. Javor and Michael Allen

I. INTRODUCTION

Developing, operating, and preserving affordable housing depend on many factors in addition to capable developers, owners, and resources. These building blocks include federal, state, and local construction and housing maintenance codes and laws that apply to all residential construction and operations. They are designed to serve important public interests, including ensuring the safety of residents and the general public and sometimes balancing competing demands of social and financial concerns. They can be problematic, however, because in their development and application, they also may serve other legitimate but less appropriate purposes.[1]

Building and maintenance codes regulating the construction and operation of housing are derived from a number of sources, both public and private. Knowledge of the sources and purposes of these requirements ensures that their application is a benefit to residential developments, their residents, and their owners. However, like any other building block, there may be inconsistent requirements that need reconciliation, ambiguities requiring clarification, or erroneous advice or enforcement requiring appropriate resolution. These problems may be exacerbated by the variety of building types; variation in standards across city, county, or state jurisdictions; or inadequate development of the codes. Failure to comply with these codes and standards can have significant financial consequences, delay or impede rentals or sales, or even result in owners or renters being prohibited from using the completed structure. In addition, failure to comply may prevent the housing from

---

1. *See* discussion *infra* at Section IV.F.

serving its purpose: providing decent, safe, affordable, and accessible residential opportunities for households that have one or more financial, physical, social, or other limitations.

Section II explains how construction and maintenance codes serve valuable public purposes. Section III provides an overview of general state and local building and housing codes, describing their purposes, content, and enforcement. Finally, Section IV gives an overview of federal, state, and local housing codes designed to serve special purposes, such as enabling access for persons with disabilities, codes applied to manufactured housing, and codes associated with public housing finance programs.

II. VALUE OF CONSTRUCTION AND MAINTENANCE CODES

How do federal, state, and local construction and housing maintenance codes and laws serve the safety of residents and the general public? Building codes governing structural strength are intended to ensure that homes will sustain regular safe use and help protect against events like earthquakes, flood damage, snow loads, or windstorms. Similarly, plumbing codes ensure a potable water supply and a sanitary liquid effluent flow into drains and sewers while preventing contamination and leakage (which may cause mold or other health hazards). Fire codes prevent fires and, in the event of a fire, protect both occupants and their property as well as first responders while assisting escape and fire suppression. Electrical codes ensure that electrical power is safe for occupant use and electrical appliances and other devices function properly. "Green" codes establish both mandatory and voluntary building standards that enhance energy and water conservation (with both societal and individual cost savings), reduce impacts on the environment (by reducing the "carbon footprint" or greenhouse gases), provide for healthier indoor living conditions, and promote recycling and reuse of materials. These construction codes also include provisions to ensure that persons with disabilities or activity limitations have access to livable housing that will meet their specific needs or is adaptable to meet them. Other codes, such as maintenance or abatement codes, establish minimum housing use requirements to preserve the health of residents, improve quality of life, and provide government enforcement procedures.

Building codes serve a number of other common and necessary purposes, almost all of which add to construction costs. In many states, structural codes are enhanced to better protect against extraordinary windstorms, flooding, and earthquakes. Energy codes, impacting all elements of a building, address the conservation of energy by limiting climate effects and increasing livability by becoming more energy efficient. In response to wildland fires, building exteriors and interiors are including more expensive fire-resistant or -retardant materials and design.

Construction standards also serve the public interest, rather than just the interests of residents and building owners. Federal and state funding agencies may require construction standards in excess of local building codes to ensure the long-term availability and sustainability of affordable housing. These requirements also ensure that the building, as well as secured loans and grants, have adequate value in case of foreclosure. Local governments may impose requirements to reduce the costs of public services, passing on the costs to the developer. Local governments also may impose "design enhancements" to respond to neighborhood opposition, address perceived stereotypes of proposed lower-income residents and their families, upgrade neighborhoods, or merely add barriers to development.

Housing maintenance codes also play a critical role. They protect occupant health by ensuring adequate heat, air circulation, and water supply, for example. They prevent illness by prohibiting mold and lead exposure, requiring weatherproof conditions, and mandating repairs of defects. Through code enforcement procedures, they ensure that tenants have administrative recourse for complaints and repairs rather than having to rely only on judicial action when negligent or unscrupulous landlords refuse to perform necessary repairs.

Altogether, building and maintenance codes (see Section III, *infra*), when used properly, can help create safe occupancies at reasonable costs.[2] However, as these codes are modified to serve greater actual or perceived societal purposes, construction costs are increased, and fewer direct benefits may flow to the most vulnerable and needy members of the community. A critical part of the legal review of proposed affordable housing development and maintenance standards is understanding the purposes, source, development, and proper application of building codes. This review will ensure that design, construction, and use comply with legal requirements while providing appropriate living standards for residents, benefits for the public, long-term use, and financial feasibility.[3]

III. OVERVIEW OF GENERAL STATE AND LOCAL BUILDING AND HOUSING CODES

A variety of types of laws and ordinances regulate the construction, use, maintenance, and repair of residential structures. These may be categorized as building codes, government design standards, private design standards, and maintenance standards. Different standards may exist and may be applicable to a specific structure depending on the nature of the occupancy, the means of construction, the source of financing, or the location of the development.

A. Conventional Housing Construction Codes

The most common types of building codes imposed by state or local governments are conventional construction codes. These codes promote consistent safe standards (as opposed to individually approved designs) and reduce planning, construction, and inspection costs. Generally, these codes allow use of current methods and materials, and are flexible enough to allow the use of new technology and to eliminate problems for builders and owners.

---

2. Under the auspices of its Reducing Regulatory Barriers program, the U.S. Dep't of Housing and Urban Development (HUD) has published reports such as "Why Not in Our Community: Removing Barriers to Affordable Housing" (2005), http://www.huduser.org/portal/publications /affhsg/whynotourComm.html. Also in 2005, HUD published a study on code development and impacts on housing construction and rehabilitation (https://www.huduser.gov/periodicals/cityscpe /vol8num1/ch2.pdf) and a response to that study (https://www.huduser.gov/periodicals/cityscpe /vol8num1/res1.pdf) (both last accessed on January 1, 2020). The White House Council on Eliminating Regulatory Barriers to Affordable Housing issued a Request for Information regarding "barriers" on November 22, 2019, https://www.federalregister.gov/documents/2020/01/14/2020-00441/white -house-council-on-eliminating-regulatory-barriers-to-affordable-housing-request-for-information, and issued a report in January 2020, https://www.huduser.gov/portal/portal/sites/default/files/pdf /eliminating-regulatory-barriers-to-affordable-housing.pdf (last accessed January 1, 2020).

3. See Chapters 2–5, *supra*, for discussions of planning and zoning requirements.

Conventional construction codes are used by architects and engineers during building design. Subsequently, local building officials use these codes to ensure compliance when the plans are reviewed, during construction, and at the final inspection to ensure consistency with the approved building plans. Generally, the building codes also include provisions for "alternate approvals," which require that the structure meet code standards for functionality and safety but allow variations after government approvals for purposes of funding, aesthetics, or other requirements.[4]

The primary and original purpose of these building standards is to ensure the health and safety of residents and the public.[5] In the United States, building and maintenance codes initially were enacted in larger cities to avoid or reduce widespread fires, disease, and injury. Over time, several regional model building standards codes were developed by private organizations for use in different jurisdictions.[6]

A state's or locality's building standards code generally comprises numerous parts or subcodes, including a building code (structural requirements and materials), an electric code, a plumbing and mechanical code, a fire code, and a model energy code. Disabled access requirements usually are inserted either in the building code or as parts of other specific codes (e.g., the height of electrical receptacles may be in the electric code rather than the building code). Other subcodes address additional issues, such as housing maintenance and use, sewage disposal, and fuel gas requirements.

Other potential threats to health and safety are not necessarily addressed by all building codes. Radon is a radioactive gas found in soil beneath houses that seeps into housing through cracks and other fissures and can cause lung cancer. The U.S. Environmental Protection Agency is promoting "Radon-Resistant New Construction" (RRNC). According to the EPA, many states do not have statewide RRNC codes, and other states allow local

---

4. Discussed *infra*; *see* notes 15–16 and accompanying text.

5. Most American building codes trace their genesis to the 18th and 19th centuries, although the earliest known building code was in *Hammurabi's Code of Laws*, which stated, "If a builder builds a house for someone and does not construct it properly, and the house which he built fall and kill its owner, then that builder shall be put to death." Analogous penalties were imposed if a slave or property were lost. The first fire codes apparently were developed around AD 64 after the burning of Rome. The London Building Act (1894) addressed both fire-related issues (e.g., access, height, etc.) as well as building materials and differentiated between three general uses (residential, commercial/manufacturing, and congregate or gathering places). Tenement house safety acts were adopted by various states, including a series of New York Tenement Acts (1867, requiring fire escapes and a window; 1887, requiring interior privies; and 1901, requiring better construction, indoor toilets, windows, and other improvements) and in California in 1909 (after the immense damage from the San Francisco earthquake in 1906).

6. These were the International Conference of Building Officials (ICBO), which published the first Uniform Building Code and related codes used in the western United States; the Southern Building Code Congress International (SBCCI), which published the Standard Building Code for use primarily in the southeastern areas of the country; the Building Officials and Code Administrators International (BOCA), which published the Basic/National Building Code used predominantly in the northeast areas; and the National Fire Protection Association (NFPA), which published fire safety standards impacting all parts of the codes. Another commonly used code, the Council of American Building Officials (CABO) One- and Two-Family Code, was used extensively in many states for many years as a single-family housing building code.

governments to adopt RRNC codes.[7] Other indoor air quality issues may include formaldehyde off-gassing from certain products, mold from inadequate venting, and particulates from inadequate ventilation.

In 2000, after a merger of three general model code groups, the International Code Council (ICC) published its first International Code, a family of codes now consisting of 15 individual codes, including two building codes (the International Building Code, or IBC, for multifamily structures and the International Residential Code, or IRC, or one- and two-family residential structures), a plumbing code, an energy conservation code, a residential construction code that combines several codes and is applicable to single-family and two-family residential structures, and, since 2018, the International Green Conservation Code. Subsequently, the National Fire Protection Association (NFPA), with partners such as the International Association of Plumbing and Mechanical Officials (IAPMO), published a family of codes called the Comprehensive Consensus Code (C3). The ICC now publishes the primary family of codes. NFPA publishes more than 300 codes, including fire, life safety, fuel gas, and electrical codes. IAPMO primarily publishes plumbing and mechanical codes as well as a uniform solar energy code and a "Green Plumbing and Mechanical Supplement." Each family of codes has different approaches to the standards and their development. These differences may impact housing costs and construction when architects or designers from other jurisdictions utilize different codes.[8]

The panoply of building standards and codes applicable to a particular construction or rehabilitation project is jurisdiction-specific and can be derived from a number of model codes that are published by one or more national code groups. How particular codes are selected and adopted, and whether they are applied as written, depends on state laws or local government ordinances. Adoption of non–model code standards may be based on specific local conditions that are unique to a particular geographic area.

Local modifications to the model codes may include (1) additional energy conservation standards; (2) extensive internal fire-suppression requirements (such as requiring both firewalls and expansive sprinkler systems); (3) prohibitions on certain materials or methods of construction that are adequate for general code requirements, such as certain types of plastic piping; or (4) requirements to use certain materials or methods of construction that are excessively expensive and may not have benefits to residents that are consistent with their costs. In contrast, the use of uniform construction standards generally decreases the costs of construction and code enforcement.

---

7. For building standards, see https://www.epa.gov/radon/building-codes-and-standards-radon-resistant-new-construction-rrnc (last accessed Jan. 1, 2020).

8. As of 2010, all or parts of the ICC family of codes had been adopted in 50 states, the District of Columbia, and Puerto Rico, and these codes also have been endorsed by HUD. For a list of which ICC codes are adopted in which jurisdictions, see http://www.iccsafe.org/advocacy (last accessed Jan. 1, 2020) and click on the link to "Online Building Codes." The NFPA fire code and electric code (National Electric Code) also have been adopted as standards in many localities (*see* http://www.nfpa.org and click on "Codefinder" for state information) (last accessed Jan. 1, 2020), along with the Uniform Mechanical Code and Uniform Plumbing Code published by IAPMO (*see* http://www.iapmo.org) (last accessed Jan. 1, 2020). Some states, cities, and counties continue to use and update the older codes, particularly specific subcodes, even though they are not updated by the model code organization to address new construction materials, designs, and techniques.

States can regulate whether and how local modifications are made. In California, for example, the state Department of Housing and Community Development proposes residential building codes for adoption by the California Building Standards Commission with a number of statewide amendments or modifications to the model codes in order to address California conditions that impact on affordability.[9] After adoption by the Building Standards Commission, California's 600 or so cities and counties have six months to take one of three actions: (1) enforce the approved California Building Standards Code; (2) enforce the approved statewide code with local amendments (but those local amendments must be supported by findings identifying unique local climatic, geologic, or topographical conditions); or (3) take no action, resulting in the California Building Standards Code being adopted by operation of law after the six-month period.[10]

Building code requirements, adoptions, and procedures in other states and localities vary widely. In particular, there are especially large variations between statewide and local codes, as well as differences in base model codes. In Colorado, state building codes apply to certain state-owned buildings, and local building codes apply to most dwellings. The state and localities rely on the International Building Code, the International Mechanical Code, the International Plumbing Code, either International or NFPA fire codes, and the National Electrical Code, among others.[11]

Illinois has a statewide plumbing code; it adopts a fire/life safety code (except for one- and two-family structures) and the International Energy Conservation Code statewide, and it enforces a statewide accessibility code that localities must adopt as minimum standards. Chicago had written its own building and mechanical codes but now uses the current ICC Building Code as a model for the Chicago Building Code.

Pennsylvania has had a statewide Uniform Construction Code (UCC) that, since December 10, 2009, has been based on the International Code Council's family of codes. Local governments may elect to enforce the UCC, and more than 90 percent of Pennsylvania's 2,562 municipalities have chosen to do so.[12]

Texas adopts a few statewide building codes, leaving building code adoption to localities, which adopt a variety of uniform codes for all buildings, including residential occupancies.[13] Similarly, Arizona does not adopt a statewide residential building code; however, all but one jurisdiction, Yuma County, adopts the International Building Code, and most jurisdictions enforce the International Residential Code. One impetus for adoption of statewide codes is a significant natural disaster: Florida adopted one after Hurricane Andrew in 1992, and Mississippi and Louisiana adopted statewide codes after Hurricane Katrina in 2005.

---

9. CAL. HEALTH & SAFETY CODE § 18930(a) (2020).

10. *Id.* § 17958.

11. COLO. REV. STAT. §§ 9-5-104, 30-28-201 (2020).

12. *See* https://www.dli.pa.gov/ucc/Pages/default.aspx (last accessed Jan. 1, 2020). *See* 35 PA. STAT. §§ 7210.101, *et seq.*, Pennsylvania Construction Code Act, 2017 Pub. L. 352, No. 36 (directing Department of Labor & Industry to promulgate regulations adopting the UCC); *id.* at § 7210.303 and § 7210.501, *et seq.* (concerning municipal adoption and enforcement); and information on adoptions and links to specific jurisdictions at https://www.dli.pa.gov/Individuals/Labor-Management-Relations/bois/Documents/UCCMUN.HTM (last accessed Jan. 1, 2020).

13. *See* ICC code adoption page for Texas, https://www.iccsafe.org/advocacy/adoptions-map/texas/ (last accessed Jan. 1, 2020).

Other states, cities, and counties have a variety of other combinations. Currently, there is no *public* resource available to provide general information on building codes in all states. The applicable codes for a particular jurisdiction can be found through a local building department, the state agency responsible for building codes, if any, or by checking with the model code bodies.[14]

In lieu of using the official building codes, developers may use other methods, materials, designs, and installations through a process called "alternate approvals" if they can demonstrate that the utilized variation is functionally equivalent to the code requirement.[15] This option is useful if certain design features are necessary but may be too costly using current codes, or the codes may not be conducive to the design feature.[16]

Once building standards are identified and employed by architects or engineers, the most important regulatory requirements should have been resolved, but often this is not the case. More major physical requirements may be imposed as "design standards."[17] Another problem may arise at the time of plan review by the local building department. While plan review should be almost ministerial—comparing plans to building codes—requirements in excess of code standards may be inadvertently or intentionally mandated. This may be attributable to inadequate training, lack of current or correct code reference books, misunderstanding about standards, or objections to affordable housing. This will result in increased costs and complexity of a project, potentially delaying both the commencement of construction and its completion.[18]

While building codes may be perceived to be firm standards, they can evolve in response to new safety concerns, inadequate performance, technological improvements, or unique local conditions. One example of the continuing modifications in building codes affecting builders, designers, and building departments relates to fire safety and

---

14. The ICC may be contacted at its headquarters, 500 New Jersey Ave., NW, 6th Floor, Washington D.C. 20001, (telephone: (888) 422-7233; facsimile, (202) 783-2348; e-mail: carecenter@iccsafe.org). NFPA's website is http://www.nfpa.org, and may be contacted at its headquarters, 1 Batterymarch Park, Quincy, MA 02169-7471 (telephone: (800-344-3555), e-mail: wdc@nfpa.org); IAPMO may be contacted at 4755 E. Philadelphia St., Ontario, CA 91761 (telephone: (909) 472-4100; e-mail: iapmo@iapmo.org) (all last accessed Jan. 1, 2020).

15. *See* I.B.C. § 1.8.7; I.R.C. § 1.8.6; CAL. HEALTH & SAFETY CODE § 17951(e)(2) (2020).

16. Alternate approvals also permit the use of new technology or special systems before the codes adopt them, although some building officials may be reluctant to approve them until they have been tested and used by other jurisdictions or building code experts. Alternate approval authority is located either in state law (*see, e.g.,* CAL. HEALTH & SAFETY CODE § 17923 (2020) (for statewide alternate approvals) or § 17951(c) (for local government alternate approvals)) or in the model codes themselves (I.B.C. §§ 104.10 and 104.11 and I.R.C. §§ R104-10 and R104.11) (2020).

17. *See infra,* Section III.F.

18. Delays of commencement and completion not only affect future residents; they can also impact financing partners or investment dates, costs of the construction loans, and deferral of rental income.

suppression.[19] Other examples include wildland urban interface exterior fire protections,[20] increased seismic construction and retrofit requirements, and improved standards for protection from hurricane-force winds.

When architects, builders, and planning departments do not rely on the same codes, a common result is that design, time, and cost can escalate rapidly. This is especially true in rural areas where, for example, changes in certain parts of plans may require additional review by other local public agencies, such as a health department. This lack of code coordination may also require additional reviews by funding agencies. Some of these extra costs can be avoided if the developer's construction, design, and legal personnel have current information about building code requirements and they meet in advance with their public counterparts to ensure their correct application.

B. Responding to Environmental Concerns: Health, Conservation, and Climate

Housing has evolved through the ages from mere shelter to both a nurturing site and equity investment, so too have the standards evolved from mere structural protections and minimum physical safety to today's growing recognition that "safety" is more than prevention of physical injury. Florence Nightingale once said, "Badly constructed houses do for the healthy what badly constructed hospitals do for the sick."[21] Coupled with the increased concern about internal environment is the more recent concern about housing becoming more responsive and compatible with external environmental concerns: air quality, resource conservation, and energy savings. Finally, over time, housing developers have increased efforts to make housing more impervious to external natural disaster and climate damage. Each of these developing movements adds to housing costs while ostensibly reducing long-term direct (e.g., utility bills) and indirect (medical bills) consumer costs.

1. Healthy Homes

As knowledge about pollutants continues to increase, and diagnostic practices become more precise, building codes and health advocates have begun to work together to address more than the traditional ventilation, light, and heat issues in housing codes. By one means or another, codes enhance the ability in homes to address dryness, cleanliness, ventilation, fire safety and unintentional accidents, contaminants, allergens and asthma, insects and rodents, pests such as bedbugs, radon, combustible sources, mold, and asbestos. Some of

---

19. The International Building Code, adopted throughout most of the country, includes many changes in sprinkler and fire protection requirements from earlier codes' standards. It has adopted the theory of allowing reductions in certain fire safety requirements when sprinklers are added, such as less fire-resistant corridor walls, longer exit distances, and narrower doors (see I.B.C. §§ 901, *et seq.* (2020)). In addition, the International Residential Code mandates fire sprinklers in one- and two-family structures (I.R.C. § R313). To the extent that a local fire department's first responders want more protection for themselves as well as occupants, they may seek local changes to the reductions recommended by the model code.

20. *See infra*, Section III.D.

21. For an excellent overview of the development of the housing-health relationship, see Chapters 1–3 of Housing Reference Manual (2006) published by the National Center for Healthy Housing, https://nchh.org/resource-library/2006_HHM_FINAL_chapter_01-03.pdf (last accessed Jan. 1, 2020).

these opportunities are in building codes and maintenance codes and some occur as a result of public education.

Not including a variety of state and local government agencies, a number of federal government and national nongovernment organizations have developed policies, procedures, and remedies for these indoor problems to prevent them or treat them. These include HUD Healthy Homes,[22] the National Center for Healthy Housing (which has a vast library of resources),[23] the National Healthy Homes Partnership,[24] and Green and Healthy Homes Initiative.[25]

a. Indoor Air Quality

Indoor air quality involves a number of factors, including building material off-gassing, carbon monoxide, mold, radon, and asbestos, and the U.S. EPA has estimated that the level of indoor air pollutants may be two to five times higher than outdoor levels.[26] For example, the U.S. EPA and some state laws also regulate the use and removal of asbestos, often found in older heating system furnace ducts, floor tiles, roof tiles, and decorative or soundproofing materials sprayed on walls.[27] Additional code response to indoor air quality include mandating carbon monoxide alarms as well as smoke alarms[28] and radon control protections.[29]

b. Lead-Based Paint

While lead-based paint manufacturing has been banned for residential spaces since 1971,[30] the paints continue to exist in homes. Lead in this paint is exposed either through the passage of time or by repairs and rehabilitation, although there are various laws and regulations governing disclosures, lead-safe work procedures, and training. Federal regulations include a Lead Disclosure Rule (applicable to housing, whether publicly or privately owned, built before 1976) and the Lead-Safe Housing Rule (applicable to HUD-assisted housing built before 1976).[31]

---

22. See https://www.hud.gov/program_offices/healthy_homes/hhi (last accessed January 1, 2020).

23. See https://nchh.org/ (last accessed Jan. 1, 2020).

24. See https://extensionhealthyhomes.org/ (last accessed Jan. 1, 2020).

25. See https://www.greenandhealthyhomes.org/ (last accessed Jan. 1, 2020).

26. For an assessment of issues related to mitigation of indoor air quality issues, *see* the Environmental Law Institute's "Indoor Air Quality in Homes" (2017), https://www.eli.org/research-repor t/indoor-air-quality-homes-state-policies-improving-health-now-and-addressing-future-risks -changing-climate (last accessed Jan. 1, 2020).

27. See http://www.epa.gov (search "asbestos") (last accessed Jan. 1, 2020) for federal information and consult state codes for state regulations, certification, and penalties.

28. I.B.C. § 915 and I.R.C. § R315 (2020).

29. I.R.C. App. F (although none in the IBC) (2020).

30. Lead Based Paint Poisoning Prevention Act, Public Law 91-695; *see also* CAL. HEALTH & SAFETY CODE
§ 17920.10 (2020), establishing California standards and linking lead hazards to the "substandard housing" definition.

31. For a variety of information, including lead-safe work practices, *see* https://www.hud.gov /program_offices/healthy_homes/lbp/hudguidelines1995. *See also infra* Section III.C., lead-safe work practices.

2. *Green Building Movement*

An example of environmental imperatives and improved technology clashing with social and financial goals is the sometimes required and sometimes voluntary "green" or "sustainable" building initiative, which includes energy conservation standards, sustainable building materials, and other factors being incorporated in all housing, including affordable housing. A number of organizations exist with unique perspectives, methods, and materials used to implement green housing and which provide written studies and examples of this concept.[32]

Considerable study has occurred with regard to the costs and benefits of green housing.[33] While some green standards are costly to implement, greater efficiency and cost savings can be achieved with careful energy design and planning.[34]

---

32. These organizations include the U.S. Green Building Council (which sponsors LEED standards), https://www.usgbc.org/leed; Enterprise (green communities), https://www.enterprisecommunity.org/solutions-and-innovation/green-communities; Build It Green (GreenPoint), https://www.builditgreen.org/greenpoint-rated/; HUD, and https://files.hudexchange.info/resources/documents/GreenHousingDevelopmentGuide.pdf; U.S. EPA (energy efficiency), https://www.energystar.gov/; and NetZero Build Summit, http://www.netzerobuildsummit.com/ (all last accessed Jan. 1, 2020).

33. The increase in design and construction costs associated with these improvements should be balanced against long-term operating savings to the owner and the residents. For one discussion of costs and benefits related to 16 affordable housing projects around the country, see *The Costs and Benefits of Green Affordable Housing*, published by New Ecology Inc. at http://www.newecology.org/publications (last accessed Jan. 1, 2020) and "Building Green in Low Income Housing Tax Credit Developments" (2020), https://www.huduser.gov/portal/pdredge/pdr_edge_featd_article_061614.html (last accessed Jan. 1, 2020). Other studies are available at the U.S. Green Building Council (USGBC) website, http://www.usgbc.org/ (last accessed Jan. 1, 2020). Typically, many jurisdictions have increased requirements for wall and roof insulation, window sizes and materials, and various appliances. However, these and other improvements, while creating some long-term savings and demonstrating adherence to "green principles," may have unintended consequences. Adding solar panels for electrical generation and/or heating water may require additional structural integrity and may increase the cost of future roof repairs and replacement. Vinyl plastic window frames, which conduct less heat, may create new fire hazards from external wildland fires. Sealing units better to block air flow in and out of a unit may exacerbate problems for those with environmental sensitivities, the so-called sick building syndrome. And roofing with lighter-color materials may reflect more summer heat, but also may result in reduced winter heat absorption. See Chapter 10, *infra*, for a brief discussion of the Energy Star program.

34. Colorado Court in Santa Monica, California, constructed by the Community Corporation of Santa Monica, is a 44-studio-unit structure with almost 100 percent of the power needed by residents generated by on-site solar photovoltaic panels and an on-site gas turbine. In addition, both passive energy design strategies (e.g., orientation of the building and windows) and energy-efficiency improvements (window shading; energy-efficient appliances; and integrated water heating, space heating, and cogeneration waste-heat systems) are expected to save over $10,000 each year in energy costs. For more information, see http://www.communitycorp.org/sustain (last accessed Jan. 1, 2020). Another recent California example is Mutual Housing at Spring Lake, the first certified zero net energy rental housing in the nation, mostly financed by USDA-RD among other sources with a majority of farmworker residents. For more information, including a "white paper" describing features, development issues, and benefits, see http://www.mutualhousing.com/yolo-communities/spring-lake/ (last accessed Jan. 1, 2020).

The "greening" of building codes and building methods and materials has accelerated rapidly. States and cities take various approaches to greening their codes.[35] In 2008, California adopted "CalGreen," a Green Building Standards Code, the first such state green code in the nation, and recently adopted a 2018 version.[36] This code consists of a number of voluntary standards and incorporated mandatory standards that already are in California's building codes as well as additional options. The ICC adopted the 2018 Green Building and Conservation Code, but it is only for commercial structures. Loans, grants, and tax credits are available from various federal and state agencies for specific housing types or purposes.

a. Solar Panels

The use of solar energy products for water heating and on-site electricity is rapidly expanding. Sold initially as a consumer product to merely save on electrical bills, it has become a "climate issue" with the goal of developing "zero-net energy" or "energy plus" homes that actually sell electricity back to utilities.[37] The building codes are involved not only for connections to a home but also to ensure that supporting roofs and roofing are structurally safe. In addition, to reach zero net energy, the homes generally require additional insulation, high efficiency appliances, high efficiency windows, passive temperature assistance, and heat pumps rather than standard heaters. Solar panels also involve civil issues, such as addressing factors that may interfere with roof placements and easements for access to sunlight.[38]

b. Energy Efficiency

Energy efficiency takes many forms in the building and rehabilitation codes and these requirements increase with each triannual update of the codes. Energy-efficient appliances, from refrigerators to lighting to water heaters, are part of increasingly standard construction specifications. When coupled with building standards, such as 2×6 studs allowing more wall insulation, increased attic and/or roofing material insulation, and measures to reduce heat and cooling loss such as dual pane windows and weatherization of all openings, these add minor costs to construction but long-term savings for consumers and the environment.[39]

---

35. For a comprehensive list of approaches, see http://www.usgbc.org/DisplayPage.aspx ?CMSPageID=1852 (last accessed July 6, 2020).

36. https://codes.iccsafe.org/content/CAGBSC2019/cover (last accessed Jan. 1, 2020).

37. California requires solar panels on most newly constructed low-rise single family and multifamily residential structures, as of January 1, 2020; see 2019 California Energy Code, Cal. Code Regs., tit. 24, pt. 6, § 150.1(a)14 (2020).

38. Solar easements and other "solar rights" have been enacted in California [(Cal. Civ. Code § 801) (2020)], Hawaii, Massachusetts, and New Mexico, among other states.

39. To see additional options, see the U.S. Department of Energy Energy-Efficient Home Design Scorecard at https://www.energy.gov/energysaver/design/energy-efficient-home-design (last accessed Jan. 1, 2020). See also "Energy Star Tools and Resources Applicable to Affordable Housing and Low-Income Housing Communities", https://www.energystar.gov/sites/default/files/tools /ES_affordablehousing_factsheet.pdf (last accessed Jan. 1, 2020).

c. Water Conservation

Water conservation has become a necessity almost everywhere, and the building codes and housing suppliers have taken steps to facilitate this. Low-flow or dual-flush toilets often are required, as well as flow regulators for water efficient appliances, faucets, and showers. The use of treated water for external irrigation reduction and for toilet flushing means fresh water use may be reduced by the adoption of recycled water systems installed during new construction.[40] In addition, contrary to the normal code rule that no changes in construction requirements can be mandated in existing buildings unless an existing item becomes substandard, California required replacement of toilets and fixtures in all buildings constructed before January 1, 1994, with specified water conservation items whenever a building permit is issued or, by January 1, 2014, for single-family homes and by January 1, 2019, for multifamily homes.[41]

d. Other Climate Change Issues

Ingenuity and perseverance to meet climatic necessities will continue to generate large and small changes to building and use codes. Electric vehicle charging stations not only are permissible but now may be required in many situations.[42] In mid-2019, two California cities, Berkeley and San Jose, banned natural gas appliances in all new buildings, requiring all-electric operations. California also in effect amended its existing housing maintenance codes by mandating that tenants may erect and use clotheslines or drying racks in their outdoor private areas subject to several conditions, including landlord permission.[43]

C. Preservation, Rehabilitation, and Repair

A state's or local jurisdiction's laws or ordinances governing repairs and rehabilitation may provide opportunities or cause problems for the owner (or prospective owner) of multifamily or single-family affordable housing developments.[44] The primary issues to consider are the extent to which more than a defective component itself must be repaired and the extent to which rehabilitation triggers additional unrelated work.[45]

Like construction codes, state or local jurisdictions regulate rehabilitation and repairs through general or specific codes and ordinances. Many jurisdictions merely adopt the various new construction codes to apply to any construction activity that exceeds a certain value or volume of activity. This approach may result in prohibitive costs and disincentives for adequate maintenance, consequently impacting affordability, health, and safety.

In California, for example, state law defines the attributes of a substandard or unsafe building.[46] State law also provides that local ordinances governing alteration and repair of

---

40. 2019 California Plumbing Code, CAL. CODE REGS., tit. 24, pt. 5, ch. 15 (2020).
41. CAL. CIV. CODE §§ 1101.11101.9 (2020).
42. See 2019 California Green Building Standards Code, CAL. CODE REGS., tit. 24, pt. 11, §§ 4-106.4–4-106.4.3.6 (2020).
43. CAL. CIV. CODE § 1940.20 (2020).
44. See Chapter 15, *infra,* for a discussion of legal issues concerning preservation of affordable housing.
45. See Chapter 9, *infra,* for a discussion of federal funding programs that include rehabilitation as an eligible activity.
46. CAL. HEALTH & SAFETY CODE §§ 17920.3, 17920.10 (2020).

existing buildings (as well as the moving of apartment houses and dwellings) must permit the replacement, retention, and extension of original materials and the continued use of original methods of construction. This is true as long as the dwelling complies with the building standards in effect at the time of construction, and the building (or relevant portion thereof) does not become or continue to be a substandard building.[47] If a residential structure becomes substandard and the owner fails to repair it, California remedies include direct repairs by the jurisdiction with temporary or permanent relocation payments (from owner to occupants) pursuant to a court order, receiverships to repair the building, and expedited repairs of vacant single-family dwellings in certain cities.[48]

Georgia takes a different approach, establishing a very low threshold triggering current codes. It defines a "renovated building" as either one in which the cost of alteration of the exterior envelope, or of specified utility systems, exceeds 10 percent of the assessed value of the building immediately prior to that alteration, or one in which the cost of alteration of the physical configuration or interior spaces exceeds one-fourth of the assessed value of the building immediately prior to that alteration.[49]

Other states may use model repair and maintenance codes. For example, Appendix J of the 2018 International Residential Code addresses the repair, renovation, and reconstruction of existing one- and two-unit homes while maintaining existing code compliance where appropriate. The ICC also has published the International Existing Building Code to replace the previous model code, the Uniform Code for Building Conservation. This international model code provides both prescriptive as well as performance standards and is intended to encourage the use and reuse of existing buildings by including standards that do not unnecessarily increase construction costs and do not restrict the use of new methods of construction or materials. It covers changes of occupancy, repairs, and three levels of alterations and additions.[50] In addition, in 1997 HUD published the National Applicable Recommended Rehabilitation Provisions (NARRP), a model rehabilitation code, to encourage the continued use or reuse of existing buildings and structures.[51] Portions of NARRP were adopted by the model code entities, with ICBO publishing the Uniform Code for Existing Buildings in 2000, and the ICC publishing the International Existing Building Code in 2003.

New Jersey has taken a proactive and coordinated approach to preservation, repairs, and rehabilitation. In 1998, the state adopted a rehabilitation subcode, which modified standards to encourage and assist housing rehabilitation, including work to effect a change of use.[52] State law previously applied new construction standards to rehabilitation work on existing buildings.[53] The subcode establishes three types of projects—rehabilitation,

---

47. *Id.* §§ 17922, 17958.8.

48. *See id.* §§ 17980, *et seq.*

49. GA. CODE ANN. § 8-2-20(8) (2020).

50. For an extensive discussion of the benefits and uses of this code, see https://www.nibs.org/files/pdfs/NIBS_NCGBCS_IEBC_WhitePaper_2016.pdf (last accessed Jan. 1, 2020).

51. For the NARRP text, see https://www.huduser.gov/Publications/pdf/HUD-7842.pdf (last accessed Jan. 1, 2020).

52. N.J. ADMIN. CODE, tit. 5, ch. 23, subch. 6, located at https://www.nj.gov/dca/divisions/codes/offices/rehab.html (last accessed Jan. 1, 2020).

53. The construction standards for new buildings applied if the rehabilitation work exceeded a certain cost (the ratio of the work on the building), whether or not floor space was added, or at the

change of use, and additions—and four categories of rehabilitation work: repair, renovation, alteration, and reconstruction.[54] The amount of work required varies with each type of project and category. The owner can determine the scope of work in advance by tailoring the project to the appropriate category.[55] All the necessary codes are in one document, clearly separated from requirements for new construction. Several years later, New Jersey adopted The Multifamily Housing Preservation and Receivership Act, which focuses on blighted properties as neighborhood problems. It enhances the ability to use both public funds and receiverships to repair these buildings and to provide for the transfer of properties to responsible owners if the noncomplying owner does not reimburse the costs of repair.[56] Since New Jersey's adoption of a rehabilitation subcode, the concept has been endorsed by HUD[57] and adopted in Rhode Island, Maryland, New Jersey, and Minnesota, among other states, and in Wichita, Kansas, and Wilmington, Delaware, among other cities.[58] In 2016, Texas adopted detailed administrative regulations, the "Texas Minimum Construction Standards," in order to assist in identifying and rehabilitating homes.[59]

A related effort that is used to create additional affordable housing is "adaptive reuse," the transformation of commercial or industrial buildings into residential structures. This rehabilitation activity results in a "change of occupancy," which usually triggers compliance with current codes, but there are both benefits and challenges to this approach.[60] California's approach to adaptive reuse allows a city or county to adopt alternative building regulations for the conversion of all or portions of commercial or industrial buildings to joint live-work residential quarters. The alternative building code need not follow the model codes adopted by California, but merely must impose standards that will protect

---

building department's discretion (based on its opinion regarding the impact of the improvements on the structure or components of the building). *See id.*

54. *Id.*

55. *Id.*

56. N.J. Stat. Ann. § 2A, 114–42 (P.L. 2003 c. 295).

57. *See, e.g., Smart Codes in Your Community: A Guide to Building Rehabilitation Codes*, Bldg. Tech., Inc., 2001, https://www.huduser.gov/portal//Publications/pdf/smartcodes.pdf (last accessed Jan. 1, 2020). See also *Best Practices for Effecting Rehabilitation of Affordable Housing* (2006), https://books.google.com/https://books.google.com/books?id=aKGgNv5RG5QC&pg=PA81&lpg =PA81&dq=nationally+applicable+recommended+rehabilitation+provisions&source=bl&ots=zQ 53fcFn9p&sig=ACfU3U1DR2RowD3r1XGVqyULzOQb43vYrg&hl=en&sa=X&ved=2ahUKEw jEuO2FspHnAhXCTN8KHb1KBvgQ6AEwBXoECAoQAQ#v=onepage&q=nationally%20appli- cable%20recommended%20rehabilitation%20provisions&f=false (last accessed Jan. 1, 2020).

58. *Smart Codes, supra* note 57, at 3.

59. See https://www.tdhca.state.tx.us/single-family/training/docs/14-TMCS.pdf (last accessed Jan. 1, 2020).

60. Rehabilitation, compared to new construction, often provides some cost savings. In addition, the current building standards codes are becoming more conducive to rehabilitation, approving materials that allow for cost savings, such as corrugated stainless steel tubing (CSST) for gas lines, which reduces the intrusions into walls for new gas lines. However, the challenges also are greater due to potential prior contamination issues, probable prior use of lead-based paint and asbestos products, and structural designs common for nonresidential structures that are difficult to adapt into residential structures.

the public health, safety, and welfare, in the determination of the local legislative body.[61] However, there may be special statewide rules.[62]

Special rules apply to the rehabilitation of historic structures. Generally, to qualify for historic preservation tax credits under various state or federal programs, substantial rehabilitation is necessary. However, state and local laws and ordinances may restrict either the quantity or quality, or both, of rehabilitation in order to retain the historic nature of the structure. In addition, building or rehabilitation codes may require specified upgrades inconsistent with some of the historic structure requirements.[63] Counsel should ensure that all applicable federal, state, and local rules and requirements are identified and complied with and become part of appropriate contracts with the architect or builder.[64]

Other laws may affect rehabilitation. Federal laws impose a number of health-related requirements. There are lead-safe work practices generally applicable to pre-1976 homes where lead-based paint commonly was used.[65] The federal standards often are enforced through state laws, which include worker certification for lead-safe practices and penalties. In addition, the U.S. Environmental Protection Agency issued a rule, 40 C.F.R. Part 745, requiring lead-safe work practices, which took effect on April 22, 2010. It applies to renovation, repair, and painting activities, but does not apply to minor maintenance or repair where less than six square feet of lead is disturbed in a room or less than 20 square feet is disturbed on the exterior, excluding window replacement.

In many states and local jurisdictions, new green construction and energy conservation requirements may be imposed on almost any type of rehabilitation. These requirements or standards may involve adding elements such as passive solar energy efforts; water conservation; building and glass requirements; use of special appliances or components; and recycling requirements or eliminating environmental hazards causing or contributing to poor health or other dangers such as lead, asbestos, or poor air circulation.[66] As previously discussed, these may add to construction costs. However, some of these capital costs may be offset by public and private subsidy programs for energy conservation improvements

---

61. CAL. HEALTH & SAFETY CODE § 17958.11 (2020).

62. For example, California Civil Code sections 1101.1 through 1101.9 (2020), enacted in 2009, mandate the replacement of noncompliant plumbing fixtures (that do not have specified water-conservation features) with fixtures meeting current use rates in 1994-or-older residential and commercial structures. These requirements apply at the time of building modifications, upon transfer, and for unmodified buildings by various deadlines starting in 2014.

63. To avoid this, California has developed guidelines in a State Historical Building Code that facilitate the preservation of original or restored architectural elements and features in a cost-effective and safe manner. *See* CAL. HEALTH & SAFETY CODE §§ 18951, *et seq.* (2020).

64. The National Trust for Historic Preservation website provides a wealth of technical, financial, and experiential information ranging from "greening" historic structures to making them accessible to persons with disabilities. https://www.preservationdirectory.com/PreservationBlogs/Library Articles.aspx#miscellaneous (last accessed Jan. 1, 2020).

65. *See* HUD's *Lead Paint Safety: A Field Guide for Painting, Home Maintenance, and Renovation Work*, https://www.hud.gov/sites/documents/DOC_11878.PDF (last accessed Jan. 1, 2020). For a list of various federal requirements and nongovernment resources related to lead, see https://www .hud.gov/sites/documents/20230_LPDRESOURCES.PDF (last accessed Jan. 1, 2020).

66. *Infra*, Section III.B.

and reductions in operating or utility costs for residents.[67] In addition, any major rehabilitation of a structure with federal or state funds may create the nexus to trigger a variety of laws, such as relocation obligations,[68] and laws related to adding Rdisabled access, such as the Rehabilitation Act of 1973.[69]

D. Conventional Housing Maintenance Codes

Just as various states and localities adopt national model codes to govern construction, the use, maintenance, and repair of residential structures are also subject to model codes. Some states, such as California, adopt their own regulations and use portions of the Uniform Housing Code (UHC), last published in 1997, as a model code.[70] The ICC has published a replacement for the Uniform Housing Code, the International Property Maintenance Code (IPMC), which may be adopted by states and local governments to establish standard rules for use, maintenance, and general repairs.[71] In addition, federal subsidy programs might include additional requirements.[72]

The IPMC, or any other statutory or regulatory maintenance code, is adopted and enforced by public entities, generally in the same manner as building and construction codes. Its standards cover the maintenance of a structure's exterior and interior areas and structural and interior components. The IPMC also addresses handrails, rubbish and garbage, vector and vermin extermination, and minimum light and ventilation requirements. It establishes minimum maintenance requirements for plumbing and mechanical facilities and fixtures, as well as fire safety and occupancy standards.[73]

These government maintenance code requirements for use and repair of an affordable residential structure have obvious overlapping requirements with public and private financing regulatory agreements and security agreements.[74] On one hand, the government maintenance code requirements provide minimum standards, which may be lower than those imposed by lenders or equity investors. However, they also include, directly or indirectly, standards for enforcement that may include options for receiverships, civil injunctions, major financial penalties, and other forms of major government involvement in the ongoing

---

67. *Id.*

68. See Chapter 16, *infra*, for a discussion of federal relocation laws.

69. *Infra*, Section IV.A.1.

70. Cal. Code Regs., tit. 24, pt. 1, ch. 1, subch. 1 (commencing with § 1) and § 32 (2020).

71. Like building codes, information on what housing maintenance code has been adopted—the IPMC or another code—can be obtained from the local building department or state department responsible for code adoptions, or the organizations listed in note 8, *supra*.

72. See Chapter 9, *infra*, for a discussion of federal subsidy programs.

73. Owners and developers should be aware that 2018 IPMC § 404.1 (2020) changes the objective maximum numerical occupancy standards previously used in the Uniform Housing Code, and now allows only one person in a bedroom with at least 70 square feet and 50 additional square feet in a bedroom for each additional person. The 2018 IPMC § 404.4.5 (2020) allows up to five persons to "occupy" a living room with at least 120 square feet and up to five persons to "occupy" a dining room of up with 120 square feet, with more allowed for larger living rooms and bedrooms. Section 404.4.5.1 (2020) expressly states that the "occupancy" limits in § 404.4.5 do not apply for sleeping purposes, unlike the Uniform Housing Code's more flexible standards.

74. See Chapters 9, 10, and 14, *infra*.

operation of the development.[75] Thus, ensuring a high quality of management and compliance with both sets of requirements is critical to avoid unwanted government intrusion.

A variety of federal laws and rules apply to housing maintenance as well. For a discussion of some of these, see Section III.B, *supra*.

E. Special State and Local Government Code Requirements

In addition to general building codes, residential construction, maintenance, and rehabilitation activities are subject to special state and local government (as well as lender or investor) requirements and restrictions relating to the site and construction standards of the affordable housing and any unique or dangerous conditions in that location.

For example, both model building codes and local government agencies adopt provisions relating to earthquakes and other seismic activity.[76] Some building standards are adopted by state or local governments and are included in the International Building Code (IBC) and the International Residential Code (IRC) published by the ICC, and in the ICC's International Existing Building Code (IEBC) for rehabilitation and remodeling of existing buildings.[77] Compliance with these standards enhances personal and property safety, affects the setting of earthquake insurance premiums, and may be a determinant of private investment in a housing development.

Similarly, construction in floodplains and special flood areas is subject to special regulation, including special alternative code requirements, and is closely tied to insurance under the National Flood Insurance Program (NFIP).[78] Minimum federal requirements exist for construction in flood-prone areas. These requirements are incorporated by local

---

75. See 2018 IPMC §§ 104.1–111.8 or local code enforcement codes (2020).

76. Most of these directly or indirectly relate to the National Earthquake Hazards Reduction Program (NEHRP), created by Congress in 1977. 42 U.S.C. §§ 7701, *et seq.* (2020), *reauthorized* by Pub. L. 101-614 (2005) and amended several times thereafter. The U.S. Geological Survey (USGS) developed national seismic hazard maps that are part of the basis of the design maps in the *NEHRP Recommended Provisions*, published by the Federal Emergency Management Agency (FEMA) and the Building Seismic Safety Council. For various related publications, see https://www.fema.gov /index-earthquake-publications-alphabetical-list-publications (2020).

77. The 2018 International Building Code, Chapter 16, and the 2018 International Residential Code, Section R-301, address a number of structural threats including snow and wind loads, flood and earthquake loads, and ice and tsunami loads (2020). The 2018 International Existing Building Code adopts or references standards for seismic retrofits under various circumstances including rehabilitation of unreinforced masonry buildings in Chapter 34 (2020). Cities such as Los Angeles have adopted ordinances mandating seismic retrofit improvements for about 15,000 pre-1978 wood-framed and other specified "soft-story" buildings with weak lower floors, such as multistory apartments with tuck-under parking spaces, and vulnerable concrete buildings (LOS ANGELES MUNICIPAL CODE Divisions 93 (commencing with § 91.9301) and 95 (commencing with § 91.9501) (2020).

78. The National Flood Insurance Act of 1968, as amended, and the Flood Disaster Protection Act of 1973, as amended. 42 U.S.C. §§ 4001, *et seq.* (2020). FEMA identifies flood hazard areas throughout the United States with various types of maps, including Flood Boundary and Floodway Maps (FBFMs), Flood Insurance Rate Maps (FIRMs), and Flood Hazard Boundary Maps (FHBMs). HUD adopts floodplain construction standards for HUD-assisted or -financed housing, including mortgage insurance, in 24 C.F.R. pt. 55 and § 200.926 (2020) and establishes floodplain development permit requirements outlined at https://www.fema.gov/permit-floodplain-development (last acccsscd Jan. 1, 2020).

government ordinances to maintain national flood insurance in their jurisdictions or to ensure federal financing of these structures.[79]

In addition, FEMA's National Hurricane Program promotes safety of residential buildings by assessing building performance after hurricanes and coastal storms, and by developing recommendations for hazard-resistant construction in new buildings and for retrofitting existing buildings. Similar programs are operated for other potential natural disasters, such as tornados, severe winter storms, and fires. In all cases, a local government in an area subject to these hazards is required to adopt FEMA recommendations or other ordinances, any of which may be either reasonably or unreasonably expensive compared to the residents' and owners' potential losses.[80]

The threat of damage and injury to property, residents, and firefighters in areas with high fire danger has spawned a number of local and state requirements for special exterior building construction standards, such as nonflammable siding, nonflammable window and door frames, smaller attic air vents or screens, and fire-resistant window glass materials. Some states, such as California, have adopted Wildland–Urban Interface Fire regulations.[81] Other states and localities may adopt the ICC's 2018 Wildland–Urban Interface Code or adopt NFPA publications.[82]

F. Enforcement

Local building departments generally enforce public building and maintenance codes. In most cases, prior to obtaining building department approval for housing, the sponsor must obtain a series of approvals, including plan review and the issuance of a building permit.[83] Depending on local ordinances and the type of proposed construction, the plan review step may also include approvals from the local health or water and sewerage department, proof of land-use approval from the planning department (including any design standards), and local fire department approval.

Code enforcement to seek correction of existing maintenance violations or prevent deterioration or creation of maintenance violations may be reactive or proactive. A reactive approach merely involves responding to tenant or neighbor complaints. A proactive approach includes public education and, in many jurisdictions, registration of rental housing coupled with periodic inspections by local government building departments and/or

---

79. Section 25.01 of the St. Louis (Mo.) City Revised Code includes an Appendix G, § 25.01.620, which governs a special floodplain development permit before any development or substantial improvement in a floodplain area, enforced by a denial of building permit. The 2018 International Building Code includes Appendix G, "Flood Resistant Construction," which may be adopted by states or municipalities for identified flood hazard areas and the 2018 International Residential Code addresses flood hazard construction in section R-301.2.4.

80. For more information on the federal requirements and assistance available for various types of natural disaster mitigation planning, *see* https://www.fema.gov/hazard-mitigation-planning (last visited Jan. 1, 2020).

81. CAL. CODE REGS., tit. 24, pt. 2, ch. 7A, and pt. 2.5, § R-302 (2020).

82. NFPA publishes numerous guides, standards, and practices related to fire prevention and suppression. See https://www.nfpa.org/Codes-and-Standards/All-Codes-and-Standards/List-of-Codes -and-Standards (last accessed Jan. 1, 2020).

83. See Chapters 2–5, *supra*, for discussions of planning and zoning issues.

annual recertifications by property owners.[84] In addition, the Section 8 Housing Choice Voucher Program requires initial and biennial inspections of vouchered units or homes.[85] Violations of housing maintenance codes may result in criminal or civil penalties;[86] government abatement procedures include mandates to repair or demolish and appointment of receivers to perform ordered work[87] and extensive tenant rights, often in conjunction with the local government code enforcement agency.[88]

Construction, maintenance, repair, and operation of housing may trigger enforcement of other maintenance codes, such as fire and health codes. The applicable state and local laws provide guidance to affordable housing operators as to the standards, procedures, and enforcement penalties for violations. In some cases, local government zoning, land-use, or development agreement approvals may include maintenance standards addressing potential problems with affordable housing. These usually deal with "crime" (e.g., increased and operative lighting and fences), "building maintenance" (e.g., paint and repaving schedules), and "occupancy impaction" (e.g., on-site and off-site parking requirements and community room schedules).[89]

IV. OVERVIEW OF FEDERAL, STATE, AND LOCAL HOUSING CODES FOR SPECIAL PURPOSES

A. Disability Access Requirements

Beyond the structural integrity and public health and safety justifications for building and housing codes just outlined, there are a number of federal and local requirements with respect to architectural and program accessibility that may be applicable to multifamily housing developments. application to"application to"HUD has been involved, at least since 1988,[90] in ensuring that construction and rehabilitation of certain housing meets federal standards requiring that people with disabilities have meaningful access to private and public housing. Three federal civil rights laws—Section 504 of the Rehabilitation Act,[91]

---

84. See Sacramento, California, Rental Housing Inspection Program, Sacramento Munici-pal Code, ch. 8.120 (2020) and https://www.cityofsacramento.org/Community-Development/Code-Compliance/Programs/Rental-Housing (last accessed Jan. 1, 2020). See also two City of Los Angeles programs, the Systematic Code Enforcement Program (interior and exterior inspections of all rental properties every two or four years or in response to complaints) and the Rent Escrow Account Program (LAMC § 162.00) (2020) in which the city establishes reduced rents based on the nature of code violations and allows the reduced rents to be paid into a city escrow program where they can be used by the building owner for repairs.

85. 42 U.S.C. § 1437f (o)(8) (2020).

86. Cal. Health & Safety Code §§ 17995–17995.4 (2020).

87. *Id.* §§ 17980–17980.10.

88. *See* Cal. Civ. Code §§ 1940–1940.1 (tenantability standards); 1942 (tenant self-help repairs and rent deduction), 1942.3 (statutory "habitability defense" for eviction lawsuits); 1942.4 (civil actions and injunctions for tenants subject to uninhabitable conditions); and 1942.5 (retaliation protection after tenant report to public agency and civil penalties) (2020).

89. *See also* Chapter 14, *infra*, regarding maintenance requirements linked to funding.

90. Although section 504 and the Rehabilitation Act itself were passed by Congress in 1973, HUD did not promulgate regulations until 1988. *See* 53 Fed. Reg. 20,216 (June 2, 1988).

91. 29 U.S.C. § 794 (2020); 24 C.F.R. §§ 8.1, *et seq.* (2020).

the Fair Housing Amendments Act of 1988,[92] and the Americans with Disabilities Act of 1990[93]—provide that covered housing units must comply with specific accessibility standards.

1. Section 504 of the Rehabilitation Act of 1973

HUD recognized the discrimination inherent in the construction of new dwellings or alteration of existing dwellings without making some of them accessible, and therefore promulgated accessibility requirements that apply when "federal financial assistance"[94] is used in housing units. Section 504 applies to funding recipients and imposes numerical minimum criteria concerning accessibility. With respect to new construction or substantial alteration of existing structures, federal regulations require that at least 5 percent of the dwelling units be accessible for people with mobility disabilities and at least 2 percent for persons with visual and hearing disabilities.[95] These requirements have important implications both for individual owners of federally assisted housing and for broader affordable housing programs operated by state or local entities receiving HUD funding under programs like Community Development Block Grants and the HOME Investment Partnership Program.

The Section 504 regulations define an "accessible dwelling unit" as a unit that is located on an accessible route and can be approached, entered, and used by individuals with physical disabilities.[96] A unit that is on an accessible route, is "adaptable," and is otherwise in compliance with the standards set forth in 24 C.F.R. § 8.32 is considered "accessible."[97] HUD's Section 504 accessibility standards require compliance with the Uniform Federal Accessibility Standards (UFAS),[98] which are promulgated by the Federal Access Board. The UFAS provides specific standards for virtually every aspect of residential units and their common areas. As a result, UFAS-compliant units provide a significantly higher level of accessibility that is not applicable to units unassisted by federal funds.

The HUD regulations require that "[a]ccessible dwelling units . . . shall, to the maximum extent feasible and subject to reasonable health and safety requirements, be distributed throughout projects and sites and shall be available in a sufficient range of sizes and amenities so that a qualified individual with handicap's choice of living arrangements is, as a whole, comparable to that of other persons eligible for housing assistance under the same program."[99] Furthermore, "[a]ny housing units newly constructed or rehabilitated for

---

92. 42 U.S.C. §§ 3601, *et seq.* (2020); 24 C.F.R. §§ 100.1 *et seq.* (2020). See Chapters 2, 3, and 8 for additional coverage of the federal Fair Housing Act.

93. 42 U.S.C. §§ 12131, *et seq.* (2020); 28 C.F.R. §§ 35.101, *et seq.* (2020).

94. 24 C.F.R. § 8.3 (2020).

95. *Id.* §§ 8.22, 8.23. HUD specifically recognized that ensuring such access would be neither difficult nor expensive for new construction, finding that "[i]n view of the low cost of making units accessible in newly constructed multifamily housing projects HUD sees no need ever to waive the five percent requirement in the context of new construction." 53 Fed. Reg. 20,216, 20,223 (June 2, 1988). HUD "may prescribe [that] a higher percentage or number of units" be made highly accessible on request by a recipient or state or local government provided the need for additional units is adequately documented. *Id.* § 8.22(c).

96. *Id.* § 8.3.

97. *Id.* § 8.22(b).

98. *Available at* https://www.access-board.gov/aba/ufas.html (last accessed Dec. 30, 2020).

99. 24 C.F.R. § 8.26 (2020).

purchase or single-family units to be constructed or rehabilitated in a program or activity receiving Federal financial assistance shall be made accessible upon request of the prospective buyer if the nature of the handicap of an expected occupant so requires."[100]

As a result of the demanding architectural accessibility standards, recipients of federal funds are cautioned to use architects, designers, and builders who are well acquainted with section 504 requirements.[101] Failure to do so has subjected owners to liability for retrofitting, which is substantially more expensive than incorporating accessibility in the design stage.[102] Recipients of federal funds should consult a notice issued by HUD's Office of Community Planning and Development, which provides substantial breadth and detail concerning compliance with accessibility and other requirements of section 504.[103]

Recent litigation suggests that municipalities operating affordable rental housing programs may face liability under section 504 and the Americans with Disabilities Act for their failure to ensure that third-party owners and managers of city-funded housing comply with UFAS and related accessibility standards. For instance, in settlement of litigation brought by two disability rights organizations and a private fair housing enforcement agency, the city of Los Angeles agreed in 2016 to spend at least $200 million to provide 4,000 units of UFAS-compliant housing and required owners and managers to comply with robust disability rights policies governing tenant selection, unit assignment, and operations.[104] Similar litigation against the city of Chicago has survived a motion to dismiss,[105] and seeks similar remedies.

In response to the private litigation in Los Angeles, the federal government has stepped up its own enforcement efforts. In July 2017, the U.S. Department of Justice intervened in a lawsuit claiming that the city of Los Angeles and a successor to the Community Redevelopment Agency (CRA/LA) had violated the False Claims Act in connection with receipt

---

100. *Id.* § 8.29.

101. *See, e.g.*, Shaw, et al. v. Cherokee Meadows, LP, et al., 431 F. Supp. 3d 1336, 1348 (N.D. Okla. 2019) (denying architect's motion for summary judgment because of dispute in material facts concerning compliance with UFAS requirements).

102. *See, e.g.*, News Release, Bush Administration Increasing Housing for People with Disabilities: HUD Announces Boston Housing Authority Will Make Nearly 700 Units Available (Apr. 5, 2002). *Available at* http://archives.hud.gov/news/2002/pr02-040.cfm (last accessed Dec. 30, 2020). *See also* DOJ consent decree in *United States v. Housing Auth. of Baltimore City*, Case No. JFM 02-CV-225 (D. Md. Sept. 29, 2004), *available at* https://www.justice.gov/sites/default/files/crt /legacy/2010/12/14/habc3settle.pdf (last accessed Dec. 30, 2020) (requiring Housing Authority of Baltimore City to make substantial modifications to its public housing developments and administrative offices to make them more accessible for persons with physical disabilities, and enjoining the Authority from violating Section 504).

103. Accessibility Notice: Section 504 of the Rehabilitation Act of 1973 and The Fair Housing Act and their applicability to housing programs funded by the HOME Investment Partnerships Program and the Community Development Block Grant Program (Nov. 3, 2005) *available at* https:// www.hud.gov/sites/documents/DOC_15259.PDF (last accessed Dec. 30, 2020).

104. *See* Disability Rights California, *Independent Living Center of Southern California, et al. v. City of Los Angeles, et al.*, *available at* https://www.disabilityrightsca.org/cases/independent-living -center-of-southern-california-et-al-v-the-city-of-los-angeles-et-al (last accessed Dec. 30, 2020); *see also* https://www.relmanlaw.com/cases-ilcsc-v-los-angeles (last accessed Dec. 30, 2020).

105. Access Living of Metropolitan Chicago v. City of Chicago, 372 F. Supp. 3d 663 (N.D. Ill. 2019); *see also* https://www.relmanlaw.com/cases-access-living (last accessed Dec. 30, 2020).

of HUD block grant funds.[106] The CRA recently settled those claims, agreeing to pay $3.1 million.[107] In August 2019, in its role as funder and regulatory authority, HUD also insisted that the city enter into a voluntary compliance agreement ensuring remediation and future compliance.[108]

2. *Fair Housing Amendments Act*

In 1988, people with disabilities obtained express congressional protection of their rights to housing without discrimination, regardless of the presence of federal funding. Congress enacted the Fair Housing Amendments Act, which "extends the principle of equal housing opportunity to handicapped persons [recognizing that] handicapped persons . . . , like other classes protected by Title VIII [the Fair Housing Act], have been the victims of unfair and discriminatory housing practices."[109]

Among its other provisions, the Fair Housing Amendments Act requires that all "covered multifamily dwellings"[110] built for first occupancy after March 13, 1991, meet minimal accessibility standards. These standards, described in the Fair Housing Act Accessibility Guidelines (FHAAG),[111] are significantly less stringent than UFAS, requiring only that covered dwellings be designed and constructed:

> in such a manner that (i) the public use and common use portions of such dwellings are readily accessible to and usable by handicapped persons; (ii) all the doors designed to allow passage into and within all premises within such dwellings are sufficiently wide to allow passage by handicapped persons in wheelchairs; and (iii) all premises within such dwellings contain the following features of adaptive design: (I) an accessible route into and through the dwelling; (II) light switches, electrical outlets, thermostats, and other environmental controls in accessible locations; (III) reinforcements in bathroom walls to allow later installation of grab

---

106. U.S. Department of Justice, "United States Intervenes in False Claims Act Lawsuit Against the City of Los Angeles and CRA/LA for Knowingly Failing to Provide Accessible Housing," June 7, 2017, *available at* https://www.justice.gov/opa/pr/united-states-intervenes-false-claims-act-law suit-against-city-los-angeles-and-crala (last accessed Dec. 30, 2020).

107. U.S. Department of Justice, "CRA/LA Agrees to Pay $3.1 Million to Resolve Alleged Misuse of Federal Funds for Inaccessible Housing," February 6, 2020, *available at* https://www .justice.gov/opa/pr/crala-agrees-pay-31-million-resolve-alleged-misuse-federal-funds-inaccessible -housing#:~:text=CRA%2FLA%20agreed%20to%20pay,federal%20funds%2C%20the%20Depart ment%20of (last accessed Dec. 30, 2020).

108. U.S. Department of Housing and Urban Development, "Fact Sheet on HUD's Historic Voluntary Compliance Agreement with the City of Los Angeles," *available at* https://www.hud.gov/sites /dfiles/Main/documents/Fact-Sheet-and-QA-HUD-City-of-Los-Angeles-VCA.pdf (last accessed Dec. 30, 2020).

109. H.R. REP. 100-711 (1988), *reprinted in* 1988 U.S.C.C.A.N. 2173, 2174.

110. 42 U.S.C. § 3604(f)(3)(C) (2020); 24 C.F.R. § 100.201 (2010) (defining term as "buildings consisting of 4 or more dwelling units if such buildings have one or more elevators; and ground floor dwelling units in other buildings consisting of 4 or more dwelling units").

111. Fair Housing Act Accessibility Guidelines, 56 Fed. Reg. 9472 (Mar. 6, 1991) (codified at 24 C.F.R. ch. I, subch. A, app. II) (2009), *available at* https://www.hud.gov/program_offices/fair_hous ing_equal_opp/disabilities/fhefhag (last accessed Dec. 30, 2020).

bars; and (IV) usable kitchens and bathrooms such that an individual in a wheel-chair can maneuver about the space.[112]

Enforcement of the FHAAG has become a much higher priority for HUD and the U.S. Department of Justice.[113]

Private enforcement of the Fair Housing Act's "design and construction" accessibility standards has grown in importance since 2005. Private fair housing enforcement groups and disability advocacy groups have taken advantage of the act's broad standing provisions to pursue litigation in federal courts around the country.[114] One of the significant issues that has arisen is the statute of limitations governing such actions, with some federal courts taking the cramped view that no design and construction claim can be brought more than two years after a certificate of occupancy has been issued on a unit;[115] others have read the issue more expansively to permit later-filed claims.[116] Some have explicitly held that, where a continuous pattern and practice of noncompliant design and construction can be shown over a series of developments, the "continuing violation" theory first articulated by the U.S. Supreme Court in *Havens Realty Corp. v. Coleman*[117] can be applied to include all post-1991 buildings that are part of that pattern.[118]

The accessibility requirements imposed on new residential structures by the Fair Housing Amendments Act are established for some builders in model codes. Otherwise, they are separately adopted by localities and states adopting building codes (see *supra*, Section III). In other cases, builders must use the HUD regulations[119] and the regulations found in American National Standards Institute (ANSI) A117.1.[120] For example, the 2018 International Building Code includes a "Chapter 11," which provides design and construction requirements consistent with the act and the Fair Housing Act Accessibility Guidelines. This chapter previously has been given a "Fair Housing Act Safe Harbor Review" and tentative approval by HUD.[121] Some states, such as California, adopt slightly different

---

112. 42 U.S.C. § 3604(f)(3)(C) (2020).

113. *See* Department of Justice Fair Housing Act case list, *available at* https://www.justice.gov/crt/housing-and-civil-enforcement-section-cases-1#disabil (a significant number of cases listed there concern the FHAA design and construction accessibility requirements) (last accessed Dec. 30, 2020).

114. In January 2010, the National Fair Housing Alliance and four of its members announced the settlement of one of the biggest design and construction cases under the Fair Housing Act. That agreement with the A.G. Spanos Companies is valued at $14.75 million, and requires retrofits of 12,300 units and common areas at 81 complexes in 11 states. *See* https://www.relmanlaw.com/cases-spanos (last accessed Dec. 30, 2020).

115. *See, e.g.*, Garcia v. Brockway, 526 F.3d 456 (9th Cir. 2008).

116. Fair Hous. Council v. Vill. of Olde St. Andrews, 210 Fed. App. 469 (6th Cir. 2006), *cert. denied sub nom.*, WKB Assocs. v. Fair Hous. Council, 552 U.S. 1130, 128 S. Ct. 880 (2008).

117. 455 U.S. 363 (1982).

118. *Id. See also* Alliance v. A.G. Spanos Constr., Inc., 542 F. Supp. 2d 1054 (N.D. Cal. 2008).

119. 24 C.F.R. § 100.205 (2020).

120. Am. Nat'l Standards Inst. for Buildings and Facilities—Providing Accessibility and Usability for Physically Handicapped People. *See* 42 U.S.C. § 3604(f)(4) (2020); 24 C.F.R. § 100.201 (2020).

121. Notice of Draft Report, 65 Fed. Reg. 151 (Aug. 6, 2004). On December 8, 2020, HUD adopted a final rule granting safe harbor status to the 2009 edition of International Code Council (ICC) Accessible and Usable Building and Facilities (ICC A117.1-2009) standard and to designate

fair housing accessibility requirements, which provide one source for all disabled access requirements.[122]

3. Americans with Disabilities Act

While Title III of the Americans with Disabilities Act does not apply to residential dwellings, it does require compliance with accessibility standards applicable to the portions of a housing community that are construed to be "public accommodations" or "commercial facilities,"[123] such as rental offices, facilities held out to the general public, and adjacent parking and arrival areas. For example, homeless shelters are considered "public accommodations" for the purposes of the ADA.[124]

Title II of the Americans with Disabilities Act applies to state and local governments and requires that all of their programs and activities (including affordable rental housing programs) be meaningfully accessible to people with disabilities. As discussed earlier, Title II and Section 504 together oblige cities to ensure that housing developers and managers receiving city assistance comply with strict architectural and program accessibility requirements, and courts are beginning to recognize the enforceability of those requirements.

4. Universal Design and Visitability

A growing worldwide movement affecting the design and use of multifamily and single-family housing involves recommending or imposing standards on the design of exterior and interior areas to afford better access, safety, and ease of use for persons with disabilities and other activity limitations without imposing the full array of disabled access requirements established under the Fair Housing Act. These standards, similar to ergonomic standards found in workplace settings, permit persons with disabilities or restrictions to visit more homes and use their own better. They allow continued use of a home in the event of a family member's temporary or permanent disability. And they permit full "life-cycle" use of a home for family members from pregnancy or birth through older age.

Incorporation of universal design standards, often also called "inclusive design," is particularly appropriate for affordable housing because many low- and moderate-income households (1) have, or desire to have, multigenerational households; (2) have one or more household members with temporary or permanent disabilities; or (3) are economically unable to deal with the cost of either moving, rehabilitating, or acquiring assistive devices for the duration of a temporary or permanent disability to address the activity limitations.

---

the 2009, 2012, 2015, and 2018 editions of the International Building Code (IBC) as safe harbors under the Fair Housing Act. 85 Fed. Reg. 78957-63 (Dec. 8, 2020).

122. In California, a "covered multifamily dwelling" covers three rental units and four condominium units, a higher standard than the federal requirements. *See* CAL. GOV'T CODE § 12955.1 (2020). The building standards are established entirely in two chapters of the California Building Code, Chapter 11A (CAL. CODE REGS. tit. 25, §§ 1101A, *et seq.*) for housing without public funding, and Chapter 11B (CAL. CODE REGS. tit. 25, §§ 1101B, *et seq.*) for housing with public funding and for public areas in privately funded residential structures (2020).

123. 42 U.S.C. § 12183 (2020). Congress recognized that under such circumstances the major benefit of accessibility outweighs any minimal costs associated with ensuring accessibility. *See, e.g.*, 28 C.F.R. §§ 36.401, 36.402 (2020).

124. *See* https://www.ada.gov/pcatoolkit/chap7shelterchk.htm (last accessed Jan. 1, 2020).

One model that embodies these standards is called "visitability." This term was coined by Concrete Change, a Georgia organization that was a pioneer in the field of general accessibility. It encouraged the use of home design that incorporates zero-step entry, wider hallways, and an accessible bathroom on the primary floor. Visitability standards primarily address mobility impairments, including the activity limitations of seniors.[125]

The other leading model is "universal design," conceived at North Carolina State University. Universal design goes beyond visitability, looking at the ergonomic possibilities of improving all parts of a home, not merely providing for accessibility into portions of the home. Universal design encourages maximum feasible use of all rooms and considers all types of activity limitations (sight, hearing, environmental, cognitive, etc.) rather than just mobility impairments.[126]

Various laws and ordinances impose different standards of universal design requirements. For example, according to recent reports, ordinances in Atlanta (Georgia), Urbana (Illinois), and Long Beach (California) and laws in the states of Michigan, Oregon, and Minnesota link compliance with the design requirements to receipt of public assistance from or through the jurisdiction.[127] Georgia and Kansas as well as San Antonio (Texas) and Iowa City (Iowa) apply the requirements to most publicly funded new housing.[128] Minnesota applies the requirements to any housing receiving assistance from the Minnesota Housing Finance Agency.[129] Pima County (Arizona), Sacramento (California), and Naperville (Illinois) apply the requirements in unsubsidized single-family homes.[130] Many other jurisdictions have adopted universal design ordinances or laws.

California has three universal design laws. First, the state Department of Housing and Community Development has the authority to develop model ordinances for voluntary adoption by cities and counties. These ordinances impose universal design requirements on some or all newly constructed or rehabilitated housing in jurisdictions adopting them.[131] Second, since July 1, 2004, California law has required builders to offer a list of specified universal design options (which are available at the option of the builder and the cost of the buyer) to new home buyers purchasing single-family homes during the construction period.[132] Also, in 2019, California enacted a new law authorizing adding specified universal

125. The work on visitability has been taken up by the National Council on Independent Living which can be seen on its sponsored website, https://visitability.org/ (last accessed Jan. 1, 2020).

126. Sources of information on this concept can be obtained from websites at AARP (https://www.aarp.org/content/dam/aarp/ppi/2017/06/expanding-implementation-of-universal-design-and-visitability-features-in-the-housing-stock.pdf) (last accessed Jan. 1, 2020), the National Institute of Building Sciences (https://www.wbdg.org/resources/visitability) (last accessed Jan. 1, 2020) and the Center for Universal Design at North Carolina State University (https://projects.ncsu.edu/ncsu/design/cud/pubs_p/docs/UDinHousing.pdf) (last accessed Jan. 1, 2020), among others. Another leading resource is the Center for Inclusive Design and Environmental Access (IDEA) at the State University of New York at Buffalo, http://idea.ap.buffalo.edu/ (last accessed Jan. 1, 2020.

127. Kate Spegal & Phoebe Liebig, *Visitability: Trends, Approaches, and Outcomes* (Nat'l Resource Center on Supportive Housing and Home Modification, U.S.C. Andrus Gerontology Center), 5–6 (2003), and Jennifer Evans-Cowley, *Zoning for Universal Design and Visitability* (2006).

128. Spegal & Liebig, *supra* note 127, at 7–8.

129. *Id.* at 8.

130. *Id.* at 9.

131. CAL. HEALTH & SAFETY CODE § 17959 (2020).

132. *Id.* § 17959.6.

design features into the 2022 California Residential Code if they do not significantly increase the cost of construction.[133]

Programs exist in other states and localities that could impact affordable housing construction. Some provide subsidies.[134] Visalia (California) has a certification program for homes that incorporate specified visitability features. Pittsburgh (Pennsylvania) has a visibility features tax credit.[135] Austin (Texas) requires that all new homes be accessible with specified visitability standards.[136] Other jurisdictions waive building permit fees or provide other fiscal and non-fiscal benefits to builders or buyers of homes with visitable or universal design features.

B. Codes Governing Manufactured and Modular Housing

The use of various types of factory-built housing is often consistent with the goals and objectives of affordable housing developers. Building housing in factories reduces overall housing costs by reducing construction and financing costs compared to site-built homes, by increasing efficiency through using limited plans, and by taking advantage of subdivision and infill opportunities.[137] As technology continues to improve, these products are being used more often as single-family or multifamily developments with single-story or multiple-story structures.[138]

Three types of homes are built partially or completely in factories and assembled or installed on real property sites: manufactured homes, modular homes, and panelized homes. Each is subject to specific construction and installation rules and regulations, with some modifications in specific states. Because they are moved in large sections, state or local laws may limit their lengths, heights, and widths. And their transportation may require highway permits or accompanying escort vehicles.

1. Manufactured Homes

Manufactured homes—also called "mobile homes" or "HUD-code homes"—are single-family homes built entirely in a factory with one or more sections. California also allows for construction of "multifamily manufactured homes" of two or more units, constructed to

133. *Id.* § 17922.15.

134. For example, an Accessible Housing Demonstration Grant Program in Illinois provides $5,000 in subsidies to builders of "spec" homes, single-family residences constructed for sale and not built for an individual for immediate occupancy, with specified universal design features, including zero-step entries, accessible electrical receptacles, and bathroom walls reinforced for grab bars. http://www.ilga.gov/legislation/ilcs/ilcs3.asp?ActID=1441&ChapterID=29 (2020) For its regulations, see https://www.ihda.org/wp-content/uploads/2016/04/368_Accessible_Housing_Demonstration_Grant_Program.pdf (2020).

135. https://pittsburghpa.gov/dcp/vtc (last visited Jan. 1, 2020).

136. The Austin Residential Code § R-320; the standards can be seen at https://www.aiaaustin.org/sites/default/files/visitability_presentation2016.pdf (last accessed on Jan. 1, 2020).

137. See Chapter 5, *supra*, for discussion of siting issues concerning manufactured housing.

138. An excellent study, *Affordable Manufactured Housing Best Practices: Opportunities for California Affordable Housing Developers* (https://aeae507d-e90c-449b-9332-a6e33d13c0ca.filesusr.com/ugd/8d7a46_19981fe480194efbb284206190cadc9f.pdf (last accessed Jan. 1, 2020) was published in 2010 by the California Coalition for Rural Housing. It provides in-depth and valuable case studies demonstrating the cost-effectiveness, quality, and versatility of manufactured housing as an affordable housing option.

HUD-code standards augmented by applicable laws such as those governing multifamily housing disabled access.[139] These homes are constructed according to federal laws and regulations governing minimum building standards, design and inspection procedures, warranties, and installation.[140] With minor exceptions, they are completely constructed upon delivery, unless multiple sections are connected to create a "double-wide" or "triple-wide" home or a multistory home. On-site construction usually is limited to exterior utility connection and installation either on permanent foundations as a fixture to real property or on support systems ("piers and pads") as personal property or chattel.[141] They are constructed on, and travel on, a permanent chassis, but the wheels, axles, and hitches can be removed upon installation, so that they are not readily "mobile" after installation.

The installations (connections and support system or foundation) are inspected in most states.[142] However, because HUD's building standards are preemptive and inspections occur in a factory before attachment of a HUD insignia, local governments may not inspect the home itself.[143] Other related structures (such as a garage, a storage building, a cabana, or a deck) are constructed on-site according to state or local building codes and are inspected by the state or local government responsible for that type of installation.

Many manufactured homes produced today in most states are not installed in traditional "mobile home parks,"[144] but rather on individually owned private lots. Thus, they may be subject to design and safety features not preempted by the HUD regulations (e.g., fire sprinklers, floodplain requirements, aesthetic features, etc.).[145] Therefore, in any state,

---

139. CAL. HEALTH & SAFETY CODE § 18008.7 (2020).

140. *See* National Mobile Home Construction and Safety Standards Act of 1974, 42 U.S.C. §§ 5401, *et seq.* (2020); 24 C.F.R. §§ 3280.1, *et seq.* and 3282.1, *et seq.* (2020) (as amended in 2000 by the Manufactured Housing Improvement Act of 2000, Pub. L. 105-569).

141. In California, an additional option exists: installation of a manufactured home on a permanent foundation may be deemed "chattel" rather than a fixture for the purposes of financing. CAL. HEALTH & SAFETY CODE § 18551(b) (2020).

142. HUD has some preemptive installation requirements. See https://www.manufacturedhous inginstallation.com/ (last accessed January 1, 2020). See also the 2018 IRC, Appendix E, for manufactured housing installation standards subject to state or local government adoption (2020).

143. *See, e.g.*, Scurlock v. City of Lynn Haven, 858 F.2d 1521, 1525 (11th Cir. 1988) (finding local zoning ordinance that excluded any mobile home that did not meet either Southern Standard Building Code, the National Electrical Code, or the city's own electrical code, or that did not bear seal of Florida Department of Community Affairs, was preempted by both federal law and state law). Regulations prohibit any state or locality from establishing and enforcing rules or taking any action that "impair[s] the Federal superintendence of the manufactured home industry." 24 C.F.R. § 3282.11 (2020). HUD standards do not preempt state or local regulation "over any manufactured home construction or safety issue with respect to which no Federal manufactured home construction and safety standard has been established." 42 U.S.C. § 5422(a) (2020). Some states and localities impose additional requirements, particularly on mobile home parks, especially where government subsidies are involved. *See, e.g.*, MICH. COMP. LAWS §§ 125.2301, *et seq.* (2020) (establishing Mobile Home Commission, which, inter alia, reviews local mobile home park regulations). *See generally* William G. Phelps, *Preemptive Effect of Construction and Safety Standards of National Manufactured Housing Construction and Safety Standards Act of 1974*, 172 A.L.R. FED. 349 (updated July 2004).

144. These are sometimes known as "manufactured housing communities" or "land lease communities."

145. States adopt the federal standards for implementation, as well as authority to enforce those manufactured housing matters not preempted by HUD, such as fire sprinklers, installation standards, and requirements for rehabilitation and alteration of manufactured homes. *See, e.g.*, CAL. HEALTH &

developers planning to use or occupy manufactured homes on private property or in mobile home parks should be aware of that state's authority.

September 15, 1976, marks a critical date in dealing with existing mobile homes and manufactured homes, as this is the date when the federal laws and regulations governing manufactured housing standards took effect. Before that, mobile home standards varied widely, depending on the manufacturer and the state of construction or installation. Some states restrict local governments from imposing special conditions, design requirements, roof overhangs, or permit procedures on the use of manufactured housing on permanent foundations in certain areas or neighborhoods if the housing was constructed on or after September 15, 1976.[146]

2. Modular and Panelized Homes

Modular homes—also called "factory-built homes" or "pre-fab homes"—generally are almost entirely built in a factory. However, they are constructed to comply with the state or local building codes where they will be installed. Modular homes also are built in sections to be put together and installed on-site. If local codes differ from the state codes, they apply only to foundations and to any applicable utility hookups, and only those components are subject to inspection by local inspectors. Consistency with state or local building codes is indicated by a decal or other label affixed to the unit by private or public inspection agencies working at the factory, even if the home's eventual location will be in a different state.[147]

Because modular homes are constructed in accordance with state and local building codes,[148] their designs can be more compatible with the proposed use and area, whether built as single-family homes on small lots, as large multifamily complexes, or as a subdivision.[149] Consistency with state or local conventional building codes helps those living in manufactured homes to avoid negative perceptions by local officials, buyers, or neighbors that are often associated with these types of homes. This consistency also permits after-installation alterations to be subject to local building department approvals.

Panelized homes are constructed using factory-built panels. The panels may represent an entire wall or part of a wall, and may include windows, doors, electrical wiring, plumbing, and other components. They may have external walls or sheathing already installed as

---

SAFETY CODE §§ 18025–18032.5 (2020) and 430 ILL. COMP. STAT. 115/1, *et seq.*, 117/1, *et seq.* & 120/1 *et seq.* (2020). *See also* Chapter 5, *supra.*

146. *See, e.g.*, CAL GOV'T. CODE §§ 65852.3–65852.5 (2020).

147. See, for example, CAL. HEALTH & SAFETY CODE §§ 19960–19997, CAL. CODE REGS., tit. 25, §§ 3000–3082 (2020); COLO. C.R.S. §§ 24-32-3301, *et seq.* (2020).

148. *See, e.g.*, CAL. HEALTH & SAFETY CODE §§ 19980, *et seq.* (2020) (governing factory-built housing construction, along with state and local government rights and obligations). *See also* FLA. ADMIN. CODE §§ 9B-1.002, *et seq.* (2020) (covering all manufactured housing units). In some states, modular homes must have approval from the state as consistent with state building codes prior to a local government considering the unit for the permit approval process.

149. While most modular homes are single-family structures, there is a growing market of multi-unit modular housing, as stacked or attached modular units built either to state codes or, at a state's option, to HUD-Code standards. Depending on the state's specific requirements, an affordable housing developer with an opportunity to add duplexes or small multifamily developments on an infill basis, or larger multifamily developments on larger parcels, should investigate these options because they often have the same cost benefits as manufactured housing.

well. They generally are constructed in accordance with the state code where they are to be installed, but are subject to whatever inspections are permitted or required by local laws, including proper connection and installation.

C. Other Federal Building and Maintenance Requirements

Other federal construction and maintenance standards may apply to the development, preservation, or operation of affordable housing, whether single-family or multifamily. These include the following.

1. HUD Financing and Insurance — General Requirements

While some special standards may apply to specific types of housing programs, such as supportive or senior housing, the primary HUD construction design standard is the Minimum Property Standards (MPS), covering new single-family homes, multifamily housing, and health care–type facilities. The MPS requirements are located in HUD Handbook No. 4910.1, 1994 edition, with updates.[150]

The MPS provisions applicable to single-family and duplex homes (in Appendix K of the Handbook) virtually have been replaced by local building codes that are consistent with approved national building codes and Mortgagee Letter 2001-27, allowing reliance on local building permits and certificates of occupancy under state building codes as alternate proof of MPS compliance. For multifamily housing, there is reliance on local codes, but there are also dozens of MPS durability and livability requirements, such as minimum room sizes and dimensions and allowable building methods, materials, and finishes. The primary difference between MPS and model codes relates to minimum standards for the durability of items. These items include windows and doors, painting and wall coverings, kitchen cabinets, carpeting, and other similar items that ensure that the value of a Federal Housing Administration–insured home is not unreasonably reduced by premature deterioration or excessive wear of these improvements.[151]

HUD financing or insurance for various types of factory-built and modular housing relies on a similar protocol, the Technical Suitability of Products Program, with procedures for acceptance of products and materials detailed in HUD Handbook No. 4950.1.[152] In

---

150. The Handbook includes chapters on the program's policy, including requirements for elderly and disabled residents; general criteria for the property site (e.g., streets, utilities, and access); site design (building design, location on the property, groundwater, yards, grading, walks, and parking); building design (space planning, access, circulation, stairs, elevators, ventilation, etc.); the kind and quality of materials acceptable to ensure durability, economy, resistance to weather, moisture, corrosion, and fire, etc.; and construction standards (site development, construction materials, elevators, water and sewer supply, various mechanical items, energy, etc.). *See* https://www.hud.gov /program_offices/housing/rmra/mps/mpshome (last accessed Jan. 1, 2020). The Handbook was superseded in part by HUD Handbook 4000.1, effective September 14, 2015. https://www.hud.gov /program_offices/housing/sfh/handbook_4000-1 (last accessed Jan. 1, 2020).

151. In addition, in those areas where there are no—or incomplete—building codes, the appropriate HUD Field Office will specify a building code to be utilized, usually from the ICC family of codes. More information on MPS and applicable building codes is available from HUD's website, www.hud.gov (last accessed Jan. 1, 2020)). *See also* 24 C.F.R. §§ 200.927, *et seq.* (2020).

152. The program provides for prompt technical approval of new and innovative materials, components, and structural systems under HUD mortgage insurance programs. The program provides for formal, three-year approvals through Structural Engineering Bulletins for structural systems such

addition, HUD can accept state approvals of modular housing so that manufacturers do not have to obtain Structural Engineering Bulletins, as long as the housing is constructed in accordance with state building code requirements and receives state labels.[153]

2. *USDA Rural Development Housing in Rural Areas or for Agricultural Workers*[154]

Rural Development Instruction 1924-A, enacted pursuant to 7 C.F.R. section 1924.4(h),[155] provides that housing financed by the USDA-RD must comply with either a standard adopted by Rural Development for specific states, a voluntary national model building code, or HUD's Minimum Property Standards for Housing, Handbook No. 4910.1, 1984 edition (For One- and Two-Family Dwellings and Multi-Family Housing). The housing also must comply with Thermal Performance Construction Standards (energy conservation requirements) prescribed by USDA-RD, as well as other prescribed standards, although USDA-RD accepts the HUD-code thermal standards for manufactured homes.[156]

Another critical USDA-RD building standard is located in RD Instruction 1944-3, beginning with 7 C.F.R. section 1944.215.[157] These special conditions deal with "cost containment," addressing amenities deemed appropriate by USDA-RD as well as the cost/benefit ratio and life-cycle costs for materials and construction methods. It also establishes standards for site development work, project site densities, and exterior design restrictions. It lists "nonessential" facilities, unless required by local codes or ordinances, which include garages/covered parking, bay or box picture windows, fireplaces, sliding glass/atrium doors, saunas, and swimming pools, among others.[158]

D. Other Housing Formats

1. Farmworker Housing Standards

Housing accommodations for agricultural workers—migrant, seasonal, and permanent—have been accorded a special protective status by the federal government and some state governments for a number of years.[159] These protections establish a minimum level of habitability and fair dealing for traditional farmworkers and others who work with raw agricultural materials (such as forestry workers and aqua-farmers).

---

as modular housing or panelized construction and for subsystems such as roof or wall systems; Mechanical Engineering Bulletins for separate utility cores or nonstandard mechanical systems such as modular kitchens and baths; Use of Materials Bulletins for generic acceptances of materials, products, or systems; and Materials Releases for specific materials, products, or systems. See the HUD Handbook at https://www.hud.gov/program_offices/administration/hudclips/handbooks/hsgh/4950.1 (last accessed Jan. 1, 2020).

153. More information can be obtained from the HUD Program Office at (202) 708-6423.
154. See Chapter 5, *supra*, for a discussion of siting issues related to farmworker housing.
155. *See also generally* 7 C.F.R. § 1924, subpt. A (2020) for standards.
156. The thermal standards are found in 7 C.F.R. pt. 1924, Exhibit D to subpart A. Exhibits A through I in 7 C.F.R. pt. 1924, subpart A cover a variety of standards.
157. *See* 7 C.F.R. § 1944.215 (2020).
158. 7 C.F.R. § 1944.215(a)(11) (2020). For more information on USDA-RD legal requirements, *see* https://www.rd.usda.gov/ under "Programs and Services" (last accessed Jan. 1, 2020).
159. See Chapter 5, *supra*, for a discussion of legal issues concerning the siting of farmworker housing.

Federal law provides housing and health requirements pursuant to the Migrant and Seasonal Agricultural Worker Protection Act (AWPA or MSPA).[160] While AWPA does not require the provision of housing for migrant workers, the act[161] requires that each person operating real property used as housing for two or more migrant or seasonal farmworkers, other than an "innkeeper" providing commercial improved lodging facilities, is responsible for ensuring that the real property complies with AWPA's health and safety standards as set forth in the AWPA regulations at 29 C.F.R. § 500.130–.135.[162]

The federal standards apply to almost all aspects of the facilities.[163] Permits must be obtained at the nearest Department of Labor-Wage and Hour Division Office, and information including the permit, the name and address of the housing provider, and terms and conditions of the housing must be posted in a conspicuous place at the facility.[164]

State standards governing housing for agricultural workers vary from no protections to well-regulated and -enforced requirements.[165] Some examples of this range include California's Employee Housing Act (EHA),[166] which provides operating and maintenance standards for all employee housing consisting of (1) five or more employees of the housing provider, or (2) in rural areas, for housing used by five or more farmworkers on terms not available to the general public;[167] Illinois' Migrant Labor Camp Law, enforced by the Public Health Department, which includes general requirements governing water supply, sewage, sanitary facilities, solid-waste disposal, fire protection, and communicable disease reporting;[168] New Jersey's Seasonal Farm Labor Act, which requires that every farmworker camp shall provide "sleeping places in reasonably good structural condition";[169] North Carolina's Migrant Housing Act, which requires, among other things, heating equipment, fire

160. 29 U.S.C. §§ 1801–1872 (2009); 29 C.F.R. §§ 500.130, *et seq.* (2020).

161. 29 U.S.C. § 1823 (2020).

162. *See also id.* § 1910.142 (2020) (applicable federal standards for housing constructed after April 3, 1980, are those issued by the Occupational Safety and Health Administration for temporary labor camps).

163. *Id.* Kitchens and mess halls, when provided; electrical wiring; fire safety; garbage and refuse; handwashing, bathing, and laundry; heating; structural safety; toilet and bathing facilities; bed spacing and storage; water standards; and lighting are all covered.

164. 29 C.F.R. § 500.75(f) (2009). *See generally id.* § 500 (2020).

165. See Chapter 5 also.

166. Cal. Health & Safety Code §§ 17000, *et seq.* (2020); Cal. Code Regs. tit. 25, §§ 600, *et seq.* (2020).

167. Cal. Health & Safety Code § 17008(a)–(b) (2020). The state regulations cover drainage, cleanliness, and spacing of structures, maintenance, floor and sleeping area, bathing, toilet and water facilities, and other safety and cleanliness features. The act requires an annual permit to operate, which is coupled with annual inspections, although building permits for repairs and construction are obtained from local governments. *See* Cal. Code Regs. tit. 25, §§ 700–792 (2020).

168. 210 Ill. Comp. Stat. 110/1, *et seq.* (2020); Ill. Admin. Code tit. 77, §§ 935, *et seq.* (2020).

169. N.J. Stat. Ann. § 34:9A-22 (2020) (including provisions on communicable diseases (A-12), shelter and sleeping places requirements (A-22), air and privacy (A-24), food preparation (A-25), water (A-26), bathing and toilet facilities (A-27 and A-28), garbage and waste (A-29), and penalties (A-34)).

safety and clean food preparation facilities, and kitchen facilities;[170] and Washington's state laws, which also provide broad protections to migrant and seasonal workers.[171]

As more and more migrant and seasonal farmworkers are employed by farm labor contractors rather than the growers themselves, a concurrent trend has been the increased use of H2A workers[172] imported for short periods from other countries as farmworkers. Pursuant to the immigration law and regulations, the employing farm labor contractor must provide housing at no cost to the H2A workers, and the housing conditions must comply with applicable local standards; if there are no local standards, then state standards apply.[173] Noncompliance with the housing requirements may result in debarment of the farm labor contractor to import and provide the H2A farmworkers to growers.[174] Several important provisions of California's Employee Housing Act were amended effective January 1, 2020, specifically related to H2A farmworker housing construction, maintenance, and use issues.[175]

2. Mobile Home Parks and Special Occupancy Parks

Other common sources of affordable rental housing throughout the United States are mobile home parks and special occupancy parks (permanent housing in recreational vehicle or "trailer" parks). Both manufactured homes and recreational vehicles have utility components (e.g., electrical, water, sewage, etc.) that are unique to their structures rather than consistent with conventional building codes. Thus, the laws and regulations governing parks tend to be a combination of standard building and maintenance codes as well as standards unique to either the HUD code for mobile homes and manufactured homes or the standards applicable to recreational vehicles. Most states have their own unique standards for mobile home parks and special occupancy parks, and special enforcement provisions.[176]

3. "Tiny Homes"

A move toward constructing and living in "tiny homes" burgeoned as a result in increased ecological sensitivities and the 2008 recession, although examples preceded those periods, with some saying that it dates back to Henry David Thoreau's *Walden*. While there is no express definition of size, they generally are less than 400 square feet and may or may not be constructed and used on wheels and a chassis. Depending on cost and creativity, many

---

170. N.C. Gen. Stat. §§ 95-222 to 95-229 (2020).

171. Wash. Rev. Code §§ 70.114A-010 to 70.114A.901 (2020) (including consistency with AWPA (§ 70.114A.100), housing operation standards (§ 70.114A.045), housing on rural worksites (§ 70.114A.050), and inspection of housing (§ 70.114A.060)).

172. Section 218 of the Immigration and Naturalization Act and 20 C.F.R. § 655.122(d) (2020).

173. 20 C.F.R. § 655.122(d)(1)(iii) (2020).

174. *Id.* § 655.122.

175. In order to see the specific amendments, see Cal Chap. 866, Stats. of 2019, at https://leginfo.legislature.ca.gov/faces/billTextClient.xhtml?bill_id=201920200AB1783; click "Today's Law as Amended" for changes (last visited Jan. 1, 2020).

176. A number of states regulate mobile home parks with statewide standards. *See, e.g.*, Fla. Stat. ch. 513.05–513.051 (2009); Fla. Admin. Code Ann. r. 64E-15 (2020). *See also* Cal. Health & Safety Code §§ 18200, *et seq.* (2020) (for mobile home parks); Cal. Code Regs. tit. 25, § 1000, *et seq.* (2020); Cal. Health & Safety Code §§ 18865, *et seq.* (2020) (for special occupancy parks); Cal. Code Regs. tit. 25, §§ 2000, *et seq.* (2020*). See also* 210 Ill. Comp. Stat. 115/1, *et seq.* (2020).

are constructed without reliance on any fixed standards. The classic tiny home was and remains the small trailer or recreational vehicle, constructed today to standards adopted by the Recreational Vehicle Industry Association.[177]

As the expansion of use of nonconventional tiny homes increased, state and local building officials required guidance to distinguish between adequately safe structures that were both "tiny" and affordable, and the panoply of other structures reaching the market (Google "tiny home" for examples). Generally, any structure for residency must meet applicable construction codes and if a residential structure fails to do so, it may be condemned for occupancy by the local building official or have utilities disconnected.[178]

The potential uses of tiny homes from a counterculture option to legitimacy are increasing. They are being used as temporary and permanent housing for homeless people in many cities, including Seattle, Washington; Austin, Texas; Eugene, Oregon; Ithaca, New York; and other cities.[179] They also are being explored for use as accessory dwelling units or ADUs in many communities. Placement remains difficult; if they are on wheels, most zoning codes ban them, and if they are too small, they similarly run afoul of zoning and housing codes.[180] In response to the demand for assistance to establish reasonable standards for tiny homes, the ICC added Appendix Q to the 2018 International Residential Code, which may be adopted by state and local governments.[181] This, along with community acceptance, may lead to the next expansion of this concept.

4. Accessory Dwelling Units (ADUs)

Accessory dwelling units, or ADUs, have existed for many years. They are sometimes known as "granny units," "in-law quarters," "second units," or even "carriage houses." In recent years, they have taken on greater importance as a source of affordable housing, as a means to increase housing density with a limited "footprint," and as a resource for multigenerational housing. They may be attached to a primary house, detached, internal, under or over a primary house, or inside or over a garage.[182] As with tiny homes, the primary issues are code (health and safety) standards and both community acceptance and zoning, although housing finance (for both the primary house and ADU) may play a limiting role in some situations.

---

177. See standards at https://www.rvia.org/standards-regulations/standards-compliance/associa tion-and-ansi-standards (last accessed Jan. 1, 2020).

178. The California Department of Housing and Community Development, lead state agency on various housing codes, issued an Information Bulletin in 2016 explaining how to differentiate between the various types of legal and illegal "tiny homes." https://www.hcd.ca.gov/docs/IB2016 -01.pdf (last accessed Jan. 1, 2020).

179. See the THIMBY (Tiny Homes In My Backyard) model, https://www.laneysiegner.com /blog/2018/5/15/from-thimby-1-to-thimby-2-tiny-houses-in-east-bay-ca (last accessed Jan. 1, 2020).

180. *But see* Home Builders of So. New Jersey, Inc. v. Twp. of Berlin (1979) 81 N.J 127, 405 A.2d 381, holding invalid minimum floor area zoning requirements for residential dwellings invalid.

181. https://codes.iccsafe.org/content/IRC2018P3/appendix-q-tiny-houses (last accessed Jan. 1, 2020).

182. See two HUD studies, https://www.huduser.gov/portal/publications/adu.pdf and https:// www.huduser.gov/portal/casestudies/study-09082016.html (last accessed Jan. 1, 2020).

California has led the way in establishing requirements for ADUs in various zoning ordinances, and New Hampshire and Oregon impose similar requirements in single-family zoned neighborhoods.[183]

Building standards must be considered in designing and constructing an ADU, the most critical of which include maximum/minimum size, fire suppression systems, and energy code.[184] Generally, because an ADU is a residential unit, existing single-family housing building codes must be complied with, unless otherwise provided by state laws or ordinances.

5. *"Emergency Residential Shelters"*

Many states, cities, and counties are struggling to balance the need—now often an accelerating emergency—to construct inexpensive temporary shelter, transitional housing, and permanent housing opportunities for the tens of thousands of homeless individuals and households living on their streets, in cars, or other nonresidential situations. Federal funds were redirected from transitional housing, which is designed to provide several months for assistance with identifying and overcoming housing barriers, to "rapid rehousing," which merely provides funding to put households into housing subsidized for a period or to new permanent housing with supportive services. However, in many areas, there is not enough low-rent market rate housing even for the existing populations. Thus, these jurisdictions and their housing developers must balance speed and cost of development with the urgency for action while creating accommodations consistent with the goal of implementing "housing first" programs helping homeless people move from temporary shelters or transitional housing to permanent housing.[185]

Some states, such as California, adopted laws to provide local governments with the means to bypass some of the barriers to quick shelter development. California's "shelter crisis ordinance" law[186] allows cities and counties to adopt shelter ordinances while waiving general land use and construction standards[187] and for specified cities, even greater latitude in waiving state-mandated building standards.[188] In order to provide technical standards and guidance to local governments, the California Department of Housing and Community Development adopted two voluntary appendices in the California Building Standards Code governing special reduced emergency housing standards.[189]

---

183. An excellent overview of ADU issues was published by AARP, "The ABC's of ADU's," found at https://www.hcd.ca.gov/policy-research/docs/ADU-guide-web-singles.pdf (last accessed on Jan. 1, 2020); see also State of Oregon 2019 standards, https://www.oregon.gov/lcd/Publications/ADU_Guidance_updatedSept2019.pdf (last accessed Jan. 1, 2020).

184. See advice generally at https://www.hcd.ca.gov/policy-research/AccessoryDwellingUnits.shtml#booklet and specifically at https://www.hcd.ca.gov/policy-research/docs/StateStandardsChecklist.pdf for compliance with California standards (last accessed Jan. 1, 2020).

185. See, for example, a report by the United States Interagency Council on Homelessness, https://www.usich.gov/resources/uploads/asset_library/emergency-shelter-key-considerations.pdf (last accessed Jan. 1, 2020) and https://endhomelessness.org/resource/housing-first/ (last accessed Jan. 1, 2020).

186. CAL. GOV'T. CODE §§ 8698–8698.4 (2020).

187. *Id.* § 8698.1.

188. *Id.* §§ 8698.3–8698.4.

189. For Appendix O in the California Building Code, see https://codes.iccsafe.org/content/CABCV22019/appendix-o-emergency-housing, and for Appendix X in the California Residential

Notwithstanding the relaxation of many state and local standards, emergency shelters remain subject to the ADA.[190]

E. Other State and Local Building and Maintenance Requirements

Construction financed in whole or in part by loans or grants provided by a federal government or state housing finance agency generally must be consistent with applicable state or local building design and permit requirements, inspections, and certificates of occupancy. In addition, they may be subject to special requirements imposed by the agency or by a specific program operated by that agency.

Various state and local agencies finance both single-family and multifamily housing construction. They may or may not impose special development standards on construction but generally do impose cost-containment provisions, which may conflict with local land-use and design approval requirements.[191]

F. Local Design Requirements

Other requirements applicable to multifamily housing construction—and often particularly to affordable housing—are local government design and operational standards that exceed government building and housing code standards. These requirements have limited benefits for the residents or owners and merely address the perceptions of the immediate neighborhood, the larger community, or the political jurisdiction. They are generally rationalized as (1) enhancing compatibility with neighborhood values and surrounding properties; (2) improving the environment for the development's residents; (3) improving public health, welfare, and safety; or (4) providing objective standards for design review. However, in practice they threaten the feasibility of construction and/or operating budgets with limited benefit to the development.[192]

Code, see https://codes.iccsafe.org/content/CARC2019/cover. See https://www.hcd.ca.gov/docs /IB2018-01.pdf for a discussion of these codes (all last accessed Jan. 1, 2020).

190. See Section IV.A.e., *supra*.

191. *See* CAL. CODE REGS. tit. 25, § 7314 (2020) stating: "Except where required to secure local government approvals essential to completion of the Project, or where necessary to receive tax credits for historic preservation, costs associated with the following items [which exceed costs for similar features in modestly designed housing] are ineligible for funding with Program loan proceeds, and cannot be paid for from syndication proceeds or loans supported by Rents from Assisted Units: . . . ." It then lists building and roof shapes, ornamentation, and exterior finish schemes; fireplaces and tennis courts; and custom windows, ceramic tile floors and counters, and similar features (unless those materials have lower life-cycle costs due to lower maintenance and replacement costs).

192. *See, e.g.*, the detailed local requirements titled "Central City Neighborhood Design Guidelines, 2nd Edition" http://www.cityofsacramento.org/-/media/Corporate/Files/CDD/Planning /Major-Projects/Central-City-Specific-Plan/Section-4--Central-City-Neighborhood-Design-Guid elines.pdf?la=en (last visited Jan. 1, 2020). They are divided into various categories each of which includes significant detail of desired enhancements, and many of which likely to increase construction costs. None of these is required by local building codes. None is necessarily cost-effective nor even desired by future residents. None may be sought by investors and lenders. However, all can be imposed as discretionary design standards even when property is already properly zoned and the proposed project otherwise meets all building code requirements.

An affordable housing developer could invoke the federal Fair Housing Act in response to these demands for excessive design and operational improvements.[193] Other options may also be available.[194] If there are statewide preemptive building or maintenance codes, and any portion of the design or use standards intrudes into that preemptive authority, the standard may be invalid.[195] Finally, some of the maintenance requirements may be so costly as to preclude receipt of favorable financing; this may provide an opportunity to negotiate less onerous requirements.

193. See Chapters 2, 3, and 8 for more discussion of the federal Fair Housing Act.

194. In the case of the Sacramento ordinance, many of the public benefit improvements required by the ordinance may violate the city's housing element, which requires the removal, rather than imposition, of barriers to the construction of affordable rental housing. See Chapter 2, *supra*, for an overview of California's (and other states') housing element requirements.

195. *See* Briseno v. City of Santa Ana, 8 Cal. Rptr. 486 (App. 4th Dist. 1982).

Regulation and Provision of Affordable Housing Finance

II

Using the Qualified Opportunity Zone Incentive with Affordable Housing

7

Glenn A. Graff, Megan Murphy, and John Sciarretti

I. INTRODUCTION

The Tax Cuts and Jobs Act of 2017 introduced the opportunity zone (OZ) regime, a tax incentive designed to encourage long-term investment in low-income areas to spur economic growth and job creation.[1] The incentives are threefold and are designed to increase in value the longer an opportunity zone investment is held. We discuss the benefits further *infra*. At a very high level, by timely investing eligible gains in a fund that has a purpose of investing in OZs (a "qualified opportunity fund," or QOF), an eligible taxpayer can defer taxation of the gains until 2026, exclude as much as 15 percent of these gains from taxation, and the taxpayer's investment in the fund can grow tax free if held for at least ten years. The requirements to qualify for these benefits, including what constitutes a "timely" investment, "eligible gains," an "eligible taxpayer," and a "QOF," are discussed in the pages that follow.

While these tax benefits are valuable, they are designed to be complementary to an investor's economic return on investment along with other federal and state tax incentives, particularly tax credit incentives. For example, OZ investing can be paired with projects that are eligible for the low-income housing tax credit, the historic tax credit, or, less commonly, the new markets tax credit. Such real estate OZ projects will generally take a legal structure in which a partnership QOF invests in an operating partnership that will own

---

1. The OZ provisions are contained in Internal Revenue Code Sections 1400Z-1 (Designation of Qualified Opportunity Zones) and 1400Z-2 (Special Rule for Capital Gains Invested in Opportunity Zones). The Internal Revenue Service (IRS) has issued lengthy regulations implementing Section 1400Z-2 and such regulations are located at Treasury Regulation Sections 1.1400Z2-0 through 1.1400Z2-(f).

and operate the real estate. That lower-level partnership will need to meet the requirements to be a Qualified Opportunity Zone Business (QOZB). See Figure 7.1; statutory and regulatory requirements of QOZBs discussed *infra*. Fortunately, as we will discuss, the QOZB requirements are generally compatible with developing affordable housing.

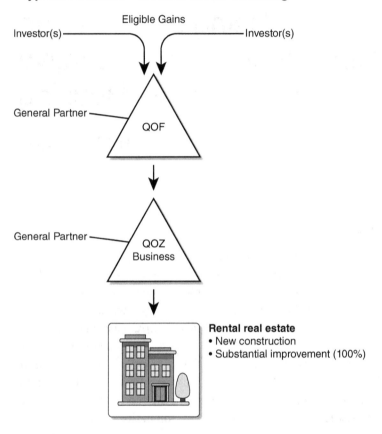

Typical Structure - OZ Real Estate Investing

Figure 7.1

The Internal Revenue Code sections that constitute the opportunity zones statute are about 2,250 words long. The final Treasury regulations, finalized in December 2019, are over 60,000 words long, with further Treasury commentary in the preamble to the final regulations and additional correcting regulation amendments issued as recently as August 2021. The incentive took considerable time and effort to implement and continues to develop today, including proposed legislation around QOF reporting and deferral of the 2026 gain recognition date to 2029. Even so, with many of the early uncertainties resolved and with businesses looking toward post-COVID plans, opportunity zone investment appears to be increasing in 2021.

This chapter first provides a brief overview of how the OZ incentive can be used with affordable housing. The second part of the chapter discusses the very detailed rules involved in using the OZ incentive. As used in this chapter, "Code" or "I.R.C. §" refers to the Internal Revenue Code of 1986, as amended. "Treas. Reg." and "Regulations" mean the Income Tax Regulations issued under the Code and preceding federal tax laws; and "IRS" or "Service" means the Internal Revenue Service.

II. OVERVIEW OF USING THE OZ INCENTIVE TO PROMOTE AFFORDABLE HOUSING

The OZ incentive can be leveraged to create affordable housing in a number of ways. OZs can be used with the Low-Income Housing Tax Credit (LIHTC) under Code Section 42, with historic rehabilitation tax credits (HTC) under Code Section 47, and sometimes with New Markets Tax Credits (NMTC) under Code Section 45D. It is also possible for OZ equity to be a separate layer of financing for projects with or without tax credits, or even for the developer/sponsor of affordable housing to provide OZ equity. The use of OZ equity for workforce housing has also been shown to be popular.

A. Structures for Investors to Receive Both LIHTC and OZ Benefits

Structurally, OZs can be used with LIHTC. The benefit from coupling OZs with LIHTC is very dependent on the structure involved and can range from a modest benefit to a more significant benefit. However, the benefit from LIHTCs in most cases will significantly outweigh the OZ benefit with the OZ incentive providing incremental value.

The structure of using OZs with LIHTC is not much different from the typical LIHTC structure. In a typical LIHTC structure, a tax credit investor invests in a syndication fund. That fund then invests in one or more partnerships that will own and operate low-income housing. This tiered partnership structure provides tax credit investors with LIHTCs and flow-through of depreciation expenses. Because affordable housing is real estate- and fixed asset-heavy, the businesses and projects incur large depreciation expenses.

The OZ structure is the same. Under the OZ incentive, an eligible taxpayer (defined *infra*) with eligible gains invests in a QOF (which is a fund), and that QOF invests in a partnership that will qualify as a QOZB. It is important to note that the OZ rules do not allow for additional layers of ownership. The taxpayer has to invest directly in the fund and the fund has to invest in a partnership that owns and operates the real estate.[2] Fund management will be very similar, with the exception that a QOF manager needs to ensure that it invests at least 90 percent of its assets in qualifying partnerships, and provide oversight and assistance to the QOZB partnerships so that they will initially meet the QOZB requirements and continue to meet those requirements for the duration of the investment.

In order to receive depreciation deductions and tax credits and to have a valid OZ investment, the investment needs to be respected as equity, rather than debt. Preferred interests are permitted, as are partnership interests with special allocations,[3] but features such as a set return known in advance are problematic.

---

2. Technically the QOF can invest in a corporation, but that is unlikely to be a useful structure for investments in affordable housing. Real estate investments generally benefit from the tax flow-through ability allowed by partnerships.

3. Treas. Reg. § 1.1400Z2(a)-1(b)(12)(i).

1. How OZ Requirements Relate to LIHTC Projects

As shown by the hundreds of pages of regulations, the OZ requirements are quite complex. Fortunately, they are generally compatible with LIHTC projects.

Location. The most basic OZ requirement is that the investment must be in a Qualified Opportunity Zone (a QOZ). QOZs, defined in more detail *infra*, are designated low-income communities. Many LIHTC projects are located in low-income census tracts, so it is possible for a LIHTC project to be in a QOZ. However, because states were limited to nominating 25 percent of their low-income census tracts and certain adjacent tracts, it is critical in planning to pair the OZ incentive with LIHTCs to ensure that a proposed LIHTC project is in fact in a QOZ.

Related Party Restrictions. OZs have related party restrictions, which generally complicate a QOZB's acquisition of property where the seller of property has more than a 20 percent interest in the QOZB partnership. LIHTC projects have a very similar restriction, but the related party threshold is 50 percent. While the OZ related party rules are more restrictive, these rules can be managed in similar ways as LIHTC projects with their 50 percent restriction. Features such as seller financing, deferred developer fees, loans from related parties, and a nonprofit right of first refusal under Section 42 may mitigate the impact of the related party rules by allowing economics to be paid out to related parties in the form of legitimate fees and debt repayment or a right of first refusal rather than distributions to partners.

50 Percent Gross Income from QOZ. QOZBs need to have 50 percent of their income come from the active conduct of a trade or business within the QOZ. As a real estate–based business, meeting such requirements should not be difficult for a LIHTC project located in a QOZ.

Timeline. Another similarity between LIHTC and OZ investing is the timeline involved. LIHTC investments are commonly held for at least 15 years, although sometimes investors may exit after ten years of operations. For OZ investments, the timeline is generally at least ten years of investment, with such time including the construction period. As a result, the OZ timeline is less restrictive than the typical LIHTC investment window.

QOF Must Acquire QOZB Partnership Interest as Original Issue—Syndicator Structuring. In LIHTC transactions, it is common for a syndicator to purchase a LIHTC partnership interest in its own name and then transfer that interest to a LIHTC syndication fund at a later date when investors for the fund have been secured. However, such a structure would not work for an OZ investment. In order for the syndication fund to qualify as a QOF, the QOF will likely need the LIHTC partnership interest to qualify as qualified opportunity zone property (QOZP). One of the requirements of Code Section 1400Z-2(d)(2)(C)(i) for a QOZB partnership interest to be QOZP is that such partnership interest has to be acquired directly from the partnership in exchange for cash. As a result, acquisition of the partnership interest by the syndicator and followed by a transfer to a fund would not qualify. Therefore LIHTC-OZ syndicators need to arrange for a "direct closing" in which the syndicator's QOF directly invests cash in the LIHTC partnership in exchange for the partnership interest.

2. Benefits of Pairing OZ and LIHTC

The benefits of pairing OZ with LIHTC can vary from light to significant. For QOF investments that have been held for seven or five years as of December 31, 2026, that is, investments made by the end of 2019 or 2021, 15 percent or 10 percent of the deferred capital gains tax that would be due can be avoided. In addition, there are the following benefits.

Tax-Free Appreciation. After meeting a ten-year OZ holding period, QOFs that invest in LIHTC projects that are QOZBs can benefit from the OZ incentive either from tax-free appreciation or avoidance of exit taxes. LIHTC projects in areas with increasing rents or projects with project-based Section 8 contracts may experience significant appreciation over the project life. For such projects, the ability to step up their basis to fair market value and then sell the project after ten years (often 15 years for LIHTC projects due to their 15-year compliance period[4]) can result in no taxes on the profits and can be a significant benefit.

Avoidance of Exit Taxes. The appreciation of many other LIHTC projects may be small or nonexistent due to limited cash flow from low-income rents. These low-appreciation QOZB projects may still benefit from the OZ incentive by being able to avoid exit taxes. Due to limited equity in some LIHTC projects, especially projects financed with tax-exempt bonds, such projects may have LIHTC investors that are allocated losses in excess of their capital contributions resulting in a negative capital account. Normally such investors would owe tax upon exit from a LIHTC partnership, and often the general partner in the LIHTC partnership may bear the cost of the exit taxes. However, the OZ incentive can avoid these exit taxes where the LIHTC partnership is a QOZB. As discussed in more detail later in this chapter, after satisfying a ten-year OZ holding period, OZ investors can step up the tax basis of their QOF interest (or their basis in the QOZB partnership interest or the basis of the QOZB's assets). Special OZ rules provide that the step up to fair market value includes debt on a QOZB project.[5] The result can be a significant basis step-up that results in the avoidance of exit taxes, thus saving investors or general partners a significant cost when the project is sold.

Reduced Taxes Due on December 31, 2026, for Projects with Low Fair Market Value. While it is commonly said that the deferred capital gains tax is due no later than December 31, 2026 (or 85 or 90 percent of such tax for investments held seven or five years), there is a technical way that less tax can be due. As discussed in more detail later, if the QOF has lost value, then the amount of taxes due can be reduced. This appears to be a commonsense result to the effect that if a QOF investment has lost value, then the deferred capital gains taxes due from an investor should be similarly reduced.

Because many LIHTC projects have little value other than their tax credits, it could be possible for the fair market value of a LIHTC project on December 31, 2026, to be significantly lower than the cost to construct it. For example, a project completed and rented up in 2021 could have already delivered six of the ten years of LIHTC. Thus, 60 percent of the value of the project may no longer exist. This could significantly reduce the capital gains taxes due no later than December 31, 2026. However, as discussed in more detail later in this chapter, when a QOF is a partnership, the Regulations interpret the statutory fair market value in a way that narrows this ability to avoid some of the deferred capital gains taxes where QOFs or QOZBs use debt to finance distributions or taxable losses.[6] While this special rule can diminish the reduction in taxes due no later than the end of 2026, it is

---

4. I.R.C. § 42(i)(1).
5. Treas. Reg. § 1.1400Z2(c)-1(b)(2)(i).
6. Treas. Reg. § 1.1400Z2(b)-1(e)(4).

still possible that a low fair market value could lead to less taxes being due in 2026 than the deferred capital gains taxes (less 10 or 15 percent in basis earned at years five and seven).

Early Equity Can Lead to Possible Reduced Construction Interest. As discussed later, OZ Investors are required to invest their capital earlier than is normal for LIHTC or affordable housing development more generally. While the partnership agreement for the QOZB entity will likely include milestones for when the equity can be spent, it may be possible to negotiate with investor to allow some of that early capital to be used for construction, thus reducing interest on construction loans.

Pricing and Expanded Investor Base. The authors' experience has been that having a LIHTC project also qualify for OZ has led to modest or no change to the price per tax credit. There have been some situations where the OZ incentive availability did make a project appeal to a wider investor base than would have been available for a LIHTC project without OZ. There have also been situations where adding OZ to a transaction was a way to recapture yield for the investor where such yield may have suffered due to other changes in the project as it headed toward a closing with the investor.

3. Difficulties of Pairing OZs with LIHTC

Capital Contribution Timing Issues. The investor requirement to invest eligible gains within 180 days of realization of those gains, will often mean OZ investors fully fund their capital upfront. This works against the common LIHTC structure of deferring capital contributions to maximize investor yield/credit pricing.

Few LIHTC Investors with Capital Gain. One of the hardest parts of using OZ with a LIHTC investor is that the typical LIHTC investor is a financial institution, often a bank. Although there are exceptions, most banks do not generate capital gains as a regular part of their business and thus it can be hard to find a LIHTC-OZ investor. However, some banks have occasional capital gains that can be used. LIHTC exit gains can also provide a small pipeline of capital gains that could work with the OZ incentive.

4. What LIHTC Projects Work Best with OZ

The complex combination of OZ and LIHTC rules limits the types of LIHTC Projects for which OZs would be beneficial. Some general rules of thumb follow.

New Construction. New construction avoids the OZ-specific doubling of basis requirement for substantial rehabilitations, and is therefore more likely to work with OZs.

Very Substantial Rehabilitation. For existing buildings, the OZ rules require the owner to double the basis of an acquired building. This means that light or even some moderate rehabilitations are not compatible with OZ, but buildings requiring significant rehabilitation may be compatible.

Projects That Need Debt. A significant part of the return a LIHTC investor receives is from the ability to utilize taxable losses (often from large depreciation expenses) generated by a LIHTC partnership. Under the mechanics of the OZ incentive (discussed in detail *infra*), OZ investors initially receive $0 in basis in their interests in the QOF until December 31, 2026, when the deferred capital gains tax is due. Due to this lack of tax basis, tax rules around allocation of partnership losses often result in OZ investors not being able to use taxable losses unless there is project debt that could be allocated to them and give them tax basis. Thus, debt may allow the investor to use the taxable losses. Such debt would generally need to be third-party non-recourse debt, which is not guaranteed by the general partner of the LIHTC partnership.[7]

B. LIHTC Developers' Use of OZ

LIHTC developers who have capital gain can also benefit from the OZ incentive if they are investing capital. The developer would form its own QOF, making sure the QOF is a partnership with at least two partners.[8] That QOF would then be the general partner or a special limited partner in the LIHTC partnership that would be the QOZB. In this way, taxes can be deferred on capital gains that the developer contributes to the QOF and that the QOF contributes QOZB. In addition, profits that the developer receives when the project is sold after at least ten years (and usually 15 years for LIHTC deals) could be received tax free. Using the foregoing structure can be very attractive to developers. Unlike most LIHTC investors, LIHTC developers value long-term appreciation of projects.

Caution and careful structuring are important in trying to maximize OZ benefits for developers. Developers commonly receive their interest in a LIHTC partnership for rendering services to the partnership. However, such a structure—services for a partnership interest—would not qualify as a proper investment by a developer's QOF because QOFs have to receive QOZB partnership interests solely in exchange for cash. If the developer's QOF receives an interest in the LIHTC QOZB for both cash contributed and for services rendered, then a portion of the investment would not qualify for OZ benefits. In such cases it might be prudent to structure the developer QOF's cash investment as a special limited partner interest in the LIHTC-QOZB partnership. The interest in the LIHTC-QOZB partnership that is received for service rendered could be classified as the general partner interest in the LIHTC-QOZB partnership and could be owned by the developer directly rather than through the QOF. It would also be recommended to do financial modeling or engage a valuation professional to demonstrate that the expected back-end value to be received by the QOF is commensurate with the capital invested and isn't disguised remuneration for services rendered.

C. OZ Equity as Non-LIHTC Investor

It can be possible to bring in OZ equity as its own layer of equity in both LIHTC projects and non-LIHTC projects. The QOF is just a partner in the housing partnership that will be the QOZB and will receive an economic return for its participation. Generating sufficient return to be inviting for an OZ investor can be difficult for affordable housing projects given their low rents. This can be especially difficult for LIHTC projects as they tend to have even less cash flow. One possible approach might be to have the OZ equity take the place of secured debt in an OZ-LIHTC project. The OZ investors, through their interest in the QOF, could then get a preferred return and there could be a cash out refinance after 10 to 15 years. However, care must be used in this approach. A QOF's investment in a QOZB

---

7. *See* Glenn A. Graff, *Why Does My Tax Lawyer Keep Saying We Need Nonrecourse Debt for My Low-Income Housing Tax Credit Project*, 27 J. AFFORDABLE HOUS. 435 (2018).

8. The partners must be separate entities that are not disregarded into a common entity. Thus, for example, they cannot be two single-member LLCs treated as disregarded entities that are owned by the same person or entity.

partnership must be a capital contribution and cannot be classified as a loan for tax purposes. Therefore, using OZ equity as a replacement for debt must be carefully structured so that the QOF's rights are not so similar to a lender's rights that the investment might be classified as debt by the IRS.

D. OZ with Historic Tax Credits

The OZ incentive can pair nicely with the historic rehabilitation tax credit (HTC) available under Code Section 47. This can work for both residential rental housing or for commercial developments. Similar to OZ-LIHTC structures, an investor could receive the benefit of HTCs and the OZ incentive. This can increase the return to the investor resulting in a noticeable increase in equity invested in the project. However, because HTC projects often have more substantial economic returns than LIHTC projects, there is a greater ability for other non-HTC users to participate by investing OZ equity. An HTC developer might want to set up its own QOF to invest in the HTC-QOZB partnership, thus deferring capital gain and allowing some long-term profits to escape taxation. There may also be sufficient return to incentivize an OZ investor to invest as a separate layer of financing and allow the HTCs to be allocated to a different investor.

Some historic tax credit transactions are structured as lease passthroughs, where the building is owned by one entity but is leased to a master tenant partnership and the tax credits are passed through to the master tenant partnership.[9] Such leases are generally structured as triple-net leases where the terms of the lease provide that the tenant bears the cost of taxes, insurance, and maintenance. However, as discussed later in this chapter, under the OZ regulations, a business cannot qualify as a QOZB if it is merely a landlord entering into a triple-net lease.[10] Because of this, care must be used in lease passthrough structures so that the leases are not triple-net leases.

E. OZ with New Markets Tax Credits

It is theoretically possible to use the OZ incentive with New Markets Tax Credits (NMTC). However, successfully structuring this can be very difficult; NMTC investments are generally structured as loans, but the OZ incentive is available only for equity investments. There are sometimes NMTC investments structured as equity rather than a loan, however such structures are very rare and create some negative implications for NMTC investors.[11] Another restriction is that NMTC is only available for nonresidential rental housing. As

---

9. *See* Treas. Reg. § 1.48-4 (Election of lessor of new Section 48 property to treat lessee as purchaser). "A Master Tenant Partnership is a Partnership that leases a Building from Developer Partnership (Head Lease) and for which an election is made pursuant to Treas. Reg. Section 1.148-4(a)(1) to treat the Master Tenant Partnership as having acquired the Building solely for purposes of the § 47 rehabilitation credit)." Rev. Proc. 2014-12.

10. Treas. Reg. § 1.400Z2(d)-1(d)(3)(iii)(B).

11. The reasonable expectations test under Treas. Reg. § 1.45(D)-1(d)(6)(i) is not available if the community development entity (CDE) has control of the qualified active low-income community business (QALICB). Control exists if the CDE has 50 percent or more of the value of the QALICB or 50 percent or more of voting or management rights. Treas. Reg. § 1.45(D)-1(d)(6)(i)(B). In an OZ transaction, the QALICB would also be the QOZB partnership. However, if the OZ investor invests OZ equity in the QALICB/QOZB partnership but also receives NMTCs thorough an investment in the CDE, then it may be deemed to have control if it has 50 percent or more of the equity or voting/management rights in the QALICB/QOZB.

a result, an OZ-NMTC project needs to be a nonresidential commercial development or a residential rental development with significant commercial portions such that less than 80 percent of the gross rent would come from dwelling units.

F. OZ with Workforce Housing

A popular use of OZ equity is for workforce housing. Workforce housing is commonly referred to as housing for people with up to 80 percent of area median gross income. Such housing generally doesn't qualify for LIHTCs, but because of increased rental income, there can be enough economics to be a viable OZ investment. Workforce housing also can generate Community Reinvestment Act[12] (CRA) credit and therefore this can be an attractive investment for banks generally where at least half of the units will qualify as workforce housing. Workforce housing can also work well in combination with HTCs or NMTCs.

G. Socially Motivated Investors

In all of the preceding types of transactions involving affordable housing and OZ investing, it can be very helpful to look for investors who are "socially motivated" investors. While such investors generally still look for a significant economic return on their investment, they are often willing to take a lower return than other non-socially motivated investors. While banks looking for CRA investments are one such investor, there are also other non-CRA investors who are socially motivated.

III. DETAILED ANALYSIS OF OPPORTUNITY ZONE INCENTIVE

A. Qualified Opportunity Zones

As previously stated, the Tax Cuts and Jobs Act (TCJA) of 2017 created the OZ incentive in order to spur long-term economic investment in low-income areas. The TCJA specified the criteria and designation process for these low-income areas, called qualified opportunity zones (QOZs).[13] These are census tract-based designations. To be eligible for designation as a QOZ, a census tract had to be a low-income community as determined by the 2010 census. A tract is low-income if its residents have a poverty rate of 20 percent or higher; or if the median family income within the tract is not more than 80 percent of the statewide or metropolitan area median.[14] A limited number of tracts adjacent to low-income communities could also be designated as QOZs if that tract's median family income was not more than 125 percent of the adjacent low-income tract's median family income, and the adjacent low-income tract was designated as a QOZ.

The reasonable expectations test allows an entity to be treated as a QALICB during the duration of a CDE's investment if, at the time of investment, the CDE reasonably expects the entity will satisfy QALICB requirements throughout the period of investment or loan. Where the reasonable expectations test is not available, the purported QALICB must meet various tests throughout the period of CDE control. For further discussion, see NOVOGRADAC & COMPANY LLP, NEW MARKET TAX CREDITS HANDBOOK: A TAX CREDIT PRACTITIONERS GUIDE TO USING NEW MARKET TAX CREDITS TO PROVIDE INVESTMENTS IN LOW-INCOME COMMUNITIES Ch. 2.08[1][e] (2019 ed.).

12. 12 U.S.C. § 2901.

13. *See* I.R.C. § 1400Z-1.

14. This is the same definition for a "low-income community" as in the New Markets Tax Credit program.

In the 2010 census, there were 74,001 census tracts, with 31,680 meeting the low-income definition. Generally, from the low-income census tracts therein, the chief executive[15] of each U.S. state, possession, and territory was permitted to nominate as QOZs as many as 25 percent of the number of low-income tracts (but at least 25 low-income tracts). The exception, under 2018 legislation, is that every low-income census tract in Puerto Rico is a QOZ,[16] which is the vast majority of the island.

Between December 22, 2017, and March 22, 2018, governors nominated tracts as QOZs by notifying the Secretary of the Treasury of the nomination via an online nomination tool. After this, the Secretary of the Treasury had 30 days to certify the nominations and designate the tracts. Governors could request a 30-day extension for either or both of the determination period and the Secretary's consideration period. Notice 2018-48, as modified by Notice 2019-42, lists all of the census tracts that have been designated as QOZs. Whether an address is within a QOZ can be determined by going to https://oppor tunityzones.hud.gov/resources/map.

The designation of a census tract as a QOZ remains in effect until December 31, 2028. The ability for investors to qualify for the ten-year hold benefit is not hurt by the expiration of the zone designations at the end of 2028: despite zone designation expiration, a qualified QOF investment can still grow tax free to an investor through 2047. However, if a QOF sold a QOZB investment after December 31, 2028, it appears that it would not be able to make a new QOZB investment because the QOZ status of the census tracts would have expired.

The 2020 census led to some census tract boundaries changing, the merging of some census tracts, and the split of other census tracts. IRS Announcement 2021-10 confirmed that the census tract boundaries in effect when the QOZ designations were made are the boundaries that control and are not subject to change. As a result, changes in the 2020 census do not impact whether or not a location is considered to be in a QOZ.

B. Gain Deferral and Exclusion Benefits

The term "investor" is used in this chapter to describe an eligible taxpayer that has timely invested eligible gains in a QOF and elected to defer capital gains taxation of the invested gains. This section will first will discuss each of these terms—eligible taxpayer, eligible gains, and timely investment—and then the election an eligible taxpayer must make in order to take advantage of the OZ incentive.

1. Requirements to be Eligible for the OZ Incentive

Eligible Taxpayers. The OZ incentive is available to "eligible taxpayers," as defined in the final Treasury regulations. Generally, an eligible taxpayer is defined as a person who is required, under federal income tax principals, to report the recognition of gains during the taxable year. This can include individuals, C corporations, regulated investment companies

---

15. This is generally a governor; in the case of Washington, D.C.'s QOZ nominations, it was the mayor.

16. I.R.C. § 1400Z-1(b)(3).

(RICs), real estate investment companies (REITs), partnerships, S corporations, trusts, and decedents' estates.[17]

Under the OZ rules, the party that has the capital gain generally has to be the party that makes the investment in a QOF. However, the final OZ Regulations provide an important exception whereby one consolidated corporate group member can invest the eligible gains of a different member.[18] This is critical in the LIHTC industry, where the largest investors tend to be banks. Many banks organize their LIHTC investments in a single corporate subsidiary, which is a community development corporation (CDC).[19] However, bank capital gains generally come from other members of the bank consolidated group. Thus, for such bank consolidated groups and other consolidated groups operating in heavily regulated industries, it was a significant help that the final Regulations allow one consolidated member to have a capital gain but for a different member to make an investment in a QOF.

Eligible Gain. To be an "eligible gain" the gain (1) must be a capital gain, (2) from an unrelated party,[20] and (3) would have be recognized and subject to tax by December 31, 2026. The Regulations have interpreted capital gains to include qualified gains under Code Section 1231 (certain gains from the sale of real property or depreciable business property). Gains can be invested on a gross basis; that is, without reducing gains for any losses incurred or carried over to the tax year.[21]

Timing Requirements. An eligible taxpayer's investment of eligible gains must be timely in order to benefit from the OZ incentive. For gains directly realized by an eligible taxpayer, the eligible gain must be invested in a QOF within a 180-day period beginning on the day on which the gain would otherwise have been recognized for federal income tax purposes.[22]

Where a gain is realized by a partnership, itself an eligible taxpayer, the Regulations provide significant flexibility. First, the partnership entity may invest the gain within 180 days of the gain being realized. If the partnership does not invest the gain, the partners may invest some or all of their distributive share of the gain instead. Where partners invest the gain, the 180-day period generally begins on the last day of the partnership's tax year. Alternatively, the owner may elect to treat the beginning of their 180 period as

- the same as the partnership's 180-day period; or
- the 180-day period beginning on the due date for the partnership's tax return, without extensions, for the tax year in which the partnership realized the gain.

---

17. Non-U.S. taxpayers with effectively connected eligible gains to which the taxpayer does not elect to apply a treaty exemption can benefit from OZ investing. Treas. Reg. § 1.1400Z2(a)-1(b)(11)(ix)(A)(1). Similarly, resident individuals of U.S. territories (e.g., Puerto Rico) who file a U.S. tax return can make a deferral election, but only with respect to gains not derived within their territory of residence. Proposed regulations address FIRPTA withholding mechanics, though this remains an area of uncertainty.

18. Treas. Reg. § 1.1502-14Z.

19. See https://www.occ.gov/publications-and-resources/publications/community-affairs/community-developments-fact-sheets/ca-fact-sheet-bank-owned-comm-dev-corp-sep-2011.html for a discussion of the use of CDCs.

20. For purposes of OZs, two legal entities can be considered related parties if there is more than 20 percent common ownership. I.R.C. § 1400Z-2(e)(2). Familial relationships can also cause parties to be considered related. See cross reference to I.R.C. § 267 in I.R.C. § 1400Z-2(e)(2).

21. Treas. Reg. § 1.1400Z2(a)-1(b)(11).

22. *Id.* § 1.1400Z2(a)-1(b)(7).

Similar rules apply to S corporations, non-grantor trusts, and estates.[23]

With the COVID-19 pandemic, investors were provided additional time to invest eligible gains in a QOF. The IRS released Notice 2021-10, which allowed taxpayers until March 31, 2021, to invest gains where the taxpayer's last day of their 180-day window was between April 1, 2020, and March 31, 2021.

Deferral Election. Qualification for OZ tax benefits is not automatic; an eligible taxpayer must elect to defer tax on capital gains invested in a QOF.[24] Interestingly, there is no tracing of funds. There is no need to show that the exact funds that created the capital gain are the same funds that are invested in a QOF. It is enough merely to have a gain, to make a timely investment in a QOF, and then to elect to defer taxation of some or all of the capital gain. The election to defer taxation of the capital gain is considered a regulatory election and is initially made on Form 8949, with QOF holdings reported on Form 8997, to be filed with the taxpayer's return for the year in which the gain would otherwise be included.[25] The investor must continue to include Form 8997 with its return in every year in which the investor owns an interest in a QOF.

2. Tax Benefits of Opportunity Zones Investing

By investing in a QOF, an investor can realize three tax benefits:

- Deferred taxation on the invested gain;
- Permanent exclusion of some of the invested gain from taxation; and
- Unrecaptured losses and tax-free growth of the QOF investment.

Deferred Taxation of Invested Gain. An investor defers taxation of invested gain until the earlier of an inclusion event or December 31, 2026.[26] Numerous events can result in an inclusion event. Where an investor transfers all or a portion of its investment in a QOF, this is an inclusion event to the extent the investor's equity interest is reduced. Thus, if an investor sells, exchanges, or gifts part or all of its qualifying investment in a QOF prior to having recognized all of the deferred gain associated with that investment, the sale or exchange is an inclusion event, which the investor should generally report via Form 8949, with changes to QOF investment amounts reported on Form 8997.

Distributions of Property or Cash as an Inclusion Event. Generally, if a taxpayer receives property (including money) from a QOF, and that property receipt is treated as a distribution for federal income tax purposes, it is an inclusion event.[27] This is generally the case regardless of whether the receipt of property reduces the investor's ownership in the QOF. However, distributions from a QOF partnership that do not exceed a QOF partner's adjusted basis in its QOF partnership interest are not inclusion events.[28] An example of

---

23. *Id.* § 1.1400Z2(a)-1(b)(7)(iii).

24. *Id.* § 1.1400Z2(a)-1(a)(2).

25. The election made on Form 8949 is a regulatory election. The IRS has, in one circumstance at the time of writing, granted Treas. Reg. § 301.9100 relief to an investor who erred in filing or completing its initial Form 8949. PLR 202021009. Thus, missing the election may be fixable, but at the time of writing, the fix is to request a private letter ruling—a time-intensive and expensive process.

26. At the time of writing, legislative proposals exist to extend this date to allow later investments in QOFs to have a long enough investment timeline to benefit from the five- and seven-year gain exclusion provision.

27. Treas. Reg. § 1.1400Z2(b)-1(b).

28. *Id.* § 1.1400Z2(b)-1(c)(1)(i).

this would be a debt-financed distribution of cash to an investor, where the additional debt creates basis for the taxpayer, thus sheltering the distribution from taxation and inclusion. However care must be taken with respect to debt-financed distributions, as special OZ rules can treat such distributions as a disguised sale rather than capital contributions.[29] Such treatment would result in a portion of the investment in the QOF not qualifying for OZ treatment. It is generally recommended that debt-financed distributions occur more than two years after the last investor contribution into a QOF in order to avoid the presumption of a disguised sale.[30]

Worthless Stock or QOF Cessation as Inclusion Event. If an investor claims a loss for worthless stock under Section 165(g) or otherwise claims a worthlessness deduction with respect to its QOF investment, the investor is treated as disposing of that portion of the taxpayer's qualifying investment.[31] Finally, if an eligible entity ceases to be a QOF, that is an inclusion event to the investors, and triggers recognition of previously deferred gain with respect to qualifying investments in the QOF.[32]

Calculation of Capital Gains Recognized. When an inclusion event or the December 31, 2026 date triggers gain recognition, the amount of gain an investor includes in their income is limited to the remaining amount of deferred gain reduced by the 10 or 15 percent basis adjustments discussed later.[33] The gain recognized may be further limited where the QOF investment lost value: If the fair market value of the portion of the investment disposed of (or of the QOF investment as a whole at December 31, 2026) is less than the remaining proportional amount of deferred gain, the amount recognized upon the inclusion event is the fair market value of the portion of the qualifying investment disposed of less the investor's basis in the portion of the disposed investment.

Regulation 1.1400Z2(b)-1(e)(4) provides a special rule that applies to QOF partnerships and S corporations when computing the amount gain from an inclusion event. Investors must compare the remaining amount of deferred gain (possibly reduced 10 to 15 percent for timely holding QOF investments for five to seven years) to gain that would be recognized on a fully taxable disposition of the investment or portion of investment disposed.[34] This modification to the fair market value limitation appears to be intended to prevent investors from intentionally reducing the fair market value of investments in QOF partnerships through debt-financed distributions that would not otherwise trigger an inclusion event or from using the tax basis provided by debt to allow deductions that the investors would not otherwise have been able to access.

Short-Term versus Long-Term Capital Gain. The attributes of the capital gain deferred as long- or short-term are preserved when eventually included in an investor's income.[35] So, if an investor defers short-term capital gain, the gain remains short-term capital gain when it is later included, regardless of how long the investor holds the QOF investment. However, the tax provisions and rates that apply at inclusion are those that prevail at

---

29. *See id.* § 1.1400Z2-(a)-1(c)(5)(iii)(A).
30. *See id.* § 1.707-3(c).
31. Treas. Reg. § 1.1400Z2(b)-1(c)(iii) & (c)(14).
32. *Id.* § 1.1400Z2(b)-1(c)(iv).
33. I.R.C. § 1400Z-2(b)(2); Treas. Reg. § 1.1400Z2(b)-1(e)(1).
34. Treas. Reg. § 1.1400Z2(b)-1(e)(4).
35. *Id.* § 1.1400Z2(a)-1(c)(i).

the time of inclusion.[36] That is, gain realized in 2018 and timely invested in a QOF, if held by the investor through December 31, 2026, will be taxed at 2026 rates. This presents some investor risk that their invested gains may be taxed at a higher rate than they would have been were the OZ investment not made. However, this risk is offset by the deferral benefit, the possible avoidance of 10 to 15 percent of capital gain tax, and the potential for tax-free growth at higher rates.

3. Ten to Fifteen Percent Permanent Exclusion of Some Invested Gains from Taxation

When an investor first invests its deferred-tax gain into a QOF, its federal tax basis in its QOF interest is zero.[37] If, by December 31, 2026, an investor has held its interest in the QOF for at least five years, the investor receives a basis increase in its investment equal to 10 percent of the deferred gains invested.[38] This permanently excludes 10 percent of the original deferred gain from taxation.[39] If, by December 31, 2026, an investor has held its interest in the QOF for at least seven years, the investor receives an additional basis increase of 5 percent of the deferred gains invested, permanently excluding a total of 15 percent of the original deferred gain from taxation.[40]

As of the date of writing, a new QOF investor would not have sufficient time before the gain inclusion date of December 31, 2026, to benefit from the seven-year basis increase (unless Congress were to extend the gain inclusion date). However, this does not detract from what many view as the most attractive benefits of long-term Opportunity Zone investment—unrecaptured depreciation and tax-free growth.

4. Unrecaptured Depreciation and Tax-Free Growth of the QOF Investment—The 10-Year Hold Benefit

Where an investor holds its QOF investment at least ten years, the investor can elect to have the basis of its QOF interest equal the fair market value of its QOF interest on the date the QOF interest is sold or exchanged.[41] This benefit permanently excludes from taxation any unrecaptured depreciation and post-acquisition gain in the QOF investment. Where an investor holds its QOF investment in a QOF partnership or QOF S corporation for at least ten years, and the QOF, or any partnership that is owned directly or indirectly by the QOF solely through one of more partnerships, sells or exchanges property, the investor can elect to exclude from its gross income all gains and losses allocable to the disposal of qualifying investment.[42]

In LIHTC transactions, an additional boon can be had. As mentioned *supra*, it is not uncommon for the LIHTC investor to incur "exit taxes" when getting out of a LIHTC investment, due to the investor having taken losses—generally related to large depreciation deductions—in excess of the amount invested, leading to a negative capital account (i.e., debt-financed losses). This is especially common for projects qualifying for 4 percent

---

36. *Id.* § 1.1400Z2(a)-1(c)(ii).
37. I.R.C. § 1400Z-2(b)(2)(B)(i).
38. *Id.* § 1400Z-2(b)(2)(B)(iii).
39. *See id.* § 1400Z-2(b)(2)(A)(ii) (basis in investment reduces amount of gain).
40. I.R.C. § 1400Z-2(b)(2)(B)(iii).
41. *Id.* § 1400Z-2(c).
42. Treas. Reg. § 1.1400Z2(c)-1(b)(2).

tax credits through the use of tax-exempt bond financing because such projects have less investor capital to debt than projects that are allocated 9 percent tax credits. However, the OZ rules provide that the step up to fair market value of the interest is tax free and thus exit taxes are avoided. In addition, even if the fair market value of the LIHTC project is low, as often may be the case of LIHTC projects that have limited economics, the OZ rules provide that the fair market value computation includes debt on the LIHTC project.[43] This rule means that even low-value projects can avoid exit taxes.

The Treasury Regulations provide that investors can only make fair market value basis step-up elections until December 31, 2047. There is no such provision in the Code. This regulatory deadline may create an OZ market sell-off with potential diminishing effects on the OZ communities as large numbers of investors may choose to sell their investment in 2047 in order to benefit from the fair market value basis adjustment. Congress is aware of this issue, and is considering potential "fixes," including the ability of investors to declare a date for basis step-up without requiring actual sale or exchange of their QOF interest.

5. Mixed Funds Investments

Only a qualifying investment, that is, an investment of deferred gain, is eligible for Opportunity Zone tax benefits. A taxpayer is permitted to make a nonqualifying investment in a QOF—an investment made with something other than deferred gain—but the tax benefits are available only with respect to an investment made with deferred gain.[44] If a taxpayer makes investments in a QOF and only a portion of those investments are investments of deferred gain, the taxpayer is treated as owning two separate investments in the QOF: a qualifying portion and a nonqualifying portion that must be tracked separately over the life of the investment. Only the qualifying portion is eligible for the OZ tax benefits.

C. Qualified Opportunity Funds

To qualify for opportunity zone tax benefits, a taxpayer must timely invest eligible gain in a QOF.[45] A QOF is defined as an investment vehicle organized as a corporation or partnership for the purpose of investing in QOZP, and that holds at least 90 percent of its assets in QOZP.[46] At the time of writing, a fund-of-funds structure is not permitted, as interests in a QOF do not constitute QOZP. We discuss QOZP in greater detail *infra*.

A QOF must self-certify its status as such by filing Form 8996 with its tax return each year.[47] In the first year of operation, it is generally advisable that the QOF select the month during which it first received a qualified investment as its first month as a QOF; this ensures that the investor's qualified investment is treated as having been made to a QOF, and permits the maximum amount of time before the QOF's first testing date (testing dates discussed further *infra*). The IRS considers the Form 8996 certification to be a regulatory election and has, in specific circumstances, granted Regulation 301.9100 relief to a QOF that erred in filing or completing its initial Form 8996.[48] Thus, missing the QOF

---

43. *Id.*
44. I.R.C. § 1400Z-2(e)(1).
45. *Id.* § 1400Z-2(a)(1)(A).
46. *Id.* § 1400Z-2(d)(1).
47. Treas. Reg. § 1.1400Z2(d)-1(a)(2).
48. *See, e.g.*, PLRs 202019017, 202116011, 202103013, and 202119003.

certification may be fixable, but at the time of writing, the fix is to request a private letter ruling—a time-intensive and expensive process.

1. The 90 Percent Investment Standard ("90 Percent Test")

A QOF must maintain the 90 percent investment standard, which is reported annually via Form 8996. The measurement is an average of the QOZP percentage held at two testing dates: the last day of the first six-month period of the QOF's tax year and the last day of the QOF's tax year.[49] By way of example, this means that a QOF first certifying as a QOF for May 2021 has a testing date each at October 31, 2021, and at its December 31, 2021 tax year end. If an eligible entity becomes a QOF in the seventh or later month of a taxable year, the 90 percent investment standard would only take into account the assets held on the last day of the QOF's taxable year.[50]

At each testing date, the fund determines the percentage of its assets held in QOZP. Where a QOF fails to meet the 90 Percent Test and does not establish reasonable cause for the failure, the QOF is required to pay a penalty which accrues monthly.[51] In theory, repeated failures may allow the IRS to take action to decertify a fund, though the mechanics of such a forced decertification are not specified in the Code or Treasury Regulations, and have not yet been tested.

For purposes of the 90 Percent Test, a QOF has the option to disregard contributions received not more than six months before a testing date, if those contributions are held continuously in cash, cash equivalents, or debt instruments with a term of 18 months or less.[52] This provides a QOF time to deploy contributions and could yield as much as nearly a year to deploy contributions, depending on receipt. To illustrate, suppose a December 31 year-end QOF receives a contribution on January 2. This contribution can be disregarded at the June 30 testing date, in which case the QOF has until December 31 to invest those newly contributed funds into QOZP.

At their first testing date, new QOFs may need to choose to disregard all contributions received to-date if the funds have not yet been invested.[53] This yields two potential problems. first, the ratio at the first testing date of QOZP over total assets may be $0/$0, an undefined number. Second, to the extent those contributions were deposited into an interest-bearing account and earned interest, might those earnings create assets that cannot be disregarded, such that the QOF's percentage of assets invested in QOZP is zero percent? The IRS has yet to provide formal guidance on these issues but has indicated informally that a QOF should report 100 percent for the $0/$0 situation, and should be permitted to exclude interest earned on contributions received within six months prior to a testing date.

---

49. I.R.C. § 1400Z-2(d)(1).

50. *Id.* § 1400Z-2(d)(1).

51. *Id.* § 1400Z-2(f)(1). Notice 2021-10 provides reasonable cause penalty relief for QOFs impacted by the COVID-19 pandemic where a testing date falls between April 1, 2020, and June 30, 2021. Form 8996 must still be completed in full, including computations of penalty amounts, but with $0 entered as the penalty total.

52. Treas. Reg. § 1.1400Z2(d)-1(b)(2)(B).

53. *Id.*

2. Valuation Method

To measure for the 90 Percent Test, a QOF may value its assets according to financial statements (the "applicable financial statement method"), or using the "alternative valuation method,"[54] under which the unadjusted cost basis of assets is generally used.[55] Financial statement valuation is only available if the financial statements provide GAAP-based valuations, and if the financial statements value assets at least annually, recognize "mark-to-market" income arising from these valuations, and require a mark-to-market based realization of income on the disposal of assets.[56]

Unadjusted cost basis means that for valuation purposes one would look at the original basis (generally the original cost) of the asset without adjusting for subsequent depreciation.[57] Unadjusted cost basis valuation tends to be more attractive for a number of reasons. First, not all QOFs will have financial statements meeting the applicable financial statement method requirements. Perhaps more importantly, using unadjusted cost basis provides longer-term dependability. Using the unadjusted cost basis approach, a QOF does not have to worry about depreciation or fluctuations in the value of assets impacting the 90 Percent Test. However, if property was not purchased or constructed for fair market value (for example, contributed property), the unadjusted cost basis approach to valuation cannot be used; instead, the asset's value for purposes of the 90 Percent Test is the asset's fair market value on each testing date.

In the case of leased property, the value under the alternative valuation method is the present value of each payment to be made under the lease, inclusive of amount-certain payments that would be made under any lease extension terms available at the time the lease is entered into.[58] The value under this approach is determined at the time the lease is entered into and holds for the duration of the lease. That is, a new value does not need to be determined as time passes (and therefore the number of lease payments to be made decreases).

D. Qualified Opportunity Zone Property

QOZP includes (1) QOZ stock, (2) QOZ partnership interests, and (3) QOZ business property (QOZBP).[59] While it is possible for a QOF to directly own QOZBP and directly operate a trade or business, this is extremely rare. The reason is twofold: first, a qualified opportunity zone business (QOZB) can benefit from working capital safe harbor periods that generally permit a QOZB up to 31 months to use the cash that is invested in the QOZB. This 31-month working capital rule (discussed *infra*) does not apply where the QOF directly owns property rather than indirectly owning property by investing in a corporation or partnership that owns the property used in a trade or business. Second, where a QOF must maintain a 90 percent investment standard, a QOZB must maintain a more forgiving 70 percent tangible property standard (discussed *infra*).

54. *Id.* § 1.1400Z2(d)-1(b)(3).
55. *Id.* § 1.1400Z2(d)-1(b)(4).
56. *Id.* § 1.1400Z2(d)-1(b)(3)(ii).
57. *Id.* § 1.1400Z2(d)-1(b)(4).
58. *Id.* § 1.1400Z2(d)-1(b)(4)(iii).
59. I.R.C. § 1400Z-2(d)(2)(A).

1. QOZ Stock

QOZ stock is stock in a domestic entity classified as a corporation for federal tax purposes, acquired after December 31, 2017, at its original issue from the corporation solely in exchange for cash.[60] To qualify, the issuer must be a QOZB or, if the corporation is newly formed, it must have been organized for purposes of being a QOZB. Further, during substantially all (at least 90 percent) of the QOF's holding period for the stock, the corporation must qualify as a QOZB.

Although QOZ stock constitutes QOZP and is thereby a "good" asset for purposes of a QOF's 90 percent investment standard, QOZ stock is rarely used in real estate investing: The corporate form does not allow for investors to receive passthrough depreciation deductions.

2. QOZ Partnership Interest

QOZ partnership interests are the principal method of investing in OZ-sited real estate projects. A QOZ partnership interest is a capital or profits interest in a domestic entity classified as a partnership for federal tax purposes, acquired after December 31, 2017, from the partnership solely in exchange for cash.[61] Similar to QOZ stock, at the time the QOF acquired the interest, the partnership must be a QOZB or, if the partnership is newly formed, it must have been organized for purposes of being a QOZB. Again, during substantially all (at least 90 percent) of the QOF's holding period for the interest, the partnership must qualify as a QOZB.[62]

For both QOZ stock and QOZ partnership interests, the interest needs to be equity. Preferred stock is permissible, as are partnership interests, which receive special allocations. However, the rights associated with the interest should not bear too many similarities to debt, such as a fixed rate of return or repayment date.

3. QOZBP

QOZBP is defined as tangible property, purchased or leased, used in a trade or business that meets the following requirements:[63]

- Purchased after December 31, 2017, from an unrelated person;
- Original use of the property in the QOZ commences with the QOF (or the QOZB), or the QOF (or QOZB) substantially improves the property; and
- During at least 90 percent of the QOF's (or QOZB's) holding period for the property, at least 70 percent of the use of the property is in the QOZ.

The substantial improvement requirement is met if, during any 30-month period beginning after the date of acquisition of the property, additions to the basis of the property in the hands of the QOF (or QOZB) exceed an amount equal to the adjusted basis of the property at the beginning of the 30-month period in the hands of the QOF (or QOZB).[64]

---

60. *Id.* § 1400Z-2(d)(2)(B).
61. *Id.* § 1400Z-2(d)(2)(C).
62. *Id.*
63. *Id.* § 1400Z-2(d)(2)(D).
64. I.R.C. § 1400Z-2(d)(2)(D)(ii).

In affordable housing, it is not uncommon for the developer to be related to the project-owning partnership (the project-owning partnership serving as the QOZB entity in the OZ context). The regulations are not clear as to whether reasonable payments from the QOZB to the related developer for the development or construction of tangible property constitute QOZBP.

Land generally does not need to be substantially improved.[65] That said, an unimproved piece of land does need to be used in a trade or business. Land will not be QOZBP if it is unimproved or minimally improved and was purchased with an expectation or intention not to improve it by more than an insubstantial amount within 30 months of acquisition.[66] It is not completely clear what "more than insubstantial" means: presumably something less than a doubling of the basis, with acceptable improvement examples in the final Treasury Regulations including clearing, remediating, and grading the land in preparation for its use.

Leased QOZBP must meet all of the following requirements:[67]

- Lease entered into after December 31, 2017, from a related or unrelated person;
- Generally, the lease terms must be market-rate;[68] and
- During at least 90 percent of the QOF's (or QOZB's) holding period for the property, at least 70 percent of the use of the property is in the QOZ.

Leased property is not subject to the "original use" or "substantial improvement" requirements; that is, a QOF or QOZB may lease property that had previously been used by another party within the QOZ. Improvements that a lessee makes to leased property satisfy the original use requirement as purchased property.

In the case of nonqualified property, the Code and Treasury Regulations are silent as to the treatment of improvements: Though the existing property is not QOZBP, might the improvements thereto qualify as QOZBP? Interestingly, one must look to the preamble to the final Treasury Regulations for an answer. A commenter pointed out that improvements to leased property are treated as separate property and reasoned that the same standard should apply to owned property. The Treasury did not agree, having "determined that the administrative burdens that would arise for taxpayers and the IRS from tracking improvements made to such non-qualified property would significantly exceed those arising from the tracking of lessee improvements."[69] At present, a QOZB or QOF should understand that improving nonqualified property may add to its non-QOZBP or non-QOZP assets, and threaten its ability to meet the 70 Percent Test (discussed *infra*) or 90 Percent Test. However, land is considered a separate asset from a building constructed on it. Thus, nonqualified land could have a new building constructed on it and that new building should not be considered nonqualified property merely because it was built on nonqualified land.

---

65. Treas. Reg. § 1400Z2(d)-2(b)(4)(iv)(B).

66. *Id.* § 1.1400Z2(d)-(2)(b)(4)(iv)(C).

67. *Id.* § 1400Z2(d)-2(c).

68. For leases between unrelated parties, the rebuttable assumption is that the terms are market rate. Related party leases must meet several additional requirements specified in the final Treasury regulations. In the case of leases of tangible property from a state, local, or Indian tribal government, the lease is treated as not between related parties.

69. IRS, Treasury Decision, TD 9889, 85 FR 1866, Investing in Qualified Opportunity Funds (2020).

E. Qualified Opportunity Zone Businesses (QOZB)

A business must meet several criteria at the end of its tax year to be a QOZB for that taxable year:

- A QOZB can be a new or existing entity but must be classified as a partnership or corporation for federal income tax purposes and organized under the laws of the United States.[70]
- The QOZB must be engaged in the active conduct of a trade or business.[71]
- The QOZB must meet the 70 percent tangible property standard; that is, at least 70 percent of the tangible property owned or leased by the QOZB must be QOZBP.[72]
- At least 50 percent of the QOZB's total gross income must be derived from the active conduct of a trade or business in the QOZ, or in multiple QOZs.[73]
- At least 40 percent of the QOZB's intangible property must be used in the active conduct of a trade or business in a QOZ.[74]
- Nonqualified financial property (NQFP) must constitute less than 5 percent of the QOZB's property.[75]
- The business of the QOZB may not involve operation of what is commonly called a "sin business": operating a private or commercial golf course, a country club, a massage parlor, a hot tub facility, a suntan facility, a racetrack, a gambling establishment, or a store if the principal business is the sale of alcohol for consumption off premises.[76]

1. Active Conduct of a Trade or Business

The Regulations specifically focus on the ownership and operation of real property and discuss what the bounds are for leasing activity to be considered the active conduct of a trade or business. Owning and leasing real property can constitute the active conduct of a trade or business, but "merely entering into a triple-net-lease" does not.[77]

The Regulations provide examples of this. In one, a company constructs, places into service, and leases out a building to one tenant, and the tenant is responsible under the lease for all taxes, insurance, and maintenance expenses related to the building. The company maintains a staffed office to address issues that may arise with respect to the lease but has no other property. The company is not engaged in the active conduct of a trade or business for purposes of Code Section 1400Z-2(d)(3)(A).[78] By contrast, the facts in a second example have a QOZB company that leases three different floors of a building to three different

---

70. Treas. Reg. §§ 1.1400Z2(d)-1(a)(1)(iii), 1.1400Z2(d)-1(a)(1)(i).

71. I.R.C. § 1400Z-2(d)(3)(A), Treas. Reg. § 1.1400Z2(d)-1(d)(3)(iii).

72. I.R.C. § 1400Z-2(d)(3)(A)(i), Treas. Reg. § 1.1400Z2(d)-1(d)(2)(i).

73. Treas. Reg. § 1.1400Z2(d)-1(d)(3)(i).

74. *Id.* § 1.1400Z2(d)-1(d)(3)(ii)(A).

75. *Id.* § 1.1400Z2(d)-1(d)(3)(iv).

76. *Id.* § 1.1400Z2(d)-1(d)(4)(i). De minimis amounts (less than 5 percent) of gross income attributable to sin business activity is permitted. In a rental context, de minimis means that less than 5 percent of rentable square feet and less than 5 percent of the value for all other tangible property. *Id.* § 1.1400Z2(d)-1(d)(4)(ii)–(iii).

77. *Id.* § 1.400Z2(d)-1(d)(3)(iii)(B).

78. *Id.* § 1.1400Z2(d)-1(d)(3)(iii)(C), Example 1.

tenants. One floor is triple-net leased to a tenant, with the other two floors having leases that are not triple-net. For the non-triple-net leased floors, the company manages and operates the floors. The Regulations conclude that under these facts, the company is engaged in the active conduct of a trade or business for purposes of Code Section 1400Z-2(d)(3)(A).[79]

2. Seventy Percent Tangible Property Standard ("70 Percent Test")

Whether a trade or business of the entity satisfies the 70 Percent Test is determined by using a fraction, the numerator of which is the total value of all QOZBP owned or leased by the QOZB and the denominator of which is the total value of all tangible property owned or leased by the QOZB, whether located inside or outside of a QOZ.[80] The valuation methods available for this purpose are the same as those applied under the 90 Percent Test and discussed *supra*: the applicable financial statement method or the alternative valuation method.

3. Gross Income Test

In order for a business to be considered a QOZB, with respect to any tax year, at least 50 percent of its total gross income must be derived from the active conduct of a trade or business within QOZs.[81] By meeting any one of the following three safe harbors, a QOZB is considered to have met its Gross Income Test requirement.[82]

1. *Hours performed.* This safe harbor is met if, over the course of the year, at least 50 percent of services performed for the business by employees and independent contractors are performed within a QOZ. A ratio is used to determine whether this safe harbor is met, with the numerator equaling the number of hours services are performed for the QOZB within QOZs, and the denominator equaling the total number of hours services are performed for the QOZB within and without QOZs.[83]

2. *Cost of services.* This safe harbor is met if, over the course of the year, at least 50 percent of the amounts paid for services performed for the business by employees and independent contractors are for services performed within QOZs. Similar to the preceding, a ratio is used to determine if this safe harbor is met. In this case, the numerator is the amount paid by the QOZB for services performed in QOZs, and the denominator is the total amount paid by the QOZB for services performed both within and without QOZs.[84]

3. *Property and management functions.* This safe harbor is met if, over the course of the year, the QOZ-sited tangible property and management or operational functions performed within QOZs are necessary for the generation of at least 50 percent of the business's gross income.[85]

---

79. *Id.* § 1.1400Z2(d)-1(d)(3)(iii)(C), Example 2.
80. *Id.* § 1400Z2(d)-1(d)(2).
81. *See* I.R.C. § 1400Z02(3)(3)(A)(ii) (cross-reference to I.R.C. § 1397C(b)(2)).
82. Treas. Reg. § 1.1400Z2(d)-1(d)(3)(i).
83. *Id.* § 1.1400Z2(d)-1(d)(3)(i)(A).
84. *Id.* § 1.1400Z2(d)-1(d)(3)(i)(B).
85. *Id.* § 1.1400Z2(d)-1(d)(3)(i)(C).

In lieu of meeting these tests, general facts and circumstances are considered.[86] However, note that in the case of rental real estate–based investments and the characteristic of non-moveable assets to the generation of income, the third safe harbor is likely to be met.

4. Intangibles Test

Where a QOZB owns intangible assets, at least 40 percent of the use of the intangibles must be in the active conduct of the QOZB's trade or business within a QOZ.[87] Intangible property is generally considered to be used in the active conduct of a trade or business in a QOZ where:

- The use of the intangible property is normal, usual or customary in the conduct of the trade or business; and
- The intangible property is used in QOZs in the performance of an activity of the trade or business that contributed to the generation of gross income for the trade or business.[88]

In the affordable housing context, this test is generally either irrelevant or easily met: Such businesses are generally real estate focused and have few intangible assets. What intangible assets affordable housing businesses do have are likely to be related to the real estate, which will need to be located in a QOZ.

5. NQFP Test

A business will not qualify as a QOZB if 5 percent or more of the average of the aggregate unadjusted bases of property owned by the business is NQFP.[89] NQFP includes debt, stock, partnership interests, options, futures contracts, forward contracts, warrants, notional principal contracts, annuities, and other similar property specified in the final Treasury Regulations. Although Section 1397C(e) does not explicitly say cash and cash equivalents are NQFP, the fact that they are NQFP is commonly understood based on the reasonable working capital exclusion principals and the working capital safe harbor.

In measuring the amount of NQFP held by a QOZB, reasonable amounts of working capital held in cash, cash equivalents, or debt instruments with a term of 18 months or less is excluded from the definition of NQFP.[90] In addition, accounts or notes receivable acquired in the ordinary course of business for services rendered or from the sale of property are also excluded.

Because real estate projects require a large amount of available liquid assets during construction periods, the NQFP rules had the potential to create significant problems for such projects. Thankfully, the Regulations contain a working capital safe harbor that allows reasonable amounts of working capital to be excluded from the calculation of NQFP if the working capital is to be used within 31 months to construct/rehabilitate a building or invest in a trade or business.[91] A QOZB may benefit from more than a single overlapping or sequential application of the 31-month working capital safe harbor period, provided each

---

86. *Id.* § 1.1400Z2(d)-1(d)(3)(i)(D).
87. *Id.* § 1.1400Z2(d)-1(d)(3)(ii)(A).
88. *Id.* § 1.1400Z2(d)-1(d)(3)(ii)(B).
89. I.R.C. § 1400Z-2(d)(3)(A)(ii) cross-references the NQFP rules of I.R.C. § 1397C(b)(8).
90. *Id.* § 1.1400Z2(d)-1(d)(3)(iv).
91. *Id.* § 1.1400Z2(d)-1(d)(3)(v).

application satisfies all of the requirements discussed next.[92] However, the maximum time for all applications cannot exceed 62 months. Not more than an additional 24 months can also be available for a working capital safe harbor period where a QOZB is located in a federally declared disaster.[93] In the case of the COVID-19 pandemic in 2020–2021, QOZBs nationwide generally have up to an additional 24 months' use working capital assets, if they need it.[94]

For working capital amounts held by a QOZB to be treated as reasonable under the safe harbor, all of the following requirements[95] must be met:

- The amounts are designated in writing for the development of a trade or business in a QOZ, including, when appropriate, the acquisition, construction, and/or substantial improvement of tangible property in a QOZ.
- There is a written schedule consistent with the ordinary start-up of a trade or business for the expenditure of the working capital assets that shows consumption of the working capital assets within 31 months of the date on which the business received the assets. The written designation and schedule should include provision for overlapping or sequential safe harbor periods, if such additional safe harbors are anticipated to be needed.
- The QOZB must actually use the working capital assets in a manner that is substantially consistent with the written plan and written schedule.[96]

In the case of a new OZ LIHTC project, it is typical to include the written designation and written schedule as an addendum to the partnership's limited partnership agreement.

6. Start-Up QOZB Safe Harbors

The final Treasury Regulations provide for several safe harbors, designed to allow a business to satisfy QOZB requirements through certain common business start-up issues and working capital safe harbor periods, particularly:

- Safe harbor for property on which working capital is being expended;
- Gross income safe harbor; and
- Intangible property safe harbor.

The final Treasury Regulations provide if there is a valid working capital safe harbor period in effect, the assets that are intended to be covered by the safe harbor are deemed to satisfy QOZBP requirements.[97] The QOZBP requirements directly apply to tangible property—not to the business entity—so there is a lack of consensus among practitioners as to how to interpret this rule. One interpretation of this language is that as long as the entity

---

92. *Id.* § 1.1400Z2(d)-1(d)(3)(v)(E).

93. See Notice 2021-10, which extends relief to QOZBs with working capital assets intended to be covered by the working capital safe harbor before June 30, 2021.

94. *Id.*

95. Treas. Reg. § 1.1400Z2(d)-1(d)(3)(v).

96. *Id.* § 1.1400Z2(d)-1(d)(3)(v)(A)–(C). Proposed Treasury regulations outline the permissibility, in the event of a federally declared disaster, of revised written plans and schedules, and require that such revisions must be adopted within 120 days of the end of close of a disaster period. Prop. Reg. § 1.1400Z2(d)-1(d)(3)(v)(D).

97. Treas. Reg. § 1.1400Z2(d)-1(d)(3)(vi)(D)(1).

holds working capital assets that are covered by the working capital safe harbor, then the entity is deemed to satisfy the 70 Percent Test discussed earlier.

Informal conversations with the IRS have confirmed the intent to provide this safe harbor and suspend the 70 percent tangible property standard during a valid working capital safe harbor period. This safe harbor is helpful to affordable housing businesses in particular; it provides time to purchase or construct qualified property, and time to use property in a trade or business, during which a QOZB needn't worry that these assets—not yet placed in service—are not being used in the active conduct of a trade or business.

Additionally, any gross income derived from working capital assets that are subject to a working capital safe harbor period, counts toward meeting the 50 Percent Gross Income Test.[98] During a working capital safe harbor period, a business's only income may be from interest earned on its cash deposits. This safe harbor allows a business to make the prudent business decision to deposit working capital funds into interest-bearing accounts without running afoul of the QOZB 50 Percent Gross Income Test.

Finally, intangible property (IP) purchased or licensed by a business under a valid working capital safe harbor satisfies the use requirement during any period in which the business is proceeding in a manner that is substantially consistent with its written plan. This allows a business to purchase or license the IP it may need for its business before the business is necessarily in a position to ensure that the IP's use in a trade or business is at least 40 percent conducted within QOZs.[99]

IV. AN ILLUSTRATION

Some of the concepts discussed in the preceding pages are illustrated in the following very simplified scenario: Stanley and Helen Roper are the owners of Threes Company, LLC ("Threes Co."). Threes Co. is classified as a partnership for federal tax purposes and uses a calendar year end.

Threes Co. realized $10 million of eligible gain on December 31, 2020. Threes Co. has until June 29, 2021 (180 days from December 31, 2020) to invest the gain into a QOF. If Threes Co. does not invest the gain, the Ropers have until September 11, 2021 (180 days from Threes Co.'s March 15, 2021, tax return due date without extension) to invest the gain into a QOF.

On July 15, 2021, the Ropers timely invest $10 million into a QOF organized primarily to invest in Affordable Santa Monica, LLC, a QOZB that will own and operate an affordable housing development located in a QOZ and eligible for LIHTCs. On their 2021 tax return, the Ropers elect to defer recognition of the gain on Form 8949 and report their interest in the QOF on Form 8997.

The Ropers will initially receive a $0 basis in their interests in the QOF. If the Ropers hold their QOF interests, on July 15, 2026, the Ropers will receive a basis increase equal to 10 percent of the deferred gain, or $1 million. There is not enough time before the gain realization date of December 31, 2026, for the additional 5 percent basis increase for holding the QOF investment for seven years. On their 2026 tax return, the Ropers will include gain in the amount of

---

98. *Id.* § 1.1400Z2(d)-1(d)(3)(vi)(B).
99. *Id.* § 1.1400Z2(d)-1(d)(3)(vi)(C).

- The lesser of the fair market value of the QOF interest[100] or the amount of gain deferred, less
- $1 million basis.

This gain will take the same character (i.e., long-term versus short-term) as the gain had at December 31, 2020. Starting July 15, 2031, and through December 31, 2047, the Ropers will be permitted to sell or dispose of their interests in the QOF and elect to have their basis in the QOF interests equal fair market value at the time of the sale or disposal.

Assuming the investment from the Ropers is the QOF's first receipt of a qualifying investment from an investor, the QOF will certify as a QOF effective July 2021. The QOF's first testing date for the sake of the 90 Percent Test will be December 31, 2021 (the last day of the first sixth-month period as a QOF). In order to provide it time to deploy recently received funds, the QOF is able to disregard the contribution from the Ropers for purposes of this first 90 Percent Test. Assuming the QOF's only assets are the cash from the Ropers (and perhaps additional subsequent investors) and interest earned on that cash, the QOF's 2021 Form 8996 will reflect 100 percent for the 90 Percent Test, with no resulting penalty.[101]

The QOF should deploy the cash from the Ropers by no later than the next testing date, June 30, 2022. On April 1, 2022, the QOF invests in newly formed Affordable Santa Monica, LLC. As an addendum to its Operating Agreement, Affordable Santa Monica, LLC adopted a written plan and schedule under which funds will be spent for the construction of the development. The written plan and schedule anticipate a second capital infusion into Affordable Santa Monica, LLC at approximately December 2024, and call for two consecutive 31-month working capital periods. This written plan should include expenditures by November 1, 2024, of amounts specified in the first 31-month period—at least equal to the amount of funds received from the QOF on April 1, 2022.

V. CONCLUSION

The Opportunity Zone incentive can pair well with affordable housing. The OZ tax benefits of delayed capital gains taxation, avoidance of 10 percent to 15 percent of capital gain tax, and tax-free appreciation are helpful to investors and developers. For OZ-LIHTC transactions in particular, OZs can also avoid exit taxes and increase the appeal of a project to investors. While there is additional complexity from including OZs, because affordable housing is real estate based, the complexity is less than it would be with other types of investments. As a result, OZ can be a positive impact on affordable housing in QOZs. However, the OZ incentive is currently structured so that no capital gains can be deferred after December 31, 2026, and thus new investments in QOF would no longer be possible. Without congressional action, new investments in QOFs can only be made for the next few years. Congress is considering extension and modification of the incentive, which would allow a longer opportunity for the incentive to impact affordable housing.

---

100. *See supra* note 34 and accompanying text for special rule for determining fair market value of QOF Partnership interests.

101. *See supra* note 54 and accompanying text for a discussion of the issue of $0 of QOZBP divided by $0 total assets.

Federal Regulation of Financing for Affordable Housing

8

Maeve Elise Brown

I. INTRODUCTION

This chapter explains a wide range of federal laws[1] that regulate financing of affordable housing development.[2] Section II provides context for these laws. Section III discusses laws that promote community investment in affordable housing, with a focus on the Community Reinvestment Act of 1977 (CRA).[3] The CRA is a regulatory incentive that encourages the private sector to invest in low- and moderate-income communities and affordable housing development. It has had a considerable effect on affordable multifamily and single-family development and may be revised in some fashion in the future. This section also briefly discusses other federal laws promulgated by the Office of the Comptroller of Currency (OCC) and the Federal Deposit Insurance Corporation (FDIC) that encourage, but do not require, financial institutions to invest in low-income communities, including by promoting affordable housing development.

Section IV focuses on the Fair Housing Amendments Act of 1988[4] (FHAA), the primary federal law prohibiting discrimination in housing. The FHAA's impact has been most noticeable in the single-family home mortgage

---

1. Brief mention of state laws is made in Section III.C, *infra*.

2. The focus of this chapter is affordable *multifamily* rental housing.

3. Housing and Community Development Act of 1977, Pub. L. No. 95-128, Title VIII, § 802, 91 Stat. 1147 (Oct. 12, 1977), (codified as amended at 12 U.S.C. §§ 2901, *et seq.* (known as the Community Reinvestment Act of 1977) (2010)).

4. Civil Rights Act of 1968, Pub. L. No. 90-284, 82 Stat. 73 (1968) (as amended through Pub. L. No. 113-14 (2013)), and the Fair Housing Amendments Act of 1988, Pub. L. No. 100-430, 102 Stat. 1619 (Sept. 13, 1988). For more information on the legislative history of the Fair Housing Act of 1968, *see* Robert G. Schwemm,

and rental arena. This section also discusses antidiscrimination regulations promulgated by the Office of Thrift Supervision (OTS), which, although not focused on affordable housing, could have an impact through regulation of secondary market activities.

Section V covers laws pertaining to Government-Sponsored Enterprises (GSEs) that are still significant participants in the secondary housing market—the Federal National Mortgage Association (Fannie Mae), the Federal Home Loan Mortgage Corporation (Freddie Mac), and the Federal Home Loan Bank System. All three invest heavily in the housing market, focusing primarily on single-family housing, but increasingly on multifamily housing. This section will also touch on the financial failure of both Fannie Mae and Freddie Mac in 2008, the subsequent creation of the Federal Housing Finance Agency that same year, and subsequent regulatory changes affecting the role of the GSEs in affordable housing development.

Section VI discusses new funding released to stabilize neighborhoods with high rates of foreclosure, which is funding primarily for purchase and rehabilitation of foreclosed-on properties. Section VII touches briefly on the landmark creation of a new federal agency that is dedicated to the protection of consumers—the Consumer Financial Protection Bureau (CFPB).

Finally, Section VIII touches on climate change–related insurance, construction regulation, and utility access concerns as well as the role of the Environmental Protection Agency (EPA) and Federal Emergency Management agency (FEMA) in the evolving affordable housing arena.

II. FEDERAL AFFORDABLE HOUSING REGULATIONS IN CONTEXT

Climate change, a global pandemic, and significant economic hardship resulting from COVID-19 pandemic–related emergency orders provide critical context for this chapter in the third edition of this book. The foreclosure crisis, which affected many countries in addition to the United States, was barely in the rear-view mirror before the current pandemic-related crises arrived. These crises might ultimately cause significant tenant displacement as well as foreclosures.[5] States, cities, and counties nationally imposed eviction moratoria to limit tenant displacement for at least a period of time.[6] Federal mortgage insurers issued

---

Housing Discrimination Law and Litigation (updated July 2020), Westlaw HDISLL [hereinafter Schwemm].

5. *See* Brian Menickella, *COVID-19 Worldwide: The Pandemic's Impact on the Economy and Markets*, Forbes (Apr. 8, 2020, 2:57 PM), https://www.forbes.com/sites/brianmenickella/2020/04/08/covid-19-worldwide-the-pandemics-impact-on-the-economy-and-markets/#524c08cd28c3 [https://perma.cc/RR23-WXSL].

6. *See* Laurie Goodman, Karaan Kaul, & Michael Neal, *The CARES Act Eviction Moratorium Covers All Federally Financed Rentals—That's One in Four US Rental Units*, Urban Inst. (Apr. 2, 2020), https://www.urban.org/urban-wire/cares-act-eviction-moratorium-covers-all-federally-financed-rentals-thats-one-four-us-rental-units [https://perma.cc/ZSJ6-53NA]; *see* Center for Disease Control, *Temporary Halt in Residential Evictions to Prevent the Further Spread of COVID-19* (Sept. 4, 2020), https://www.govinfo.gov/content/pkg/FR-2020-09-04/pdf/2020-19654.pdf; and Maya Brennan, *When Moratoria Lift, How Can State and Local Governments Avoid a COVID-19 Eviction Surge?*, Urban Inst. (May 20, 2020), https://housingmatters.urban.org/articles/when-moratoria-lift-how-can-state-and-local-governments-avoid-covid-19-eviction-surge [https://perma.cc/UPJ8-Z6G6].

foreclosure moratoria and moratoria on evictions from properties with federally insured mortgages.[7] Some states negotiated temporary moratoria on foreclosures on some nonfederally insured mortgages.[8] However, for multifamily property owners not being paid rent and the small property owners (homeowners renting out rooms in their homes; duplex, triplex, and quadraplex owners), there has not been any mortgage relief offered at the local, state, or national level. In addition, emergency rental assistance programs have been slow to provide funds with rules baked in that will result in a substantial amount of funds never being distributed unless rules are changed. It is not clear how many small or large landlords applied or could have applied for the federal Paycheck Protection Program, which was intended to encourage small businesses to keep employees on their payrolls.[9] It does appear that the demand for the program outstripped its availability.[10]

With the financial, health, and housing uncertainties created by the current crises, some have wondered whether we are poised to see a new foreclosure crisis unfold. Certainly, one difference between the run up to that crisis and the current time period is that the pandemic has been a primary driving force behind our current crises. In contrast, the foreclosure crisis that ran from approximately 2006 to 2014 was born of abusive mortgage lending practices that included steering consumers into loans that were more costly than what they were qualified to receive, lending money to consumers that they clearly did not have the income to repay (setting them up for the ultimate loss of their home), and financial institutions' almost literally betting on and contributing to a housing bubble that was unsustainable.[11] The widespread failure of financial institutions was one of the results, including the largest bank closure and second largest savings and loan closure in U.S. history.[12] Lax

---

7. *See Summary of National Foreclosure Moratoria and Forbearance Programs,* CONFERENCE OF STATE BANK SUPERVISORS, https://www.csbs.org/sites/default/files/2020-04/FederalMoratoriumConsumerForeclosuresFactSheet%28updated4-3-2020%29.pdf [https://perma.cc/XMZ6-52B4] (last updated Apr. 3, 2020).

8. *See Covid-19 State Foreclosure Moratoriums and Stays,* NAT'L CONSUMER LAW CTR. (Apr. 20, 2021), https://www.nclc.org/issues/foreclosures-and-mortgages/covid-19-state-foreclosure-moratoriums-and-stays.html [https://perma.cc/2HSH-PW4Q].

9. *See* Paycheck Protection Program Flexibility Act of 2020, Pub. L. No. 116-142, 134 Stat. 641-43.

10. Lisa Desjardins, *It Took 13 Days for the Paycheck Protection Program to Run Out of Money. What Comes Next?,* PBS (Apr. 16, 2020, 2:43 PM), https://www.pbs.org/newshour/politics/it-took-13-days-for-the-paycheck-protection-program-to-run-out-of-money-what-comes-next [https://perma.cc/2X64-FXHM].

11. See Congressional Oversight Panel, March 2009 Oversight Report, *Foreclosure Crisis: Working Toward a Solution,* (Mar. 6, 2009), https://fraser.stlouisfed.org/files/docs/historical/fct/cop.senate.gov/documents/cop-030609-_report_20090306.pdf. [https://perma.cc/G9EM-5WZE].

12. Kathy M. Kristoff & Andrea Chang, *Federal Regulators Seize Crippled IndyMac Bank,* L.A. TIMES (July 12, 2008, 12:00 AM), https://www.latimes.com/archives/la-xpm-2008-jul-12-fi-indymac12-story.html [https://perma.cc/499K-Y4Q3]; Robin Sidel, David Enrich, & Dan Fitzpatrick, *WaMu Is Seized, Sold Off to J.P. Morgan, In Largest Failure in U.S. Banking History,* WALL. ST. J. ONLINE (Sept. 26, 2008, 12:01 AM), https://www.wsj.com/articles/SB122238415586576687 [https://perma.cc/SX83-3NR4].

and otherwise inadequate regulatory oversight contributed to this financial crisis.[13] Lending on multifamily dwellings slowed as a result.[14]

What the full economic impact will be from COVID-19 emergency orders remains to be seen, but data so far shows the orders have caused widespread closures of small businesses, and a disproportionate impact on small businesses owned by people of color.[15] The pandemic itself has had a disproportionately negative health impact on households of color and all residents age 75 and older.[16] Unemployment claims filed by approximately 55 million Americans have outstripped the 37 million filed during the most recent foreclosure crisis.[17] With business closures and loss of income comes the possibility of imminent population migration on what may be a significant level. We already know that 52 percent of young adults (age 18–29) now live at home with their parents—the greatest percentage since the Great Depression.[18] How many relocated a significant distance to move back in with parents, how many will continue to live there and for how long are all open questions.

Changes to household size and location and residents' financial circumstance are drivers of affordable housing need that must be considered. In addition, given the evolution of climate change, we must consider more than ever where affordable housing can be built safely, as well as the cost and risks of building related to location. For example, climate change may be increasing the severity and frequency of hurricanes in the United States.[19]

---

13. *See* U.S. Gov't Accountability Office, GAO-10-555T, *Financial Crisis Highlights Need to Improve Oversight of Leverage at Financial Institutions and Across System*, (May 6, 2010), https://www.gao.gov/products/gao-10-555t [https://perma.cc/XSY8-AFHG]; Michael M. Phillips & Jessica Holzer, *Regulator Let IndyMac Backdate Infusion*, Wall. St. J. (Dec. 23, 2008, 12:01 AM), http://online.wsj.com/article/SB122998621544328009.html [https://perma.cc/LDT6-X7P9]; *Report to Congress on the Root Causes of the Foreclosure Crisis*, U.S. Dep't of Housing & Urban Dev., Office of Pol'y Dev. & Rsch. (Jan. 28, 2010), http://www.huduser.org/Publications/PDF/Foreclo sure_09.pdf [https://perma.cc/Q3Q8-CQYL] [hereinafter *Root Causes of the Foreclosure Crisis*].

14. Jerry Ascierto, *MBA Reports Dismal 4Q for Multifamily Originations*, Affordable Housing Finance (Jan. 1, 2009), housingfinance.com/news/mba-reports-dismal-4q-for-multifamily -originations_o [https://perma.cc/48R5-B3H2].

15. Claire Kramer Mills, Ph.D. & Jessica Battisto, Double Jeopardy: Covid-19's Concentrated Health and Wealth Effects In Black Communities, (Federal Reserve Bank of New York, Aug. 2020), https://www.newyorkfed.org/medialibrary/media/smallbusiness/Doubl eJeopardy_COVID19andBlackOwnedBusinesses [https://perma.cc/M8UL-AWGR].

16. *See COVID-19 Hospitalization and Death by Age*, Center for Disease Control, https:// www.cdc.gov/coronavirus/2019-ncov/covid-data/investigations-discovery/hospitalization-death-by -age.html [https://perma.cc/TGW9-RDLU] (last updated Feb. 18, 2021).

17. Jack Kelly, *1.2 Million Americans File For Unemployment—Roughly 55 Million Filed since March*, Forbes (Aug. 6, 2020, 12:43 PM), https://www.forbes.com/sites/jackkelly/2020/08/06/12 -million-americans-file-for-unemployment-roughly-55-million-filed-since-march/#208db3374531 [https://perma.cc/GXF9-2HLN].

18. Richard Fry, Jeffrey S. Passel, & D'Vera Cohn, *A Majority of Young Adults in the U.S. Live with Their Parents for the First Time since the Great Depression*, Pew Research Center (Sept. 4, 2020), https://www.pewresearch.org/fact-tank/2020/09/04/a-majority-of-young-adults -in-the-u-s-live-with-their-parents-for-the-first-time-since-the-great-depression/ [https://perma.cc /BZ82-MB2A].

19. Allison Chinchar & Brandom Miller, *Climate Change Didn't Cause Hurricane Laura but It Did Make the Storm Worse*, CNN (Aug. 30, 2020, 4:00 AM), https://www.cnn.com/2020/08/30/weather /weather-hurricane-laura-climate-impacts-scope/index.html [https://perma.cc/X4YK-8SUR].

III. LAWS THAT PROMOTE COMMUNITY INVESTMENT IN AFFORDABLE HOUSING

A. The Community Reinvestment Act

1. Overview

This section will first explain the Community Reinvestment Act (CRA) generally and then focus on how it affects finance for affordable housing development.

The CRA grew out of widespread, hard-fought community organizing and advocacy in response to disinvestment by financial institutions in low-income communities and communities of color.[20] For the past 34 years, the CRA has been the only federal law that affirmatively requires private financial institutions to serve the credit and deposit needs of the local communities in which they are chartered to do business.[21] The CRA applies to any "regulated financial institution," which is defined as a depository institution covered by the Federal Deposit Insurance Corporation (FDIC).[22] Almost all U.S. banks and savings associations are FDIC members.[23] Credit unions and mortgage companies are not subject to the CRA.[24]

Since the act's passage in 1977, several amendments to the statute and changes to the implementing regulations significantly changed the nature of CRA enforcement and have increased public participation in the process. In 1989, the CRA was amended to allow public access to bank ratings and accompanying written evaluations.[25] Such access changed the nature of consumer advocacy by opening a window to the regulatory process. In 1989, regulators denied a merger application,[26] engendering a new sense of seriousness in the industry about CRA obligations.[27] In 1995, regulators improved enforcement by changing the way in which they evaluate the banking industry's compliance with CRA obligations. Institutions' performance, rather than just effort, became the focus, and a series of general tests were introduced to guide the examination process.[28] Notably, from 1993 to

---

20. For a fuller discussion of the historical context out of which the CRA grew, see GREGORY D. SQUIRES ED., ORGANIZING ACCESS TO CAPITAL: ADVOCACY AND THE DEMOCRATIZATION OF FINANCIAL INSTITUTIONS (2003).

21. 12 U.S.C. §§ 2901, *et seq.*

22. *Id.* § 2902.

23. Since the year 2000, as mortgage companies' share of home mortgage lending increased, consumer groups advocated increasingly for them to be covered by the CRA.

24. Banks and savings associations have been advocating vigorously for credit unions that do not have a low-income community charter to be governed by the CRA.

25. 12 U.S.C. § 2906 (2001).

26. *See* Continental Ill. Bancorp, Inc., 75 Fed. Res. Bull. 304 (1989). *See also* 1989 Fed. Res. Interp. Ltr. LEXIS 69, a subsequent opinion letter.

27. See William C. Apgar & Mark Duda, *The Twenty-Fifth Anniversary of the Community Reinvestment Act: Past Accomplishments and Future Regulatory Challenges*, 9 FRBNY ECON. POL'Y REV. 169 (2003), http://www.ny.frb.org/research/epr/03v09n2/0306apga.pdf [https://perma.cc/3F7Y-4R9P] [HEREINAFTER *Twenty-Fifth Anniversary Study*].

28. 60 Fed. Reg. 22,192 (May 4, 1995) (codified at 12 C.F.R. § 228.22 (2010); and, the regulators gave institutions permission to include CRA activity of affiliates and subsidiaries in the primary institutions' exam process. *See also* Joint Center for Housing Studies, Harvard Univ., *The 25th Anniversary of the Community Reinvestment Act: Access to Capital in An Evolving Financial*

1998, single-family mortgage lending to low- and moderate-income families increased by 80 percent.[29]

In 1999, an amendment to the CRA loosened oversight of financial institutions with aggregate assets of $250 million or less ("small institutions") by reducing the frequency of CRA examinations based on their prior CRA rating.[30] The amendment also expanded the financial activities that depository institutions may undertake while simultaneously requiring that institutions have satisfactory CRA ratings before they, their holding companies, affiliates, or subsidiaries may engage in such broader activities.[31] A 2017 amendment to the CRA conformed the definitions of home mortgage and consumer loan to changes the CFPB made to the Home Mortgage Disclosure Act provisions with no significant impact on affordable housing finance.[32] However, a 2019 amendment changed definitions of the types of activities for which financial institution can get CRA credit.[33] How the impact will play out remains to be seen, but community groups have cautioned that it may incentivize lenders to invest in large-scale infrastructure projects rather than affordable housing development.[34]

One trend to keep an eye on is the rise of increased state-level regulation of financing, including the possible increased regulation of and bolstering of fair housing and financing regulation in the face of federal deregulation and reduced enforcement.[35] For example, in

---

Services System 41–42 (2002), https://www.jchs.harvard.edu/sites/default/files/media/imp/cra02-1.pdf [https://perma.cc/UTL4-VZAM] [hereinafter *The 25th Anniversary of the* CRA].

29. Robert E. Litan, Nicolas P. Retsinas, Eric S. Belsky, & Susan White Haag, *The Community Reinvestment Act after Financial Modernization: A Baseline Report* 15 (U.S. Dep't of Treasury 2000) [hereinafter *After Financial Modernization Study*], https://www.treasury.gov/press-center/press-releases/Pages/report3079.aspx [https://perma.cc/H2R3-R6QK].

30. Gramm-Leach-Bliley Act of 1999, Pub. L. No. 106-102, § 713, 113 Stat. 1338; *see also* 12 U.S.C. § 2908.

31. Pub. L. No. 106-102, *supra* note 30. Thus, starting in 1999, while Congress relaxed oversight of smaller financial institutions, it also introduced a new incentive to meet CRA obligations, coming at a time when the "merger-mania" of depository institutions that had begun in 1990 was still in full swing. *See* Robert Oshinsky, *Merging the BIF and SAIF: Would a Merger Improve the Funds' Viability?* FDIC, Div. of Research & Stats., Working Paper 99-4, 11–15 (1999), https://www.fdic.gov/bank/analytical/working/wp99-04.pdf [https://perma.cc/HNL4-UT9R].

32. *Agencies Amend CRA Regulations to Conform to HMDA Regulation Changes and Remove References to the Neighborhood Stabilization Program*, Office of the Comptroller of the Currency (Nov. 20, 2017), https://www.occ.gov/news-issuances/news-releases/2017/nr-ia-2017-137.html [https://perma.cc/F47L-LB7N].

33. *FDIC and OCC Propose to Modernize Community Reinvestment Act Regulations*, Office of the Comptroller of the Currency (Dec. 12, 2019), https://www.occ.gov/news-issuances/news-releases/2019/nr-ia-2019-147.html [https://perma.cc/ESU7-5ZLL]. *See also OCC Finalizes Rule to Strengthen and Modernize Community Reinvestment Act Regulations*, Office of the Comptroller of the Currency (May 20, 2020), https://occ.treas.gov/news-issuances/news-releases/2020/nr-occ-2020-63.html [https://perma.cc/GP4J-K6YX].

34. Nancy Marshall-Genzer, *An Updated Community Reinvestment Act Faces Criticism*, Marketplace (June 18, 2020), https://www.marketplace.org/2020/06/18/an-updated-community-reinvestment-act-faces-criticism/ [https://perma.cc/2DF4-KELM].

35. Christopher L. Peterson, *Dormant: The Consumer Financial Protection Bureau's Law Enforcement Program in Decline*, Consumer Federation of America (Mar. 12, 2019), https://consumerfed.org/wp-content/uploads/2019/03/CFPB-Enforcement-in-Decline.pdf [https://perma.cc/HBL7-S6M9].

California, the largest housing market in the United States, a so-called state level CFPB has been developed— the Department of Financial Protection and Innovation.[36] If other similar entities are created in various states, affordable housing developers may have an additional layer of regulation to comply with and may be operating in an environment of uncertainty as litigation regarding federal preemption of state regulation is likely. On the other hand, it may result in greater state-level support for creation of affordable housing developments. In another example, New York has its own New York Community Reinvestment Act, Section 28-b of the New York Banking Law (NYBL), which was recently strengthened.[37]

2. CRA Enforcement

The CRA requires "each appropriate Federal financial supervisory agency to use its authority when examining financial institutions, to encourage such institutions to help meet the credit needs of the local communities in which they are chartered consistent with the safe and sound operation of such institutions."[38] The CRA's statutory provisions are broadly worded and do not provide specific guidance about the examination process. The regulations drafted by the agencies entrusted with enforcement provide greater substance; the heart of CRA enforcement lies in the federal regulations.[39] Pursuant to these regulations, federal financial supervisory agencies review institutions' record of meeting the credit and deposit needs of low and moderate-income communities.[40] Regulators have defined examination protocols, creating written uniformity via regulations that implement their shared statutory obligations under the act.

---

36. *See* S.B. 819, 2019-20 Leg., Reg. Sess. (Cal. 2020), https://leginfo.legislature.ca.gov/faces /billStatusClient.xhtml?bill_id=201920200SB819 [https://perma.cc/3RAY-YRAY].

37. Letter from Brian H. Montgomery, Deputy Superintendent of N.Y. State Dep't of Financial Services to All Banking Institutions Subject to the N.Y. State Community Reinvestment Act, *Industry Letter: Alert Regarding Amendments to the New York Community Reinvestment Act* (June 30, 2020), https://www.dfs.ny.gov/industry_guidance/industry_letters/il20200630_alert_amends_nycra [https://perma.cc/CW9M-9R4N].

38. 12 U.S.C. § 2901 (2020). The "appropriate Federal financial supervisory agenc[ies]" are the Office of the Comptroller of the Currency (OCC) (with respect to national banks), the Federal Reserve Board (FRB) (with respect to state-chartered banks that are members of the Federal Reserve System and bank holding companies), the Federal Deposit Insurance Corporation (FDIC) (with respect to state-chartered banks and savings banks that are not members of the Federal Reserve System and the deposits of which are FDIC-insured), and the director of the Office of Thrift Supervision (OTS) (with respect to FDIC-insured savings associations and savings and loan holding companies).

39. 12 C.F.R. §§ 228.11–228.45 (also known as Reg. BB) (FRB regulations), 12 C.F.R. §§ 25.11– 25.45 (OCC regulations), 12 C.F.R. §§ 563e.11–563.45 (OTS regulations), and 12 C.F.R. §§ 345.11– 345.45 (FDIC regulations). CRA regulations of each agency mirror each other in numbering system, location in part 12 of the Code of Federal Regulations, and content. Hereafter in this chapter, all references to CRA regulations will use the FRB's numbering only.

40. 12 U.S.C. § 2903. Examinations are annual for most institutions and up to every five years under some circumstances for small institutions. Regulators may examine more frequently at their discretion. For each institution reviewed, regulators must prepare a written report of their CRA findings, a portion of which is required to be public, and a portion of which is confidential. The public section must disclose the agencies' conclusions for each assessment factor in the enabling regulations, the rating given to the institution, and data supporting the agencies' conclusions. Ratings may be "outstanding," "satisfactory," "needs to improve," or "substantial noncompliance." See 12 U.S.C. § 2906 & 12 C.F.R. § 228.21(c).

3. CRA Compliance

A key regulatory incentive for institutions to comply with the CRA stems from the regulators' power to consider the CRA record of a bank when the bank proposes to conduct particular business transactions, specifically (1) open a new branch; (2) merge with another bank; (3) become a bank holding company or acquire ownership, a controlling share, or most of the assets of a bank; (4) become a subsidiary of a bank holding company; or (5) own, control, or operate a savings association.[41] The regulator must take public comment and may deny or condition approval of any of the foregoing activities based on CRA performance.[42] An additional compliance incentive is that any bank holding company seeking to become a financial holding company may do so only if the Board of Governors of the Federal Reserve System finds that all of the subsidiary insured depository institutions of the bank holding company achieved at least a "satisfactory" rating at their most recent examination.[43]

The accelerated pace of consolidation within the financial services industry helped make these incentives meaningful over the years.[44] Most contested mergers ended in a settlement between the depository institution and community groups, yielding CRA commitments from the institution.[45] The 1989 CRA amendment mandating public access to ratings information and supporting documentation, along with the public comment element of the 1999 amendment, helped promote CRA compliance by subjecting banks to the potentially intense scrutiny of the public and investors.[46]

4. The Impact of CRA on Investment in Affordable Housing

Regulators have focused traditionally on the availability of single-family home mortgages to underserved communities and on low-income consumers' lack of access to retail consumer credit services.[47] That focus left it to advocacy groups and financial institutions themselves to promote affordable housing finance as a valued means for fulfilling CRA obligations.[48]

The effect of the CRA on investment in affordable housing depends on the complex interplay between (1) current CRA regulations and regulators' examination protocols and

---

41. 12 C.F.R. § 228.29.

42. *Id.*

43. 12 U.S.C. § 2903(c). Please note that the statute lists certain exceptions.

44. See FDIC, *A Statistical Profile of the United States Banking Industry, Chart A-2, Statistics on Banking* (2004), showing that the number of main offices of FDIC-insured institutions from 1985 to 1988 decreased from 14,407 to 13,123. Dramatically, from 1988 through December 31, 2003, that number decreased by almost 41 percent, to 7,782.

45. Joseph Moore, *Community Reinvestment Act and Its Impact on Bank Mergers*, 1 N.C. BANKING INST. 412, 427 (1997).

46. Robert B. Avery, Raphael W. Bostic, & Glenn B. Canner, *CRA Special Lending Programs*, 86, FED. RES. BULL. 711, 711–12 (2000).

47. *Twenty-Fifth Anniversary Study, supra* note 27, at 6, 41–42. These problems may be caused by banking policies that make services inaccessible (high minimum balances, stringent credit requirements, high fees) or due to physical withdrawal from low-income communities via branch closures.

48. *After Financial Modernization Study, supra* note 29, at 58. A year 2000 study states that there is anecdotal evidence to suggest that affordable housing activity is increasing but notes that there appear to have been no comprehensive studies to date verifying the true state of such investment and lending.

practices; (2) banks' awareness of and responses to CRA regulations and regulators' examination protocols and practices; (3) the effectiveness of advocacy by the financial industry and community groups to change the regulations and examination practices; and, possibly, (4) the profitability of CRA loans in affordable housing development. Each will be discussed in turn.

The majority of financial institutions subject to the CRA are reviewed under three tests—investment, service, and lending.[49] The first and third tests are the two categories under which institutions may receive credit for affordable housing finance.

The investment test "evaluates a bank's record of helping to meet the credit needs of its assessment area(s) through qualified investments that benefit its assessment area(s) or a broader statewide or regional area that includes the bank's assessment area(s)."[50] The amount, innovativeness, or complexity of the investment and its responsiveness to community need are among the examiners' considerations under this test, in addition to whether the qualified investments are not routinely provided by private investors. Since many affordable housing financing deals are innovative and complex, banks could, in principle, earn CRA credit for lending credit in these transactions.

Under the lending test, "community development" (CD) is defined to include "[a]ffordable housing (including multifamily rental housing) for low- or moderate-income individuals."[51] The CD element of the lending test is more flexible than other sections of the test, allowing financial institutions to get CRA credit for loans originated by a third party, provided (1) the financial institution under CRA examination has invested in the loans in some fashion; (2) the loans meet the definition of CD loans; and (3) they comply with other limited restrictions.[52] The number, amount, and complexity of CD loans are also evaluated.[53] In 2005, the CRA was somewhat weakened by the adoption of a rule that exempted so-called small banks from certain aspects of CRA reporting and oversight.[54] One study found that the quality of investments—the innovation and complexity—had a

---

49. 12 C.F.R. §§ 228.22–228.24. Wholesale and limited-purpose banks are subject to the community development (CD) portion of the lending test and strategic plan review only. *See* 12 C.F.R. § 228.21(a)(2), § 228.21(a)(4), and § 228.25.

50. *Id.* § 228.23.

51. *Id.* § 228.22 (The term "low-income" is defined as individual or family income at or below 50 percent of area median income (AMI). "Moderate-income" refers to individuals or families whose income is between 50 and 80 percent of AMI); *see id.* §§ 228.12(m)(1) and (2)(2020); *Twenty-Fifth Anniversary Study, supra* note 27, at 170. Those accustomed to working on federally subsidized housing should not confuse this definition with the 80 percent of AMI-or-below definition of low income typically utilized in such programs. The 1995 CRA amendment increased emphasis on affordable housing finance by its clear inclusion of that activity in its definition.

52. 12 C.F.R. § 228.22(a)(4).

53. For both the lending and investment tests, the bank's assessment area circumscribes the geographic scope of the examination. *See* 12 C.F.R. § 228.22(b) and § 228.41. The assessment area encompasses the region or neighborhoods where the institution's main office, branches, and deposit-taking ATMs are located, as well as neighboring areas in which the institution originates or purchases substantial portions of its loans.

54. *See Inactive Financial Institutions Letters, Community Reinvestment Act, Joint Final Rules*, FDIC (Aug. 9, 2005), http://www.fdic.gov/news/news/financial/2005/fil7905.html [https://perma .cc/WRB8-CFS9] (Small bank is defined to mean a bank with assets between $250 million and $1 billion, in 2005, and as adjusted upward annually thereafter.).

greater positive impact on CRA ratings than the number or volume of investments.[55] Such evaluation favors affordable housing development. However, there have also been charges of inconsistency in evaluations or arbitrariness in the examination process.[56] Affordable housing development may suffer more than other qualifying CRA activities from erratic evaluations due to the complexity of the activity.[57] If institutions are not confident that their innovativeness will be rewarded by regulators, then they may not pursue investment in affordable housing. Regulators' focus on mortgage lending as the primary way to meet CRA goals may result in less investment in affordable housing in the long run because banks and savings institutions may turn away from affordable housing lending in frustration over not receiving proper CRA credit for this complex work.[58] Some additional guidance about whether an activity might be considered CRA-eligible can be found in an interagency publication.[59]

Throughout CRA's history, community groups have been essential to its enforcement.[60] Their primary enforcement strategies include challenging mergers and conducting public education campaigns. In the past 15 years, national, statewide, and local advocacy groups[61] have increased their participation in the merger review process.[62] Groups are also manifest-

55. Ryan Trammell, *Understanding the Relationship between Investment Test Examination Criteria and Investment Test Ratings*, Federal Reserve Bank of San Francisco, Center for Community Development Investments (2004) (many of the investments analyzed in this study were in affordable housing development).

56. A lack of understanding by regulators of complex investments or lending is a reason for inconsistent CRA ratings, adding another disincentive for financial institutions that may otherwise seek to participate in complex, affordable housing investments or lending. Conversely, lenders have "also noted that regulators continually raise the bar for what constitutes acceptable lending levels and 'innovativeness' in investment, service, and community development lending activities." *Twenty-Fifth Anniversary Study, supra* note 27, at 107–08 (also finding that some lenders do not attempt to deliver the best possible CRA performance because of that perception).

57. For more information on variations in scoring and weighting of examination categories across supervisory agencies, see Michael Stegman, Kelly Cochran, & Robert Faris, *Policy Brief 96: Creating a Scorecard for the CRA Service Test*, THE BROOKINGS INSTITUTION (Mar. 2003), https://communitycapital.unc.edu/wp-content/uploads/sites/340/2002/03/CRAScorecard.pdf [https://perma.cc/7Z8P-5Z22].

58. *Id.*

59. See Community Reinvestment Act; Interagency Questions and Answers Regarding Community Reinvestment; Notice, 75 Fed. Reg. 11,641 (Mar. 11, 2010).

60. Judicial enforcement of the CRA has proven to be difficult. Unlike antidiscrimination statutes (see Section III, *infra*, regarding antidiscrimination laws affecting finance), the CRA does not create civil or criminal sanctions for violations. And there is no private right of enforcement. Lee v. Bd. of Governors. of the Fed. Res. Sys., 118 F.3d 905, 912–13 (2d Cir. 1997).

61. *See* California Reinvestment Coalition, http://calreinvest.org/ [https://perma.cc/RA94-33VF] (last visited June 6, 2021); National Community Reinvestment Coalition (NCRC), http://www.ncrc.org [https://perma.cc/J5MX-55YV] (last visited June 6, 2021); the National Congress for Community Economic Development, https://www.nacced.org/ [https://perma.cc/VZ4Y-RBQB] (last visited June 6, 2021).

62. The number of consumer challenges to merger applications at the FRB rose from an estimated 1–2 percent of merger applications from 1988 to the early 1990s, to approximately half of approved merger applications in 1996. *See* Moore, supra note 45, at 412, citing to John R. Wilke, *Home Loans to Blacks, Hispanics, Soared in '94*, WALL ST. J., July 19, 1995, at A1, and Laura T. Beyer, Comment, *The Community Reinvestment Act: Boost to Low- and Moderate-Income Communities; Setback for Minority-Owned Banks*, 1 N.C. BANKING INST. 387, 394–95 (1997).

ing their presence through negotiating CRA commitment agreements. Regulatory changes increasing the leverage of the public during proposed mergers and regulators' reluctance to deny proposed mergers on the basis of CRA performance have been factors contributing to the increase in deal-making.[63] Community group advocacy has had a significant effect on investment in affordable housing, albeit with inconsistent objectives and outcomes.[64] For example, community groups' focus on single-family mortgage loans and individual access to branch services rather than directly on affordable housing finance may reinforce regulators' similar focus. By the same token, abundant evidence of discrimination in single-family mortgage lending indicates that there is a tremendous and continuing need for advocacy regarding fair access.[65]

As financial institutions have developed experience and partnerships, profitability of investments and lending has become a significant motivator for CRA lending.[66] In 1999, the Federal Reserve Board of Governors conducted a survey of the 500 largest retail banking institutions in the country to evaluate profitability and performance of lending related to the CRA.[67] While not focused on affordable housing lending, the survey results in the "community development" lending category (which would include affordable housing lending) strongly support CRA's profitability.[68] An Office of the Comptroller of the Currency (OCC) report states that national banks made $600 million in LIHTC investment in

---

63. Alex Schwartz, *From Confrontation to Collaboration? Banks, Community Groups, and the Implementation of Community Reinvestment Agreements*, 9 Hous. Pol'y Debate 631, 633 (1998).

64. *Twenty-Fifth Anniversary Report*, *supra* note 27, at 99. See Schwartz, *supra* note 63, at 633, 638–39.

65. *See* Policy Development and Research, Housing and Urban Development Discrimination in Metropolitan Housing Markets: National Results from Phase 1, Phase 2, and Phase 3 of the Housing Discrimination Study (HDS), HudUser (Mar. 31, 2005), https://www.huduser.gov/portal/publica tions/hsgfin/hds.html [https://perma.cc/64UR-EAFZ]. Though the CRA does not prohibit discrimination in lending, its affirmative investment and lending requirements are an effective vehicle for addressing the problem.

66. Achieving a high CRA rating, improving service to the local community and their public image are all motivators for financial institutions to engage in CRA activity. National institutions have taken to declaring and publicizing their community investment goals. Schwartz, *supra* note 63, at 632.

67. Board of Governors of the Federal Reserve System, *The Performance and Profitability of CRA-Related Lending*, Federal Reserve (July 17, 2000), https://www.federalreserve.gov/BoardDocs /Surveys/CRAloansurvey/cratext.pdf [https://perma.cc/W3WU-3BPH]. The survey was mandated by Congress, Gramm-Leach-Bliley Act. Results were reported to the Senate and House Banking Committees and general results were released to the public.

68. The Federal Reserve Board survey found that 54 percent of banks found their CRA loans to be profitable; 39 percent found those loans to be marginally profitable; and 4 percent reported breaking even on such loans. Only 2 percent found the loans to be marginally unprofitable, and only 1 percent found them to be unprofitable. *Id.* at xxiii. In addition, "[m]ore than two-thirds of the respondents report[ed] that their CRA-related lending has led to new, profitable opportunities . . . [and/or resulted in] some other benefit not related to loan profitability from CRA-related lending, such as promoting a good image in the community." *Id.* at 64.

2002.[69] A 2020 break down by state shows over $600 million in LIHTC allocations.[70] A more recent study provides updated information on multifamily loan volume.[71]

Some opponents of the CRA have claimed in recent years that the CRA helped create the foreclosure crisis and ensuing financial meltdown nationally by encouraging lending to underserved consumers.[72] Such claims have, however, been discredited. In fact, studies done by the Federal Reserve Board have found that "lending to lower-income individuals and communities has been nearly as profitable and performed similarly to other types of lending done by CRA-covered institutions."[73]

While the CRA has been in place for over 34 years, the foreclosure crisis arose rapidly over a five-year time period, driven largely by high-priced, high-risk loans and ancillary investments in those loans by Wall Street, issued by private mortgage companies that are not even regulated by the CRA.[74] If anything, the strong performance of CRA-regulated loans compared to the foreclosure rate on loans issued by unregulated entities has been pointed to as potentially indicative of a need to extend coverage of the CRA, with all of its oversight requirements, to all entities that issue mortgages as a part of the CRA updating.[75]

5. The Future of the CRA

The future of the CRA will largely continue to depend on the interplay of the four factors just discussed. In particular, industry and consumer advocacy has led to statutory revision and changes in enforcement of the CRA over the years. Financial institutions argue that the CRA (and other consumer and fair housing–type laws) impose overly burdensome reporting obligations that have increased their costs of providing services, to the detriment of the public. The result of the 1999 amendments supported by the industry is that smaller institutions are subject to less monitoring.[76] Though the change drastically reduced the number

---

69. Comptroller of the Currency, Administrator of National Banks, *2002 Directory of National Bank Community Development Investments* 3 (2002), http://www.occ.treas.gov/topics/consumers-and -communities/community-affairs/resource-directories/public-welfare-investments/2002directory -part24.pdf [https://perma.cc/8V4X-VPW3].

70. *2020 Federal LIHTC Information by State*, Novogradac, https://www.novoco.com/resource -centers/affordable-housing-tax-credits/application-allocation/state-lihtc-allocating-agencies/2020 -federal-lihtc-information-state [https://perma.cc/ZK32-XJ6E] (last visited June 7, 2021).

71. Laurie Goodman, Jun Zhu, & John Walsh, *The Community Reinvestment Act Lending Data Highlights*, Urban Inst. (Nov. 2018), https://www.urban.org/sites/default/files/publication/99427 /community_reinvestment_act_lending_data_highlights_update.pdf [https://perma.cc/Z6EN-6ZWD].

72. Stan Liebowitz, *The Real Scandal-How Feds Invited the Mortgage Mess*, N.Y. Post, excerpt published by Free Republic (Feb. 5, 2008), http://www.freerepublic.com/focus/f-news/196523 9/posts [https://perma.cc/5AZ9-CTDD].

73. Randall Kroszner, Booth School of Business, Univ. of Chicago, *The Community Reinvestment Act and the Recent Mortgage Crisis* (Dec. 3, 2008), http://www.frbsf.org/publications/com munity/cra/cra_recent_mortgage_crisis.pdf [https://perma.cc/8YJL-RATM] (This article is an excerpt from a speech given by Federal Reserve Governor Randall Kroszner titled "The Community Reinvestment Act and the Recent Mortgage Crisis." The speech was delivered at the Confronting Concentrated Poverty Policy Forum at the Board of Governors of the Federal Reserve System in Washington, D.C. on December 3, 2008.).

74. *Root Causes of the Foreclosure Crisis*, *supra* note 13, at x, 41–42.

75. *Id.* at xiv.

76. Under OTS's regulation, institutions with assets of up to $1 billion (instead of the previous $250 million) will now qualify for "streamlined review" as "smaller institutions." The final

of institutions subject to annual CRA examination, it is difficult to determine its impact on CRA investments. The 2020 changes to the CRA are too recent for their impact to be clear. At least one national organization, however, believes that it is likely to result in substantial damage to the CRA's impact by virtue of expanding eligible activities to include middle-income and larger developments with no apparent connection to housing, by measuring amounts invested rather than impact, and removing the brick and mortar location of the bank from consideration of its provision of access to credit.[77]

Consumer groups have been waging their own campaigns to revise CRA regulations to increase its reach and enforcement mechanisms. Advocates argue that the CRA does not go far enough in effectuating its original intent because its most effective protections are triggered only by mergers of financial institutions. They have been working to expand the CRA's reach to other financial institutions not currently covered, such as mortgage companies, credit unions, and other new participants that provide financial services in an increasingly deregulated market, and to increase the number and types of CRA compliance incentives beyond the merger trigger.[78] In their view, if the CRA is not modified to match the changing face of financial services in the United States, it will lose its effectiveness, which may decrease affordable housing investment. Issues flagged by federal regulators that will probably continue to be in play even after the most recent rule changes include (1) whether the CRA's strictures should differ depending on the geographic location and coverage of the financial institution in question; (2) whether performance criteria should be revised; (3) whether activities by affiliates of institutions should be considered: (4) how small business and consumer lending data should be evaluated; (5) how access to services for the unbanked should be considered; (6) how to encourage community development investments; (7) whether and how to improve the ratings themselves to recognize good performance and better define substandard performance; and (8) how unsafe, unsound, and unfair lending practices should be factored into the ratings process.[79]

B. Other Federal Programs Promoting Investment in Affordable Housing

Each agency that has oversight of the banking industry has developed regulations pertaining to affordable housing investment. In addition, as a result of climate change and increased concerns over the location and physical structure (construction techniques, materials, design features) of multifamily buildings, the Environmental Protection Agency

---

rule, 69 Fed. Reg. 51,155 (Aug. 18, 2004), became effective on Oct. 1, 2004. The higher threshold stemmed from financial services industry complaints that the cost of regulatory compliance was forcing smaller institutions to merge. Complaints were directed toward regulatory compliance generally, but it was the fair housing portion of compliance and other consumer-friendly regulations that the industry particularly targeted for removal or loosening.

77. FAIR HOUSING IN JEOPARDY: TRUMP ADMINISTRATION UNDERMINES CRITICAL TOOLS FOR ACHIEVING RACIAL EQUITY, NATIONAL FAIR HOUSING ALLIANCE (2020), https://nationalfairhousing.org/wp-content/uploads/2020/09/NFHA-2020-Fair-Housing-Trends-Report.pdf.

78. *See Twenty-Fifth Anniversary Study*, supra note 27.

79. *See* Agencies Announce Public Hearings on Community Reinvestment Act Regulations, FEDERAL RESERVE SYSTEM (June 17, 2010), http://www.federalreserve.gov/newsevents/press/bcreg/20100617b.htm [https://perma.cc/K342-P7A7] (follow "Topics and questions excerpt from hearings notice" hyperlink to see examples of questions remaining).

(EPA) and the Federal Emergency Management Agency (FEMA) may play a role. HUD has itself undertaken an examination of environmental considerations affecting housing development.[80]

1. Office of the Comptroller of the Currency, Public Welfare Investment Regulation

While the CRA and its implementing regulations are reasonably general in their definition of acceptable community investment activity, the Office of the Comptroller of the Currency's (OCC) "public welfare investments" definition is even broader.[81]

The OCC's regulations authorize national banks to make public welfare investments.[82] The most essential requirement is that the investments primarily benefit low- and moderate-income people or areas (at or below 80 percent of AMI) or areas targeted for redevelopment, or constitute a "qualified investment" under the CRA.[83] Investment in affordable housing is specifically defined as one of four categories of "qualifying public welfare investment."[84] Affordable housing activities include (but are not limited to):

> (1) Investments in an entity that finances, acquires, develops, rehabilitates, manages, sells, or rents housing primarily for low- and moderate-income individuals; (2) Investments in a project that develops or operates transitional housing for the homeless; (3) Investments in a project that develops or operates special needs housing for disabled or elderly low- and moderate-income individuals; and (4) Investments in a project that qualifies for the Federal low-income housing tax credit.[85]

The regulations state that it is OCC's policy to encourage such investments, but the regulations do not require or set any suggested target levels for such investment. Rather, there is a cap on investments of 5 percent of a bank's capital and surplus, or, under special circumstances and with OCC's written approval, up to 15 percent of its capital and

---

80. *See Climate Change Resilience*, HUD, https://www.hud.gov/program_offices/economic_development/resilience/about [https://perma.cc/S9RM-YF8Y] (last visited June 7, 2021).

81. According to an OCC publication, it has approved over 2,000 investments under the Public Welfare Investments provision "and predecessor provisions" since 1965. *See* OCC, 2002 Directory of National Banks Community Development Investments 114 (2002). *See* 12 C.F.R. § 228.21–228.24 for pertinent CRA regulations. *See also* National Bank Community Development Investments Third Quarter 2018 (July 1, 2018–Sept. 30, 2018) At-a-Glance Chart, OCC (2018), https://www.occ.treas.gov/topics/consumers-and-communities/community-affairs/resource-directories/public-welfare-investments/public-welfare-investments-at-a-glance-2018-3q.pdf [https://perma.cc/9FVY-3JJ4], showing over 3.7 billion in this category of investment in the third quarter of 2018 alone [hereinafter *National Bank Community Development Investments*].

82. 12 C.F.R. § 24.3. Low income is defined as less than 50 percent of AMI, while moderate income is defined as between 50 and 80 percent of AMI, per 12 C.F.R. § 25.12.

83. *Id.* § 24.3.

84. *Id.* § 24.6.

85. *Id.*

surplus.[86] Public welfare investments are another way in which banks regulated by the OCC can obtain CRA credit.[87]

2. Federal Reserve Board, Regulation

The Federal Reserve Board (FRB) also permits a similarly limited amount of public welfare investments, but does not include language in its regulations encouraging such investments.[88] The FRB's definition of investments not requiring prior FRB approval encompasses the OCC's public welfare investment definition, as well as a broad range of affordable housing activities.[89] The FRB provides that bank holding companies may invest in "corporations or projects designed primarily to promote community welfare, such as the economic rehabilitation and development of low-income areas."[90] Affordable housing activities are highlighted in the regulations as permissible.[91]

3. The FDIC's Affordable Housing Program

The Federal Deposit Insurance Corporation (FDIC) has a property disposition program that it refers to as its "affordable housing program." In disposition of multi- and single-family properties, the FDIC gives preference "among substantially similar offers to the offer that would reserve the highest percentage of dwelling units for occupancy or purchase by very low-income and low-income families and would retain such affordability for the longest term." The program is intended to serve very low-income, low-income, and moderate-income families.[92] The FDIC may provide financing and may sell a multifamily property below market value to enable a public agency or nonprofit to achieve the FDIC's low-income occupancy requirements for such a property.[93] There is an annual dollar limit to losses resulting from the sale of properties under this provision up to annual appropriation levels or a maximum of $30 million. However, there is no minimum investment level or goal for the program's production of affordable housing units.[94] And, there are no additional fair housing requirements regarding the composition of occupying families or the location of the housing.

---

86. *Id.* § 24.4.

87. See OCC, *2002 Directory of National Banks Community Development Investments* 3 (2002). The public welfare category permits national banks to engage in a range of community development investments that would not otherwise be permitted under the National Bank Act. *See also National Bank Community Development Investments, supra* note 81.

88. 12 C.F.R. § 225.127.

89. *See id.* § 208.22; *see* 12 U.S.C. § 338a.

90. 12 C.F.R. § 225.127.

91. The regulations permit "investments in projects to construct or rehabilitate multifamily low- or moderate-income housing with respect to which the mortgage is insured under . . . the National Housing Act . . . ," as well as other affordable housing projects. *Id.* § 225.127.

92. *Id.* § 1831q.

93. *Id.* § 1831q(g).

94. *Id.*

4. The American Jobs Proposal

The new federal administration is proposing significant investment in affordable housing via a comprehensive infrastructure and jobs proposal.[95] Though not reduced as yet to implementing legislation approved by Congress, the Biden administration plan speaks to the need for more affordable housing, as well as the need to rehab and maintain existing affordable housing stock. The proposal also notes energy efficiency as an important element of housing, which could have implications as to funding that could become available and support if not a federal mandate to take into consideration climate change in affordable housing development. The plan proposes an investment of $213 billion in preservation, retrofitting, and production of two million affordable units through tax credits, formula funding, grants, and rental assistance. In addition to calling out the need for affordable housing for middle income as well as low income residents, the plan also calls out the need to eliminate exclusionary zoning and land-use policies. How and whether these proposals get moved forward, and the important details regarding implementation remain to be seen. However, the federal administration has requested a significant increase in funding for existing affordable housing programs nationally.[96]

IV. LAWS THAT PROHIBIT UNFAIR TREATMENT

A. Federal Fair Housing Act

1. Overview

In 1968, the Fair Housing Act was passed, outlawing private discrimination, with a particular focus on racial discrimination in housing.[97] The law resulted from community organizing and outrage over widespread, rampant discrimination in the sales and rental of housing in the United States. Building on the framework of the Fair Housing Act of 1968, the Fair Housing Amendments Act (FHAA) of 1988 was also landmark legislation in its own right.[98] The FHAA expanded the protections of the original act[99] and strengthened the ability of the public to enforce its terms.[100] The FHAA also ushered in expanded coverage of housing finance transactions by including the secondary market within its ambit.[101] Over the next ten years, claims and complaints concerning fair lending rose but remained at less than 10 percent of all fair housing complaints filed with either the U.S. Department of

---

95. *See FACT SHEET: The American Jobs Plan,* WH.GOV (Mar. 31, 2021), https://www.whitehouse.gov/briefing-room/statements-releases/2021/03/31/fact-sheet-the-american-jobs-plan/ [https://perma.cc/W7US-6LTZ].

96. *See* Letter from the Executive Office of the President, Office of Management and Budget, to the Committee on Appropriations regarding the President's request for fiscal year (FY) 2022 discretionary funding, (Apr. 9, 2021), https://www.whitehouse.gov/wp-content/uploads/2021/04/FY2022-Discretionary-Request.pdf [https://perma.cc/A3DP-L8NA].

97. Civil Rights Act of 1968, *supra* note 4; see SCHWEMM, *supra* note 4 (Chapter 3 includes a discussion of the federal Fair Housing Act's application to zoning.).

98. Pub. L. No. 100-430, 102 Stat. 1619 (1988).

99. 42 U.S.C. §§ 3604–3603.

100. *Id.* § 3613(a)(1)(A).

101. 42 U.S.C. § 3605(b)(1) (2010).

Housing and Urban Development (HUD) or its equivalent, fair housing assistance program (FHAP) agencies.[102]

2. Application to Affordable Housing Finance

Only one provision of the FHAA, Section 3605 (Discrimination in Residential Real Estate–Related Transactions) specifically governs finance and housing:

> It shall be unlawful for any person or other entity whose business includes engaging in residential real estate–related transactions to discriminate against any person in making available such a transaction, or in the terms or conditions of such a transaction, because of race, color, religion, sex, handicap, familial status, or national origin.[103]

"Residential real estate-related transaction" is defined to include, in relevant part:

> (1) The making or purchasing of loans or providing other financial assistance—
> (A) for purchasing, constructing, improving, repairing, or maintaining a dwelling; or
> (B) secured by residential real estate.[104]

The term "dwelling" is defined under the act to include all buildings designed, intended for, or occupied as a residence, "and any vacant land which is offered for sale or lease for the construction or location thereon of any such building, structure, or portion thereof."[105] Thus, affordable housing development (both new construction and rehabilitation) is covered under this definition.[106]

The scope of Section 3605 appears to be reasonably broad and still evolving.[107] The FHAA also effectively extended the reach of Section 3605 to the secondary lending market by including entities that purchase loans or provide other types of financial assistance.[108] The only flexibility allowed to mortgage purchasers in the interpretation of this clause is the ability to take factors affecting "business necessity" into account.[109]

3. Enforcement of Section 3605

Complaints under the FHAA may be pursued via three avenues: a complaint to HUD (Section 3610), a direct lawsuit (Section 3613), or suit by the U.S. attorney general (Section 3614).[110] A complaint may be brought under Sections 3610 or 3613 by any "aggrieved

---

102. Michael H. Schill & Samantha Friedman, *The Fair Housing Amendments Act of 1988: The First Decade*, 4 CITYSCAPE: A JOURNAL OF POL'Y DEV. & RSCH. 57, 63–64 (1999), http://www.huduser.org/periodicals/cityscpe/vol4num3/schill.pdf [https://perma.cc/9FSV-LLVS].
103. 42 U.S.C. § 3605.
104. *Id.*
105. *Id.* § 3602(b).
106. In contrast to other sections of the act, there are no exemptions to the coverage of Section 3605 (other than an exemption for appraisers, not relevant to this chapter's discussion).
107. *See* United States v. Mass. Indus. Fin. Agency, 910 F. Supp. 21 (D. Mass. 1996).
108. *See* Section IV *infra* for a discussion of regulation of the secondary lending market.
109. *See* SCHWEMM, *supra* note 4, at Section 18.
110. *See* 42 U.S.C. §§ 3610, 3613, & 3614.

person,"[111] defined as any person who "claims to have been injured by a discriminatory housing practice, or believes that such person will be injured by a discriminatory housing practice that is about to occur."[112] Statutory standing requirements are broad: An aggrieved "person" may include not only individuals but "corporations, partnerships, associations, labor organizations, legal representatives, mutual companies, joint-stock companies, trusts, unincorporated organizations, trustees, trustees in cases under title 11, receivers, and fiduciaries."[113] Article III of the U.S. Constitution's "injury in fact" minimum standard applies to FHAA claims under these sections. Under the Article III standard, the claimant must show actual or threatened injury, proximately caused by the defendant, along with a good probability of redress by the court.[114]

A "discriminatory housing practice" means any act that is unlawful pursuant to Sections 3604, 3605, 3606, or 3617.[115] HUD's regulations had not previously indicated clearly whether discriminatory intent is required for a violation.[116] Instead, the regulations set forth three examples of activities it would deem to be a violation of Section 3605:

> (1) Purchasing loans or other debts or securities which relate to, or which are secured by dwellings in certain communities or neighborhoods but not in others because of the race, color, religion, sex, handicap, familial status, or national origin of persons in such neighborhoods or communities.

> (2) Pooling or packaging loans or other debts or securities which relate to, or which are secured by, dwellings differently because of race, color, religion, sex, handicap, familial status, or national origin.

> (3) Imposing or using different terms or conditions on the marketing or sale of securities issued on the basis of loans or other debts or securities which relate to, or which are secured by, dwellings because of race, color, religion, sex, handicap, familial status, or national origin.[117]

A HUD regulation advises that lenders may offer a legitimate business reason for their actions as a defense.[118]

---

111. *See id.* § 3610(a)(1)(A)(i) and § 3613(a)(1)(A).

112. 42 U.S.C. § 3602(i)(1).

113. *Id.* § 3602(d). For a discussion of fair housing organizations' standing to sue in their own right under the Fair Housing Act, see Arkansas ACORN Fair Housing Inc. v. Greystone Dev. Co., 160 F.3d 433, 434 (8th Cir. 1998), citing Havens Realty Corp v. Coleman, 455 U.S. 363 (1998).

114. See Havens Realty Corp. v. Coleman, 455 U.S. 363, 372–73 (1998).

115. 42 U.S.C. § 3602(f).

116. Some courts have found that discriminatory effect is sufficient in redlining cases. A claimant in such a case would probably have to produce a significant amount of statistical evidence to support its claim of disparate treatment. *See* Margery Austin Turner & Felicity Skidmore, *Mortgage Lending Discrimination, A Review of Existing* Evidence, Urban Inst. (June 1, 1999), http://webarchive.urban.org/publications/309090.html [https://perma.cc/MEB9-VS3Y] (follow "Read Complete Document" hyperlink for a PDF of the publication).

117. 24 C.F.R. § 100.125(b)(1)–(3). The list is not intended to be exhaustive but to illustrate how HUD interprets the application of the statute.

118. The regulation states that in evaluating a claim of discrimination in loan purchases, business necessity could be considered: "[...] including requirements of Federal law, relating to a transaction's financial security or to protection against default or reduction of the value of the security. Thus, this provision would not preclude considerations employed in normal and prudent transactions,

The liability implications of Section 3605 in the context of affordable housing finance are significant for affordable housing investors, for financial institutions, and for the secondary lending market. First, the owner of a LIHTC development risks loss of its tax credits if it violates the FHAA.[119] Second, an affordable housing developer, a fair housing agency, a community-based organization, or individual residents could file an FHAA claim under Section 3605 against a lender for discriminating in the terms or conditions of an investment in an affordable housing development "because of race, color, religion, sex, handicap, familial status, or national origin."[120] For example, assume that the lender's investment in the development was at a higher rate of interest or with less favorable terms than those the lender provided to another developer. If the aggrieved party could prove that the difference in terms resulted from the development's intended use as housing for people of color or those with disabilities, the aggrieved party could have a colorable FHAA claim against the lender. A servicer of such loans could also conceivably be liable under this section.[121] Inaction by a lender or delayed action on a loan application for an affordable housing development may be grounds for a claim under the FHAA because financing for affordable housing developments can be complex, with little allowance for significant cost overruns. Even potential violations of the FHAA's finance protections in Section 3605 may be actionable if brought by someone who anticipates being harmed, provided he or she meets the constitutional and statutory requirements for standing.

Finally, for the secondary market, other interesting scenarios are possible. Assume that an actor in the secondary market has a practice of offering less favorable terms for (or not purchasing) loans financing affordable housing developments in certain neighborhoods. If those neighborhoods consist predominantly of people of color, this could be viewed as "redlining,"[122] simply transferred to an affordable housing mortgage purchase context. The FHAA would give aggrieved parties the opportunity to seek a remedy, provided the party meets the minimum "injury in fact" standard.

There have been landmark decisions against lenders under Section 3605 with regard to single-family home mortgages, but only a handful of published appellate cases utilize this section in connection with affordable housing development.[123] The key concern in such

provided that no such factor may in any way relate to race, color, religion, sex, handicap, familial status or national origin." *Id.* § 100.125(c). *See also* Cartwright v. Am. Savings & Loan Ass'n, 880 F.2d 912 (7th Cir. 1989).

119. In 2000, HUD, the Department of Justice, and the Department of Treasury signed a memorandum of understanding to better coordinate enforcement of the FHAA in LIHTC developments. See Memorandum of Understanding Among the Department of the Treasury, The Department of Housing and Urban Development and the Department of Justice (Aug. 9, 11, 2000), (ON FILE WITH TREASURER.CA.GOV, https://www.treasurer.ca.gov/ctcac/compliance/manual/appendix1/understanding.pdf [https://perma.cc/MLE6-FB34]. See Chapter 9 for a discussion of the LIHTC program.

120. 42 U.S.C. § 3605.

121. *See* Preamble to Final Rule Implementing Fair Housing Amendments Act of 1988 (published Jan. 19, 1989), 24 C.F.R. ch. 1, subch. A, app. I, Implementation of the Fair Housing Amendments Act, 54 Fed. Reg. 3232, 3241–42 (Jan. 23, 1989).

122. The term "redlining" refers to the practice of not making loans to particular neighborhoods or other geographic areas based on the personal characteristics of the inhabitants.

123. Cartwright v. Am. Savings & Loan Ass'n, 880 F.2d 912 (7th Cir. 1989) (noting the FHAA did not eliminate a lender's ability to use its legitimate business judgment); Simms v. First Gibraltar Bank, 83 F.3d 1546 (5th Cir.), *cert. denied*, 519 U.S. 1041 (1996) (finding no Section 3605

cases is proving whether or not the financial institution based its actions on legitimate business factors.

In 2020, HUD issued regulations that make proof of disparate impact far more difficult for aggrieved parties. The recently finalized rules carve out an enormous exception for businesses that have discriminated based on the use of third-party algorithms. In our modern housing market in which third-party credit scoring, and a wide variety of other lending-related algorithms are in place, this exception encompasses a critically important and widely used decision-making tool. The revised rule has faced widespread criticism, including by some major players in the private housing industry, for its insensitivity to America's history of racism and for its potential to ". . . hinder further progress toward addressing ongoing systemic racism."[124] Some of this industry commentary echoes the critique by fair housing advocates that the rule actually guts a key and invaluable tool that helps the public and advocates address systemic racism.[125] The rule would establish a tremendously high hurdle in order to successfully pursue disparate impact-based discrimination claims. Plaintiffs would have to satisfy a new, five-part test, with the burden of proving up front that a policy is (1) "arbitrary, artificial, and unnecessary" to achieve a valid interest; (2) with a "robust causal link" between the practice and the disparate impact; (3) negatively affecting "members of a protected class" based on race, color, religion, sex, family status, or national origin; (4) with significant impact; and (5) directly causing the "complaining party's alleged injury."[126]

The Biden administration has already taken steps to undo this rule and to simultaneously restore HUD's 2013 rule that formalized application of a discriminatory effects standard in assessing potential discrimination.[127] This prior rule consists of three steps, the first of which called for the complaining party to prove that a challenged practice caused or predictably will cause a discriminatory effect.[128] If the plaintiff successfully makes this prima facie showing, then the defendant had the burden of proving that the ". . . challenged practice is necessary to achieve one or more of its substantial, legitimate, nondiscrimina-

---

violation); Ring v. First Interstate Mortg., Inc., 984 F.2d 924 (8th Cir. 1993) (discussing pleadings requirements for an FHA case which included a 3605 claim).

124. Phil Hall, *HUD Responds to Fair Housing Act Criticisms*, DSNews (July 16, 2020), https://dsnews.com/daily-dose/07-16-2020/hud-responds-to-criticism-to-fair-housing-act [https://perma.cc/Q9AD-V9NQ]; *see* Mike Sorohan, *MBA Asks HUD to Withhold Publication of Final Disparate Impact Rule*, Mortg. Bankers' Ass'n (July 20, 2020), https://newslink.mba.org/mba-newslinks/2020/july/mba-newslink-monday-july-20-2020/mba-asks-hud-to-withhold-publication-of-final-disparate-impact-rule/ [https://perma.cc/USM8-2RR7].

125. *See National Fair Housing Alliance Condemns HUD's Evisceration of Civil Rights Tool to Address Systemic Racism*, National Fair Housing Alliance (Sept. 4, 2020), https://natio nalfairhousing.org/2020/09/04/national-fair-housing-alliance-condemns-huds-evisceration-of-civil -rights-tool-to-address-systemic-racism/ [https://perma.cc/B7AK-V55K], *see Preliminary Analysis of HUD's Final Disparate Impact Rule*, Nat'l Low Income Hous. Coal. (Sept. 14, 2020), https://nlihc.org/resource/preliminary-analysis-huds-final-disparate-impact-rule [https://perma.c c/C3LA-BBG7].

126. HUD's Implementation of the Fair Housing Act's Disparate Impact Standard, 84 Fed. Reg. 42,854 (2019).

127. *See* Notice of Proposed Rulemaking, 86 Fed. Reg. 33590 (June 25, 2021).

128. Implementation of the Fair Housing Act's Discriminatory Effects Standard, 78 Fed. Reg. 11460 (2013).

tory interests."[129] If the defendant meets that burden, then the plaintiff has one more chance to establish liability by proving that ". . . the substantial, legitimate, nondiscriminatory interest could be served by a practice that has a less discriminatory effect."[130]

HUD's 2020 proposed revision of the three-part test would not only impose a more onerous proof standard for disparate impact, but the entire weight of providing proof would rest on the shoulders of the aggrieved party. Without the burden shifting of the 2013 rules, the new rule would essentially require those who presumably have the least power, with the longest history of experiencing discrimination, with the obligation to somehow gather sufficient information to meet this almost impossible to prove standard.

On October 25, 2020, however, before this new and onerous rule could take effect, a district court in Massachusetts issued a stay and nationwide preliminary injunction against Secretary Ben Carson and the U.S. Department of Housing and Urban Development (HUD), halting HUD's overhaul of the disparate impact protections of the Fair Housing Act. This ruling was in response to a suit filed by a fair housing center, claiming that the proposed rule violates the Administrative Procedure Act. Most notably, the court noted plaintiffs will likely succeed on their claim that the rule is arbitrary and capricious.[131]

In a momentous reversal, with the change in federal administration, HUD announced it would withdraw its appeal of the district court's decision.[132] Two months later, acting in alignment with Executive Orders issued by the Biden administration,[133] HUD announced it is moving to reinstate the 2015 fair housing rules in ostensibly their original form.[134] This rapid action by the Biden administration restores an invaluable framework for fair housing protection and enforcement nationally.

4. General Enforcement of Section 3608

Section 3608 of the FHAA provides that:

> All executive departments and agencies shall administer their programs and activities relating to housing and urban development (including any Federal agency having regulatory or supervisory authority over financial institutions) in a manner

---

129. *Id.*

130. *Id.*

131. *See* Memorandum and Order Regarding Plaintiffs' Motion for Preliminary Injunction under 5 U.S.C. § 705 to Postpone the Effective Date of Hud's Unlawful New Rule, Massachusetts Fair Housing Center and Housing Inc. v. US Department of Housing and Urban Development, Civil Action No. 20-11765-MGM, U.S. District Court, Massachusetts, (filed Oct. 25, 2020) http://law yersforcivilrights.org/wp-content/uploads/2020/10/Nationwide-PI-Against-HUD.pdf [https://perma .cc/E49Z-LVY7].

132. Alex Roha, *HUD Withdraws Appeal in Fair Housing Case*, Hous. Wire (Feb. 10, 2021, 1:46 PM), https://www.housingwire.com/articles/hud-withdraws-appeal-in-fair-housing-case/ [https:// perma.cc/4LND-79Z6].

133. *See FACT SHEET: President Biden to Take Action to Advance Racial Equity and Support Underserved Communities*, WH.gov (Jan. 26, 2021), https://www.whitehouse.gov/briefing-room /statements-releases/2021/01/26/fact-sheet-president-biden-to-take-action-to-advance-racial -equity-and-support-underserved-communities/ [https://perma.cc/N5W7-AJCN].

134. Tracy Jan, *Trump Gutted Obama-Era Housing Discrimination Rules. Biden's Bringing Them Back*, Wash. Post (Apr. 13, 2021, 3:39 AM), https://www.washingtonpost.com/us-policy /2021/04/13/hud-biden-fair-housing-rules/ [https://perma.cc/C8BC-ASL7].

affirmatively to further the purposes of this subchapter and shall cooperate with the Secretary [of HUD] to further such purposes.[135]

In other words, all of the federal agencies discussed in this chapter—the FRB, the OTS, the FDIC, the OCC—are covered by this section of the FHAA and must affirmatively further fair housing in the administration of their programs.[136] Because violations of Section 3608 are not included in the FHAA's definition of "discriminatory housing practices,"[137] claimants must find other statutes to provide jurisdiction. Courts have found jurisdiction over Section 3608 claims under 28 U.S.C. §§ 1331 and 1343(a)(4). More recently, courts have usually found that there is no private right of action to bring a 3608 claim, and so those federal provisions could not be used.[138] However, the Administrative Procedure Act (APA) is available under some circumstances as a basis for judicial review of actions by federal agencies and could be employed in pursuit of a 3608 claim.[139]

The question becomes what "affirmatively to further" means and how these agencies may satisfy that mandate. The statute does not shed much light on the meaning of "to affirmatively further," but the courts have offered interpretations. The first appellate court to review this language interpreted it within the context of the Housing Act of 1949 and the Civil Rights Act of 1964 and 1968, finding that it was connected to an obligation to ensure that community improvement and community development plans be nondiscriminatory in their effects.[140] Several other courts have found that the "to affirmatively further" language "establishes an affirmative duty to take action that directly results in 'the implementation of the dual and mutual goals of fair housing and the elimination of discrimination in that housing.'"[141]

---

135. 42 U.S.C. § 3608(d) (emphasis added). *See also id.* § 3608(e)(5).

136. The level of HUD enforcement and monitoring has been uneven. While Section 3608 of the FHAA has been litigated almost exclusively with regard to HUD and HUD-funded programs, it has been extended by some courts to other entities that receive federal funding, including public housing authorities (PHAs). *See* Otero v. N.Y.C. Housing Auth., 484 F.2d 1122 (2d Cir. 1973); United States v. Charlottesville Redev. & Housing Auth., 718 F. Supp. 461 (W.D. Va. 1989); Reese v. Miami-Dade Cnty., 210 F. Supp. 2d 1324 (S.D. Fla. 2002). *See* SCHWEMM, *supra* note 4, at §§ 21:2, 21-10 to 21-11.

137. 42 U.S.C. § 3602(f).

138. *See* Jones v. Office of Comptroller of Currency, 983 F. Supp. 197, 202 (D.D.C. 1997), citing to NAACP v. Sec'y of Hous. & Urban Dev., 817 F.2d 149, 154 (1st Cir. 1987); Latinos Unidos de Chelsea v. Sec'y of Hous. & Urban Dev., 799 F.2d, 774, 792–93 (1st Cir. 1986); Lee v. Pierce, 698 F. Supp. 332, 342 (D.D.C. 1988). *See generally* SCHWEMM, *supra* note 4, at 21.

139. 5 U.S.C. § 706(2)(A) and § 701(a)(2). According to one published decision, while Section 701(a)(2) of the APA prohibited review of an agency's specific decision, it permitted review of the agency's general compliance with the 3608(d) obligation to affirmatively further fair housing in its program administration. Jones v. Office of Comptroller of Currency, 983 F. Supp. 197 (D.D.C. 1997) (finding no violation). Evidence of compliance included a declaration stating that OCC examines institutions periodically for FHAA compliance, guidelines developed by the OCC for detecting unlawful discriminatory practices during examinations, a declaration stating that it refers all fair housing complaints to HUD for investigation and a determination, and refers any evidence of a pattern and practice of discrimination to the attorney general, participation in banking industry education efforts, and publications on the topic. *Jones*, 983 F. Supp. at n.10.

140. Shannon v. United States Dep't of Hous. & Urban Dev., 436 F.2d 809, 820 (3d Cir. 1970).

141. Albany Apts. Tenants' Ass'n v. Veneman, 2003 U.S. Dist. LEXIS 3720, at *10–11 (D. Minn. Mar. 11, 2003), citing Clients' Council v. Pierce, 711 F.2d 1406, 1425 (8th Cir. 1983); Little

Enforcement of the "to affirmatively further" requirement has resulted in three approaches: (1) do no wrong;[142] (2) know what is going on, and provide data so that HUD can monitor it;[143] and (3) fulfill your affirmative obligation to promote fair housing and avoid discrimination, including promoting integration.[144]

In one landmark decision, a district court found that HUD had failed to fulfill its 3608(e)(5) duty to affirmatively further fair housing when it failed "adequately to consider a regional approach to desegregation of public housing."[145] The court's findings suggest that HUD and any other agency obligated under 3608 to affirmatively further fair housing must take a broader and more proactive view on how to fulfill that duty.[146] Although the court's decision discusses HUD's obligation under 3608(e)(5), the decision should be viewed as relevant to 3608(d) obligations, which extend to federal agencies having regulatory or supervisory authority over financial institutions.

In another historic case brought under the False Claims Act, the court found that a county's failure to analyze race-based impediments to fair housing (among other failures) constituted a failure to meet its duty to affirmatively further fair housing a (pre-condition to receipt of funds from HUD), and that its certifications to HUD that it had met its duty to affirmatively further fair housing were false.[147] As a result of this case, recipients of HUD dollars should have no doubt that a pro forma, rubber-stamp certification of having met their duty to affirmatively further fair housing could result in having to repay grant funds to HUD.

A Section 3608 enforcement claim may not need to prove discriminatory intent.[148] Thus, in a claim against the FRB over the effect of its regulations or regulatory activity, the

---

Earth of United Tribes, Inc. v. U.S. Dep't of Hous. & Urban Dev., 675 F. Supp. 497, 534 (D. Minn. 1987) (quoting *Pierce*).

142. *See Shannon*, 436 F.2d at 820.

143. See Albany Apts. Tenants' Ass'n, 2003 U.S. Dist. LEXIS, at *11–12 (finding that the statute leaves "agencies with broad discretion in deciding which policies will best further the objectives of the programs established by Congress" in a claim invoking Section 3608(d) as protection for minority residents against displacement).

144. *See* Clients' Council v. Pierce, 711 F.2d 1406, 1425 (8th Cir. 1983); *see Little Earth*, 675 F. Supp. at 534 (quoting *Pierce*). For further discussion regarding the meaning and interpretations of the duty to affirmatively further fair housing, see Schwemm, *supra* note 4, at § 21.1, 21-1 to 21-10.

145. Thompson v. U.S. Dep't of Hous. & Urban Dev., 348 F. Supp. 2d 398 (D. Md. 2005). The court found that it was incumbent on HUD to look beyond the borders of a local housing authority's jurisdiction (Baltimore City) in attempting to address the issue of segregation. The fact that HUD's jurisdiction is national and yet it continued to apply a piecemeal, city-focused approach to addressing desegregation was particularly irksome to the court. *Id.* at 409.

146. For example, OTS and OCC as covered agencies may wish to consider whether reductions in CRA oversight are consistent with their duty to affirmatively further fair housing.

147. United States *ex rel.* Anti-Discrimination Center of Metro N.Y., Inc. v. Westchester Cnty., 668 F. Supp. 2d 548 (S.D.N.Y. 2009).

148. Shannon v. U.S. Dep't of Hous. & Urban Dev., 436 F.2d 809, 820 (3d Cir. 1970); *Pierce*, 711 F.2d at 1425; *Little Earth*, 675 F. Supp. at 534. *See also* Texas Dep't of Hous. & Community Affairs v. Inclusive Communities Project, Inc., 576 U.S. 519, 545 (2015), in which the U.S. Supreme Court affirmed that "disparate-impact claims are cognizable under the Fair Housing Act. . .".

claimant may only need to show that the FRB's actions or inactions resulted in discrimination in housing against the FHAA's protected classifications.[149]

In 2015, the Obama administration issued an Affirmatively Furthering Fair Housing (AFFH) rule that provided strong guidance on what would constitute compliance with AFFH. The 2015 rule introduced standardization into the governmental process of determining fair housing need, introducing an Assessment of Fair Housing (AFH) tool, with guidance about factors that participants were required to consider in the assessment process, to undertake fair housing priorities into governmental decision making on community development, encouraging regional approaches and collaboration across jurisdictions to address fair housing concerns, with a meaningful community participation requirement in the planning process.[150] The rule also sought to assist program participants in reducing disparities in housing choice and access to housing and opportunity based on race, color, religion, sex, familial status, national origin, or disability, thereby expanding economic opportunity and enhancing the quality of life.

In 2020, under the rubric of the larger framework of reduction of oversight by federal agencies, HUD reverted to its weaker, more generic, pre-1994 interpretation of "affirmatively further fair housing." Under the new "Preserving Community and Neighborhood Choice" rule, jurisdictions funded by HUD need only certify they will use HUD funds to actively promote fair housing, with a requirement only to take some form of action beyond statutory minimums statutes to promote fair housing.[151] The rollback was, on its face, a complete repudiation of the substantive guidance created in 2015 that gave clarity and made it more difficult for jurisdictions to claim that they did not understand the meaning of AFFH.

On June 10, 2021, the Biden administration addressed this problem. HUD published an interim final rule that reinstated the Affirmatively Furthering Fair Housing (AFFH) definitions and certification requirements from the 2015 AFFH rule while revoking the 2020 Preserving Community and Neighborhood Choice (PCNC) rule.[152]

5. The Low-Income Housing Tax Credit Program

The country's largest current source of financing for low-income rental housing is the Low-Income Housing Tax Credit (LIHTC) program.[153] This section will discuss how fair housing requirements apply to the LIHTC program.

---

149. How the regulatory agencies supervising financial institutions show that they actively have taken steps to promote integration and what HUD has required of them in this regard is worthy of research.

150. Affirmatively Furthering Fair Housing, 80 Fed. Reg. 42,272 (July 16, 2015) (codified at 24 C.F.R. pts. 5, 91, 92, 570, 574, 576, 903), https://www.govinfo.gov/content/pkg/FR-2015-07-16/pdf/2015-17032.pdf [https://perma.cc/4A6U-L67S].

151. *See* 24 C.F.R. pts 5, 91, 92, 570, 574, 576, 903.

152. *See Restoring Affirmatively Furthering Fair Housing Definitions and Certifications* (June 20, 2021), 86 FR 30779.

153. Established under the Tax Reform Act of 1986, and codified at 26 U.S.C. §§ 42, *et seq*. See Chapter 9 for an overview of the LIHTC program.

Private investors are the primary source of equity financing for LIHTC projects.[154] The Internal Revenue Service (IRS) is responsible for oversight of the program, issuing regulations and conducting periodic audits. Pursuant to Section 3608 of the FHAA, the IRS has an affirmative duty to further fair housing.[155] States also have responsibility for monitoring and compliance oversight of the program, and, therefore, may be subject to the same Section 3608 duty.[156] IRS regulations mandate that states must adopt Qualified Allocation Plans (QAP), which must provide for a monitoring process that includes notification of the IRS in case of noncompliance.[157] In addition, LIHTC program regulations prohibit discrimination generally for LIHTC units, stating that a unit of a building does not qualify for tax credit if it is rented in a manner that violates HUD's antidiscrimination regulations.[158] IRS regulations reference fair housing obligations,[159] but it is the FHAA's Sections 3604, 3605, and 3608 (discussed *supra*) that provide the bulwark of fair housing obligation for the LIHTC program.

LIHTC project location has been cited as an indicator of a lack of fair housing oversight by the IRS and state agencies administering tax credits.[160] Studies on LIHTC show that "more than half of tax credit units are in central cities," in areas of high poverty with high numbers of people of color. Half the units in the suburbs are in high-poverty areas, and 20 percent of units are in areas where more than half of the residents are people of color.[161] The result is a housing pattern that is highly segregated racially.[162]

More clarification is needed regarding how to interpret the FHAA's obligations in the LIHTC program.[163] The need for Congress or HUD to provide additional guidance for courts and agencies regarding the application of FHAA's Section 3608 duty to affirmatively further fair housing in LIHTC projects is evident in the handful of court decisions addressing it. Four nonprofit organizations in the case of *In re Adoption of the 2003 Low Income Housing Tax Credit Qualified Allocation Plan* challenged the New Jersey Housing Mortgage Finance Agency (HMFA) Qualified Allocation Plan (QAP) on the grounds that it concentrated low-income housing in urban neighborhoods with substandard schools,

---

154. See U.S. Gov't Accountability Office, GAO/GGD/RCED-97-55, Tax Credits: Opportunities to Improve Oversight of the Low-Income Housing Program 27 (1997), https://www.gao.gov/assets/ggd/rced-97-55.pdf [https://perma.cc/M5JY-3XML].

155. *Id.* at 29.

156. *Id.* at 30.

157. 26 U.S.C. § 42(m)(1)(B)(iii).

158. 26 C.F.R. § 1.42-9(a).

159. 26 U.S.C. § 1.42-5; 26 C.F.R. § 1.42-9(a).

160. *See* Florence Wagman Roisman, *Mandates Unsatisfied: The Low Income Housing Tax Credit Program and the Civil Rights Laws*, 52 U. Miami L. Rev. 1011 (1998).

161. *Id.* at 1019–22, citing ABT Assocs. Inc., Development and Analysis of the National Low-Income Housing Tax Credit Database: Final Report 1–2, 4–16 (July 1, 1996).

162. *Id.* at 1021.

163. The IRS could take affirmative steps to meet the obligations imposed by these statutes, including amending IRS regulations to "A. . . . acknowledge the authority of Title VIII (the FHAA), as well as HUD's Title VIII regulations, and the tax credit statute's non-discrimination requirements; B. specify what housing credit agencies must do to satisfy civil rights obligations; and C. . . . specify what tax credit developers must do to satisfy civil rights obligations." Roisman, *supra* note 160, at 1031. The author offers further detailed suggestions about how FHAA obligations could be satisfied. *Id.* at 1032–49.

thereby perpetuating segregation and violating the FHAA.[164] The court found that the HMFA has a duty under the FHAA to affirmatively further fair housing, but that this obligation "must be defined congruent with its express statutory powers and far-reaching housing agenda as defined under federal and state law."[165] In this case, the court found that focusing on racial composition of a community could "compromise HMFA's fundamental mission."[166] The court emphasized the fact that the selection criteria set forth in the governing LIHTC statute, 26 U.S.C. § 42(m)(1)(A), do not require an analysis of the racial composition of the proposed project site.[167]

As discussed *supra*, Section 3608 of the FHAA does not offer a definition of affirmatively furthering fair housing. Courts have interpreted the language to include a duty to promote racial integration, which can best be implemented when the agency entrusted with this duty has "before it the relevant racial and socio-economic information necessary for compliance with its duties under the 1964 [Civil Rights Act and 1968 Fair Housing Act]."[168] It is not clear whether the court is suggesting that the LIHTC's statutory language takes precedence over the FHAA's requirement to affirmatively further fair housing. Reading *In re Adoption* in combination with the *Jones* and *Veneman* cases,[169] perhaps the most consistent thread is that the courts in these cases did not want to substitute their judgment for that of the controlling state agency on the definition of affirmatively furthering fair housing. The court in the *In re Adoption* case found that "the agency's judgment must be an informed one; one which weighs the alternatives and finds that the need for physical rehabilitation or additional minority housing at the site in question clearly outweighs the disadvantage of increasing or perpetuating racial concentration."[170]

However, whereas siting and development of LIHTC may have shifted in light of the relaxed interpretation of the AFFH in the final year of the Trump administration, the Biden administration's return to ostensibly if not exactly 2015 language regarding AFFH offers an opportunity to argue for application of that standard to LIHTC programs, thereby increasing the ability of communities and affordable housing developers to overcome resistance

---

164. *In re* Adoption of the 2003 Low Income Housing Tax Credit Qualified Allocation Plan, 848 A.2d 1, 15–16 (N.J. Super. Ct. App. Div. 2004).

165. *Id.* at 10, 24–25, citing 26 U.S.C.A. § 42(m)(1)(B) & (C) and the N.J. Housing and Mortgage Finance Agency Law of 1983, N.J.S.A. 55:14K-1 to 81.

166. *Id.* at 26.

167. *Id.* In a more recent case, a nonprofit claimed that a state's department of housing and community affairs "perpetuates housing segregation by disproportionately allocating tax credits for proposed developments in low-income, predominantly minority areas and denying tax credits for proposed developments in higher-income, predominantly Caucasian areas." The published decision did not address the substantive issue, however, of how the QAP was being implemented.

168. Shannon v. U.S. Dep't of Hous. & Urban Dev., 436 F.2d 809, 821 (3d Cir. 1970); *see also* NAACP v. Sec'y of Hous. & Urban Dev., 817 F.2d 149, 156 (1st Cir. 1987); Langlois v. Abington Hous. Auth., 234 F. Supp. 2d 33, 77–78 (D. Mass. 2002).

169. *See* Jones v. Office of Comptroller of Currency, 983 F. Supp. 197, 202 (D.D.C. 1997), *citing to* NAACP v. Sec'y of Hous. & Urban Dev., 817 F.2d 149, 154 (1st Cir. 1987); Albany Apts. Tenants' Ass'n v. Veneman, 2003 U.S. Dist. LEXIS 3720, at *10–11 (D. Minn. Mar. 11, 2003), *citing* Clients' Council v. Pierce, 711 F.2d 1406, 1425 (8th Cir. 1983).

170. *In re* Adoption of the 2003 Low Income Housing Tax Credit Qualified Allocation Plan, 848 A.2d at 20, citing *Shannon*, at 822.

to siting of affordable housing in lower poverty areas, and their general ability to obtain approval for affordable housing development in municipalities that are resistant.[171]

B. Additional Federal Provisions

1. Office of Thrift Supervision Antidiscrimination Regulations

The Office of Thrift Supervision (OTS has) established general, nondiscrimination regulations, prohibiting "arbitrary refusals to consider loan applications on the basis of the age or location of a dwelling" and prohibiting discrimination based on race, disability, and other protected categories in considering loan applications as well as "in fixing the amount, interest rate, duration, application procedures, collection or enforcement procedures, or other terms or conditions of housing related loans."[172] "Such discrimination is also prohibited in the purchase of loans and securities."[173] This last provision is applicable to OTS-regulated institutions operating in the secondary market. In addition, the regulations explain that "[r]efusing to lend, or offering less favorable terms (such as interest rate, down payment, or maturity) to applicants because of the income level in an area can discriminate against minority group persons."[174] Complaints regarding violation of these provisions must be referred to the Assistant Secretary for Fair Housing and Equal Opportunity of HUD.[175]

2. The U.S. Housing Act Duty to Affirmatively Further Fair Housing

The U.S. Housing Act[176] provides that HUD and "any other departments or agencies of the Federal government having powers, functions, or duties with respect to housing, shall exercise their powers, functions, or duties . . . in such manner as will encourage and assist . . . the development of well-planned, integrated, residential neighborhoods."[177] The language of the various federal statutes and regulations discussed thus far in this chapter makes it clear that the federal agencies supervising financial institutions have duties with regard to housing. As of this writing, there are no published appellate cases discussing the application of the statute to these agencies. Cases thus far have found no private right of action to enforce this statute.[178]

3. Executive Order No. 12.892

Executive Order No. 12.892, adopted January 17, 1994, requires that each executive agency administer its programs in a manner that furthers fair housing.[179] To that end, the order

---

171. The New Jersey decision offered a new wrinkle—that perhaps the FHAA's affirmatively furthering fair housing mandate could be circumscribed or satisfied by another statutory system's requirement (LIHTC), or by the conflicting mission of the agency subject to the obligation.

172. 12 C.F.R. § 390.142.

173. *Id.*

174. *Id.* § 390.150.

175. *Id.* § 528.8.

176. U.S. Housing Act of 1937, 42 U.S.C. §§ 1437 *et seq.*; Title V of Pub. L. No. 105-276, 112 Stat. 2461, 2518 (Oct. 1998) as amended by the Quality Housing and Work Responsibility Act of 1998.

177. 42 U.S.C § 1441.

178. *See* Burroughs v. Hills, 741 F.2d 1525 (7th Cir. 1984), *cert. denied*, 471 U.S. 1099 (1985).

179. 59 Fed. Reg. 2939, § 2-201 (Jan. 17, 1994).

established a Fair Housing Council.[180] The Council is entrusted with an ambitious agenda, which includes a requirement that it "review the design and delivery of Federal programs and activities to ensure that they support a coordinated strategy to affirmatively further fair housing. The Council shall propose revisions to existing programs or activities, develop pilot programs and activities, and propose new programs and activities to achieve its goals."[181] Theoretically, such a coordinated approach to resolving fair housing problems could yield significant results, but to date the Council has not been noticeably active.

C. State Fair Lending Laws

Most states and many cities have fair housing laws that are substantially similar to the FHAA. Partly because of preemption concerns, states and cities have not contributed fair housing–type regulations targeting lenders that invest in affordable housing. When states or other localities have focused on fair lending in the housing context, however, they have focused primarily on single-family mortgages. For example, several states and a few cities imposed laws aimed at stopping predatory mortgage lending[182] in the single-family market.[183] States have not focused on beefing up state mortgage–focused laws much since implementation of the federal Dodd–Frank Act in 2010, which created the Consumer Financial Protection Bureau and mandated substantial changes to mortgage-lending regulation at the federal level.[184] Debate ensued at the federal and local levels and within financial supervisory agencies regarding whether such laws should be (or already are) federally preempted.[185]

In 2009, President Obama issued an Executive Order announcing "the general policy of [his] Administration that preemption of State law by executive departments and agencies should be undertaken only with full consideration of the legitimate prerogatives of the

---

180. Council members are the secretary of HUD, the secretaries of Health and Human Services, Transportation, Education, Labor, Defense, Agriculture, Veterans Affairs, Treasury, and the Interior, along with the attorney general, the chair of the Federal Reserve, the Comptroller of the Currency, the director of the OTS, and the chair of the FDIC. The president may, at any time, designate other officials to participate.

181. 59 Fed. Reg. 2939, § at 3-302 (Jan. 17, 1994).

182. "Predatory mortgage lending" is a term that refers to unscrupulous or abusive mortgage lending practices that currently occur predominantly in the subprime mortgage refinance market, targeting seniors and people of color in particular. For more information on practices and their impact, *see* Center for Responsible Lending, http://www.responsiblelending.org [https://perma.cc/N368 -MXKR] (last visited June 8, 2021). Note that "predatory lending" also refers to abusive lending practices in the arena of smaller, personal loans, such as payday lending and refund anticipation loans.

183. States that have enacted such laws include Arkansas, California, Colorado, Connecticut, Georgia, Nevada, New York, North Carolina, and Wisconsin. *See Mortgage Lending Practices, Subprime and Predatory Mortgage Lending*, NAT'L CONFERENCE OF STATE LEGISLATURES, https:// www.ncsl.org/research/financial-services-and-commerce/mortgage-lending-practices-state-statutes .aspx [https://perma.cc/NTA4-QZJA] (last visited June 8, 2021).

184. Dodd-Frank Wall Street Reform and Consumer Protection Act, Pub. L. No. 111-203, 124 Stat. 1376 (2010), https://www.congress.gov/bill/111th-congress/house-bill/4173/text [https://perma .cc/M8FM-YHBC].

185. Since local or state laws may have better remedies or a broader range of protections, it may be strategic to bring an action under local or state laws in addition to federal laws when both are available.

States and with a sufficient legal basis for preemption."[186] The order provides specifically that:

1. Heads of departments and agencies should not include in regulatory preambles statements that the department or agency intends to preempt state law through the regulation except where preemption provisions are also included in the codified regulation.

2. Heads of departments and agencies should not include preemption provisions in codified regulations except where such provisions would be justified under legal principles governing preemption, including the principles outlined in Executive Order 13,132.

3. Heads of departments and agencies should review regulations issued within the past ten years that contain statements in regulatory preambles or codified provisions intended by the department or agency to preempt state law, in order to decide whether such statements or provisions are justified under applicable legal principles governing preemption. Where the head of a department or agency determines that a regulatory statement of preemption or codified regulatory provision cannot be so justified, the head of that department or agency should initiate appropriate action, which may include amendment of the relevant regulation.

To the extent that any federal regulator attempts to restrict the ability of a private person or entity to enforce state or federal laws as they pertain to multifamily housing development, practitioners may still be able to cite to this executive order when the preemption claim is not explicitly grounded in legislation.

With regard to state preemption of local laws, ". . . states have prohibited many cities, towns and villages from being able to implement housing policies to effectively respond to local housing markets. For instance, six states currently have preemption inclusionary zoning programs, twenty-nine states preempt rent control, and two states preempt source of income nondiscrimination ordinances."[187] Practitioners must navigate the array of state laws affecting fair housing concerns in the development process.

V. LAWS GOVERNING THE SECONDARY MARKET

A. Fannie Mae and Freddie Mac

1. Overview

In the secondary market, investors purchase assets from other investors. Among the myriad of investments available in this market are affordable housing loans, which are pooled and securitized before sale. Banks and other institutions sell these loans in the secondary market because the sale provides cash for further lending and relieves the risk of carrying a

---

186. *See* Memorandum for the Heads of Executive Departments and Agencies, 74 Fed. Reg. 24,693 (May 20, 2009), https://www.govinfo.gov/content/pkg/FR-2009-05-22/pdf/E9-12250.pdf [https://perma.cc/S8QN-TYW9].

187. *Navigating Preemption during COVID: Four Steps Cities Can Take to Increase Affordable Housing*, NAT'L LEAGUE OF CITIES (July 14, 2020), https://www.nlc.org/article/2020/07/14/navigating-preemption-during-covid-four-steps-cities-can-take-to-increase-affordable-housing/ [https://perma.cc/B6MS-W9W8].

defaulted loan. Institutional investors also buy these loans and hold them in their portfolios rather than selling them to other investors.

Two significant participants in the secondary market are the Federal National Mortgage Association (Fannie Mae)[188] and the Federal Home Loan Mortgage Corporation (Freddie Mac). Both are government-sponsored enterprises (GSEs) formed specifically to facilitate the flow of funds to residential mortgages.[189] In 1968, Fannie Mae became a publicly owned GSE and expanded the scope of its secondary market work.[190] Two years later, Freddie Mac, whose service focus was the savings and loan industry, was formed as part of the former Federal Home Loan Bank system. In 1989, Freddie Mac became a publicly owned GSE as well.[191] The regulatory and tax exemptions that GSEs receive function as subsidies, and the perception that they have a special relationship with the federal government enhances their ability to conduct business profitably.[192] In 2008, Fannie Mae and Freddie Mac were put into receivership due in part to the severity of their financial losses.[193] Some have blamed their financial failure on the regulatory mandate that these institutions support affordable housing,[194] but it appears that a strong drive by Fannie Mae and Freddie Mac executives for profits and poor decision making on their part is more likely to have been the root cause of the companies' financial failure.[195]

Fannie Mae and Freddie Mac are prohibited from discriminating in the purchase of mortgages.[196] They also have "an affirmative obligation to facilitate the financing of afford-able housing for low- and moderate-income families in a manner consistent with their

---

188. Fannie Mae was created by Congress in 1938 as part of the Federal Housing Administration (FHA) in order to bolster the housing industry after the Great Depression of the 1930s by buying FHA-insured mortgages. Fannie Mae came at a time when mortgage interest rates were prohibitively high. By borrowing funds from investors at a reduced rate, Fannie Mae was able to infuse the housing market with a stream of cheaper capital, translating into lower costs for consumers.

189. See discussion, *infra*, Section 3 for a discussion of the Fair Housing Act's application to the secondary market, specifically 42 U.S.C. § 3605(b)(1).

190. See the Federal National Mortgage Association Charter Act (12 U.S.C. §§ 1716, *et seq.*). That same year, a new entity—the Government National Mortgage Association (Ginnie Mae)—was created to take over Fannie Mae's FHA support work and take on similar work for Veterans Administration mortgages.

191. See the Federal Home Loan Mortgage Corporation Act (12 U.S.C. §§ 1451, *et seq.*).

192. *See* Kent W. Colton, Joint Center for Housing Studies, *Housing Finance in the United States: The Transformation of the U.S. Housing Finance System* (July, 2002) (describing the history of the secondary market in the United States), https://www.jchs.harvard.edu/sites/default/files/media/imp/w02-5_colton.pdf [https://perma.cc/43BA-B4W3].

193. Gretchen Morgenson, *They Left Fannie Mae but We Got the Legal Bills*, N.Y. Times (Sept. 5, 2009), http://www.nytimes.com/2009/09/06/business/economy/06gret.html [https://perma.cc/4PEP-MDFG].

194. Peter J. Wallison, *Barney Frank: Predatory Lender*, Wall St. J. Online (Oct. 15, 2009, 9:45 PM), https://www.wsj.com/articles/SB10001424052748704107204574475110152189446 [https://perma.cc/8G7X-4UK8].

195. *See* Eric Dash, *Fannie Mae Ex-Officers Sued by U.S.*, N.Y. Times (Dec. 19, 2006), http://www.nytimes.com/2006/12/19/business/19fannie.html [https://perma.cc/F3V6-SAPR]. *See also* Sarah Hansard, *Why Fannie Mae Failed: Ex-CEO Blames Conflicting Mandates*, AOL, (Apr. 9, 2010, 10:15 AM) https://www.aol.com/2010/04/09/why-fannie-mae-failed-ex-ceo-blames-conflicting-mandates/ [https://perma.cc/72BR-MELY].

196. 12 U.S.C. § 4545. Protected classifications are race, color, religion, sex, disability, familial status, age, and national origin. Fannie Mae and Freddie Mac are also prohibited from considering

overall public purposes, while maintaining a strong financial condition and a reasonable economic return. . . ."[197] In addition, upon request, they must submit data to HUD to assist in fair housing and credit discrimination investigations of lenders with whom they do business. And they must take action against lenders found guilty of such unlawful behavior.[198] HUD is charged with reviewing the underwriting and appraisal guidelines of Fannie Mae and Freddie Mac to make sure they comply with the FHAA.[199]

Fannie Mae and Freddie Mac must also meet Federal Housing Finance Agency (FHFA)–established low- and very low-income housing goals and a "multifamily special affordable housing" goal. The GSEs are required to serve underserved markets, defined to include very low-, low-, and moderate-income families; to preserve affordable housing (which includes most federal, state, and local affordable housing programs); and to serve rural communities.[200] To meet the housing goals established by FHFA, the GSEs must engage in a range of specific activities, including "develop[ing] relationships with nonprofit and for-profit organizations that develop and finance housing and with State and local governments, including housing finance agencies"; "assist[ing] primary lenders to make housing credit available in areas with concentrations of low-income and minority families"; and "assist[ing] insured depository institutions to meet their obligations under the Community Reinvestment Act of 1977 [12 USCS §§ 2901 *et seq.*]."[201] FHFA must evaluate and rate the GSEs' compliance with the housing goals.[202] Given the depleted reserves of the GSEs due to financial losses that drove them into conservatorship, FHFA had proposed that the GSEs not pursue any new lines of business for underserved markets in the early years of exiting the foreclosure crisis.[203] In early 2018, FHFA established updated affordable housing goals for the GSEs for the 2018–2020 time period.[204] Please note that these housing goals grew steadily from 2010 to 2018.[205] Given the emergence of Fannie and Freddie from conservatorship, the modest increases in goals may be appropriate, despite the substantial need for affordable housing nationally. Proposed 2021 goals represent a 5 percent increase on the multifamily front in terms of the total number of units financed.[206]

---

the location or age of a dwelling or the neighborhood or census tract where it is located if that results in a discriminatory effect.

197. *Id.* § 4501(7).

198. *Id.* § 4545.

199. *Id.*

200. *Id.* § 4565.

201. *Id.*

202. *Id.*

203. *Id.* §§ 4561 and 4563 (2010). *See also* Federal Housing Enterprises Financial Safety and Soundness Act of 1992, Pub. L. No. 102–550 (1992), and as amended. *See* Duty to Serve Underserved Markets for Enterprises, Federal Register (Aug. 4, 2009), https://www.federalregister .gov/documents/2009/08/04/E9-18515/duty-to-serve-underserved-markets-for-enterprises [https:// perma.cc/5BV2-54UT].

204. 83 Fed. Reg. 5,878 (2018).

205. *Housing Goals Performance, Multifamily Housing Goals*, FHFA (last updated Dec. 16, 2020), https://www.fhfa.gov/PolicyProgramsResearch/Programs/AffordableHousing/Pages/Fannie -Mae-and-Freddie-Mac-Housing-Goals-Performance.aspx [https://perma.cc/E93A-KJYN].

206. *FHFA Proposes 2021 Housing Goals for Fannie May and Freddie Mac*, FHFA (July 20, 2020), https://www.fhfa.gov/Media/PublicAffairs/Pages/FHFA-Proposes-2021-Housing-Goals-for -Fannie-Mae-and-Freddie-Mac.aspx [https://perma.cc/ZTV2-UCEB].

2. Oversight of Fannie Mae and Freddie Mac

The Office of Federal Housing Enterprise Oversight (OFHEO) was an independent entity within HUD[207] that used to regulate the safety and financial soundness of Fannie Mae and Freddie Mac.[208] HUD, in turn, was responsible for ensuring that these entities adhered to their charters and met affordable housing mandates.[209] That task is now under the purview of FHFA, the newly created regulator of the GSEs. If FHFA finds that the GSEs have fallen, or are substantially likely to fall, short of achieving any of the required housing goals, and if those goals were feasible in FHFA's estimation, FHFA must require the GSEs to develop a plan that sets forth exactly how they plan to meet those goals.[210]

3. GSE Performance and Influence on Affordable Housing

Fannie Mae and Freddie Mac have a lengthy history of investment in affordable multi-family housing and, over the years, have expanded their presence in that market.[211] Their support is credited with helping create investor acceptance of the LIHTC program from its inception in 1986.[212]

Since 1992, the federal government has increased the role of Fannie Mae and Freddie Mac in supporting the affordable multifamily and home mortgage markets by establishing housing goals for the GSEs and increasing required investment levels regularly.[213] However, Fannie Mae and Freddie Mac's fair housing performance vis-à-vis affordable multifamily housing has oscillated over the years. For example, in proposed changes to the mandatory housing goals for Fannie Mae and Freddie Mac in 2004, HUD criticized the two GSEs for not having achieved their potential in the purchase of affordable multifamily mortgages as well as home mortgages for underserved markets, including those where the population is predominantly people of color.[214] HUD proposed to increase housing goals steadily from 2005 to 2008, with single-family mortgages still to receive the lion's share of investment dollars.[215] Fannie Mae and Freddie Mac's investment in affordable multifamily housing did,

---

207. 12 U.S.C. §§ 4511–12.

208. *Id.* § 4513.

209. *Id.* §§ 4541 & 4545.

210. *Id.* § 4566(c). The plan must be approved by FHFA before it is implemented. FHFA has the discretion to issue charges and call upon the GSEs to cease and desist their unlawful conduct for failure to submit in a timely fashion or implement a plan in good faith. *See* 12 U.S.C. § 4581 (2010). The GSEs may request judicial review of such an order, and FHFA may request civil money penalties and call upon the attorney general to assist in enforcement. See 12 U.S.C. §§ 4581 & 4585 (2010).

211. One study that acknowledges the strong presence of Fannie and Freddie in this market also faults the secondary market for not investing in affordable multifamily housing other than that funded through the LIHTC program. William Segal & Edward J. Szymanoski, *The Multifamily Secondary Mortgage Market: The Role of Government-Sponsored Enterprises* 11 (Office of Policy Development and Research, Housing and Urban Development, Working Paper No. HF-002, 1997), http://www.huduser.org/Publications/pdf/mf_002wp.pdf [https://perma.cc/CBL8-7X7H].

212. *Id.*

213. *See, e.g.*, Housing Goals 2000 Final Rule, 65 Fed. Reg. 65,044–65,229 (Oct. 31, 2000), establishing, across the board, increased investment goals for 2000–2003, including temporary bonus points for purchase of mortgages for small multifamily properties.

214. 69 Fed. Reg. 24,228, 24,231 (May 3, 2004).

215. 69 Fed. Reg. at 24,232 (May 3, 2004).

in fact, increase from 2005 to 2007.[216] However, the investment by Fannie Mae and Freddie Mac in the single-family market through purchase of subprime mortgage-backed securities peaked in 2004 and declined markedly through 2006, even as the subprime mortgage market expanded rapidly.[217]

Lenders have become increasingly dependent on the secondary market as a source of funding for their loans.[218] As a result, the GSEs' influence has increased to the extent that they can exercise significant control on portions of the housing market by setting parameters on how loans get originated by lenders and the terms of those loans. Proposed 2021 housing goals for the GSEs are now available.[219] These goals represent a 5 percent increase over 2019–2018 goals; it is hard to say whether this is appropriate given the current financial status of the GSEs, but it seems a modest, conservative increase compared to national affordable multifamily housing needs.

B. The Federal Housing Finance Agency

In 2008, not long after Fannie Mae and Freddie Mac failed financially and were put under a conservator, the Federal Housing Finance Agency was created to oversee both entities, along with the Federal Home Loan Banks and the Office of Finance. FHFA's goals include ensuring that:

> (ii) the operations and activities of each regulated entity foster liquid, efficient, competitive, and resilient national housing finance markets (including activities relating to mortgages on housing for low- and moderate-income families involving a reasonable economic return that may be less than the return earned on other activities).[220]

To assist with oversight, the Federal Housing Finance Oversight Board was also created, consisting of the Secretary of the Treasury, the Secretary of Housing and Urban Development, the chairman of the Securities and Exchange Commission, and the director of the FHFA itself.[221] As referenced earlier in this chapter, FHFA is responsible for setting both single-family and multifamily affordable housing mortgage purchase goals annually for the GSEs.[222] A GSE may petition the agency to adjust those goals during the year, and

---

216. Overview of the GSEs' Housing Goal Performance 2000–2007, HUD 4 (2008), http://www.huduser.org/Datasets/GSE/gse2007.pdf [https://perma.cc/9AGQ-LMJS].

217. *Root Causes of the Foreclosure Crisis*, *supra* note 13, at 43.

218. Ronald K. Schuster, *Lending Discrimination: Is the Secondary Market Helping to Make the "American Dream" a Reality?*, 36 Gonz. L. Rev. 153, 157–58 (2000), citing to U.S. Dep't of Housing & Urban Dev., Stage 3: The Loan Approval or Disapproval Decision, https://archives.hud.gov/news/1999/newsconf/stage3.html [https://perma.cc/GP4K-P7UF] (last modified Sept. 8, 2000). According to HUD, "[t]he GSEs' purchases between 1999 and 2002 accounted for . . . 30 percent of the multifamily units that received financing during this period." 69 Fed. Reg. 24,228, 24,235 (May 3, 2004).

219. 85 Fed. Reg. 49,312 (2020).

220. Housing and Economic Recovery Act of 2008, Pub. L. No. 110–289, July 30, 2008, §1101 (amending Sections 1311 and 1312 of the Federal Housing Enterprises Financial Safety and Soundness Act of 1992) (codified at 12 U.S.C. §§4501, *et seq*.), http://www.govtrack.us/congress/bill.xpd?bill=h110-3221 [https://perma.cc/JE2B-L5M4].

221. Housing and Economic Recovery Act of 2008, Pub. L. No. 110–289, § 1102.

222. Housing and Economic Recovery Act of 2008, Pub. L. No. 110–289, § 1128.

for any reduction in goals, FHFA must seek public comment.[223] The GSEs have a duty to serve underserved markets (including very low-, low-, and moderate-income families) in the arena of manufactured homes and affordable housing preservation, and in rural areas FHFA must consider a specified set of factors in determining whether the GSEs have met that duty.[224] FHFA has broad enforcement powers as to GSE compliance with their housing goals.[225]

In 2008, a national Housing Trust Fund (HTF) was established under the purview of HUD, one of the goals of which is to "increase and preserve the supply of rental housing for extremely low- and very low-income families, including homeless families."[226] All financial assistance from the fund is defined as federal financial assistance,[227] which made it subject to the FHAA's requirements regarding the duty of recipients of federal funding from HUD to affirmatively further fair housing. With the 2020 withdrawal of the affirmatively furthering fair housing language, it is not clear whether the HTF is now covered by the substitute provisions recently enacted. Assistance from the fund can go to states or designees of the state, such as a housing and community development agency. HUD was required to develop a formula in accordance with statutory guidelines (that create some measure of renter need compared to affordable housing availability) to distribute trust funds to provide affordable housing to extremely and very low-income households.[228] States are required to develop an allocation plan for every year of housing trust funds received.[229] Trust funds must be used in a fashion that complies with local tenant protections, laws requiring public participation, and fair housing laws.[230]

The HTF had no funding for a period of years when FHFA, as conservator for Fannie Mae and Freddie Mac, directed them not to provide money to the trust fund until they become better capitalized.[231] In 2014, however, funds were mandated for the first time to be allocated, and continue to be allocated to the HTF and provided to states.[232]

---

223. *Id.*
224. *Id.* § 1129.
225. *Id.* § 1130.
226. *Id.* § 1131.
227. *Id.*
228. *Id.*
229. *Id.*
230. *Id.*
231. *Maloney Applauds FHFA for Finally Funding Federal Housing Trust Fund*, Rep. Carol B. Maloney (Dec. 11, 2014), https://maloney.house.gov/media-center/press-releases/maloney-applauds-fhfa-for-finally-funding-federal-housing-trust-fund [https://perma.cc/D8LT-9JCB].
232. *See* Housing Trust Fund, Interim Rule FR-5246-I-03, 80 Fed. Reg. 5,200 (2015), https://www.govinfo.gov/content/pkg/FR-2015-01-30/pdf/2015-01642.pdf [https://perma.cc/RS9C-XJV6]. *See also* Housing Trust Fund Federal Register Allocation Notice, 84 Fed. Reg. 22,512 (2019) https://www.govinfo.gov/content/pkg/FR-2019-05-17/pdf/2019-10337.pdf [https://perma.cc/AEL5-CPMQ].

C. The Federal Home Loan Bank System

1. Overview

The Federal Home Loan Bank (FHLB) system is a GSE chartered in 1932[233] to support the primary business of thrifts, which was mortgage lending. After the savings and loan scandal and financial disaster of the 1980s, the FHLB diversified its membership to include financial institutions other than thrifts. The FHLB system is composed of 12 banks responsible for different regions of the country. The system functions as a cooperative, with each retaining some autonomy.

By purchasing loans from member banks, the FHLB serves a role similar to Fannie Mae and Freddie Mac. It also provides other forms of financing, such as advances to member institutions. The expansion in FHLB's membership after the savings and loan disaster broadened the reach of FHLB's program to include financing activities other than housing.[234] The FHLB is required to establish "community" mortgage lending and affordable housing programs.

One such program is the Community Investment Program (CIP), promoting community-oriented mortgage lending and lending for rehabilitation of housing. Lending under the CIP must be to (or for) the benefit of families with an income at 115 percent of AMI or less.[235]

An additional FHLB program, the Affordable Housing Program (AHP), provides subsidization of interest rates "on advances to members engaged in lending for long-term, low- and moderate-income, owner-occupied and affordable rental housing. . . ."[236] For the AHP, multifamily lending is eligible when 20 percent or more of the units will be "occupied by and affordable for very low-income households for the remaining useful life of such housing or the mortgage term."[237]

Under the authorizing statute, neither the CIP nor AHP are subject to any fair housing requirements beyond meeting the targeted income levels of beneficiaries.[238] The CIP is governed under the Community Investment Cash Advance (CICA) regulations, which require that each FHLB develop a targeted community lending plan.[239] Regulations require the FHLBs to take a number of steps in creating the plan, including conducting market research and setting quantitative "targeted community lending performance goals." The regulations do not require a fair housing assessment as part of developing the plan. Since

---

233. Federal Home Loan Bank Act, 12 U.S.C. §§ 1421, *et seq.*

234. *See* Federal Subsidies and the Housing GSEs, CONG. BUDGET OFFICE, 3-4 (2001), https://www.cbo.gov/sites/default/files/107th-congress-2001-2002/reports/gses.pdf [https://perma.cc/L7XW-LKVX].

235. 12 U.S.C. § 1430(i).

236. *Id.* § 1430(j)(1).

237. *Id.* § 1430 (j)(2)(b) (2010). For purposes of the AHP, very low-income is defined as a household with an income at or below 50 percent of AMI. Low or moderate income refers to households with an income at 80 percent of AMI or below. *See* 12 U.S.C. § 1430(j)(13).

238. Compliance with federal and state fair housing laws is one of the minimum standards that applicants to the AHP must meet. 12 C.F.R. § 951.5(b)(9) (2010).

239. *See* 12 C.F.R. §§ 952.4 and 944.6.

the AHP is an important non-tax funding source for affordable housing in the United States, the lack of fair housing regulation is significant.[240]

2. Oversight of the FHLB System

The former Federal Housing Finance Board (FHFB) had the same powers to require the FHLB to take corrective action that the OFHEO had vis-à-vis Fannie Mae and Freddie Mac.[241] In 2008, the FHFB (along with OFHEO) was merged out of existence under the newly formed FHFA. FHFB had been criticized for not fulfilling its oversight responsibilities for the FHLB System and for immersing itself in FHLB operations to such an extent that it may have lost some of the independence necessary to function properly as a regulator.[242] Among numerous problems cited in a 1998 General Accounting Office report is the fact that in the nine years since it was established, FHFB still had not met its duty to review the FHLB system.[243]

Starting in 2010, FHFA, the new regulator over the GSEs, was tasked with setting housing goals for the FHLB with regard to the purchase of mortgages, both single-family and multifamily, as discussed *supra*.[244] The initial proposed goals were published for public comment in February 2010.[245] The goals of 2019 were similar to those of 2018.[246] However, amounts allocated have grown with the earnings of the FHLB. "FHLBank AHP Funding Contributions and Allocations: An FHLBank's annual AHP statutory funding contribution must equal at least 10 percent of its net earnings for the prior year (subject to a $100 million minimum combined contribution by all of the FHLBanks collectively)."[247] Overall, FHLB funding for affordable housing remained stable in 2018 compared to 2017.

> The FHLBanks awarded approximately $458 million in total AHP funds in 2018, about 15 percent more than in 2017. This funding assisted over 49,000 low- or moderate-income households, including about 25,900 very low-income

---

240. From its inception in 1990 to 2002, FHLB institutions have invested $1.7 billion in the AHP. See *Testimony of John T. Korsmo, Chairman, Federal Housing Finance Board, Before the Housing Representatives' Committee on Financial Services, Wash., D.C.* 5 (Sept. 25, 2003), https:// archives-financialservices.house.gov/media/pdf/092503jk.pdf [https://perma.cc/3WXM-EWRD]. In 2019, AHP investments were at approximately $404 million nationally. See *Affordable Housing Program*, Federal Housing Finance Authority, https://www.fhfa.gov/PolicyProgramsResearch /Programs/AffordableHousing/Pages/Affordable-Housing-Home-Loan-Banks.aspx [https://perma .cc/94GU-YJWH].

241. 12 U.S.C. § 1422b(a)(5).

242. *See* U.S. Gov't Accountability Office, GAO/GGD-98-203, GAO, Actions Needed to Improve Regulatory Oversight 6 (Sept. 1998), https://www.gao.gov/products/ggd-98-203 [https://perma.cc/WDD7-FR6E].

243. *Id.* at 9.

244. Housing and Economic Recovery Act of 2008, Pub. L. No. 110–289, § 1205.

245. *Id.* § 1128. *See also* Proposed Federal Home Loan Bank Housing Goals, 75 Fed. Reg. 9034 (Feb. 26, 2010), http://edocket.access.gpo.gov/2010/2010-12849.htm [https://perma.cc/PDN8 -9VWC].

246. 85 Fed. Reg. 38,031 (2020). *See also 2019 Low-Income Housing And Community Development Activities Of The Federal Home Loan Banks, Federal Housing Finance Agency* (Oct. 2020), https://www.fhfa.gov/AboutUs/Reports/ReportDocuments/2019_Low-Income-Housing-and -Comm-Dev-Activities-of-the-FHLBanks.pdf [https://perma.cc/X4L9-4HDJ].

247. *2019 Low-Income Housing and Community Development, supra* note 246, at 5.

households. Through the CIP, the FHLBanks funded approximately $3.1 billion in targeted housing and economic development advances in 2018, about 33 percent less than in 2017. The CIP assisted about 26,000 households in 2018, a decline of approximately 36 percent from 2017. The FHLBanks' CICA funding, which supports targeted economic development, was about $3.1 billion in 2018, approximately 18 percent less than in 2017.[248]

VI. FUNDS TO REBUILD NEIGHBORHOODS

The Neighborhood Stabilization Program (NSP1) was created in 2008, from funds appropriated from the U.S. Department of Treasury, "for the redevelopment of abandoned and foreclosed upon homes and residential properties."[249] Funds were made available to states and other eligible units of local government under a formula developed by HUD for use within 18 months of receipt.[250] The legislation provided that "amounts appropriated, revenues generated, or amounts otherwise made available to States and units of general local government under this section shall be treated as though such funds were community development block grant funds under title I of the Housing and Community Development Act of 1974 (42 U.S.C. § 5301 *et seq.*)."[251] Thus, activities conducted under this funding stream cannot be discriminatory on the basis of race, gender, religion, national origin, color, or age, per the Age Discrimination Act of 1975 [42 U.S.C. §§ 6101 *et seq.*], or with respect to an otherwise qualified handicapped individual as provided in section 794 of title 29.[252] Furthermore, funded activities must affirmatively further fair housing,[253] and cannot violate Title VI of the Civil Rights Act of 1964.

NSP1 funds could only be used to benefit households with an income of 120 percent of area median income or less; no less than 25 percent of funds could be used to benefit households with income not exceeding 50 percent of area median income.[254]

A second round of NSP funding for the same purpose of redevelopment of foreclosed-on properties was provided in 2009 for entities that were funded in 2008; funding was subject to the same nondiscrimination and duty to affirmatively further fair housing requirements listed *supra*.[255] A third and final round of NSP was issued in 2010.[256]

---

248. 2018 Low-Income Housing And Community Development Activities Of The Federal Home Loan Banks, Federal Housing Finance Agency (Oct. 2019), https://www.fhfa.gov/AboutUs/Reports/ReportDocuments/2018%20Low-Income%20Housing%20and%20Community%20Development%20Activities%20of%20the%20Federal%20Home%20Loan%20Banks%20Report.pdf [https://perma.cc/RZ8P-GADB].

249. Housing and Economic Recovery Act of 2008, Pub. L. No. 110–289, § 2301.

250. *Id.*

251. *Id.*

252. *See* 42 U.S.C. § 5309 (2010).

253. *See id.* § 5304.

254. Housing and Economic Recovery Act of 2008, Pub. L. No. 110–289, § 2301(f).

255. American Recovery and Reinvestment Act of 2009, Pub. L. No. 111-5 (Feb. 17, 2009), http://www.govtrack.us/congress/bill.xpd?bill=h111-1 [https://perma.cc/M2PM-SYMU]. The federal government has established a website to track Recovery Act activities at https://www.treasury.gov/about/organizational-structure/ig/Pages/ig_recoveryact.aspx [https://perma.cc/Q6DX-E96V].

256. Wall Street Reform and Consumer Protection Act of 2010. Pub. L. No. 111–203, § 1497 (approved July 21, 2010).

VII. THE CONSUMER FINANCIAL PROTECTION BUREAU

One of the byproducts of the foreclosure crisis and ensuing revelations regarding the predatory, fraudulent, and sometimes discriminatory nature of residential mortgage lending practices in the United States has been the realization that regulators and regulatory protections failed the average consumer. The resulting push for consumer protection yielded a historic bill that created a new Consumer Financial Protection Bureau (CFPB) "[t]o promote the financial stability of the United States by improving accountability and transparency in the financial system, to end 'too big to fail,' to protect the American taxpayer by ending bailouts, to protect consumers from abusive financial services practices, and for other purposes."[257] The Bureau's mandate is "to seek to implement and, where applicable, enforce Federal consumer financial law consistently for the purpose of ensuring that all consumers have access to markets for consumer financial products and services and that markets for consumer financial products and services are fair, transparent, and competitive."[258] The legislation gives broad authority to the bureau in terms of how it is to achieve this monumental task, but what remains to be seen is how implementing regulations further define its powers and duties, and how the Bureau will interface with other federal financial regulatory agencies. One of the positive aspects of its broad mandate is the potential for the CFPB to address the reality of the market that consumers face as a whole instead of being relegated to a piecemeal approach to problem solving on behalf of the public. Its effect on affordable housing development will take many months to be realized. Under the new administration, we are seeing increased focus on analysis of housing needs by the CFPB.[259] The CFPB is housed as an independent agency within the Federal Reserve System.[260]

The bill also included several provisions pertaining to multifamily housing. One such provision established the Multifamily Mortgage Resolution Program (MMRP), which required HUD to develop a program to help stabilize at-risk multifamily properties by employing various strategies, including maintaining government subsidies, providing funding for rehabilitation of the properties, and facilitating transfers of the property to owners who are able to maintain the affordability of the units for tenants.[261] Another provision authorized additional funding for the NSP for the "redevelopment of abandoned and foreclosed homes."[262] What is currently in place instead of the MMRP are protections extended by the FHA and FHFA related to the COVID-19 pandemic. Owners of multifamily properties (as well as single-family homes) with a federally insured mortgage were allowed to

---

257. See Dodd-Frank Wall Street Reform and Consumer Protection Act, H.R. 4173, Pub. L. No. 111-203, https://www.congress.gov/bill/111th-congress/house-bill/4173/text.

258. *Id.*

259. For example, Housing insecurity and the COVID-19 pandemic (March 2021), CFPB, https://files.consumerfinance.gov/f/documents/cfpb_Housing_insecurity_and_the_COVID-19_pandemic.pdf.

260. https://www.consumerfinance.gov/.

261. Dodd-Frank Wall Street Reform and Consumer Protection Act, Pub. L. No. 111-203, 124 Stat. 1376 (2010), https://www.congress.gov/bill/111th-congress/house-bill/4173/text [https://perma.cc/M8FM-YHBC].

262. *Id.* § 1497.

seek a forbearance of up to one year on their mortgage payments.[263] Properties with such a forbearance in place are prohibited from evicting tenants for the length of the forbearance.

VIII. CLIMATE CHANGE AND ENVIRONMENTAL, INSURANCE, AND CONSTRUCTION CONSIDERATIONS

With climate change as a well-established phenomenon, insurance, construction standards, and utility access concerns are incorporating planning for disasters. In this same vein, the Environmental Protection Agency (EPA) and Federal Emergency Management agency (FEMA) now have an increased significance in the affordable housing arena. Climate change also raises new questions about the siting of affordable housing (both existing and proposed new construction), and equity in access to such housing. Population shifts can come quickly in the face of disaster and may significantly affect local housing markets receiving evacuees from disaster areas.[264] From the current COVID-19 pandemic alone, population shifts have been caused in some substantial part by related job losses and resulting inability to pay rent despite eviction moratoria widely in place nationally. The extent of the COVID-19 pandemic's impact on housing and its long-term impact remain to be seen. Though a decline in market rate rental prices is already evident in higher cost parts of the country, the need for affordable housing is likely to be more significant than ever in the months and years of recovery to come.

The cost of building housing using current methods is affected by climate change, raising the question of how to build safe dwellings at a price point that supports affordable rent or below market purchase.[265] Delays from heavy rain, strong winds, and extreme temperatures cost the construction industry billions of dollars.[266] In 2019, there were at least six major storms that caused about $1 billion of losses each, and, the frequency of such events has increased significantly since 1998.[267] New construction will need to withstand extreme weather, yet still be affordable.[268]

---

263. *See* Coronavirus Aid, Relief, and Economic Security Act, Pub. L. No. 116-136 (2020).

264. Tim McDonnell & Amanda Shendruk, *It's Time to Prepare Cities for People Uprooted by Climate Change*, QUARTZ (Sept. 1, 2020), https://qz.com/1895263/how-cities-can-prepare-to -support-climate-migrants/ [https://perma.cc/47NW-XT6D].

265. Jennifer Freeman, *Climate & Construction*, NAT'L OCEANIC & ATMOSPHERIC ADMIN. (Sept. 27, 2017), https://www.climate.gov/news-features/climate-and/climate-construction [https:// perma.cc/KB93-RMTD].

266. Kimberly Hegeman, *How Changing Climate Is Changing the Construction Industry*, FOR CONSTRUCTION PROS (Mar. 7, 2019), https://www.forconstructionpros.com/busines s/article/21049882/changing-weather-is-changing-the-construction-industry [https://perma.cc/9HJD -VC4S].

267. Teresa Wiltz, *Climate Change Is Making the Affordable Housing Crunch Worse*, PEW CHARITABLE TRUSTS (Aug. 30, 2019), https://www.pewtrusts.org/en/research-and-analysis/blogs /stateline/2019/08/30/climate-change-is-making-the-affordable-housing-crunch-worse [https://perma .cc/K4B2-36QU].

268. Guillermo Ortiz, Heidi Schultheis, Valerie Novack, & Aleah Holt, *A Perfect Storm, Extreme Weather as an Affordable Housing Crisis Multiplier*, CTR. FOR AM. PROGRESS (Aug. 1, 2019, 9:01 AM), https://www.americanprogress.org/issues/green/reports/2019/08/01/473067/a-perfect -storm-2/ [https://perma.cc/K5TQ-MPZC].

In accordance with the National Environmental Policy Act, the Council on Environmental Quality (CEQ) released a draft report in 2010, updated in 2014, with final guidance in 2016, providing a framework for federal agencies to understand, incorporate, and coordinate activities regarding the impact of greenhouse gases and ensuing climate change on the subject areas each agency governs.[269] An updated final rule was published in 2020.[270] This guidance provides only the starting point for agencies to determine which climate change impacts warrant consideration in their environmental assessments and environmental impact statements.

A. HUD, Climate Change, and Affordable Housing

Per the CEQ guidance, HUD must consider the particular impacts of climate change on vulnerable communities.[271] HUD's Office of Environment and Energy maintains its environmental regulations and guidance on HUD Exchange, along with a variety of web-based tools that can help builders, community groups, and policy makers to better plan for possible environmental impacts on projects.[272]

HUD has been evolving into a source of resources for unmet disaster needs through the Community Development Block Grant (CDBG) program. The CDBG Disaster Recovery program was first provided in 1992.[273] More funds have been appropriated annually since then for subsequent disasters to help municipalities and states recover from presidentially declared disasters, especially in low-income areas.[274] This flexible funding can include help to address housing needs.[275] Another funding program created by HUD in 2018 to help states recover from disasters occurring in 2015 through 2017 is the CDBG Mitigation (CDBG-MIT) Program.[276] As with some Federal Emergency Management

---

269. *Final Guidance for Federal Departments and Agencies on Consideration of Greenhouse Gas Emissions and the Effects of Climate Change in National Environmental Policy Act Reviews*, Executive Office of the President, Council on Environmental Quality (2016), https://obamawhitehouse.archives.gov/sites/whitehouse.gov/files/documents/nepa_final_ghg_guidance.pdf [https://perma.cc/6Z4H-6EKR].

270. Update to the Regulations Implementing the Procedural Provisions of the National Environmental Policy Act, 85 Fed. Reg. 43,304 (July 16, 2020), https://www.federalregister.gov/documents/2020/07/16/2020-15179/update-to-the-regulations-implementing-the-procedural-provisions-of-the-national-environmental [https://perma.cc/J86F-A7G6].

271. *See* 24 C.F.R. pt. 50; *Environmental Justice*, HUD Exch., https://www.hudexchange.info/programs/environmental-review/environmental-justice/ [https://perma.cc/PAC9-7V29] *citing to* Executive Order 12898, "Federal Actions to Address Environmental Justice in Minority Populations and Low-income Populations" (1994) (last visited June 8, 2021).

272. *See Environmental Review*, HUD Exch., https://www.hudexchange.info/programs/environmental-review/ [https://perma.cc/PQR7-YCC3] (last visited June 8, 2021); *see Environmental Assessments*, HUD Exch., https://www.hudexchange.info/programs/environmental-review/environmental-assessments/ [https://perma.cc/6879-ZQTR] (last visited June 8, 2021).

273. *See CDBG-Disaster Recovery Grant History 1992–2017*, U.S. Dep't of Hous. & Urban Dev. (2017), https://files.hudexchange.info/resources/documents/CDBG-DR-Grant-History.pdf [https://perma.cc/5Z9S-Z9VT].

274. *See Community Development Block Grant Disaster Recovery CDBG-DR Overview*, U.S. Dep't of Hous. & Urban Dev. (Mar. 2020), https://files.hudexchange.info/resources/documents/CDBG-Disaster-Recovery-Overview.pdf [https://perma.cc/WP5Z-5ZHZ].

275. 24 C.F.R. § 570.201.

276. 84 Fed. Reg. 45,838 (Aug. 30, 2019).

Agency (FEMA) funding, grantees must conduct a broad spectrum risk assessment as the foundation for projects and programs. "Grantees must also assess how the use of CDBG–MIT funds may affect members of protected classes under fair housing and civil rights laws, racially and ethnically concentrated areas, as well as concentrated areas of poverty; will promote more resilient affordable housing and will respond to natural hazard related impacts."[277] In addition, any proposed mitigation programs must prioritize and describe how they will prioritize protection of low- and moderate-income residents.[278] If housing "resiliency" is a goal, the mitigation plan must describe how it will be achieved for housing for vulnerable populations, ". . . including the following housing: Transitional housing, permanent supportive housing, permanent housing serving individuals and families (including subpopulations) that are homeless and at-risk of homelessness, and public housing developments."[279]

B. FEMA and Affordable Housing

As households are displaced by disasters—permanently or temporarily—whether they will have access to affordable housing is critically important. Related questions are the quality and siting of that housing, and who will have access to it. FEMA was directed in 2006 to create a national disaster housing strategy, amongst other disaster mitigation and avoidance mandates.[280] In addition to coordinating with key federal agencies and organizations, the law mandated that the strategy developed ". . . outline the most efficient and cost effective Federal programs that will best meet the short-term and long-term housing needs of individuals and households affected by a major disaster, . . . [and] describe programs directed to meet the needs of special needs and low-income populations and ensure that a sufficient number of housing units are provided for individuals with disabilities. . . ."[281] The authorizing statute also requires the following: minimum disaster housing assistance requirements for residents with vision, hearing, or mobility impairments (localities can request higher amounts); taking into account the needs of special needs residents; and that all federal entities administering disaster services (including housing related) maintain interpretation and translation assistance.[282]

FEMA's most recent report on disaster preparedness, published in May 2020, calls out the need for disaster planners to account for the housing needs of those most vulnerable who are affected by disaster, including homeless, precariously housed and incarcerated populations, and people with disabilities.[283] It is clear that the federal government will be called upon to provide increasing amounts of disaster relief to house residents, especially for those who are low-income and communities of color more likely to have been in the path of climate disaster. Affordable housing developers will also have to evolve and design

---

277. *Id.* at 45,847.
278. *Id.*
279. *Id.*
280. Pub. L. No. 109–295, title VI, § 683, 120 Stat. 1446 (Oct. 4, 2006). *See also* 6 U.S.C. § 772.
281. 6 U.S.C. § 772.
282. *Id.*
283. Planning Considerations: Disaster Housing Guidance for State, Local, Tribal and Territorial Partners. FEMA (May 2020), https://www.fema.gov/sites/default/files/2020-07/planning-considerations-disaster-housing.pdf [https://perma.cc/GW7C-F7M5].

housing to address the emerging patterns of extreme weather and other climate change–related damage. Competition for land located in safer zones will likely increase dramatically in years to come, which will affect affordability of housing and development costs.

C. Insurance, Climate Change, and Affordable Housing

Siting of housing and insurance concerns have a relationship with climate change in a number of different ways. A great deal of affordable housing is sited currently in locations prone to flooding from rising sea levels.[284] The likely future for affordable housing includes avoiding building in flood zones and rebuilding from areas that are more frequently experiencing climate impact. Insurance costs will undoubtedly help drive selection of building materials and building site selection as insurers assess the true cost of climate change. Insurers are already taking into account the increased costs of construction caused by severe weather.[285] Equity in siting of affordable housing from an environmental standpoint is a growing fair housing concern.[286] A related issue is access to affordable energy as a component of affordable housing, both in terms of siting and construction methods and materials.[287]

Recently, perhaps in response to large numbers of claims on federal flood protection funds due to climate change, the federal government has shifted from buying out residents who own homes in flood plains to requiring localities, in exchange for access to federal flood protection funds, to exercise eminent domain to force those property owners to sell their homes to localities.[288] Whether this has a disparate impact on owners historically shut out of access to affordable homeownership remains to be seen, but it seems unlikely that homeowners forced to sell under such circumstances are recovering the true value that the home had for them.

For over 50 years, there has been federal law (e.g., the National Flood Insurance Act of 1968[289] and Flood Disaster Protection Act of 1973[290]) creating then expanding access to the National Flood Insurance Program, which has made federally subsidized flood insurance available to homeowners and requires that owners obtain flood insurance when obtaining financing from a government insured lender when the home is in a special flood hazard

---

284. Wiltz, *supra* note 267.

285. *Climate Change in Construction: 5 Things You Should Know*, Zurich Am. Ins. Co. (Aug. 23, 2019), https://www.zurichna.com/knowledge/articles/2019/08/climate-change-in-construction-5-things-you-should-know [https://perma.cc/E7EB-C7ZN].

286. *See* Jeremy Deaton, *Climate Change Is Creating an Affordable Housing Crisis in Miami*, Huffpost (Aug. 29, 2018, 12:12 PM), https://www.huffpost.com/entry/climate-change-is-creating-an-affordable-housing-crisis_b_5b85b639e4b0f023e4a60441 [https://perma.cc/KAH8-J8CP]; *see Adapting to Climate Change: Cities and the Urban Poor*, Int'l Hous. Coal. (Aug. 2011) https://ihcglobal.org/wp-content/uploads/2016/04/Climate-Change-and-the-Urban-Poor.pdf [https://perma.cc/2H28-S8WG].

287. *Uncovering Energy Inequity*, Cmty. Climate Collaborative (July, 2020), https://static1.squarespace.com/static/5a0c67f5f09ca475c85d7686/t/5f2071d39eb94c7ad741a90d/1595961851763/C3%27s+Uncovering+Energy+Inequity.pdf [https://perma.cc/RJK9-9SW5].

288. Christopher Flavelle, *Trump Administration Presses Cities to Evict Homeowners from Flood Zones*, N.Y. Times (Mar. 11, 2020), https://www.nytimes.com/2020/03/11/climate/government-land-eviction-floods.html [https://perma.cc/C9GJ-2WKB].

289. Pub. L. No. 90-448, tit. XIII, 82 Stat. 572 (42 U.S.C. 4001 *et seq.*) (Aug. 1, 1968).

290. Pub. L. No. 93-234; 87 Stat. 975 (1973).

area.[291] Most insurers, in fact, exclude flood coverage from standard homeowners insurance because of claims costs.[292] Further federal legislation was passed over the ensuing decades implementing a range of natural disaster responses (e.g., coastal protection, purchase of properties damaged by natural disasters).[293]

In 2012, Congress extended federal flood insurance laws and expanded requirements, including mandating further flood plain mapping to make sure insurance rates more accurately reflect loss risk in flood zones, with the goal of transitioning subsidized flood insurance rates into risk-based rates.[294] Given concerns raised by localities regarding the likely significant increase in insurance costs to homeowners in flood plains, including some homeowners not previously required to have such coverage, implementation of this law was slowed.[295] Through 2019 amendments to the act, regulated lending institutions were required to accept policies that meet the statutory definition of "private flood insurance" in the updated Biggert–Waters Act, as well as plans issued by mutual aid societies that do not meet the statutory definition of "private flood insurance," subject to certain restrictions; federal agencies supervising financial institutions issued joint regulations implementing this new law.[296] This change may increase the ability of affordable housing developers and the public to find flood insurance that is somewhat more affordable, but loss rates may ultimately drive most insurers away from providing homeowners' insurance in flood prone areas.

291. James M. Wright, The Nation's Response to Flood Disasters: A Historical Account (Wendy L. Hessler ed. 2000), Association of State Flood Plain Managers, https://biotech.law.lsu.edu/blog/hist_fpm.pdf [https://perma.cc/6YUA-KQ3E].

292. *What Is Covered by Standard Homeowners Insurance?* Ins. Information Inst., https://www.iii.org/article/what-covered-standard-homeowners-policy [https://perma.cc/NU7B-7WZV] (last visited June 8, 2020).

293. *See* Wright, *supra* note 289.

294. Biggert-Waters Flood Insurance Reform Act of 2012, Pub. L. No. 112-141, 126 Stat. 916 (2012).

295. *The Biggert-Waters Flood Insurance Reform Act of 2012*, Municipal Ass'n of S.C. (Mar. 2014), https://www.masc.sc/Pages/resources/The-Biggert-Waters-Flood-Insurance-Reform-Act-of-2012.aspx.

296. *New Rule Covers Private Flood Insurance*, Office of the Comptroller of the Currency (Feb. 12, 2019), https://occ.gov/news-issuances/news-releases/2019/nr-ia-2019-15.html [https://perma.cc/C84C-CUST].

Federal Sources of Financing

9

Rochelle E. Lento

I. INTRODUCTION

The Department of Housing and Urban Development (HUD) defines housing as "affordable" if not more than 30 percent of a family's income goes toward housing costs.[1] However, this is a goal often unmet by the market alone, which has no mechanism by which to ensure that housing is priced at a level that families can afford.[2] Generally, for "low-income households" (defined as those with incomes at or below 50 percent of area median income) and even for many "moderate income households" (defined as those with incomes at or below 80 percent of area median income), housing can be affordable under HUD's definition only if it is subsidized by government or other sources.

The term "subsidized housing" means that some form of private or government financing is included in the development sources of revenue that offsets the overall costs of the development, and makes the housing "affordable" as just defined. There are a few types of subsidy: public housing, federally supported mortgages, Section 8 project-based subsidies, Section 8 certificates or vouchers, Veteran Affairs Supportive Housing (VASH) vouchers, and tax credit projects.[3] These subsidies include those provided for rental housing and those provided to create homeownership opportunities. The subsidy may be provided in any of three ways: (1) directly to a developer to build the housing; (2) directly to the tenant to subsidize the rent so that the housing is more affordable; or (3) directly to the homeowner in the form of down-payment assistance or mortgage insurance.

This chapter discusses some of the numerous sources of federal financing that are available as subsidies to make housing "affordable" under HUD's

---

1. HUD, Defining Housing Affordability (June 2021), https://www.huduser.gov/portal/pdredge/pdr-edge-featd-article-081417.html.

2. *Id.*

3. Tiffany C. Wright, *What Does Subsidized Housing Mean?*, POCKETSENSE.COM (last updated Dec. 12, 2019).

definition.[4] Most of the sources referenced share the criteria of being long-standing, well-established, highly regulated, based on statutory or regulatory guidance, and dependent on annual federal budget appropriations. A key distinguishing characteristic is how the various sources are administered: some flow through participating jurisdictions (which may be local, county, or state governments); others are directly administered by HUD. The primary focus is on federal sources for rental housing, with limited coverage of homeownership sources or programs.

Section II discusses the Low-Income Housing Tax Credit (LIHTC) Program. This program remains the backbone of affordable rental housing being developed in this country during the past 15 years and has continued to evolve and develop over the last few years. Because of its complexity and emergence as the most significant source of affordable rental housing support, the LIHTC program is discussed most thoroughly. Section III discusses the HOME Investment Partnership Program. Section IV describes the Community Development Block Grant (CDBG) Program and the CDBG-COVID or CDBG-CV Program. Section V discusses bond financing of multifamily housing. Section VI describes a variety of direct HUD funding programs, including Supportive Housing for the Elderly, Supportive Housing for People with Disabilities, Section 8 rental assistance, certain programs benefiting homeless people, and selected environmental/energy programs. Section VII describes Rural Housing Service Programs. Section VIII discusses Homeownership Initiatives.[5]

II. LOW-INCOME HOUSING TAX CREDITS[6]

A. Overview

The low-income housing tax credit (LIHTC) is an indirect federal subsidy for qualified low-income rental housing, made available under Section 42 of the Internal Revenue Code

---

4. Besides the funding programs covered in other chapters in Part II, additional housing programs are sponsored by the federal government that are either discussed in other chapters or may be accessed from other resources. Chapter 5, *supra*, discusses some state funding programs for affordable housing. Chapter 8, *supra*, discusses the Federal Home Loan Banks' two primary affordable housing programs. Although not a federally financed program, the Federal Home Loan Banks wholesale banks chartered by Congress in 1932 have become a prime source of funding for affordable housing development. *See* http://www.fhlbanks.com (last accessed Apr. 5, 2021). Chapter 13, *infra*, discusses sources of financing for mixed-use developments. Chapter 15, *infra*, discusses some federal and state housing preservation funding programs. See COVID-19 Pandemic Response in Cities: Ensuring Housing Stability for All Residents, National League of Cities Report, https://covid19.nlc.org. For general legislative and policy updates on affordable housing initiatives, *see* http://www.novogradac.com or www.housingfinance.com (last accessed Apr. 13, 2021).

5. Chapters 10 and 11, *infra*, provide similar information regarding state and local financing sources, respectively.

6. For purposes of this section, Low-Income Housing Tax Credit, or LIHTC, is used; however, the IRS often refers to this program as Low-Income Housing Credit in some publications. *See* INTERNAL REVENUE SERVICE, MARKET SEGMENT SPECIALIZATION PROGRAM: LOW-INCOME HOUSING CREDIT, http://www.irs.gov (last accessed April 5, 2021). *See also* What Is the Low-Income Housing Tax Credit Program and How Does It Work?, http://www.taxpolicycenter.org.

of 1986, as amended (Section 42).[7] The Tax Reform Act of 1986[8] created the LIHTC program.[9] The LIHTC is designed to create an incentive for investors, such as private corporations and banks, to invest in affordable housing. The LIHTC creates "tax credits" that investors can take advantage of, and in turn those investors provide equity for affordable housing development. The tax credits offset the investor's federal income taxes on a dollar-for-dollar basis for a ten-year period. The equity provided by the investor covers a significant portion of the construction expenses of the housing and also reduces rents for low-income tenants.

For tax and oversight reasons, these investors will become a part of the ownership structure for LIHTC projects. There is not a standard structure for a LIHTC transaction, as it will depend on the various types of financing that are combined to develop the project. Financing is usually layered with other HUD programs (i.e., CDBG, HOME) or Tax Exempt Bonds, each of which will have its own requirements and restrictions. Also, as a general rule, the most onerous program requirements will apply. Regardless of the financing sources, in a LIHTC transaction structured as a limited partnership, the investor will be the limited partner and the developer will be the general partner. In a LIHTC transaction structured as a limited liability company, all parties will be members, with the investor as the investor member and the developer usually designated as the managing member. (Ownership structures are discussed further in Section D *infra*.) Investors earn tax credits by investing in low-income housing, primarily through the use of tax syndicates.

Although the LIHTC was initially a temporary program, the Omnibus Reconciliation Act of 1993[10] extended the LIHTC permanently. Since 1986, the LIHTC has become the primary tool for the creation of affordable rental housing in the United States.[11] Although federal loans and other subsidies have suffered from federal budget cuts and other changes in federal housing policy, the LIHTC has been a stable source of financing for affordable housing.

B. Mechanics of the LIHTC Program

1. The Basics

The federal government annually authorizes the amount of tax credits available to the LIHTC program. These tax credits are distributed to the states through an allocation formula, which is based on population of the states. Pursuant to IRS regulation, state

---

7. I.R.C. § 42 (2010); Treas. Reg. § 1.42 (2010). See Chapter 8, *supra*, for a discussion of the application of the federal Fair Housing Act to the LIHTC program.

8. Tax Reform Act of 1986, Pub. L. No. 99-514, 100 Stat. 2085 (1986) (codified as amended at I.R.C. § 42 (2010)).

9. Senator Alan Cranston and Representative Alan Gonzalez introduced the Cranston-Gonzalez National Affordable Housing Act, Pub. L. No. 101-625, 104 Stat. 4079 (1990) (codified at 42 U.S.C. §§ 12701 *et seq.* (2010)).

10. Omnibus Budget Reconciliation Act, Pub. L. No. 103-66, 107 Stat. 312 (1993) (codified at 26 U.S.C. §§ 1391–1397D (2010) (amended by the Taxpayer Relief Act of 1997, Pub. L. No. 105-34, 111 Stat. 788, 885 (1997)).

11. Substantially all of the affordable rental housing that has been built since 1986 has been created with the use of low-income housing tax credit[s]. *Id.* HUD-User Database claims that 1,843,000 housing units were placed in service between 1987 and 2010. HUD, Low-Income Housing Tax Credits, http://www.huduser.org/datasets/lihtc.html (last accessed Apr. 5, 2021).

governments must develop and adopt Qualified Allocation Plans (QAPs), which provide guidelines for their programs on how they will allocate their tax credits.[12] The federal Low-Income Housing Tax Credit Program requires each state agency that allocates tax credits, which are generally called housing finance agencies or housing authorities, to have a QAP. The QAP sets out the state's eligibility priorities for awarding federal tax credits to housing developers for affordable housing developments.[13] States review applications under their QAPs to make awards of tax credit allocations to qualifying housing developers[14] who compete for the tax credits. There are a variety of criteria that states must use in allocating LIHTCs among potential low-income housing projects.

Pursuant to the terms of Housing and Economic Recovery Act (HERA) of 2008[15] (discussed in further detail later in this chapter and in Chapter 7 *supra*), there are two additional criteria that states must use in allocating LIHTCs among potential low-income housing projects: "energy efficiency of the project" and "the historic nature of the project."[16] Through a review titled *Energy Efficiency for All*, it was reported that State Housing Agencies are using a variety of strategies to promote energy efficiency, including Green Capital or Physical Needs Assessment, Energy and Water Audits, Water Conservation, Renewable Energy Incentives as mechanisms to preserve affordable rental housing's energy and water efficiency.[17] An explanation prepared by the Joint Tax Committee clarifies that "historic nature" relates to encouraging rehabilitation of certified historic structures. Once LIHTCs are awarded to the housing developers, the developers identify investors and then negotiate a price for the credits and other essential business terms for the transaction. (See Figure 9.1, General Accounting Office chart.)

Tax credits will likely only fund a portion of the total development costs, requiring the developer to seek other sources of funding for the development. After they have assembled the rest of the financing, received all necessary land-use and other approvals, and complied with all the due diligence of the development funders, the developer builds the project and rents it up. As long as the project is in compliance with all program regulations, the tax credit investors take advantage of the tax credits in succeeding years against their federal income tax liability until they are exhausted, or for up to ten years.

---

12. All states have adopted QAPs, which provide guidelines for applications and scoring for LIHTC awards. States generally administer the LIHTC as a competitive program and award credits in two annual rounds. A state's QAP may include special set-asides and incentive scoring systems.

13. Qualified Allocation Plan, by Ed Gramlich, Director of Regulatory Affairs, National Low Income Housing Coalition, https://nilhc.org.

14. The terms *developer*, *partnership*, and *owner* are used in this chapter interchangeably and refer to the same party.

15. H.R. 3221 on July 30, 2008, included a package of housing legislation that incorporated a number of modifications to the LIHTC credit, rehabilitation and tax-exempt bond programs, temporary cap increases, and a number of other provisions intending to encourage the financial and housing markets. H.R. 3221, 110th Cong. § 3002, Pub. L. 110-289 (2008).

16. H.R. 3221, 110th Cong. § 3004(d), Pub. L. 110-289 (2008).

17. Energy Efficiency Program Guide, https://www.hud.gov/sites/documents/21647_GUIDE .PDF (last accessed October 2021).

Transferring Tax Credits from the Federal Government to the Private Sector

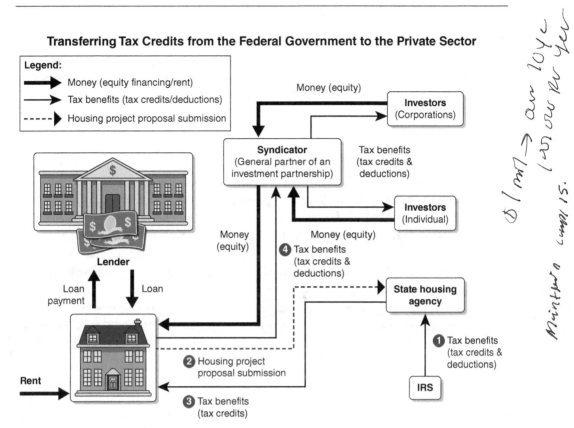

Figure 9.1 Transferring Tax Credits from the Federal Government to the Private Sector

2. Compliance and Extended-Use Period

Although the credit is claimed annually for only a ten-year period, the project must be maintained as low-income housing for a 15-year "compliance period," and the project must continue to be restricted for low-income households for an "extended use" period of at least 15 additional years.[18]

The LIHTC is a housing program governed under the Treasury Department and the Internal Revenue Service (IRS) through required annual tax returns. State housing agencies monitor compliance with IRC Section 42 during the 15-year compliance period with notice to the IRS.[19] In addition to the 15-year compliance period, all projects receiving credits after 1989 must comply with an extended low-income housing use or regulatory agreement entered into between the state credit agency and the project owner at the end of the first year in which the credit is claimed.[20] This extended use agreement binds the owner (and its successors) to maintain the low-income use during a defined "extended use period," which period is the greater of 30 years or a date specified by the state credit allocation agency. Generally, there are provisions for termination of the extended-use period, but

---

18. Part I Section 24—Low Income Housing Credit, §§ 1.42-5, 1.42-15, 1.103 and I.R.C. § 42(h) (6)(D).

19. Internal Revenue Forms 1065, 8586, 8609 and Form 8609m Schedule A must be filed annually.

20. I.R.C. § 42(h) (2010).

those must comport with the Internal Revenue Code (IRC or the Code) Section 42.[21] The extended use period may also terminate due to foreclosure by a lending institution.[22] However, the lender must assure tenants are not displaced and must continue certain restrictions for a minimum three-year period.[23] In practice, private lenders that provide construction or permanent loans for these projects generally must subordinate their loans to the extended-use agreements.

3. *Applicable Percentages*

The applicable percentage of credit awarded will depend on the type of project, with the present value of the credit equal to either 70 percent or 30 percent of the cost of the low-income units. The 70 percent subsidy (corresponding to the 9 percent credit[24]) is available for new construction or substantial rehabilitation that is not otherwise federally subsidized. For those projects that qualify for the 70 percent subsidy, the amount of annual credit will equal approximately 9 percent of the "qualified basis" (as defined *infra*) or building costs for ten years.[25] The 30 percent subsidy (corresponding to the 4 percent credit) is generally available for acquisition of existing buildings or for new building construction that are federally subsidized with the same general rules of applicability as the 9 percent credit.[26] In all states, the 4 percent credit is also available for those projects supported by bond financing.[27]

While the 9 percent LIHTC rate has been fixed as such since 2013, only recently, on December 27, 2020, legislation was signed into law fixing the rate for the 30 percent present value LIHTC rate at 4 percent. To qualify to the 4 percent floor, however, under the new law, buildings must be placed in service after December 31, 2020, and either (1) receive a LIHTC allocation after December 31, 2020, or (2) be financed by a tax-exempt bond issued: after December 31, 2020 that is subject to a State's applicable bond volume cap. There are many key questions that must be addressed to determine a project's feasibility as

---

21. *Id.* § 42(h)(6)(F) allows for the termination of an extended use period if the state housing agency is unable to find a purchaser for the project in an amount equal to a minimum statutory price as defined in the Code.

22. I.R.C. § 42(h)(6)((D)(2010).

23. *Id.* § 42(h)(6)(E)(ii). Some tax attorneys believe that a three-year minimum no eviction rule and no increase in gross rent applies.

24. The applicable percentage rate is that which is prescribed by the Dep't of Treasury for either the month in which the building is placed in service (i.e., occupied) or at the election of the taxpayer, the month in which the taxpayer and the state housing finance authority enter into a binding agreement designating the credit amount to be allocated to the building. (I.R.C. § 42(b)(2)(A) (2010)). The applicable percentage for nonfederally subsidized new buildings places in service after July 30, 2008, and before December 31, 2013, shall be not less than 9 percent. For more information, see I.R.S. Notice 2008-106, which provides greater guidance on the 9 percent floor, or the Housing and Economic Recovery Act of 2008, as discussed in Chapter 7, *supra*.

25. Rev. Rul. 2004-44. 2004-19 I.R.B. 885, Table 4.

26. *Id.*

27. *See, e.g.*, Michigan State Housing Development Authority, Qualified Allocation Plan 2009 at 21, http://www.michigan.gov/mshda/0,1607,7-141--31750--,00.html (last accessed Apr. 12, 2021).

to whether a project will qualify for the 4 percent floor, and projects should be evaluated on a case-by-case basis to assure eligibility for this floor.[28]

The result is significant additional equity, however, there may be unintended tax consequences to the tax credit investor that must be closely evaluated, such as a reallocation of tax benefits if an investor's capital account goes negative, and/or the state housing agency may view the additional equity as a windfall and reduce its bond financing or gap financing for a project as a way to offset the increased revenue from additional equity. At this writing, there is uncertainty in the industry as to whether bonds are deemed "issued" on the date they were subject to a volume cap or on the date they are actually drawn, and whether an additional 2021 bond issuance will qualify a project awarded tax credits in 2020 can qualify for the 4 percent floor. Additional guidance is needed.

Under previous law, projects receiving below-market loans, defined as those with interest rates less than the applicable federal rate (AFR) were not allowed to make use of the 70 percent subsidy and were limited to the 4 percent credit, however with the changes from HERA, that has changed. Additionally, projects receiving any federal subsidies other than tax-exempt bonds, such as HUD HOME or HOPE VI (both discussed *infra*) subsidies are now eligible to qualify for the 9 percent tax credit under HERA.[29]

There are special rules under the Code and Regulations that apply to the 4 percent credit, which is available for rehabilitation expenditures and for acquisition costs utilizing LIHTCs. Rehabilitation expenditures may be treated similar to new construction provided (1) the expenditures during a 24-month period equal at least the greater of (a) 20 percent of the building's "adjusted basis" (defined *infra*) as of the first day of the period or (b) $6,000 or more for each low-income unit, indexed for inflation.[30] To receive acquisition credits, existing buildings must be substantially rehabilitated,[31] and buildings must not have been placed in service under the LIHTC program in the ten-year period prior to acquisition.[32] However, even though most properties placed in service within the past ten years could not be acquired using the credit with a few very limited exceptions to this rule, a provision of HERA creates an exception for federally or state-assisted properties. This exception applies to properties substantially assisted, financed, or operated under Section 8, 221(d)(3), 221(d)(4), or 236 of the National Housing Act; Section 515 of the Housing Act of 1949, or "any other housing program administered by the Department of Housing and Urban Development or by the Rural Housing Service."[33]

Finally, the building has to be purchased from an unrelated seller.[34] The previously existing LIHTC related party rule requiring that there be no more than a 10 percent relationship between the taxpayer claiming acquisition credits and the seller of the property

---

28. Kimberly C. Moore, *Congress Establishes the 4 Percent Floor to Support Affordable Housing*, Gʀᴀᴠᴇʟ2Gᴀᴠᴇʟ (Jan. 21, 2021), https://www.gravel2gavel.com/congress-four-percent-floor-affordable-housing/.

29. *Id.*

30. I.R.C. § 42(e)(3)(A)(ii)(TI) (2010); Rev. Rul. 91-38, 1991-2 C.B. 3; H.R. 3221, 110th Cong. § 3003, Pub. L. 110-289 (2008).

31. I.R.C. § 42(d)(2)(B)(iv) (2010).

32. *Id.* § 42(d)(2)(B)(ii).

33. H.R. 3221, 110th Cong. § 3003(f), Pub. L. 110-289 (2008).

34. *See* I.R.C. § 42(d)(2)(B)(i) (2010).

has been amended by HERA, in that this number is increased to 50 percent, conforming it to the related party rule for the rest of the IRC.[35] This means that a member in the purchasing entity that was also in the selling entity won't be deemed to be a related party unless this member has more than a 50 percent membership interest in the entity. This provision will make it easier to preserve LIHTC properties in need of recapitalization by allowing a wider group of multi-investor funds to acquire those properties. Additionally, this change should enable and encourage the transfer and sale of more existing properties for syndication with tax credits for the first time, and re-syndication and rehabilitation with new tax credits, including old HUD and tax credit properties.

4. Calculation of the LIHTC, Basis Rules and Depreciation

LIHTCs can only be used on the residential low-income portion of a building. If the building is mixed use, other sources will have to fund the commercial or retail components. Buildings do not have to be 100 percent low-income, and more often there is a mixed-income approach with some units as affordable and others as market rate in the same development. There is not a minimum number of units for a project to be eligible for LIHTC funding, however, the more low-income units included in the development, the more tax credits the development can be awarded and the more financially feasible the project will be. In addition, deeper targeting will garner more points on a LIHTC proposal for the competitive 9 percent program.[36] The amount of LIHTC a building owner may claim in the initial year is the building's "qualified basis" multiplied by the applicable percentage of the available credit.[37] To qualify for the credit, a project must be a qualified low-income building.[38]

The terms "eligible basis" and "qualified basis" are distinct and are defined in relation to each other. The "eligible basis" for a building is the adjusted basis, which is generally the cost of new construction, acquisition, and the costs of improvements to the property.[39] The eligible basis can include certain amenities (i.e., the cost of certain personal property and site improvements such as appliances, air conditioning, or parking areas) at the end of the first taxable year of the credit.[40] Land costs are not allowable in eligible basis.[41] The "qualified basis" of any building is equal to that portion of the building's eligible basis attributable to low-income tenants. The "qualified basis" for a taxable year is equal to an amount based on the applicable fraction for the tax credits multiplied by the "eligible basis." To determine the applicable fraction, one must determine the percentage of low-income occupancies within a building. The formula is equal to the lesser of (1) the number of low-income units divided by the total number of units (or unit fraction) or (2) the floor space of the low-income units divided by the floor space of all of the residential units (floor space fraction). Whenever 100 percent of the units in a LIHTC development are low-income, this

35. H.R. 3221, 110th Cong. §3003(e), Pub. L. 110-289 (2008).

36. C.P. Scully, A. Gold & N. DuBois, *The Low Income Housing Tax Credit: How It Works and Who It Serves*, http://www.urban.org (July 2018).

37. I.R.C. §42(a) (2010).

38. *See id.* §42(a)(2) and (c)(2), which state the building must remain low-income during the 15-year compliance period.

39. *See* I.R.C. §103(b)(2010) and Reg. §1.103-8(b)(4)(iii).

40. *Id.*

41. *See* Tech. Adv. Mem. 200043017 (Oct. 27, 2000).

becomes a simple formula, since the applicable percentage will allow the qualified basis to equal the eligible basis. The types of costs that can qualify for the credit are acquisition, rehabilitation expenses, construction, and construction-related costs.[42]

The IRS has issued regulations, letter rulings, and Technical Advice Memoranda that have addressed what can and cannot be included in "eligible basis."[43] Soft costs[44] are generally includable. However, they will be subject to greater scrutiny, especially if related parties[45] are involved. Developers' fees are always includable. However, the fair value of those fees and the percentage that is earned at a particular point in time are often subject to greater scrutiny.[46] Guidance from the IRS has resulted in certain costs for environmental remediation, soil correction, landscaping, and surveys being questionable for inclusion in eligible basis, unless those cost items are depreciable.

Under previous law, eligible basis would generally need to be reduced if the project received federal grants prior to the end of the compliance period. The only exceptions to this requirement were certain federal rental assistance programs such as Section 8. A new provision in HERA clarifies the treatment of federal grants to make clear that the basis reduction rule only applies to federally funded grants received prior to the compliance period. The explanatory language accompanying the bill clarifies that no basis reduction is required for (1) federally funded rental, operating, or interest rate payment assistance programs that involve ongoing payments used to support operation of the property; and (2) loans (regardless of interest rate) made from the proceeds of federally funded grants. This provision will make it easier to combine LIHTC assistance with Section 236 interest rate payments, as well as federal rental and operating assistance under a variety of programs (Native American Housing Assistance and Self-Determination Act of 1996 (NAHASDA),[47] McKinney-Vento Act, etc.) not currently allowed under Treasury regulations.[48]

Depreciation rules depend on when a LIHTC building is "placed-in-service," which is defined as the point in time when a building is ready for occupancy by low-income tenants, and generally marks the beginning of the tax credit compliance period.[49] Generally, for buildings placed in service before January 1, 2018, the deprecation is 40 years, versus 27.5 years under general depreciation rules; whereas for buildings placed in service after December 31, 2017, the alternative depreciation period is 30 years, not 40.[50] Bonus depreciation for a qualified property, which is generally property with a recovery period

---

42. I.R.C. § 42(d) (2010). *See* Novogradac, Low Income Housing Tax Credit Handbook (2010 ed.) §§ 3:1–3:3, at 56–59.

43. *See* Rev. Rul. 2004-82, 2004-35 I.R.B. 350, http://www.irs.gov/pub/irs-irbs/irb04-35.pdf (last accessed Apr. 26, 2021).

44. Soft costs refer to professional fees for architects and environmental consultants, title and recording fees, developer's fees, insurance costs, payment/performance bonds, permit fees, and so on.

45. *See* I.R.C. § 49(a)(1)(D)(v), which incorporates at-risk rules contained at I.R.C. § 465(b)(3)(C) to determine whether someone is a related party.

46. Tech. Adv. Mem. 200043017 (Oct. 27, 2000); Tech. Adv. Mem. 200044004 (Nov. 3, 2000).

47. 25 U.S.C. § 4101 (2010).

48. H.R. 3221, 110th Cong. § 3003, Pub. L. No. 110-289 (2008).

49. https://www.novoco.com/resource-centers/affordable-housing-tax-credits/lihtc-basics /about-lihtc (last accessed Apr. 26, 2021).

50. *End-of-Year Planning for LIHTC Properties*, http://www.novoco.com (Aug. 6, 2019).

of 20 years or less, can be claimed by a LIHTC property owner, and this is governed under IRC Section 168(k). These rules were recently modified to allow 100 percent of the depreciable basis to be expensed for a qualifying property that is placed in service after September 27, 2017, and before January 1, 2023.[51]

5. *Rent Restrictions and Other Requirements*

The LIHTC program requires that a minimum number of units must be rented to low-income tenants at reduced rates. Section 42 of the Code requires a building to satisfy three specific tests: (1) the minimum "set-aside test,"[52] (2) the rent restriction test,[53] and (3) the building must be suitable for residential occupancy.[54]

Under the minimum set-aside test (often referred to as the 20/40 or 40/60 test), either:

(i) 20 percent or more of the units in a project must be rented and occupied by tenants whose incomes are 50 percent or less of the area median gross income (AMI);[55] or

(ii) 40 percent or more of the units in a project must be rented and occupied by tenants whose incomes are 60 percent or less of the area median gross income.[56]

An irrevocable election of the minimum set-aside must be made at the time of the submission of the IRS Form 8609, or Low-Income Housing Credit Allocation Certification, or, more simply put, the owner's tax return for the first year of the credit period. Generally, most developers will establish these rental targets at a much earlier point, and include them in the application for tax credits submitted to the relevant state housing tax credit authority. Often, to make an application more competitive, owners will target a higher percentage of the units to a high percentage of low-income renters than is required under this minimum set-aside test.

More recently, the IRS has implemented a new approach to income targeting known as income averaging, which allows LIHTC owners to elect to serve tenants with incomes of up to 80 percent of AMI, and have these households qualify for LIHTC units. The key is that the LIHTC owner must be able to demonstrate that the average income/rent limit of the development remains at or below 60 percent AMI.[57] Even if a LIHTC owner elects to use the income averaging approach to allow greater opportunity to rent to a broader range

---

51. Tax Cuts and Jobs Act (TCJA), Pub. Law No. 115-97, Section 113 Stat. 2054, November 2, 2017.

52. I.R.C. § 42(g) (2010).

53. *Id.*

54. Suitability for rental occupancy does not imply that LIHTC developments cannot incorporate mixed-use developments. It only implies that the tax credit can be used to finance only the residential portion of the development. The retail or commercial space must have another financing source, and all costs associated with the development or rehabilitation of the retail/commercial space must be excluded from eligible basis.

55. Area Median Income or AMI is established by the U.S. Census Bureau and periodically updated with each census. "Area" usually refers to a county or multicounty area.

56. I.R.C. § 42(g)(1) (2010). If a project is located in NYC, then a special 25/60 test is used instead of the 40/60 test, *id.* § 42(g)(4) and (g)(6).

57. *What Do Advocates Need to Know About the New Income Averaging Rules for LIHTC Properties?*, https://www.nhlp.org/wp-content/uploads/2018/06/LIHTC-Properties-Webinar-Slides.pdf (Apr. 3, 2018). Or see the Consolidated Appropriations Act of 2018, (P.L. 115-141, Dec. 31, 2020).

of tenants, that owner must still ensure that 40 percent of the units are rented to tenants at or below 40 percent.[58] Some have referred to this income averaging as the "third income test."[59]

For the 2009 calendar year and later, the measurement of area median income to determine income eligibility and rents for a LIHTC and/or tax-exempt housing bond–financed property will not be permitted to decline from the previous calendar year, codifying current HUD policy.[60] In addition, the area median income for a LIHTC or tax-exempt housing bond–financed property will rise with annual area median income increases, even if HUD freezes the area median income.[61]

The rent restriction test requires that rents charged to low-income tenants must be affordable under HUD guidelines for low-income renters, and cannot exceed 30 percent of the tenant's income reduced by a utility allowance and adjusted for family size.[62] Obviously, this rental restriction test must be calculated taking into consideration the minimum set-aside test. If rents are subsidized through Section 8, then the IRS will only consider the tenant's portion of the rent to determine if rents are affordable. Historically, LIHTC units require a six-month lease. However, general practice is to require a one-year lease for tenants to stabilize a development.[63]

The IRS has not explicitly defined the requirement that a building be "suitable for residential occupancy," but it appears to state a policy guideline that ensures that LIHTCs are utilized for quality affordable housing projects. Minimally, units must have a kitchen and bathroom to meet these criteria.[64] There are applicable local and state building code requirements (see Chapter 6). Historically, HUD has also imposed housing quality standards in addition to those requirements.[65]

Under the general public use requirement, tenant selection preferences that violate fair housing, restrict eligibility to employees of certain employers or members of social organizations are prohibited. However, the IRS audit office released guidance in January 2007 that appeared to expand the interpretation to cover any housing that targeted certain groups. Under this provision of HERA, the general public-use rule is clarified to provide that it permits buildings to restrict occupancy or have preferences that favor tenants with special needs, or who are members of a specified group under a federal or state housing program, or who are involved in artistic or literary activities.[66]

6. *Further Restrictions on Types of Housing*

In addition to the rent restrictions, the IRS has limited the use of LIHTCs to certain types of housing, and has restricted their use in other types of housing. Ineligible

---

58. *Id.*

59. *An Introduction to the Low Income Housing Tax Credit*, http://fas.org (updated Jan. 26, 2021).

60. H.R. 3221, 110th Cong. § 3009, Pub. L. No. 110-289 (2008).

61. *Id.*

62. I.R.C. § 42(g)(2) (2010).

63. Section 42 regulations, § 1.1038.

64. *See* Treas. Reg. § 1.103-8(b)(8)(i) (2005).

65. In Detroit, for example, the City's Housing & Revitalization Department has a manual entitled "Contractor's Performance Standards," which is modeled on HUD's Housing Quality Standards, and generally exceeds local and state code requirements.

66. H.R. 3221, 110th Cong. § 3004(9), Pub. L. No. 110-289 (2008).

types of housing include the following: student housing;[67] hospitals, nursing homes, and sanitariums;[68] elderly, retirement, or other housing that provides "significant services other than housing";[69] mobile homes not on "permanent foundations";[70] nursing homes or psychiatric facilities;[71] and housing that is not available to the general public.[72] None of these exclusions implies that tax credit developments cannot be targeted to certain populations or categories of tenants. For example, a market study may determine that the area being redeveloped has a need for senior housing units. Thus, a project may market and target its units toward that population, provided it is allowable by the HUD Handbook.[73]

More recently, the student restrictions in LIHTC properties have been reevaluated; and, in 2013, the Department of Housing and Urban Development revised regulations governing the HOME program for student housing; and some of these revisions have been adopted by the IRS for the LIHTC program. These policies have very specific exception criteria and if a LIHTC developer is considering developing housing for students, he or she needs to consult a professional or legal counsel.[74]

7. *State Credit Allocations*

Each state is awarded a certain amount of credits based on a minimum per person allocation.[75] States receive the equivalent of nearly $5 billion nationally in annual budget authority to issue tax credits for acquisition, rehabilitation, or new construction.[76] A project is selected to receive tax credits by the state housing authority through a competitive process. Under Section 42 of the Code, each state can determine its own system of allocation; however, certain minimal requirements are imposed.[77] All states must ensure projects meet a "locally identified housing need"[78] that must be evidenced by credible data in the form of a

---

67. Student housing is generally ineligible, except that which is for government-sponsored job training program participants, those receiving AMC payments or Title IV of the Social Security Act, or certain heads of household and their children and certain married students. I.R.C. § 42(i)(3)(D) (2010); Priv. Ltr. Rul. 200339022 (Sept. 26, 2003); I.R.S. Info. Ltr. INFO 2002-0067 (June 28, 2002); I.R.S. Info. Ltr. INFO 2000-0088 (June 30, 2000). Additionally, the exception to the prohibition on renting LIHTC units to students is expanded in HERA to include students who formerly received foster care. H.R. 3221, 110th Cong. § 3004(e), Pub. L. 110-289 (2008).

68. Treas. Reg. § 1.42-11(b)(3) (2010).

69. Treas. Reg. § 1.42-11(b)(3)(i) (2010); Notice 89-6, 1989-1 CB 625 and Ltr. Rul. 891035.

70. I.R.C. § 42 (i)(3)(A) (2010).

71. Rev. Rul. 98-47, 1998-2 C.H. 399.

72. Treas. Reg. § 1.42-9 (2010).

73. HUD, HUD Handbook 4350.3.

74. A. Champine, *Student Restrictions: HUD vs LIHTC vs HOME/US Housing Consultants*, http://www.us.hc.com (Jan. 25, 2016).

75. In 2020, the amount per credit was the greater of $2.8125 multiplied by the state population or $3,245,625. According to recent publications, this per capita calculator will remain the same for 2021. *LIHTC Per-Capital Multiplier Remains Same for 2021*, http://www.novoco.com (Oct. 26, 2020).

76. *See* HUD, Low-Income Housing Tax Credits Database, http://www.huduser.gov/portal /datasets/lihtc.html (last accessed Apr. 26, 2021).

77. One such requirement is that each state must set aside a certain percentage of its credits for projects involving qualified nonprofit organizations. The nonprofit must be a 501(c)(3) entity, and must "materially participate in the projects' development and operation." I.R.C. § 42(h)(5) (2010).

78. *Id.* § 42(m)(1)(A)(iii).

market study submitted with the application. All states must comply with the "automatic" allocation of tax credits for bond-financed projects.[79] Those projects that are bond and tax credit financed, despite being "automatic," must still satisfy state allocation requirements, submit an application, and obtain state approval.[80] Beyond these minimum requirements, states may set their own priorities for allocating their tax credits, resulting in diverse state programs.[81]

8. Carryover Allocations

After a state provides an allocation or award of credits, the investor must claim the credits on his or her (or a corporate) tax return in the year the project is placed in service (i.e., occupied). If the investor does not do this, the project sponsor must request a carryover allocation by application to the state housing authority in order for the investor to begin to claim the credits in the year(s) beyond the year the credits were allocated.[82] A carryover allocation is discretionary on the part of a state housing authority. It may occur for new construction or rehabilitation if at least 10 percent of the "reasonably expected basis"[83] (which can include land costs) has been incurred either (1) by a date six months after the date of allocation of tax credits or (2) by the close of the calendar year in which the credit was allocated for a building placed in service on or before July 30, 2008.[84] Pursuant to HERA, for buildings placed in service after July 30, 2008, the carryover allocation rule restrictions are modified so that an allocation that is more than 10 percent of the taxpayer's expected basis in the project is incurred as of 12 months after the allocation is made.[85] Typically, the applicant must provide the state agency with an accountant's or lawyer's opinion that the 10 percent test has been satisfied.

---

79. If 50 percent or less of a project is financed with tax-exempt bonds issued under a state volume cap allocation of bonding authority, the project will be eligible for tax credits up to 50 percent without going through the competitive process. If more than 50 percent is bond financed, then the project is eligible for 100 percent tax credits. These bond-financed projects are considered "federally subsidized," and thus are only eligible for the 4 percent credit. I.R.C. § 142(a) (2010). Certain types of bonds, such as 501(c)(3), essential function and taxable bonds do not qualify for this "automatic" credit allocation. *See* Section V.A. *infra* for a discussion of bond financing; *and see* Section II.C.2 *infra* for a discussion on LIHTC limitations regarding use of other federal grants or subsidies.

80. I.R.C. § 42(m)(1)(D) (2010).

81. In Michigan, for example, pursuant to the 2021 draft Qualified Allocation Plan, in addition to the requisite nonprofit set-aside, there are rural, elderly and eligible distressed set-asides, and eligible distressed area set-asides. https://www.michigan.gov/mshda/0,4641,7-141-5587_5601-556787--,00.html.

82. I.R.C. § 42 (h)(1)(D) (2010); *id.* § (h)(1)(E)(i); Reg. § 1.42-6.

83. The calculation of "reasonably expected basis" differs from qualified eligible basis. It can include adjusted basis in land or depreciable property that is "reasonably" expected to be part of the project. *See* I.R.C. § 42 (h)(1) (2010); *see also* Ltr. Rul. 8941035 and I.R.S. Information Letter 2001-0292.

84. I.R.C. § 42(h)(1)(E)(ii) (2010). There are specific rules for eligible costs that can be included in a carryover allocation application. There are also guidelines for documentation to demonstrate that the costs have been "incurred" by the date. One of the most common costs included in carryover allocation applications are construction materials or construction-related costs. If those guidelines are not followed, the I.R.S. may deem a carryover allocation as improper.

85. H.R. 3221, 110th Cong. § 3004(b), Pub. L. No. 110-289 (2008); but note that this does not change the two-year placed in service guidelines.

Although the state housing authority has the discretion to deny carryover allocations, states will readily approve carryover allocations that have proper documentation. As discussed *supra*, bond-financed projects are not subject to credit allocation rules because Congress excepted those projects from this requirement since they are limited by an annual volume cap on tax-exempt bond financing.[86]

C. Layering Other Financing Sources with LIHTCs

A traditional tax credit transaction will have multiple funding sources. Each source must be evaluated and structured so as to be compatible with other funding sources and the LIHTC. A typical LIHTC transaction is likely to have a private construction loan, public loans or grants, and other "gap" sources that may be short or long term. It is generally the role of counsel working with the developer to structure these financing sources, to negotiate their terms to ensure compliance with Section 42 of the Code, and to serve the financial and project needs of the developer. This subsection discusses two important issues related to secondary or gap financing and how they are generally handled.

1. Non-Recourse Loans

A private construction loan will generally be a recourse loan, but when converted to a permanent loan, most limited partners will require loans to be structured as non-recourse to minimize their risk. The investor,[87] often a limited partner or an investor member depending on the form of ownership entity created, in LIHTC transactions, cannot receive allocations of losses in excess of its capital account unless it restores a deficit balance or the losses result from allocations of deductions relating to minimum gain.[88] Minimum gain generally results if non-recourse debt is secured by the project and it equals the excess of the debt over the partnership's depreciated basis in its property securing the debt. One common structure employed by financial institutions is to provide a short-term construction loan, which will be a recourse loan during construction, with the expectation that it is paid in full and discharged at the completion of construction. Any remaining debt at the end of construction converted to a permanent loan will generally be structured as a non-recourse loan, and will have to subordinate to the state housing authorities' regulatory or use agreement. Non-recourse financing can be included in eligible basis as long as the investor contributes cash to the deal and recognizes a minimum gain.

2. Federal Grants or Subsidies

There are special considerations for federal grants coupled with LIHTCs. Examples of federal grants typically combined with LIHTC financing are those under the HOME Program,[89] Supportive Housing Grant program,[90] or HOPE VI program.[91] Without excep-

---

86. I.R.C. § 42(h)(4) (2010).

87. An investor in a LIHTC transaction is typically a limited partner or a limited liability member, and, thus, has to comply with partnership tax considerations.

88. The minimum gain rule is the minimum amount of debt the partnership will have to recognize in a foreclosure situation. Treas. Reg. § 1.704-2(b)(2) (2010) http://www.sec.gov.

89. HOME Program is authorized under 42 U.S.C. § 12742 (2012).

90. 2 U.S.C. § 1701q (2010).

91. See Chapter 12, *infra*, for further discussion of the HOPE VI program.

tion, the amount of federal grants received during the construction stage or the compliance period must be deducted from the eligible basis.[92]

There are several ways to structure the financing of federal grants in a LIHTC project to avoid this deduction. One option is to restructure the grant as a loan by providing it to a party other than the partnership.[93] This intermediate party can then loan the funds to the partnership. However, this loan must be at the AFR and any interest against the loan must be compounded interest.[94] This option necessitates an analysis of the project's debt service feasibility because a loan will not be respected as debt for tax purposes unless the value of the obligor's property exceeds the amount of the partnership's debts, including accrued but unpaid interest on the loan. Second, a grant can be directed to a general partner, which can in turn provide a capital contribution to the owner or partnership. Third, the grant can be structured as a grant with no debt service, and can be utilized for costs other than those related to the building, making it not an eligible basis cost item.

Under the federal stimulus legislation as discussed in Chapter 7 *supra,* federal subsidies[95] no longer have to be deducted from eligible basis if the taxpayer wants to remain qualified for the 9 percent credit.[96] There are exceptions to this rule, particularly as it relates to subsidies from the HOME Program or the Native American Housing Assistance and Self Determination Act of 1996, CDBG Funds,[97] and the Affordable Housing Program of the Federal Home Loan Bank.[98] The exception for the HOME Program is the most fully developed, and applies as long as 40 percent of the units are occupied by renters earning 50 percent or less of AMI. In addition, if the project utilizes HOME funds as a subsidy loan with an interest rate below AFR, it cannot also take advantage of a 30 percent basis boost if

---

92. I.R.C. §§ 42(h)(5), (k)(2)(A) (2010).

93. The term "sponsor" is used here to refer to the owner or developer. This will likely be a limited partnership or limited liability company that will own the LIHTC development during the compliance period.

94. Priv. Ltr. Rul. 8813024 (Dec. 30, 1987), https://www.novoco.com.

95. Federal subsidies are either loans that have exempt interest under Section 103 or a federally funded loan with interest that is below AFR then in effect under Section 1274 (d)(1) as of the date of the loan. I.R.C. § 42(i)(2) (2010).

96. Without the deduction, the project will only be qualified for the 4 percent credit. I.R.C. § 42(b)(1)(B) (2010). For more guidance on this issue, visit http://www.law.cornell.edu (last visited on Apr. 30, 2021).

97. I.R.C. § 42 (i)(2)(D) (2010).

98. AHP loans are made by private institutions pursuant to Section 721 of the Financial Institutions Reform, Recovery and Enforcement Act of 1989 (FIRREA). Their treatment as federal subsidies in a LIHTC transaction is covered at Treas. Reg. § 1.42-3 (2010).

in a qualified census tract.[99] There are also interest rate considerations and other tax rules that must be factored in when structuring subsidy financing in an LIHTC transaction.[100]

D. Ownership Structures for LIHTC Transactions

Ownership of a housing development project financed under the LIHTC program is usually organized as either a limited partnership (LP) or a limited liability company (LLC). Both types of legal entities are treated as partnerships for tax purposes. In these structures, the general partner in an LP (or the managing member in the case of an LLC) has a management and oversight role, while the limited partner agrees to invest in the LP or LLC, thereby infusing capital into the transaction in exchange for an allocation of 99 percent or more of the tax credits with limited liability. In December 1996, the IRS enacted the "Check-the-Box" rule[101] that allows a newly formed entity to be classified as a partnership if it has at least two members, unless it affirmatively elects to be treated as an association, that is, taxed as a corporation. This simplified an important aspect of investments in housing. It is critical for the ownership entity in a LIHTC transaction—whatever its form—to be taxed as a partnership to ensure that the partnership's tax characteristics (i.e., credits, deductions, income, gains, or losses) will be "passed through" to its partners. Despite these IRS rules, the LP or LLC structure will be governed by the state law of the jurisdiction where the project is located. Thus, the operational documents will vary somewhat from transaction to transaction.

A number of major issues control the venture and transcend even the state differences. These issues present the most central dimensions of the transaction; they must be negotiated and addressed in either the LP Partnership Agreement or the LLC Operating Agreement.[102] These major issues may include the price on the dollar for each tax credit,[103] pay-in

---

99. Normally a project can take 100 percent of eligible basis to calculate the available credit; however in a difficult to develop area or qualified low-income census tract (QCT) as determined by HUD, the project may be eligible to calculate the credit on 130 percent of basis. When using federal funds, taking the boost is considered double-dipping, and is not available under I.R.C. § 42(d)(5)(C) (2010). However, under HERA, credit-allocating agencies will be able to provide basis boosts to projects outside difficult-to-develop areas and QCTs that are designated by the state allocating agency as requiring an increase in the credit amount to be financially feasible. H.R. 3221, 110th Cong. § 1001 *et seq.*, Pub. L. No. 110-289 (2008); *see also* Rev. Rul. 2004-82, 2004-35 I.R.B. 350.

100. *See* Priv. Ltr. Rul. 200035016 (Sept. 1, 2000) (interest rate is one factor supporting a loan); I.R.C. § 118 (2010) (grants to partners contributed as capital to the partnership may or may not be grant income). *See also* passive loss rules for limited partnerships generally.

101. Treas. Reg. §§ 301.7701-1 to 301.7701-3 (2010).

102. Major issues listed in the text are common; however, issues may vary according to local conditions, specific characteristics of a transaction, and other factors.

103. The average equity syndicator in December 2020 was offering an average equity price of $.90. These prices were as high as $1.06 in June 2016. See Novogradac & Company, LLP, *LIHTC Equity Pricing Trends, January 2016–December 2020*, Vol. XII(III) Novogradac Journal of Tax Credits (March 2021).

schedule for equity contributions,[104] tax credit adjusters,[105] guaranties,[106] provisions involving removal or default of the general partner,[107] scope of fees to be paid,[108] representations and warranties,[109] indemnification procedures, and reserves.[110]

An equally important issue, but one that is not consistently negotiated, arises when there is a nonprofit sponsor that is either directly the general partner, or that has formed a for-profit subsidiary to function as the general partner. In these instances, there are issues concerning management control and ensuring that the nonprofit does not jeopardize its IRC Section 501 (c)(3) status. In order to get a special allocation of tax credits under a nonprofit set-aside for qualified nonprofits, the nonprofit (or its wholly owned subsidiary) must "materially participate"[111] in the development and operations of the project during the compliance period. In addition, during this compliance period, the nonprofit must maintain its status as a "qualified non-profit organization"[112] under Section 42 of the IRC provided, however, it may do so by maintaining its own qualification[113] or by having 100 percent of stock owned by a qualified nonprofit organization.[114] Often, funders will require evidence through stock ownership certificates or a resolution to demonstrate that a subsidiary is wholly owned by the nonprofit.

If the tax credits were awarded to a project under the nonprofit set-aside, and the nonprofit involved is a Community Housing Development Organization (CHDO),[115] then

---

104. The schedule or the timing of equity contributions is a heavily negotiated item, which can affect the price on the dollar, and can vary greatly from transaction to trans-action.

105. Generally, the equity syndicator will prefer latitude in imposing an adjuster to their price on the dollar in the event there is a reduction in available credit or a delay in realization of their equity, generally caused by construction delays or lease-up/placed-in-service delays.

106. Guaranties often include a construction completion guaranty, an operating deficit guaranty, a tax credit guaranty, and a guaranty of replacement or debt service reserves. The duration of the guaranties is negotiable and often will "burn off" at break-even level for operations.

107. Removal issues focus on the standard for such removal, consequences in the event of removal, and right to cure a default to avoid removal.

108. Fees may be earned for development services, and may be assessed against the partnership for property management, partnership incentive management, limited partner oversight fee, guaranty loan fee, and other services that are negotiated.

109. This section of a Partnership Agreement is likely to cover environmental issues and indemnities, tax credit compliance, insurance requirements, property management, property conditions, securities issues, accounting/bookkeeping and compliance with local, state or other applicable codes, ordinances, regulations, and licenses.

110. Reserves will be required for operations, debt service, development deficit, replacement costs, and others negotiated by the parties. Reserves may be for the entire compliance period or they may be for a shorter period dependent upon the nature of the reserve.

111. I.R.C. § 469(h) (2010).

112. *See id.* § 42 (h)(5)(C).

113. *See id.* § 42 (h)(5)(D)(ii).

114. *Id.*

115. CHDO is defined as a nonprofit organization that has as a central purpose the development of decent affordable housing for low- to moderate-income people. To qualify, the CHDO must contain this purpose in its articles and bylaws; it must maintain representation on its governing board of low-income residents and/or beneficiaries of the housing to be provided, or those representing low-income organizations; and it must restrict government, or government-related individuals, from serving on its board. Finally, it must have a demonstrated capacity for serving the local community, and the potential to implement affordable housing projects. *See* 42 U.S.C. § 12704 (2010).

the CHDO must be the managing general partner of the partnership, and must maintain "effective project control" during the compliance period.[116] Further, in the event that a CHDO that is the managing general partner is subject to removal in the Partnership Agreement, the Partnership Agreement must provide that any replacement of this general partner must satisfy Section 42 (h)(5)(c) by ensuring that the replacement is a "qualified non-profit organization."

E. Current Developments in LIHTC Transactions

The LIHTC is a complex regulatory program. Many issues have been resolved over the years through IRS regulations, revenue rulings, private letter rulings, and tax court cases that decide issues through administrative or judicial proceedings. The Housing and Economic Recovery Act (or HERA) of 2008[117] followed Revenue Ruling 2004-82[118] and addressed certain questions concerning low-income housing tax credits under Section 42 of the Code that had been plaguing the industry for many years. More specifically, this ruling addressed issues related to eligible qualified-basis, first-year low-income unit use, extended low-income housing compliance, HOME Investment Partnership Act Loans, vacant unit rules, record-keeping and record retention, and tenant income documentation.

This IRS revenue ruling provides an overview of the law and legislative history of Section 42, with particular emphasis on the applicable sections of the law that impact the issues addressed. It also provides a detailed discussion of each of these issues, and provides direct guidance to housing tax credit agencies, developers, and management companies on the proper procedures for administration of tax credit properties.[119]

HERA includes nearly two dozen provisions modernizing the LIHTC and tax-exempt housing private activity bond programs. The changes are aimed at improving the LIHTC program and enabling more types of developments to be financially feasible. Many provisions of HERA have been incorporated into this chapter, however please see Chapter 7 *infra* for an in-depth look at HERA. A few other interesting points to note with respect to the HERA provisions are outlined next.

Under HERA there was a temporary LIHTC allocation increase, wherein the state per capita allocation volume cap was increased from $2 to $2.20 for 2008 and 2009 except for the nine states subject to the small-state minimum, in which case the cap was raised by 10 percent (from $2,325,000 to $2,557,500). In 2010 and thereafter, both allocations returned to what they would have been if HERA had not been enacted (i.e., inflation-adjusted from $2.00 today to $x in 2010 dollars). As of August 2020, each stated Housing Finance Agency received approximately $0.275 per capita or the minimum small population states received an allocation of $3,166,875.[120] Since 2004, annual allocations have been tied to inflation and increase at a nominal rate each year.[121]

---

116. 24 C.F.R. § 92.300(a)(1) (2010).

117. Pub. L. No. 110-289, 122 Stat. 2654 enacted July 30, 2008.

118. *See also* Rev. Rul. 2004-82.

119. In addition to review of Rev. Rul. 2004-82, the I.R.S. Office of Associate Chief Counsel (Passthroughs and Special Industries) may be contacted at (202) 622-3040 for further information.

120. 2020 Federal LIHTC Information by State, Novogradac, https://www.novoco.com /resource-centers/affordable-housing-tax-credits/2021-federal-lihtc-information-state.

121. http://taxfoundation.org (Aug. 11, 2020).

Under HERA, investors may now use LIHTCs, tax-exempt housing private activity bonds, and historic rehabilitation tax credits against alternative minimum tax (AMT) liability.[122]

Under previous law, investors wanting to sell their interest in LIHTC properties were required to post a bond so that the IRS could access funds for recapture if the property was found to be out of compliance. In HERA, that requirement is repealed and replaced with a change in the statute of limitations for any tax recapture so that the three-year period does not begin to run until the IRS is notified by the taxpayer of a recapture event.[123] Despite that change, however, the requirement of a recapture bond is still discretionary on the part of a LIHTC investor upon exit.[124]

Previously projects were able to include up to 10 percent of eligible basis to finance community service facilities in qualified census tracts, even if those facilities primarily serve nonresidents. Under HERA, the community service space rule is liberalized to permit such space to equal up to 25 percent of eligible basis on the first $15 million of a project, with 10 percent thereafter.[125] This provision will make it easier to finance community services facilities, especially for smaller LIHTC developments; however, the rules governing community facilities in LIHTC developments must be closely evaluated, because if not handled correctly, could result in noncompliance finding during an IRS audit. Also, consulting with a state agency may be prudent.[126]

Additionally, HERA implements new requirements for LIHTC tenant data collection by requiring state allocating agencies to report LIHTC tenant data to HUD annually, including tenant race, ethnicity, family composition, age, income, use of rental assistance or other similar assistance, disability status, and monthly rental payments.[127]

On February 17, 2009, President Obama signed the American Recovery and Reinvestment Act of 2009 (ARRA) into law.[128] The primary focus of ARRA is creating and saving jobs in the near term and investing in infrastructure that will provide long-term economic benefits. The full title is an act making supplemental appropriations for job preservation and creation, infrastructure investment, energy efficiency and science, assistance to the unemployed, and state and local fiscal stabilization, for the fiscal year ending September 30, 2009, and for other purposes. ARRA includes two economic incentives for LIHTC developers. The LIHTC-related provisions are (1) competitive grants through $2.25 billion of gap financing under the HOME Program, which will be allocated to states through the HOME Program formula and will be dispersed to projects on a competitive basis by the state LIHTC allocating agencies, also known as the Tax Credit Assistance Program (TCAP); and (2) under Section 1602 of ARRA, state housing credit agencies are eligible to receive Section 1602 grants to states for low-income housing projects in lieu of low-income housing credits under Section 42 of the IRC for 2009, which essentially means the state

---

122. H.R. 3221, 110th Cong. § 3022 (2008).

123. *Id.* § 3004(c)(6)(B).

124. *LIHTC Recapture Bonds for Affordable Housing*, http://www.scottins.com (Aug. 31, 2020).

125. H.R. 3221, 110th Cong. § 3003(c), Pub. L. No. 110-289 (2008).

126. Compliance Corner: Community Rooms and Public Use Buildings, http://travois.com (Mar. 15, 2015).

127. H.R. 3221, 110th Cong. § 2835, Pub. L. No. 110-289 (2008).

128. 123 Stat. 115, Feb. 17, 2009.

housing credit agency is electing to take a portion of its 2009 state housing credit ceiling in the form of grant amounts and agreeing to the terms and conditions applicable to the Section 1602 program. Section 1602 is also referred to as the "Tax Credit Exchange Program," the "Section 1602 Program," and the "Monetized Tax Credit Program."

Even more recently, there have been some changes to the Tax Credit Program to allow for the "twinning" of 4 percent and 9 percent credits on a single project. This involves separating a single project with multiple funding sources into two distinct projects with separate revenue streams. Each project will have to allocate costs and be funded separately. While IRS guidance on this "twinning" process has not been complete, industry guidance from developers who have implemented this process has been helpful. The legal framework for these projects will include having two of everything from the financing documents, construction and architectural agreements, third-party studies and reports.[129]

III. HOME INVESTMENT PARTNERSHIP ACT[130]

A. Purpose and Activities

The HOME Investment Partnership Act (HOME or HOME Program) was authorized in 1990 under Title II of the Cranston-Gonzalez National Affordable Housing Act.[131] In general, the purpose of the HOME Program is to increase the supply of decent, safe, and affordable housing for families, to ensure expansion of the long-term supply of affordable housing, and to promote public–private partnerships in the development of affordable housing.[132] The amendments published in the Final Rule on July 24, 2013, represent the most sweeping changes in the program in 17 years.[133] In this Final Rule, HUD established regulatory changes to address certain operational obstacles facing local units of government, or participating jurisdictions (PJs) that administer the HOME program. More specifically, the Final Rule updated definitions and added new terminology relevant in real estate nomenclature, modified eligibility requirements for community housing development organizations or CHDOs to ensure that these organizations are capable of carrying out their responsibilities under the HOME program, provided more teeth to the conflict of interest provisions, and removed some ambiguities relative to expectations of those who

---

129. *See The Hybrid: A New Deal Design*, RedStone Equity Partners, http://www.mdahc.org (Oct. 2019); and Steve Paul & Katie Day, *The Low-Income Housing Credit*, https://www.kleinhornig.com/2019-edition-of-low-income-housing-tax-credit-outline/ (2019 edition); or see Erik Hoffman, *"Twinning" a 9% Credit Project with Tax Exempt Bond/4% Project*, KLEIN HORNIG LLP, https://www.handhousing.org/wp-content/uploads/HAND-TE-Bond-Financing-Panels-9-4-Twinning-2.pdf.

130. *See* http://www.hud.gov.home program (last accessed July 13, 2010) for a complete overview of the HOME Program and links to new developments in the HOME Program. Much of the information contained in this section is derived from that website.

131. 42 U.S.C. §§ 12741–12774 (2010). Program regulations are contained at 24 C.F.R. § 92 (Final Rule published on July 24, 2013).

132. *Id.*

133. *Id.*

utilize this source of funding.[134] HOME provides formula block grants to states and localities. HOME dollars are generally administered by participating jurisdictions (PJs), which can be local, county, or state governments; however, there is oversight by the HUD regional offices.

There is a wide range of eligible activities under HOME, including developing single-family homeownership or rental units, multifamily rental units, tenant-based rental assistance, and down payment assistance to first-time home buyers.[135] PJs must reserve at least 15 percent of their allocations to fund housing owned, developed, or sponsored by CHDOs. In addition, HOME dollars can provide operational support for CHDOs that have active HOME-funded projects. PJs must ensure that HOME-funded units remain affordable for a specified period: 20 years for new rental construction and 5 to 15 years for construction of homeownership units and rehabilitation, depending on the amount of HOME subsidy. A PJ does have the discretion to require a longer period of affordability if there is a mandate by the local governing body to maintain affordability for a longer period.

Although HUD monitors and sets general parameters for the HOME Program, PJs can develop policy guidelines within those parameters for the administration of their HOME Programs.[136] These policies allow local communities to tailor their HOME Programs to local needs established through planning processes.[137] Up to 10 percent of a PJs allocation can be dedicated to program planning.

B. Eligible Grantees and Costs

States are eligible for HOME funds and can receive their formula allocation or $3 million dollars, whichever is greater. In some states, cities over a certain size and counties that serve smaller cities will be eligible for a direct HOME allocation.[138]

Eligible costs include (1) acquisition of land[139] and improvements, (2) demolition,[140] (3) site improvements, (4) new construction, (5) rehabilitation, (6) reconstruction, (7) tenant rent and security deposits, (8) relocation,[141] (9) operating costs of CHDOs, (10) soft costs related to the eligible development, and (11) administrative overhead costs for the PJ. HOME funds that can be structured as grants, direct loans, loan guarantees, equity investments, or advances, with the PJ maintaining a great deal of flexibility on terms of the financing. As part of its application, a developer must provide a breakdown of its project

---

134. For a complete summary of this Final Rule, see HOME Investment Partnerships Program: Improving Performance and Accountability: Updating Property Standards (July 24, 2013), https://www.federalregister.gov/documents/2013/07/24/2013-17348/home-investment-partnerships-program-improving-performance-and-accountability-updating-property.

135. 24 C.F.R. § 92.205 (2013).

136. The city of Detroit provides as part of its HOME Application a set of guidelines that govern its program.

137. *See* Part I, Chapter 2, *supra*, for more discussion of HUD's required planning requirements.

138. See http://www.hud.gov, The HOME Program Formula.

139. Acquisition of publicly owned land, owned by the PJ, may not be an eligible cost for HOME dollars administered by that PJ.

140. Both acquisition and demolition costs must be related to the particular housing project for which HOME dollars will be used to develop.

141. Some PJs, for example, Detroit, Michigan, have determined by policy for its HOME Program that relocation expenses are not eligible costs.

costs, or a pro forma outlining both the overall sources and uses of funds, and specifically how it will utilize HOME dollars within these eligibility guidelines. The PJ has to accept and approve the project pro forma, and is responsible for how the HOME dollars are being utilized in the project.

C. Limitations on Use of HOME Funds

HUD has set maximum limits on the amount of HOME funds that can be spent on a per-unit basis. For multifamily rental units, the limit cannot be less than the per-unit dollar limitation of the Section 221(d)(3) program, adjusted upwards to 140 percent of those amounts for multifamily housing in areas where such construction costs exceed the national average.[142] Cost limits on single-family for sale units are set on a market-by-market basis, and will vary widely from state to state. A guiding principle is that HOME-funded housing is not luxury housing; however, it should be durable and offer suitable amenities.[143]

Rental housing must also meet six specific criteria under the HOME Program to be considered "affordable housing":

- Rents cannot exceed the lesser of the existing fair market rents as established for the Section 8 program, or 30 percent of the adjusted income of a family whose income equals 65 percent of the median income for the area, adjusted by the number of bedrooms per unit.[144]
- At least 20 percent of the units must be occupied by families that do not exceed 50 percent of the HUD-adjusted level for median income.[145]
- The housing must be occupied only by households that qualify as low-income families (80 percent or less of AMI).
- No Section 8 certificate holder can be refused an opportunity to become a resident because of his or her status as a holder of a certificate or voucher.
- The rents must remain affordable for the remaining useful life or for the longest period of time according to the Affordable Housing Restriction agreement entered into with the participating jurisdiction.[146]
- For new construction, projects must comply with energy efficiency standards.[147]

D. Matching Requirements

Under current HOME rules, with the exception of administrative costs, PJs must match dollars of HOME funds used, with 25 percent coming from nonfederal sources. These nonfederal sources may include donated materials or labor, donated property, proceeds from

---

142. 42 U.S.C. § 12742(e) (2013).

143. *Id.*

144. 42 U.S.C. § 12745(a)(1)(A) (2010). Note that per the provisions of HERA, projects with HOME assistance are no longer required to have the increased unit set-aside.

145. Restrictions on rents for rental units under HOME are generally consistent with those under the LIHTC program. *See* I.R.C. § 42(g)(2) (2013).

146. 24 C.F.R. § 92.252(e) (2013).

147. 2 U.S.C. §§ 12745(a)(1)(A)–(F) (2013). See discussion of the Energy Star Program, *infra*, at F.3.

bond financing, and other resources. This matching requirement may be reduced if the PJ is distressed or has suffered a program-declared disaster.[148]

HOME administrative costs can be paid from CDBG funds.[149] CDBG funds may be used for housing counseling related to tenant-based rental assistance, actual rental assistance to tenants, energy auditing, loan processing, direct development costs, and other services.[150]

E. Current Developments in the HOME Program

Participating jurisdictions can set policy guidelines for their programs, but those must be consistent with HUD guidelines.[151] Included are guidelines for ensuring equal treatment of faith-based organizations participating in the HOME Program.[152]

HUD has also developed its "Consortia Builder" program, a tool to provide guidance on how to combine the demographics of proposed member governments for the purpose of qualifying for a HOME formula allocation that may be greater than an individual allocation.[153] Finally, HUD periodically evaluates the program from a policy perspective, and in 2004 conducted a study of the choices governments are making through the HOME Program that impact homeownership opportunities.[154]

IV. COMMUNITY DEVELOPMENT BLOCK GRANT PROGRAM

A. CDBG Generally

Created in 1974, the CDBG is similar to the HOME Program in that the federal government, through HUD, provides dollars to cities, counties, and states each year. Under the Housing and Community Development Act of 1974, CDBG funds should be used "to aid in the prevention or elimination of slums and blight or to address community development needs that present a serious and immediate threat to the health or welfare of a community."[155] The CDBG program has broad guidelines, allowing the funds to be directed to a wide range of activities involving neighborhood revitalization, supporting economic development, improving community facilities, and providing social services. The threshold for receiving annual allocations is metropolitan cities of more than 50,000 people, or certain urban counties that will serve smaller cities. State governments may also receive allocations for communities not entitled to receive CDBG funds from the county or local governments in

---

148. *See* https://www.hud.gov/sites/documents/19652_98-8.PDF (last visited Dec. 13, 2021).

149. Section 205 of the 1994 Housing Reform Act.

150. *Id.* In fact, the city of Detroit has amended its standard HOME Development and Loan Agreement to allow for substitution of CDBG funds for HOME dollars it commits.

151. *See* HUD, HOME Investment Partnerships Program, https://www.hud.gov/program_offices /comm_planning/home (last visited Dec. 13, 2021).

152. HUD, HOME Investment Partnership Program—HUD Exchange, https://www.hudex change.info/programs/home/ (last visited Dec. 13, 2021).

153. HUD, Home Investment Partnerships Program, https://www.hud.gov/program_offices /comm_planning/home (last visited Dec. 13, 2021).

154. *See* HUD, *Study of Homebuyer Opportunities through the HOME Investment Partnership Program* (Jan. 2004), www.huduser.org/Publications/pdf/Homebuy.pdf.

155. Title I of Housing & Community Development Act of 1974, Public Act 93-383, as amended, codified at 42 U.S.C. §§ 5301 *et seq.* (2010).

which they are located.[156] As with the HOME Program, communities have broad discretion to develop their own programs and to determine how to spend their CDBG dollars. A more specific directive is that all CDBG activities must benefit low- and moderate-income people, and not less than 70 percent of the funds must be used for activities that benefit low- and moderate-income people over a time period not to exceed three years.

B. Eligible Activities, Grantees, and Administration

CDBG activities must fit within the broad parameters defined *supra*. Specific types of eligible activities include acquisition of real property; new construction or rehabilitation of residential and nonresidential property; infrastructure or public improvements or facilities such as sidewalks, lighting, curb or street replacement or repair, or water and sewer systems; neighborhood or community centers; loan guarantees or Section 108 loans; and economic development activities.[157] CDBG funds can also be used for administrative costs for community-based organizations engaged in either development or social services.

CDBG funds are distributed by PJs and may be in the form of grants, forgivable loans, or loans. The funds may be provided directly to community-based organizations or individuals that are furthering a community's CDBG goals. Often, PJs will allocate CDBG funds to support affordable housing development projects that are being assisted with other public or private funds. One advantage of CDBG funding for affordable housing is that grants and loans obtained from CDBG and HOME are not considered "federal subsidy" for purposes of the LIHTC program because of exceptions in the tax credit laws. One drawback is that CDBG expenditures must comply with applicable program requirements and are subject to audit by the granting agency.[158]

C. Loan Guarantees or Section 108 Loans

Another important use for CDBG funds is to provide loan guarantees for housing rehabilitation, economic development, and larger-scale residential or commercial development. These loan guarantees are provided against future block grant allocations. Section 108 of the Housing and Community Development Act (as amended) outlines this loan guarantee provision of the CDBG program. Section 108 allows the community to pledge its future or current CDBG funds as a loan guarantee or security for a private or a public loan. The types of projects that the loan guarantee can secure cover similar eligible activities to the CDBG program generally, with the addition of relocation assistance, clearance or demolition, interest payment of the guaranteed loan, debt service costs, or reserves.[159]

---

156. 42 U.S.C. § 5306(d) (2010). *See also* http://uscode.house.gov.

157. 24 C.F.R. § 570.200 (2010); *id.* § 570.202(a)(2).

158. For information on auditing and regulation of HUD programs, see Chapter 8, *infra*.

159. Bennett L. Hecht, Developing Affordable Housing: A Practical Guide for Nonprofit Organizations 93 (2d ed., New York, John Wiley & Sons 1999).

V. BOND FINANCING OF MULTIFAMILY HOUSING

A. Bond Financing in General

Bonds issued by local or state governments and their administrative agencies provide another source of financing for affordable housing because the tax-exempt feature creates a less expensive source of financing than bank loans.[160] Bond financing can be used for multifamily housing, and will include rules and regulations similar to those for tax credits governing use restrictions, affordability requirements, and repayment obligations. In very general terms, jurisdictions have authority to issue two kinds of bonds: (1) revenue bonds, which are secured by and payable from the revenues generated from the financed project; and (2) general obligation bonds, which are secured by the full faith and credit of the government issuer.

In the context of affordable housing, private activity bonds (often referred to as revenue bonds) are generally utilized. They must be secured by, or derived from, payments from the project's revenues.[161] Bonds can be combined with other sources of financing for affordable housing. The user will have to be cognizant of how the bond obligations mesh with other sources, however. Technically, revenue bonds usually fall into two categories: (1) bonds issued for projects owned by IRC Section 501(c)(3) organizations and (2) bonds issued for projects owned by private owners, usually partnerships with for-profit limited partners that make substantial capital investments. As described, the latter will usually be eligible for low-income housing tax credits.

Every year pursuant to IRC Section 146, the IRS announces bond caps for the states' limitations on the amount of new tax-exempt bonds that will be issued by the IRS for the states. States also have bond volume caps that limit the amount of private-activity bonds that can be issued for affordable housing projects. Each state's cap is determined by multiplying its population by a number; thus, it will change annually. The IRS reviews the inflation rate to determine if the multiplier should be raised each year.[162] Although the IRS controls a state's total private-activity tax-exempt bond cap, states decide how to prioritize their bond cap or allocation between housing and other priorities. For example, in 2021, Illinois had a $500,000 state ceiling bond cap, of which $100,000 was available for multifamily allocations on a first-come, first-served basis; and Texas had a $3,200,000 state ceiling bond cap, and directed $840,000 toward its multifamily allocation.[163]

It is important to note that pursuant to HERA, the following rules for the multifamily bond program are conformed to that of the LIHTC program when combined: (1) "next available unit" (which requires property managers of mixed income LIHTC developments to rent the next available unit that becomes vacant in any assisted building to an income-eligible tenant once an existing tenants' income increases beyond 140 percent of qualifying income standard), (2) definition of student (newly expanded), and (3) Single Room Occupancy (SRO) units.[164]

---

160. See Chapter 11, *infra,* for a discussion of local bonds.

161. 26 U.S.C. § 141 generally; and § 141(b)(2), http://law.cornell.edu.

162. 26 U.S.C. § 146(d)(2) (2010).

163. See *2021 Federal Bond Information by State*, page 25, vol. XII(III) Novogradac Journal of Tax Credits (March 2021).

164. H.R. 3221, 110th Cong. § 3008, Pub. L. No. 110-289 (2008).

B. Tax-Exempt Bonds

Generally, the interest paid to bondholders from bonds that are issued by state or local governments for government facilities or operations is tax exempt. Bonds issued to finance privately owned housing sponsored by nonprofit or for-profit entities will be taxable, unless they meet the criteria of Section 142 of the Code.[165] In general, the standards applicable to bond-financed housing projects are quite similar to the rules that apply to tax credit projects. In particular, the following apply: the 20/40 and 40/60 tests (discussed *supra* at II.B.5), however, given the recent modification allowing for an income averaging approach as discussed previously that would apply to the tax exempt bond-funded projects as well; the requirement that the facilities have cooking, sleeping, and bathroom facilities; and that leases not be on a transient basis.[166]

To qualify for tax-exempt bonds, privately owned projects must be subject to a public hearing,[167] and receive an allocation from the state volume cap. One important benefit of bond financing is that a project that is tax-exempt bond financed will qualify for tax credits in the same proportion as the project's bond financing; that is, if the project is more than 50 percent bond financed, then the entire project will qualify for tax credits.[168] In each case, the issuing agency has to make certain findings.[169] State agencies may also provide gap financing to these types of projects in the form of HOME dollars, housing trust fund dollars.[170]

C. Taxable Bonds

Although much less common, local jurisdictions can issue taxable bonds.[171] These bonds will carry a higher interest rate than qualified private activity bonds. However, they may not carry as many restrictions on use, because they are subject only to local government rules. With the onset of the LIHTC program since 1986, taxable bonds have become a more common vehicle for financing multifamily affordable housing. There will, of course, be debt service associated with bond financing, and the projects may not automatically qualify for tax credits.

VI. OTHER SOURCES OF FEDERAL FINANCING

A. Supportive Housing for the Elderly

Section 202 of the Housing Act of 1959 provides funding for the development of housing for the elderly. Under this program, HUD provides a capital advance to a nonprofit housing developer and/or consumer cooperative and a rental subsidy under a multiyear Project

---

165. 26 U.S.C. § 141 (2010).

166. *Id.* § 142(d) as it relates to qualified residential rental projects.

167. *Id.* § 147(f).

168. How Do Affordable Housing Bonds Work, http://www.millionacres.com (last visited Dec. 13, 2021).

169. 26 U.S.C. § 42 (m)(2)(d) (2010).

170. Housing trust funds are distinct funds established by local, county, or state governments, and are generally supported by public and private sources. *See* http://housingtrustfundproject.org.

171. See Chapter 11, *infra*, for a discussion of local government bonds.

Rental Assistance Contract (PRAC) between HUD and the owner. The capital advance,[172] although secured by a mortgage with HUD, is interest free, and repayment will not be required if the housing remains rented to eligible low-income elderly persons for 40 years. The capital advance funds can be used for new construction, rehabilitation, reconstruction, and acquisition from the FDIC.[173] As with most federally financed housing, HUD 202 projects are likely to have other sources of financing, and their requisite requirements will have to mesh with the HUD 202 project requirements.

In 2019, the Section 202 program underwent some major revisions. If a developer owned an "old law" Section 202 property, that is, one developed with a HUD 202 direct loan between 1959 and 1974, which is considered the program's first phase, HUD has provide new tools for these projects to receive project-based rental assistance through the Project-Based Voucher or PBV program.[174] Informally called the Rental Assistance Demonstration or RAD for PRAC, this new direction for the HUD 202 properties could revive many aging elderly housing developments. HUD estimates more than 125,000 units of senior housing could be eligible for RAD for PRAC.[175] At this writing, it has been estimated that 94,000 units have been converted utilizing this RAD for PRAC program.[176]

To be eligible, low-income elderly must be 62 years or older and must earn less than 50 percent of the area's AMI for a family unit with at least one person 62 years old or older.[177] Section 202 housing is not a program for assisted living or nursing home-type developments. It is a program for independent senior living, where residents must be able to feed, bathe, and dress themselves. Section 202 projects may supply housekeeping and transportation services, occasional assistance for difficult meal preparation, and grooming or dressing needs. However, tenants must not be required to pay for these supportive services as a condition of occupancy. PRAC funds may be used to hire a service coordinator.[178] Rent limits for 202 projects are established by HUD's current per-unit operating standard, as established for a project based on its location. Tenants are required to pay no more than 30 percent of their adjusted gross income toward their monthly rent. The PRAC subsidy is reserved for payment of 75 percent of the unit cost. PRAC terms previously were

---

172. The program is codified at 12 U.S.C. § 1704 (2010). For the purposes of the capital advance, HUD establishes per unit development cost limits annually, which are published in the Section 202 Notice of Funding Availability (NOFA), http://www.nls.gov/offices/adm/grants/nofa09/grpsec202e.cfm (last accessed May 5, 2021). Capital advance funds are made available for average reasonable and necessary costs for projects developed with a "modest design" as referenced in the HUD description of such advances.

173. For a current analysis, history, and overview of the past 50 years of the HUD 202 Program, see *A Great Place to Call Home: A Representative Portfolio of HUD's Section 202 Program (195902009)*, a publication of the U.S. Department of Housing and Urban Development, www.hud.gov.

174. See Preservation Options for Pre-1974 Section 202 Direct Loan Projects, http://www.hud.gov.

175. RAD for PRAC Overview, http://tidwellgroup.com (Jan. 14, 2020).

176. The Promise and Peril of HUD's RAD Program, http://shelterforce.org (July 30, 2018).

177. *See* HUD, *Programs*, https://www.hud.gov/rad/ (last accessed May 8, 2021); *see also* HUD, *Multifamily Housing,* https://www.hud.gov/program_offices/housing/mfh (last visited Dec. 13, 2021).

178. 12 U.S.C. § 1701q(j)(6) (2010).

authorized for 20 years; currently, the terms are set at five years, with renewals subject to appropriations.[179]

Unlike other HUD-supported programs, which are administered by local, county, or state governments, the HUD 202 program is administered directly by HUD through its regional field offices, and HUD Washington. Sponsors must apply for a HUD 202 Capital Advance by submitting a Section 202 Application, accessed through the HUD Notice of Funding Availability (NOFA) issued annually.[180] Funding for the HUD 202 is part of the annual HUD budget bill and for 2010, HUD requested $765 million, which was the same level as provided in the 2009 fiscal year Omnibus Appropriations Act. In addition, the budget provides $522 million for "expansion grants," that is, to expand existing HUD 202 developments. Also, the budget provides for $153 million into renew and/or amend Project Rental Assistance Contracts or PRACs and $90 million to support hiring service coordinators—a new direction for the program. Finally, planning grants and conversion to assisted living grants are no longer separate line items, but eligible activities under the main program.[181] Similarly, albeit smaller appropriations are available for the Section 811 Housing for Persons with Disabilities.[182]

Until recently, HUD 202 projects could only be developed and owned by Section 501c(3) or c(4) organizations, which had to be single-purpose entities.[183] Under the American Homeownership and Economic Opportunity Act of 2000 (AHEO),[184] Section 202 projects can be owned by for-profit limited partnerships, provided that the sole general partner is either a qualified nonprofit or a wholly owned entity controlled by the nonprofit.[185]

This allows HUD 202 projects to become mixed-financed developments, which is an important change since often the capital advance with its limitations on per-cost of units is insufficient to construct quality senior housing.[186] HUD has authorized a Mixed Finance Program combining HUD 202 funds with tax credits to create for-profit developments, and HUD has developed underwriting instructions which were incorporated into a HUD Handbook in 2009.[187] As of this writing, approximately 46 mixed-finance projects utilizing 202 and LIHTC financing have been funded, with many others in the queue for closing under this financing structure.[188] Several other issues, such as treatment of PRAC assistance as a

---

179. *See* HUD, Information for Senior Citizens, http://www.hud.gov/groups/seniors.cfm (last accessed July 13, 2010).

180. *See id.*

181. *See* U.S. Dep't of Hous. & Urban Dev., FY 2010 Budget, https://archives.hud.gov/budget /fy10/budgetsummary.cfm (last checked May 8, 2021).

182. *Id.*

183. 24 C.F.R. § 891.805 (2010).

184. The American Homeownership and Economic Opportunity Act of 2000, Pub. L. No. 106-569, 114 Stat. 2944 (2000).

185. Since the HUD 202 program is administered by field offices, HUD offices have not necessarily been consistent in their treatment of the wholly owned affiliate requirement. *See* Scott Fireison, *Section 202 Basics*, in materials from ABA Forum on Affordable Housing and Community Development Law's 13th Annual Conference, Washington, D.C. (May 20–21, 2004).

186. *See* Ruth Sparrow, *Heard from HUD: Mixed-Finance Section 202 and Section 811 Housing*, 13 J. Affordable Hous. & Cmty Dev. L., 171–75 (2004) for comprehensive overview of issues surrounding combining HUD 202 or 811 funds with other financing programs.

187. 24 C.F.R. § 891.800 (2010).

188. See HUD Portfolio on the 202 Program, *supra* note 173.

federal grant and what are allowable rent restrictions have been resolved and are addressed in the 2009 HUD Handbook.[189]

HERA changes include requiring delegated processing of all new Section 202 elderly housing grants that also use funding sources not associated with HUD and allowing qualified and willing housing finance agencies to underwrite Section 202 program transactions.[190] HUD has continued its funding of the Section 202 Program with NOFAs issued in 2020 and 2021, with approximately $150 million available in 2021.[191]

B. Supportive Housing for People with Disabilities

Under the HUD Section 811 program, HUD provides financing to nonprofit housing developers to increase the supply of housing that offer supportive services to very low and extremely low income persons with disabilities.[192] The Section 811 program enables persons with disabilities to live independently in their community by offering subsidized housing with access to appropriate services.[193] The HUD 811 program is almost identical to the HUD 202 program, providing a capital advance and rental assistance to eligible private nonprofit sponsors to finance the development of rental housing, only the housing must include supportive services for persons with disabilities. Similar to the 202 program, the 811 capital advance is interest free and need not be repaid providing that the housing remains available to very low-income people (i.e., at or below 50 percent of AMI), who are between the ages of 18 and 62 and who have disabilities. Similarly, project rental assistance is also available.

The Section 811 program is authorized by HUD to operate in two ways: (1) the traditional way by providing interest-free capital advances and operating subsidies to nonprofit developers of affordable housing; and (2) by providing project rental assistance to state housing agencies, which is also known as Section 811-PRA.[194] The clear difference here is that the traditional program provides support from HUD to the nonprofit developer, while the Section 811-PRA awards funds to state housing agencies, which must then develop their own rules to structure and administer the PRA Program. There is guidance from HUD on how the PRA-funded units are structured.[195]

C. Section 8 Rental Assistance

As exclusively a source of rental assistance for tenants, the multiple sub-programs under Section 8, or what is also called the Housing Choice Voucher Program, are qualitatively different from other programs discussed *supra*; they are a major source of federal financing

---

189. 24 C.F.R. § 891.800 (2010).

190. H.R. 3221, 110th Cong. § 2835(b), Pub. L. No. 110-289 (2008).

191. Section 202 Supportive Housing for the Elderly Program (Jan. 27, 2021), https://www.hud.gov/program_offices/spm/gmomgmt/grantsinfo/fundingopps/fy20_section202.

192. The program is codified at 42 U.S.C. § 8013 (2010). For definition of "persons with disabilities" *see* HUD, Evaluation of Supportive Housing Programs for Persons with Disabilities (1996), http://www.huduser.org/portal/publications/suppsvcs/shp.html (last accessed July 13, 2010).

193. Section 811 Portal, https://www.hud.gov/program_offices/housing/mfh/grants/section811ptl (last visited Dec. 13, 2021).

194. Section 811 Supportive Housing for Persons with Disabilities, https://www.hud.gov/program_offices/housing/mfh/progdesc/disab811 (last visited Dec. 13, 2021).

195. Section 811 PRA Program—HUD Exchange, https://www.hudexchange.info/programs/811-pra/ (last visited Dec. 13, 2021).

for affordable housing. Authorized under the 1937 Housing Act,[196] there are two main categories of Section 8: tenant-based assistance[197] and project-based assistance.[198] The primary distinction is whether the funds are portable by family (tenant-based) or tied to a unit (project-based). The essence of the Section 8 program is that funds are made available by the federal government to Public Housing Authorities (PHAs), which in turn provide rental subsidy payments directly to landlords. In other words, the PHA pays the landlord the difference between 30 percent of the household's adjusted income and the unit's rental amount. The administering PHA must inspect any housing units before renting to ensure compliance with HUD quality standards.[199] The current trend in the past 40 years has been to shift away from "project-based"[200] to "tenant-based" assistance, and to eliminate or sharply reduce the availability of Section 8 as a tool for new construction or substantial rehabilitation of housing.[201] Landlords in turn must agree to charge only the fair market rent for the rental housing in the area.[202]

Section 8 is a program designed to assist very low-income families,[203] with rental assistance limited to "very low-income" or those at or below 50 percent of AMI, while 75 percent of all families assisted by Section 8 in any PHA fiscal year must be to "extremely low-income" families, those at or below 30 percent of AMI.[204] In general, families should be paying only 30 percent of adjusted income for rent, which should include an allowance for utilities.[205]

As indicated, the program is designed to provide rental payments to landlords by the PHA. Landlord/owners have certain responsibilities to maintain quality housing, comply with all federal fair housing rules and regulations, provide a lease compliant with HUD

196. 1937 Housing Act, 42 U.S.C. § 1437f, including significant amendments at Pub. L. No. 106-377, 114 St. 1441 (2000). *See also* www.hudclips.org and www.hud.gov generally. Other useful links for current developments include National Low Income Housing Coalition, http://www.nlihc.org (last accessed May 8, 2021).

197. 24 C.F.R. § 982.1 (2010).

198. *Id.* § 983.1; *see also* 66 Fed. Reg. 3605-02 (Jan. 16, 2001) for revisions to the PHA Project-Based Assistance Program. In addition, there is a special Section 8 voucher called "enhanced Section 8 voucher," which relates to affordable housing preservation programs. See Chapter 15, *infra*, for a discussion of these.

199. HUD, Housing Choice Voucher Program Section 8, Housing Choice Vouchers Fact Sheet, https://www.hud.gov/topics/housing_choice_voucher_program_section_8 (last visited Dec. 13, 2021).

200. There was limited authority established in 2001 for "project-based" vouchers. Departments of Veterans Affairs and Housing and Urban Development-Appropriations Pub. L. No. 106-377, § 232 (2000).

201. Pub. L. No. 98-181, § 209(a)(3); 97 Stat. 1183 (1983).

202. *Supra* note 199.

203. Originally, Section 8 was designed for low-income families or those at or below 80 percent of AMI. Previous amendments have lowered the income targeting.

204. 24 C.F.R. § 982.201(b)(2)(i) (2010).

205. For minimum rent calculation, check 24 C.F.R. § 5.630 (2010) and 42 U.S.C. § 1437a(a)(3) (2010), which prescribe minimum rental amounts for project-based and tenant-based assistance. For the formula to determine the correct "adjusted amount" for income, *see generally* 24 C.F.R. pt. 5. The intent of the Section 8 program is to cover housing costs inclusive of rent and a utility allowance. HUD determines an amount that would be considered reasonably prudent for utility usage, which is based on utility usage of comparable units in the area, and not based on actual costs. I.R.S. Notice 89-6, 1989-1 C.B. 625.

regulations, ensure lead-paint compliance, and conduct periodic reporting to the PHA regarding income verification.[206] The PHA also has responsibilities under Section 8 to enforce all landlord/owner obligations, to ensure payment of rents to owners, to address tenant grievances, and to report to HUD.[207] The responsibilities of the tenant in a Section 8 unit are comparable to those of any tenant, with the additional responsibility of regularly reporting updated income, and the avoidance of criminal activity.[208]

Both the tenant-based assistance and project-based assistance programs under Section 8 continue to undergo considerable reform. Significantly, for the tenant-based program, the voucher and certificate programs have been merged, and the tenant's voucher is portable. Similarly, the project-based program has undergone considerable changes to address the vast number of expiring Section 8 projects, increased notice requirements, and the impact of the mark-to-market program.[209]

HERA increases project-based voucher program flexibility by (1) increasing the maximum Section 8 project-based voucher contract from 10 to 15 years; (2) codifying existing regulations allowing project-based voucher rents in LIHTC developments to reach normally allowed voucher payment standard-based maximum rent, even if greater than LIHTC rent; (3) eliminating HUD's subsidy layering review for project-based vouchers if a state or locality has completed such review for LIHTC purposes; (4) repealing environmental review for existing housing unless otherwise required; and (5) clarifying standards for voucher rent reasonableness for LIHTC developments.[210]

D. Homeless Assistance Grants (McKinney-Vento Act)

The Stewart B. McKinney Homeless Assistance Act[211] was passed by Congress in July 1987 to fund community-based efforts to address homelessness, and originally consisted of 15 different programs such as emergency shelters, transitional housing, job training, primary health care, and education to address homelessness.[212] Over the years, this act has been amended, and received less funding, but is the landmark bill creating programs to address homelessness.[213] This act provides rights and services to children and youth experiencing homelessness, with a focus on providing educational opportunities.[214] The McKinney-Vento Act defines homeless children and youth as "individuals who lack a fixed, regular, and

---

206. 24 C.F.R. § 245 (2010).

207. *Id.* § 982.

208. *Id.* § 982.553.

209. Roberta Rubin & Jonathan Klein, *Nonprofit Guaranties Redux*, 9 J. Affordable Hous. & Cmty. Dev. L. 317 (2000); Roberta Rubin & Jonathan Klein, *Nonprofit Guaranties in Tax Credit Transaction*, 9 J. Affordable Hous. & Cmty. Dev. L. 302 (1999); Roberta Rubin, *Public Housing Occupancy-Related Issues in Mixed-Finance Transactions*, course materials from the 13th Annual ABA Forum on Affordable Housing Conference (1999). See Chapter 15, *infra*, for a discussion of preservation issues.

210. H.R. 3221, 110th Cong. § 2835(a), Pub. L. No. 110-289 (2008).

211. 42 U.S.C. ch. 119 § 11301 *et seq.*, commonly known as the Stewart B. McKinney Homeless Assistance Act of 1987, as amended in 1988, 1990, 1992, and 1994.

212. On October 30, 2000, President Bill Clinton renamed the legislation the McKinney-Vento Homeless Assistance Act.

213. For a good summary of the McKinney-Vento Act, see National Homeless Coalition's report published in June 2006, https://www.nationalhomeless.org/publications/facts/McKinney.pdf.

214. http://schoolhouseconnection.org (last visited May 2021).

adequate nighttime residence."[215] Homeless assistance grants are divided into two main categories: formula (or noncompetitive) and competitive. A major component of the competitive program is that funds are awarded competitively based on a "Continuum of Care" system developed by the community for which assistance is sought.[216] The Continuum of Care approach is predicated on the understanding that homelessness is not caused merely by a lack of shelter, but involves a variety of underlying unmet needs—physical, economic, and social.[217] Funding is announced through an annual NOFA. Through the Continuum of Care plans, the community is supposed to develop systems and strategies that identify the needs of homeless people and to design programs to address those needs. The amount of money allocated will depend on the local needs identified and the quality of the Continuum plan. HUD provides the funding, but allows the local community some discretion in how it is allocated.[218]

There are two competitive programs and two formula programs. The two competitive programs are the Supportive Housing Program and the Shelter Plus Care Program.[219] The Supportive Housing Program funds individual housing units and group homes (congregate living projects). The Shelter Plus Care Program provides grants for rental assistance either directly to the tenant, the sponsor, and the project or through funding for single-room occupancy (SRO) facilities. HERA changes include the authorization of 15-year terms for renewal of Shelter Plus Care permanent housing assistance contracts and extends the time period for completion of Shelter Plus Care projects utilizing LIHTCs to five years.[220]

One formula program,[221] the Emergency Shelter Grants (ESG) program, provides homeless persons with basic shelter and essential supportive services. Under ESG, the grantees are government entities with funds channeled through large cities, urban counties, or state agencies. Those entities in turn fund recipient agencies and organizations that implement the homeless assistance projects. Funding can be spent on the development of new shelter facilities, rehabilitation or remodeling of existing buildings, essential supportive services, homelessness prevention, and grant administration.[222]

The other formula program falls under Title V of the McKinney-Vento Act. Under this program, federal properties that are considered unutilized, underutilized, excess, or surplus can be used to assist homeless people. Such properties are made available to local or state units of governments and other eligible organizations. These properties are leased at no charge, but a homeless advocacy organization must support the operational and repair

215. http://www.ccsid.net (last visited May 2021).

216. The "Continuum of Care" (COC) approach is an approach to homelessness that focuses on various types of housing that homeless people might need as they move from living on the street to self-sufficiency, for example, emergency shelter, transitional housing, supportive housing, and so on.

217. HUD, Evaluation of Continuums of Care for Homeless People: Final Report, http://www.huduser.org/portal/publications/povsoc/continuums.html (last visited May 10, 2021).

218. Hecht, *supra* note 159.

219. *See* HUD, Shelter Plus Care (S+C), https://www.hud.gov/hudprograms/spc (last visited Dec. 13, 2021).

220. H.R. 3221, 110th Cong. § 2835(c), Pub. L. No. 110-289 (2008).

221. Formula grants are awarded based on HUD's review and approval of a locality's Consolidated Plan.

222. HUD, Emergency Shelter Grants (ESG) Program, https://www.hud.gov/hudprograms/esg (last visited Dec. 13, 2021).

costs, as there is no separate funding for this program and properties are made available "as is." HUD publishes a weekly list of available properties, and the Department of Health and Human Services accepts applications and handles administration of the program.[223]

E. Housing Opportunities for People with AIDS

Beginning in 1992, the Housing Opportunities for People with AIDS (HOPWA) program, which is managed by HUD's Office of HIV/AIDS Housing, was established to provide housing assistance and supportive services related to that housing for low-income persons with HIV/AID and their families.[224] The 2020 president's budget requested $330 million for HOPWA, which was $45 million less than that awarded in the 2019 Continuing Budget Resolution.[225] HOPWA has provided funds to support community efforts to create housing opportunities for people with HIV/AIDS and family members who reside with them. Eligible activities under the HOPWA program include rental assistance, supportive or social services, acquisition/rehabilitation or new construction of housing units, short-term payments to prevent homelessness, and costs for facility operations. Similar to McKinney Homeless Assistance grants, HOPWA funds are awarded to states, local communities, and nonprofit organizations engaged in projects to benefit people with HIV/AIDS. HOPWA funds are awarded utilizing a formula program (noncompetitive) and competitive program. HOPWA funding for housing and related services are part of HUD's Consolidated Planning initiative. HUD has a division of HIV/AIDS Housing that works with area Community Planning Development offices to coordinate HUD programs and initiatives for people with HIV/AIDS. There is a special Tenant Based Rental Assistance Program (TBRA), which is a federally funded HOPWA program that provides rental assistance to persons with HIV/AIDS.[226]

F. Environmental/Energy Programs

HUD has recognized that older industrial cities are burdened with environmental contamination that challenges redevelopment strategies. Much of the vacant land in cities that is abandoned, idle, or underutilized is complicated by the presence, or potential presence, of environmental contamination.[227] To redevelop these sites successfully, the environmental condition must be identified, a clean-up or remediation plan devised, and funds to cover that clean-up accessed. The following describes program initiatives designed for such remediation.[228]

---

223. HUD, Title V - Federal Surplus Property for Use to Assist the Homeless, https://www.hud exchange.info/programs/title-v/ (last visited Dec. 13, 2021).

224. 42 U.S.C. §§ 12901–12912. *See also* HOPWA Eligibility Requirements, https://www.hud exchange.info/programs/hopwa/hopwa-eligibility-requirements/ (last visited Dec. 13, 2021).

225. HUD, Housing Opportunities for People with AIDS (HOPWA), https://www.hud.gov/hud programs/hopwa (last visited Dec. 13, 2021).

226. *Id.*

227. HUD, Brownfields FAQs (Dec. 2012), https://www.hudexchange.info/resource/3180 /brownfields-frequently-asked-questions/.

228. See Part I, Chapter 2, *supra*, for a discussion of how environmental programs relate to affordable housing development.

1. Brownfield Economic Development Initiative

The Brownfield Economic Development Initiative (BEDI) was a competitive grant program administered by HUD to "stimulate and promote economic growth and community development. BEDI is designed to assist cities with the redevelopment of abandoned, idled or underused industrial and commercial facilities where expansion and redevelopment is burdened by *real or potential* environmental contamination."[229] This site clean up initiative is no longer active. Brownfield redevelopment can now be financed through CDBG program, Section 108 Loan Guarantees, and Renewal Communities/Empowerment Zones and Enterprise Communities. (As of this writing, BEDI and Economic Development Initiative (EDI) grants are no longer available.)[230] CDBG entitlement communities and non-entitlement communities are eligible to receive loan guarantees.[231]

2. Lead-Based Paint Grants

For nearly 35 years, addressing lead-based paint hazards in existing housing has been a major area of concern for affordable housing development, and it continues to be important.[232] HUD has established the Office of Healthy Homes for Lead Hazard Control programs and issued new regulations to protect children from these hazards in all federally assisted housing.[233] In 1999, HUD established requirements for control of and remediation of lead-based paint hazards under the "Lead Safe Housing Rules" (also known as the "Notification, Evaluation and Reduction of Lead-Based Paint Hazards in Federally Owned Residential Properties and Housing Receiving Federal Assistance" guidelines).[234] Generally, these requirements apply to housing built before 1978, the year lead-based paint was banned in the United States. Depending on the plan for housing development or rehabilitation, the requirements provide for dust testing after any lead-based paint is disturbed, and for a plan to dispose, remove, or remediate. There are many statutes and regulations pertaining to lead-paint hazards and the rules that HUD has established to address them. HUD has established a link on its website, and developed a manual on guidelines for the evaluation of lead-based paint for affordable housing developers.[235]

---

229. HUD, BEDI: *Brownfields Economic Development Initiative,* https://archives.hud.gov/hud programs/bedi.cfm (last visited May 2021).

230. *Id.*

231. https://www.hud.gov/program_offices/comm_planning/section108.

232. In 2005, HUD announced a settlement of a major lawsuit against a midwestern company for its failure to warn tenants of lead-based paint hazards in over 4,500 apartments. This settlement resulted in complete removal of lead-based paint by the property owner of apartments in four states. *See U.S. Announces Settlements Against Two Minnesota Landlords—250 Apartments in Minnesota, Wisconsin and Indiana to Become Lead Safe* (Mar. 30, 2005), http://archives.hud.gov/news/2005/pr05-039.cfm. *See* Part I, Chapter 2, *supra*, for a brief discussion of how such environmental requirements affect review of affordable housing development proposals.

233. Lead-Based Paint and Lead Hazard Reduction Grant Program, https://www.hud.gov/program_offices/healthy_homes/lbp/lhc (last visited Dec. 13, 2021).

234. 24 C.F.R. § 35, subpts. B–R (2010).

235. Lead Regulations, https://www.hud.gov/program_offices/healthy_homes/enforcemen/reg ulations (last visited Dec. 13, 2021); *see also* GUIDELINES FOR THE EVALUATION AND CONTROL OF LEAD-BASED PAINT IN HOUSING, OFFICE OF HEALTHY HOMES AND LEAD HAZARD CONTROL, 2d ed., July 2012, https://www.hud.gov/program_offices/healthy_homes/lbp/hudguidelines.

All federally assisted housing programs must comply with these requirements. Grant programs are available to state and local governments to address and control this problem.[236] These grants are usually provided to local or state governments and administered by the local health departments in collaboration with the appropriate housing agency or department.

3. Energy STAR Program

A unique HUD program, the Energy Star Program, involves the cooperation of the Environmental Protection Agency (EPA), the Department of Energy (DOE), and HUD to promote the use of energy-efficient products in federally assisted housing, either public housing or other housing assisted by HUD programs such as CDBG and HOME.[237] Although not a direct subsidy, this program supports affordable housing development. The Energy Star is a voluntary labeling program designed to promote and identify energy-efficient appliances and products in order to promote energy-saving building systems and conservation and Energy Star-qualified new homes. The potential benefits include savings by HUD on utility allowances and renters saving dollars on utility bills. Also, new homeowners can save significantly on heating/cooling systems. Energy Star is now a widely recognized benchmark of energy efficiency.[238]

Pursuant to Section 154 of the Energy Policy Act of 2005, HUD is required to submit a progress report to Congress every two years on HUD's implementation of its energy strategy. In HUD's August 2016 report, *Moving to the Next Level: Increasing Energy Efficiency in Affordable Housing*, HUD renewed energy efficiency and green building as a top priority.[239] The underlying goals of HUD's Energy Action Plan, more recently reiterated in this 2016 report, were to provide information, incentives, and technical assistance to HUD consumers, partners, and other housing providers to assist in the development or design of new housing and in the management, maintenance, or operation of existing stock.

In addition to the energy-related activities in the 2008 report, HUD has begun to address a broader green building agenda that addresses indoor environmental air quality, siting and location, materials selection, and water conservation. The activities are intended to complement the growing number of national green housing initiatives, such as the Enterprise Green Communities program, LEED for Homes, the Energy Star Plus Indoor Air Package, and the National Association of Home Builders' (NAHB) Green Building Guidelines.

---

236. Lead-based paint control grants are part of Title X of the Housing and Community Development Act of 1992, Pub. L. No. 102-550, 106 Stat. 3672.

237. HUD, Energy STAR program, https://www.energystar.gov/ (last visited Dec. 13, 2021); HUD, Office of Env't & Energy, https://www.hud.gov/topics/energy (last visited Dec. 13, 2021).

238. HUD, *Implementing HUD's Energy Strategy,* http://portal.hud.gov/portal/page/portal/HUD/topics/energy (last accessed May 2021).

239. HUD, *Moving to the Next Level: Increasing Energy Efficiency in Affordable Housing*, August 2016, https://www.hud.gov/sites/documents/REPORT_CONGRESS8-9-16.PDF.

VII. RURAL HOUSING DEVELOPMENT

Historically, rural rental housing was developed under the Section 515 program of the U.S. Department of Agriculture Rural Rental Housing Service (USDA-RRHS).[240] The Section 515 program administered by RHS provides competitive mortgage loans to build and maintain multifamily housing for very low-, low- and moderate-income families, elderly persons, and persons with disabilities in rural communities. Loans are generally for a 30-year term at 1 percent interest and are amortized over a 50-year term. USDA-RRHS puts out an annual Notice of Funding Availability (NOFA) for its program.[241]

Beginning in 2012, USDA has not issued NOFAs for Section 515 loans, but instead has used its funds for preservation purposes. Despite this drop in production, housing preservationists and advocates are concerned about the existing stock of Section 515 properties, some of which are aging and experiencing physical deterioration, because their reserves and cash flow may be insufficient to complete necessary repairs and maintenance. RHS is cognizant that the properties may be in jeopardy, and it has issued guidelines for revitalization and preservation.[242] Congress also attempted to prevent prepayment on Section 515 loans for these properties. However, depending on the date of origination of the 515 properties, while some loans contain restrictive use provisions that will mandate long-term low-income occupancy, making prepayment a difficult option, others may not contain such restrictions.[243] RHS is evaluating multifaceted strategies to address the long-term future of its Section 515 portfolio.[244] More recently, RHS developed the Rural Development Voucher Program, providing house vouchers to low-income tenants of RD-financed multifamily properties with Section 515 loans that have either been prepaid or foreclosed upon prior to maturity.[245]

In addition, U.S. Department of Agriculture (USDA) operates the Section 538 loan guarantee program for affordable housing developments in rural communities. This program has undergone some regulatory changes. For a Section 538 loan, a developer of affordable housing will have to identify an approved FHA lender to provide the loan.[246]

In 1994, HUD developed the Rural Housing and Economic Development Program (RHED) to advance rural housing and economic development initiatives by state and local governments.[247] For purposes of this program, HUD defines rural communities with five criteria: (1) a locality with fewer than 2,500 inhabitants; (2) a county with fewer than 25,000 inhabitants; (3) a territory, persons, and housing units in rural portions of "extended

---

240. For additional information, *see* U.S. Dep't of Agriculture (USDA), *Rural Rental Housing Loans*, http://www.ruralhome.org (last visited May 2021).

241. *Rural Rental Housing (Section 515)*, https://www.rd.usda.gov/programs-services/multi family-housing-programs/multifamily-housing-rental-assistance (last visited May 2021).

242. *See USDA Rural Rental Housing Programs, Report of the National Low Income Housing Coalition*, https://nlihc.org/sites/default/files/AG-2019/04-13_USDA-Rural-Rental-Housing-Pro grams.pdf (last visited May 2021).

243. *See Rural Housing: RHS Leader Faces $1 Billion Preservation Price Tag*, 13 AFFORDABLE HOUSING FINANCE MAGAZINE (January 2005).

244. *Id.*

245. Rural Development Voucher Program, Section 542 of the Housing Act of 1949, Fed. Reg., Vol. 75, No. 71, Apr. 14, 2010.

246. USDA 538 Loans—Multifamily Loans, https://www.multifamily.loans/usda-538-loans (last visited Dec. 13, 2021).

247. Rural Housing and Economic Development-Archive, archives.hud.gov/funding/2009/rhe dsec.doc.

cities"; (4) open country that is not connected to an urban area; or (5) any locality with a population under 20,000 that is not located in a Metropolitan Statistical Area.[248] The HUD website contains a complete description of eligible grantees, which are generally local rural nonprofits or community development corporations, state housing finance agencies, other state or local government agencies, and federally recognized Indian tribes. In addition, HUD issues an annual NOFA outlining eligible activities for funding, levels of funding available, and applicable deadlines and rating factors utilized for determining awards.[249]

Rural housing development may also receive funding under the LIHTC program, and often these rules are intended to complement the funding available under the programs available through HUD and the Department of Agriculture. Under the majority of state QAPs for LIHTC programs nationwide, there is a set-aside for rural housing development projects to be developed in rural parts of the state.[250]

One change from HERA provides for tenant income and rent limits for LIHTC units for projects in rural areas to be based on the greater of the (1) HUD area median gross income or (2) the national non-metropolitan median income, for determinations after July 30, 2008, for new and existing buildings.[251] The prior tenant income and rent limits were tied to the HUD median income. Additionally, with the elimination of the below-market loan concept in HERA, projects with 1 percent USDA Rural Housing Service Section 515 loans are now eligible for the 9 percent tax credit, which is a major shift from the previous restrictions.[252] More recently, however, HUD has announced a $10 million allocation in capacity-building grants for rural America.[253]

VIII. HOMEOWNERSHIP PROGRAMS

There are numerous federal grant programs, all of which have had varying degrees of success, that have been created to stimulate the development of affordable single-family homes.[254] Those programs encompass a variety of approaches: some assist state and local governments to support single-family developments;[255] others provide direct

---

248. *Id.*

249. *Id.*

250. For example, the state of Michigan's QAP has created set-asides based on housing needs within the state to ensure that low-income housing tax credits will be used to create and preserve housing within both urban and rural areas of the state. Under the Michigan QAP draft for 2011, 10 percent of the LIHTCs must be awarded to projects that are (1) financed by a loan guaranteed by RHS; (2) funded by a federal program for the development of rural housing; or (3) is located in an area other than a metropolitan area. *See* MICH. STATE HOUSING DEV. AUTH., *supra* note 27.

251. H.R. 3221, 110th Cong. § 3004(f), Pub. L. No. 110-289 (2008).

252. *Id.*

253. HUD No. 21-001, HUD Public Affairs, HUD Announces $10 Million in Capacity Building Grants for Rural America (Jan. 5, 2021), https://www.hud.gov/press/press_releases_media_advisories/HUD_No_21_001#:~:text=WASHINGTON%20%2D%20The%20U.S.%20Department%20of,(CDCs)%2C%20Community%20Housing%20Development.

254. HUD provides a comprehensive list of programs for single-family homeownership development both through the basic Federal Housing Administration or FHA-insured loans. For a description of such programs, see Paul Esajian, *Struggling to Buy a Home? Find Out If You Qualify for One of These 12 Homeownership Programs*, http://www.fortunebuilders.com (last accessed May 2021).

255. Both the HOME Program and the CDBG Program, discussed *infra*, can support homeownership development.

down-payment assistance to eligible home buyers or provide mortgage insurance to first-time home buyers;[256] and still others provide grants to nonprofit development organizations to develop and sell housing to low- to low-to-moderate income home buyers.

Although there are many initiatives for homeownership, a few more recent programs will be specifically discussed: Homeownership Zone Initiative (HOZ) and Self-Help Homeownership Program (SHOP), the Affordable Housing Program (AHP) of the Federal Home Loan Bank (FHLB), and the newly proposed homeownership tax credit.

Established in 1996, the Homeownership Zone Initiative (HOZ) allows communities to reclaim vacant, blighted, or underutilized properties to promote homeownership "zones" consisting of several hundred new homes concentrated in neighborhoods close to major employment centers. This initiative provided HOZ grants to local governments to reduce the costs of building new housing, thereby stimulating investment in those areas. At least 51 percent of the homebuyers assisted with HOZ funds must be at or below 80 percent of AMI, as adjusted for family size. Eligible uses are broad, ranging from site acquisition, direct housing development, infrastructure improvements, direct home buyer assistance and administrative costs. HOZ funds were made available in FY 1996 and 1997 with grantees awarded in 1997 still active. In 2013, the Federal Housing Administration did an evaluation of HUD's affordable homeownership programs to assess major obstacles toward achieving long-term affordable homeownership.[257]

Through its FY 2020 Notice of Funding Opportunity, or NOFO, HUD is making $10,000,000 in "sweat equity" grant funds to national and regional nonprofit organizations and consortia to produce affordable homes for low-income families, through HUD's SHOP Program. SHOP Grants are only provided to national and regional nonprofits (i.e., not directly to an individual homeowner), which have experience administering self-help programs. These funds can be used to buy land and install or improve infrastructure, but must not exceed an average investment of $15,000 per home. Homeowners must contribute a minimum of 100 hours of sweat equity toward the construction of their home.[258] Two of the main recipients of SHOP grants include the Housing Assistance Council and Habitat for Humanity International.[259]

The Federal Home Loan Bank's Affordable Housing Program (AHP)[260] (or home-ownership initiatives) was previously simplified. There are now two major programs: the

---

256. HUD defines a first-time home buyer as someone who has not owned a principal residence for the last three years, a single parent or displaced homemaker who has only owned a home with an estranged spouse, a person who has owned either a nonpermanent structure or a structure not in compliance with local applicable codes. *See What Is a First-Time Homebuyer?*, FHA, http://www.fha.com.

257. Edwin and Brian Stromberg, *The Federal Housing Administration and Long-Term Affordable Homeownership Programs*, CITYSCAPE, Vol. 15 No. 2 (2013), https://www.huduser.gov/portal/periodicals/cityscpe/vol15num2/ch21.pdf.

258. Self-Help Homeownership Opportunity Program (SHOP), https://www.hud.gov/hudprograms/shop (last visited Dec. 13, 2021). The legal authority for this program is under Section 11 of the Housing Opportunity Program Extension Act of 1996, 42 U.S.C. 12805.

259. Self-Help Homeownership Opportunity Program/Community, http://community-wealth.org (last visited May 2021).

260. Although not a federally financed program, the Federal Home Loan Banks, wholesale banks chartered by Congress in 1932 have become a prime source of funding for affordable housing development. *See* https://fhlbanks.com (last accessed May 2021).

Neighborhood Impact Program (NIP) and the Homeownership Opportunity Program (HOP). Both programs provide funding for homeownership to assist with down payment and closing cost assistance and rehabilitation assistance. Maximum grants per household are $5,000 for each program, and are offered on a first-come, first-served basis.

More generally, the AHP subsidies can be used to finance the purchase, construction, and/or rehabilitation of rental housing with at least 20 percent for very low-income households available for the mortgage term.[261] AHP funds can also be used to finance the purchase, construction, and/or rehabilitation of owner-occupied housing for very low-, low-, and low-to-moderate income households.[262] The FHLB (which is set up in 12 regions) channels its funds through its member banks, which review and fund qualified projects that meet criteria established by the Federal Housing Finance Agency of the FHLB.[263] Specifically, in the area of homeownership, funds will be directed to nonprofit developers, and AHP funds can be available for closing costs, down payment assistance, and homeownership counseling to households with incomes at 80 percent or less of AMI. The period of affordability for AHP funding for individual home buyers is five years.[264]

IX. NEIGHBORHOOD STABILIZATION PROGRAM

The Neighborhood Stabilization Program (NSP) was established to provide emergency assistance to stabilize communities experiencing high rates of abandonment and foreclosure, and to assist households with annual incomes of 120 percent of AMI. This NSP assistance was provided to state and local governments to acquire and redevelop these foreclosed properties for the purposes of resale or redevelopment to help communities stem a decline in housing values.[265] The U.S. Congress appropriated three rounds of funding under the NSP Program beginning in 2008. The first round was NSP1 under the Housing and Economic Recovery Act of 2008 (HERA);[266] a second round of NSP2 was awarded in 2009 under the American Recovery and Reinvestment Act;[267] and a third round, or NSP3, was awarded in 2010 under the Dodd-Frank Wall Street Reform Act.[268] Congress has not allocated any additional NSP funds since that third round, and grantees are in the process of completing activities and completing any and all compliance reports.[269]

In conclusion, federal financing for affordable housing is dynamic, ever-changing, and evolving. Clearly dependent on congressional action, and shaped by the political forces in Congress, financing programs come and go, and are often modified. The most important

---

261. AHP subsidies are generally in the form of forgivable loans, that is, loans that need not be repaid if certain conditions such as the housing remaining affordable are met.

262. Federal Housing Finance Agency, *Affordable Housing Program*, http://fhfa.gov/Default.aspx?Page=102 (last visited May 2021).

263. *Id.*

264. *Id.*

265. NSP is authorized under Title III of the Housing and Economic Recovery Act, H.R. 1, 111th Cong., Pub. L. No. 111-5 (2009).

266. *Id.*

267. American Recovery and Reinvestment Act of 2009, 123 Stat. 115, effective February 17, 2009.

268. Neighborhood Stabilization Program Data, https://www.huduser.gov/Portal/datasets/nsp.html (last visited Dec. 13, 2021).

269. *Id.*

agency in this arena is the Department of Housing and Urban Development, and the HUD website is an excellent resource, easy to navigate, consistently updated, and highly informative. Despite efforts to make this chapter timely and current, changes will occur the day after it is submitted for publication, but this will provide a base of knowledge and a starting point for your understanding of these programs. HUD has also started regular webinars to further update on current trends, as well as legislative and policy initiatives.

State Sources of Housing Finance

10

Carlie J. Boos with Peter Salsich*

I. INTRODUCTION

Governments at local, state, and federal levels are the primary engines of affordable housing development. This chapter focuses on the role of state governments in financing and supporting affordable housing development.[1] Section I contains a brief discussion of states' increasing involvement in funding affordable housing and an explanation of the two primary institutional forms through which states conduct their financing of affordable housing. Subsequent sections discuss the major sources of state housing financial assistance, including housing bond programs (Section II), state allocation of low-income housing tax credits (Section III), housing trust funds (Section IV), and property tax relief programs (Section V).[2] The chapter concludes with a brief discussion of emerging innovations in funding (Section VI) and some practice considerations (Section VII).

---

* Initially authored by Peter Salsich. Updated and edited by Carlie J. Boos, with contributions by law student Anna Bulkowski.

1. See Chapter 5 for a discussion of additional state regulatory measures that support the development of certain types of affordable housing.

2. Because of space limitations, no attempt will be made to review programs in all 50 states. Rather, programs in a few states will be highlighted as examples of the major state programs across the country. PrezCat, NATIONAL HOUSING TRUST & KLEIN HORNIG LLP, prezcat.org [https://perma.cc/SYA2-7PF3] (last visited June 11, 2021) (PrezCat is an "online, searchable catalog of state and local affordable housing preservation policies" hosted by the National Housing Trust and Klein Hornig, LLP). More detailed information about specific state activity may be obtained from the websites of the respective state agencies responsible for administering state tax credit and bond program activities. *Housing Assistance for Low Income Households: States Do Not Fill the Gap*, NAT'L LOW INCOME HOUSING COALITION (Oct. 1, 2008), https://nlihc.org/resource/housing-assistance-low-income-households [https://perma.cc/6SWY-AJ7U] (summarizing state and local programs).

A. Increasing State Involvement

States developed a sophisticated range of programs to help finance affordable housing development. The first vehicle was the tax-exempt revenue bond. Originally a Depression-era strategy to help cities and states in the South encourage economic development and fund the construction of public housing units, the state of New York in the 1960s began using tax-exempt revenue bonds to fund the construction of privately owned affordable housing.[3] From this beginning, a major nationwide program developed. In 2014 alone, states issued $13 billion in single and multifamily housing bonds.[4] Proceeds from these bonds fund a sophisticated range of programs supporting first-time homebuyers as well as nonprofit and limited-profit rental housing producers.[5]

Experience gained from administering the housing bond programs enabled states to take on additional responsibilities in the housing field. States now administer federal low-income housing tax credits (LIHTC) by designating housing finance agencies (HFAs) or other state agencies as "housing credit agencies,"[6] and allocate federal community development block grant (CDBG) funds,[7] housing block grant (HOME)[8] funds for rural areas, and National Housing Trust Fund (NHTF) dollars for extremely low-income households. Most states make additional public funds available for housing production and operating subsidies, either directly or through housing trust funds. Each year, the National Council of State Housing Agencies publishes the State HFA Factbook, a compilation of state housing programs and statistics. States also support efforts to provide affordable housing by adjusting the state property tax system in a variety of ways. This may include limiting property tax assessments on low- and moderate-income housing or granting tax abatements for such projects.

Some states assume a large role in offering and administering housing subsidy programs like the Section 8 Housing Choice Voucher program and the reformed Section 811 Project Rental Assistance program, which provides integrated and affordable housing options for people with disabilities.[9] Some state-funded rental assistance programs also exist, such as the place-based Elderly Rental Assistance Program administered by the Connecticut Department of Housing[10] and Pennsylvania's Nursing Home Transition Tenant-Based Rental Assistance[11] to help individuals with disabilities transition out of institutional settings to more independent living.

---

3. N.Y. Priv. Hous. Fin. Law §§ 10–37 (McKinney 2010) (Mitchell-Lama Limited-Profit Housing Companies Law, L.1961, c.803).

4. David Ho, *Tax-Exempt Housing Bonds: Municipals and Mortgages Intersect*, First Principles Capital Management, LLC (Oct. 2015), https://www.fpcmllc.com/content/dam/fpcm/america-canada/us/documents/white-paper-tax-exempt-housing-bonds-october-2015-brochure.pdf [https://perma.cc/NH5B-SEXQ].

5. *Id.*

6. I.R.C. § 42(m) (2020).

7. 42 U.S.C. §§ 5301–5321.

8. *Id.* §§ 12741–12756.

9. Cranston-Gonzalez National Affordable Housing Act of 1990, Pub. L. No. 101-625 104 Stat. 4079 (codified as amended at 42 U.S.C. § 8013, Sec. 811 (2011)).

10. Conn. Gen. Stat. § 8-119kk (2013).

11. *Guidebook for the Nursing Home Transition Program*, Pennsylvania Dep't of Human Services (Dec. 2016) https://www.dhs.pa.gov/providers/Providers/Documents/NHT%20Providers/NHT%20Guidebook.pdf [https://perma.cc/3TDC-TXRF].

In recent years, some states increased their roles in the housing policy arena, acting as researchers and thought leaders for the housing industry. For example, the South Carolina State Housing Finance and Development Authority recently published its Housing Needs Assessment to distribute reliable housing market information to residents and stakeholders while promoting data-driven policy making in the housing finance sector.[12] The Ohio Housing Finance Agency's Office of Housing Policy hosts the "Stories of Home" podcast, featuring snapshots of housing innovation, like a conversation on the intersections of housing affordability and mental health stigma.[13]

During the Great Recession, many states considerably expanded their portfolios to include foreclosure prevention and mitigation programming. The economic downturn that began around 2007 led to a glut in the U.S. housing market and a substantial collapse in property values. Lenders and investors began to see massive defaults on loans while many families lost their homes. Most of the legislative action in response to the housing market collapse came from the federal government, with states and localities largely responsible for implementing the federal initiatives.[14]

Eighteen states[15] participated in the Hardest Hit Fund (HHF), a component of the Troubled Asset Relief Program, to prevent foreclosure. Michigan, for example, used the funding to provide mortgage payment assistance to those receiving unemployment compensation, offered rescue funds for homeowners who fell behind on their mortgage payments, and made principal reductions for homeowners who could no longer afford their mortgage payments as a result of reduced income.[16] Michigan was also one of eight states to institute a blight elimination program with HHF funding, which, by the first quarter of 2020, resulted in the elimination of 42,259 nuisance properties that suppressed surrounding home values and elevated the foreclosure risk of communities.[17] Oregon offered foreclosure avoidance programs like counseling and public information forums, issued innovative mortgage refinancing products for underwater homeowners, and provided emergency housing and

---

12. South Carolina Housing Needs Assessment Volume 1: State Overview, S.C. Housing (Aug. 2019), https://issuu.com/schousing/docs/sc_needs_assessment_report_finalweb?fr=sY2QzYzE3MTk1MQ [https://perma.cc/SB7G-MKLV].

13. *Stories of Home—Podcasts*, Ohio Housing Financing Agency, https://ohiohome.org/news/storiesofhome-podcast.aspx [https://perma.cc/NF5B-2E7W] (last visited June 11, 2021).

14. Bruce Arthur, *Housing and Economic Recovery Act of 2008*, 46 Harv. J. on Legis. 585 (2009).

15. Press Release, U.S. Dep't of Treasury, Treasury Announces Additional Investment in Hardest Hit Fund, (Feb. 19, 2016), https://www.treasury.gov/press-center/press-releases/Pages/jl0358.aspx [https://perma.cc/HJ6Q-5QSL].

16. *About the Michigan Hardest Hit Fund Program*, U.S. Dep't of Treasury, https://home.treasury.gov/sites/default/files/initiatives/financial-stability/TARP-Programs/housing/hhf/Documents/Michigan%20Fact%20Sheet.pdf (last visited June 11, 2021).

17. *Hardest Hit Fund, First Quarter 2020 Performance Summary*, U.S. Dep't of Treasury, https://www.treasury.gov/initiatives/financial-stability/reports/Documents/Q1%202020%20Hardest%20Hit%20Fund%20Program%20Performance%20Summary.pdf [https://perma.cc/3VJN-Q3CZ] (last visited June 11, 2021).

shelter assistance for those facing homelessness.[18] All states' Hardest Hit Fund programs closed in 2021 after distributing $9.8 billion in aid to 418,156 homeowners.[19]

States took locally funded foreclosure prevention action, as well. Indiana created the Indiana Foreclosure Prevention Network, a coalition of housing professionals, lenders, and nonprofits, to provide counseling and funding relief for homeowners at risk of foreclosure.[20] Many states increased access to housing counseling and loss mitigation resources, including 26 HFAs that acted as funding intermediaries in the National Foreclosure Mitigation Counseling program administered by NeighborWorks America. The program ultimately served 2.14 million homeowners before ending in 2018.[21]

Some of these foreclosure prevention and recovery programs continued after the end of federal funding initiatives and, as COVID-19 spurred a second major market disruption in 2020, provided states a dependable distribution platform to release emergency housing relief funds.[22] In March 2020, the CARES Act deployed billions of housing relief dollars through state mechanisms, including the Emergency Solutions Grant deconcentrating shelters and preventing homelessness, the CDBG program responding to emergency needs, tenant-based rental relief initiatives providing medium-term housing stability, and the highly elastic Coronavirus Relief Fund for a variety of other local needs.[23] This was followed by the Consolidated Appropriations Act of 2021 and the American Rescue Plan Act, each more fully investing in these mitigation measures and adding new aid for homeowners and other distressed populations. Some states also advanced companion legislation to protect and ameliorate renters from COVID's economic impacts, like local eviction moratoriums,[24] right to

18. Oregon Housing and Community Services, https://www.oregon.gov/OHCS/pages/index.aspx [https://perma.cc/FPV5-EV4H] (last visited June 11, 2021).

19. *Hardest Hit Fund Second Quarter 2021 Performance Summary*, U.S. Dep't of Treasury (Sept. 22, 2021) https://home.treasury.gov/system/files/256/Q2-2021-Hardest-Hit-Fund-Program-Performance-Summary.pdf [https://perma.cc/KA29-HFB6].

20. *HHF Frequently Asked Questions,* Indiana Foreclosure Prevention Network, https://www.877gethope.org/faq [https://perma.cc/V8EQ-U9U5] (last visited June 11, 2021).

21. *Responding to a Crisis: the National Foreclosure Mitigation Counseling Program Capstone Evaluation,* NeighborWorks America (Dec. 2018), https://www.neighborworks.org/NFMCCapstoneReport [https://perma.cc/E7JD-PX4N].

22. For example, in May 2020, the Pennsylvania General Assembly approved at least $150 million in CARES Acts funding to be distributed by the Pennsylvania Housing Finance Agency to assist struggling renters and homeowners impacted by the COVID-19 pandemic. Pennsylvania Housing Financing Agency, https://www.phfa.org/pacares/ [https://perma.cc/8L9X-TGDD] (last visited June 11, 2021).

23. Coronavirus Aid, Relief, and Economic Security Act (CARES Act), Pub. L. No. 116-136, 134 Stat. 281 (2020).

24. COVID-19 and Changing Eviction Policies Around the Nation, Eviction Lab (Mar. 19, 2020), https://evictionlab.org/covid-eviction-policies/ [https://perma.cc/QLM9-EX8P] (As of this writing, 13 states had statewide eviction moratoria in effect, and current tracking information can be found on the Eviction Lab's website).

counsel laws that guaranteed legal representation in eviction cases,[25] and eviction sealing[26] rules that phased out public access to eviction records.

B. State Department of Housing and Community Development Programs

Many states organize all their housing assistance programs under one department.[27] California and New Jersey provide representative examples. California's Department of Housing and Community Development administers a wide variety of programs, including crafting the state housing plan and related housing planning activities;[28] grants to nonprofit housing sponsors and local public entities for planning, developing, and operating assisted housing;[29] a farmworker housing grant program;[30] a predevelopment loan program;[31] a jobs-housing balance improvement program;[32] a workforce housing rewards program providing grants and loans to encourage housing for working-class households;[33] deferred-payment housing rehabilitation loans;[34] a multifamily housing program;[35] a rental housing construction program;[36] an emergency housing and assistance program;[37] the state's share of the federal Small Cities CDBG program;[38] a mechanism for the state to fulfill the required matching share of the federal HOPE and HOME programs;[39] a state housing trust fund, including a matching grant program for local housing trust funds;[40] a neighborhood

---

25. WASH. REV. CODE § 59.18 (2021). Washington is the first state to adopt a right to counsel law which guarantees legal representation for households receiving public assistance or earning 200 percent of the federal poverty line or less.

26. Doug Livingston, *Bipartisan State Proposal Would Allow Renters to Seal Eviction Cases Tracked by Landlords*, AKRON BEACON JOURNAL (April 16, 2021 5:56 AM), https://www.beacon journal.com/story/news/2021/04/16/renters-could-expunge-seal-evictions-proposed-ohio-senate -bill/7226991002/ [https://perma.cc/F9JN-GGER].

27. While states operate a variety of housing programs that fall squarely in the housing sector, like Housing Trust Funds, other programs may also serve industries outside the housing world, like bond financing program, which leads to variety in each state's organizational structure. In addition to consolidated agencies, like those in California and New Jersey, and Housing Finance Agencies described below, aspects of housing programming can also be found within agencies that focus on economic development, commerce, human services, rural affairs, urban development, or health and Medicaid.

28. CAL. HEALTH & SAFETY CODE §§ 50450–50459 (2009).

29. CAL. HEALTH & SAFETY CODE § 50504 (2019). Comprehensive annual reports, as well as individual reports on implementation of new programs, are required to be submitted by the department to the legislature. *Id.* § 50408. These are available from the department's website, www.hcd .ca.gov (last visited Sept. 7, 2020).

30. *Id.* §§ 50550–50550.2.

31. *Id.* §§ 50530–50532.

32. *Id.* §§ 50540–50546.

33. *Id.* §§ 50550–50550.2.

34. *Id.* §§ 50660–50671.6.

35. *Id.* §§ 50675–50675.14.

36. *Id.* §§ 50735–50771.3.

37. *Id.* §§ 50800–50804.

38. *Id.* §§ 50825–50834.

39. *Id.* §§ 50835–50836.5.

40. *Id.* §§ 50842.1–50843.5.

development program (BEGIN);[41] the state's allocation of federal HOME funds;[42] and the Homekey program to address health and social service needs of individuals facing homelessness during COVID-19.[43]

New Jersey's Department of Community Affairs, created in 1966 as one of the first such state agencies in the country, includes a division of Housing and Community Resources, which is responsible for programs supporting housing production, housing services, and housing code enforcement.[44] Its programs include a revolving and demonstration grant fund for non-interest-bearing loans to nonprofit and mutual housing sponsors to defray development costs of housing for families of moderate income;[45] a revolving loan and grant program to assist local governments in preserving neighborhoods through housing rehabilitation;[46] temporary rental or housing assistance for persons who are homeless or in "imminent danger" of becoming homeless because of "inability to pay rent or other housing costs;"[47] the *Mt. Laurel* "fair share" housing program;[48] and grants for housing rehabilitation under the national Neighborhood Housing Services program of the Neighborhood Reinvestment Corporation.[49]

State agencies administer federal and state housing and community development programs in accordance with regulations and guidelines published occasionally. Regulations and guidelines for receipt of assistance, as well as necessary application forms, may be accessed through agency or state websites.[50]

C. Housing Finance Agencies

All states, as well as the District of Columbia and four U.S. territories, have established HFAs. These entities can take a variety of forms, dictated both by legal composition and local custom. In Minnesota, HFA "members" are appointed by the governor and confirmed with advice and consent of the state Senate while the agency's commissioner is a member of the governor's cabinet.[51] The South Dakota Housing Development Authority is a "self-

---

41. *Id.* §§ 50860–50866.

42. *Id.* §§ 50896–50896.3.

43. Press Release, Office of Governor Gavin Newsom, Governor Newsom Visits Project Roomkey Site in Bay Area to Announce "Homekey," the Next Phase in State's COVID-19 Response to Protect Homeless Californians Office of Governor (June 30, 2020), https://www.gov.ca.gov/2020/06/30/governor-newsom-visits-project-roomkey-site-in-bay-area-to-announce-homekey-the-next-phase-in-states-covid-19-response-to-protect-homeless-californians/ [https://perma.cc/LN9W-BC2X].

44. N.J. Rev. Stat. § 52:27D-1 (2019).

45. *Id.* § 52:27D-64 . In a report, *Department of Community Affairs 2008 Year in Review*, the department briefly summarized active housing and related development programs and reported distributing over $1 billion in state and federal funds through grants and loans to municipalities, community groups, organizations, and individuals., *Department of Community Affairs 2008 Year in Review*, N.J. Department of Community Affairs, http://www.state.nj.us/dca/announcements/approved/081002_yearinreview.html (last visited June 11, 2021).

46. N.J. Rev. Stat. §§ 52:27D-155 (2019).

47. *Id.* §§ 52:27D-280–52:27D-287.

48. *Id.* §§ 52:27D-301–52:27D-329.4.

49. *Id.* §§ 52:27D-366–52:27D-380.

50. *See, e.g., Forms and Applications,*, N.J. Dep't of Community Affairs, http://www.state.nj.us/dca/divisions/dhcr/forms/ [https://perma.cc/8V65-CWAN] (last visited June 11, 2021).

51. Minn. Stat. § 462A.04 (2019).

supporting, nonprofit entity that uses no State tax dollars to fund its operating budget" and is overseen by a bipartisan, seven-member commission appointed by the governor.[52] An agency's operating structure, funding mechanism ("on budget" or "off budget"), leadership culture, and portfolio scope will affect its ability to influence policy and operate within a politicized atmosphere.

Born of the need for more creative and reliable housing finance tools, New York created the first such HFA in 1960 after voters rejected a series of general obligation bond issues for housing in the 1950s.[53] At the time, the use of revenue bonds to finance housing was problematic because of the uncertainty that rental income streams would be available in sufficient amount and regularity to enable bond interest and principal requirements to be met. To ease public and investor concerns over bond repayment risks, a controversial provision known as "moral obligation" was added to the legislation establishing the New York State Housing Finance Agency; this obligation committed the state to consider making up any deficit in funds when interest and principal payments were due.[54] In 1967, New Jersey followed with its Housing Finance Agency, now known as the Housing and Mortgage Finance Agency (HMFA).[55] Within a few years, most states created housing finance agencies. By 2003, all states had done so.[56]

The National Council of State Housing Agencies (NCSHA) is the national membership organization for state housing agencies. NCSHA represents the interests of state housing agencies in Washington; produces industry best-practices; compiles data on state housing

---

52. S.D. CODIFIED LAWS §§ 11-11-1, *et seq.* (2019).

53. *See* John R. Nolon, *Shattering the Myth of Municipal Impotence: The Authority of Local Government to Create Affordable Housing*, 17 FORDHAM URB. L.J. 383, 405–06 (1989).

54. The bonds are secured in part by a reserve fund that is funded by bond proceeds and legislative appropriations. The state legislature may maintain the fund but does not have a legal obligation to do so. N.Y. PRIV. HOUS. FIN. LAW § 47 (McKinney 2019) (originally contained the housing bond "moral obligation" language). In 2001, the statutes were reorganized and provisions for the state to consider supporting revenue bond issue payments for several authorities, including the state housing finance agency, were collected in a new Article 5-C-Revenue Bond Financing Program, N.Y. STATE FIN. LAW §§ 68-a to 68-c (2010). The obligation is called "moral" because N.Y. STATE FIN. LAW § 68-b(e) (2010) provides that revenue bonds and any agreements to make payments out of a special fund to support revenue bond payments "shall not be a debt of the state." The major case upholding use of moral obligation language by state housing finance agencies is *State ex rel. Warren v. Nusbaum*, 208 N.W.2d 780 (Wis. 1973). The moral obligation concept is discussed in Janice C. Griffith, *"Moral Obligation" Bonds: Illusion or Security?*, 8 URB. LAW. 54, 70–93 (1976). To the question whether a legislative body would respond to a request to honor its "moral" obligation to make up a shortfall in bond or note payments, the Pennsylvania General Assembly answered "yes" in 1976, but imposed additional conditions on the borrowing powers of the Pennsylvania Housing Finance Agency. 35 PA. STAT. & CONS. STAT. ANN. § 1680.401a (West 1976), discussed in Peter W. Salsich, Jr., *Housing Finance Agencies: Instruments of State Housing Policy or Confused Hybrids?*, 23 ST. LOUIS U. L.J. 595, 608–10 (1978). In 1984, these restrictions were removed. Pub. L. 364, No. 73, § 1, amending 35 PA. STAT. & CONS. STAT. ANN. § 1680.401a (West 1984).

55. N.J. REV. STAT. §§ 55:14K-1 to 55:14K-93 (2010). In 2008 and 2009, New Jersey added the Mortgage Stabilization Relief Act, N.J. REV. STAT. §§ 55:14K-82 to 55:14K-87 (2019), and the Housing Assistance and Recovery Program Support Fund, N.J. REV. STAT. §§ 55:14K-88 to 55:14K-93 (2019).

56. *See* Find a State Housing Finance Agency, NATIONAL COUNCIL OF STATE HOUSING AGENCIES, https://www.ncsha.org/housing-help/ [https://perma.cc/4C6G-R9RR] (last visited June 11, 2021).

programs, including their eligibility criteria and their accomplishments; and provides links to state and local housing websites through its website.[57]

II. BOND-FINANCED PROGRAMS

One core function of HFAs is to market housing revenue bonds. Proceeds from housing bonds are used to provide low-cost loans to developers of multifamily affordable rental housing and to provide mortgage loans to first-time homebuyers through financial institutions. The tax-exempt nature of the bonds[58] coupled with low-default risks enables issuers to sell the bonds at lower rates because the purchaser/investors do not have to pay income tax on their investment income. While the tax-exempt revenue bond was a staple of state and municipal public infrastructure finance throughout our nation's history, using the technique for privately owned housing only began in the 1960s.[59]

While the tax-exempt revenue bond remains central to their activities, state HFAs, alone or in cooperation with state housing community development agencies, now administer many state and federal programs with funds generated by state and federal appropriations and general obligation bonds.[60]

The tax-exempt nature of bond financing brings state HFA programs into close contact with the Internal Revenue Code (IRC). The Tax Reform Act of 1986 amended the IRC and ushered in a new era of regulation of state bond financing with the institution of the private activity bond volume cap and targeting requirements,[61] along with restrictions on the amount of interest income that issuing agencies can earn by investment of bond proceeds (arbitrage limitations).[62] The bond volume cap is perhaps the most significant limitation. Originally set at the greater of $50 per capita or $150 million for each state, it was increased

---

57. *See* National Council of State Housing Agencies, http://www.ncsha.org (last visited June 11, 2021).

58. While these bonds were traditionally tax exempt, some states also authorize taxable bonds. *See, e.g.*, the Delaware State Housing Authority's taxable bond first-time homebuyer mortgage assistance program, originally funded in 1998, at Delaware State Housing Authority. Single Family Mortgage Revenue Bonds Quarterly Disclosure Statements, Delaware State Housing Authority (June 30, 2020), http://www.destatehousing.com/FormsAndInformation/FinancialReports/ds_quarterlydisclosurereport_0620220.pdf [https://perma.cc/K26R-5SJQ]. The sale of $3 million in zero-coupon taxable bonds made possible a $10,000 down payment and closing costs mortgage loan program. 26 [Curr. Dev] Hous. & Dev Rep. 54 (West 1998).

59. For discussions of the origins of housing bond finance, see Peter Morris, State Housing Finance Agencies: An Entrepreneurial Approach to Subsidized Housing (1974); Committee on Housing and Urban Development, *Development of State Housing Finance Agencies*, 9 Real Prop., Prob. & Tr. J. 471 (1974); Griffith, *supra* note 54, at 54; Nolon, *supra* note 53, at 409–12; Salsich, Jr., *supra* note 54, at 595; Peter W. Salsich, Jr., *Urban Housing: A Strategic Role for the States,* 12 Yale L. & Pol'y Rev. 93, 101–03 (1994).

60. For example, California voters approved Proposition 1: Housing Programs and Veterans' Loans Bond in 2018 that provided $4 billion in general obligation bond funds for housing programs, projects, grants, and loans including programs that facilitate transit-oriented design, veterans home ownership, and matching funds for local housing trust funds. Veterans and Affordable Housing Bond Act of 2018, SB 3 (Chapter 365, Statutes of 2017), Beall, Legislative Analyst's Office, https://lao.ca.gov/BallotAnalysis/Proposition?number=1&year=2018 [https://perma.cc/665K-B37K] (last visited June 12, 2021).

61. 26 U.S.C. §§ 141, 145 & 146 (2018).

62. *Id.* § 148.

in stages until 2003, when it was indexed for inflation. In 2020, the volume cap was the greater of $105 per capita or $321,775,000.[63] In 2018, $25 billion in private activity bonds were issued, with an additional $51 billion carried forward to 2019.[64]

The bond volume cap applies to a variety of bonds used to fund private activities that have a public purpose, for example, student loans, small manufacturing facilities, and redevelopment activities in blighted areas, in addition to housing production.[65] As a result, states may need to choose among competing bond-funding priorities, often by establishing elaborate allocation systems.[66] Georgia's allocation system provides an example of the way states administer their multifamily housing bond proceeds. The following statements were taken from the Georgia Department of Community Affairs (GDCA) website in August 2020:

> Allocation amounts are set aside for economic development purposes, housing purposes, and purposes such as solid waste disposal. To receive an allocation, the local issuing authorities must approve the project, hold a public hearing, have local government approval, and general financing in place. [. . .] Multi-family housing projects must demonstrate that a minimum number of units will be set aside for low to moderate income families and single-family proposals must demonstrate the ability to turn allocations into cost-effective mortgages for first-time low and moderate income homebuyers. The bottom line is that use of this scarce resource allows for lower than normal financing costs, resulting in the creation or retention of jobs and expansion of affordable housing.[67]

In 2020, GDCA's private activity bond allocation cap was fully subscribed for the first time in 20 years, reflecting a nationwide trend toward greater private activity bond utilization.[68] As this resource grows scarcer, states are increasingly called to evaluate not just the financial feasibility and technical programmatic requirements of a project pro-

---

63. Jennifer Schwartz, *IRS Releases 2020 Housing Credit and Private Activity Bond Volume Cap Levels*, NCSHA (Nov. 8, 2019), https://www.ncsha.org/blog/irs-releases-2020-housing-credit-and -private-activity-bond-volume-cap-levels/ [https://perma.cc/S26X-4DYE].

64. *An Analysis of 2018 Private Activity Bond and Volume Cap Trends*, COUNCIL OF DEV. FINANCE AGENCIES (CDFA): https://www.novoco.com/sites/default/files/atoms/files/cdfa_annual _bond_volume_cap_2018_report_101519.pdf [https://perma.cc/7JPD-TTLM] (last visited June 11, 2021).

65. The volume cap applies to all private-activity bonds. 26 U.S.C. § 146(a) (2006). Private-activity bonds are defined in 26 U.S.C. § 141 (2018). However, multi- and single-family housing bonds constitute a large majority of bond activity, accounting for 92 percent of all private activity bond issuances in 2018. CDFA, *supra* note 64.

66. For example, Nebraska funds an agricultural program in addition to its mortgage revenue bond program., *Welcome Farmers and Ranchers*, NEBRASKA INVESTMENT FINANCE AUTHORITY, https://www.nifa.org/farmer [https://perma.cc/VLL6-79SY] (last visited June 11, 2021).

67. *Bond Allocation Program*, GEORGIA DEP'T OF CMTY. AFFAIRS, https://www.dca.ga.gov /local-government-assistance/research-surveys/bond-allocation-program [https://perma.cc/CS9L -MGEF] (last visited June 11, 2021).

68. Memo from Kyle Hood, Community Development Division Director, to Program Participants and other interested Parties regarding the Private Activity Bond (PAB) Volume Cap Allocation Program (Feb. 10, 2020) (on file with Georgia Department of Community Affairs; https://www.dca .ga.gov/sites/default/files/2020_original_allocation_memo.pdf [https://perma.cc/NVD4-2UN5].

posal but also to review adherence to the state's public policy agenda. For example, New Jersey, which saw an increase in bond funding demand following Hurricane Sandy, considers a variety of factors when awarding allocations, including community needs, developer capacity, proximity to amenities, local employment access, and the ability of the project to make payments in lieu of local property taxes to the local jurisdiction.[69]

In 2017, the U.S. House of Representatives passed a version of the Tax Cuts and Jobs Act that proposed eliminating tax exemption for housing bonds.[70] This was not adopted in the Senate version, saving a critical piece of the housing finance toolkit.

As it relates to housing, the two most common bond programs states offer are multifamily rental housing programs and the single-family Mortgage Revenue Bond, which are described next.

A. Multifamily Rental Housing Programs

All states have active multifamily rental housing programs. States typically distribute funds from bond proceeds (both tax-exempt and taxable) as construction loans or permanent take-out financing.[71] The state may provide construction loans to eligible private for-profit and nonprofit developers. The state may structure these loans to convert to permanent financing or to local housing authorities for turnkey developments.[72] To be eligible for tax-exempt status, the state must distribute bond proceeds in accordance with the Internal Revenue Code's targeting requirements. Funds may be used only to finance "qualified residential rental projects" in which at least 20 percent[73] of the units in the development will be occupied by persons with incomes of 50 percent or less of area median gross income (AMI), or at least 40 percent of the units will be occupied by persons with 60 percent or less of AMI.[74]

---

69. *General Info for Multifamily Developers*, New Jersey Hous. & Mortg. Finance Agency, https://www.njhousing.gov/dca/hmfa/developers/multifamily/generalinfo/index.shtml [https://perma.cc/SSW4-L4JE] (last visited June 11, 2021).

70. H.R. 1, 115th Cong. tit. 1, § 13404 (2017) (codified at Pub. L. No. 115-97, 131 Stat. 2054 (2017)).

71. "Take-out financing" is a financing technique in which a financial institution commits to providing permanent financing for a project upon the completion of construction. For a discussion of mortgage loan commitments, *see* Grant S. Nelson, Dale A. Whitman, Ann M. Burkhart, & R. Wilson Freyermuth, Real Estate Finance Law § 12.3 (6th ed. 2014).

72. *See, e.g.*, N.J. Rev. Stat. § 55:14K-6 (2010); Selection, Underwriting & Financing Guidelines & Policy, Multifamily Programs and Lending, New Jersey Housing and Mortgage Finance Agency, https://www.nj.gov/dca/hmfa/developers/docs/multifamily/mf_rental_financing_under writing_guidelines.pdf [https://perma.cc/4J6T-HTUD] (last visited June 11, 2021).

73. For a great discussion of how multifamily housing bonds can promote mixed-income housing, see Carol Galante, Carolina Reid & Nathaniel Decker, *Section G-29. Rebuilding the Bond Market for Mixed-Income Housing*, *in* What Works to Promote Inclusive, Equitable Mixed-Income Communities (Mark L. Joseph & Amy T. Khare, eds., Nat'l Initiative on Mixed-Income Communities, Case Western Reserve University 2019).

74. 26 U.S.C. § 142(d)(1) (2018). Units must meet the income-targeting tests during the "qualified project period," which begins on the date that 10% of the units are occupied and ends on the latest of (1) 15 years after the date on which 50% of the units are occupied, (2) the first day no tax-exempt private activity bonds are outstanding, or (3) the date on which any Section 8 assistance to occupants of the units terminates. *Id.* at § 142(d)(2) (2006). These are nearly the same targeting

The National Council of State Housing Agencies (NCSHA) reported in 2020 that since the inception of the mortgage revenue bond (MRB) states "have made first-time homeownership possible for over 3.25 million lower-income families, historically 100,000 every year" and multifamily housing bond programs financed 1.2 million rental units for low-income households.[75] To achieve this large-scale effect and deep income targeting, multifamily housing bonds often are used in conjunction with federal and state housing tax credits, discussed *infra*, as well as the federal CDBG, HOME, and Section 8 programs and local gap financing.

In response to the financial crisis, Congress in 2008 permitted HFAs to use funds received through bond repayments to finance additional housing developments without having the second transaction count against the bond volume cap, thereby increasing multifamily housing bond authority.[76] A special program, the New Issue Bond Program, initiated in 2009 by the federal government helped state and local HFAs weather the financial crisis enabled the Treasury Department to facilitate the sale through Fannie Mae and Freddie Mac of $15 billion in housing bonds from 49 states and more than 50 local HFAs.[77]

B. Single-Family Mortgage Revenue Bond Programs

The mortgage revenue bond (MRB) program is another state housing program funded by housing bonds. MRBs are private activity bonds subject to similar volume caps and targeting rules of the IRC.[78] The IRC refers to MRBs as "qualified mortgage bonds," and subjects them to several targeting restrictions. In general, at least 95 percent of the net proceeds of a bond issue must finance single-family home purchases by "first time home buyers."[79] All owner financing must be directed to mortgagors whose family income does not exceed 115 percent of the AMI.[80] Income may be as high as 140 percent of AMI if the residence is in a targeted area, defined as a "census tract in which 70 percent or more of the families have income which is 80 percent or less of the statewide median family income,"[81] or an "area of chronic economic distress" as defined by the state and approved by HUD.[82] Acquisition costs of residences financed through MRBs may not exceed 90 percent of the average purchase price of single-family residences within the applicable statistical area over the previous year.[83] The purchase price in targeted areas, as just defined, may be as

---

requirements as the Low Income Housing Tax Credit except that the income averaging test does not apply to bond financing, discussed *infra* Section III.C.

75. *Housing Bonds*, NATIONAL COUNCIL OF HOUSING FINANCE AGENCIES, https://www.ncsha .org/advocacy-issues/housing-bonds/ [https://perma.cc/XV86-PB96] (last visited June 11, 2021).

76. Housing and Economic Recovery Act of 2008, Pub. L. No. 110-289, 122. Stat. 2654 Div. C., Title I, § 302(a), adding new subsection (6) to 26 U.S.C. § 146(i).

77. *Housing Government Sponsored Enterprise* Programs, U.S. DEP'T OF TREASURY, https:// www.treasury.gov/about/budget-performance/Documents/CJ_FY2012_GSE_508.pdf [https://perma .cc/9FYH-VZDZ] (last visited June 11, 2021).

78. 26 U.S.C. §§ 141, 143 (2018).

79. First-time homebuyers are "mortgagors who had no present ownership interest in their principal residences at any time during the 3-year period ending on the date their mortgage is executed." 26 U.S.C. § 143(d) (2006).

80. 26 U.S.C. § 143(f) (2018).

81. *Id.* §§ 143(f)(3), 143(j)(2).

82. *Id.* § 143(j)(3).

83. *Id.* § 143(e).

high as 110 percent of the average price.[84] MRBs are subject to the volume cap and arbitrage limitations described earlier.

The National Low Income Housing Coalition reported that almost $6 billion[85] was raised through the sale of MRBs in 2016, enabling 31,157 single-family home loans, down considerably from 2007, when $17.8 billion was raised, enabling 127,000 single-family home loans to be made to eligible households.[86] By 2018, the average income of MRB borrowers was $47,600,[87] approximately 75 percent of the national median family income.

The decreased MRB activity is forcing states to become more creative and competitive in their home-buyer enterprises. The Maryland Department of Housing and Community Development website, for instance, describes a number of homeownership programs with competitive interest rates and/or down payment assistance, including Maryland SmartBuy, a first-time homeowner program that helps pay off student loan debt while purchasing a home; Maryland HomeAbility for homebuyers with disabilities; programs customized to regions of the state that pair state assistance with locally run programs; and partner match initiatives that leverage the investments made by employers, home builders, and community organizations.[88] Many states also elect to convert a portion of their private activity bond authority into Mortgage Credit Certificates to pair with their home purchase products to offer qualified buyers a nonrefundable tax credit to further their annual housing costs.[89]

As with the multifamily programs just described, all states have similar homeownership programs, with details adjusted to fit local conditions. Virginia Housing offers a homeownership grant for educators and first responders;[90] Florida created the Hurricane Michael Recovery Loan Program;[91] and Ohio hosts the Next Home program to help empty nesters and victims of the foreclosure crisis, among others, maintain or return to

---

84. *Id.* § 143(e)(5).

85. Greg Zagorski, *Housing Bonds*, NAT'L LOW INCOME HOUS. COAL., https://nlihc.org/sites /default/files/AG-2019/05-03_Housing-Bonds.pdf [https://perma.cc/TM8A-TDE2] (last visited June 11, 2021).

86. NAT'L COUNCIL OF STATE HOUSING AGENCIES, STATE HFA FACTBOOK (2008), available at www.ncsha.org, at 61–62 (last visited June 14, 2010).

87. NCSHA *supra* note 57.

88. *Maryland Mortgage Program*, MARYLAND DEP'T OF HOUS. & CMTY DEV., https://mmp .maryland.gov/Pages/1stTimeAdvantage.aspx [https://perma.cc/6TWF-3W7P] (last visited June 11, 2021).

89. *Mortgage Tax Credit Certificate (MCC)*, FED. DEPOSIT INS. CORP. (FDIC), https://www.fdic .gov/consumers/community/mortgagelending/guide/part_2_docs/mortgage_tax_credit.pdf [https:// perma.cc/3EFS-STHG] (last visited June 11, 2021).

90. Press Release, Virginia Housing, VHDA Announces Community Heroes Grant to Help Educators and First Responders Buy Homes (May 13, 2019), https://www.vhda.com/about/NewsCe nter/Pages/Community-Heroes-May132019.pdf#search=community%20hero%20program [https:// perma.cc/4VWK-KCLK].

91. News Release, Ron DeSantis, 46th Governor of Florida, *Ron DeSantis Announces Relaunch of Hurricane Michael Homebuyer Program* (Aug. 17, 2020), https://www.flgov.com/2020/08/17/gov-ernor-ron-desantis-announces-relaunch-of-hurricane-michael-homebuyer-program/ [https://perm a.cc/VA2N-XVWJ].

homeownership.[92] Detailed information, eligibility standards, applicable regulations, and application forms are found on agency websites.

III. HOUSING TAX CREDITS

A. Federal Low Income Housing Tax Credit Programs

Congress delegated the responsibility for administering the federal Low Income Housing Tax Credit (LIHTC)[93] program to state housing agencies. Created in 1986,[94] the LIHTC first acted as a temporary replacement for various deductions that were controversial "tax shelters."[95] The LIHTC became permanent in 1993.[96] Since then, it has become the main federal housing production subsidy program.[97] The credit focuses on the equity side of the development equation, providing a dollar-for-dollar credit against a taxpayer's income tax obligations in return for investment in qualified housing development projects.[98] (The LIHTC as a source of financing for affordable housing is discussed in detail in Chapter 9.)

States also administer federal Historic Preservation Tax Incentives[99] together with state preservation programs, which are a valuable source of financing for some affordable housing projects. Between 1977 and 2019, the federal programs supported the rehabilitation of construction of over 600,000 residential housing units, including 172,416 that are affordable to low- and moderate-income residents.[100]

B. State Tax Credit Programs

Many states enacted companion state housing tax credit programs. For example, California's state tax credit program is like the federal program in many respects and is available only to projects receiving the federal credit. However, it differs in some important ways. The California Tax Credit Allocation Committee (TCAC) gives priority to projects that are in a qualified census tract or difficult development area and also (1) include special needs units, (2) request 4 percent LIHTC and State Farmworker Credits, or (3) request 4 percent LIHTC and propose new construction.[101] The applicable percentages for determining the amount of state credits are 30 percent for projects not federally subsidized (in contrast to 9 percent for the federal credit) and 13 percent for projects that are federally subsidized (in contrast to 4 percent for the federal credit). Any surplus revenues generated above a state

---

92. *Next Home*, OHIO HOUSING FINANCE AGENCY, https://myohiohome.org/nexthome.aspx [https://perma.cc/4XGC-XAN2] (last visited June 11, 2021).

93. 26 U.S.C. § 42(h)(3)(b) (2018). Formally, the name is "Low Income Housing Credit," but it is colloquially known as the "Low Income Housing Tax Credit" program or LIHTC.

94. Pub. L. No. 99-514, 100 Stat. 2189, tit. II, § 252(a) (1986).

95. House Conf. Rep. No. 99-841 (Sept. 18, 1986).

96. Pub. L. No. 103-66, 107 Stat. 312, tit. XIII, § 13142, (1993) (codified at 26 U.S.C. § 42).

97. *See, e.g.*, Charles J. Orlebeke, *The Evolution of Low-Income Housing Policy, 1949 to 1999*, 11 HOUS. POL'Y DEBATE 489, 511 (2000), *quoting* James Wallace, *Financing Affordable Housing in the United States*, 6 HOUS. POL'Y DEBATE 785, 793 (1995).

98. 26 U.S.C. §§ 38(b)(5), 42(a) (2018).

99. *Id.* § 47.

100. *Federal Tax Incentives for Rehabilitating Historic Buildings, Annual Report for Fiscal Year 2019*, NATIONAL PARK SERV. U.S. DEP'T OF THE INTERIOR, https://www.nps.gov/tps/tax-incentives /taxdocs/tax-incentives-2019annual.pdf [https://perma.cc/2SEP-UWTA] (last visited June 11, 2021).

101. CAL. CODE REGS. tit. 4 § 10317 (2020).

limitation on rates of return must be applied to rent reduction.[102] In 2018, $98.6 million was authorized for the state tax credit program, with 85 percent of awarded state credits supplementing the 9 percent LIHTC.[103]

State tax credits are gaining popularity, including in Nebraska where the legislature approved the Nebraska Affordable Housing Tax Credit (AHTC) in 2016, which may be taken against state income tax liability and is claimable over a six-year period.[104] Nebraska will award AHTCs up to 100 percent of the federal competitive LIHTC allocation a project receives. In August 2020, six states were considering state tax credit proposals: Minnesota, Arizona, Indiana, Kentucky, Pennsylvania, and Maryland.[105] Missouri, however, demonstrated the fragility of state funding programs when, in 2017, the Missouri Housing Development Commission voted to suspend its state LIHTC matching program.[106]

C. Qualified Allocation Plans

As noted earlier, the LIHTC statute delegates responsibility to state housing agencies to administer the allocation of federal housing tax credits to developers. To accomplish this allocation, state housing agencies must prepare "qualified allocation plans" (QAPs) that establish benchmarks for the allocation. These plans must include criteria to implement housing priorities that are (1) "appropriate to local conditions," (2) give preference to projects serving the lowest-income tenants for the longest periods, (3) are located in targeted low-income areas, and (4) contribute to a "concerted community revitalization plan."[107] Qualified allocation plans must establish a procedure by which the agency or its delegate can monitor compliance with the statute. Any evidence of noncompliance must be reported to the Internal Revenue Service.[108] Housing credit agencies also must (1) notify the mayor (or other local chief executive officer) of a pending tax credit project and provide an opportunity to comment, (2) require tax credit developers complete a comprehensive market study by an agency-approved "disinterested party," and (3) provide a written public

---

102. CAL. REV. & TAX. CODE § 12206(c)(1) & (2) (West 2018), described in *California Tax Credit Allocation Committee Program Overview*, OFFICE OF THE STATE TREASURER, CALIFORNIA http://www.treasurer.ca.gov/ctcac/program.pdf [https://perma.cc/UWV5-XGJX] (last visited June 11, 2021).

103. *Id.*

104. NEB. REV. STAT. § 77-2501 to 77-2507 (2016).

105. *State LIHTC Program Descriptions*, NOVOGRADAC, https://www.novoco.com/resource-centers/affordable-housing-tax-credits/application-allocation/state-lihtc-program-descriptions#az [https://perma.cc/ZF8A-8QVL] (last visited June 11, 2021).

106. Opponents argued the state tax credit program benefitted developers and created inefficiencies. *See* Joe Gamm, *Missourians Push to Reinstate Low-Income Housing Tax Credits*, NEWS TRIBUNE (Feb. 20, 2020, 8:50 PM), https://www.newstribune.com/news/local/story/2020/feb/21/missourians-push-reinstate-low-income-housing-tax-credits/817589/ [https://perma.cc/3A72-BHBV]. *See also* Maria Benevento, *Low-Income Tax Credit Debate Reignited in Senate*, COLUMBIA MISSOURIAN (Feb. 25, 2020), https://www.columbiamissourian.com/news/state_news/low-income-tax-credit-debate-reignited-in-senate/article_48803000-57ff-11ea-8d36-ef1284537b0d.html [https://perma.cc/T5ZZ-4DVG].

107. 26 U.S.C. §§ 42(m)(1)(B)(i)–(ii) (2018).

108. *Id.* § 42(m)(1)(B)(iii).

explanation for any allocation not in accordance with agency-established priorities and selection criteria.[109]

In addition to regulatory requirements, NCSHA compiles QAP best practices.[110] In its most recent guidance, it recommends states consider how QAP requirements impact up-front development costs and long-term operating expenses, reduce local barriers to affordable housing development, create policies that promote housing choice and access to high opportunity neighborhoods, and facilitate the development of supportive housing and consider the funding implications of the Olmstead decision.[111] It also recommends states take administrative steps to make their QAPs usable, including cross referencing related policies and procedures, reviewing and revising QAPs annually, and engaging stakeholders in the development process.

QAPs can change annually, sometimes significantly. Small changes are common to adopt new tools (e.g., a neighborhood walkability score), correct unintended consequences (e.g., if a large city fails to receive any competitive awards), or to leverage a new funding (e.g., a HUD Choice Neighborhood grant). In some states, more substantial changes are also routine. For example, a state that currently divvies up funding by geographic regions may wish to convert to a policy that sets aside credits for different population pools to better balance the needs of seniors and families.

States policy prerogatives vary significantly with need and HFA structure, with some adopting a clear policy prerogative while others emphasize technical and administrative expediency. Ohio's 2020 QAP[112] is a representative example of the multiple, competing policy needs that must be accommodated in the LIHTC program. In 2020, the state received nearly $33 million in ten-year tax credits. Those credits are split into four policy pools: developments that are newly affordable, developments that preserve affordability (usually rehabilitation of a project with place-based subsidy), service-enriched housing for formerly homeless individuals, and single-family rental housing. Some of these policy pools are subdivided by the population they serve or the extent to which the location is urbanized.

Ohio exemplifies the varied ways that state QAPs can influence the development type. For example, Ohio "sets aside" credits for high-need projects, such as those serving homeless youth. Because OHFA guarantees funding to these set-asides, therefore making them more likely to get funded, developers adapt their behavior to pursue these comparatively easy opportunities. Similarly, OHFA calculates the maximum amount of fee a developer can charge to the project based, in part, on the value it delivers to the community, increasing the developer fee by $75,000 for projects that pay prevailing wages to contractors. Finally, awarding basis boost[113] can help steer housing development toward needed but

---

109. *Id.* § 42 (m)(1)(A)(ii)–(iv).

110. *Recommended Practice in Housing Credit Administration*, NAT'L COUNCIL OF STATE HOUS. AGENCIES (Dec. 2017), https://www.ncsha.org/wp-content/uploads/2018/04/NCSHA-Rec ommended-Practices-in-Housing-Credit-Administration-Updated-Forms-1.pdf [https://perma.cc /3CHF-TKJX].

111. Olmstead v. L.C. *ex rel.* Zimring, 527 U.S. 581, 587 (1999).

112. The Ohio QAP is a two-year governing document. Major policy changes are generally launched in the first year of the plan, and smaller "technical amendments" are adopted in the second year.

113. 26 U.S.C. §§ 42(d)(5)(v) (2018). Basis boost increases the eligible basis a taxpayer can claim resulting in additional credits to the project. Basis boost can be statutorily awarded for projects

difficult development projects, such as those in rural areas that preserve U.S. Department of Agriculture Rural Development subsidies.

To further refine a policy agenda, most QAPs award credits through a complex point system. Some of the most common priority areas are listed here, some of which are derived from the IRS criteria specified earlier:

- Promoting housing for lower income households. Example: Tennessee's 2019–20 QAP provides five points to developments that restrict at least 20 percent of units to serving those at 50 percent of the area median income.[114]

- Preserving affordability in already-subsidized projects. Example: Alabama's 2020 QAP provides eight points for the rehabilitation of a project with an existing HOME loan.[115]

- Balancing the unique needs of urban, suburban, and rural residents. Example: Kentucky's 2020 QAP creates funding based on the geography, with $1.4 million in credits reserved for urban preservation projects and $2.8 in credits reserved for urban new construction developments.[116]

- Ensuring sufficient construction for families and seniors, including a variety of housing configurations. Example: the Ohio QAP's new affordability pool includes a sub-pool for family-oriented developments in high-opportunity neighborhoods.[117]

- Promoting green technologies and emergency efficiency. Example: the Pennsylvania QAP offers ten points for developments meeting the Passive House requirements.[118]

Beyond policy, points can achieve administrative objectives such as containing development costs, rewarding high-performing partners, and maximizing leveraged funding sources. Ohio also uses points to target communities that are most in need of LIHTC investment, such as census tracts with severe housing problems or a large demand for affordable housing.

---

in a Qualified Census Tract or Difficulty Development Area, or it can be awarded by the discretion of the allocator for projects that would not be financially feasible but for the boost.

114. *2019–2020 Low-Income Housing Credit Qualified Allocation Plan*, TENNESSEE HOUS. DEV. AGENCY (THDA), https://s3.amazonaws.com/thda.org/Documents/Business-Partners/Multi-Family-Developers/LIHTC-Program/Allocations-QAPs-Statistics/2019-2020-QAP-AMENDED-01.29.2020-CLEAN_1.PDF [https://perma.cc/84Y3-9FTW] (last visited June 11, 2021).

115. *2020 Housing Credit Qualified Allocation Plan*, ALABAMA HOUS. FIN. AUTH., https://www.ahfa.com/Content/Uploads/ahfa.com/files/MF%20Allocation/2020%20docs/AHFA%202020%20QAP_Publication%20after%20Gov%20Approval.pdf [https://perma.cc/567T-M3AT] (last visited June 11, 2021).

116. *2019–2020 Qualified Allocation Plan*, KENTUCKY HOUS. CORP. https://www.novoco.com/sites/default/files/atoms/files/kentucky_2019-2020_final_qap_053118.pdf [https://perma.cc/GJ22-BCMH] (last visited June 11, 2021).

117. *2020–2021 Qualified Allocation Plan*, OHIO HOUS. FIN. AGENCY, https://ohiohome.org/ppd/documents/2020-21-QAP-BoardApproved.pdf [https://perma.cc/F7CC-ZZWJ] (last visited June 11, 2021).

118. *Allocation Plan for Program Years 2019–2020 Low Income Housing Tax Credit Program*, PENNSYLVANIA HOUS. FIN. AGENCY, https://www.phfa.org/forms/multifamily_news/news/2018/2019-2020-qap-final-news.pdf [https://perma.cc/PJT5-UUU5] (last visited June 11, 2021).

In some states, flexible funding is reserved to support innovative developments that do not fit into the narrowly defined point categories in order to correct funding imbalances caused by the point system, or to advance strategic priorities that have a significant community impact. Tennessee's Innovation Round is "an opportunity for applicants to propose unique development approaches that address unmet housing needs including; hard to serve populations, distinctive design and construction concepts, underserved regional or geographical areas, etc.; without being competitively disadvantaged in the regular competitive allocation round."[119]

Beyond helping select winners and losers in the tax credit competition, the QAP often sets the procedural rules for the state, interpreting and expanding on the Internal Revenue Code. Common provisions include deadlines for completing the construction period, the site approval processes, how to seek carryover allocation relief extending the time to place the project in service, reporting requirements before and after credit allocation, the inspection and monitoring process for active units, and the fees assessed to the project for underwriting and monitoring. Some QAPs may also include guidelines for ancillary programs, such as gap funding or credit bridge financing.

Some states use QAPs to expand tenant rights, often by notifying applicants about the rights and obligations that will appear in the land-use restriction agreement. Examples include waiving a right to a qualified contract, tenant notification and eviction protections during a decontrol period, antidiscrimination protections protecting a class on the basis of "sexual orientation or gender identity or expression," and guidelines for implementing Violence Against Women Act protections.

In recent years, some states increasingly flexed the QAP power to address emerging or entrenched housing challenges in innovative ways. The Ohio Housing Finance Agency's (OHFA) 2019 QAP[120] provides a useful case study to see how a variety of housing barriers can be addressed through creative allocation plan techniques. Due to the codified basis boost advantage for projects located in qualified census tracts and because of long-standing opposition of well-resourced communities to accepting affordable housing, LIHTC projects are disproportionately concentrated in low-income areas and racially concentrated areas of poverty.[121] To counteract this and significantly expand housing in high opportunity locations, OHFA partnered with the Kirwan Institute for the Study of Race and Ethnicity to map "opportunity" and then used scoring and funding incentives to direct tax credits to these amenity-rich communities. OHFA also launched an anti-gentrification pilot program called the FHAct50 program that vested local municipalities with greater power in influencing affordable housing locations, provided they used this new authority to combat gentrification or exclusion in rapidly growing communities. Finally, acknowledging the linkage between housing and population, OHFA awarded points and increased the developer fee for family housing projects "that enter[ed] into a partnership with an infant mortality prevention partner to provide education or services to development residents and/or

119. THDA, *supra* note 114.

120. *Qualified Allocation Plan 2019 Technical Revisions*, Ohio Hous. Fin. Agency, https://ohiohome.org/ppd/documents/2018-19-QAP-TechnicalRevisions.pdf [https://perma.cc/6MD5-CWRP] (last visited June 11, 2021).

121. Texas Dep't of Hous. & Cmty. Affairs v. Inclusive Cmtys. Project, Inc., 576 U.S. 519 (2015).

the surrounding neighborhood."[122] A growing body of research[123] suggests that income integration where unrestricted units are in the same building as affordable units can be a powerful driver of more equitable, prosperous neighborhoods. However, states struggle to craft an incentive for mixed-income housing that is powerful enough to overcome structural LIHTC barriers.[124] OHFA's 2019 QAP included the evaluation criteria "Market Rate Integration," which operated as a stretch goal for developers, awarding both scoring points and additional developer fee if 15 percent of units were not income restricted. Finally, OHFA used the QAP as one way to meet the state's Olmstead[125] obligation to provide deinstitutionalized housing settings for people with disabilities by providing points, and in some cases double points, for developers that committed to accepting Section 811 Supportive Housing subsidies in their housing developments.

QAPs can be supplemented by other HFA requirements, such as those contained in an underwriting manual, a design or architectural standards document, or a compliance handbook. In response to COVID-19 and the resultant run-up in construction costs, at least one state augmented its QAP with a procedure for approved LIHTC developments to seek additional credits to close funding gaps.[126] Because these documents change often and are not always intuitively located on state websites, affordable housing practitioners should meet with HFA staff prior to submitting a funding application to ensure they satisfy all local requirements.

IV. STATE HOUSING TRUST FUNDS

A major addition to state and local funding sources for affordable housing is the housing trust fund, a dedicated source of money administered by a state or local agency and made available to sponsors of affordable housing.[127] The decline in federal housing subsidy

---

122. Another excellent example of how QAPs can incorporate the social determinants of health is the Vital Brooklyn program, which New York State describes as "a model for community development and wellness, breaking down barriers to health and wellbeing through eight (8) integrated areas of investment" including affordable housing. This is integrated in the 2020 New York 9% LIHTC Request for Proposals as a set-aside. *See HCR Multifamily Finance 9% RFP—Summer 2020*, New York Homes & Cmty Renewal, https://hcr.ny.gov/system/files/documents/2020/07/summer-2020-hcr-multifamily-finance-9pct-rfp_0.pdf [https://perma.cc/9LEH-GKAT] (last visited June 11, 2021).

123. *See also Housing National Initiative on Mixed-Income Communities*, Case Western Reserve University, https://case.edu/socialwork/nimc/ [https://perma.cc/U4BD-TY7H] (last visited June 11, 2021).

124. Bryan P. Grady & Carlie J. Boos, *Qualified Allocation Plans as an Instrument of Mixed-Income Placemaking, in* What Works to Promote Inclusive, Equitable Mixed-Income Communities (Mark L. Joseph & Amy T. Khare, eds., Nat'l Initiative on Mixed-Income Communities Case, Western Reserve University 2019). Some of these structural barriers that stem from serving a very large range of incomes include the complexity in pricing debt and tax credits, straddling different architectural expectations, and meeting a wider band of property management needs.

125. Olmstead v. L.C. *ex rel.* Zimring, 527 U.S. 581 (1999).

126. *Additional Tax Credit (LIHTC) Allocations for 2020 9% LIHTC Awards*, Georgia Dep't of Cmty. Affairs, https://www.dca.ga.gov/sites/default/files/additional_credits_policy_2019-2020_awards-5-10-2021-final.pdf (last visited June 11, 2021).

127. See Chapter 11 for a discussion of local housing trust funds. An earlier version of this history of housing trust funds appeared in Charles E. Daye, et al., Housing and Community

programs and increased congressional pressure on the use of tax-exempt bond financing that occurred during the 1980s led state and local advocates of affordable housing to seek alternative sources of funding. A device that became popular—in part because it avoids the "bottomless pit" of direct appropriations of state and local general tax revenues for housing subsidies—is the housing trust fund (HTF).[128] Housing trust funds are dedicated funds that are administered by state or local public agencies. They can take a variety of forms, including subordinate debt, "soft" debt (e.g., a cash-flow or forgivable loan), or grant funding. Moneys are received from various sources and invested; the resulting investment income is used to provide various types of housing subsidies.

A. Housing Trust Fund Characteristics

Created by state legislation or local ordinances, HTFs generally have four characteristics: (1) a regular source of revenue; (2) dedicated to housing assistance; (3) targeted to low- and moderate-income beneficiaries; and (4) designed to establish a permanent source of funding for affordable housing.[129] Funding sources generally include special excise taxes, such as real estate transfer taxes, surplus funds, litigation settlements, gambling revenues, and, in some cases, appropriations from general revenue as seed money for the fund.[130]

For example, the California Local Housing Trust Fund Program[131] receives appropriations from the state legislature, as well as bond proceeds and other funds made available to it, for matching funds to local housing trust funds established by cities, counties, Native American Tribes, and 501(C)(3) nonprofit organizations. In 2000, the California legislature

---

DEVELOPMENT, 3d ed. 281–82 (1999), copyright © Charles E. Daye, and is used with permission.

128. For additional information on housing trust funds, *see* Mary Brooks, *Housing Trust Funds: A New Approach to Funding Affordable Housing*, in AFFORDABLE HOUSING AND URBAN REDEVELOPMENT IN THE UNITED STATES (Willem Van Vliet ed., 1997). An earlier work by the same author is A SURVEY OF HOUSING TRUST FUNDS (Center for Community Change, Wash., D.C. 1988). The Center for Community Change (CCC), an advocacy organization, maintains information about housing trust funds on its website, https://housingtrustfundproject.org/ [https://perma.cc/TPZ6-U9MK] (last visited June 11, 2021) which claims that "[m]ore than 800 housing trust funds in cities, counties and states generate more than $2.5 billion a year to support critical housing needs, underscoring the integral role these funds play in the world of affordable housing."

A National Housing Trust Fund was created as a provision of the Housing and Economic Recovery Act of 2008 and fund were first allocated to the states in 2016. Pub. L. No. 110-289, 122 Stat. 2654, tit. I, § 1131, (2008). Information about the National Housing Trust Fund is available from the National Low Income Housing Coalition, https://nlihc.org/explore-issues/projects-campaigns /national-housing-trust-fund [https://perma.cc/QSS6-DBRR] (last visited June 11, 2021). *See also* Peter W. Salsich, *National Affordable Housing Trust Fund Legislation: The Subprime Mortgage Crisis Also Hits Renters,* 16 GEO. J. ON POVERTY L. & POL'Y 11, 33–50 (2009).

129. For an uncommon combination of a state trust fund that supports affordable housing development and land conservation, see VT. STAT. ANN. tit. 10, § 301 (2012).

130. *See, e.g.*, Phillip Kolbe, Sonya Schenk, Luchy S. Burrell & Steve Redding, *Affordable Housing in Memphis: Revenue Sources and Cost-Benefit Analysis*, REGIONAL ECONOMIC DEVELOPMENT CENTER, UNIVERSITY OF MEMPHIS TENNESSEE (Jan. 1998) (discussing using lotteries and gambling funds to fund housing trust funds); NORTH CAROLINA HOUSING FINANCE AGENCY, http:// www.nchfa.com/About/financingfrom.aspx [https://perma.cc/49AE-XEAR] (discussing how the N.C. Housing Trust Fund was created through a legal settlement with oil company) (last visited June 11, 2021).

131. CAL. HEALTH & SAFETY CODE §§ 50842.1–50843.5 (2019).

enacted an amendment to the authorizing legislation stating that the principal should be invested rather than spent and that it intended to make "a significant appropriation" to the trust fund to provide "a permanent source of financing . . . [and] significant ongoing resources" for the trust fund.[132] The 2020 Notice of Funding Availability released $57 million in matching funds for the following activities:[133]

> Funds may be used for construction loans and/or permanent financing loans to pay for predevelopment costs, acquisition costs, and other costs associated with development or rehabilitation of Affordable rental housing projects, Emergency Shelters, Permanent Supportive Housing, Transitional Housing, or Affordable homebuyer/homeowner projects, including assistance to income-eligible households to purchase for-sale units. Funds may also be used for the construction, conversion, repair, reconstruction or rehabilitation of Accessory Dwelling Units or Junior Accessory Dwelling Units.[134]

The Missouri Housing Trust Fund had about $3 million available for 2020 from a $3 recording fee on all real estate documents filed in Missouri.[135] The Ohio Housing Trust Fund also receives real estate recordation fees.[136] Administered by the Ohio Department of Development, the 2019 state budget increased the allocation for the first time in 16 years, increasing the allocation by $2.5 to $3 million per year.[137] Since its creation in 1991, the Ohio Housing Trust Fund leveraged over $3.5 billion in federal and private funding sources.[138] The Texas Housing Trust Fund, administered by the Housing Finance Division of the Texas Department of Housing and Community Affairs, receives and invests funds from appropriations or transfers made to the fund, unencumbered fund balances, and public or private gifts and grants.[139]

---

132. *Id.* § 50840.

133. Jennifer Seeger, *Local Housing Trust Fund Program Notice of Funding Availability*, CALIFORNIA DEP'T OF HOUS. & CMTY. DEV., https://www.hcd.ca.gov/grants-funding/active-funding/lhtf/docs/1LHTF_NOFA.pdf [https://perma.cc/XL4E-JY78] (last visited June 11, 2021).

134. *Local Housing Trust Fund Program Final 2020 Guidelines*, CALIFORNIA DEP'T OF HOUS. & CMTY. DEV. (April 2020), https://www.hcd.ca.gov/grants-funding/active-funding/lhtf/docs/2020_Final_Guidelines.pdf [https://perma.cc/9W2G-LNQ7].

135. MO. REV. STAT. § 215.034 (2020); Missouri Housing Trust Fund, MISSOURI HOUSING DEVELOPMENT COMMISSION, http://mhdc.com/housing_trust_fund/index.htm [https://perma.cc/V43K-U7AD] (follow links to 2021 "MHTF Allocation Plan" and "2021 MHTF NOFA" to view the allocation plan and the notice of funding availability which lays out the money available and where the money came from) (last visited June 11, 2021).

136. OHIO REV. CODE ANN. § 174.01–07 (West 2019).

137. Am. Sub. H. B. No. 166, 133rd Gen. Ass. (Ohio 2019); Mark Ferenchik, *Ohio Housing Trust Fund Get First Budget Increase In 16 Years*, COLUMBUS DISPATCH (July 18, 2019, 8:08 PM), https://www.dispatch.com/news/20190718/ohio-housing-trust-fund-get-first-budget-increase-in-16-years [https://perma.cc/2MH2-7MNU].

138. *Home Matters to Ohio*, COALITION ON HOMELESSNESS AND HOUSING IN OHIO, https://cohhio.org/wp-content/uploads/2019/02/Brochure8.5x11_v7-digi.pdf [https://perma.cc/X72U-XHWU] (last visited June 11, 2021).

139. TEX. GOV'T CODE ANN. § 2306.201 (West 2015).

B. Allocation Procedures

States establish allocation procedures and eligibility criteria for their housing trust fund programs. For example, the Oklahoma Housing Finance Agency (OHFA) administers the Oklahoma Housing Trust Fund (OHTF).[140] As of July 2019, OHFA has over $4 million trust funds available for distribution, including at least $2.6 million for rural areas and $1 million for urban areas.[141] Signed in 1998, the OHTF statute creates an advisory committee to develop program rules and oversee policy development. OHFA's executive director appoints committee members, which must include representation from "housing development, sales, and finance industries; nonprofit housing development organizations; and economic development agencies or organizations."[142] In 2017, the committee issued a final rule[143] that identified eligible OHTF funding activities as:

1. New construction of rental and homeownership units;
2. Conversion of nonresidential buildings or structures into rental or homeownership units;
3. Acquisition and/or rehabilitation of rental and homeownership units;
4. Infrastructure development, when it is part of an affordable housing development;
5. Rental assistance; and
6. Supportive services directly related to providing housing.

Pursuant to the rule, these funds can be distributed as either grants or sub-market loans. The rule empowers OHFA to establish an application packet with development selection criteria, which may evaluate elements such as the development description, applicant capacity, financial strength and feasibility, and readiness to proceed.

OHFA's 2021 Application Packet specifies that OHTF funds are for construction finance and are issued as a loan with 2 percent simple interest for a 24-month term.[144] The project must serve households at or below 120 percent of the Area Median Income and the assistance carries a three-year affordability term, which may be eclipsed by more stringent funding requirements such as those from LIHTCs. Funding is open to political subdivisions, nonprofit and for-profit developers, and Native American Tribes for new construction of rental or homeownership units, adaptive reuse projects that create housing, rehabilitation and acquisition-rehabilitation developments, and infrastructure investments that support affordable housing development.

Staff review, score, and underwrite an application before making a funding recommendation to the OHFA board of trustees who has discretion to accept or reject the

---

140. Okla. Stat. tit. 74 § 74-2901.2 (2015).

141. *Id.* ("A minimum of sixty-five percent (65%), but not to exceed seventy-five percent (75%) of all annual expenditures from the Oklahoma Housing Trust Fund shall be made for the purpose of providing affordable housing in counties with a population of less than four hundred ninety thousand (490,000) according to the latest federal decennial census.").

142. Okla. Stat. tit. 74 § 74-2901.3 (2015).

143. Okla. Admin. Code § 330:60-1-1 (2017).

144. Application Materials & Program Resources, Oklahoma Housing Finance Agency, https://www.ohfa.org/oklahoma-housing-trust-fund/ [https://perma.cc/67XX-V6GN] (follow link to "2021 OHTF Application" which opens a Microsoft Word document with the specifications of the loan) (last visited June 11, 2021).

recommendation. Applicants must meet threshold criteria such as providing (1) a detailed development description (including partner roles, financing structure, and management control) and (2) a market study showing project sustainability, financial feasibility, and a readiness to proceed (for instance showing site control and conforming zoning regulations). If insufficient funding is available to support all applications, OHFA will recommend projects serving "the most low-income families."[145]

V. STATE TAX EXPENDITURES

In addition to bond financing, tax credit allocation, and trust fund administration, states make significant use of tax relief programs to assist affordable housing development efforts. This is achieved primarily through modifications to the state and local real property tax system.[146]

A. Property Tax Abatement

The classic urban redevelopment tax relief program involves foregoing a portion of the real property taxes that ordinarily would be generated by new development. For example, Missouri's Chapter 353 program abates property taxes for ten years on improvements made pursuant to an approved urban redevelopment plan for a blighted area, and provides that such improvements be assessed at only 50 percent of true value for the next 15 years.[147] Oregon authorizes a ten-year abatement of property taxes on new single-family housing structures, except manufactured structures or floating homes, that were constructed in distressed urban areas between January 1, 1990, and July, 1, 2025, and which have a market value (land and improvements) of no more than 120 percent of the median sales price of single-family homes within the applicable city.[148]

California authorizes local government agencies to exempt from local taxes, fees, or assessments, for up to 20 years, housing that is owned or operated by nonprofit or for-profit entities, limited equity cooperatives, and other entities receiving federal HOME or HOPE funds.[149] Washington, D.C., offers an abatement for mixed-income development in higher-cost areas that have historically excluded affordable housing where 15 percent of housing units are affordable to households at 50 and 60 percent of area median income.[150] The city also offers abatements for certain affordable multifamily housing and substantial rehabilitation of single-family homes in enterprise zones.[151]

---

145. *Id.*

146. The research for an earlier version of this section was provided in part by members of the Edwin F. Mandel Legal Aid Clinic and Jeff Leslie, Assistant Clinical Professor of Law, University of Chicago Law School, as well as a survey by Kenneth Lore, Harold Levy & Robert Knight, Swidler Berlin Sheriff Friedman, LLP, Wash., D.C., Tax Assessment of Affordable Housing Projects, Oct. 7, 2002.

147. Mo. Rev. Stat. § 353.110 (2018).

148. Or. Rev. Stat. §§ 307.651–.687 (2020).

149. Cal. Health & Safety Code § 50836 (2019).

150. D.C. Code § 47-857.07 (2020).

151. *Id.* §§ 47-857.01–.10; 47-858.01–.05; 47-864.

Originally enacted in conjunction with the old federal urban renewal program,[152] property tax abatement programs are controversial because of the impact foregone property tax revenue has on institutions such as local public schools, public libraries, water and sewer districts, and other local agencies that depend on the property tax. One report estimated that tax abatements cost Ohio schools $125 million in 2017.[153] Abating agencies often counter that cities that use property tax abatement and other tax expenditure techniques to foster redevelopment will be able to recover lost revenue through increased sales and/or income tax revenues not generally available to special districts.[154]

In addition to tax abatement programs, some states offer property tax exemption for rental housing owned and operated by nonprofit organizations. For example, California provides a partial property tax exemption for rental housing owned by qualified nonprofits if the development was financed with tax-exempt bonds or other governmental loans or grants, or the development is receiving federal low-income housing tax credits, or 90 percent or more of the occupants are lower-income households. The exemption is equal to the "percentage of the value of the property that the portion of the property serving lower-income households represents of the total property."[155] Michigan has a special statute to exempt taxes for senior housing developments wherein the state pays the local jurisdiction for the forgone property taxes. To be eligible for the exemption, the housing must be owned by a nonprofit or a public organization; must be for persons 62 years of age or older or disabled persons; and must be qualified, built, or financed under the main federal housing programs for elderly and disabled people.[156]

---

152. 42 U.S.C. § 5316 (2018) (The Housing and Community Development Act of 1974 terminated authority to make new grants or loans under the urban renewal program after Jan. 1, 1975 including grants and loans under Title I of the Housing Act of 1949, 42 U.S.C. §§ 1450, *et seq.*).

153. Zach Schiller & Grace Chu, *Tax Abatements Cost Ohio Schools at Least $125 Million*, POLICY MATTERS OHIO (Oct. 2, 2018), https://www.policymattersohio.org/research-policy/quality -ohio/revenue-budget/budget-policy/tax-abatements-cost-ohio-schools-at-least-125-million [https:// perma.cc/34DE-FJ2N]. *See also* Bruce McDonald, John Decker, & Brad Johnson, *You Don't Always Get What You Want: The Effect of Financial Incentives on State Fiscal Health*, PUB. ADMIN. REV. (Feb. 2, 2020) https://ssrn.com/abstract=3376991 [https://perma.cc/F8HA-D7LB].

154. For a discussion of those issues in the context of tax increment financing, discussed *infra* Section V.B., *see* Fred A. Forgey, *Tax Increment Financing: Equity, Effectiveness, and Efficiency* (Dec. 1992) (Dissertation In Land Use, Planning, Management and Design for Doctor of Philosophy at Texas Tech University) (on file at https://www.researchgate.net/publication/265206058_TAX _INCREMENT_FINANCING_AN_EVALUATION_BASED_ON_CRITERIA_RELATING_TO _EQUITY_EFFECTIVENESS_AND_EFFICIENCY#fullTextFileContent [https://perma.cc/5AK6 -MVK8].; *see also* Joseph Parilla & Sifan Liu, *Examining the Local Value of Economic Development Incentives*, METROPOLITAN POLICY PROGRAM AT BROOKINGS (Mar. 2018), https://www.brookings .edu/wp-content/uploads/2018/02/report_examining-the-local-value-of-economic-development -incentives_brookings-metro_march-2018.pdf [https://perma.cc/CC58-G3T5].

155. CAL. REV. & TAX. CODE § 214(g) (2019).

156. MICH. COMP. LAWS SERV. § 211.7d (2010) ((citing several federal housing subsidy programs: Section 202 (12 U.S.C. § 1701q), Section 236 (12 U.S.C. § 1715z-1), or Section 811 (42 U.S.C. § 8013)). See Chapter 9 for a description of these programs.

B. Tax Increment Financing[157]

An alternative that became quite popular, but also controversial, is tax increment financing (TIF). First developed in California,[158] TIF channels new property tax revenues rather than abating them. As with traditional tax abatement programs, TIF-enabling statutes require local governments to prepare plans for the redevelopment of blighted areas[159] or areas in which the development "will further the public purpose of encouraging increased residential, industrial and commercial activity."[160]

Some states require these plans to adhere to a broader plan to benefit the community. Maine, for instance, requires localities to consider how the Affordable Housing Development District will contribute to the "health, welfare or safety of the inhabitants of the municipality" and "meets an identified community housing need."[161] Municipalities seeking to establish such a TIF district in Maine must provide proof of public notice and comment, a description of the area and all planned activities, a relocation plan for displaced individuals, and a plan for meeting affordability requirements.[162]

Tax increment financing of urban redevelopment was upheld against a variety of constitutional challenges, including lack of public purpose, equal protection, non-uniform tax, and impairment of contracts.[163] A number of courts have held that TIF bonds are subject to state constitutional debt limitations.[164]

Some states make special arrangements for affordable housing. Illinois, for example, requires the preparation of a housing impact study if a TIF redevelopment plan indicates that residents of ten or more inhabited units will be displaced, and school districts may receive payments if the addition of assisted housing units to a TIF redevelopment project results in increased costs to the school districts.[165] Iowa prohibits use of TIF funds for public improvements "related to" housing and residential development in an "economic development area" unless the plan includes "assistance for low and moderate income family housing."[166] Michigan established a brownfield redevelopment TIF available for

---

157. See Chapter 11 for a discussion of tax increment financing at the local government level.

158. Cal. Health & Safety Code §§ 33000–37910 (2019); American Planning Association, Growing Smart Legislative Guidebook: Model Statutes for Planning and Management of Change 14–53 (Stuart Meck ed., 2002).

159. *See, e.g.*, Cal. Health & Safety Code §§ 33037, 33330 (2019).

160. Mass. Gen. Laws ch. 40Q, § 2(a) (2019).

161. Me. Rev. Stat. Ann. tit. 30-A, § 5247 (2003).

162. *Affordable Housing Tax Increment Financing Application*, Maine State Housing Authority, https://www.mainehousing.org/docs/default-source/applications/tif-application.pdf ?sfvrsn=f173a915_6 [https://perma.cc/69LY-98LD] (last visited June 11, 2021).

163. Denver Urban Renewal Auth. v. Byrne, 618 P.2d 1374 (Colo. 1980); Richards v. City of Muscatine, 237 N.W.2d 48 (Iowa 1975); Tax Increment Fin. Comm'n v. J.E. Dunn Constr. Co., 781 S.W.2d 70 (Mo. 1989); Dennehy v. Dep't of Revenue, 756 P.2d 13 (Or. 1988); Meierhenry v. City of Huron, 354 N.W.2d 171 (S.D. 1984).

164. Okla. City Urban Renewal Auth. v. Med. Tech. and Research Auth. of Okla., 4 P.3d 677 (Okla. 2000); City of Hartford v. Kirley, 493 N.W.2d 45 (Wis. 1992); *Meierhenry*, 354 N.W.2d 171.

165. 65 Ill. Comp. Stat. 5 / 11-74.4-3–74.4-9 (2011).

166. Iowa Code § 403.22(1) (2010); Knudson v. City of Decorah, 622 N.W.2d 42, 51 (Iowa 2000) (public street improvements that lead directly to a proposed residential development are related to that development because they have "a reasonable nexus or logical connection" with the development and thus must "be included in calculating the amount of money to be provided for

residential or commercial development involving some environmental remediation resulting from a brownfield. Eligible activities include (1) infrastructure improvements directly
benefiting property subject to a brownfield plan; (2) baseline environmental assessments;
(3) environmental compliance activities pursuant to a brownfield plan; (4) demolition of
certain structures; and (5) site preparation that is not in response to state environmental law
requirements to protect the public health, safety, or welfare, or the environment or natural
resources.[167]

C. Property Tax Assessment

A third way that states give favorable tax treatment to affordable housing developments is
by recognizing the impact of federal and state subsidies when assessing the value of the
property for property tax purposes. For example, a Florida statute provides:

> [I]n assessing the property for ad valorem taxation . . . neither the [Federal nor
> state] tax credits, nor financing generated by tax credits, shall be considered as
> income to the property, and the actual rental income from rent-restricted units in
> low-income tax credit development shall be recognized by the property appraiser.
> In considering or using the market or cost approaches . . . neither the costs paid by
> tax credits nor the costs paid for by additional financing proceeds received because
> the property is in the program shall be included in the valuation.[168]

Illinois statutes exclude federal low-income housing tax credits from the definition of
property for tax assessment purposes and direct that property receiving such tax credits
"be valued at 33 and one-third percent of the fair market value of their economic productiv-
ity to the owners . . . to help insure that their valuation for property taxation does not result
in taxes so high that rent levels must be raised. . . ."[169]

In states that do not have legislation specifically addressing the impact of subsidies
on property value, courts have reached different results. Many courts require that both the
benefits (subsidies) and burdens (regulations) of assisted housing be taken into consideration.[170] Others consider the benefits of the subsidy as an aspect of property value,[171] while
a third group does not consider the subsidies.[172]

---

assistance for low and moderate income family housing"). *See also* DANIEL P. MANDELKER, ET
AL., STATE AND LOCAL GOVERNMENT IN A FEDERAL SYSTEM 430–43 (6th ed. 2006) (discussing tax
increment financing, cases cited, and the Illinois and Iowa statutes).

167. MICH. COMP. LAWS §§ 125.2651, 125.2652, 125.2663, and 125.2664 (2010).

168. FLA. STAT. §§ 420.5093(5), 420.5099(5) (2018).

169. 35 ILL. COMP. STAT 200 / 10-235 (2010).

170. Glenridge Dev. Co. v. City of Augusta, 662 A.2d 928 (Me. 1995); Supervisor of Assessments v. Har Sinai West Corp., 95 Md. App. 631 (Md. Ct. Spec. App. 1993); Meadowlanes Ltd. Dividend Housing Ass'n v. City of Holland, 437 Mich. 473 (Mich. 1991); Steele v. Town of Allenstown,
471 A.2d. (N.H. 1984); Alta Pacific Assocs. v. Utah State Tax Comm'n, 931 P.2d 103 (Utah 1997).

171. Penns Grove Gardens, Ltd. v. Penns Grove Borough, 18 N.J. Tax 253 (N.J. Tax Ct. 1999);
Parkside Townhomes Assocs. v. Bd. of Assessment Appeals, 711 A.2d 607 (Pa. Commw. Ct. 1998).

172. Maryville Props., L.P. v. Nelson, 83 S.W.3d 608 (Mo. Ct. App. 2002); Alliance Towers, Ltd.
v. Stark County Bd. of Revision, 523 N.E.2d 826 (Ohio 1988); Piedmont Plaza Investors v. Dep't
of Revenue, 18 P.3d 1092 (Or. 2001). *See also* Wis. *ex rel.* Heartland-Beloit Watertower v. Bd. of
Review, 235 Wis. 2d 276 (Wis. Ct. App. 2000) (this is an unpublished opinion applying WIS. STAT.
§ 70.32 prohibiting consideration of federal low-income housing tax credit on value of property). *See*

Because low-income housing developments can be single-family rentals as well as multifamily developments, property tax exemptions for single-family homes can implicate affordability and provide operating cost predictability to developers. "Circuit breaker" programs are a common mechanism to ensure that property tax obligations do not exceed a certain portion of a household's income.[173] They operate like an emergency override system so that when property tax bills grow too quickly, like in gentrifying neighborhoods, they cap the amount of tax liability homeowners must pay for a period of time.[174] These can be further adapted to certain populations, like seniors,[175] individuals with a permanent disability,[176] or low-income households. Circuit breakers can be available to both homeowner- and tenant-occupied homes. States fund these programs through two primary methods: a refundable income tax credit to the eligible household or direct reimbursement to the local property tax administrator for the foregone assessment amount.

VI. EMERGING INNOVATIONS

In addition to established funding programs, states are exploring innovative financing tools to help meet their affordable housing needs. The programs identified next are in their infancy compared to housing bonds or housing tax credits, but they represent an emerging prospect for some communities.

A. Alternate Loan Programs

States may use general funds to provide low-cost multifamily loan options, including construction loans, credit bridge loans, or permanent loans. As with State Housing Trust Fund programs, the revenue earned from these investments can help support deeper affordability and creative pilot programing. The Ohio Housing Finance Agency's Multifamily Loan Program (MLP) was endowed with $60 million in general funds and Recycled Tax Credit Assistance Program funds; it now operates to provide below-market long-term financing to projects that primarily work in conjunction with the 9 percent LIHTC. However, some funds are also available for "Choice MLP Loans," unique projects that help meet a compelling affordable housing goal without twinning the LIHTC.[177]

---

also Heron Lake II Apartments, LP. v. Lowndes County Board of Tax Assessors, 833 S.E.2d 528, 533 (Ga. 2019) finding LIHTCs are not "actual income."

173. John E. Anderson, *Income-Based Property Tax Relief: Circuit Breaker Tax Expenditures* (Lincoln Institute of Land Policy, Working Paper, Lincoln Institute Product Code: WP13JA3 2012), https://www.lincolninst.edu/sites/default/files/pubfiles/2278_1617_Anderson_WP13JA3.pdf [https://perma.cc/HQX7-WL55].

174. Karen Lyons, Sarak Farkas & Nicholas Johnson, *The Property Tax Circuit Breaker: An Introduction and Survey of Current Programs*, CENTER ON BUDGET AND POLICY PRIORITIES (Mar. 21, 2007), https://www.cbpp.org/research/the-property-tax-circuit-breaker [].

175. Massachusetts' Senior Circuit Breaker Tax Credit; MASS. GEN. LAWS ch. 62, § 6 (2020).

176. Missouri Property Tax Credit Claim; MO. REV. STAT. §§ 135.010–135.096 (2020).

177. *2020 Multifamily Lending Program Guidelines*, OHIO HOUSING FINANCE AGENCY, https://ohiohome.org/ppd/documents/2020-MLP-Guidelines.pdf [https://perma.cc/3BCX-X4CD] (last visited June 11, 2021).

B. Social Impact Bonds

A social impact bond is a contractual agreement between a government and a private organization in which the government agrees to pay for certain outcomes, such as reduced street
homelessness, that the private organization produces. The funding for these "pay for success" agreements comes from the costs savings associated with reducing a social ill. For
instance, eliminating homelessness is shown to reduce policing costs, emergency medical
service calls, and public maintenance costs.[178] Ohio entered an outcome-based arrangement with senior and supportive housing developer National Church Residences that would
leverage anticipated Medicaid savings gained from diverting seniors from skilled nursing
facilities to more need-appropriate assisted living communities. The agreement is backed
by a guarantee from the Kresge Foundation.[179] The Denver Social Impact Bond program
leveraged the LIHTC to provide housing to 330 people that were previously homeless and
through 2019 had received three investor "success payments" totaling $2.5 million for
delivering the agreed social outcomes.[180]

C. Shared Equity Housing

Shared equity housing is a broad term encompassing a range of housing models that seek to
bolster community control and shared wealth through partial public ownership of housing.

> While the practice of shared equity housing is flexible and context-dependent, pro-
> grams often achieve these outcomes by limiting the sale or rental price of homes
> in their portfolios, requiring the sharing of home appreciation gains, and provid-
> ing homeownership assistance to program residents. Residents and community
> members build community control by participating in governance of shared equity
> housing organizations through democratic decision-making and/or cooperative
> ownership structures.[181]

States can support the creation of shared equity housing by enacting enabling legislation, by conducting research and providing thought leadership to the growing field of study,
by offering technical assistance to practitioners, and by using flexible funding streams such
as HOME Investment Partnership fund to support the development of shared equity housing. For example, Maryland signed into law the Affordable Housing Land Trust Act, which

---

178. Jeremy Keele & Sara Peters, *How Outcomes-Based Funding Models Can Improve the
Effectiveness of State and Local Governments, in* WHAT MATTERS: INVESTING IN RESULTS TO BUILD
STRONG, VIBRANT COMMUNITIES (Investing in Results ed., 2017).

179. Kimberlee R. Cornett, *The Kresge Foundation's Social Impact Transactions*, U.S. DEPART-
MENT OF HOUSING & URBAN DEVELOPMENT, PD&R ONLINE MAGAZINE, https://www.huduser
.gov/portal/pdredge/pdr_edge_hudpartrpt_120513.html [https://perma.cc/P6DG-AR9Q] (last visited
June 11, 2021).

180. *Three Years into Denver's Innovative Social Impact Bond Program, Independent Report
Points to Continued Success*, CITY OF DENVER MAYOR'S OFFICE (Nov. 12, 2019), https://www.de
nvergov.org/content/denvergov/en/mayors-office/newsroom/2019/three-years-into-denver-s-innova
tive-social-impact-bond-program-.html [https://perma.cc/2JUJ-HBQQ].

181. Anna Carlsson, *Shared Equity Housing: A Review of Existing Literature*, JOINT CENTER
FOR HOUSING STUDIES OF HARVARD UNIVERSITY, https://www.jchs.harvard.edu/sites/default/files/ha
rvard_jchs_shared_equity_housing_lit_review_carlsson_2019.pdf [https://perma.cc/VF4B-P3U2]
(last visited June 11, 2021).

creates a registry of housing land trusts and authorizes activities such as the acquisition, improvement, and sale of properties under control of a land trust.[182]

D. Disaster Recovery Funding

Disaster readiness was long on the radar of state housing agencies, particularly as it relates to funding sustainable housing locations (for example, curtailing state-funded construction in flood plains). Other, more inventive, templates for state engagement are also emerging. After Hurricane Florence, for instance, North Carolina created the Back@Home program to use a "cost effective rapid rehousing model" to help residents return to normalcy through housing location assistance, financial assistance, and housing stabilization services.[183] In the midst of the COVID-19 pandemic, states are responding to the swelling housing crisis using a variety of funding pools, including pledging Coronavirus Relief Funds to emergency housing assistance, redirecting Community Development Block Grant funds to housing and homeless needs, and facilitating the deployment of FEMA resources to homeless and congregate housing settings.[184]

E. Public–Private Partnerships

As states achieve deeper understanding of the interdependent nature of housing and economic development gains, states are eager to partner with major regional employers in win–win agreements that expand the affordable housing stock while steadying workforce capacity and readiness. For example, the state of California and Facebook teamed up in a $1 billion partnership to create 20,000 new housing units for essential workers.[185]

VII. PRACTICE CONSIDERATIONS

Developing and financing housing for low-income households is a complex process. By definition, the economic circumstances of the people being served means their low incomes cannot support the development and operational costs of housing available through private market activity. In response to this reality, our elected officials and policy makers developed funding programs that seek to balance the development's need for financial support against the government's desire for strong oversight and compliance mechanisms. Some argue this complexity ensures that only experienced project developers with exceptional capacity are entrusted with public funds and that public–private partnerships create a superior product that is highly targeted to the end-user. Others argue that this complexity creates artificial access barriers, perpetuates a profit motive in meeting a fundamental human need, and unduly increases the administrative costs of supporting housing thereby reducing overall access. At least one state, Minnesota, tries to ease some of this difficulty with

---

182. MD. REAL PROP. CODE ANN. §§ 14-501–14-511 (2018).

183. BACK AT HOME NORTH CAROLINA, https://www.backathome.org/about [https://perma.cc/6ZXA-K6JK] (last visited June 11, 2021)..

184. *NLIHC COVID-19 Rental Assistance Database*, NATIONAL LOW INCOME HOUSING COALITION, https://docs.google.com/spreadsheets/d/1hLfybfo9NydIptQu5wghUpKXecimh3gaoqT7LU1JGc8/edit#gid=79194074 [https://perma.cc/L79B-357V] (last visited June 11, 2021).

185. David Wehner, *Facebook Commits $1 Billion and Partners with the State of California to Address Housing Affordability*, FACEBOOK (Oct. 22, 2019), https://about.fb.com/news/2019/10/facebook-commits-1-billion-to-address-housing-affordability/ [https://perma.cc/LET7-HY83].

a consolidated request for proposals process that simultaneously evaluates eligibility for tax credits, mortgages, deferred loans, and other partners' funding programs, including the Greater Minnesota Housing Fund and the Metropolitan Council Local Housing Incentive Account.[186]

In developing housing for people with low incomes, developers are highly constrained in their architectural choices, project location, and amenity offerings. Prior to creating project specifications, developers must have a general understanding of what funding streams they will use, what income restrictions those will carry, and what the local rent receipts will be for those residents. This information helps them calculate the amount of debt that a project can carry, if any. Knowing this information will then inform the number of units that are needed to support construction estimates, which will further inform how much can be budgeted to land acquisition costs. Beyond price constraints, locations will often be further circumscribed by whether the site scores high enough under a funder's priorities to be competitive. The cumulative effects of this process severely restrict where and how affordable housing can be created. While a market-rate developer must also design for their intended customer, because costs can be passed on to the consumer, they have significantly more flexibility in design decisions and addressing unexpected cost overruns.

The housing programs discussed in this chapter are designed to help meet those challenges and fill those financial gaps in several ways. Gaps on the *development expenses* side can be filled through debt-oriented programs, such as tax-exempt bonds and tax increment financing, or equity-oriented programs, such as the low-income housing tax credit. Additional gap-filling sources of funds, usually for relatively short periods of time, include (1) federal CDBG and HOME funds, allocated through state and local agencies; (2) the increasingly important state and local housing trust funds; (3) charitable contributions; and (4) "sweat equity," as pioneered by Habitat for Humanity. For gaps in *operating expense budgets*, rental subsidies such as Section 8 vouchers and property tax abatements, assessments, and exemptions become important.

Since none of the financing programs discussed in this chapter have enough available funds to meet demand,[187] putting this all together becomes an arduous task. It is common to have multiple funders, all with their own application procedures, required documents, and program priorities, resulting in layered financing. Strict observance of allocation criteria, deadlines, and standards is critical. In this environment, attorneys function as team leaders and must master the intricacies of the programs in order to help their clients compete for the scarce dollars necessary for successful affordable housing development. Moreover, attorneys are also well positioned to use their analytical and advocacy skills to help shape funding programs and state policy agendas to ensure they adhere to their clients' and the community's needs.

---

186. *Application Resources for Multifamily Financing*, Minnesota Housing, http://www.mnhousing.gov/sites/multifamily/applicationresources [https://perma.cc/P8FC-GFXE] (last visited June 11, 2021).

187. The *Gap: A Shortage of Affordable Homes*, National Low Income Housing Coalition (Mar. 2020) https://reports.nlihc.org/sites/default/files/gap/Gap-Report_2020.pdf [https://perma.cc/8XWG-FPSP] (As of 2020, the U.S. only had 36 affordable and available housing units for every 100 extremely low-income renter households).

Local Government Financing Powers and Sources of Funding

11

Barbara E. Kautz with Roy J. Koegen*

I. INTRODUCTION

A. Overview

Depending on their state's law, local governments offer a variety of programs that provide financial assistance for affordable housing development. This chapter does not contain a comprehensive survey of the programs but provides information and examples of programs from select states.[1] Section I discusses the legal parameters of local government authority to finance affordable housing and a common local government finance structure, the housing trust fund. Section II describes local taxes that are set aside for

---

* Rick Judd co-authored the first edition of this chapter and is largely responsible for its organization and structure and the selection of many of the specific examples. Vincent L. Brown assisted with the second edition. Roy J. Koegen updated Section VI for the third edition. The authors also wish to thank Minda Bautista Hickey and Amy Metzgar, who updated many of the referenced sources in this third edition, and to John Cuerva, who updated the sources in the second edition, arduous undertakings involving many different states and cities.

1. *See* Opening Doors to Homes for All: The 2016 Housing Trust Fund Survey Report, The Center for Community Change, https://housingtrust-fundproject.org/wp-content/uploads/2016/10/HTF_Survey-Report-2016-final.pdf [https://perma.cc/WVN3-JVZH] [hereinafter 2016 Housing Trust Fund Report]; *see* Michael A. Steman, Urban Land Institute, State and Local Affordable Housing Programs: A Rich Tapestry (1999), for an excellent, if outdated, overview of these programs. These reports include state and local programs that depend on state, federal, or private funding, as well as resources generated locally, which are the focus of this chapter. *See also* Bruce Katz et al., The Brookings Institution and the Urban Institute, Rethinking Local Affordable Housing Strategies: Lessons from 70 Years of Policy and Practice (2003).

affordable housing. Section III discusses commercial linkage fees. Section IV explains in-lieu fees from inclusionary housing programs. Section V describes land transfer programs. Section VI discusses the issuance of government-sponsored bonds for housing development. Section VII describes fee-waiver programs. Finally, Section VIII explains tax increment financing.[2] This survey is not exhaustive, but focuses on forms of government support found in multiple jurisdictions that provide quantifiable, locally generated financing. Programs from most regions of the country, as well as a variety of innovative local approaches, are described. The housing efforts of major cities with extensive programs, such as New York, Boston, and San Francisco, are not represented, while rural and small city programs are probably underrepresented.

This description of local government housing finance programs illustrates a wide variety of local approaches, tailored to local resources and initiatives and to varying state law, political conditions, and development parameters. The nationwide reach of these efforts signals the depth and breadth of the challenge of meeting Americans' housing needs. While local governments do not command financial resources on the scale of the federal or many state governments, the creativity and variety of local approaches testify to the concern of individuals and groups in all parts of the country and to the persistence of the tradition of local self-reliance in trying to solve problems close to home. Even after the dramatic drop in home prices that occurred in many markets beginning in 2007, communities for the most part maintained their commitment to their locally funded programs. As the price of homes in many parts of the country have more than recovered from the Great Recession, with skyrocketing homelessness and housing cost–burdened households, local communities' efforts are even more important.

B. Parameters of Local Government Authority

States vary in the extent to which they extend "home rule" or police power authority to local governments, and thus enable those governments to independently establish housing assistance programs. Local governments' authority to institute new or increased taxes also differs from state to state.

Most U.S. local governments operate under some form of broad home rule grant; in 1990, such grants were identified in 41 states.[3] While the scope of home rule authority typically depends on general enabling statutes or state constitutions,[4] the extent to which an individual city is authorized to use a particular means to assist affordable housing development may also depend on other state legislation. Further, the extent of authority afforded by a typical broad home rule grant is not easily determined.[5]

---

2. See Chapters 4 and 5 for local government regulatory programs that support affordable housing.

3. Richard Briffault, *Our Localism: Part I—The Structure of Local Government Law*, 90 COLUM. L. REV. 1, 11, n.25 (1990); *see also* NESTOR DAVIDSON ET AL., PRINCIPLES OF HOME RULE FOR THE 21ST CENTURY, NAT'L LEAGUE OF CITIES 13 (2020).

4. DAVIDSON ET AL., *supra* note 3.

5. "Each case must turn on its own facts. . . . [E]xamples of the traditional application of the police power to municipal affairs . . . merely illustrate the scope of the power and do not delimit it." Berman v. Parker, 348 U.S. 26, 32 (1954). *See generally* DAVIDSON ET AL., *supra* note 3, at 9–13.

In some states, lack of authority has been an issue for programs that impose fees on nonresidential development to support affordable housing or use tax increment districts to support affordable housing.[6] The legal question is frequently whether a program conflicts with or is limited by established state or other law. Examples of potentially conflicting laws include (1) constitutional or statutory prohibitions on gifts of public lands or funds, which may restrict preferential disposition of land for affordable housing; (2) restrictions on imposition of inclusionary housing, including in-lieu fee requirements; or (3) voter approval requirements for bonds. In addition, local governments' taxing abilities depend on their authority under state law, which may be more limited than other municipal powers and is often affected by limitations on new or increased taxes or spending or revenue ceilings. A disturbing trend is increasing action by state legislatures to restrict local authority, including in the area of housing policy.[7] Further discussion on these questions follows.

C. Local Housing Trust Funds

The housing trust fund movement has been a driving force in expanding and institutionalizing local affordable housing funding. A local housing trust fund is established by a city or a county when a source of revenue is dedicated to a distinct fund with the express purpose of providing affordable housing.[8]

Many of the funding programs discussed *infra* are part of, or linked to, housing trust funds. Proceeds of local taxes set aside for housing, linkage fees, inclusionary in-lieu fees, and tax increment funds are often placed in local housing trust funds. Other sources of revenue can include property taxes, bond proceeds, transient occupancy taxes, land sales, and bond revenues.[9]

According to the Center for Community Change, as of 2016, there were over 770 housing trust funds across states, counties, and in cities that produced more than $1 billion a year in housing support.[10] New Jersey alone had 304 local trust funds.[11] In 2015, state housing trust funds accounted for the largest amount of revenue, at over $790 million. County housing trust fund revenue exceeded $385 million dollars, while city housing trust fund revenue topped $100 million.[12] Twelve cities collected more than $5 million in 2015.[13]

---

6. *See, e.g.,* Leonard v. City of Spokane, 897 P.2d 358, 359 (Wash. 1995) (holding that Washington's Community Redevelopment Financing Act was inconsistent with the state constitution).

7. *See, e.g.,* Nestor M. Davidson & Timothy M. Mulvaney, *Takings Localism*, 121 COLUM. L. REV. 215, 251–53, 253 n.165 (Mar. 2021) (describing limitations on local adoption of rent control and inclusionary ordinances); Richard Briffault, *The Challenge of the New Preemption*, 70 STAN. L. REV. 1997, 2002 (June 2018) (noting that 26 states bar local rent control and 11 bar local inclusionary ordinances).

8. *See* 2016 HOUSING TRUST FUND REPORT, *supra* note 1, at 23. *See also* Chapter 10 for a discussion of State Housing Trust Funds. This chapter does not discuss the allocation or administration functions of housing trust funds, nor the establishment, governance, or operation of the funds. For a discussion of the administrative functions of local housing trust funds, *see* 2016 HOUSING TRUST FUND REPORT, *supra* note 1, at 18, 26.

9. *See* 2016 HOUSING TRUST FUND REPORT, *supra* note 1, at 17.

10. *Id.* at 1.

11. *Id.*

12. *Id.* at 2.

13. *Id.* at 17.

The most common revenue sources utilized by city housing trust funds were general funds and developer impact fees, collected by all 304 New Jersey communities under the New Jersey Fair Housing Act.[14] For county trust funds, document recording fees were the primary revenue source, including 54 Pennsylvania counties and 39 Washington counties.[15] On average, city trust funds leveraged $6 in additional public and private funds for each trust fund dollar, while county trust funds leveraged $8.50 for each trust fund dollar.[16]

As one example, the San Diego Affordable Housing Fund was established in 1990 to receive commercial linkage fees, which are impact fees assessed on nonresidential development. In 2003, the authorizing ordinance was amended to state that funding would include inclusionary in-lieu fees charged to residential development.[17] Despite the COVID pandemic, revenues to the Affordable Housing Fund in Fiscal Year 2020 totaled $1.8 million from commercial linkage fees and almost $19.8 million from inclusionary in-lieu fees.[18] While the Fund is required to achieve 2:1 leveraging, in 2020 its leveraging ratio was over 11:1.[19] The majority of the funds are expended to finance rental housing, with 946 units assisted in 2020.[20]

II. SET-ASIDES OF LOCAL TAXES

Local governments' primary funding sources are taxes, and a number of cities have approved tax increases whose proceeds are specifically targeted for affordable housing. The extent of a locality's taxing authority depends on state law and, in some cases, on a locality's own charter. In California, for instance, instituting or increasing a general tax requires majority approval at a local election, and instituting or increasing a tax for a particular purpose (as opposed to a tax that may be used for any legal purpose) requires two-thirds voter approval.[21] However, subject to the voter approval requirement, local governments in California have broad general authority to impose taxes of all types.[22]

In other states, local taxes imposed specifically to fund affordable housing have generally been based on specific state authorization. The most common tax for such purposes

---

14. *Id.* at 24.

15. *Id.* at 32.

16. *Id.* at 17, 26.

17. *City of San Diego Affordable Housing Fund Fiscal Year 2020 Annual Report*, SAN DIEGO HOUSING COMMISSION (Sept. 5, 2020) at 5.

18. *Id.* at 7, 10.

19. *Id.* at 5.

20. *Id.* at 11, 13.

21. See Santa Clara Cnty. Local Transp. Auth. v. Guardino, 902 P.2d 225 (Cal. 1995) (holding that a 1986 California initiative validly imposed a voter approval requirement, after seven years of conflicting judicial opinions) CAL. CONST. art. XIIIC, § 1(b) (extending the voter approval requirement to charter cities). *See also* Howard Jarvis Taxpayers Ass'n v. City of Roseville, 132 Cal. Rptr. 2d 1, 4–5 (Cal. Ct. App. 2003).

22. Charter cities have largely unrestricted "home rule" authority to impose taxes without specific authorization by type of tax under the California Constitution art. XI, § 5; *see* Rivera v. City of Fresno, 490 P.2d 793 (Cal. 1971). General law cities (i.e., those without their own charters) have roughly equivalent statutory authority (CAL. GOV'T CODE § 37100.5). Counties, which have responsibilities equivalent to those of cities in areas not within an incorporated city but limited responsibilities in incorporated areas where the vast majority of Californians live, are legal subdivisions of the state and generally have more limited powers (*see* CAL. CONST. art. XI, §§ 1(a), 4).

is a real estate transfer tax, typically imposed on recordation of transfer documents. The following are examples of such taxes.

A. Pennsylvania

In 1992, Pennsylvania's General Assembly passed the Optional County Affordable Housing Funds Act,[23] which authorized almost all Pennsylvania counties to increase fees for recording deeds and mortgages if an ordinance were adopted by the county commissioners. The total of each county's fee increases could not exceed the preexisting recording fee,[24] and 85 percent of the funds raised by the fee increase were required to be used for "affordable housing efforts," with a maximum of 15 percent of the funds used for administration.[25]

By 2005, 49 of the 66 eligible counties in the state had established housing trust funds. Thirty percent of the counties with programs had raised recording fees more than once, and six counties had collected total funds estimated at more than $5 million (Allegheny, Bucks, Chester, Delaware, Lancaster, and Montgomery).[26] Per-county revenue averaged over $325,000 per year. Program satisfaction was very high, with 94 percent of counties strongly agreeing that the housing trust funds were a valuable tool in promoting affordable housing. In 2005, the state legislation was recodified and extended to the city of Philadelphia.[27] For counties, the definition of "affordable housing efforts" was modified to limit expenditures to housing serving residents whose income was less than the median income of the county;[28] Philadelphia was allowed to serve residents earning up to 115 percent of median income in the metropolitan statistical area.[29] In 2011, the statute was further amended to allow Philadelphia to increase its recording fee.[30]

The permitted uses of the funds are very broad, allowing the funds to be used for any sales or rental project that "increases the availability of quality housing," including supportive services. In Philadelphia, for instance, half of the funds are targeted to low-income households earning 30 percent of annual median income or less and half are targeted to households earning between 30 percent and 115 percent of annual median income. At least half the funds are used for new or substantially rehabilitated homes, with the rest supporting homelessness prevention and rehabilitation.[31] The city's 2019–2020 Action Plan showed annual revenues of $12 million.[32]

---

23. Former 35 PA. CONS. STAT. §§ 1690.1–1690.6 (repealed 2005; recodified at 53 PA. CONS. STAT. §§ 6001–6023).

24. Former 35 PA. CONS. STAT. § 1690.4.

25. *Id.* § 1690.5.

26. CENTER FOR SURVEY RESEARCH, INST. OF STATE & REGIONAL AFFAIRS, PENN STATE HARRISBURG, UPDATE ON THE IMPLEMENTATION OF PENNSYLVANIA'S COUNTY HOUSING TRUST FUND LEGISLATION (Mar. 2005), http://housingtrustfundproject.org/wp-content/uploads/2011/10/2005-report-on-the-progress-of-Act-137.pdf [https://perma.cc/3SEE-ZF2V].

27. 53 PA. CONS. STAT. §§ 6001–6023 (2005).

28. *Id.* § 6013.

29. *Id.* § 6023.

30. *Id.* § 6021(b).

31. CITY OF PHILADELPHIA, DIVISION OF HOUSING AND COMMUNITY DEVELOPMENT, ANNUAL ACTION PLAN 2019–2020 41–42 (June 2019) https://www.phila.gov/media/20190928080141/Annual-Action-Plan-2019-2020.pdf [https://perma.cc/573B-QC5U].

32. *Id.* at 37.

B. St. Louis, Missouri

Missouri state law authorizes local governments to levy local use taxes on purchases from out-of-state vendors if a majority of local voters approves.[33] The city of St. Louis collects a 2.725 percent local use tax under this authority, reserving a substantial portion for development and preservation of affordable and accessible housing, pursuant to two city ordinances, 65609 (2002) and 65132 (2001). Ordinance 65609 divides the first $10 million of annual tax proceeds between an Affordable Housing Trust Fund and a Health Care Trust Fund. Finally, any additional annual proceeds can be used for a variety of purposes, including development and preservation of affordable housing, demolition of derelict buildings, health care services, public safety, and neighborhood preservation.

The Affordable Housing Trust Fund is administered by an 11-member Affordable Housing Commission whose members are appointed by the mayor and approved by the board of aldermen. Funds from the Affordable Housing Trust Fund must benefit households earning no more than 80 percent of local median income, and 40 percent of Affordable Housing Trust Fund expenditures must benefit households earning no more than 20 percent of local median income.[34] The funds may be used for low- or no-interest development loans and for grants to local housing or neighborhood organizations for a wide variety of purposes, including accommodations for people with disabilities, lead paint abatement, emergency home repairs, services to prevent homelessness, emergency and transitional housing, security or utility deposits, and down-payment and closing cost assistance.[35] As of November 14, 2019, the city of St. Louis had created 2,790 public housing units within the affordable housing inventory and made up to 532 emergency shelter beds available each night.[36] In 2020, the Commission awarded approximately $6 million dollars, marking its largest distribution of trust funds in ten years. The funds distributed in 2020 built 134 new single-family and rental homes, and provided homeless prevention and shelter services for 18,401 people.[37]

A separate Missouri statute authorizes certain counties, including St. Louis County, to charge a $3 fee on all recorded instruments to be used for assistance to homeless persons. This assistance can include repair or replacement of housing. In certain cases, an additional

---

33. Mo. Rev. Stat. § 144.757 (2007).

34. St. Louis, Mo., Ordinance 65132, § 3(G).

35. *Id*. at § 3(D)(2). The same state statute authorizes St. Louis County to charge a similar use tax. While initially half of the proceeds were to be deposited into a "community comeback trust" to be used for a variety of community development purposes, including residential development, the use tax measure failed to get voter approval, and the provision currently permits the funds to be used for a broader range of local needs. *See* Mo. Rev. Stat. §§ 144.757(2)(a), 144.759(2) (2007); Phil Sutin, *St. Louis County Rejects Tax; City OKs Measure to Fund Housing, Health Care*, St. Louis Post-Dispatch, Apr. 4, 2001, at 10.

36. City of St. Louis Cmty. Dev. Admin., Consolidated Plan for the Five-Year Period 2020–2024, 82–106, 121–22 (Nov. 14, 2019) https://www.stlouis-mo.gov/government/departments/community-development/documents/upload/CityofStLouis_2020-2024ConsolidatedPlan_and_2020AnnualActionPlan_2019-11-15.pdf [https://perma.cc/YWE8-6X77].

37. Report to the Community 2020, Affordable Housing Commission, https://www.stlouis-mo.gov/government/departments/affordable-housing/documents/upload/2020-Annual-Report-FINAL.pdf [https://perma.cc/FN3B-SR6Q] (last visited June 12, 2021).

$3 may be imposed to fund renovation or rehabilitation of market-rate for-sale housing.[38] Both fees require voter approval, and all three counties eligible to implement the fee have done so.[39]

C. Seattle, Washington

Washington state law expressly authorizes counties, cities, and towns to increase property taxes by securing voter approval[40] and specifically authorizes imposition of an additional property tax levy up to $0.50 per $1,000 of assessed value for a period of up to ten years to finance affordable housing for very low-income households.[41] Voter-approved levies may exceed applicable maximum tax levies. The additional levy for very low-income housing may further cause the local property tax rate to exceed otherwise applicable statutory maximums[42] and requires, in addition to voter approval, an emergency declaration concerning local availability of very low-income housing[43] and an affordable housing financing plan.[44] Seattle approved levies for affordable housing under these statutes in 1986, 1995, 2002, 2009, and 2016.[45] The 2016 levy, submitted to the voters by Seattle Ordinance No. 125028, authorizes the City to levy additional taxes for low-income housing for up to seven years, from 2017 through 2023.[46]

The 2016 ordinance (approved by over 70 percent of the voters[47]) authorized a total of $290 million in additional tax levies over a seven-year period, with an estimated tax rate in the first year of $0.25 per $1,000 of assessed value,[48] to be deposited in a Low-Income Housing Fund.[49] About two-thirds of the funds are designated for rental housing production and preservation, while the remainder is divided among operating and maintenance subsidies, rental assistance, home buyer assistance, and property acquisition.[50] An oversight

---

38. *See* Mo. Rev. Stat. § 67.1063 (2000).

39. *See* The Ctr. for Cmty. Change, The Housing Trust Fund Progress Report 2002: Local Responses to America's Housing Needs 18 (2002). The report noted that 78 percent of St. Louis County voters approved the fee increase, and that the county collected more than $800,000 annually from the increase. *See also* 2016 Housing Trust Fund Survey Report, *supra* note 1, at 37.

40. Wash. Rev. Code § 84.55.050 (2018), amended by 2021 Wash. Sess. Laws 1069-S2).

41. Wash. Rev. Code § 84.52.105 (extended Oct. 10, 2020 for ten years).

42. The limitations are in Wash. Rev. Code §§ 84.52.043 and 84.55.010, *et seq.*; exemption of the very low-income levy from the § 84.52.043 limitation is provided by § 84.52.105(4).

43. Very low-income households are defined as those at or below 50 percent of Average Median Income (AMI).

44. Wash. Rev. Code § 84.52.105(1)–(3) (2020).

45. Seattle, Wash., Ordinance 112904 (1986); Ordinance 117711 (1995); Ordinance 120823 (2002); Ordinance 123013 (2009); and Ordinance 125028 (2016).

46. Seattle, Wash., Ordinance 125028, § 3.

47. Election Results, Primary and Special Election: City of Seattle: Proposition One (Aug. 2, 2016) https://aqua.kingcounty.gov/elections/2016/aug-primary/results/results.pdf [https://perma.cc/7TMN-NY6D].

48. Seattle, Wash., Ordinance 125028, §§ 3, 11.

49. "Low-income households" are those with income less than or equal to 80 percent of median income. *Id.* § 2. For the 2016 levy, Seattle relied on Wash. Rev. Code § 84.55.050, rather than the special provisions regarding levies for very low-income housing. *Id.* § 3.

50. Seattle, Wash., Ordinance 125028, at Exhibit 1—2016 Housing Levy Programs.

committee approves fund expenditures.[51] Since the approval of the first levy in 1986, as of 2016, the levies had funded construction of more than 12,500 rental units and assisted 800 home buyers and 6,500 renter households at risk of homelessness.[52]

Seattle also benefits from a Washington statute that provides for a statewide surcharge of $10 on each recorded document.[53] Sixty percent of the proceeds of this surcharge is retained by the recording county for housing affordable to very low-income persons and must be deposited into a fund shared by the jurisdictions within the county and allocated according to an agreement reached among the participants.[54] The funds may be used for acquisition, rehabilitation, construction, operation and maintenance costs, rental assistance, and operating costs for emergency and overnight shelters, with priority given to extremely low-income households.[55]

D. Massachusetts

The Massachusetts Community Preservation Act[56] (CPA) is statewide enabling legislation that allows voters in cities and towns to approve a surcharge of not more than 3 percent of real property levies by majority vote. (Localities may, but are not required to, exempt certain specified categories of property, such as low-income housing and the first $100,000 in taxable value for residences.[57]) At least 10 percent of the revenues from the surcharge must be directed to community housing serving households earning less than 80 percent of the area-wide median income.[58] The state of Massachusetts provides matching funds to communities that adopt the surcharge from a statewide recording fee.[59] According to records

---

51. *Id.* § 9.

52. Letter from Edward B. Murray, Mayor of the City of Seattle to Honorable Bruce Harrell, President of Seattle City Council (Mar. 1, 2016) (on file https://seattle.legistar.com/View .ashx?M=F&ID=4372076&GUID=B3F1D6A1-BC6D-49AF-91CD-E1574347B512 [https://perma .cc/T7YM-GWG8].

53. WASH. REV. CODE § 36.22.178 (2018) (to be updated in 2021, amended by 2021 Wash. Sess. Laws 1277-S2). Florida has a similar program, which sets aside a portion of document recording fees for deposit into a statewide Local Government Housing Trust Fund. FLA. STAT. § 201.15(9)(b) (2020). The funds are distributed from the Local Government Housing Trust Fund by the Florida Housing Finance Corporation to all eligible counties and cities pursuant to a statutory formula (FLA. STAT. § 420.9073 (2020)); eligibility depends on meeting certain housing planning requirements. FLA. STAT. § 420-9072 (2020).

54. WASH. REV. CODE § 36.22.178(2) (2018), amended by 2021 Wash. Sess. Laws 1277-S2). The remaining funds are transmitted to the state for housing affordable to extremely low-income households (incomes at or less than 30 percent of median income). *Id.*

55. *Id.*

56. MASS. GEN. LAWS ch. 44B, § 1, initially adopted in 2000. Massachusetts Property Tax Bureau Informational Guideline Release No. 00-209 (superseded by Bureau of Municipal Finance Law Informational Guideline Release No. 19-14) explains the administration and implementation of Community Preservation Funds resulting from such surcharges.

57. MASS. GEN. LAWS ch. 44B, § 3 (2006).

58. *Id.* §§ 2, 6.

59. MASS. GEN. LAWS ch. 44B, § 10 (2006). Through 2007, all communities received a 100 percent match. However, the average match was reduced to 76.62 percent in 2008, to 34.81 percent in 2009, and to 27.2 percent in 2010, and rose slightly in 2020 to 28.63 percent. *See What Is the CPA Trust Fund?* COMMUNITY PRESERVATION COALITION, https://www.communitypreservation.org /trustfund [https://perma.cc/YUC2-WWGF] (last visited May 5, 2021).

compiled by the Community Preservation Coalition, as of May 5, 2021, 187 communities in Massachusetts had adopted surcharges ranging from 0.5 to 3 percent.[60] Between 2000 and June 2006, more than $68 million was appropriated for housing purposes, approximately 32 percent of total CPA appropriations. A Harvard study estimated that 70 percent of the housing funds were used to purchase existing units.[61]

III. COMMERCIAL LINKAGE FEES

Linkage fees are impact fees charged to new commercial, office, and other nonresidential developments to offset the impact of commercial growth on the demand for affordable housing. Local governments have also imposed mitigation fees on commercial projects that directly cause the loss of low-income housing through change of use or demolition.

Linkage fees are usually imposed as a flat cost per square foot of new construction, depending on the expected use of the building. Developers may be given the option of constructing affordable housing rather than paying the fee. The fees are based on a "nexus" study, an economic report establishing how much housing demand is created by each square foot of nonresidential space.[62] The fees go into a dedicated fund and pay for affordable housing.

A. Authority

Commercial linkage fees were overturned in New Jersey and Boston as ultra vires until state action was taken to authorize the fees.[63] Developers in other states have successfully challenged all types of impact fees as unconstitutional taxes, as exceeding statutory authority, or as conflicting with state law.[64] Almost half of the states have adopted legislation specifically authorizing impact fees, and many strictly limit the types of impact fees that can be imposed. For instance, the state of Washington prohibits all involuntary fees except for specifically authorized public facilities, including only roads, parks, schools, and fire

---

60. *See* Community Preservation Coalition, CPA: An Overview, https://www.communit ypreservation.org/about [https://perma.cc/VL76-9RGB] (last visited June 13, 2021).

61. *See* Robin Sherman & David Luberoff, The Massachusetts Community Preservation Act: Who Benefits? Who Pays? 17–18 (July 2007), https://www.hks.harvard.edu/sites /default/files/centers/rappaport/files/cpa_final.pdf [https://perma.cc/C5U2-NDZ3].

62. *See* references to specific nexus studies *infra* Section III.C.

63. In New Jersey, the State Supreme Court found that the state's Council on Affordable Housing had to promulgate a comprehensive set of regulations authorizing the fees before cities could impose commercial linkage fees. *See* Holmdel Builders Ass'n v. Twp. of Holmdel, 583 A.2d 277, 290 (N.J. 1990). A Boston superior court found Boston's linkage fee invalid because the city did not have express statutory authority to adopt it. The court's decision was overturned on procedural grounds. Bonan v. City of Boston, 496 N.E.2d 640, 641–42 (Mass. 1986). Ultimately the program required state authorizing legislation. *See* 1956 Mass. Acts 610–17.

64. *See, e.g.*, Home Builders Ass'n v. City of West Des Moines, 644 N.W.2d 339, 350 (Iowa 2002); Home Builders Ass'n v. Apache Junction, 11 P.3d 1032, 1039 (Ariz. Ct. App. 2000) (statutory authority to finance "necessary public services" does not authorize county to impose school impact fees); R/L. Assocs., Inc. v. City of Seattle, 780 P.2d 838, 842 (Wash. 1989) (Seattle ordinance requiring relocation payments "invalid on its face" as in conflict with statutory limitations on indirect development charges.).

stations.[65] This statute was used to invalidate a city of Seattle ordinance that required either replacement housing or payment of an in-lieu fee when low-income housing was removed for nonresidential uses.[66] Consequently, localities' authority to impose commercial linkage fees may be constrained by both the usual limitations on home rule and specific conflicting state statutes.

B. Constitutional Issues

Litigants have filed numerous cases in the federal and state courts alleging that impact fees of all types, including commercial linkage fees, violate the Takings Clause of the U.S. Constitution.[67] A key issue is the appropriate standard of review.

A government's demand for property from a land-use permit applicant has long been required to satisfy the "essential nexus" and "rough proportionality" requirements established in *Nollan v. California Coastal Commission*[68] and *Dolan v. City of Tigard.*[69] In *Nollan* and *Dolan*, the Supreme Court imposed intermediate scrutiny to determine whether required *dedications* of land to public agencies constituted a taking. The *Nollan/Dolan* test requires an "essential nexus" between the specific impact of the project and the required dedication,[70] and places the burden of proof on the local agency to demonstrate that the "nature and extent" of the dedication is "roughly proportional" to the project's impact.[71]

An unresolved issue, however, had been whether the *Nollan/Dolan* test applied to a government's demand for payment of *money*, such as payment of an impact fee.[72] In *Koontz v. St. Johns River Water Mgmt. Dist.*,[73] the U.S Supreme Court held in a 5–4 decision that a demand for payment of money was similarly subject to the *Nollan/Dolan* test.[74] Thus a public agency imposing an impact fee on an individual applicant bears the burden of

---

65. WASH. REV. CODE §§ 82.02.050(4), 82.02.090(7) (2018). Charges for water, sewer, drainage, and natural gas facilities are also permitted. *Id.* §§ 82.02.020(3).

66. San Telmo Assocs. v. City of Seattle, 735 P.2d 673, 673–74, 675 (Wash. 1987). Similarly, the state of Texas allows impact fees to be collected only for water, sanitary sewer, storm water, and road facilities. *See also* TEX. LOC. GOV'T CODE ANN. 395.011-395.012 (West 2011) (prohibiting local impact fees unless specifically authorized); Davidson & Mulvaney, *supra* note 7, at 250 nn.155 & 156 (describing state laws limiting local adoption of impact fees).

67. U.S. CONST. amend. V (". . . nor shall private property be taken for public use, without just compensation").

68. Nollan v. California Coastal Comm'n, 483 U.S. 825 (1987).

69. Dolan v. City of Tigard, 512 U.S. 374 (1994).

70. *Nollan*, 483 U.S. at 837.

71. *Dolan*, 512 U.S. at 391.

72. For lists of cases that considered the applicability of *Nollan/Dolan* to impact fees and other money payments, *see* Nancy E. Stroud, *A Review of Del Monte Dunes v. City of Monterey and Its Implications for Local Government Exactions*, 15 J. OF LAND USE & ENVTL. L. 195, 203–04 (1999). For an extensive discussion of the issue, *see also* Commonwealth Edison Co. v. United States, 46 Fed. Cl. 29, 37–42 (Fed. Cl. 2000). The California Supreme Court had determined in 1996 that the *Nollan/Dolan* test applied to impact fees imposed on individual projects. *See* Ehrlich v. Culver City, 911 P.2d, 429, 444, (Cal. 1996) (applying *Nollan/Dolan* to a recreational mitigation fee because it was imposed on a single landowner who applied to convert his private recreational facility into an office building).

73. Koontz v. St. Johns River Water Mgmt. Dist. 570 U.S. 595 (2013).

74. *See id.* at 612.

proof to demonstrate that the fee bears an "essential nexus" to the project's impacts and is "roughly proportional" to those impacts.

A remaining unresolved issue is whether the *Nollan/Dolan* test applies to impact fees imposed by "generally applicable legislation" that provides for limited discretion in imposing the fees, as most commercial linkage fees are structured, or only to impact fees imposed on an ad hoc basis on individual applicants, as was the case in *Koontz*.[75] Prior to *Koontz*, the majority of state and federal courts that had considered the issue held that the *Nollan/Dolan* test does not apply to generally applicable legislation.[76] Their rationale in part, as expressed by an Oregon appeals court, was that:

> [W]hen government action is taken pursuant to a legislatively adopted standard . . . , and when there is no need for adjudication or the exercise of discretion at the time that the standard is applied to a particular property, there is far less danger of a governmental entity attempting to use its power to extort unconstitutional conditions from persons seeking governmental approval of a specific proposal.[77]

A review of post-*Koontz* cases found that eight of ten courts to address the issue had affirmatively declined to extend *Nollan/Dolan* to generally applicable legislation, maintaining this as the majority view of the courts. The rationale in the cases reviewed was based generally on (1) the disputes in *Nollan*, *Dolan*, and *Koontz* involved requirements imposed on individual parcels; and (2) the Supreme Court has repeatedly referenced the applicability of its tests to "adjudicative," rather than legislative, decisions.[78] For instance, in *Lingle v. Chevron U.S.A. Inc.*,[79] the examples given by the Court in reference to *Nollan/Dolan* were all "adjudicative [i.e., case-by-case] exactions."[80]

State enabling legislation may require a more rigorous means-ends test on legislative enactments than imposed by the courts.[81] The majority of courts, however, apply a "rational nexus" or "reasonable relationship" test to legislatively imposed impact fees, requiring only

---

75. Prior to *Koontz*, the issue had been raised in at least 15 petitions for certiorari. *See* Timothy M. Mulvaney, *The State of Exactions*, 61 Wm. & Mary L. Rev. 169, 194 (2019). *See* Calif. Building Industry Ass'n v. City of San Jose, 577 U.S. 1179 (2016) (In a concurring opinion to the denial of certiorari, Justice Thomas noted a conflict regarding the standard of review applicable to legislative v. adjudicative decisions, but the Court has not granted certiorari to resolve this asserted conflict.).

76. *See, e.g.*, McClung v. City of Sumner, 548 F.3d 1219, 1227–28 (9th Cir. 2008); Santa Monica Beach, Ltd. v. Superior Court, 968 P.2d 993, 1001 (Cal. 1999); Parking Ass'n of Ga. v. City of Atlanta, 450 S.E.2d 200, 203 n.3 (Ga. 1994). For lists of cases that considered the applicability of *Nollan/Dolan* to legislative acts pre-*Koontz*, *see* Edward H. Ziegler, *Development Exactions and Permit Decisions: The Supreme Court's Nollan, Dolan, and Del Monte Dunes Decisions*, 34 Urb. Law. 155, 164–65, nn.48 & 51 (2002).

77. Dudek v. Umatilla Cnty., 69 P.3d 751, 755–56 (Or. Ct. App. 2003).

78. See Mulvaney, *supra* note 75, at 194–207. *See, e.g.*, Dabbs v. Anne Arundel Cnty., 182 A.3d 798, 813 (Md. 2018) ("Impact fees imposed by legislation applicable on an area-wide basis are not subject to Nollan and Dolan scrutiny.").

79. Lingle v. Chevron U.S.A. Inc., 544 U.S. 528 (2005).

80. *See id.* at 546–48; Daniel L. Siegel, *Exactions after Lingle: How Basing Nollan and Dolan on the Unconstitutional Conditions Doctrine Limits Their Scope*, 28 Stan. Envtl. L.J. 577, 607–12 (July 2009) (discussing applicability of *Nollan* and *Dolan* to legislative enactments after *Lingle*).

81. *Compare* 605 Ill. Comp. Stat. 5 / 5-904 (2018) (impact fees must be "specifically and uniquely attributable to the new development paying the fee"), *with* Cal. Gov't Code §§ 66001 (2007) (requiring a "reasonable relationship between the fee's use and the type of development

that the fees be limited to an amount that "bears a *rational nexus* to the needs created by, and benefits conferred upon" a project.[82]

C. Applicability to Linkage Fees

Very few published cases have considered a takings claim in relation to linkage fees. Those that have done so have utilized the "reasonable relationship" test. In *Commercial Builders of Northern California v. City of Sacramento*,[83] the Ninth Circuit Court of Appeals in 1991 found Sacramento's linkage fee to be constitutional. The city had adopted the fee after completing a detailed study of the effects of commercial development on the need for low-income housing and designed the fee to raise only 9 percent of the cost of the needed housing.[84] Although the court discussed the "indirectness of the connection between the creation of new jobs and the need for low-income housing,"[85] it concluded that the fee "bears a *rational relationship* to a public cost closely associated with" new development, in part because such a low percentage of the costs was assessed against the developers.[86]

In *Holmdel Builders v. Township of Holmdel*,[87] the New Jersey Supreme Court also concluded that *Nollan*'s rational nexus test was "not apposite" to commercial linkage fees.[88] Instead, the court stated:

> We find a sound basis to support a legislative judgment that there is a *reasonable relationship* between unrestrained nonresidential development and the need for affordable residential development. We do not equate such a reasonable relationship with the strict rational-nexus standard. . . . [T]he relationship [between commercial development and linkage fees] is to be founded on the actual, albeit indirect and general, impact that such nonresidential development has on both the need for lower-income residential development and on the opportunity and capacity of municipalities to meet that need.[89]

The California Supreme Court further explicated the "reasonable relationship" test in relation to a housing replacement fee intended to mitigate loss of low-income housing resulting from converting a residential hotel to tourist use. The fee was based on 80 percent of the cost of the replacement housing and resulted in a fee of $567,000 for conversion of 30

---

project" and a "reasonable relationship between the need for the public facility and the type of development project."

82. *See, e.g.*, Longridge Builders, Inc. v. Planning Bd., 245 A.2d 336, 337 (N.J. 1968). *See also* San Remo Hotel, L.P. v. City & Cnty. of San Francisco, 41 P.3d 87, 102–03 (Cal. 2002); Home Builders Ass'n v. City of Scottsdale, 930 P.2d 993, 999 (Ariz. 1997).

83. Commercial Builders v. City of Sacramento, 941 F.2d 872 (9th Cir. 1991), *cert. denied*, 504 U.S. 931 (1992).

84. *Id.* at 873.

85. *Id.* at 876.

86. *Id.* at 874 (emphasis added). The Ninth Circuit did not explicitly hold that *Nollan* was inapplicable to Sacramento's linkage fee but instead found that *Nollan* did not "materially change[ ]" the scrutiny to be applied to the fee. *Id.*

87. Holmdel Builders Ass'n v. Twp. of Holmdel, 583 A.2d 277 (N.J. 1990).

88. *Id.* at 288.

89. *Id.* (emphasis added). Since *Commercial Builders* and *Holmdel Builders* were decided, there appear to be no published cases that directly address the constitutionality of commercial linkage fees or the methodology used to justify them.

hotel rooms. The plaintiffs argued that the mechanism for counting the number of rooms being converted was faulty. However, the court agreed that a showing had not been made that the fees were unreasonable in the *generality* or *great majority* of cases, and consequently that the fees did bear a reasonable relationship to the loss of housing.[90]

Some economists believe it is a fallacy to assert that commercial development creates a need for low-income housing.[91] In *Commercial Builders*, the developer presented an expert witness who "testified" that "employers follow the workforce" rather than vice versa.[92] The dissenter argued that commercial linkage fees are "nothing more than a convenient way to fund a system of transfer payments."[93] But researchers supportive of the programs have concluded that most linkage programs "dramatically understate" a development's impact on housing.[94] As noted by the New Jersey Supreme Court in *Holmdel*, "Land must be viewed as an essential but exhaustible resource; any land that is developed for any purpose reduces the supply of land capable of being used to build affordable housing."[95]

Where linkage fees are authorized by state law, all communities have completed studies demonstrating a reasonable relationship between the fee and the development's impact on affordable housing, as shown in the following examples of existing programs.

D. Local Examples

1. Boston, Massachusetts

After Boston's original 1983 program was challenged as exceeding the city's home rule powers,[96] Boston submitted a home rule petition to the state legislature and in 1987 received statutory authority to adopt an ordinance.[97] Another home rule petition, adopted by the legislature in 2001, raised the linkage fee to $7.18 per square foot and allowed increases every three years.[98] In 2020, further amendments were made to allow Boston flexibility to adjust the payment and program guidelines.[99] On March 11, 2021, after several years of feasibility

---

90. Compare San Remo Hotel, L.P, v. City & Cnty. of San Francisco, 41 P.3d 87, 107 (Cal. 2002), *with* San Telmo Assocs. v. City of Seattle, 735 P.2d 673, 675 (Wash. 1987) ("The Housing Preservation Ordinance would apparently require San Telmo to either build a new, comparable housing project, or contribute approximately $1.5 million to the low-income housing fund. We seriously question whether faced with that potential levy, San Telmo would be in a position to make any profitable use of its property. If not, the ordinance would constitute a taking. . . .").

91. *See* Teresa R. Herrero, *Housing Linkage: Will It Play a Role in the 1990s?*, 13 J. OF URB. AFF. 1, 14–16 (1991).

92. Commercial Builders v. City of Sacramento, 941 F.2d 872, 876 (9th Cir. 1991).

93. *Id.* at 877 (Beezer, J., dissenting). *See also* Timothy M. Tesluk, *Commercial Builders of Northern California v. City of Sacramento: Commerce Creates Poverty*, 42 CASE W. RES. L. REV. 1339 (1992) (criticizing *Commercial Builders* for similar reasons).

94. Jane E. Schukoske, *Housing Linkage: Regulating Development Impact on Housing Costs*, 76 IOWA L. REV. 1011, 1026 (1991); 24 LAND USE & ENV'T L. REV. 141–95 (2009).

95. Holmdel Builders Ass'n v. Twp. of Holmdel, 583 A.2d 277, 285 (N.J. 1990).

96. Bonan v. City of Boston, 496 N.E.2d 640, 641–42 (Mass. 1986).

97. 1956 MASS. ACTS ch. 665, §§ 15–20, added by 1987 MASS. ACTS ch. 371 § 3. In 1991, the Massachusetts Legislature approved a similar home rule petition for the City of Cambridge. *See* 1991 MASS. ACTS ch. 482.

98. 1956 MASS. ACTS ch. 665, §§ 15–21, amended and added by 2001 MASS. ACTS ch. 170 §§ 2-8 and 2001 MASS. ACTS ch. 203 § 13.

99. 1956 MASS. ACTS ch. 665, § 15–21, amended by HN No. 4115, §§ 2-21 (2020).

assessments and conversations with developers and advocates, fees were increased to equal $13 per square foot for housing contributions, and to $2.39 per square foot for jobs contribution, for a total of $15.39.[100]

Boston's fees apply only to commercial square footage exceeding 100,000 square feet in large commercial projects that require some sort of "zoning relief," such as a variance, use permit, or rezoning.[101] Developers have the choice of paying the linkage fee or using equivalent funds to create new housing affordable to households earning up to 80 percent of area median income.[102] In either case, developers must enter into Development Impact Project contracts with the Boston Redevelopment Authority (BRA) to ensure that the linkage fees are paid.[103]

Commercial linkage fees are generally paid in seven equal annual installments to the Neighborhood Housing Trust (NHT), commencing either 24 months after issuance of an occupancy permit or, in the downtown area, upon issuance of a building permit.[104] The governing body of NHT consists of seven trustees: the president of the City Council or designee, the city of Boston's collector-treasurer, and five members appointed by the mayor. The collector-treasurer is responsible for administering the NHT and managing its finances.[105] The city's Department of Neighborhood Development reviews and administers grant applications.[106]

From 1986 through the end of 2012, the NHT had spent nearly $133 million in linkage fees (over $5 million per year) and created or preserved 10,176 affordable housing units.[107] Since 2014, the program had generated $80 million, and new development approved in 2020 alone was expected to generate over $43 million in housing fees.[108] Virtually any entity may apply to the NHT for funds to construct or rehabilitate housing affordable to households earning up to 80 percent of the median income. Ownership units must remain affordable for at least 50 years; rental units must remain affordable in perpetuity.[109] Ten percent of the linkage fees from downtown projects and 20 percent of the fees from other projects are targeted to the neighborhood affected by the project.[110]

---

100. BOSTON, MASS.— REDEVELOPMENT AUTHORITY, §§ 80B-7(4)(a)(1), 80B-7(5)(a)(1) (2021).

101. *Id.*

102. *Id.* §§ 80B-7(3)(a), 80B-7(4)(a), (b); *see Mayor Walsh Signs 42 Percent Increase in Linkage Fees into Law*, CITY OF BOSTON, BOSTON PLANNING AND DEVELOPMENT AGENCY (Mar. 11, 2021), http://www.bostonplans.org/news-calendar/news-updates/2021/03/11/mayor-walsh-signs-42-percent-increase-in-linkage-f [https://perma.cc/YY9B-6HD7].

103. BOSTON, MASS.—REDEVELOPMENT AUTHORITY, § 80B-7(3).

104. BOSTON, MASS.—REDEVELOPMENT AUTHORITY, §§ 80B-7(1)(a), (4)(a)(iii) (2010).

105. *See* NEIGHBORHOOD HOUSING TRUST, CITY OF BOSTON (2017) at 6, https://www.boston.gov/sites/default/files/embed/n/nht_report_2017_170102.pdf [https://perma.cc/9PDF-BMCQ].

106. *See Mayor Walsh*, *supra* note 102.

107. *See* NEIGHBORHOOD HOUSING TRUST, *supra* note 105, at 3.

108. *See Mayor Walsh*, *supra* note 102.

109. *See* NEIGHBORHOOD HOUSING TRUST, *supra* note 105, at 5.

110. BOSTON, MASS.—REDEVELOPMENT AUTHORITY, §§ 80B-7(4)(a)(ii) (2021).

The Boston Redevelopment Authority concluded in a 2000 study that its program was the "best in the nation" in terms of raising money for housing while encouraging continued commercial development.[111]

2. Sacramento, California

The city of Sacramento adopted its commercial linkage fee in 1989. No state legislation was required; California's Constitution delegates the police power to its cities.[112] Sacramento's fee was immediately challenged but was upheld by the Ninth Circuit in the *Commercial Builders* case discussed earlier in this section.

A city of over 500,000 located in the inland Central Valley and California's state capitol, Sacramento imposes fees that are much lower than those in Boston. Fees effective July 1, 2020, ranged from $0.76 per square foot for warehouses to $2.76 per square foot for offices.[113] Linkage fees apply to all new commercial and industrial construction.[114] Developers have the option of constructing housing of any type, affordable or not, to house the required number of employees and pay 40 percent of the linkage fee. A formula determines the number of units that must be built. For instance, a 100,000 square foot office building must provide 13 units, while a 100,000 square foot warehouse must provide only three units.[115]

Between the program's inception in 1989 and June 2019, Sacramento collected over $32 million in linkage fees and used them to develop more than 3,590 affordable homes and apartments.[116] Annual revenues, including interest on fund balances and loan repayments, were approximately $3 million from 2015 through 2019.[117] The fees are placed in a Housing Trust Fund and allocated to projects by the Sacramento Housing and Redevelopment Agency.[118] The city originally attempted to locate the affordable housing within commuting distance (defined as seven miles) of the projects contributing linkage fees; a 2004 survey found that 99 percent of the assisted housing was located within that radius.

---

111. *See* Boston Redevelopment Authority, Survey of Linkage Programs in Other U.S. Cities with Comparisons to Boston (May 2000), http://www.bostonplans.org/getattachment/8440bf23-afa7-40b0-a274-4aca16359252/ [https://perma.cc/954S-K9ZM].

112. Cal. Const. art. XI, § 7. California courts have held that the police power of cities is as broad as that of the state, as long as local laws are not in conflict with state laws. *See* Candid Enters., Inc. v. Grossmont Union High School Dist., 705 P.2d 876, 882 (Cal. 1985).

113. *See* City of Sacramento, Community Development., Fee Notice, Housing Trust Fund (HTF) Fee Increase Effective July 1, 2020, http://www.cityofsacramento.org/layouts/Corporate/FC_Search/GetAttachment.aspx?filename=21000123137982020-07-01Housing_Trust_Fund_Notice_FY21.pdf (last visited June 13, 2021).

114. *See* Sacramento, Cal., City Code § 18.56.410 (2021).

115. *Id.* § 18.56.460.

116. League of California Cities Policy Committee, City of Sacramento Housing Trust Fund (June 13, 2019) at 8, https://www.cacities.org/Resources-Documents/Policy-Advocacy-Section/Policy-Development/Policy-Committees/Housing,-Community-and-Economic-Development/City-of-Sacramento-Housing-Trust-Fund.aspx [https://perma.cc/NUS7-AZEH].

117. *See* 2021–2029 Sacramento Housing Element, at H-4-8 (May 2021) A [https://perma.cc/9GNZ-88YD].

118. Sacramento, Cal., City Code § 18.56.430(A),(B) (2021).

Projects ranged from new apartments on vacant lots to rehabilitation of boarded, vacant, and dilapidated apartments.[119]

The city's original 1989 nexus study, used to defend against the court challenge, was updated in 2004 and 2006.[120] The 2004 update found that the subsidy cost for each unit of very low-income housing had nearly doubled since 1989, from $33,131 to $60,077 per unit.[121] Of the new jobs created since 1990, the majority paid low-income or very low-income wages: 28 percent low-income wages and 36 percent very low-income wages.[122] Nonetheless, to ensure that the fees did not inhibit economic development, the city chose to limit its fee increase to 44 percent, resulting in fees that were only 10 to 30 percent of the maximum permissible fees under the *original* 1989 study.[123]

3. Colorado Resort Communities

Many Colorado communities located near ski resorts, including Telluride, Basalt (near Aspen), and Eagle County (which includes Vail), require the payment of linkage fees or the construction of employee housing for all new development, both residential and commercial. The ordinances were adopted in the 1990s in response to the demand for relatively low-paid workers created by new resorts and the construction of luxury second homes. The second-home industry not only increased housing costs but also acted as "an industry creating a demand for workers."[124] Unlike the Sacramento and Boston programs, the Colorado ordinances give strong preference for the actual construction of employee housing and limit the use of linkage fees.

Colorado communities have the authority to adopt linkage fees.[125] Communities with home rule charters (Telluride and Basalt)[126] and without (Eagle County) have adopted commercial linkage fees. All three jurisdictions have completed nexus studies to determine the

---

119. *See* REAL ESTATE ANALYTICS, A PERIODIC REVIEW OF ECONOMIC NEXUS BETWEEN EMPLOYMENT-GENERATED DEMAND AND AFFORDABLE HOUSING AND OF THE HOUSING TRUST FUND OF THE CITY AND COUNTY OF SACRAMENTO, at 66, 70 (Mar. 2004).

120. *Id.*; *Housing Trust Fund*, CITY OF SACRAMENTO, http://www.cityofsacramento.org /Community-Development/Planning/Long-Range/Housing-Programs/Housing-Trust-Fund [https:// perma.cc/J8TW-EKAA].

121. REAL ESTATE ANALYTICS, *supra* note 119, at 57.

122. *See* CITY OF SACRAMENTO, STAFF REPORT TO CITY COUNCIL, *Housing Trust Fund Increase*, Sept. 30, 2004, at 2, 5.

123. *Id.* at 9. Note that linkage fees in Sacramento were originally increased by 81 percent in October 2004. After an outcry, the percentage increase was reduced to 44 percent, as discussed in the text. *See also Housing Trust Fund*, *supra* note 120.

124. LINDA VENTURONI, NW. COLO. COUNCIL OF GOV'TS, THE SOCIAL & ECONOMIC EFFECTS OF SECOND HOMES, EXECUTIVE SUMMARY 6 (June 2004).

125. *See* discussion of the authority of both statutory and home rule cities and counties to adopt linkage fees and other affordable housing programs in RRC ASSOCS. TEAM & HEALTHY MOUNTAIN COMMUNITIES, FINAL REPORT: REGIONAL HOUSING INITIATIVE 101–03 (Jan. 1, 2000).

126. *See* TELLURIDE, COLO., HOME RULE CHARTER (adopted 1977; current through election of November 5, 2013); BASALT, COLO., HOME RULE CHARTER (adopted Nov. 5, 2002).

need for affordable workforce housing created by new development,[127] although Basalt also requires that each project complete an Employee Impact and Housing Mitigation Report.[128]

The programs vary substantially in the proportion of housing demand that new development must meet. Telluride requires that new development provide housing for 40 percent of the employees generated;[129] Basalt, 15 percent;[130] and Eagle County, 45 percent of employees earning less than 140 percent of the median income.[131] All three programs allow applicants to provide employee housing through a variety of mechanisms (such as on- and off-site construction, land dedication, and acquisition of existing units) and characterize linkage fees as "in-lieu fees." The fee amounts are set per square foot of affordable employee housing that is not constructed or otherwise provided and are intended to approximate the cost of providing that housing. Telluride's fee in 2021 was set at $502 per square foot of required affordable housing;[132] Eagle County in 2020 estimated payments to be $171 per square foot.[133]

Both Eagle County[134] and Basalt allow a developer to pay an in-lieu fee rather than provide on-site housing. Basalt allows in-lieu fees to be paid for the first 7,000 square feet of required housing and for 75 percent of the remainder; in-lieu fees may be paid for all of the need through a special review procedure.[135] Telluride, however, permits in-lieu fees to be paid for only 10 percent or less of the developer's total obligation.[136]

The nexus studies prepared by these relatively small Colorado communities are quite sophisticated and can serve as a model for other communities considering linkage fees.[137]

IV. IN-LIEU FEES FROM INCLUSIONARY ZONING PROGRAMS

Inclusionary zoning requires a developer of new residences to make a certain percentage of the homes affordable to low- and/or moderate-income households.[138] It is most commonly imposed in high-cost areas to provide a supply of affordable housing. Communities

---

127. *See, e.g.*, TOWN OF BASALT, COLORADO, COMMUNITY HOUSING-STRATEGY SUPPORT STUDY (Rees Consulting/RRC Assocs., Inc., January 2009); EAGLE COUNTY, COLORADO, NEXUS/PROPORTIONALITY ANALYSIS FOR COMMERCIAL DEVELOPMENT/WORKFORCE HOUSING LINKAGE (Rees Consulting/RRC Assocs., Inc., January 2008).

128. *See* BASALT, COLO. CODE, Art. xix § 16-413 (2021). The ordinance contains a complicated formula for calculating the housing needed, normally assuming that 3,000 sq. ft. of commercial space would generate a need for 959 sq. ft. of affordable housing. *See id.* § 16-417(d).

129. TELLURIDE, COLO. CODE, Art. 3, Div. 7, § 3-720.C.1.b (2021).

130. BASALT, COLO. CODE § 16-417(a) (2021).

131. EAGLE COUNTY, COLO. AFFORDABLE HOUSING GUIDELINES § 3-02 (amended October 6, 2020).

132. TOWN OF TELLURIDE, DEVELOPMENT FEES, EFFECTIVE JANUARY 1, 2021.

133. EAGLE COUNTY, COLO., AFFORDABLE HOUSING GUIDELINES: ADMINISTRATIVE PROCEDURES (amended October 6, 2020) at 19, Table 7-5.

134. AFFORDABLE HOUSING GUIDELINES, *supra* note 131, at § 4.07.

135. BASALT, COLO. CODE, Art. xix, § 16-415 (2021).

136. TELLURIDE, COLO., CODE, Art. 3, Div. 7, § 3-740.A.5 (2021).

137. *See* studies referenced *supra* note 127.

138. See Chapter 4 for a general discussion of inclusionary zoning programs.

with inclusionary zoning usually allow developers to pay a fee in lieu of constructing the housing.[139]

A. Inclusionary Zoning and Fees: Exactions or Land-Use Requirements?

Commercial linkage fees are clearly characterized as impact fees, a type of exaction, and are based on nexus studies showing that new commercial development creates additional demand for affordable housing. The development community and some published analyses of inclusionary zoning have often asserted, without analysis, that inclusionary requirements are development exactions and must be justified by a nexus study, sometimes pointing to the in-lieu fee option as evidence that an inclusionary requirement is equivalent to a monetary exaction. Supporters of inclusionary zoning, however, argue that inclusionary ordinances are land-use ordinances, rather than exactions, with the in-lieu fee alternative simply an accommodation to the development community.[140] How the inclusionary requirement is characterized determines how in-lieu fees are calculated.

In 1990, the New Jersey Supreme Court firmly adopted the "land-use ordinance" position. The court explained that "inclusionary-zoning devices," including inclusionary in-lieu fees, are land-use ordinances that bear a "real and substantial relationship to the regulation of land" because they are specifically designed to help create affordable housing and will therefore affect "the nature and extent of the uses of land and of buildings. . . ."[141] Further, inclusionary in-lieu fees are *not* exactions similar to impact fees, because the affordable housing requirements are not based on the *impact* of a project but rather on "the relationship that . . . development has on both the need for lower-income residential development and on the opportunity and capacity of municipalities to meet that need. . . ."[142]

---

139. *See, e.g.*, Non-Profit Housing Ass'n of Northern California, Affordable by Choice: Trends in California Inclusionary Housing Programs 17 (2007) (89 percent of inclusionary programs in California have an in-lieu fee option).

140. Despite the case results described below, the issue continues to be disputed. *Compare* Richard P. Epstein, *The Unassailable Case Against Affordable Housing Mandates, in* Evidence and Innovation in Housing Law and Policy 64, 66 (Lee Ann Fennell & Benjamin J. Keys, eds., 2017) (asserting that inclusionary programs are takings), *with* Audrey G. McFarlane & Randall K. Johnson, *Cities, Inclusion and Exactions*, 102 Iowa L. Rev. 2145, 2180–84 (2017) (noting that while a consensus has not been reached, inclusionary ordinances should survive scrutiny under both the *Penn Central* and *Nollan/Dolan* tests). *See also* Barbara Ehrlich Kautz, *In Defense of Inclusionary Zoning: Successfully Creating Affordable Housing*, 36 U.S.F. L. Rev. 971, 975 (2002); William W. Merrill III & Robert K. Lincoln, *Linkage Fees and Fair Share Regulations: Law and Method*, 25 Urb. Law. 223, 274 (1993); Thomas Kleven, *Inclusionary Ordinances—Policy and Legal Issues in Requiring Private Developers to Build Low Cost Housing*, 21 UCLA L. Rev. 1432, 1490 (1974). Some commentators simply assume that inclusionary housing is an exaction. *See, e.g.*, James S. Burling & Graham Owen, *The Implications of Lingle on Inclusionary Zoning and Other Legislative and Monetary Exactions*, 28 Stan. Envtl. L.J. 397, 405–07 (2009); Mark Fenster, *Takings Formalism and Regulatory Formulas: Exactions and the Consequences of Clarity*, 92 Cal. L. Rev. 609, 657 (2004).

141. Holmdel Builders Ass'n v. Twp. of Holmdel, 583 A.2d 277, 286–97 (N.J. 1990).

142. *Id.* at 288.

A concerted litigation strategy by the Pacific Legal Foundation and California Building Industry Association to characterize inclusionary requirements as exactions[143] culminated in the California Supreme Court's decision in *California Building Industry Association [CBIA] v. City of San Jose.*[144] The CBIA asserted that San Jose's recently adopted inclusionary ordinance violated the unconstitutional conditions doctrine, because it imposed an exaction—the inclusionary requirement—upon developers without showing that housing development caused a need for the required affordable housing.[145] The court, however, held that:

> [T]here is no exaction—the ordinance does not require a developer to give up a property interest for which the government would have been required to pay just compensation under the takings clause. . . . Instead, like many other land use regulations, this condition simply places a restriction on the way the developer may use its property by limiting the price for which the developer may offer some of its units for sale. . . . Contrary to CBIA's contention, such a requirement does not constitute an exaction for the *Nollan/Dolan* line of decisions.[146]

San Jose's ordinance also allowed a developer to pay an in-lieu as an alternative to providing affordable units, and the CBIA argued that the U.S. Supreme Court's decision in *Koontz v. St. Johns River Water Management District*[147] required that the fee could only imposed if needed to mitigate impacts of the project. The California court held, however, that *Koontz* would not apply if San Jose offered a means of satisfying the ordinance that did not violate the takings clause. Because the inclusionary requirement itself did not violate the takings clause, the unconstitutional conditions doctrine described in *Koontz* did not apply to the in-lieu fee.[148] Under the court's ruling, no nexus study is required to justify an in-lieu fee offered as an alternative to an on-site construction requirement.

The California Supreme Court's reasoning has been favorably cited in two published federal District Court decisions, one challenging an in-lieu fee imposed by the City of Chicago[149] and the other challenging Washington D.C.'s Inclusionary Zoning Program.[150] Nonetheless, at least two additional petitions for certiorari challenging inclusionary in-lieu fees have been filed, both denied by the U.S. Supreme Court.[151] It is clear that the effort to characterize inclusionary requirements as exactions continues.

---

143. Home Builders Ass'n v. City of Napa, 108 Cal. Rptr. 2d 60 (Cal. Ct. App. 2001); Action Apt. Ass'n v. City of Santa Monica, 82 Cal. Rptr. 3d 722 (Cal. Ct. App. 2008); Mead v. City of Cotati, 2008 U.S. Dist. LEXIS 4963048; Kamaole Pointe Dev. L.P. v. Cnty. of Maui, 573 F. Supp. 2d 1354 (D. Haw. 2008), all cases seeking to apply *Nollan/Dolan* to an inclusionary ordinance were litigated by the Pacific Legal Foundation (PLF), as was the *San Jose* case discussed *infra*, note 144, 148.

144. *Calif. Bldg. Industry Ass'n [CBIA] v. City of San Jose*, 351 P.3d 974 (2015); *cert. denied*, 577 U.S. 1179.

145. *See id.* at 977–79.

146. *Id.* at 990–91 (citations omitted).

147. Koontz v. St. Johns River Water Mgmt. Dist., 570 U.S. 595 (2013).

148. *See* CBIA v. San Jose, 351 P.3d at 996–1006.

149. Home Builders Ass'n v. City of Chicago, 213 F. Supp. 3d 1019 (N.D. Ill. 2016).

150. 2910 Georgia Ave. LLC v. District of Columbia, 234 F. Supp. 3d 281 (D.D.C. 2017).

151. 616 Croft Ave. LLC v. City of West Hollywood, 207 Cal. Rptr. 3d 729 (Cal. Ct. App. 2016); *cert. denied*, 138 S. Ct. 377 (2017); *Cherk v. Cnty. of Marin*, 2018 WL 6583442 (Cal. Ct. App. 2018) (unpublished opinion); *cert. denied*, 140 S. Ct. 652 (2019).

B. Calculating In-Lieu Fees

Where in-lieu fees are considered to be land-use requirements, the amount of the in-lieu fee is not based on the impact of the development, but instead is determined by the dollar subsidy required to provide the same number of inclusionary units, at the same income levels, as would otherwise be constructed on the site. This is typically calculated in one of two ways. Most simply, the in-lieu fee for each inclusionary unit can be calculated as the difference between the affordable price (or value as a rental) and the unit's fair market value. Alternatively, the in-lieu fee can be calculated to equal the difference between all costs of creating the unit (land, construction, financing, fees, etc.) and the affordable sales price (or value as a rental).[152] This cost is usually translated into a cost per affordable unit or cost per square foot of market-rate construction and may vary in different geographic areas.[153]

Most inclusionary in-lieu fees are not set high enough to build the same amount of housing as would have been constructed if the underlying inclusionary requirement were imposed on the project.[154] Many communities imposing in-lieu fees initially set rather low fees but then raise them substantially after finding that they are inadequate to construct the same amount of housing as would have been provided on-site.

Where communities have treated inclusionary in-lieu fees as impact fees, they have completed detailed nexus studies to quantify the demand for *affordable* housing created by new *market-rate* housing. These nexus studies quantify the low-wage local service employment for sales clerks, teachers, health care workers, household workers, and other local service workers generated by new housing construction, calculate the amount of affordable housing needed by those workers and the subsidy needed to create that housing, and translate that into an amount per unit or per square foot of market-rate housing.[155] In general, the wealthier the community, the higher the fees that can be justified. This is because wealthier residents have more disposable income and create a need for more local service employment.

Affordable housing advocates have at times disfavored nexus studies, in part because they fear that they may result in reduced affordable housing requirements or serve to undermine the "land-use" position. However, where communities have completed nexus studies, they have found that the fees justified by the nexus study are often substantially in

---

152. *See* LOCAL GOVERNMENT COMMISSION, MEETING CALIFORNIA'S HOUSING NEEDS: BEST PRACTICES FOR INCLUSIONARY HOUSING 6 (Nov. 2018), https://www.lgc.org/wordpress/wp-content/uploads/2018/11/inclusionary-factsheet_v2.pdf [https://perma.cc/BW3R-D3V2].

153. *See generally* AARON SHROYER, DETERMINING IN-LIEU FEES IN INCLUSIONARY ZONING POLICIES: CONSIDERATIONS FOR LOCAL GOVERNMENTS, URBAN INSTITUTE (May 2020), https://www.urban.org/sites/default/files/publication/102230/determining-in-lieu-fees-in-inclusionary-zoning-policies.pdf [https://perma.cc/8QVY-ZSNG].

154. *See* LOCAL GOVERNMENT COMMISSION, *supra* note 152, at 6. Where fees are set below the developer's cost to provide the units, developers will pay the fee rather than build the units, resulting in fewer units built.

155. *See, e.g.*, KEYSER MARSTON ASSOCS., AFFORDABLE HOUSING NEXUS ANALYSIS PREPARED FOR CITY OF ENCINITAS (Nov. 2019); RESIDENTIAL NEXUS ANALYSIS, RICHMOND, CALIFORNIA (July 2016); RESIDENTIAL NEXUS ANALYSIS, INCLUSIONARY HOUSING ORDINANCE, FREMONT, CAL. (Apr. 2010).

excess of the in-lieu fees previously charged.[156] Nexus studies may still be desirable in some cases, even where not required. Some communities, especially those where most housing development consists of single-family homes, may want to impose a fee requirement rather than an on-site requirement as a more practical way to accumulate funds for an affordable development. Some communities are also concerned about the continued litigation over inclusionary housing and desire to obtain a nexus study as an additional defense.

C. California Communities

Monterey County and the city of Santa Monica represent two views of in-lieu fee programs, with Monterey County treating its program as a land-use ordinance and Santa Monica treating its program as an impact fee.

1. Monterey County

Monterey County's program, adopted on October 28, 1980, initially required that developers either build 15 percent of new units as affordable housing or pay an in-lieu fee of $1,000 per unit or lot. Five years later the in-lieu fee was substantially increased to equal 15 percent of the median sales price of each home in the development.[157] Developers of three- to four-unit homes may pay in-lieu fees, while developers of five homes or more must demonstrate that characteristics of the development, such as large lot development or potentially high maintenance costs, make the site unsuitable for affordable housing. Fees for each market-rate unit are set at one-fifth of the difference between the affordable price for a home affordable to a median-income household and the cost of developing a three-bedroom home.[158]

The inclusionary in-lieu fee varies by planning area and is based on the difference between the median sales price in the planning area and an affordable price of $130,000. It ranges from a high of $145,864 per market-rate unit in the exclusive Big Sur area to $4,590 per market-rate unit in the agricultural South County area.[159] Between 1980 and 2001, the county collected a total of $5.3 million in inclusionary in-lieu fees and assisted 981 affordable units. Most of these units also received funding from other sources.[160]

In evaluating the inclusionary housing program in 2002, the county concluded that its in-lieu fees were inadequate to produce the same number of units as would have been

---

156. *See, e.g.*, Residential Nexus Analysis, Inclusionary Housing Ordinance, Fremont, Cal. (Apr. 2010).

157. *See* County of Monterey, How Did We Do? An Evaluation of the Inclusionary Housing Program 1980–2001 11–14 (2002). It is not clear how an "affordable" unit was defined in the early years of the program.

158. *See* County of Monterey, Cal. Code § 18.40.090 (2021). The County has also increased the inclusionary percentage, requiring that new developments set aside 8 percent of units for moderate-income households, 6 percent for low-income households, and 6 percent for very low-income households. *Id.* § 18.40.110.

159. *See* County of Monterey, Cal., Administrative Manual: County of Monterey Inclusionary Housing Program (amended July 12, 2011) at Appendix G, p. 54 (fees effective Dec. 8, 2000), https://www.co.monterey.ca.us/home/showpublisheddocument?id=81001 [https://perma.cc/LF5M-UTAY].

160. *See* How Did We Do?, *supra* note 157, at 13.

created on-site.[161] In-lieu fees, which had averaged $233,000 per year from 1980 to 2001, generated approximately $2 million in fees after 2003, or about $285,000 per year.[162] Where the county agrees to allow payment of in-lieu fees, substantial sums can be collected. One development alone, the single-family Ferrini Ranch project, approved in December 2014, generated an in-lieu fee of $4 million for 26 lower income units not provided on-site, although the project did provide 17 moderate-income units.[163]

2. City of Santa Monica

Santa Monica's ordinance was the result of an initiative amendment adopted on November 6, 1990, which mandated that at least 30 percent of new multifamily housing in the city be affordable to low- and moderate-income families.[164] However, an economic study concluded that the requirement acted as a constraint on the construction of new housing, and the city determined that a fee would permit it to comply with the voter initiative without rendering multifamily housing economically infeasible.[165]

A nexus study completed in 1998 computed the demand for goods and services created by residents of market-rate housing, the number of low- and moderate-wage workers needed to satisfy that demand, and the cost of producing the affordable housing needed by those low-wage workers. The 1998 report concluded that an impact fee of $5.41 to $8.01 per square foot would be supportable,[166] and Santa Monica initially adopted a fee of $7.13 per square foot for condominiums and $6.14 per square foot for apartments, providing revenues of less than $500,000 per year.[167]

As in Monterey County, city staff found that the fees were much too low to produce as much housing as would a requirement to construct the housing on-site. In 2006, the city

---

161. *Id.* at 32–33.

162. *See* COUNTY OF MONTEREY, 2015–2023 HOUSING ELEMENT B-12 (Jan. 26, 2016), https://www.co.monterey.ca.us/home/showdocument?id=12511 [https://perma.cc/9JAW-R3QB]; HOW DID WE DO?, *supra* note 157, at 13. However, only $50,000 was expected in fiscal year 2010–11 because the housing market had collapsed in the county. *See* MONTEREY COUNTY, ANNUAL HOUSING REPORT 2010 44 (filed Mar. 2, 2010), https://monterey.legistar.com/LegislationDetail.aspx?ID=1339293&GUID=1AECF3AF-CD3A-4281-94C1-CADC6A32BB6D&Options=&Search=&FullText=1 [https://perma.cc/T4WM-UT2W] (follow link to "2010 – Annual Housing Report" to view a copy of the report).

163. COUNTY OF MONTEREY, 2015–2023 HOUSING ELEMENT, *supra* note 162, at 104–05, B-12.

164. *See* SANTA MONICA, CAL. CHARTER § 630 (2004). The definitions of "low income" and "moderate income" included in the charter provision are not consistent with usual HUD guidelines. "Low income" households are defined as those with incomes at 60 percent of area median income or below (compared with the HUD standard of 80 percent of median), while "moderate income" households are defined as those with incomes at 100 percent of median or below (compared with the standard 120 percent of median).

165. *See* SANTA MONICA, CAL., STAFF REPORT TO CITY COUNCIL (Apr. 14, 1998), https://www.smgov.net/departments/council/agendas/1998/19980414/s1998041406-I.html [https://perma.cc/A2D8-K2D3].

166. *See* HAMILTON, RABINOVITZ & ALSCHULER, INC., THE NEXUS BETWEEN NEW MARKET RATE MULTI-FAMILY DEVELOPMENTS IN THE CITY OF SANTA MONICA AND THE NEED FOR AFFORDABLE HOUSING (July 7, 1998). The study was updated in 2005.

167. *See* e-mail from Steve Goldmaker, Housing Analyst, City of Santa Monica, to Rebecca Blanda (Nov. 9, 2004) (on file with author); e-mail from Jim Kemper, Senior Administrative Analyst, City of Santa Monica, to Rebecca Blanda (Nov. 10, 2004) (on file with author).

amended its inclusionary ordinance to require the actual provision of affordable units in all for-sale projects of four or more units.[168] It also updated its nexus study. While current fees, as of June 2021, are $35.70 per square foot for apartments and $41.70 per square foot for condominiums,[169] payment of in-lieu fees is only available for projects of three units or less or for fractional unit requirements.

V. LAND TRANSFER PROGRAMS

Programs to transfer land to affordable housing developers on advantageous terms appear to be widely available but have not been comprehensively surveyed. New York City's program and new California legislation are discussed here.[170]

A. City of New York Third Party Transfer Initiative

The city of New York operates a Third Party Transfer Initiative, which transfers properties subject to foreclosure for unpaid property taxes to new owners for rehabilitation. The program was created to reduce a large inventory of foreclosed buildings owned and managed by the city as landlord of last resort; by 1994, the inventory had grown to 5,458 buildings containing 51,672 units.[171] Between 1996 and 2008, 436 properties, containing approximately 4,600 units, were included in the Third Party Transfer Initiative. With the assistance of federal funds, the city was able to provide roughly $74,000 per unit for rehabilitation.[172]

The program derives its authority from the city's discretion to carry out an in rem foreclosure action on "distressed property," defined as property subject to a tax lien[173] equal to 25 percent of the property's value, or equal to 15 percent off the property's value if there are hazardous conditions,[174] and then to transfer the property to qualified third parties designated by the Commissioner of Housing Preservation and Development.[175] Foreclosure proceedings can begin based on as little as one year of tax delinquencies for most buildings, although three years of delinquency are a prerequisite for smaller buildings.[176] The New York City Administrative Code limits the tax-defaulting owner's right to redeem

168. SANTA MONICA, CAL. CODE § 9.64.040 (2021).

169. *See* Fee—Affordable Housing, CITY OF SANTA MONICA, CAL., https://www.smgov.net /Departments/HED/content.aspx?id=20938 (last visited June 13, 2021).

170. Other cities that have reported active programs to transfer land for affordable housing include Boston, which saw almost 400 city-owned parcels in use for new affordable housing between 2001 and 2004, according to LEADING THE WAY II, A REPORT ON BOSTON'S HOUSING STRATEGY FY 2004–FY 2007 (May 2004), 4–15. See Chapter 4 for a discussion of land banking.

171. The program and its history and implementation are described in CHRISTOPHER J. ALLRED, BREAKING THE CYCLE OF ABANDONMENT: USING A TAX ENFORCEMENT TOOL TO RETURN DISTRESSED PROPERTIES TO SOUND PRIVATE OWNERSHIP (Pioneer Inst.-Better Gov't Competition No. 10, 2000).

172. *See* JERILYN PERINE, HAROLD SHULTZ & STEFANI MARAZZI, THE INVISIBLE TRANSFORMATION: TURNING DEBT INTO REVENUE 20 (Citizens Housing & Planning Council 2010).

173. A tax lien in New York City may include delinquent water and sewer charges. NEW YORK CITY, N.Y., ADMIN. CODE § 11-301 (2021).

174. *Id.* § 11-401(4).

175. *Id.* § 11-412.1(b). Discretion is exercised by the commissioner of finance, subject to a right of the City Council, within 45 days after notification, to disapprove transfer to a third party (§ 11-412.2).

176. *Id.* § 11-319.

the foreclosed property to a four-month period after the final judgment awarding posses-sion to a new owner,[177] but the Commissioner of Housing Preservation and Development has the authority to remove "distressed" property from this tax lien disposition process.[178] Foreclosed-upon properties are then transferred to the nonprofit Neighborhood Restore Housing Development Fund Corporation, which works with both nonprofit and for-profit developers to rehabilitate and manage the properties.[179]

The program's goals include collection of delinquent taxes and water and sewage charges for properties where the city has expended funds to repair hazardous conditions.[180] The Third Party Transfer program (TPT) targets properties needing substantial rehabilita-tion. TPT's aim is to provide an alternative to tax sales, which, though yielding tax pro-ceeds for the city, could lead to loss of housing.

A task force established by the city in 2016 sought to reduce the number of proper-ties sold with tax liens by providing payment plans, earlier notices of delinquencies, lower interest rates, and more outreach.[181] Nonetheless, the last round of the TPT program, cul-minating in the transfer of 65 properties to Neighborhood Restore,[182] resulted in substantial criticism. A city council oversight report found that some of the selected properties did not properly qualify as "distressed property," properties selected were primarily in com-munities of color, and homeowners were not always notified and had little opportunity to redeem their properties.[183] The report concluded that changes in the housing market since 1996 may justify a review of the viability and purpose of the TPT.[184]

VI. BOND PROCEEDS

Local governments issue two types of bonds to finance affordable housing: revenue bonds and general obligation bonds. This section briefly discusses revenue bonds and then focuses primarily on general obligation bonds.

A. Revenue Bonds

A revenue bond is generally issued as a private activity bond to finance a particular single or multifamily project, and is payable from the revenues generated by that particular proj-ect. There are two main types of revenue bonds that can be issued to finance affordable housing: (1) single-family mortgage revenue bonds, which finance single-family home pur-chases for qualified low-income home buyers; and (2) multifamily housing bonds, which

---

177. *Id.* § 11-412.1(d).

178. *Id.* § 11-401.1.

179. *See* COUNCIL OF THE CITY OF NEW YORK, OVERSIGHT—TAKING STOCK: A LOOK INTO THE THIRD PARTY TRANSFER PROGRAM IN MODERN DAY NEW YORK 8 (filed July 22, 2019), https://legi star.council.nyc.gov/LegislationDetail.aspx?ID=3968976&GUID=30748786-B223-49B9-A6E5 -D381B3FAF5F7 (follow link to "Committee Report").

180. *See* CITY OF NEW YORK, REPORT OF THE LIEN SALE TASK FORCE 8–12 (Sept. 2016), https:// www1.nyc.gov/assets/finance/downloads/pdf/reports/lien_sale_report/lien_sale_task_force_report .pdf [https://perma.cc/5S6H-PPJ4].

181. *Id.* at 13–16.

182. TAKING STOCK, *supra* note 179, at 9.

183. *Id.* at 9–16.

184. *Id.* at 16.

finance the acquisition, construction, and rehabilitation of multifamily developments for low-income renters.

State and local governments sell tax-exempt housing bonds, commonly known as Mortgage Revenue Bonds (MRBs) and Multifamily Housing Bonds, and use the proceeds to finance low-cost mortgages for lower-income first-time home buyers or the construction of apartments at rents affordable to lower-income families.

Multifamily housing projects consist of acquiring and developing rental housing facilities, which are revenue-producing assets. Projects are generally financed on a secured, non-recourse basis, meaning that the borrower is obligated to make payments on the debt only from project revenues (subject to certain standard carve-outs), and the lender's primary security for the financing is the asset itself. The capital structure for a typical bond-financed project includes the following: (1) senior loan funded with tax-exempt bonds; (2) one or more grants and/or subordinate loans from state or local government; and/or (3) equity from limited partners, often tax-credit investors.

MRBs are tax-exempt bonds that state and local governments issue through housing finance agencies to help fund below-market-interest-rate mortgages for first-time qualifying home buyers. Eligible borrowers are first-time home buyers with low to moderate incomes below 115 percent of median family income.

B. General Obligation Bonds

Although general obligation bonds are less common than revenue bonds due to the constitutional and statutory approval requirements, their issuance can result in a larger amount of money because they are repaid from ad valorem property taxes rather than from revenues from a particular project. The constitution and statutes of each state contain requirements for their issuance. Although each state's constitution and statutes are different, they normally require an election authorizing the issuance of such bonds and approving the authority to levy ad valorem property taxes for their repayment. Depending on the state, a majority (50 percent plus one) or a super majority (60 percent to 66 percent) is required to approve a general obligation bond and the imposition of a dedicated property tax. General obligation bond elections can be challenging because proponents must raise money to conduct an election campaign to explain to voters the need and benefits of the affordable housing project to be financed by general obligation bonds. Depending on the jurisdiction, campaigns can cost hundreds of thousands to millions of dollars. However, once approved, the general obligation bonds can be sold to provide money for a particular project or projects or to fund a housing trust fund.[185] An advantage of general obligation bonds is, since they are not dependent on revenues of a particular project for repayment, their proceeds can be treated as equity. Examples of general obligation bond issues for affordable housing projects are set forth next.

C. Polk County, Iowa

Polk County, which includes Des Moines, has periodically earmarked bond funding for affordable housing, typically as part of an annual authorized issuance of general obligation county bonds for several purposes. Iowa general obligation bonds are payable from ad

---

185. Local housing trust funds are discussed, *infra*, Section 1.C.

valorem property tax levies,[186] and the bond-authorizing resolution may also serve to levy a tax for repayment.[187] Iowa state law governing general obligation bonds expressly establishes as an "essential county purpose" the "funding of programs to provide for or assist in providing for the acquisition, restoration, or demolition of housing, as part of a municipal housing project. . . ."[188] General obligation bonds issued for this purpose do not require voter approval.[189] Because the bonds are issued for a governmental purpose, they are not subject to state volume caps, which affect multifamily housing or mortgage revenue bonds, but interest on the bonds is exempt from federal income taxation.

The Polk County Housing Trust Fund has been a primary recipient of proceeds from such bonds. Since 2004, $1.5 million per year has been set aside for the Housing Trust Fund.[190] The Housing Trust Fund is not a governmental agency. It was formed under a state joint exercise of powers statute[191] that permits a local public agency to enter into an agreement with a private agency for cooperative action, including creation of a separate entity to carry out the purposes of the agreement.[192] The Trust Fund operates under an agreement approved in 1995; two members of the County Board of Supervisors sit on the Trust Fund board. The bond proceeds amount to about half of the Trust Fund's income; the Trust Fund also receives state housing trust fund dollars, private donations, and other state and federal funds when available.[193]

D. San Francisco, California

San Francisco voters have approved a series of general obligation bonds to raise funds for affordable housing: $100 million in 1996, approved by 67.4 percent of the voters;[194] $310 million in 2015, approved by 74 percent of the voters;[195] and $600 million in 2019, approved

---

186. IOWA CODE § 331.441(2)(a).

187. *See, e.g.*, Polk County, Iowa, Resolution Authorizing the Issuance of Essential County Purpose General Obligation Bonds, Series 2004, in the Aggregate Principal Amount of $3,770,000 and Levying a Tax for the Payment Thereof, adopted July 13, 2004. Linda Kniep, of Ahlers & Cooney, P.C., in Des Moines, kindly provided portions of the bond documents to the authors.

188. IOWA CODE § 331.441(2)(b)(10).

189. *Id.* § 331.443.

190. *See* Polk County, Iowa, Tax Exemption Certificate, § 2.2(b)(ii) (2004); *Affordable Housing Receives Support from Polk County; Supervisors Approve Renewal of 28E Agreement*, POLK COUNTY HOUSING TRUST FUND (July 2010).

191. IOWA CODE ANN. § 28E.1 (2009).

192. *Id.* § 28E.4.

193. *See* ANNUAL REPORT FOR 2008–2009 of the Polk County Housing Trust Fund, POLK COUNTY HOUSING TRUST FUND (2009) https://www.pchtf.org/about-us/publication-archive/pdf s/annual-reports/2008-2009-annual-report.pdf [https://perma.cc/9S8Q-572J] (last visited June 13, 2021).

194. The bonds were submitted to the voters pursuant to San Francisco Board of Supervisors Resolution No. 343-01 at 1–2, Res. No. 343-01: 2001 Affordable Housing Bond Sale, https://sfbos .org/ftp/uploadedfiles/bdsupvrs/resolutions01/r0343-01.pdf [https://perma.cc/WQ68-QJC2] (last visited June 13, 2021).

195. *See 2015 Affordable Housing General Obligation Bond*, SAN FRANCISCO MAYOR'S OFFICE OF HOUSING AND COMMUNITY DEVELOPMENT, https://sfmohcd.org/2015-affordable-housing-gen eral-obligation-bond [https://perma.cc/G3GS-XRPM] (last visited June 13, 2021).

by 71 percent of the voters.[196] The California Constitution requires two-thirds local voter approval before a local government can incur multiyear debt payable out of general government revenues.[197]

The 1996 bond regulations required that at least one-fourth of available bond funds be set aside for down-payment assistance for first-time home buyers with household incomes not greater than area median income.[198] All rental units assisted by bond proceeds, and at least 51 percent of units in projects where some units receive bond proceeds, were required to be occupied by households at or below 60 percent of area median income, at rents affordable to a household with income at 60 percent of area median.[199] As of 2008, 31 projects, constituting a total of 2,179 units, had benefited from the 1996 bonds. Of the 2,179 units, 71 percent were newly constructed units, while 29 percent were the result of acquisition or rehabilitation.[200]

The $310 million generated by the 2015 bonds were allocated to public housing ($80 million) and affordable housing ($100 million), serving households with incomes up to 80 percent of median income; development in the Mission District ($50 million); and middle-income housing ($80 million) for households with incomes between 80 and 175 percent of median income, serving a broader range of income levels as housing costs soared.[201] As of December 2020, the bonds had assisted 1,520 units.[202] The $600 million authorized in 2019 was split between public housing ($150 million), low-income housing serving households with incomes up to 80 percent of median income ($220 million), senior low-income housing ($150 million), educator housing ($20 million), middle-income housing ($30 million), and affordable housing preservation ($30 million).[203]

E. Austin, Texas

In 2006, 63 percent of the voters of Austin approved a $55 million general obligation bond issue to support the development of affordable housing.[204] The city was able to leverage the $55 million to secure an additional $177 million in development expenditures.[205] The funds

---

196. *See 2019 Affordable Housing General Obligation Bond*, SAN FRANCISCO MAYOR'S OFFICE OF HOUSING AND COMMUNITY DEVELOPMENT, https://sfmohcd.org/2019-affordable-housing-general-obligation-bond-0 [https://perma.cc/5GZQ-HNPL] (last visited June 13, 2021).

197. CAL. CONST. art. XVI, § 18.

198. AFFORDABLE HOUSING AND HOME OWNERSHIP BOND PROGRAM REGULATIONS § III(A), (B)(1), Oct. 29, 1997 [hereinafter REGULATIONS] (can be obtained from the Mayor's Office of Housing). At least 25 percent of the buyers assisted from each annual allocation must be households at or below 80 percent of area median income.

199. *Id.* § II(E)(1).

200. SAN FRANCISCO MAYOR'S OFFICE OF HOUSING, REPORT TO THE BOARD OF SUPERVISORS (2008).

201. *See 2015 Affordable Housing General Obligation Bond, supra* note 195.

202. *Id.*

203. *See 2019 Affordable Housing General Obligation Bond, supra* note 196.

204. *The Economic Impact of General Obligation Bonds for Affordable Housing in Austin*, HOUSING WORKS 1 (May 2012); http://housingworksaustin.org/wp-content/uploads/2014/04/HousingWorks_Economic_Impact_Study_2012.pdf [https://perma.cc/4K9Z-N87E].

205. *Id.*

were used to develop or rehabilitate 3,055 housing units, of which 2,242 were designed for low-income affordable housing.[206]

In 2013, the qualified electors in Austin, Texas, approved $65 million in general obligation bonds to finance affordable housing.[207] Particular focus was on households earning 30 percent or less of area medium income.[208] The bond issue was designed to allow the city to partner with organizations to use bond proceeds for affordable rental and ownership housing and the preservation of existing affordable housing.[209] Eligibility was based on income. Depending on the program and the needs of the household, a family of four earning $58,550 or less in 2013 could qualify for funding.[210] The bond issue was also designed to support very low-income households of a family of four earning $36,600 or less in 2013.[211] The funding could be used to (1) create affordable rental housing by providing grants and loans; (2) provide grants and loans to acquire property, design and develop infrastructure, construct new rental housing, and rehabilitate existing rental housing; and (3) fund targeted areas of preferred investment, including access to employment opportunities and public transportation.[212]

F. Miami-Dade County, Florida

In 2004, the qualified electors in Miami-Dade County approved a multiyear Building Better Communities general obligation bond program, a portion of the proceeds of which were designated to fund affordable housing.[213] As part of this program, in 2004, the voters authorized the issuance of $194,997,000 of general obligation bonds to construct and improve affordable housing.[214] The program was designed to provide 77 new affordable family units ($10 million); 124 new affordable elderly units ($10 million); 95 new affordable housing units ($12.3 million); and additional affordable housing units (375 to 450 units). The program also provided 400 to 500 first and second mortgages to low- or moderate-income families as a means to expand home ownership ($137.7 million).[215]

Examples of projects funded by the Building Better Communities general obligation bond program include a homeless complex at the site of the former Homestead Air Force Base, which combined affordable housing with on-site case management services and a

---

206. *Id.*

207. *City of Austin Special Election Information Proposition 1: Affordable Housing Bond*, AUSTINTEXAS.GOV (Nov. 5, 2013), http://austintexas.gov/sites/default/files/files/Capital_Planning /Bond_Development/2013_Bond/FINAL_Affordable_Housing_Bond_Voter_Information_Flier.pdf [https://perma.cc/7Z6X-S68E]

208. *Id.*

209. *Id.*

210. *Id.*

211. *Id.*

212. *Id. See* TEX. GOV'T CODE ANN. § 1331 (West 1999), for authority to issue bonds.

213. See Building Better Communities Bond Program home page, https://www.miamidade.gov /global/management/building-better-communities.page. *See* MIAMI-DADE COUNTY, FLORIDA, CODE, CHAPTER 16, for authority to issue the bonds.

214. Miami-Dade County Resolution No. R-918-04 passed on July 20, 2004.

215. *Id.*

grant of $10,592,307 made to a limited liability company for the development of 87 afford-able elderly rental units.[216]

G. Portland, Oregon

In 2016, the qualified electors in Portland, Oregon, authorized the issuance of $285.4 mil-lion in general obligation bonds to create new and preserve existing affordable rental hous-ing.[217] The proceeds of the bonds were intended to be used to fund 1,300 apartments, including 600 apartments for families earning less than 30 percent of the medium family income.[218] The housing contains a mix of unit sizes.[219] Some units are accessible for low-income people with disabilities and for seniors.[220] For this program, "affordable" meant rents restricted by designated household size and income level for the dwelling.[221] "Low income" means a household making 60 percent or less of median family income, and there is also a lower income threshold for some units.[222] In 2016, 60 percent of median family income for a family of four was $43,980 per year.[223] The general obligation bonds are repaid from a tax rate that was estimated to be $0.4208 per $1,000 of assessed value.[224]

H. Alameda County, California

At an election held on November 8, 2016, Alameda County voters approved Proposition A1, which authorized the issuance of $580 million of general obligation bonds.[225] The bonds are payable solely from ad valorem taxes levied on all taxable property within the county without limitation as to rate or amount.[226] Proposition A1 provides funding for projects identified in the County's Affordable Housing Bond Program.[227] The Affordable Housing Program consists of the several programs related to homeownership and a rental housing development program designed to help with housing affordability in the county.[228]

The Affordable Housing Homeownership Program includes (1) the Down Payment Loan Assistance Program to assist middle-income first-time home buyers to stay in the county; (2) the Home Preservation Rehabilitation Program to help low-income homeowners in the county, especially seniors and people with disabilities, remain safely in their homes;

---

216. Miami-Dade County Resolution No. R-819-10 passed on July 20, 2010.

217. City of Portland Resolution No. 37220, adopted June 30, 2016, as amended, together with the exhibits attached thereto, https://www.portlandoregon.gov/auditor/article/582877.

218. June 27, 2016, Affordable Housing Bond for Portland memo from Kurt Creager, Director, Portland Housing Bureau to Portland City Council, Exhibit C to City of Portland Resolution No. 37220, page 1.

219. *Id.*

220. *Id.*

221. *Id.*

222. *Id.*

223. *Id.*

224. Exhibit A to City of Portland Resolution No. 37220, page 1.

225. Resolution No. R-2017-340, adopted by the County Council on November 7, 2017, http://www.acgov.org/board/bos_calendar/documents/DocsAgendaReg_11_07_17/GENERAL%20ADMINISTRATION/Regular%20Calendar/CAO_256646.pdf.

226. *Id.* at 2.

227. *Id.* at 2.

228. *Id.* at 2.

and (3) the Homeownership Development Program to create homeownership opportunities for lower income residents in the county.[229]

The Affordable Rental Housing Development Program includes the following two components: (1) the Rental Housing Development Fund to provide financing for the development of new, and the preservation of existing, affordable rental housing units for low-income residents in the county; and (2) the Innovation and Opportunity Fund to provide financing that promotes innovation and allows for quick responses to capture opportunities that arise in the market to preserve and expand affordable rental housing and/or prevent tenant displacement.[230]

- Home Preservation Loan Program. The goal of this loan program is to assist low-income senior citizens, people with disabilities, and other low-income homeowners to remain safely in their homes.
- Low-Income Homeowner Housing Development Program. The goal of this program is to assist in the development and long-term affordability of homeownership housing for low-income households to become first-time home buyers, while remaining in the county.
- The Rental Housing Development Program. The goal of the rental housing development program is to assist in the creation and preservation of affordable rental housing for vulnerable populations, including the county's low-income workforce, and includes two components.
- Rental Housing Innovation and Opportunity Fund. The goal of this portion of the program is to support the ability for affordable housing developers to respond quickly to opportunities that arise in the market to preserve and expand affordable rental housing and prevent displacement of current low-income tenants.[231]

The proceeds of the Series 2018A Bonds for the Affordable Housing Program were allocated as follows:[232]

Down Payment Assistance Loan Program	$18,000,000
Home Preservation Loan Program	18,000,000
Homeowner Housing Development Program	15,000,000
Rental Housing Development Fund	156,100,000
Innovation & Opportunity Fund	25,000,000
Affordable Housing Program Delivery/ Administrative Costs	7,200,000
TOTAL	**$ 239,300,000**

229. Resolution No. R-2017-340, adopted by the County Council on November 7, 2017, Exhibit 1, Measure AI Programs Description, Costs and Project Documentation, pp. I-1 to I-4.
230. *Id.*
231. *Id.*
232. Official Statement, County of Alameda, General Obligation Bonds (Measure A1) 2018 Series A, page 6.

VII. FEE WAIVER PROGRAMS

Fees payable to local governments or districts can add significantly to housing costs. In California, for instance, strict limits on local taxes have led many jurisdictions to maximize development fees in order to provide necessary infrastructure and to avoid the need to spend limited local tax revenues.[233] The following provides a sampling of cities with formally established programs to waive development fees for eligible affordable housing.

A. Fort Lauderdale, Florida

Fort Lauderdale's municipal code provides that development fees will not be charged for qualified developments sold or leased to very low-income households; similar reductions eliminating 75 percent of fees are available for low-income housing.[234] Some of the shortfalls in development fees may be covered by State Housing Initiatives Partnership (SHIP) funds, which are distributed on an entitlement basis to local governments that develop a local housing plan and incentive strategy.[235] In Fort Lauderdale, fee waivers and reductions are considered on a first-come, first-served basis in the event funds to cover shortfalls are not available. Reductions are applicable to an entire development if at least 20 percent of its units are set aside for affordable housing.[236] Recorded covenants restricting occupancy of owner-occupied units for five years and leased dwellings for 15 years are required.[237] Of the seven Fort Lauderdale projects noted in a 2007 audit of SHIP funds, two projects received fee waivers, both in the amount of $5,000.[238]

---

233. A March 2018 survey of seven large cities in California found total fees (include building permit, planning, and impact fees) ranging from $11,746 to $75,158 per unit for multifamily developments and from $21,174 to $156,614 per unit for single-family developments. *See* Sarah Mawhorter, David Garcia & Hayley Raetz, *It All Adds Up: The Cost of Housing Development Fees in Seven California Cities*, TERNER CENTER FOR HOUSING INNOVATION AT U.C. BERKELEY 20 (Mar. 2018), https://ternercenter.berkeley.edu/wp-content/uploads/pdfs/Development_Fees_Report_Final_2.pdf [https://perma.cc/G9Y5-62QR]. A 2008 survey of 14 jurisdictions in San Mateo County, south of San Francisco, California, found fees averaging approximately $28,000 per single-family home and $18,000 per multifamily unit (in an assumed project of ten units). *See* Development Fee Survey, Internal Summary, 21 ELEMENTS (Sept. 17, 2008), http://www.21elements.com/documents-mainmenu-3/housing-elements/archiving-including-rhna-4/rhna-4-2007-2014/constraints-1/fees-and-exactions/159-development-fees-summary-report-pdf/file [https://perma.cc/U8ND-5AE9]. From time to time, cities have raised questions about the legal authority to waive fees, based on the possibility that it would not be possible to make up the lost revenue. Though the authors know of no case answering this question, they believe that cities may waive fees, since they are under no legal obligation to charge developers or any particular developer the full cost of project impacts, so long as other developers are not asked to make up the lost revenue.

234. FT. LAUDERDALE, FLA., MUN. CODE § 9-343(1) (2021).

235. *State Housing Initiatives Partnership (SHIP)*, STATE OF FLORIDA HOUSING FINANCE CORPORATION, https://www.floridahousing.org/programs/special-programs/ship---state-housing-initiatives-partnership-program [https://perma.cc/YTJ2-5CKQ] (last visited June 13, 2021).

236. FT. LAUDERDALE, FLA., MUN. CODE § 9-343(1)–(3).

237. *Id.* § 9-341(5).

238. *See City of Ft. Lauderdale, Review of the State Housing Initiatives Partnership (SHIP) Program*, STATE OF FLORIDA, OFFICE OF MANAGEMENT AND BUDGET, AUDIT 06/07-XX-10 (Aug. 31, 2007), https://www.fortlauderdale.gov/home/showpublisheddocument/580/635380810151930000 [https://perma.cc/6WWH-7QZU].

B. Salt Lake City, Utah

Salt Lake City's Code exempts from impact fees housing whose rents will not annually exceed 30 percent of the income of a household earning 60 percent of the city's median income or whose annual mortgage payment will not exceed 30 percent of 80 percent of city median income.[239] Partial fee exemptions are provided for ownership housing affordable at 90 percent and 100 percent of median income.[240] Nonprofit organizations can petition for waiver or deferral of any fees required by the Building and Construction title if the sponsoring nonprofit organization furthers the goal of providing housing for persons or families earning less than 80 percent of the city's median income, as long as the project in question does not receive 75 percent or more of its funding directly or indirectly from federal or state agencies.[241]

In 2009, Salt Lake City granted fee exemptions totaling $224,220 to three developments containing 148 affordable units. The largest project included 95 affordable homes and received an exemption of $143,925.[242]

C. Tallahassee, Florida

Tallahassee authorizes the exemption of all qualifying affordable housing from water and sewer system charges and road impact fees, and of affordable owner-occupied housing from water and sewer tap fees.[243] However, projects of more than 25 units that are intended for 100 percent low-income occupancy are not exempt unless approved by the Planning Commission.[244] The city certifies those projects eligible for the fee exemption, and eligible projects are also entitled to priority processing, technical assistance, and special regulatory provisions.[245] The city funds the exemptions primarily from general funds, estimated at $150,000 per year,[246] and exemptions are limited based on funding to make up the lost fees. The maximum amount of the exemption is also limited.[247] Failure to secure a building permit within six months for ownership units, or one year for rental units, voids the exemption.[248]

Generally, rental units are eligible if affordable to households at or below 60 percent of area median income;[249] owner-occupied units may be eligible if affordable to

---

239. SALT LAKE CITY, UTAH, CODE § 18.98.060(E). The code provision does not spell out the effect, if any, of later increases in mortgage payments or rents and does not prescribe adjustments for home-ownership expenses other than mortgage payments.

240. *Id.*

241. *Id.* § 18.20.220.

242. Telephone conversation with LuAnn Clark, Salt Lake City Building Services (Sept. 30, 2010) (notes on file with author).

243. TALLAHASSEE, FLA. CODE § 21-152 (2021).

244. TALLAHASSEE, FLA. CITY COMM'N POL'Y §§ 1104, 1104.03.

245. *Id.* at §§ 1104, 1104.02.

246. CITY OF TALLAHASSEE, FLA., FIVE-YEAR CONSOLIDATED PLAN 2020–2024 6, 145 (2020) https://www.talgov.com/Uploads/Public/Documents/neighborhood/housing/consol-plan-2020-2024 .pdf [https://perma.cc/A74Y-WDZW] (last visited June 13, 2021).

247. TALLAHASSEE, FLA. CODE, § 21-152(a)(2), (n).

248. *Id.* § 21-152(g).

249. *Id.* § 21-152(b)(2).

households earning up to 80 percent of area median income.[250] Seven years of affordability are required for both rental and ownership units.[251] Enforceability is reinforced by a lien recorded against the unit, which requires the owner to repay to the city the full amount of fees exempted if the terms of the exemption are violated.[252] Between 1991 and 2010, 688 single-family homes and nine multifamily developments, totaling 528 homes, received fee waivers.[253]

VIII. REDEVELOPMENT AGENCY TAX INCREMENT FINANCING

A number of states provide mechanisms for local governments to finance housing development through tax increment mechanisms.[254] Tax increment financing is based on the observation that local government assistance, often in the form of public improvements or amenities, can be used to spur development. The "kick-started" development increases the taxable value of private property and thereby increases property-based tax revenue. The increased revenue can then be set aside to finance this kind of local government assistance. The process can be started by issuing bonds, repayable from the anticipated property tax increase, or "increment." This section provides descriptions of tax increment financing programs for housing in Oregon, Chicago, and Minneapolis.

Tax increment financing can dwarf other local sources of funds for affordable housing. California expressly authorized local government use of a tax increment mechanism in 1951[255] but in 2011 abolished the ability of redevelopment agencies to receive tax increment or to incur new debt and required the eventual dissolution of all redevelopment agencies.[256] Although pre-dissolution law required only 20 percent of tax increment to be spent on affordable housing,[257] the provision provided by far the most funds available to local government for affordable housing. In the 2007–08 fiscal year (the last year for which data is available), total housing fund tax increment deposits were slightly over $1 billion, and additional deposits were made from interest, loan repayments, and other sources, for a total deposit of over $1.8 million.[258] Redevelopment substitutes instituted since 2011 are substantially limited and cannot provide the amount of funds previously available to local agencies.[259]

---

250. *Id.* § 21-152(b)(2); City Comm'n Pol'y, *supra* note 244, §§ 1104, 1104.06(A).

251. Tallahassee, Fla. Code § 21-152(b).

252. *Id.* § 21-152(e).

253. E-mail from Donna Raffensperger, Records Management Division, Office of the City Treasurer-Clerk, City of Tallahassee (Sept. 24, 2010) (on file with author).

254. See Chapter 10 for a discussion of the state's role in tax increment financing.

255. Cal. Pub. Util. Code § 1411 (West 1951).

256. 2011 Cal. Stat. (AB1x 26).

257. Cal. Health & Safety Code § 33334.2 (West 2009).

258. Cal. Dep't of Housing and Community Development, Fiscal Year 2007–2008 Housing Activities of California Redevelopment Agencies, Exhibit A-1. This report was required to be published annually but is not available for later years. It includes Housing Fund income from all sources.

259. *See generally* Christopher Lynch & Jim Morales, *Redevelopment 2.0: Existing Laws, Pending Legislation, & Legal Theory*, League of Cal. Cities (Oct. 18, 2019), https://www.cacities.org/Resources-Documents/Member-Engagement/Professional-Departments/City-Attorneys

A. Oregon

Oregon identifies itself as the second state to authorize local government to initiate tax increment financing.[260] Local urban renewal agencies (which are legally separate from the city or county but may be run by the city or county's governing body) administer local tax increment programs. The agencies may undertake any form of housing activity that the local general governing body authorizes, including (but not limited to) construction, leasing, or management of housing.[261] Use of tax increment financing by Oregon local governments has been complicated by a series of statewide ballot measures that have limited overall government property tax collections. Under those measures,[262] property tax revenues designated as tax increment can "use up" a local entity's limited tax capacity, reducing its ability to fund regular government operations. Nonetheless, and despite a focus in practice on economic and urban development activities,[263] Oregon tax increment has been used to fund both rehabilitation of existing housing and new development.

For example, in October 2006, the Portland City Council established a set-aside of tax increment dollars for the development, preservation, and rehabilitation of affordable housing for households with incomes below 80 percent of median income.[264] Under the newly adopted ordinance, 30 percent of tax increment was to be dedicated to affordable housing over the life of an Urban Renewal District. In April 2007, the ordinance was amended to allow the 30 percent set-aside to also be used to provide assistance to home buyers with restricted incomes and for the development of home ownership units with three bedrooms or more for households earning up to 100 percent of median income.[265] As a result, $67 million for affordable housing was generated over a three-year period.[266]

On July 1, 2015, the city council further increased the housing set-aside to 45 percent of tax increment, citing the city's "housing affordability crisis."[267] The funds are to be used to develop housing affordable to residents earning median income or less and to assist

/Library/2019/2019-Annual-Conference/10-2019-AC;-Lynch-Morales-Redevelopment-2-0-Existi .aspx [https://perma.cc/G74W-UNB2].

260. Nina Johnson & Jeffrey Tashman, *Portland Development Commission, Urban Renewal in Oregon*, TASHMAN & JOHNSON, LLC. 7 (2002), https://citeseerx.ist.psu.edu/viewdoc/download ?doi=10.1.1.173.5712&rep=rep1&type=pdf [https://perma.cc/52G9-ZVZC] (noting constitutional authorization in 1960 and implementing legislation in 1961).

261. OR. REV. STAT. § 457.180(7) (2021).

262. *See* Shilo Inn v. Multnomah County, 36 P.2d 954 (Or. 2001), for a description of Measures 5 (adopted in 1990) and 50 (adopted in 1997) and their application to tax increment intended for urban renewal agencies.

263. This focus is reflected, for instance, in the ten case studies in the 2002 JOHNSON & TASHMAN report, *supra* note 260.

264. Portland, Or., Ordinance 180547; *Affordable Housing Tax Increment Financing Set-Aside Policy, Binding City Policy* HOU-1.04, THE CITY OF PORTLAND, OREGON (2006) https://www.port landoregon.gov/citycode/article/155330 [https://perma.cc/J27M-GCQJ] (last visited June 13, 2021).

265. *Id.*

266. *Tax Increment Financing Affordable Housing Set Aside Annual Report FY 2008–2009*, PORTLAND DEVELOPMENT COMM'N, PORTLAND HOUSING BUREAU 4, https://www.portlandorego n.gov/phb/article/652902 [https://perma.cc/C4QX-GSZ3] (last visited June 13, 2021).

267. *Affordable Housing Tax Increment Financing Set-Aside Policy, Binding City Policy HOU-1.06*, THE CITY OF PORTLAND, OREGON (2017), https://www.portland.gov/policies/housing /affordable-housing-production-and-preservation/hou-106-affordable-housing-tax [https://perma.cc /HB8K-79BH] (last visited June 13, 2021).

households earning 100 percent of median or less to purchase homes.[268] As of 2019, $543 million of tax increment had been set aside for affordable housing, financing 1,886 rental units.[269]

B. Chicago, Illinois

Illinois statutes authorize Illinois municipalities to pay from tax increment revenue up to 50 percent of the cost of newly created housing that is to be occupied by low-income or very low-income households in a redevelopment project area.[270] Tax increment funds (TIF) may also be used, without the percentage limitation, for rehabilitation, reconstruction, repair, or remodeling of existing buildings.[271] The statute authorizes municipalities to adopt guidelines implementing their tax increment authority.[272] Chicago's guidelines, applicable to newly constructed housing and housing created by renovation or rehabilitation of formerly nonresidential buildings, are set out in the form of a TIF Recapture Mortgage, which is recorded against tax increment–assisted units sold to low- or very low-income households. Tax increment–assisted rental units are instead subject to agreements that maintain the required affordability for 30 years.[273]

Since 1983, a total of 184 TIF districts have been created, and there were 136 active districts as of January 1, 2020.[274] Only 5.1 percent of TIF funds have been used to finance affordable housing,[275] but since 2011 more than $225 million has been set aside for development and rehabilitation of affordable units.[276] The Chicago Department of Planning and Development calculated that as of December 31, 2003, Chicago had approved a total of $244 million in tax increment financing for 36 projects with aggregate project budgets of $1.45 billion; these projects included 3,520 affordable housing units.[277] In 2019, the city's Department of Housing committed $1.1 million in TIF funds for single-family

---

268. *Affordable Housing Tax Increment Financing Set-Aside Policy, Binding City Policy HOU-1.06, Ex. A,* THE CITY OF PORTLAND, OREGON (2017) https://www.portland.gov/policies/housin g/affordable-housing-production-and-preservation/hou-106-affordable-housing-tax [https://perma. cc/HB8K-79BH] (follow link under "Related Documents" titled "HOU-1.06 Exhibits A, B, and C" to review the exhibits) (last visited June 13, 2021).

269. TAX INCREMENT FINANCING: AFFORDABLE HOUSING SET ASIDE 2019 REPORT, CITY OF PORTLAND, PORTLAND HOUSING BUREAU 4, 7 (2019) https://www.portland.gov/sites/default/file s/2020/phb-2019-tif-report.pdf [https://perma.cc/7ZLH-SHUD] (last visited June 13, 2021).

270. 65 ILL. COMP. STAT 5 / 11-74.4-3(q)(11)(F) (part of the state Tax Increment Allocation Redevelopment Act). Low-income households are those with incomes between 50 percent and 80 percent of area median; very low-income households are those at or below 50 percent of area median income. *See* 310 ILL. COMP. STAT. 65 / 3(c), (d).

271. 65 ILL. COMP. STAT. 5 / 11-74.4-3(q)(3).

272. 65 ILL. COMP. STAT. 5 / 11-74.4-3(q)(11)(F).

273. CHICAGO, ILL. MUN. CODE § 2-45-110(f).

274. DEPARTMENT OF PLANNING & DEVELOPMENT, TAX INCREMENT FINANCING PROGRAM GUIDE, CITY OF CHICAGO 4 (2020), https://www.chicago.gov/content/dam/city/depts/dcd/tif/2020 _TIF_Program_Guide.6.1.pdf [https://perma.cc/3JDN-38CJ] (last visited June 13, 2021).

275. *Id.* at 10.

276. *Id.* at 12.

277. The authors appreciate the help of Michael Gaynor, Assistant Corporation Counsel, in obtaining information about Chicago's tax increment program.

rehabilitation and $38.7 million to assist in the production of 460 units;[278] in 2020 it committed $13.9 million to assist 61 units.[279]

C. Minneapolis, Minnesota

Minnesota's tax increment financing statute authorizes formation of tax increment financing "housing districts" and "qualified housing districts"[280] (as well as districts for broader purposes), which may have a term of up to 25 years.[281] In these districts, tax increments may only be used to finance either a "housing project," public improvements directly related to the project, and administrative costs.[282] Assisted housing must meet income standards under federal statutes,[283] unless located in a "targeted area."[284] A targeted area is a census tract where at least 70 percent of the households have incomes that are 80 percent or less of the state median income.[285] Minnesota limits tax increment financing to projects that meet a "but for" test: It must be shown that, but for tax increment financing, the project would not be undertaken by a private developer and would not occur within the reasonably foreseeable future.[286] According to the March 2017 State Auditor's report, there were 541 active housing TIF districts in the state, comprising about 31.5 percent of all TIF districts.[287]

Minneapolis has used tax increment financing to assist a variety of housing developments, including substandard residences that are included in multisite housing replacement tax increment districts. The city's Tax Increment Financing Policy specifies required objectives and criteria for selecting and approving tax increment projects in general, with an objective to "[p]rovide an array of housing choices that meet the needs of current residents and attract new residents to the city, with an emphasis on providing affordable housing."[288]

Of interest is that in October 2019, the city adopted a policy allowing developers to use tax increment financing to offset revenue loss due to the city's inclusionary zoning policy. Revenue loss assistance is available to developments that provide 20 percent of the total dwelling units, or at least ten units, whichever is greater, to households earning 50 percent or less of area median income, and where no more than 20 percent of the square footage of

---

278. 2019–2023 Housing Plan, 2019 Fourth Quarter Progress Report, City of Chicago, Department of Housing 19, 41 (Dec. 2019), https://www.chicago.gov/content/dam/city/depts /doh/general/Full_Report_Q4_2019.pdf [https://perma.cc/VTD9-TQRA] (last visited June 13, 2021).

279. 2019–2023 Housing Plan, 2020 Fourth Quarter Progress Report, City of Chicago, Department of Housing 19 (Dec. 2020), https://www.chicago.gov/content/dam/city/depts/doh/ reports/Full_Report_Q4_2020.pdf [https://perma.cc/6QK7-3ZMQ] (last visited June 13, 2021).

280. Minn. Stat. §§ 469.042, 469.174 (2020).

281. *Id.* § 469.176, subd. 1(b)(5).

282. *Id.* § 469.176, subd. 4(d).

283. *Id.* §§ 469.174, subd. 11; 469.1761.

284. *Id.* § 469.1761, subd. 1.

285. *Id.* § 462C.02, subd. 9(e).

286. *Id.* § 469.175, subd. 3(b)(2)(i).

287. *See Housing TIF Districts*, Minnesota House Research Department, https://www .house.mn/hrd/issinfo/tif/hsgdist.aspx#TARG [https://perma.cc/69PT-Q2AR] (last visited June 13, 2021). It appears from the number of districts that housing districts can be established in small areas, perhaps equal to the size of an individual project.

288. *Tax Increment Financing (TIF) Policy*, City of Minneapolis, https://www2.minneap olismn.gov/business-services/business-assistance/community-development-business-assistance /tax-increment-financing/tif-policy/ [https://perma.cc/D9WL-A76J] (last visited June 13, 2021).

any building is designated for nonresidential use. The city may provide financial assistance in an amount necessary to ensure the project remains economically feasible. If this amount is greater than the projected tax increment, the city may provide additional assistance. Projects must also pay prevailing wages.[289]

---

289. *See* Inclusionary Zoning Revenue Loss Offset Assistance Policy, City of Minneapolis (Oct. 29, 2019), https://www2.minneapolismn.gov/media/content-assets/www2-documents /government/Revenue-Loss-Offset-Financial-Assistance-Policy-(PDF).pdf [https://perma.cc /5TBU-P9FH].

Mixed-Finance Development of Public Housing

12

A.M. McClain

I. INTRODUCTION

The mixed-finance method of developing public housing evolved as a tool intended to replace the nation's most severely distressed public housing stock with revitalized, sustainable communities while also promoting the leveraging of limited federal funds to develop mixed-finance and mixed-income housing. By combining federal public housing capital funds (initially including HOPE VI grant funds[1]) or operating funds[2] with private dollars (including local and state funds) to develop public housing, public housing authorities (PHAs) expanded the mixed-finance approach to modernize the nation's public housing inventory under circumstances of ever-decreasing resources from the U.S. Department of Housing and Urban Development (HUD). Mixed-finance development presents PHAs with a variety of options and opportunities to address creatively the affordable housing needs of their communities. Mixed-finance development opened new funding sources and new

---

* This chapter was adapted from a version initially drafted by the author with Paul K. Casey with the assistance of those noted in the initial footnotes of the prior editions. Mr. Casey has since retired from Ballard Spahr LLP.

1. The HOPE VI Program was first created as a demonstration program for urban revitalization under the Department of Veteran Affairs and Housing and Urban Development, and Independent Agencies Appropriations Act of 1993, Pub. L. No. 102-389, 106 Stat. 1579 (1993). HOPE is an acronym for Homeownership and Opportunity for People Everywhere.

2. This chapter focuses on mixed-finance development which combines federal capital funds with other sources. However, mixed-finance could also include the combination of federal operating funds with financing other than public housing capital funds. This alternative requires using other capital development financing sources without public housing capital funds as leverage. 24 C.F.R. 905.604(j)(2) and *Notice PIH 2004-5* (issued April 9, 2004 and extended indefinitely January 5, 2021) (describing mixed-finance projects using operating subsidy only).

possibilities for revitalizing the nation's more distressed communities. The mixed-finance method shifted away from the HOPE VI program as reduced appropriations were offset by other forms of financing and adaptation of the mixed-finance method to innovative programs approved by HUD.[3] The key characteristics of the approach rely on flexibility in federal programs using existing resources, as well as the social benefit of mixed-income communities.

The remainder of Section I explains the origin and defines the requirements of mixed-finance development, and discusses its advantages and challenges. Section II explains important business and legal considerations associated with mixed-finance development, including the roles played by principal parties, key legal concepts and documents, and critical real estate development issues. In light of HUD's focus on the disposition of public housing,[4] Section III addresses the ability of PHAs to rely on mixed-finance development of units available under a PHA's Faircloth limit[5] as an initial step in the conversion of public housing assistance to Section 8 project-based vouchers using the Faircloth-to-RAD strategy under the Rental Assistance Demonstration program.[6]

A. Origin of the Mixed-Finance Program

Federal involvement in providing affordable public housing for persons of limited income began with the enactment of the U.S. Housing Act of 1937 (the "Act").[7] During the 1980s, many of the public housing projects constructed in the early years after passage of the Act had deteriorated, as had federal financial support for public housing. In 1989, Congress created the National Commission on Severely Distressed Public Housing (the "Commission") to (1) identify public housing projects that were in a severe state of distress; (2) assess the most promising strategies to improve the condition of severely distressed public housing projects implemented by PHAs and other government agencies; and (3) develop a national action plan to eliminate unfit living conditions in the most distressed public housing projects by the year 2000.[8]

In *The Final Report*, the Commission defined severely distressed public housing as exhibiting the presence of one or more of the following: (1) families living in distress;

---

3. Mixed-finance has also continued to adapt through the adoption of relevant Public and Indian Housing notices and the creativity of members of HUD's Office of Public Housing Investments and Office of General Counsel Assisted Housing Division. For example, according to HUD's Office of Public Housing Investments, HUD has approved 248 financings under the Capital Fund Financing Program. Office of Capital Improvements, List of Transactions Approved to Date, https://www.hud.gov/sites/dfiles/PIH/documents/CFFP%20Chronological%20List.pdf (last updated Apr. 3, 2019).

4. *See* U.S. Dep't of Hous. & Urban Dev., *Notice PIH 2021-07* (issued Jan. 19, 2021).

5. 42 U.S.C. § 1437g(g)(3) (1998); *see also* U.S. Dep't of Hous. & Urban Dev., *Guidance on Complying with the Maximum Number of Units Eligible for Operating Subsidy Pursuant to Section 9(g)(3)(A) of the Housing Act of 1937*, https://www.hud.gov/sites/dfiles/PIH/images/FAIRCLOTH-GUIDANCE_rev.pdf (last visited July 6, 2021).

6. *See* U.S. Dep't of Hous. & Urban Dev., *Faircloth-to-RAD: New Pathway to Create New Deeply Affordable Housing; 227,000 Available Units of Authority Eligible for Construction* (last updated May 7, 2021).

7. 42 U.S.C. § 1437 *et. seq.* (2003).

8. Department of Housing and Urban Development Reform Act of 1989: Title V National Commission on Severely Distressed Housing, Pub. L. No. 101-235, 103 Stat. 1987 (1989).

(2) high rates of serious crimes in the development or the surrounding neighborhood; (3) barriers to managing the environment; and (4) physical deterioration of the buildings.[9] The Commission estimated that 86,000 units, or 6 percent of all public housing units, were severely distressed,[10] and estimated that at least $8.2 billion would be required to modernize these public housing units.[11] The Commission urged Congress to authorize the leveraging of public housing funds, regulatory flexibility, and private sector partnerships as means of addressing severely distressed public housing.[12] In response, Congress developed the Urban Revitalization Demonstration Program (more commonly known as HOPE VI) in 1992, which provided an initial appropriation of $300 million in funds for demolition, acquisition, and revitalization of severely distressed public housing projects.[13] Because it was originally anticipated that the federal government would provide all the development funds through appropriation grants, early grants were in amounts as high as $50 million.[14]

A 1994 opinion from HUD's General Counsel[15] marked an important shift in public housing development; it facilitated private ownership of public housing and led to the establishment of a new method of public housing development—the mixed-finance model.

B. The Mixed-Finance Method of Development

The mixed-finance model, as interpreted by the 1994 opinion and the accompanying mixed-finance regulations, added to the traditional methods of development by which a PHA could develop, own, maintain, and operate the housing units,[16] and expanded the

---

9. NAT'L COMM'N ON SEVERELY DISTRESSED PUBLIC HOUS., THE FINAL REPORT B-2 (Washington, D.C., Gov't Printing Office) (Aug. 1992).

10. *Id.* at 2.

11. *Id.* at 10–33 (summarizing estimates related to the cost of implementing the Commission's recommendations); *see also* Barry G. Jacobs, *Housing Will Be Key Priority for New Administration, Congress,* AFFORDABLE HOUSING FINANCE, January 2009, http://www.housingfinance.com/ahf /articles/2009/jan/0109-housing-priority.htm (noting an even greater need with an "estimated backlog of $32 billion in capital repair needs" for public housing); *see also* HDR CURRENT DEVELOPMENTS, August 9, 2010 (estimating public housing capital repair needs in a range of $20 billion to $30 billion).

12. NAT'L COMM'N ON SEVERELY DISTRESSED PUBLIC HOUS., *supra* note 9, at 124–33 (encouraging non-traditional approaches to public housing including alternative management strategies, alleviation of regulatory and statutory barriers, and authorization of private sector partnerships).

13. Pub. L. No. 102-389, 106 Stat. 1579 (1992). The initial HOPE VI developments anticipated no leveraging of funds from other sources, but the advent of mixed-finance developments helped to increase significantly the ability of the program to foster the development of public housing in mixed-income communities. Originally, Congress restricted HOPE VI funding availability to PHAs in America's 40 largest cities or in any city with a PHA designated by HUD as troubled. *Id. See also* U.S. DEP'T OF HOUS. & URBAN DEV., *HOPE VI Program Authority and Funding History* (last updated March 2007) http://www.hud.gov/offices/pih/programs/ph/hope6/about/fundinghistory.pdf.

14. Pub. L. No. 102-389, *supra* note 13. *See also* SUSAN J. POPKIN, ET AL., THE URBAN INSTITUTE & THE BROOKINGS INSTITUTE, A DECADE OF HOPE VI: RESEARCH FINDINGS AND POLICY CHALLENGES 1 (May 2004).

15. Memorandum from Nelson A. Diaz, HUD General Counsel, to Joseph Shuldiner, Assistant Secretary for Public and Indian Housing (Apr. 13, 1994).

16. Although mixed-finance development has become the primary method of developing public housing, PHAs may still develop public housing using more traditional methods of development, including the conventional, turnkey, acquisition and force account methods. See 24 C.F.R. § 905.600

players involved in public housing and affordable housing development.[17] This method can involve financing from both public and private sources,[18] developed or acquired in accordance with 24 C.F.R. § 905, subpart F, with specific requirements set forth at 24 C.F.R. § 905.604. Mixed-finance projects frequently involve private management of these developments.[19] Unlike HOPE VI, mixed-finance development does not require a finding that the public housing units be severely distressed.[20]

HUD defines mixed-finance development as "development (through new construction or acquisition, with or without rehabilitation) or modernization of public housing, where the public housing units are owned in whole or in part by an entity other than a PHA."[21] The mixed-finance approach was formally codified in May 1996 when HUD promulgated an interim mixed-finance rule,[22] with an update to the rule issued in 2013.[23] Through flexible private–public partnerships, PHAs can play various roles within the ownership and development structure. In addition, a mixed-finance development may be developed as a mixed-income project combining public and non-public housing with a significant number of units rented or sold at market rate.[24] This section will discuss each of these characteristics.

1. Mixed Sources of Finance

In addition to HOPE VI funds, various other public housing capital funds (including Demolition or Disposition Transitional Funding (DDTF))[25] are available for use in public housing development. Beginning in 2001, HUD began to approve the use of future capital fund

---

(defining these methods of development). 24 C.F.R. part 905 addresses public housing development, generally.

17. 24 C.F.R. pt. 905, subpt. F. The regulations set forth more formally and comprehensively the rules guiding mixed-finance development initially described in the 1994 opinion. The mixed-finance program was enacted into law through Section 539 of the Quality Housing and Work Responsibility Act of 1998, adding Section 35 to the Housing Act of 1937. Title V of Pub. L. No. 105-276 (1998). *See also* Eileen M. Greenbaum, *Quality Housing and Work Responsibility Act of 1998: Its Major Impact on Development of Public Housing*, 8 J. Affordable Hous. 310, 319, *et. seq.* (1999) (discussing mixed-finance provisions adopted in QHWRA).

18. 24 C.F.R. § 905.604(a)(3).

19. *Mixed-Finance Guidebook, supra* note 3, at 2-24 to 2-25 (discussing asset management).

20. *Cf.* 42 U.S.C. § 1437v(a)(1) (2004) (authorizing the program initially authorized as HOPE VI in connection with the FY 1993 and subsequent appropriations acts, citing as one of the purposes, "improving the living environment for public housing residents of severely distressed public housing projects") with 42 U.S.C. § 1437z-7(2004) and 24 C.F.R. pt. 941, subpt. F (2010) (failing to specifically identify severe distress as a characteristic of a mixed-finance project).

21. 24 C.F.R. § 905.604(a) (2021).

22. 61 Fed. Reg. 19,714 (May 2, 1996). This interim rule was finalized at 24 C.F.R. pt. 941, subpt. F, the predecessor to the current regulations.

23. 78 Fed. Reg. 63,786 (Oct. 24, 2013) (codified at 24 C.F.R. pt. 905).

24. Paul K. Casey, *Real HOPE at HUD*, 7 J. Affordable Hous. 18, 21 (1997).

25. The DDTF is a regulatory provision found at 24 C.F.R. § 905.400(j). DDTF is an award of special capital funding for public housing units demolished or disposed on or after October 1, 2013. DDTF are considered a subset of HUD's capital fund appropriation and are allocated to a PHA when capital funds are allocated. DDTF can be used for eligible activities under the Capital Fund Program, provided the PHA has not received funding for public housing units that are replacing the demolished or disposed units from certain other sources. *See* 24 C.F.R. § 905.400(j)(4)(ii) and (iii).

appropriations as security for either loans or bonds under the Capital Fund Financing Program (CFFP).[26]

CFFP permits a PHA to rely on its future capital fund appropriations to finance current modernization and development of public housing.[27] The CFFP is a valuable tool in addressing the backlog of significant capital improvement and development needs because it provides gap financing for mixed-finance developments. CFFP funds have the potential to leverage private investment through the use of volume cap private activity bonds, which can generate 4 percent low-income-housing tax credits.[28]

The CFFP uses two types of debt instruments: revenue bonds and bank loans that are secured by future federal appropriations of public housing capital funds and not by a security interest in the project property.[29] The bond or loan proceeds must be used for the same purposes as public housing capital funds. HUD has confirmed that payment of debt service is an eligible capital fund purpose.[30] If bonds are used, the PHA (provided it has authority to do so) or another governmental entity may serve as issuer.

Guidance on the CFFP is set forth at 24 C.F.R. part 905, subpart E, with additional detail provided in the Capital Fund Guide Book.[31] HUD directs PHAs to include the following in a proposal for CFFP funding: (1) a transmittal letter; (2) a term sheet, table of contents, and contact information; (3) financing schedules; (4) a Capital Fund Financing budget, certain PHA Plan information, an independent management assessment (required for bond issue), an independent fairness opinion (required for bond issue), and a physical needs assessment; (5) financing documents (i.e., trust indenture and preliminary official statement for bonds); and (6) certain declarations of trust.[32]

---

26. The CFFP was not originally used with mixed-finance transactions, but it has been selectively used in this way as another tool in maximizing public housing development resources for transactions for PHAs including Denver, CO, Houston, TX, King County, WA, New Orleans, LA, Philadelphia, PA, Portland, OR, Puerto Rico, Tacoma, WA, and Washington, DC.

27. *See* Section 9(d)(1) of the U.S. Housing Act of 1937, as amended by the Quality Housing and Work Responsibility Act of 1998 (Pub. L. No. 105-276, 112 Stat. 2461) (authorizing capital fund appropriations).

28. See Chapter 9 for further discussion of low-income housing tax credits. And see Chapters 8 and 11 for more discussion of bond financing of affordable housing development.

29. *See* Section 9(d)(1) of the U.S. Housing Act of 1937, *supra* note 27. Per 24 C.F.R. 905.505(n)(2), the form of Capital Fund Financing Amendment must provide: "The financing does not constitute a debt or liability of HUD or the United States, the full faith and credit of the United States are not pledged to the payment of debt service, and debt service is not guaranteed by HUD or the United States." Therefore, the CFFP debt instruments run the risk of no, or reduced, federal appropriations in future fiscal years.

30. *See, e.g.*, 24 C.F.R. § 905.505(n)(1): "Amounts payable to the PHA by HUD pursuant to the CFFP and pledged to the payment of debt service by the PHA shall be used exclusively for debt service in accordance with the debt service schedule approved by HUD and shall not be available for any other purpose."

31. U.S. Dep't of Hous. & Urb. Dev., *Notice PIH 2004-15* at 9 (issued Aug. 9, 2004) (indicating that HUD has begun to implement the CFFP, directing PHAs to contact the HUD Office of Capital Improvements for technical assistance and additional information); *see also* Use of Public Housing Capital and Operating Funds for Financing Activities, 72 Fed. Reg. 39,546 (July 18, 2007) (publishing HUD's proposed rule).

32. Office of Capital Improvements, CFFP—How Does a PHA Apply?, http://www.hud.gov /offices/pih/programs/ph/capfund/cffpphaapply.cfm (last visited Mar. 18, 2011). For the most recent

A PHA should make certain threshold determinations when considering using the CFFP, including the extent of critical unmet capital needs that could be funded with a CFFP borrowing and any additional leveraged funds (i.e., low-income-housing tax credit equity). In addition, the PHA needs to assess its own projected capital fund allocation and the portion of that allocation that can be responsibly pledged for annual debt service, without jeopardizing its ongoing capital need obligations. These determinations must consider three important risks. The first risk is the potential for a reduction in, or elimination of, capital fund appropriations. But this risk is controlled by limiting the amount of annual appropriations that can be pledged to pay the debt.[33] The second risk is congressional delay in timely appropriation of capital funds, but this risk is mitigated by the use of debt service reserve funds. The third risk is possible PHA receivership, financial mismanagement, or the risk of failure to complete the project. This risk is minimized by HUD's "intercept provision", which provides for HUD's payment directly to the creditor.[34] Because a CFFP bond issuance does not grant a security interest in the project property, HUD may require other assurances that the construction of the project will occur on time and within budget. Typically, HUD's concern is adequately addressed through the use of a tax credit investor.

In addition to the use of capital funds through the CFFP, a mixed-finance transaction relies on a variety of revenue sources including a PHA's current award of capital funds (including DDTF), low-income housing tax credit equity, state housing finance agency loan funds, conventional financing, tax-exempt bonds, and grants. The impact of these multiple sources is discussed *infra*.

2. Public–Private Partnerships

Mixed-finance development promotes a central role for the private sector in developing and managing public housing. Specifically, PHAs have worked with private affordable housing developers, tax credit equity investors and conventional lenders, and engaged management companies for mixed-finance projects. Under this method, a PHA develops public housing in collaboration with a private entity formed to develop, own, and operate the mixed-income development. What sets a mixed-finance housing project apart from traditional public housing development is the ownership of the development by a private entity generally formed as a limited partnership, a limited liability company, or, in some states, a limited liability limited partnership.[35]

With the role of private entities greatly enhanced, the transaction assumes a distinctly more privatized character. Mixed-finance development, however, does not result in the

---

requirements for submission of a capital fund financing term sheet, contact HUD's Office of Capital Improvements.

33. Debt service coverage test is a significant assessment in this regard. Requiring at least 2.5 or 3.0 times coverage of project debt service by annual appropriations mitigates the PHA risk. A bond rating agency will require that the issuer demonstrate that for a certain period of time (e.g., the last three years) immediately preceding the bond issue, the average amount of capital fund appropriations allocated to and received by the PHA met the 2.5 or 3.0 debt service coverage test.

34. HUD's approval of a CFFP financing includes an "intercept" provision in the transaction's documents which requires HUD to make a direct payment from the line of credit control system ("LOCCS") to the trustee on a bond issuance or to the lender of a bank loan. *See* U.S. DEP'T OF HOUS. & URBAN DEV., *Capital Fund Guidebook*, at 11.1 (Apr. 1, 2016).

35. 24 C.F.R. 941.600(a)(1) (2010).

elimination of PHAs from the public housing development process. Instead, a PHA performs significant roles in the development process either by (1) selecting a private developer and serving as a significant participant by providing access to funds, land, and ongoing operating subsidy for the public housing units and by enforcing applicable public housing requirements; or (2) by being its own developer or co-developer (which may include participating as a member of the ownership entity, as well as a guarantor).

3. Mixed-Income Developments

Mixed-finance developments often involve a mixed-income component in which a certain percentage of the units are public housing, while other low-income housing units are available to households with incomes at or below a prescribed level of the area median income (AMI) and additional units are market rate (i.e., have no income restrictions). These income restrictions are most often dictated by requirements linked to the source of funds supporting the development.

Based upon its character as "public housing," federal law requires that (1) public housing be made available to families at or below 80 percent of AMI;[36] (2) a PHA dedicate at least 40 percent of its public housing inventory to families with incomes at or below 30 percent of AMI at the time of initial occupancy;[37] and (3) the rent charged for public housing units cannot exceed 30 percent of the resident's income.[38]

Pursuant to Title 42 of the Internal Revenue Code, mixed-finance developments involving low-income housing tax credits must contain a certain percentage of the units that are rented to residents with incomes on average at or below 60 percent of the AMI for the duration of the extended use period.[39] And, tax credit rents must be no more than 30 percent of the imputed income limitation.[40]

---

36. *See* 42 U.S.C. § 1437a (2003) (defining low-income families as those earning 80 percent of area median income or less and very low-income families as those earning 50 percent or less of area median income).

37. 42 U.S.C. § 1437n(a) (2003).

38. *Id.* § 1437a(a)(1) (setting out three calculations, of which the highest may be charged to low-income families: 30 percent of family's monthly adjusted income; 10 percent of family's monthly income; or the portion of any welfare assistance payment specifically designated for housing costs).

39. 26 U.S.C. § 42(g)(1) (2002). *See also* 42 U.S.C. § 35(f)(2) (2003) (describing the maximum rents allowed in a mixed-finance project as the maximum tax credit rents permitted under Section 42 of the Internal Revenue Code, provided that rent levels for public housing units do not exceed levels permitted by 42 U.S.C. § 3). A project meeting the 20-50 test will provide 20 percent or more of the units to residents at or below 50 percent of AMI, while a project complying with the 40-60 test will provide 40 percent or more of the units to residents at or below 60 percent of AMI. *Id.* See Chapter 9 for an overview of the LIHTC program.

40. Therefore a tax credit unit within a project counting toward the 20–50 test (i.e., 20 percent or more of the units are rent-restricted and occupied by individuals whose income is 50 percent or less of AMI) cannot carry a rent that exceeds 30 percent of 50 percent of AMI, while the rent charged for a tax credit unit within a project meeting the 40–60 test (i.e., 40 percent or more of the units are rent-restricted and occupied by individuals whose income is 60 percent or less of AMI) cannot exceed 30 percent of the 60 percent of AMI. 26 U.S.C. § 42(g) (2002).

Additional income restrictions are frequently imposed by other sources of financing from state and local governments or special programs such as the Affordable Housing Program of the Federal Home Loan Bank (AHP).[41]

All of these income requirements must be maintained while also satisfying HUD's deconcentration rule, which requires that any site on which public housing will be constructed cannot be an area of minority or low-income concentration.[42] HUD's regulations permit construction of new public housing on an existing site, provided that it is either a HOPE VI development or one of three criteria aimed at minimizing the number of public housing units at the site is met.[43]

C. Advantages of the Mixed-Finance Method of Development

The mixed-finance approach provides three important benefits: (1) it develops needed affordable housing in a manner which is often beneficial for both residents and the surrounding community;[44] (2) it has revitalized PHAs by redeveloping portfolios and offering opportunities to be engaged in the development process through collaborations with the private investors; and (3) it offers a model for public housing development through increased access to private and public funds, greater regulatory flexibility, and involving ongoing monitoring from the private sector.

The mixed-finance program, initially fueled by HOPE VI funding and then by accelerated access to public housing capital funds, has produced successful mixed-income housing integrated into the neighborhood fabric of America's cities.[45] This living environment provides more opportunities for low-income families to move out of poverty and become self-sufficient, while it eliminates concentrated poverty and crime-stricken communities.[46]

As a result of the method's flexible combination of funding sources, mixed-finance developments may include a range of income levels, including, in some cases, units occupied by families regardless of income. This approach facilitates the social integration of

---

41. See Chapter 9 for a discussion of some of the Federal Home Loan Bank's programs financing affordable housing development.

42. 24 C.F.R. § 905.604(e) (2020). One effective solution to the problem of combining and coordinating funding sources with different income and occupancy requirements is to insert in the closing documents language stating that in the event of any such conflict, the more stringent requirements will control. HUD has approved such language for inclusion within key closing documents, provided that the more stringent requirement does not violate mixed-finance Public Housing Requirements.

43. *Id.* at § 941.202(c)(2). Note, however, recent congressional efforts to require one-for-one replacement.

44. The mixed-finance method is associated with mixed-income development, the reconnection of street grids, restoration of land to productive uses and the spurring of other development in the surrounding community. *See, e.g.*, Office of Public and Indian Housing, Mixed-Finance Public Housing Development, March 2001, http://www.hud.gov/offices/pih/programs/ph/hope6/mfph/mfdev.pdf (last visited Sept. 23, 2010).

45. *See generally* Sean Zielenbach, *Catalyzing Community Development: HOPE VI and Neighborhood Revitalization*, 13 J. AFFORDABLE HOUS. 40, 48–73 (Fall 2003) (discussing indicators of neighborhood change within certain HOPE VI neighborhoods).

46. Harry J. Wexler, *Goals, Strategies, and Midterm Lessons of HUD's Urban Revitalization Demonstration Program*, 10 J. AFFORDABLE HOUS. 195, 204–06, 210–11 (Spring 2001) (discussing the objectives of a mixed-income community to provide support to low-income residents and develop more dynamic and sustainable communities and the benefits of support services to encourage self-sufficiency).

public housing with the surrounding community and establishes a more economically integrated community framework making it difficult to discern the various income groups. This may decrease the stigma that often accompanied historic public housing developments, which concentrated the poorest of the poor.

The mixed-finance program has encouraged PHAs to participate actively in affordable housing development with private partners using other public housing resources.[47] The mixed-finance model presents experienced and capable PHAs with the opportunity to act as their own developers. While this role may expose a PHA to increased financial risk, those risks can be managed, and the PHA has an opportunity to earn a developer fee for reinvestment in other affordable housing efforts (discussed *infra* at Section II.A.4). Public housing authorities, acting as their own developers, are becoming adept at filling the funding gap and rely on the flexibility of the mixed-finance approach to develop the most difficult projects. In addition, PHAs that partner with private developers can increase their capacity for self-development by requiring that the private developer extend opportunities for the PHA to be included in the development process.

The mixed-finance paradigm helped lay the foundation for the ongoing development of public housing in spite of an uncertain future of federal appropriations.[48] The flexibility of the mixed-finance model provides an opportunity for various financing sources to be combined in one development, thus allowing for the construction of more units than would be possible if relying on public housing capital funds alone. Creativity is necessary to balance the various requirements within one development, but the public/private approach allows a development to maximize access to these funding sources. The approach also provides developers with greater regulatory flexibility (such as freedom from federal procurement rules when a private developer is involved, discussed *infra*). Finally, whether a PHA serves as its own developer or involves private sector developers, the due diligence requirements imposed by tax credit investors, conventional lenders, and state and local financing sources and HUD impose a degree of quality control that tends to ensure that the development's ownership entity will have the capacity to manage the development process, as well as the ongoing operations of the mixed-finance development.

D. Challenges in Mixed-Finance Implementation

Some of the criticisms initially associated with mixed-finance development are more appropriately identified with the HOPE VI program, such as finding fault with the implementation of the program and its approach to resident involvement,[49] relocation and displacement of public housing residents,[50] and the reduction in the overall number of public housing

---

47. H. David Prior, *Garvee Bonds for Housing: Securitizing Public Housing Capital Funds*, 11 J. Affordable Hous. 264, 265 (Spring 2002).

48. See *supra* note 13 (providing a funding history of HOPE VI).

49. Note, *When HOPE Falls Short: HOPE VI, Accountability, and the Privatization of Public Housing*, 116 Harv. L. Rev. 1477, at 1486 (2003) (asserting that HUD's emphasis on community involvement as a criterion pursuant to a HOPE VI award is hindered by denying residents status as third-party beneficiaries under the HOPE VI grant agreement).

50. Thompson v. HUD, 348 F. Supp. 2d 398, 511–12 (D. Md. 2005) (identifying as a series of supplemental factual findings related to the insufficiency of relocation support in connection with the HOPE VI program in relation to the holding that HUD failed to consider a regional approach to desegregation and integration in violation of the Fair Housing Act).

units at a revitalized site.[51] The mixed-finance regulations require, however, that a PHA include within its development proposal a description of its relocation activities, which are subject to review and approval by HUD.[52] A revitalized public housing site may include fewer public housing units than existed prior to demolition.[53] The requirement that a PHA deconcentrate the number of low-income residents within the community, while permitting the PHA to redevelop the existing site under certain parameters,[54] is an effort to undo the years of neglect and deterioration suffered at the site and the surrounding community, seeks to strike a balance between the competing public policy objectives of minimizing economic and racial concentration while ensuring that a sufficient number of public housing units remain available.[55] The HOPE VI program was also criticized for the amount of time involved in implementing and closing out a grant.[56] Often, this criticism results from the complex nature of a mixed-finance transaction, involving multiple layers of financing and regulatory requirements. While these criticisms are based upon the experiences of particular communities with the implementation of a HOPE VI or mixed-finance program, they should not detract from the valuable tool presented by the mixed-finance approach to affordable housing development that permits not only the development of public housing, but also low-income housing tax credit units that impose income restrictions in favor of low-income residents.

E. Role of Mixed-Finance Development in Neighborhood Transformation

The Choice Neighborhoods initiative, a HUD program focused on neighborhood transformation, helps address transformation of public housing developments.[57] HUD has implemented Choice Neighborhoods in an effort to build on the HOPE VI program in a number of important ways.

Choice Neighborhoods grants are awarded only to applicants that prepared a comprehensive revitalization strategy with respect to a given neighborhood.[58] The strategy

---

51. Lynn E. Cunningham, *Islands of Affordability in a Sea of Gentrification: Lessons Learned from the D.C. Housing Authority's HOPE VI Projects*, 10 J. AFFORDABLE HOUS. 353 (2001) (describing the pressure imposed upon a HOPE VI project located within a gentrifying neighborhood to implement a one for one replacement of demolished public housing units).

52. 24 C.F.R. § 941.606(i) (2010).

53. 42 U.S.C. § 1437v (2002) (identifying one of the purposes of the HOPE VI program as "providing housing that will avoid or decrease the concentration of very low-income families").

54. 24 C.F.R. § 941.202(c)(2) (2010).

55. *Id.* § 941.602(a)(3) (incorporating site and neighborhood standards, 24 C.F.R. § 941.202, into the mixed-finance regulations).

56. Beginning in FY 2002, HOPE IV appropriations have provided that if HOPE VI funds are not spent within five years of the date on which the HOPE VI funds are made available to the PHA, they must automatically be returned to the Treasury. 31 U.S.C. § 1552 (2003). Similarly, NOFAs for Choice Neighborhoods grants set forth a timeline for expenditure of grant funds and require recipients to meet certain program schedule milestones imposed by HUD. *See* U.S. DEP'T OF HOUS. & URBAN DEV., Notice of Funding Availability FY2020 Choice Neighborhoods Implementation Grant Program (FY 2020 CNI NOFA), FR-6400-N-34 at 16, 90.

57. U.S. DEP'T OF HOUS. & URBAN DEV., FY 2020 CNI NOFA at 11.

58. HUD has stated that it understands that neighborhood boundaries are not fixed like municipal or county boundaries. Applicants are responsible for identifying boundaries that are generally accepted as a neighborhood, subject to oversight by HUD. *Id.* at 3.

focuses not just on housing transformation but on neighborhood transformation, with funds available to address the three core objectives of housing, people, and neighborhood with improvements to the surrounding community, public services, facilities, and supportive services.[59] Properties eligible to benefit from the initiative include not just public housing units but also other federally assisted housing and privately owned, unassisted housing located within the distressed area.[60] A key feature of the initiative is that eligible grantees would include not only PHAs but also local governments, nonprofits, and for-profit developers that apply jointly with a public entity.[61] A threshold requirement requires one-for-one replacement of public housing and/or assisted housing, with a few exceptions.[62] This expanded grantee list is based on HUD's attempt to draw on the full range of stakeholders needed to revitalize communities.[63]

II. FORMING SUCCESSFUL PUBLIC–PRIVATE DEVELOPMENT RELATIONSHIPS

The mixed-finance model of public housing development presents a wide range of options to a PHA regarding its involvement in the development, ownership, and management of a project. A PHA may act as its own developer or as a co-developer and co-manager, lender, landlord, and regulator. This section discusses the range of options and considerations that should be taken into account (including applicable legal restrictions, preferred roles and levels of risk) as well as the consequences of these decisions on the availability of certain types of financing (e.g., the level of PHA involvement necessary to ensure eligibility for property tax exemption).

A. Assessing Capacities and Defining Roles in Ownership Structure, Development, and Management

1. Roles Permitted by State Authorizing Statutes

In determining the appropriate roles for a PHA in a mixed-finance development, it is essential at the outset to evaluate a particular PHA's state authorizing statute and/or formation documents.[64] Some states may restrict the type of entity to which a PHA may lend funds.[65] When a PHA retains an ownership interest, either as a landlord or a member/partner of the owner entity, some state laws may give the PHA the ability to extend eligibility for state property tax exemption to the ownership entity.[66] Some states have also modified their laws regulating housing authorities to permit their participation in the mixed-finance

59. *Id.* at 4–5.
60. *Id.* at 3.
61. *Id.* at 16.
62. *Id.* at 20–21.
63. Secretary of Housing and Urban Development Shaun Donovan, *From Despair to Hope: Two HUD Secretaries on Urban Revitalization and Opportunity*, National Press Club, July 14, 2009, http://www.hud.gov/news/speeches/2009-07-14.cfm (last accessed Aug. 5, 2010).
64. State authorizing statutes are available on the Internet. *See, e.g.*, www.michie.com (providing the statutes for certain states).
65. *See* 310 Ill. Comp. Stat. 10/8.4 (permitting a housing authority to make grants, loans, advances to "any non-profit corporation. . . .").
66. *See, e.g.*, Colo. Rev. Stat. § 29-4-227; Md. Ann. Code art. 44A, § 1-104(a)(1) (2003).

development strategy.[67] A PHA's formation documents, however, may limit its range of eligible activities and its jurisdictional authority within the activities and areas of operation otherwise permitted by state statute. Therefore, the authorizing law as well as the PHA's resolutions and formation documents should be carefully examined to determine its legal capacity to engage in the mixed-finance transaction and any requisite limitations in structuring the owner entity and the financing of the transaction.[68]

2. Capacity Assessment

The development of mixed-finance affordable housing is a multilayered, complex effort. Under the mixed-finance approach, a PHA has to decide which roles it can appropriately undertake, such as general partner/managing member of the owner, ground lessor, lender, and property manager. Decisions regarding structure and roles are interrelated with the relative capacity of each party for specific tasks. The mixed-finance model provides an opportunity for a less-experienced PHA to facilitate development of a complex project by collaborating with a more experienced private entity developer. Consideration should be given to the expertise each party brings to the transaction.[69]

A PHA should consider its own capacity and its objectives when assessing its role and that of any other party in relation to the development. The process for land acquisition, the structure of land ownership, and obtaining requisite public approvals are all important considerations. A developer with extensive experience in the region may have relationships with city officials, thus facilitating any required local ordinances or resolutions related to zoning, infrastructure financing, or payment in lieu of taxes designation. Likewise, the PHA may have formed strong relationships with other public entities that have access to local financing or the ability to facilitate the construction review and approval process. Moreover, the PHA has a duty to ensure that the public approval process follows applicable requirements and furthers its public mission.

An examination of these roles and an assessment of the PHA's capacities and mission will permit the PHA to decide if the mixed-finance project should be developed by a private developer or if the PHA is better suited to take on the role of developer. Past experiences with other transactions may have prepared the PHA for a particular level of complexity. Alternatively, the current level of a PHA's ongoing development activities or the overall capital needs of its broader housing portfolio may lead the PHA to procure a developer adept at the activities encompassed in the proposed development in order to avoid overextending the PHA's resources. The PHA's ability to take on an additional financial risk when considered against its current level of financial obligations may also limit the PHA's

---

67. TENN. CODE ANN. § 13-20-104 (permitting a housing authority to "[o]wn, operate, assist, or otherwise participate in one (1) or more mixed-finance projects to provide for the construction, reconstruction, rehabilitation, improvement, alteration or repair of any housing project or any part thereof." *Id.* at § 13-20-104(a)(6)).

68. If a partnership is formed, the private entity within the owner entity should provide all of the authorizations necessary for the PHA to undertake the transaction through the proper filing of organizational documents and the adoption of all necessary corporate, partnership and/or membership resolutions.

69. The private developer and/or the PHA may also take advantage of various consultants such as attorneys, financial advisors, and accountants who are experienced with HUD's mixed-finance program and can provide advice and guidance.

role within the transaction. Overall, the PHA should assess the experience and technical strengths of its staff and its accumulated expertise with sophisticated financing structures. The ultimate decision to procure a private developer or to undertake a self-development approach will shape the tasks and the implementation of the development.

3. Affiliates and Instrumentalities

PHAs often form related nonprofit and for-profit entities to assist with development of mixed-finance housing. Entities whose assets, operations, and management are legally and effectively controlled by a PHA are referred to as "instrumentalities."[70] And entities in which the PHA exerts some control, but not to the same level as with instrumentalities, are referred to as "affiliates."[71] On June 20, 2007, HUD published new guidance for the formation, procurement, and operation of affiliates and instrumentalities of PHAs for purposes of mixed-finance development.[72]

The guidance provided discussion of, among other things, whether PHAs must follow HUD's procurement requirements with respect to instrumentalities and affiliates. Generally, instrumentalities need not be procured to provide development services. In order to determine if an entity is an instrumentality, PHAs must review "indicia of control" and other factors set forth in HUD regulations. Instrumentalities themselves, however, must follow HUD's procurement regulations and competitively procure all goods and services. A different framework was set forth with respect to affiliates, however, as PHAs must procure all affiliates.[73]

The guidance also provided that public housing funds may be used (e.g., by paying legal fees) to form affiliates and instrumentalities for development purposes, but only when the entity will be used for a development that includes public housing units. For multiphase developments, the first phase must include public housing units if public housing funds are used to form a related entity. In addition, PHAs must track costs to ensure that public housing funds and resources are only used for public housing. PHAs may either use a cost allocation system or a fee-based structure. In their annual plan, PHAs must provide HUD with audited financial statements and financial performance reviews of instrumentalities and some affiliates.[74]

A number of other issues were also addressed in the notice. For example, the notice stated that PHAs must be careful to avoid conflicts of interest with affiliates and instrumentalities, including situations where an employee or board member or family member of such persons may derive a personal financial benefit from a transaction involving a PHA and a related entity. In addition, the notice provided that HUD may seek reimbursement of improperly used public housing funds and may also conduct enforcement actions if a PHA grants a security interest in public housing property without the prior written approval of HUD.[75]

---

70. *See also* 24 C.F.R. § 905.604(b)(3) for a definition of "PHA instrumentality."

71. *See also id.* § 905.604(b)(4) for a definition of "PHA affiliate."

72. *See Notice PIH 2007-15 (HA).* Pursuant to *Notice PIH 2011-47 (HA),* 2007-15 was extended indefinitely. The notice was previously extended by *Notices PIH 2008-27, 2009-24* and *2010-30.*

73. *Id.*

74. *Id.*

75. *Id.*

4. Private Development

Under the mixed-finance method of development, a PHA might procure a private developer to develop the housing units. Selection of a private developer generally offers certain benefits, including real estate development knowledge; financial capacity (including experience in assembling multiple sources of financing); assumption of the development risk (by providing guarantees of completion and operation required by lenders and tax credit investors); selection of contractors and vendors without the need to comply with federal procurement rules;[76] outreach experience and access to professional relationships; and an opportunity for a PHA inexperienced with development activity to enhance its capacity.

If a PHA decides to procure a developer to assist with the development, the selection of a developer requires an evaluation of the potential developer's experience with the mixed-finance method for developing public housing. The selected developer must have sufficient financial depth to provide the necessary guarantees required by the PHA and any investors. The developer should also have substantial experience communicating and interacting with residents and the greater community concerning the development approach and tenanting process. Many experienced developers have a preferred working relationship with particular tax credit investors, general contractors, and/or property managers. Such relationships need to be assessed prior to procuring that developer's services. If the PHA is implementing any development activities, it should also consider the developer's willingness to enhance the PHA's capacity, to permit the PHA to undertake distinct development responsibilities, and to share the developer fee with the PHA for any development functions it may perform, such as facilitating other financing and obtaining necessary local approvals (discussed *infra*).

Participating with a private developer offers the PHA access to expertise and an opportunity to build future development capacity through observation and training.[77] Some PHAs have begun a multiphased, mixed-finance HOPE VI project with a private developer and have negotiated provisions whereby the developer's role decreases and the PHA's role increases as the development proceeds into subsequent phases, with the ultimate objective being that the PHA assumes the general partner/managing member role in the last phases. In single-phased mixed-finance projects, other PHAs negotiate a partnership/operating agreement that calls for the private developer to act as the general partner/managing member through construction completion with the PHA assuming this role after stabilized occupancy. These arrangements have the benefit of providing the PHA greater input in the development and management process without extending the PHA beyond its abilities or capacities.

A PHA that elects to procure a private developer rather than act as its own developer, will negotiate and execute a Master Development Agreement (MDA), setting forth the various responsibilities of the developer and the PHA. Negotiating the MDA offers the

---

76. 24 C.F.R. § 905.604(h)(2) exempts a mixed-finance owner entity from 2 C.F.R. pt. 200 provided that the PHA does not exercise "significant functions within the owner entity with respect to managing the development of the proposed units."

77. A PHA may integrate its capacity building objectives into the development agreement negotiated with the private developer, making this a component of the contractual relationship between the PHA and the developer.

parties an opportunity to anticipate and arrange all aspects of their relationship. When the development often involves multiple phases, the MDA is critical to setting conditions and standards throughout the entire mixed-finance development process. Careful negotiation of an MDA can resolve issues such as the development schedule (performance milestones); developer fees (amount and sharing); liability and indemnification (particularly environmental issues); guarantees, reserves, and allocation of risk; the scope of each phase of the development; and default and termination conditions (including termination for convenience). At this stage, the developer and the PHA can address key provisions of critical documents such as a ground lease and the regulatory and operating agreement (R&O). For example, the MDA will set forth indemnity and liabilities provisions, and apportion environmental warranties.[78] The parties can also determine how the R&O for each phase will allocate the payment of the public housing operating subsidy provided by the PHA under its Consolidated Annual Contributions Contract (ACC) with HUD (discussed *infra*). The MDA may also determine what remedial steps will apply if the public housing units have difficulty operating on a break-even basis for an extended period of time due to a material reduction of subsidy, with such remedial steps being carried forward into the R&O.

Negotiation of these types of business and legal issues within the context of the MDA establishes a framework for each phase and saves time and legal costs that might otherwise be incurred at a later point in the transaction. If the parties do not address these issues at the outset, disagreements could lead to a difficult, expensive "breakup" and delays in development.

The amount and timing of the developer fee will also be set forth in the MDA. The developer fee is limited by HUD through the "Cost Control and Safe Harbor Standards for Rental Mixed-Finance Development."[79] A developer's fee will usually be a percentage of total development costs within a general range of 7 percent to 12 percent, with lower percentages imposed when the developer's risk is minimal. A PHA may be entitled to a portion of the developer fee if it assumes some of the developer's responsibilities (see *infra*). The amount of the developer fee may hinge on (1) the amount of risk assumed and the extent of the guaranties provided by the developer in relation to both construction and operation; (2) the responsibility for securing financing sources; (3) the need to obtain site control and any added complexity (i.e., the need to develop scattered sites); and (4) restrictions imposed or leniency afforded by the construction schedule.

5. *Self-Development*

The number of PHAs acting as their own developers in mixed-finance transactions has grown over the years.[80] A PHA with the capacity to undertake the development and

---

78. For example, the parties should consider: who bears the risk of environmental contamination at which stage of the predevelopment/development process; should environmental insurance be purchased; and should environmental liability be capped.

79. *See* U.S. Dep't of Hous. & Urban Dev., *Mixed-Finance Public Housing*, https://www.hud. gov/sites/documents/DOC_9880.PDF (providing a link to HUD's most recent version of the Cost Control and Safe Harbor Standards for Rental Mixed-Finance Development) (last accessed Aug. 2, 2010). This document was most recently updated on April 9, 2003.

80. Some examples of PHAs acting as their own developer in mixed-finance transactions include those in the following locations: Bremerton, WA; Dallas, TX; Houston, TX; King County, WA;

management of a mixed-finance development without the benefit of a private developer may choose to act as its own developer, serving as the general partner/managing member of the mixed-finance ownership entity. This type of arrangement may provide the PHA with the following benefits: (1) greater control over the development to pursue its mission; (2) enhancement of its development capacity;[81] (3) sizable developer fees, which may be recycled into the project or used by the PHA for other affordable housing purposes;[82] and (4) a more efficient development timetable because the PHA need not negotiate a MDA and other transaction-related documents with a developer.

Implementing the PHA self-developed approach requires that the PHA carefully analyze its capacity; it must also identify consultants, including attorneys, financial analysts, and accountants, to supplement its expertise. The most significant risk related to self-development is providing the construction and operating guaranties in a manner consistent with congressional and HUD-imposed limitations (discussed *infra*). As with private developers, however, those risks can be controlled by setting monetary limits on the amount of guaranties, using a portion of the development fee as the source of payment, and hiring a construction manager to assist with the timely completion of the development. Hiring experienced attorneys and financial consultants early in the process is critical to structuring the financing to maximize the leveraging of its funds and to minimize the risks. Importantly, if a PHA elects to serve as its own developer, it cannot take advantage of the exception from 2 C.F.R. part 200 provided by the mixed-finance regulations and must, instead, competitively procure its contractor, architect, engineers, management agents, and consultants.[83] Many PHAs have not found this to be an impediment, but have developed processes for successfully procuring these professionals within the regulatory requirements; and HUD will approve alternative procurement plans on a case-by-case basis.[84]

Earning development fees can be a valuable source of additional revenue for PHAs, especially in light of diminished federal support. Certain fees realized by a PHA during the development process, including developer fees, are regulated by HUD as program income.[85] The future use of this income (generally in connection with development activities associated with the grant or other affordable housing purposes) is governed by a program income certification incorporated into the project's Mixed-Finance Amendment to Consolidated Annual Contributions Contract between HUD and the PHA (the "ACC Amendment").[86]

New Orleans, LA; New York, NY; Philadelphia, PA; Portland, OR; Puerto Rico; San Francisco, CA; Seattle, WA; Tacoma, WA; Washington, DC.

81. Some PHAs are providing land, financing, and, frequently, access to other local funds and approvals.

82. Developer fee constitutes program income as defined by 2 C.F.R. § 200.307. Any use of program income generated in connection with a mixed-finance project is governed by a Program Income Certificate incorporated as Exhibit H of the Mixed-Finance Amendment to Consolidated Annual Contributions Contract (discussed *infra*).

83. State statutes and local ordinances may also impose procurement requirements that apply to a situation in which the PHA acts as the developer. A PHA should carefully document the procurement process and the resulting decisions. See *infra* for additional discussion of procurement requirements.

84. 24 C.F.R. § 905.604(h)(2) (2020).

85. 2 C.F.R. § 200.307 (2020).

86. *See* U.S. Dep't of Hous. & Urban Dev., https://www.hud.gov/sites/dfiles/PIH/documents /MixedFinanceACCAmendment.pdf (effective date Mar. 1, 2016) (providing a link to HUD's most

Other income earned following the development process, such as principal and interest payments, ground lease payments, and asset management fees, may also supplement a PHA's traditional revenues. In addition to ensuring accurate accounting for the use of program income, a PHA that acts as its own developer and creates affiliates or instrumentalities to facilitate that process must be careful to avoid conflicts of interest prohibited by its ACC, comply with federal and local procurement requirements, identify legally accessible sources of funds for guaranties, and properly allocate costs and risks amongst the entities.[87] A PHA that decides to work through an affiliated nonprofit must be certain to implement controls that respect the affiliate's existence as a distinct legal entity. These include execution of agreements between a PHA and its instrumentalities and affiliates, implementation of accounting mechanisms, and careful review of guaranty and other obligations to ensure that the work of the affiliate is properly authorized and does not expose the PHA to an inappropriate level of risk.[88]

B. Key Legal Documents

The initial document filed with HUD, which lays the foundation of a mixed-finance transaction, is the "development proposal"[89] required by 24 C.F.R. § 905.606. The development proposal (which functions like a commercial bank's underwriting term sheet) identifies the key components of the transaction, including (1) financing sources and uses; (2) the construction cost and schedule; (3) the identity of the entities comprising the owner entity; and (4) the physical elements of the project, including the number of units and their designation as public housing units, low-income housing tax credit units, and/or market-rate units. Additionally, the development proposal describes the method of allocating operating subsidy available for the public housing units, the reserves that will be maintained for the project, the management of the project, and the associated management fee.

The development proposal should be submitted to HUD's Office of Public Housing Investments 90 days prior to the proposed construction closing date.[90] HUD's review and approval of the development proposal lays the foundation for preparing and negotiating the

---

recent version of the ACC Amendment). The ACC Amendment is required to include the developed or acquired public housing units under the ACC and to receive public housing funding. It also constitutes a certification of the PHA, the PHA's partner and/or owner entity with the requirements of 24 C.F.R. Part 905, subpart F. *See* 24 C.F.R. § 905.600(a) (2020).

87. *See* U.S. Dep't of Hous. & Urban Dev., *Applicability of Public Housing Development Requirements to Transactions between Public Housing Agencies and Their Related Affiliates and Instrumentalities*, http://www.hud.gov/offices/adm/hudclips/notices/pih/files/07-15pih.doc/ (last accessed July 7, 2020).

88. *See* Office of Insp. Gen., U.S. Dept. of Hous. & Urban Dev., Public Housing Agency Development Activities Audit Report 2004-AT-0001, 8–10 (Jan. 13, 2004) (discussing deficiencies of PHAs conducting development activities with affiliated non-profits and HUD oversight of such activities). HUD noted in its comments to the Audit Report that a number of PHAs' actions would not have violated the ACC if the PHAs had obtained prior HUD approval.

89. U.S. Dep't of Hous. & Urban Dev., form HUD-50157 (exp. 04/2022). HUD may also use the form of development proposal for non-public housing development through the Choice Neighborhoods or RAD programs.

90. U.S. Dep't Hous. & Urban Dev., *Project Review Panel Protocol*, https://www.hud.gov /program_offices/public_indian_housing/programs/ph/hope6/mfph/project_review (last accessed July 8, 2021).

remaining documents evidencing the transaction, referred to as the "evidentiaries."[91] The development proposal, revised to reflect any comments made by the HUD grant manager assigned to the mixed-finance development, is evaluated by HUD's Project Review Panel, an internal review panel in the Office of Public Housing Investment that essentially functions as a loan review committee.[92] The development proposal is also the document through which the PHA requests any special variances, waivers, or approvals from HUD necessary to close the transaction.

Evidentiaries requiring HUD review and approval, which should be submitted 45 days before closing,[93] include (1) the ACC Amendment (described *infra*); (2) the HUD form of Declaration of Restrictive Covenants that will subject the fee simple property to the public housing requirements and requires HUD consent for any subsequent liens or disposition (described *infra*); (3) the R&O (described *infra*); (4) the ground lease and memorandum of ground lease or other land disposition agreement (described *infra*); (5) legal opinion from PHA counsel using the HUD form; (6) any updates to the development proposal and accompanying development proposal calculator; (7) HUD's form of certifications and assurances (form HUD-50161); (8) title policy pro forma reflecting the intended recording of the HUD Declaration of Restrictive Covenants in the order approved by HUD, along with copies of any documents slated to be recorded against the property; (9) ALTA survey; (10) the management plan, management agreement, and associated documents (including the form of tenant lease); (11) a cooperation agreement between the PHA and the local government regarding payments in lieu of taxes, local tax exemption, and the availability of local government services to be provided for the public housing units or an election to exempt the property from a payment in lieu of taxes per 24 C.F.R. § 905.606(a)(8); and (12) other documents as may be requested by HUD.[94] The HUD field office will review title and survey and the management documents. Model forms of certain pertinent evidentiary documents are available on HUD's website.[95]

C. Critical HUD Requirements

Because the mixed-finance process is another method of developing public housing,[96] HUD regulations apply to numerous development issues. Some of the most important issues (discussed *infra*) are the mix of units, construction cost limitations, procurement, subsidy layering analysis, site and neighborhood standards, environmental clearance, relocation, and HUD approval of the release of funds. In addition, other development regulations are incorporated into the mixed-finance regulations by reference at 24 C.F.R. 905.604(a).

---

91. *Supra* note 90 at § 15 (describing the evidentiary materials required for submission to HUD in connection with a mixed-finance transaction).
92. *Supra* note 90.
93. *Supra* note 90.
94. *See* U.S. Dep't of Hous. & Urban Dev., *supra* note 90 at § 15.
95. *See* U.S. Dep't of Hous. & Urban Dev., https://www.hud.gov/program_offices/public_indian_housing/programs/ph/hope6/mfph/mf_modeldocs (last visited July 8, 2021).
96. *See supra* note 16 (describing other methods of public housing development).

1. Mix of Units and Pro Rata Funding

Public housing units developed in conjunction with low-income housing tax credit units and/or market rate units must be developed so as to be indistinguishable from the non-public housing units. Specifically, 24 C.F.R. § 905.604(g) requires that the units be "comparable in size, location, external appearance, and distribution to the nonpublic housing units within the development."

It is also necessary to limit expenditure of public housing funds on costs related to the public housing units.[97] HUD confirms this by ensuring the pro rata test is met in which public housing funds committed to the project do not exceed the proportion of public housing units within the project when compared to the total units.[98] HUD may separately evaluate scenarios in which public housing funds are invested in a greater proportion of the costs for common areas to ensure the residents receive the benefits of the common area improvements.[99]

2. Construction Cost Limitations

HUD will review the budget to ensure that the amount of public housing funds invested for the construction of rental or homeownership units does not exceed the Housing Construction Cost[100] (or Housing Cost Cap or HCC, as the concept is referred to more colloquially) and the total development cost (TDC) limits.[101] The HCC limit is determined by averaging the construction costs listed in the R.S. Means cost index for construction of "average" quality and the Marshal & Swift cost index for construction of "good" quality.[102] This average cost is then multiplied by the number of units based on bedroom size and structure types. The TDC limit is calculated by multiplying the HCC limit by 1.6 for elevator type structures and by 1.75 for non-elevator type structures.[103] The TDC limit is intended to encompass the sum of HCC and Community Renewal Costs.[104] Non-public housing funds (e.g., CDBG, HOME, LIHTCs, AHP grants, and private financing) are exempt from the calculation for the TDC limit.[105] "Additional Project Costs," defined as HUD-approved costs for demolition or remediation of environmental hazards associated with public housing units that will not be replaced on the site, extraordinary site costs verified by an

---

97. 24 C.F.R. 905.604(c)(2) (2020).

98. *Id.* 905.604(c)(3).

99. *Id.* 905.604(c)(4).

100. *See id.* § 905.108 (defining "Housing Construction Cost" as the sum of "the dwelling unit hard costs . . .; builder's overhead and profit; the cost of extending utilities from the street to the public housing project; finish landscaping; and the payment of Davis-Bacon wage rates.").

101. *See id.* § 905.604(c)(4) (incorporating the definition of "Total Development Cost" and "Housing Confstructio Cost" set forth at 24 C.F.R. § 905.314(c) and (d)).

102. *Id.* § 905.314(d)(2).

103. *Id.* § 905.314(c)(2)(ii)–(iii).

104. *Id.* § 905.314(b)(1). According to the definitions at 24 C.F.R. § 905.108, Community Renewal Costs are defined to include the following costs: planning, administration, site acquisition, relocation, demolition and site remediation of environmental hazards, interest and carrying charges, off-site facilities, community buildings and non-dwelling facilities, contingency allowance, insurance premiums, any initial operating deficit, on-site streets, on-site utilities, and other costs that are not covered under the HCC.

105. *Id.* § 905.314(c)(4).

independent registered engineer, and cost effective energy-efficiency measures in excess of standard building codes, are also not subject to the TDC limit.[106]

3. Procurement

The mixed-finance regulations require that if a PHA selects a development partner that it use a competitive proposal procedure relying on competitors' qualifications.[107] The selection of a private developer entity unaffiliated with the PHA removes the need for such private developer to make future procurements in compliance with 2 C.F.R. part 200. This exemption does not apply when the PHA or its affiliate exercises "significant functions within the owner entity with respect to managing the development of the proposed units."[108] The regulations, however, permit alternative approaches to procurement subject to HUD approval, thus the procurement regulations have not posed a problem for PHAs that have acted as developers of public housing. As mentioned *supra*, self-developing PHAs have generally worked successfully within the procurement process to select professionals and construction contractors. Even with the flexibility afforded by the mixed-finance regulations, a PHA will need to determine if state and local procurement laws apply.

4. Demolition and Disposition

The demolition and disposition of public housing is authorized under Section 18 of the Act. Demolition/disposition involves the removal of public housing units from the public housing stock by razing, sale, or lease. HUD has promulgated a regulation that details the steps required to perform demolition and disposition activity in accordance with the Act.[109] While demolition and disposition has long been permitted, HUD began "to actively pursue it as a management strategy option. . . [beginning] with the HOPE VI program."[110] Reasons for this strategy include the physical deterioration of developments and the overall deterioration of surrounding communities.[111]

Importantly, dispositions for mixed-finance housing are not subject to HUD's demolition/disposition regulation described earlier.[112] These dispositions are, however, still subject to Section 18 of the Act. The Special Applications Center of HUD will process these through the MF-MOD disposition application in IMS/PIC.[113] The HUD approval letter may identify how PHAs must apply disposition proceeds.

---

106. *Id.* § 905.314(c)(3) (Additional Project Costs are defined at 24 C.F.R. § 905.108.).

107. *Id.* § 905.604(h)(1)).

108. *Id.* § 905.604(h)(2).

109. 24 C.F.R. § 970 (2010).

110. *See* Public Housing Program: Demolition or Disposition of Public Housing Projects, and Conversion of Public Housing to Tenant-Based Assistance, 79 Fed. Reg. 62,249 (Oct. 16, 2014) (publishing HUD's proposed rule) .

111. *Id.*

112. *See* 24 C.F.R. § 970.3(b)(12) (2020).

113. U.S. Dep't of Hous. & Urban Dev., Notice PIH 2021-17 (HA) (issued Jan. 19, 2021) at FN 4.

5. Funding Considerations

Public housing capital funds cannot be disbursed at an amount greater than necessary to permit the development of the project after taking into consideration other assistance.[114] A related consideration bearing on the structure of the transaction is the HUD requirement to conduct a review of the final, executed evidentiary documents before authorizing a release of the capital funds that serve as a source of funds for the development into LOCCS.[115] The PHA is generally required to submit these evidentiaries within 30 days after closing, and HUD's review tends to take an additional 30 days. Therefore, since HUD funds are not available to cover closing costs associated with recording fees and title insurance, another source of unrestricted funds will need to be accessed for these costs. Moreover, HUD will approve a draw-down schedule and the PHA will be permitted to draw funds according to a ratio that does not exceed that which is necessary to meet the PHA's pro rata share of development costs.[116] The ratio of non-public housing funds to public housing funds must correlate to the ratio of non-public housing units to public housing units constructed as part of the mixed-finance development.

D. Balancing the Interests

An inherent challenge of a mixed-finance development is the need to accommodate competing interests. The PHA often has multiple interests as ground lessor, lender, regulator, property manager, and/or general partner/managing member or other entity within the ownership structure. Each funding source brings various regulatory requirements and interests in need of protection. The low-income housing tax credit investor, for example, has multiple objectives, including the need to (1) communicate to its underlying investor or pool of investors that the development is a sound economic investment; (2) show that the development is carrying true debt that will count toward eligible basis needed to justify the tax credits allocated to the development;[117] and (3) demonstrate that the investment will not be jeopardized by a negative finding by the Internal Revenue Service during the 15-year tax credit compliance period.[118] Any AHP funds granted by the Federal Home Loan Bank also carry a set of occupancy restrictions. HUD will be concerned that the portion of the development dedicated to public housing will be maintained as public housing as required by the U.S. Housing Act of 1937,[119] and that the PHA, which may not be a member or partner of the owner entity, remains responsible for such operation. The permanent lender seeks to ensure that its investment is protected, and that it can promptly address any defaults through foreclosure rights that are not inhibited by the presence of a ground lease or any restrictive covenants with a prior recording position.

---

114. *See* 24 C.F.R. §905.610(b) (2020) (requiring a subsidy layering analysis).
115. *Id.* § 905.612(b)(2).
116. *Id.* § 905.606(a)(6)(i). HUD will approve a draw schedule included with Exhibit G of the HUD-required Mixed-Finance Amendment to Consolidated Annual Contributions Contract and may permit deviations from this standard.
117. 26 U.S.C. § 42(k)(2) (2004).
118. *Id.* § 42(j).
119. 42 U.S.C. §§ 9(d)(3)(A), 9(e)(3) (2004).

Each of these interests is set forth in various legal documents,[120] which may contain conflicting provisions requiring reconciliation. Several of these are discussed *infra*. The review and modification of these documents and the implementation of other documents presents a challenge requiring a certain level of trust, an ability to communicate and draft clearly, and a willingness to think creatively. These interests need to be balanced in a way that seeks to eliminate any ambiguity within the individual documents required by each funding source as well as within any additional documents entered into and relied upon by all of the parties.

1. Organizational Documents

The owner entity's organizational document will be either a partnership agreement or an operating agreement for a limited liability company. Among other things, this formation document will describe (1) the general partner or managing member obligations; (2) the investor partner's/member's rights to cure a default by the general partner/managing member; (3) the schedule for the pay-in of the investor's capital contribution; (4) the method for calculation net cash flow; (5) the distribution of cash flow; (6) the procedure for property disposition upon the entity's dissolution; and (7) the binding effect of certain HUD requirements on the entity and its members, including a limitation on the ability to make cash flow distributions and to satisfy guarantees and indemnifications from public housing assets.[121]

2. Ground Lease

Often, a PHA will maintain ownership of the fee simple estate upon which the mixed-finance development will be constructed. In those instances, a ground lease will be executed between the landlord PHA and the owner entity, as tenant.[122] The ground lease serves many purposes. It presents an opportunity to ensure that the property is operated according to the PHA's desired affordability levels. It serves to allocate responsibility for liability for the operation of the property during the term of the lease as well as responsibility for any environmental hazards prior to and after lease commencement. The ground lease may also be a tool that ensures that the property enjoys the benefit of a property tax exemption, by maintaining ultimate ownership in the PHA.

3. Regulatory and Operating Agreement

The PHA will also prepare the R&O with the owner entity that sets forth the requirements related to the operation of the public housing units.[123] The R&O is of significant concern for the PHA and tends to be a heavily negotiated document. This agreement establishes terms

---

120. The tax credit investor's concerns related to Section 42 of the Internal Revenue Code are generally addressed through the general partner's covenants and obligations under the partnership agreement. The state allocating agency addresses its concerns through an extended use agreement or land use restriction agreement. HUD's interests are covered in the declaration of restrictive covenants and the ACC Amendment. See *infra* for a discussion of these and other documents.

121. *See* U.S. Dep't of Hous. & Urban Dev., *Model Documents for Mixed-Finance Transactions*, https://www.hud.gov/program_offices/public_indian_housing/programs/ph/hope6/mfph/mf_modeldocs (last accessed July 8. 2021) (providing a link to a summary of HUD-required provisions for the owner partnership/operating agreements).

122. *See id.* (describing HUD-required provisions for the ground lease).

123. *Id.* (describing HUD-required provisions for the R&O).

for calculating and paying the operating subsidy that will supplement the public housing units' income. It describes the process to be implemented should the amount of operating subsidy be insufficient to support the public housing units on a break-even basis. The investor and developer are interested in establishing remedies that will provide a safety net in the event HUD diminishes the amount of subsidy to be paid to the PHA. Such remedies are necessary from the investor's and developer's perspectives to ensure that the development is financially viable. The PHA is similarly concerned with the development's economic viability, but it also seeks assurances that the development will retain its public housing character for the statutorily required time period, and that the PHA preserves and enhances the affordable housing stock available to the community's low-income residents. These concerns present a tension that must be carefully addressed.[124]

The R&O also describes the reserves that are available generally for the overall development (i.e., replacement reserve and operating deficit reserve) as well as those reserves specific to the public housing units (i.e., operating subsidy reserve and lease-up reserve). Describing how these reserves are initially funded, how they are subsequently replenished, who owns the reserves, and when these reserves can be accessed are key considerations in crafting the operating subsidy remedial language.

4. Mixed-Finance ACC Amendment

Many of the provisions within the R&O are a direct result of the PHA's regulatory obligations to HUD as evidenced by the ACC Amendment.[125] The ACC Amendment binds the PHA to operate the public housing units in accordance with the mixed-finance regulations and other HUD requirements. Any material modification of the evidentiary documents after closing requires HUD's review and approval.[126] The occurrence of a casualty or condemnation event triggers certain requirements regarding the continued operation of a certain proportion of public housing units based on the extent of the damage or eminent domain proceeding. These requirements also describe the application of casualty or condemnation proceeds if it is determined that restoration is not feasible.[127] As a party to the ACC Amendment, the PHA is under a heightened responsibility to review documents for such conflicts. Specifically, Section 6(A)(18) of the ACC Amendment requires that a PHA take all steps necessary to ensure the operation of the public housing units is not adversely effected upon a foreclosure or other adverse action against the owner entity. If a PHA fails to carefully review and negotiate all of the documents affecting the development, the PHA could unintentionally limit its rights to enforce the ACC Amendment in the future.

5. HUD Declaration of Restrictive Covenants

The Declaration of Restrictive Covenants is a HUD-required document imposing restrictions on the development and requiring that the public housing units be maintained as

---

124. Section 35(h) of the 1937 Housing Act permits a deviation from public housing requirements in the event of a reduction in operating subsidy such that the PHA is "unable to fulfill its contractual obligations with respect to those public housing units." 24 C.F.R. § 905.604(k) implements this statutory language.

125. *Supra* note 86.

126. Section 7(D) of the ACC Amendment.

127. Section 11 of the ACC Amendment.

low-income housing for the greater of a period of (1) either 40 years for new construction or 20 years for rehabilitation expenditures and (2) ten years from the last date on which the development receives operating subsidy.[128] The recording priority requires that any mortgages placed on the property be subordinated to the restrictions such that no lien foreclosures will enable the development to be subsequently operated at unrestricted, market rate rents.

6. *Other Documents*

Section 42 of the Internal Revenue Code permits the sale of a low-income housing tax credit project to a government agency or 501(c)(3) entity following the 15-year tax credit compliance period. This right is often set forth in a Purchase Option and Right of First Refusal Agreement, typically for the benefit of the PHA or its affiliate or instrumentality. Intercreditor agreements, subordination agreements, standstill agreements, nondisturbance agreements, and recording priority agreements are often used to address the competing interests of various lenders within a broader context. These documents tend to address treatment of various interests in the event of a default.

III. MIXED-FINANCE DEVELOPMENT IN CONJUNCTION WITH RAD

HUD's focus on public housing asset repositioning[129] raises the question of the efficacy of developing new public housing. As HUD has noted, however, there are over 200,000 units of housing available to PHAs under the collective Faircloth limits. A PHA's access to units available under its Faircloth limit opens resources for developing new deeply affordable public housing with the intention of transitioning it to more stable Section 8 housing assistance. The HUD Office of Recapitalization ("Recap") offers guidance on pursuing a streamlined "Faircloth-to-RAD" strategy.[130]

HUD's Rental Assistance Demonstration (RAD) program grew out of a need to address decades of disinvestment in maintaining the nation's public housing stock.[131] Converting restricted public housing assets to more flexible Section 8-supported housing, which can secure debt, expands access to financing options to help overcome capital funding shortfalls and stabilize the housing stock. Relying on the Section 8 program also provides access to a more consistent funding stream that carries broader political support, while ensuring long-term affordability through the imposition of indefinite use restrictions.

Faircloth-to-RAD offers a means to tap into a subsidy stream that supports construction of new housing under the public housing mixed-finance process, thus providing affordability for very low-income households along with the streamlined ability to convert the new units through RAD upon completion.[132] The *Faircloth-to-RAD Conversions* guide sets

---

128. *See supra* note 121.

129. *See* Repositioning Public Housing, https://www.hud.gov/program_offices/public_indian_housing/repositioning. *See also* Chapter 15 discussing affordable housing preservation, including public housing repositioning efforts.

130. U.S. Dep't of Hous. & Urban Dev., *Faircloth-to-RAD Conversions*, Apr. 7, 2021, https://www.hud.gov/sites/dfiles/Housing/documents/Faircloth_Resource_Package.pdf.

131. U.S. Dep't of Hous. & Urban Dev., *RAD Program Details for Residents*, https://www.hud.gov/RAD/program-details-residents (last visited July 9, 2021).

132. *Supra notes* 130, 131.

out the process for undertaking a dual mixed-finance and RAD conversion approach that seeks to simplify and combine the HUD mixed-finance and RAD review processes.[133] The following provides a summary of the process set out in the *Faircloth-to-RAD Conversions* guide.

A. Requesting Faircloth-to-RAD Conversion

A PHA interested in developing new units for conversion to Section 8 under RAD must notify Recap through the RAD Resource Desk by requesting a "Notice of Anticipated RAD Rents," or NARR. The NARR functions as a preliminary Commitment for Housing Assistance Payment (CHAP) to provide the PHA with a guidepost for the rents anticipated to support the project upon conversion to Section 8. Entries on the RAD Resource Desk provide details to determine the rents, provided these details are updated, as needed, at the time the PHA submits a mixed-finance development proposal.

B. Reservation of Conversion Authority

Given the RAD cap on the number of public housing units that can convert to Section 8 (currently at about 455,000 units), it is necessary for a PHA to confirm with Recap that its planned units are included within that cap through a valid reservation. A PHA effectuates a reservation by:

1. Updating an existing RAD portfolio award to add the planned units;
2. Submitting a new RAD portfolio application if the PHA does not yet have a portfolio award, but has other existing public housing units; or
3. In instances where a PHA has no other public housing units, piggy-backing on another PHA's portfolio award by increasing that award to encompass its units.

C. Reliance on Mixed-Finance Submissions

At the time submission of the mixed-finance development proposal to the Office of Public Housing Investments (OPHI) is imminent, the PAH requests a preliminary conversion call via the RRD. At this time, a RAD transaction manager is assigned and a call is scheduled with the PHA, OPHI, and other relevant stakeholders. Issues discussed during that call include:

1. The overall Faircloth-to-RAD conversion process.
2. Timing of construction delivery and occupancy lease up and whether delivery of units will occur on a phased, building by building basis or at one time. Units within a phased construction completion project (i.e., delivery on a building by building basis) require that RAD conversion only occur once the final units are completed. Additionally, a phased lease-up prior to conversion to RAD would likely trigger RAD resident engagement and public housing to Section 8 lease transition requirements. As such, timing of building delivery and lease up should be considered carefully.

---

133. *Supra note* 130 at Introduction.

3. Permanent financing terms and the timing in relation to the RAD conversion process.
4. Initial year funding considerations and timing of execution of the RAD Housing Assistance Payments contract (HAP).

D. Modified RAD Underwriting Process

Given the OPHI underwriting process, Recap only requires submission of materials to the RRD that are not otherwise submitted as required by the mixed-finance development proposal. These include:

1. Conversion overview with a description of the proposed RAD ownership structure;
2. Confirmation of which Section 8 platform is being elected (e.g., project-based vouchers or project-based rental assistance);
3. Certification of PHA board approval of the pending RAD conversion;
4. Operating pro forma;
5. Approved significant amendment to PHA Annual Plan and, if applicable, the approval of the MTW Agreement; and
6. Initial Year Funding Tool.

In light of the OPHI review of the project sources and uses, Recap considers the conversion as a no-debt conversion. OPHI also reviews the typical mixed-finance evidentiary documents, including drafts of the Mixed-Finance ACC Amendment, Declaration of Restrictive Covenants, and Regulatory and Operating Agreement. HUD advises PHAs to keep in mind the fact that these particular documents will be in place for a limited time as they will be terminated or released upon the RAD conversion, thus limiting the extent to which certain issues require negotiation.

E. Completion of Construction and Entering Units into PIC

Upon construction completion for all of the units, the PHA will prepare and submit the key documents to HUD's Office of Public and Indian Housing to verify the date of full availability (i.e., DOFA) for eligibility for public housing funds and entering of the units into the PIH Information Center (PIC). This process verifies the units' status as public housing. At this point, Recap is able to issue the CHAP and RCC, relying on its prior review of the PHA's RAD Financing Plan.

F. Engaging Recap and Proceeding to RAD Conversion

Should a PHA desire a near immediate conversion to Section 8 housing under RAD, Recap advises a PHA to alert Recap of the anticipated DOFA 60 days prior to the expected date. At this time, the PHA uploads the following to the RRD:

1. Details regarding any post-conversion work not previously approved by HUD;
2. Intention to create any additional liens against the project, keeping in mind the need for such liens to be subordinated to the long-term RAD use restrictions;
3. Description of any material changes from the transaction structure that was last approved by Recap;

4. Identification of any changes to the sources and uses previously approved by OPHI; and

5. Upon completion, certification of satisfaction of the RCCA requirements.

The PHA will also submit to the RRD for review by the RAD closing coordinator and HUD counsel the typical RAD conversion documents, along with the documents terminating the Mixed-Finance ACC Amendment and Regulatory and Operating Agreement and releasing the Declaration of Restrictive Covenants. The initial year funding tool is finalized at this time, keeping in mind that this document, rather than the Regulatory and Operating Agreement, sets the amount of subsidy received by the project during the first year following conversion. It is recommended that these materials are submitted early to minimize the passage of time between completion and conversion, noting that Recap estimates a 60-day timeframe for review of materials. This submission can occur before units have been entered into PIC.

Following Recap review of these materials, the RAD conversion can proceed, bringing the units into the Section 8 program.

IV. CONCLUSION

At a time when public–private partnerships are trending across sectors from school infrastructure to state toll road improvements as a means of extending increasingly limited public resources, mixed-finance development of public housing, particularly when coupled with RAD, will continue to serve as fertile ground for financing innovations. Not only is the mixed-finance method key to the replacement of demolished or disposed housing, but it is also a tool for the rehabilitation of existing public housing that requires significant capital improvements. All in all, the mixed-finance approach is flexible and adaptable to accommodate the varying demands and the inability of the federal appropriations process to meet the billions of dollars in backlog of capital improvement needs in the nation's public housing portfolio. The mixed-finance approach offers much upon which to build for developing new affordable housing stock, especially when considered in conjunction with the Rental Assistance Demonstration program.

Structuring Mixed-Use Developments: Financing and Real Estate Issues

13

Angela M. Christy

I. INTRODUCTION: DEFINITION OF MIXED-USE DEVELOPMENT

The first housing legislation in the early 1930s was designed primarily as a way to revive the construction industry, and it focused on the development of traditional single-family homes. As the laws changed and housing policy evolved, the focus remained on housing, jobs, and, in some cases, urban revitalization. Creativity was frequently discouraged, and many of the housing programs resulted in "cookie-cutter" housing with little consideration for transportation, commercial, and community needs. Real estate attorneys faced few challenges subdividing parcels of property since traditional, two-dimensional plats were typically used to create lots for single-family homes.

The world has changed for the real estate attorney who represents a developer, lender, investor, or governmental entity in connection with a housing development. New Urbanism and other design concepts have made the development of mixed-use projects much more common. In many ways, it is a return to the days before there was a federal housing policy, when housing was located above storefronts that could include a restaurant, the dentist, doctor, and drugstore. However, that historical development model was based on a single owner, a single financing source, and no governmental subsidies. The storefronts may now include a childcare center, convenience store, restaurant, insurance company, and coffee shop. Added considerations of sophisticated zoning and multiple financing sources, each with unique requirements, make subdividing the property much more complicated. Frequently, parcels of property and buildings must be legally separated to maximize the available financing. The determination of the correct number of parcels and the method for creating those parcels requires a thorough understanding of the developer's intended use of the property. A housing practitioner must now understand three-dimensional subdivisions and the complex interaction of multiple financing sources.

This chapter is intended to provide an overview of how the real estate and financing considerations of a mixed-use project can be structured to maximize financing sources. References in this chapter to an affordable housing practitioner can also mean an attorney who focuses on community development. The first step is to consider what is commonly included in a contemporary mixed-use development.

II. POSSIBLE COMPONENTS OF A MIXED-USE PROJECT

There are various possible components of a mixed-use project. The types of uses are virtually limitless and depend only on the creativity of the developer and its counsel. Some typical uses are:

For-Sale Housing. The units in a mixed-use development can be freestanding houses, townhouses, condominium units, or cooperative units. Affordability restrictions, including land trusts, can add to the complexity of the structure. In addition, for-sale housing may include amenities that are shared among the housing units or may be shared with adjoining rental tenants or hotel guests. These can create additional complexity.

Rental Housing. Rental housing can be market rate, affordable, or a combination of both. A single project may include a wide range of unit sizes and types and a wide range of rent levels. Inclusionary zoning requirements can impose affordability restrictions on all or a portion of a project as a condition to approving or providing benefits to a development.

1. *Market Rate.* Generally, market-rate rental housing has no construction or operating subsidy and is rented without limitation as to the income of the tenants. Market-rate housing can be combined with affordable housing in a variety of ways. Market-rate and affordable units can be combined in a single project, or luxury units could be included in a separate project with a separate entrance and amenities.

2. *Affordable.* In the most common definition of affordable housing, at least 20 percent of the units must be occupied by and affordable to persons at or below 50 percent of area median income, adjusted for family size, or at least 40 percent of the units must be occupied by and affordable to persons at or below 60 percent of area median income, adjusted for family size.[1] However, this varies based on the specific program being used to define affordability. Some income limits may be as low as 30 percent of median income[2] or as high as 120 percent of median income.[3] Some programs are based on occupancy by income eligible tenants, some on the permitted rent, and many limit tenant income and rent. Some programs may be tied to statewide rather than area incomes or have rent limits based on fair-market rents. Many programs require that the computation of affordable rent include utilities paid by the tenant. It is important to review the specific program before finalizing the structure. The permitted rent and occupancy limitations may affect

---

1. Low-Income Housing Tax Credits, I.R.C. § 42(g)(1).
2. Emergency Shelter Grant Program (ESG), 42 U.S.C. § 11302, Sec. 401.
3. Neighborhood Stabilization Program, 42 U.S.C. § 2301(b).

whether the affordable housing is included in a larger project or is physically separate and financed on its own.

Office. Small amounts of office space are typically included in a residential development for use by property management. Larger amounts of office space may be included to provide workspace for residents and to enhance the livable community concept. Live/work units are also included in a number of developments, although many zoning and planning departments have difficulty fitting this product into the traditional zoning code structure. Government officials have difficulty determining if residential or office zoning standards apply to space that is used as both. A mixed-use development may also include a larger, independent office component. Uses can be as varied as a financial institution's business office, an insurance company, a local government, or a real estate developer.

Retail. A development may include commercial retail components, such as coffee shops, office supply stores, and convenience stores, to serve the basic needs of the residents. Retail frequently extends beyond the needs of the tenants and can include major retailers, day care, and restaurants. Other developments are creating new urban or suburban centers with extensive "lifestyle" retail. Some major retailers are opening smaller-format stores that can be integrated as mixed-use urban developments.

Hotel. Hotels can be a good fit in the appropriate mixed-use development. However, hotel image, signage, and parking requirements can place demands on a project, and early decisions about layout and access may minimize conflicts. Entrances for the hotel may best be located separate and distinct from other residential uses.

Parks/Open Space. Many developments include open space and parks. Many of these amenities are included as a result of local land-use restrictions. Decisions need to be made about whether that space is publicly or privately owned. If privately owned, decisions should be made about which component of the development will own, maintain, and pay for each amenity. Some projects can include internal public spaces, including community rooms or play areas.

Transit Facilities. To create a truly livable community, projects need to address connections to transportation other than traditional parking garages. As autonomous vehicles become more common, developers need to be cognizant that parking ramps may need to be repurposed. A project may be located near mass transit and be designed to provide easy access to that facility. Some projects actually incorporate transit centers that benefit the tenants and may provide additional customers for retail business in the project. Other developments may incorporate bicycle storage and repair areas and spaces for vehicles that are available for hourly use.

III. OVERVIEW: WHAT TO CONSIDER IN STRUCTURING A MIXED-USE PROJECT

Mixed-use projects require an attorney to have a thorough knowledge of the real estate, land use, financing, and tax aspects of a project. Each aspect can impact the overall development, and the interplay of the various aspects can be quite complex. Whether the affordable housing lawyer is only representing the developer of the housing component or is representing the master developer of the entire mixed-use project, the attorney must understand the real estate, financing, operational, and construction aspects of the entire project.

First, the real estate aspects of a mixed-use project will affect the final structure of the development. The methods that can be used to subdivide the property under state and local law and the timeframes for accomplishing the subdivision may determine how many separate parcels of real estate will be included in the project and when ownership can be transferred to the various owners.

Financing considerations also play a major part in structuring how a housing project is incorporated in a mixed-use development. One type of financing may be available solely for residential property, while another source may be available only for commercial property. While in some cases it may be possible to simply allocate the funds to the various activities, other funding sources may mandate that the different projects have different legal descriptions and different ownership structures. New markets tax credits generally can't be used with low-income housing tax credits (LIHTC) in the same project, although proper structuring can result in the use of both credits in the same building.[4] Some financing sources may reduce the amount of other financing sources. For example, historic tax credits reduce the eligible basis of a project for the purpose of calculating the LIHTC allocated to the project.

Lender and investor considerations must also be taken into account when representing a housing developer. Certain investors may only be interested in residential developments, and the inclusion of a large commercial component may cause the investor to back away from a particular project. A lender may deeply discount projected parking revenue when underwriting a project. Lender underwriting criteria may result in less aggregate mortgage financing than would be available if separate mortgages were obtained for two projects.

The compatibility of uses should also be taken into account in deciding how to structure a mixed-use project. Some uses may not function well with other uses, and in those cases the physical layout of the project should make the various uses as separate as possible, including separate entrances, parking, and utilities. A hotel operator may perceive that a mixed-use residential facility does not fit with the image of a hotel, and the owner of the residential facility may not want to contribute to the upscale amenities required by a hotel franchisor. Substantial disagreements can arise as to the quality of construction materials to include in the common areas. In those circumstances, entrances may even be located on separate sides of a building to maximize the feeling of separation.

Finally, construction considerations can impact a mixed-use development. Some financing sources may require public bidding that could delay or prevent the selection of the preferred contractor for another portion of the project. Projects financed with federally insured loans must be constructed pursuant to a HUD form construction contract, a form that does not work well for other portions of the project. The ability of the contractor to file mechanic's liens against the project or individual components can also have an impact on how the project is subdivided. The creation of separate legal parcels may be necessary to prevent a contractor from filing mechanic's liens against the housing component for work done on the commercial component.

---

4. 26 C.F.R. § 1.45-1(d)(5)(ii); 26 U.S.C. § 168(e)(2)(A); 26 U.S.C. § 45D.

IV. WAYS TO DIVIDE THE REAL ESTATE

If the attorney determines that as a result of real estate ownership, financing, operational considerations, or construction the real estate must be divided into separate parcels, then the attorney must consider how to subdivide the property. The subdivision of real estate is generally governed by state and local law. Knowledge of the applicable state and local laws as well as local custom is important to be able to advise a developer about proper subdivision of the property. The following is a summary of some common subdivision techniques.

A. Traditional Plat

A traditional plat creates side-by-side lots with dedicated streets and public areas.[5] The plat subdivides the property into separate legal descriptions and is generally subject to local subdivision approval. Platting may be required to create separate parcels of land prior to other three-dimensional subdivision.

   Plats are generally governed by both state and local law. State laws set up standards for when a subdivision must be approved by a local unit of government. Local units of government enact ordinances governing the subdivision of property within that governmental unit. As a result, subdivision rules vary not only from state to state but from county to county and city to city. In addition, unwritten local procedures can also dictate methods for subdividing property. For example, some jurisdictions will recognize a subdivision based on elevation, while other jurisdictions will not permit this, even though the issue is not expressly addressed in statutes or ordinances.

B. Vertical Plat/Registered Land Survey

Vertical plats may or may not be allowed in a jurisdiction. A vertical plat splits the project on an elevation basis or may subdivide portions of floors both horizontally and vertically. The vertical plat is traditionally combined with an easement agreement that will define cross-easements for utilities and access, and address maintenance and insurance issues (similar to the terms contained in a condominium declaration).[6] Unlike the typical condominium structure, this structure does not require the establishment of a separate association.

C. Common Interest Community (CIC)

Common interest communities can include single-family detached houses, duplexes, townhomes, or other multi-unit buildings. While CICs are commonly used for creating separate units in a residential development, a CIC can also be a useful tool in subdividing a mixed-use development. In states where the Uniform Common Interest Ownership Act (UCIOA) has been adopted, local land-use requirements may not directly or indirectly prohibit the common interest community form of ownership or impose any requirement on a common interest community, upon the creation or disposition of a common interest community,

---

5. JOYCE PALOMAR, PATTON AND PALOMAR ON LAND TITLES § 119 (3d ed., Thomson West 2003).

6. Norman Geis, *Beyond the Condominium: The Uniform Common Interest Ownership Act*, 17 REAL PROP. PROB. & TR. J. 757 (1982).

or upon any part of the common interest community conversion process that it would not impose on a physically similar development under a different form of ownership.[7]

The condominium form of ownership was fairly limited until 1961, when the FHA began providing mortgage insurance for condominiums. By 1967, every state had adopted some form of condominium statute. The National Conference of Commissioners on Uniform State Laws published the Uniform Condominium Act (UCA) in 1977. Fourteen states have adopted versions of the UCA. The Uniform Planned Community Act (UPCA) was created in 1980, with the intent of bringing the same type of uniformity to laws regarding other planned communities. The UPCA has only been adopted in Pennsylvania.[8] The Model Real Estate Cooperative Act was created to deal with housing cooperatives but has only been adopted in Virginia and Pennsylvania. The broader Uniform Common Interest Ownership Act (UCIOA) was promulgated in 1982 (and amended in 1995) with the intent of superseding the UCA and the Model Real Estate Cooperative Act.

In a traditional condominium form of CIC, the unit is the airspace and improvements within the unit walls, and the common areas consist of all walls between the units, the exterior walls, the hallway and other ingress and egress areas, the roof, and the grounds. Express terms of the condominium declaration can modify the typical structure, and limited common elements can be used to allocate specific building components to a single unit or a group of units. Some state laws do not permit the formation of a condominium until the building is substantially completed,[9] which can create issues when subdivision is required to obtain separate financing for different components of a project. Except when development proceeds pursuant to Section 5-103, UCIOA requires substantial completion before a unit may be conveyed.[10] In the case of a condominium, substantial structural completion is also required before the condominium is created. As a result, in those states, it is difficult or impossible to subdivide a building for construction financing using a condominium.

A master association is an entity that coordinates the activities of several sub-associations and usually coordinates the overall site appearance and the maintenance of common amenities.[11]

In a townhouse, planned community, form of CIC, the owner typically owns the land under the dwelling together with the dwelling, and there are common areas for access, utilities, and public space. In a cooperative form of CIC, the property is owned by a corporation and the members own shares in the corporation. Cooperative shares may be characterized as real or personal property.[12]

D. Ground Lease/Air Rights Lease

Sometimes timing considerations may make it difficult to separate the residential component from the balance of the development in time for a scheduled closing. If lenders, investors, or others require that the subdivision occur before the closing, the attorney needs to think creatively about how to accomplish that subdivision. Long-term leases of land or air

---

7. Section 1-106 of the UCIOA.
8. 68 PA. C.S.A. § 51.01.
9. Section 2-101(c) of the UCIOA.
10. Section 4-120 of the UCIOA.
11. Section 2-120 of the UCIOA.
12. Section 1-105(a) of the UCIOA.

might be used to subdivide property when other methods are unavailable. It may be possible to create an airspace condominium and then amend the declaration and plat to add the completed project improvements. However, some jurisdictions may reject this approach. A 99-year lease of the air might be sufficient to subdivide the property until the condominium plat can be filed. Ground leases may avoid the requirement of government approval of a plat in those situations where plat approval is politically difficult, although this may not always be the case. However, bankruptcy and lien concerns and lender requirements may limit the use of leases to subdivide property.[13] Some lenders, including HUD, require the landlord to forfeit its fee interest in the property in the event of a foreclosure, a requirement that will not be acceptable to many landlords.

V. BALANCING MULTIPLE OBJECTIVES

After analyzing the options that are available to subdivide the property under state and local law, the attorney needs to evaluate how operational considerations impact subdivision alternatives. It may be advisable to meet with the client developing the housing component as well as the master developer, architect, and surveyor to understand the overall development. Frequently, there are conflicting considerations that must be reconciled when structuring the housing element in a mixed-use project.

A. Create Separate Legal Descriptions

First, the housing component may need to have a separate legal description. This enables the parcel to be conveyed, encumbered, and, to some extent, developed independently. While there will be various easements or restrictions that limit the independent operation of the parcels, having parcels that can be independently owned, conveyed, and encumbered is an essential element in most structures. UCIOA provides that in a condominium or planned community because "each unit that has been created together with its interest in the common elements constitutes, for all purposes, a separate parcel of real estate."[14] So UCIOA or similar statutes are frequently used to subdivide the housing component into one or more parcels. All of the units in a rental housing component may be a single unit in a CIC development, while for-sale units will typically be subdivided into multiple units within a separate residential parcel.

B. Maintain Common Areas

In addition, it is important that the attorney understand how the housing component fits into the overall plan for establishing, maintaining, and improving common areas. There are inevitably shared elements in a mixed-use development. These may be as simple as driveway and utility easements or as complicated as several stacked parcels that share elevators, stairways, utilities, green space, swimming pools, exercise rooms, dog parks, roof, walls, and other structural support. All parties will want a system for maintaining the façade of the building, the roof, and entryways. Different owners may have different standards for maintenance of the property. To complicate matters, some of the ultimate sub-developers

---

13. Jerome D. Whalen, Commercial Ground Leases (Practicing Law Inst. 2018).
14. Section 1-105 of the UCIOA.

or owners may not be identified at the time the subdivision must be completed, which mandates that some flexibility be retained in the structure.

C. Provide for an Equitable System to Share Common Expenses

To the extent that parcels share maintenance obligations, utility systems, or other items, an equitable system must be developed to allocate costs. In a simple structure, that allocation may be based on number of units, square footage, or unit cost. A more complicated structure with varied uses may require more creative allocations, and different allocations for different purposes. The permitted method of allocation may be limited by the applicable law. Under UCIOA, common expenses may be allocated equally or in any other proportion the declaration provides.[15] Some state laws may be less flexible. It is important to make sure that the allocation system does not unfairly burden the housing component.

D. Establish a System for Insurance and Reconstruction

Different components of the project may depend on other components for structural support and protection from the elements. Owners of upper floors need to know that the structural integrity of lower floors will be maintained and rebuilt in the event of a casualty. Owners on lower floors need to know that the roof will be maintained. Owners of party walls have similar concerns. The documents need to adequately address these issues for the successful development of the housing parcel.

E. Satisfy Lender and Investor Requirements for Each Portion of Development

An ownership structure that is legally feasible for the housing component may not satisfy specific lender requirements. Most lenders require a special or single-purpose entity (SPE) to own a project.[16] This means that the sole purpose of that entity must be the ownership and operation of the parcel being financed. A structure that is unfamiliar or unique may be rejected by some governmental or other lenders as "too complicated."

F. Manage Construction Issues

The attorney also needs to consider how the construction of the housing component can best be coordinated with the rest of the development. The housing developer may have a specific contractor that it wants to use for the project. Bid requirements can have an impact on the ability of a developer to use a designated contractor for specific components. Using multiple contractors on the same building can create major issues regarding coordination, insurance, and warranties. Inconsistencies in terms in construction contracts can have an adverse impact on a development. This was highlighted recently with inconsistent force majeure[17] provisions and the impact of COVID-19. In addition, the desire to use design/build, construction management, or a general contractor form of contract for different components may dictate the ownership structure. Investors or lenders may have requirements

---

15. Section 2-107 of the UCIOA.
16. HUD Notice 95-66 (July 24, 1995); Regulatory Agreement Form HUD-92466.
17. *Force majeure* is the French phrase for "superior force."

about the form of construction contract that need to be considered. For example, a project financed with a HUD-insured loan must use the HUD form of construction contract.[18]

VI. COMPATIBILITY OF LOAN/SUBSIDY SOURCES

A. HUD Programs

Various HUD programs can be used to finance affordable and mixed-income developments. The rules under these programs can determine whether and how a housing development can be integrated into a mixed-use project.

1. HUD Mortgage Insurance

The attorney needs to evaluate whether any proposed commercial space can be included in a Section 22(d) or 223(f) funded project. Section 221(d)(4) funding provides Federal Housing Authority (FHA) mortgage insurance for loans originated by private HUD-approved lenders for the construction or rehabilitation of multifamily rental or cooperative housing for moderate-income families, the elderly, and the handicapped.[19] Section 221(d)(4) generally limits commercial space to 10 percent of floor area and commercial income to 15 percent of gross income.[20] If a proposed project exceeds these percentages, the commercial space will have to be separated into a different project that is independently financed. Section 223(f) is a similar program for refinancing existing loans.[21] Section 223(f) permits up to 20 percent of a property's net rentable area to consist of commercial space or up to 20 percent of the property's income to be derived from commercial tenants.

Other financing typically used for financing affordable housing can usually be combined with a federally insured mortgage, provided that the maturity dates of secured financing extend beyond the date of the HUD lien, the loans contain certain standard HUD terms, and payments on subordinate financing are paid from available funds as approved by HUD. Note, however, that some local HUD offices are still reluctant to permit subordinate financing. Federal mortgage insurance is generally compatible with LIHTC, subject to some administrative obstacles.[22]

Under the Section 220 program, HUD provides mortgage insurance for rental housing projects located in urban renewal areas, areas with building code enforcement programs, and other areas in which local governments have undertaken certain revitalization activities.[23] Insured mortgages may be used to finance the proposed construction or rehabilitation

---

18. Form HUD-92442M, https://www.hud.gov/sites/dfiles/OCHCO/documents/92442M.pdf; *see also* HUD-92442A for a cost-plus construction contract.

19. HUD HANDBOOK 4470.1, ch. 23, https://hud.gov/program_offices/administration/hudclips /handbooks/hsgh/44701.

20. U.S. Department of Housing and Urban Development Guide to Multifamily Accelerated Processing (MAP), https://www.hud.gov/program_offices/administration/hudclips/guidebooks/hsg -GB4430.

21. HUD HANDBOOK 4566.1, https://www.hud.gov/program_offices/administration/hudclips /handbooks/hsgh/45661.

22. For an excellent discussion of combining LIHTC and HUD financing, *see* Brian Siglin, *Obstacles Encountered When Combining FHA and Other HUD Programs with Tax Credits*, 18 J. AFFORDABLE HOUS. & CMTY. DEV. L. 81 (Fall 2008).

23. HUD HANDBOOK 4555.1, 1-1, https://www.hud.gov/sites/documents/45551HSGH.PDF.

of multifamily rental housing or to finance the purchase of properties that have been rehabilitated by a local public agency. Section 220 generally permits commercial space of 20 percent of gross project area,[24] so housing projects financed with Section 220 funds may have to separate substantial commercial facilities in a separate project. The use of other financing is compatible with the Section 220 program in the same manner as described in Section 221(d) financing (discussed earlier).

2. Sections 202 and 811

Under the Section 202 program, HUD provides federal capital advances and project rental assistance for housing projects serving very low-income elderly households.[25] Initially, only private nonprofit organizations were eligible to apply to develop a Section 202 project. However, under certain circumstances, projects may now be owned by for-profit entities to permit the use of LIHTC to leverage the 202 financing. CDBG and HOME funds can be combined with 202 financing. The Section 811 program is similar to the 202 program, except that the 811 program is designed to house persons with disabilities.[26] A new Section 811 project rental assistance program was established by the Frank Melville Supportive Housing Investment Act of 2010 and is now available to provide project-based rental assistance for certain qualifying projects.

3. HOME

The HOME Investment Partnerships program provides formula-based block grants to states and local jurisdictions in need of affordable housing.[27] HOME grants fund the building, purchase, and rehabilitation of affordable housing for rent and ownership through a variety of mechanisms and can provide direct rental assistance to low-income families. Households receiving HOME assistance must meet income criteria. HOME funds may be used as a loan in combination with LIHTC and can generally be combined with other financing sources. When HOME funds are combined with other governmental assistance, the participating jurisdiction must complete a subsidy-layering review to ensure that the subsidy does not exceed the amount necessary for the financial feasibility of the project. In a mixed-use project, it is important to make sure that the HOME financing is used only for eligible project costs.

4. Rental Assistance Demonstration (RAD)

The Rental Assistance Demonstration (RAD) program allows public housing agencies (PHAs) to convert units from their original sources of HUD financing to project-based Section 8 contracts. The RAD program basically provides for the privatization of public housing while shifting to Section 8 assistance. The private owners can then leverage the Section 8 assistance to obtain private loans and investor equity, primarily from LIHTC.

---

24. MAP Guide § 3.7(B), *supra* note 20.

25. 12 U.S.C. § 1701q; 24 C.F.R. pt. 891; HUD Handbook 4571.3; *see also* Chapter 9, Section V.1.A for a detailed discussion of the 202 Program.

26. 42 U.S.C. § 8013; *see also* Chapter 9, Section VI.B for a detailed discussion of the Section 811 Program.

27. 42 U.S.C. §§ 12741–12774; *see also* Chapter 9, Section III for a detailed discussion of the HOME Program.

The owners are therefore able to address deferred maintenance issues that have caused public housing and other HUD rental stock to deteriorate. Under the RAD program, the property owner must agree to long-term renewals of the Housing Assistance Payment (HAP) contract. The RAD program also requires significant tenant protections, including provisions to prevent displacement and protect existing residents. RAD also allows rent supplement (Rent Supp), Rental Assistance Payment (RAP) Mod Rehab, and Section 202 PRAC properties to convert to project-based assistance upon contract expiration or termination.

5. Section 8

Section 8 project-based assistance is a rent subsidy program by which rental subsidies are allocated to units in specific housing projects.[28] By entering into a HAP contract with an owner, a housing authority uses federal funds to pay the landlord the difference between approved rent and 30 percent of tenant income. Families receiving assistance must meet income criteria. Section 8 is compatible with LIHTC and most other programs. The subsidies in some 202 and 811 projects (PRAC) and public housing (Section 9), while similar, are not Section 8. There are also tenant-based vouchers that eligible tenants can use to pay rent for a unit the tenant selects. The vouchers pay the difference between 30 percent of the tenant's adjusted family income and the approved rent for the unit. While helpful in providing low-income tenants housing options, vouchers do not help to finance the development of a specific project because they do not provide a reliable revenue source to support a loan.

6. CDBG

The Community Development Block Grant (CDBG) program provides grants or loans to carry out a variety of community development activities that meet one of the program's national objectives: (1) benefiting low- and moderate-income persons; (2) preventing or eliminating slums and blight; and (3) addressing conditions that present a serious and immediate threat to community health and safety.[29] Eligible activities include the acquisition of real property, relocation and demolition, and the rehabilitation of residential and nonresidential structures. In general, CDBG funds can be combined with other financing sources, including LIHTC, historic tax credits, HOME funds, FHA multifamily mortgage financing, and the 202 program. However, it is important to make sure that all necessary determinations regarding financial feasibility are obtained, that the financing is properly structured so as to not result in taxable income, and that all the competing requirements of the different financing sources can be satisfied.

B. Fannie Mae, Freddie Mac, and Ginnie Mae

There are three additional entities important in affordable housing lending. Fannie Mae and Freddie Mac are government-sponsored entities (GSEs), while Ginnie Mae is a wholly owned government corporation within HUD. Fannie Mae and Freddie Mac acquire mortgages and package them for sale. Ginnie Mae is one step removed from the lending process. It guarantees mortgage-backed securities that are backed by mortgages.

---

28. See Chapter 9, Section VI for a detailed discussion of the Section 8 Program.

29. See HUD website, http://www.hud.gov/program_offices/comm_planning/community development; see also Chapter 9, Section IV for a detailed discussion of the CDBG Program.

Fannie Mae, Freddie Mac, and Ginnie Mae are important to the development of affordable housing by making mortgage loans available for the development, acquisition, and rehabilitation of multifamily affordable housing. Both Fannie Mae and Freddie Mac acquire mortgages and package and sell them as mortgage-backed securities. Both GSEs have an affirmative obligation to facilitate the financing of affordable housing for low- and moderate-income families in a manner consistent with their overall public purposes, while maintaining a strong financial condition and a reasonable economic return.

Fannie Mae has a wide variety of loan programs. Perhaps the most common Fannie Mae program is the Delegated Underwriting and Servicing (DUS) program. Under the DUS program, Fannie works with certain approved lenders to make multifamily loans. The lenders underwrite and make the loans to developers and the DUS lenders share in the risk of default on the loans.

Freddie Mac also has a wide variety of loan programs. The basic Freddie Mac loan products include fixed rate, floating (two years), and fixed (seven years) loans with amortization up to 30 years. Another Freddie Mac program is designed for projects supported by Section 8 assistance. The borrower must have experience owning Section 8 properties. The terms vary based on whether the loan is conventional or tax-exempt bond financing.

Ginnie Mae (the "Governmental National Mortgage Association") is a government agency rather than a GSE.[30] Ginnie Mae guarantees the timely payment of mortgage bonds that include federally insured or guaranteed loans. Ginnie Mae does not make mortgage loans or buy and sell mortgages. A Ginnie Mae-approved lender makes mortgages and sells mortgages. Ginnie Mae only guarantees mortgage-backed securities (MBS) that have underlying mortgages insured by FHA, VA, RHS, or the Office of Public and Indian Housing. The Ginnie Mae guarantee enables the mortgage lenders to obtain a better price for the offerings in the capital markets.

C. Rural Housing Development

The Section 515 Rural Rental Housing Program provides loans for the construction or acquisition and rehabilitation of housing for elderly persons, persons with handicaps, and other low- and moderate-income individuals in rural areas.[31] While the 515 Program may be combined with other financing, it is important to review the special requirements of the 515 Program to determine that the programs will work together. For example, for a 515 loan, the borrower's limited partnership agreement must require that the general partners maintain a minimum 5 percent financial interest in the sale or refinancing proceeds of the partnership.[32] This may create some issues for investors, particularly in historic credit transactions, but the issues can be resolved with careful drafting.

D. Tax Increment Financing

Tax Increment Financing (TIF) is a tool that allows governmental entities to designate tax revenues from increases in a property's assessed value resulting from development within a designated TIF district to subsidize affordable housing or other specified development. TIF

---

30. 12 U.S.C. § 1716, 24 C.F.R. §§ 320–350.11.
31. https://rd.usda.gov/programs-services/multi-family-housing-direct-loans.
32. RURAL DEVELOPMENT HANDBOOK HB-1-3565, https://rd.usda.gov/files/HB-1-3565.pdf.

originated in the 1950s as an urban renewal strategy and is now one of the most common economic development tools in the country. TIF is a method of capturing the incremental taxes generated by a development project and using the increment to help the project. The rules vary across the 49 states and District of Columbia where it is authorized. There is no TIF statute in Arizona. The designation of a TIF district usually requires a finding that an area is blighted or undeveloped and that development would not take place "but for" the tax increment. Of the 50 jurisdictions (49 states and D.C.), 32 require a finding of blight. All 50 jurisdictions permit payment of increment from property taxes, but sales tax revenues are also available in 16 states. The maximum TIF district ranges from 19 years to 50 years. Many states distinguish the length of a TIF district based on the type of development. Some others determine the length of the district based on the approval of the various taxing authorities.

E. Tax-Exempt Bond Financing

There are several types of tax-exempt bond financing, including general obligation bonds, 501(c)(3) bonds, and private activity housing revenue bonds.[33] The various bond programs have different requirements. 501(c)(3) bond financing limits ownership to tax-exempt entities.[34] Housing revenue bonds impose occupancy requirements for low-income persons.[35] Obviously, ownership requirements affect the ability to combine bond financing with other funding sources.

Among the categories of exempt facilities that can be financed with tax-exempt private activity bonds are "qualified residential rental projects."[36] Qualified residential rental projects are eligible by inclusion of occupancy restrictions pursuant to which either 40 percent of residential units are required to be occupied by tenants earning not more than 60 percent of area median income, as established under HUD guidelines (the 40/60 test), or 20 percent of units are required to be continuously occupied by tenants earning not more than 50 percent of area median income.[37] There are a limited amount of these bonds available in each state, and a project must receive an allocation.[38] Private-activity bonds can typically be combined with other financing sources, such as LIHTCs and HTCs, although tax-exempt bonds are characterized as federally subsidized financing and result in a project only being eligible for the 4 percent low-income housing tax credit.[39]

501(c)(3) bonds are available to finance projects owned by charitable tax-exempt organizations whose mission is to provide housing for the poor and distressed, combating community deterioration, eliminating discrimination, lessening neighborhood dislocation,

---

33. See Chapter 9, Section V, and Chapter 10, Section II for a more detailed discussion of bond financing.
34. I.R.C. § 145.
35. *Id.* § 142(d).
36. *Id.*; Maguire, *Private Activity Bonds: An Introduction*, CRS Report for Congress (June 9, 2006), https://www.everycrsreport.com/files/20060609_RL31457_46d1ea6d5c76e77a5d6716e6f48 4ca24c7804a92.pdf
37. I.R.C. § 142(d).
38. *Id.* § 142(a).
39. *Id.* § 42(i)(2).

relieving distress of the elderly or handicapped, or lessening burdens of government.[40] The requirement that the project be owned by a 501(c)(3) entity precludes using 501(c)(3) bonds with LIHTC. At least 95 percent of the net proceeds of the issue must be spent on activities related to the exempt purpose of the 501(c)(3) group for which the bonds were issued. The "safe harbor" for a charitable corporation to qualify for the benefits of 501(c)(3) bonds for housing requires that (1) at least 75 percent of the units are made available to individuals whose incomes do not exceed 80 percent of the area median income, adjusted for family size, and (2) either (a) at least 20 percent of the units are occupied by individuals whose incomes do not exceed 50 percent of the area median income, adjusted for family size, or (b) 40 percent of the units are occupied by individuals whose incomes do not exceed 120 percent of 50 percent of the area median income, adjusted for family size.[41] Up to 25 percent of the units may be occupied by individuals whose incomes exceed these limits at market-rate rents. When using 501(c)(3) bonds, the commercial component must usually be a separate project that is financed from a source other than the 501(c)(3) bonds.

F. Conventional Financing

A housing lawyer should note that combining conventional financing with multiple subsidized sources can be challenging. Conventional lenders sometimes have trouble understanding and accepting the restrictions that accompany governmental financing, and a restrictive covenant that must have priority over a private first mortgage loan may be a deal breaker. At a minimum, additional time should be allowed to negotiate a transaction where the conventional lender does not have experience with the specific governmental program being used for the additional financing.

G. State and Local Programs

Many state and local governmental entities have programs to assist affordable housing and community development projects. While many of these programs are funded with federal sources (HOME, CDBG, etc.), some states also have programs that are sourced from state appropriations. These programs are diverse, and a careful reading of the enabling legislation or ordinance and guidelines is essential to determine whether the program is compatible with the proposed project.

VII. COMPATIBILITY OF CREDIT/TAX INCENTIVES PROGRAMS

A. Low Income Housing Tax Credit (LIHTC)

The LIHTC is a credit against federal income tax liability for certain qualified low-income housing projects.[42] There are various tax and practical aspects that an attorney must consider when the housing component in a mixed-use development is claiming LIHTC.

Commercial portions of development are generally not eligible for the LIHTC. There are special rules that permit the inclusion of certain community service facilities in eligible

---

40. *See* IRS website http://www.irs.gov/pub/irs-tege/teb_phase_1_course_11204_-10module_i .pdf.

41. Rev. Proc. 96-32, 1996-1 C.B. 717.

42. See Chapter 9, Section II for a detailed discussion of the LIHTC.

basis when the project is located in a qualified census tract. Although commercial components do not make a project ineligible for LIHTC, the commercial portion is excluded from the tax credit calculation. Investors and lenders may not like the inclusion of a commercial component in the development. Commercial components may be perceived as a significant business risk, with greater fluctuations in potential income and loss. Additional depreciation generated by the commercial portion of the project and extended depreciation schedules if the property is classified as commercial can also create adverse tax consequences for the investor. As a result, the commercial portion of the project may have to be master-leased to the developer or separated into a distinct, separately financed parcel.

Practitioners also need to investigate if there is a state low-income-housing tax credit. These can provide a significant benefit to a housing project.

B. Historic Rehabilitation Tax Credits

Prior to 2018, there were two federal credits available for qualified rehabilitation of certain historic and older buildings. While Section 47 of the Internal Revenue Code still provides for a 20 percent tax credit for the certified rehabilitation of certified historic structures, the 10 percent tax credit for the rehabilitation of certain non-historic buildings built before 1936 was eliminated. To qualify for the 20 percent credit, a building must be listed on the National Register of Historic Places or be listed as a contributing building in a historic district certified by the Secretary of the Interior. The credit is based on the amount spent on rehabilitation of the existing building and does not include costs spent on expanding the footprint of a building.[43] Prior to 2018, the 20 percent credit was taken at the time a building was placed in service. Now, the historic tax credit is determined when the building is placed in service but is claimed 4 percent each year for five years. In general, the rehabilitation expenditures must be incurred within a 24-month period, but certain phased rehabilitation can be completed over a 60-month period. Counsel for a housing developer needs to understand when the credit is available for a housing component in a mixed-use project.

The historic credit is not generally available for the for-sale units in a project. A percentage of the historic tax credit must be recaptured if the project is sold within five years of when the project is placed in service. Consequently, the for-sale units would be subject to immediate recapture of the credit. Ownership or use of the project by tax-exempt entities also may create a problem. Not more than 35 percent of the property may be leased pursuant to disqualified leases to tax-exempt entities. For-sale units and tax-exempt uses may have to be included in a separate component of the project. Subordinate financing is generally also compatible with a historic tax credit project, although care must be given to structure the financing so that grants do not reduce basis.

The historic credit may be combined with the low-income housing tax credit, but the amount of the historic credit usually reduces the eligible basis in determining the amount of the low-income credit. Historic credits can also be combined with new markets tax credits and with energy credits.[44]

Some states also have state historic credits. The structure of these credits varies greatly from state to state. Some programs provide that the credit can only be allocated to partners

---

43. Treas. Reg. § 1.47-7(a) through (f).
44. I.R.S. Notice 2002-64, 2002-41 C.B. 690.

or members in accordance with the allocation of profits or losses; other statutes permit the state credits to be transferred to non-partners independent of any partnership allocations. It is important to structure these credits to avoid income allocation or basis reduction that could adversely impact the project.

C. New Market Tax Credit

The New Market Tax Credit Program (NMTC) is designed to encourage investment in low-income communities. It is administered by a branch of the Treasury Department called the Community Development Financial Institutions Fund (the CDFI Fund), although the Internal Revenue Service also has a role in enforcing the NMTC. The NMTC gives taxpayers a tax credit for making Qualified Equity Investments (QEI) in certain eligible entities known as Qualified Community Development Entities (CDEs).

The NMTC is generally not compatible with residential development because, under the program, rental real estate cannot be used substantially for residential purposes.[45] Residential rental real estate is property that derives 80 percent or more of its income from residential tenants. However, it may be possible to use the NMTC program in connection with for-sale construction financing or residential developments that derive less than 80 percent of their income from residential tenants. On a practical basis, note that most investors will require a substantial buffer between the 80 percent limit and the projected income. As a result, the NMTC is generally not compatible with LIHTC projects unless there is a condominium or other subdivision used to separate the projects. NMTC can also be a very effective tool for developing homeless shelters, which are not classified as residential housing.

The NMTC can be used for small business lending, development of inner-city commercial and industrial space, arts facilities, development of space for childcare centers, charter schools, theaters, and a wide range of other projects. The NMTC may be effectively combined with the historic rehabilitation tax credits, HUD loans, tax increment financing, and other resources.

D. Energy Credits

A housing attorney should also be aware of when energy credits can be used to assist with the financing of the housing component or the entire mixed-use development. A federal tax credit may be available for qualified solar projects.[46] Congress continues to modify the types of renewable energy credits, so it is important to research what is currently available. Developers should also explore if there are any state incentives for the development of affordable housing with alternative energy sources. The energy credit is available for most solar power systems (such as photovoltaics or solar thermal systems; passive solar systems are not allowed), fuel cells, and small wind turbines. The solar energy facility must generate electricity, heating, cooling, hot water, or fiber-optic lighting (but cannot be used for heating swimming pools). Sale of the energy to a third party is not required.

Another developing structure is the use of solar farms in connection with developments. Some state legislatures have adopted statutes that help to facilitate the development of community solar facilities. In addition, some utility companies have developed

---

45. I.R.S. Notice 2002-64, 2002-41 C.B. 690.
46. I.R.C. § 48.

mechanisms to give customers credit when they subscribe to receive energy from a community solar garden. Some developers around the country are using community solar gardens to substantially reduce the utility bills of their tenants.

A property can take advantage of energy credits and LIHTC, but to qualify for both, the tenants cannot be charged for the utilities. In addition, the energy credit is not available for any portion of the basis of any property that is attributable to qualified rehabilitation credits for the historic tax credit.[47]

VIII. LEASE CONSIDERATIONS

As noted earlier, leases can sometimes be used to effectively separate the housing component of a mixed-use development from the commercial component. Where all or a portion of the development is subject to a master lease, there are some special issues that must be addressed.

It is important that the title insurer be provided copies of the lease so that the insurer can provide the appropriate policy for the lessee and the lessee's lender. The ALTA 13.06 (Owners) and 13.1-06 (Lenders) Leasehold Endorsements are typically used.

Frequently, the lease must also be structured so that it is financeable.[48] The lender will generally need notice and cure rights under the lease so that it can protect its interests. Negotiating the relative rights and responsibilities of the landlord and lender can be difficult and time-consuming.

The lease must be structured to the fullest extent possible to avoid the possibility that a landlord in bankruptcy could sell the property free and clear of a lease.[49] Proper drafting can minimize these concerns but may not eliminate them.

Another concern is that separating the property with leases may not adequately protect the parcels from mechanic's liens related to the other parcels. In many states, mechanic's liens apply to the fee interest of the landlord. The construction contract and lease must be carefully drafted to minimize the risk. The contractor should agree that to the extent that it has been paid on a project, it will indemnify the owner against liens filed by subcontractors on the project. The risk of mechanic's liens can also be minimized by having a coordinated disbursement mechanism for construction funds, assurances that the components are all adequately funded, and procedures for funding change orders. This will not eliminate the risk but will provide practical protection to minimize the risk of liens.

IX. CONSTRUCTION ISSUES

A. Construction Method

One important issue to be considered by the attorney for the housing developer is the structure of the construction contract.[50] Options include use of a single general contractor, the

---

47. *Id.* § 48(2)(B).

48. Jerome D. Whalen, Commercial Ground Leases (3d ed., PLI, 2018).

49. Precision Indus., Inc. v. Qualitech Steel SBQ, 327 F.3d 537 (7th Cir. 2003).

50. *See* www.aia.org for a description of the available documents. Even if you do not intend to use the AIA series of documents, the description of the forms can be helpful in understanding the various options.

use of a construction manager with multiple prime contractors, or design/build.[51] There can be some tension if the housing developer wants to or is required to use one method and the master developer wants to use another.

1. Single General Contract

There are three ways to structure a single prime contract. The first is the turnkey approach, where one owner builds the entire project and transfers components upon completion. A second option is to have one owner enter into a construction contract with the contractor and partially assign the construction contract to the other owner. The third alternative is for each owner to have a separate contract with integration provisions in each contract. The integration provisions need to address termination of the contracts, mechanics liens, change orders that impact common elements, and allocation of costs. It is essential that the separate contracts provide for completion of the entire project.

2. Construction Management

Another option is to engage a single construction manager with multiple prime contractors. The owners use the same construction manager but can select separate prime contractors. While there can still be conflicts between the separate contracts, a single construction manager can be helpful in coordinating the overall construction of the development.

3. Design/Build

A design/build arrangement involves selecting a single entity for both the design and construction of the project. This can be particularly challenging in a mixed-use project, since the developer of an upper floor needs some certainty as to the design of lower floors and the developer of lower floors may need to have knowledge of the upper floor mechanical elements. In addition, lenders and investors may not accept a design/build structure. Consequently, design/build is not frequently used for affordable housing projects.

B. Construction Form

Lender and governmental requirements for the housing component can impact the structure of the transaction. If different components have different contract requirements, the single contract with assignment model may not work, although it may be possible to amend the construction contract for a portion of the project after assignment to accommodate lender or investor requirements.

1. American Institute of Architects

The AIA forms are the most common forms and can be used in most situations. Some of the more common forms used are the A101, which provides for a fixed price, the A102, which provides for a contract fee based on costs with a guaranteed maximum price. The AIA A201 (General Conditions), which is incorporated in the AIA101 and 102, is also an important component of the contract since it sets out the rights and responsibilities of the owner, contractor, and architect.

---

51. Harvey Berman, *Understanding Project Delivery Methods*, 15 Prac. Real Estate Law. (Mar. 1999).

2. HUD Contract

Any project involving a HUD-insured multifamily loan will require use of the HUD form construction contract.[52] The contract includes fixed price and cost plus options. The HUD contract incorporates the AIA A201 General Conditions.

C. Integration

The attorney needs to make sure that the design and construction contracts provide owners assurance that HVAC, plumbing, and other systems in separate components of the mixed-use development will work together. The attorney will need to determine that the contractor cannot raise defects in the commercial or other components as a defense to warranties provided on the housing component. Finally, the housing developer needs assurance that it can pursue all necessary warranty claims. The owner of the housing component may need to pursue a warranty claim for a leaky roof even if the roof was included in the commercial construction contract.

D. Timing

Owners need to make sure that delays in the commercial component caused by the contractor are not a force majeure event for the housing component. The construction schedule must be maintained for the entire project.

A force majeure clause allocates the risk of inability to perform a contractual obligation due to unforeseen circumstances. The time for performance under a contract may be extended based on the language in a force majeure clause. A typical force majeure clause lists specific events that trigger extension of the time for performance under the contract or other remedies. Some only list specific events like war, extreme weather, or supply shortages. Other force majeure clauses have broader language like "any event beyond the reasonable control of the parties" or "acts of God." The exact language of the force majeure clause is important in determining the available remedies. Note that courts generally interpret force majeure clauses narrowly, and adverse changes in the economy have generally not been found to trigger force majeure.

E. Cost

Another challenge can be determining cost of various elements of the project. The attorney for the housing developer needs to make sure that the documents include a reasonable method for allocating change orders and construction change directives between the housing component and other components of the development.

F. Termination

Multiple owners need to determine when and how the construction contract can be terminated. What happens if the contractor is doing a superb job on one portion of the project and ignores or is incompetent on another component? This needs to be addressed in the documents.

---

52. Form HUD 92442M, hud.gov/sites/documents/92442M.pdf.

X. OPERATIONAL CONSIDERATIONS

A. General

The attorney for the housing developer must also understand how the project will operate. Proposed hours of operation, signage requirements, traffic patterns, noise and odor emissions, and utility needs must be evaluated. The attorney may develop a subdivision plan that works with respect to the financing and subdivision laws but will be inefficient or unacceptable to lenders or investors. While upper-end residential condominium purchasers may appreciate having a restaurant down the street, the persistent odor of food emanating from the first floor of the building may impair marketability of residential units.

Utility needs must also be understood to create the proper subdivision. Separate metering of utilities to different owners is preferred whenever possible. It will eliminate numerous potential disputes in the future. If utilities cannot be sub-metered, some consideration should be given by the attorney for the housing developer to compatibility of uses. Any shared use must consider proposed hours of operation, different temperature and humidity requirements, and disproportionate use of utilities by certain activities.

Government restrictions also impact how a housing component can be integrated in a mixed-use development. Zoning and fire code requirements can be triggered by the creation of separate lots. There may be additional firewalls, egress points, and window requirements that result from the subdivision of a building into separate parcels, and this can impact the construction cost of the housing components. It is important that the subdivision does not trigger additional setback requirements, window limitations, or fire suppression systems requirements. Any additional requirements can sometimes be addressed through a PUD or variances, but it is important to be aware of additional impositions and to allow time to address them appropriately.

B. Parking

Balancing the parking needs of the housing component with the other uses may be one of the greatest challenges in a mixed-use development. The inclusion of housing and commercial components in a single project may work to a development's advantage if the zoning rules permit shared parking for different uses. Some governmental entities may permit a single space to be shared for zoning purposes between a use with high daytime requirements and a use with primarily evening requirements. Some governmental bodies are also allowing less parking for mixed-use developments that include alternative transportation methods (bus shelters, transportation centers, bike racks or trails) in the development.

Dealing with the ownership and allocation of parking can also be a major challenge in structuring a development. The parking may be owned by the housing developer, the master developer, or another entity, and rights for parking may be granted to various components of the project through easements or leases. Another option is to subdivide the parking along with the subdivision of the other portions of the project. This can affect the physical configuration of the project. To do this, the attorney needs to be involved early in the process so that architectural plans are not finalized in a less than optimal configuration.

If the parking is free, it needs to be connected to a portion of the project with sufficient cash flow to support the additional mortgage principal or a subsidy source to construct the parking. If the parking generates income, the developer must evaluate the financing that will be supported by the parking income stream and then determine which portion of the project would work best economically when combined with the parking. However, it is important to remember that if the housing developer charges for parking, it will not be included in eligible basis for purposes of the LIHTC.

C. Property Tax

A housing attorney must also have a thorough understanding of the property tax laws when deciding whether to combine or separate elements. Combining a tax-exempt housing development with taxable commercial property may result in the entire project being taxable and, consequently, a substantially increase in the overall real estate taxes payable for the housing project. Combining uses may also result in the loss of favorable tax classification for a portion of the project. For example, if a favorable tax treatment is available for affordable housing, the addition of commercial space could disqualify the housing portion from the favorable tax treatment. Sometimes these issues can only be resolved by understanding the statute and meeting with the taxing authorities to review what may be a matter of first impression.

D. Insurance Issues

1. Builders Risk Coverage

Builders risk provides coverage for materials, supplies, and equipment used in construction. It is important to make sure that the coverage is provided through a single policy or that the various policies are coordinated to avoid gaps or exclusions from coverage.

2. Property

Property insurance covers repairs or replacement of building and contents from damage caused by a range of perils (fire, wind, theft, etc.). The attorney for the housing developer needs to make sure that the policy or policies provide sufficient, coordinated coverage. This can be accomplished by a single policy obtained by a condominium association. If there are separate policies, each owner needs to make sure that there is sufficient coverage to rebuild essential elements of the project and that all lender and investor requirements are satisfied. Owners may consider obtaining a single policy to insure the shell and shared components with separate policies for interior improvements. It is crucial that the attorney understand the requirements of the lenders and investors to structure the insurance coverage on a complicated mixed-use project, as failure to address insurance issues early can delay a closing.

3. Liability

Liability insurance is designed to protect against third-party bodily injury or property damage. This can present particular issues where one or more of the owners, such as a municipality, is self-insured. Again, counsel for the housing developer needs to make sure that the documents have appropriate provisions for each party to carry adequate liability insurance.

XI. CONCLUSION: CHOOSING THE APPROPRIATE STRUCTURE

After gathering all of the facts and evaluating possible legal structures, the attorney must work with the developer, the master developer, the architect, the surveyor, the lenders, and any investor to finalize the structure.

The "ultimate" real estate structure may be too complicated to be feasible. Social policy may favor having affordable units established as separate parcels, subject to a land trust and scattered throughout a development. Financing realities may require that the affordable units be included in a single contiguous development.

The attorney needs to be particularly concerned about timing issues. Subdivisions can require long lead times, and it is important to make sure that any necessary subdivision can be completed before the closing. If state law prohibits subdivision by a CIC plat before project completion, an alternative must be explored and structured early in the development process. An attorney's failure to understand and plan for the subdivision requirements of the housing component in a mixed-use project can result in loss of time-sensitive funding and make the project impossible to complete.

It seems inevitable that many housing projects will include commercial facilities or will be included as part of a master development. This trend will require the housing and community development lawyer to have a greater understanding of how the various pieces fit together and to coordinate those complex requirements to help the client maximize the funds available to complete the housing development.

After Housing Is Built

Monitoring and Enforcement in Affordable Housing

14

Rebecca Simon

I. INTRODUCTION

Overseeing the nation's affordable housing remains a critical and complex task for the federal government agencies entrusted with providing the programs and policies to develop, fund, and preserve affordable housing for low-income families and individuals. The Department of Housing and Urban Development (HUD) and the Internal Revenue Service (IRS) each have an arsenal of enforcement tools at their disposal and depend on state and local government agencies to assist in enforcing the regulatory framework of affordable housing programs.

Section I of this chapter describes how HUD and the IRS monitor and enforce the regulatory agreements and subsidy contracts that shape the enforcement framework of affordable housing programs. Developers, owners, managers, and other affordable housing participants must be aware of the enforcement mechanisms contained in the regulatory agreements and subsidy contracts, as well as the federal statutes and regulations referenced within those agreements.

Section II offers an overview of monitoring and enforcement at properties insured, subsidized, or directly funded by HUD, including administrative, civil, and criminal remedies available to HUD and its partners. Section III provides a synopsis of monitoring and enforcement by the IRS at properties benefiting from Low-Income Housing Tax Credits (LIHTC), including the delineation of responsibilities between the IRS and the states in monitoring these properties and enforcing regulatory agreements with the owners.

II. MONITORING AND ENFORCEMENT OF HUD MULTIFAMILY PROPERTIES

A. Introduction to HUD Monitoring and Enforcement

The significant variations amongst HUD programs, from insurance to block grants to rental assistance, results in a wide variety of monitoring tools and enforcement mechanisms available to different programs. Understanding the various offices involved in HUD monitoring and enforcement is critical to successful participation.

1. Enforcement by the Departmental Enforcement Center

The Departmental Enforcement Center (DEC), created in 1998, has the stated goal of ensuring that federally funded or insured programs are implemented according to program guidelines and regulations, as well as that program funds are utilized in the most efficient and effective manner possible by conducting internal and external reviews, taking suspension and debarment actions, and pursuing civil money penalties or double damages where there have been program violations.[1] The DEC and the Real Estate Assessment Center (REAC) were created at the same time as part of a plan under then-Secretary Andrew Cuomo to consolidate and reform HUD's oversight and enforcement functions.[2]

The DEC receives referrals from a variety of HUD offices, including the Office of Public and Indian Housing (PIH), the Office of Community Planning and Development (CPD), and the Office of Multifamily Housing (Multifamily).[3] The Government Accountability Office (GAO) did a review of referrals to the DEC in October 2018, focusing on Multifamily, PIH, and CPD. The GAO found that only Multifamily makes referrals to the DEC based on defined thresholds, while PIH and CPD have broad guidelines for referrals but not specific thresholds. For example, multifamily properties are referred to the DEC after a REAC physical inspection resulting in a score of less than 30, a failure to submit audited financial statements within 60 days of the end of the owner's fiscal year, or a finding of unauthorized use of project funds above a certain threshold by REAC's automated compliance review.[4]

The DEC staff sit in HUD Headquarters in Washington, D.C., and in field offices throughout the country. Upon receipt of a referral, the DEC staff perform their own review of the alleged misconduct and make a determination in regard to whether enforcement action is warranted. The DEC may then take such enforcement action, including assessment of civil money penalties (CMPs) or debarment or suspension of the participant, as more fully described in Section B.

---

1. *DEC Frequently Asked Questions*, U U.S. Dep't of Hous. & Urban Dev., https://www.hud.gov/program_offices/enforcement/faq (last visited June 1, 2021).

2. *HUD 2020 Management Reform Plan: The Six Major Reforms*, U.S. Dep't of Hous. & Urban Dev., https://archives.hud.gov/reports/2020/mrsixmaj.cfm (last visited June 1, 2021).

3. *Better Guidance and Performance Measures Would Help Strengthen Enforcement Efforts*, U.S. Gen. Accounting Office, GAO-19-38, (2018).

4. *Id.*

2. Enforcement and Affirmative Litigation by the Office of Program Enforcement

The Office of Program Enforcement (OPE) is an office within the Office of General Counsel (OGC) at HUD. In addition to providing legal services to the DEC, OPE files affirmative litigation and administrative actions against participants on behalf of HUD program offices.[5] OPE supports Multifamily, PIH, and CPD, as well as providing counsel to the Mortgagee Review Board (MRB), which is authorized to impose CMPs and other administrative actions against Federal Housing Administration (FHA)-approved lenders or mortgagees.[6] OPE also works closely with the Department of Justice (DOJ) in False Claims litigation and Qui Tam actions. OPE pursues penalties or monetary damages against participants under the False Claims Act, Program Fraud Civil Remedies Act (PFCRA), and HUD's CMPs authority, as described in more detail in Section C.

3. Real Estate Assessment Center Monitoring

HUD established REAC in the late 1990s to perform physical condition inspections of all Section 8 housing, public housing, HUD-insured multifamily housing, and other HUD-assisted housing using defined uniform physical condition standards to ensure that the housing in these programs is decent, safe, sanitary, and in good repair.[7] REAC's stated mission is to "[p]rovide our customers with independent, actionable assessments that advance risk-informed decisions about the condition of the nation's affordable housing portfolio."[8] REAC performs inspections of properties using a 3-2-1 timing system in which properties in the best condition are inspected every three years and properties in the worst condition are inspected annually.[9] HUD provides owners with 14-day notice of a REAC physical inspection—a policy implemented in February 2019.[10] In recent years, HUD released significant changes to the REAC inspection process, including expanded protocols under REAC's industry standard rules,[11] changes to owner notification timing, and updates to the consequences of receiving a failing REAC physical inspection score.[12]

---

5. *About OGC*, U.S. DEP'T OF HOUS. & URBAN DEV., https://www.hud.gov/program_offices /general_counsel/aboutogc (last visited June 1, 2021).

6. *Id.*

7. *About REAC*, U.S. DEP'T OF HOUS. & URBAN DEV., https://www.hud.gov/program_offices /public_indian_housing/reac/aboutreac (last visited June 1, 2021).

8. *Id.*

9. Properties that receive a score of 90–100 are inspected every three years. Properties that receive a score of 80–89 are inspected every two years. Properties that receive a score of less than 80 are inspected annually. Uniform Physical Condition Standards and Physical Inspection Requirements for Certain HUD Housing; Administrative Process for Assessment of Insured and Assisted Properties; Final Rule, 81 Fed. Reg. 77,233 (Dec. 8, 2000).

10. *See* U.S. DEP'T OF HOUS. & URBAN DEV., NOTICE PIH 2019-02; the COVID-19 pandemic caused REAC to suspend inspections with the exception of emergency situations. REAC resumed operations in June 2021 with expended notice periods of 28 days and prioritization of high-risk properties. Nathaniel S. Cushman, *REAC Inspections Resuming in Earnest*, NIXON PEABODY (May 6, 2021), https://www.nixonpeabody.com/en/ideas/blog/affordable-housing/2021/05/06 /reac-inspections-resuming-in-earnest?search=affordable-housing.

11. *See* U.S. DEP'T OF HOUS. & URBAN DEV., PIH INSPECTOR NOTICE 2016-03 (2016).

12. *See* U.S. DEP'T OF HOUS. & URBAN DEV., NOTICE PIH 2019-02; H-2019-04 (2019); *New HUD Inspection Guidance and New Penalties*, NIXON PEABODY (Nov. 1, 2018), https://www

REAC inspectors perform physical inspections based on a site visit that includes entering a sample of units and inspecting the building systems, building exterior, common areas, and site.[13] If the REAC inspector identifies any exigent health and safety deficiencies (EH&S) at the inspection, the owner will be alerted to these deficiencies immediately and must address and certify that all EH&S deficiencies have been corrected within three days.[14] For all other deficiencies, REAC issues a report to the owner in the weeks after the inspection that allocates an overall score on a 100-point system and identifies all deficiencies observed by the inspector.[15] Upon receipt of the inspection report, an owner is given the opportunity to review and appeal the score should the owner disagree with the results.[16] Appeals can be based on technical reviews if the owner believes an "objectively verifiable and material error occurred," or a database adjustment if the owner believes circumstances existed that affected the inspection of the property, including conditions beyond the owner's control and modernization work in progress.[17]

Properties receiving a score of 59 or less are considered failing.[18] HUD is statutorily required to issue a notice to the owner after a failed inspection and develop a "Compliance, Disposition, and Enforcement Plan" within 60 days of the inspection report release date, which generally includes a required 100 percent inspection of the project to identify all physical deficiencies and a certification that all physical deficiencies have been addressed.[19] REAC will re-inspect failing properties soon after the allocated time for the owner to address all physical deficiencies. If the owner does not comply with HUD's notice or if HUD causes a second REAC and the property's score is still failing, HUD can be expected to institute administrative sanctions, as described more thoroughly later in this chapter, including imposing civil money penalties or abating the subsidy contract.[20]

REAC uses a standardized electronic reporting system to collect data and assess property conditions. REAC creates a snapshot in time and may not always be fully reflective of property condition. As a result, HUD has created the National Standards for the Inspection of Real Estate (NSPIRE) to eventually replace REAC.[21] NSPIRE makes structural

---

.nixonpeabody.com/en/ideas/blog/affordable-housing/2018/11/01/new-hud-inspection-guidance-and-new-penalties?keyword=REAC; Richard M. Price & Rebecca Simon, *HUD Announces Major Changes to Physical Inspection Protocol*, NIXON PEABODY (Feb. 26, 2019), https://www.nixonpeabody.com/en/ideas/blog/affordable-housing/2019/02/26/hud-announces-major-changes-to-physical-inspection-protocol?keyword=zero.

13. *REAC Compilation Bulletin: Rapid 4.0 Version* 3, U.S. DEP'T OF HOUS. & URBAN DEV. 4 (2017), https://www.hud.gov/sites/dfiles/PIH/documents/newpasscb.pdf.

14. *Certification of Exigent Health and Safety*, U.S. DEP'T OF HOUS. & URBAN DEV., https://www.hud.gov/sites/documents/93332_orcf.doc (last visited June 1, 2021).

15. *Supra* note 13 at 8–9.

16. *Technical Reviews and Database Adjustments*, U.S. DEP'T OF HOUS. & URBAN DEV., https://www.hud.gov/program_offices/public_indian_housing/reac/products/pass/pass_guideandrule/trda (last visited June 1, 2021).

17. *Id.*

18. *See* U.S. DEP'T OF HOUS. & URBAN DEV., NOTICE H 2018-08 (2018).

19. *Id.* at 4.

20. *Id.* at 7.

21. *National Standards for Physical Inspection of Real Estate,* U.S. DEP'T OF HOUS. & URBAN DEV., https://www.hud.gov/program_offices/public_indian_housing/reac/nspire (last visited June 1, 2021).

inspection changes, such as requiring more-active owner participation and inspection and incorporating changes including scoring exterior and common areas separately from interior areas.[22]

The HUD REAC program office also monitors audit compliance, discussed later. Public housing authorities that administer housing choice vouchers also must meet Section Eight Management Assessment Program (SEMAP) standards.[23] SEMAP is considered an assessment and monitoring program, but poor results can trigger other enforcement, as described in this chapter.

4. Tracking Participation through the 2530 Previous Participation System

HUD's previous participation review system, sometimes referred to by the name of the Processing Form Number 2530, tracks and reports on the previous performance of applicants seeking to participate in HUD programs.[24] The forms and procedures relate back decades, with the most recent major amendment of the regulations occurring in October 2016.[25] Participants seeking to obtain HUD approval to participate in HUD multifamily programs (i.e., Section 8, Section 202 loans, FHA insurance) must submit a previous participation certification using the 2530 form or through the Active Partners Performance System (APPS). Both processes require a list of all of the previous HUD Multifamily and U.S. Department of Agriculture (USDA) Rural Development projects that the participant is affiliated with, as well as identifying information about the participant and the new participation.[26] The HUD staff member or account executive processing the application for new participation will review the participation report to determine whether the participant has any negative previous participation.

HUD uses a flagging system to assess the risk associated with a participant. A flag is placed on a participant in APPS when there is a risk concern, such as a violation or deficiency associated with that participant in the course of their involvement with a HUD

---

22. Economic Growth Regulatory Relief and Consumer Protection Act: Implementation of National Standards for the Physical Inspection of Real Estate (NSPIRE), 86 Fed. Reg. 2582 (proposed Jan. 13, 2021).

23. *Section Eight Management Assessment Program,* U.S. Dep't of Hous. & Urban Dev., https://www.hud.gov/program_offices/public_indian_housing/programs/hcv/semap (last visited June 1, 2021).

24. K. Soroka & E. Friedgut, *User Guide to HUD's Previous Participation Review Process (aka 2530 approval),* American Bar Association, 2017 [hereinafter ABA User Guide on 2530s]. *See* the ABA User Guide on 2530s for more detail about the topics covered in this chapter, as well as step-by-step directions for completing Form 2530; *Previous Participation Review for Office of Multifamily Housing and Office of Healthcare Programs Projects,* U.S. Dep't of Hous. & Urban Dev., https://www.hud.gov/program_offices/housing/mfh/prevparticipation#Overview (last visited June 1, 2021).

25. *See* Retrospective Review—Improving the Previous Participation Reviews of Prospective Multifamily Housing and Healthcare Programs Participants, 81 Fed. Reg. 71,244-75 (Oct. 14, 2016); Tatiana E. Gutierrez, *HUD Issues Final 2530 Regulation,* Nixon Peabody (Oct. 11, 2016), https://www.nixonpeabody.com/en/ideas/blog/affordable-housing/2016/10/11/hud-issues-final-2530-regulation.

26. *See* U.S. Dep't of Hous. & Urban Dev., Notice H 2016-15 (2016).

project. Flags are rated by three tiers, with Tier 1 flags representing the most egregious violations. Tier 1 flags are permanent.[27]

When a participant is made aware that a flag has been placed on them in APPS, the participant may use the procedure in the Processing Guide for Previous Participation Reviews (2530 Processing Guide) to resolve the flag.[28] While Tier 1 flags are permanent, Tier 2 and 3 flags may be removed by HUD after certain remediation actions are taken by the participant. A flag on a participant in APPS does not preclude participation in new projects with HUD; however, the participant may be required to explain the circumstances of the flag when submitting a new application. Further, HUD does retain the right to reject an applicant based on flags in APPS.

The 2530 regulations issued in 2016, and the accompanying 2530 Processing Guide for Previous, renewed HUD's focus on physical and financial compliance. The regulations clarified the definition of "covered project" to include projects subject to continuing requirements administered by HUD's Office of Housing; narrowed the definition of "controlling participant" to include individuals and entities with the ability to direct the day-to-day operations of the project as well as construction managers for Section 242 projects but not board members of nonprofits who do not control day-to-day operations; clarified that a change in controlling participation is a triggering event if HUD consent is required for the change; and established a separate definition of risk.[29]

5. HUD's Use of Administrative Sanctions

HUD uses several major tools to impose sanctions against parties with which it contracts. These are removal sanctions, such as debarments and suspensions, and fines such as CMPs,[30] claw back of funds and those available under the PFCRA.[31]

HUD rules allow the imposition of these sanctions for a variety of violations, all of which concern people contracting with HUD. However, contractors should pay the most attention to certain catchall provisions, which provide that sanctions may be applied for (1) any material breach of a contract related to a HUD project, (2) any violation of an applicable HUD regulation, or (3) the making of any false statement in connection with a HUD-financed project.

Sanctions against a person or a company generally extend to all of the subsidiaries and affiliates of that person or company. The effect of a sanction may prevent a party from participating in a covered transaction, either as a principal or as a mere participant, not only with the agency imposing the sanction but with any federal government agency throughout the executive branch. These sanctions last for a specific period of time; suspensions and LDPs last for one year, but debarments often extend up to three to five years.

HUD may consider reducing sanctions based on certain mitigating circumstances. There is a limited appeal right with a hearing officer appointed to the case, who will consider certain mitigating facts evidencing carelessness, inattention, or inefficiency rather

---

27. *Id.*
28. *Id.*
29. Gutierrez, *supra* note 25.
30. 42 U.S.C. § 1437z-1(b)(1).
31. 31 U.S.C. §§ 3801–3812.

than flagrant and intentional disregard of HUD's rules. Other significant mitigating factors are the passage of time since the events in question, the current successful operation of a property or program, the successful past course of dealings with HUD in other matters, and willingness to work out a settlement or other resolution. Circumstances vary from case to case and will dictate whether and how to raise mitigation arguments.

Sanctions such as debarment and suspension are administrative rather than civil or criminal enforcement and are intended to prevent contractors who are irresponsible from contracting with the federal government. As a result, a contractor may avoid sanctions by demonstrating that it is presently a responsible party. HUD may use past acts by the contractor to show that the contractor is not presently responsible. HUD may then still impose sanctions and pursue civil or criminal penalties.

Suspensions are imposed on participants to immediately exclude a participant from further government transactions throughout the course of an investigation or legal proceeding.[32] While temporary, suspensions are still very serious and may lead to debarment.[33] Suspensions become effective upon issuance and before any appeal may be taken, while debarments become effective only after administrative appeals are exhausted.[34] Agencies throughout the federal government use the System for Award Management (SAM) to track participants who are suspended or debarred.[35] HUD participants are required to register in SAM before doing business with HUD.

After a suspension, or in serious cases in lieu of a suspension, enforcement officials may determine that debarment is the appropriate sanction for particularly egregious infractions. A debarment is a sanction that prevents a participant from conducting business with any federal agency in the government.[36] Debarment is the most serious compliance sanction and is generally imposed for a three-year period. However, debarment officials can opt to impose a longer sanction in the interest of protecting the public interest. Debarments may be imposed for violations such as use of false documents to originate FHA-insured mortgages, diversion of project assets, embezzlement, theft, forgery, false statements or claims, or bribery.[37]

In addition to suspensions and debarments, officials in HUD field offices are able to impose a Limited Denial of Participation (LDP) for lesser offenses, such as failure to comply with HUD program standards.[38] In these cases, the participant will be prevented from participation in HUD programs within a certain geographic area, generally for a period of one year.[39]

---

32. *Suspensions*, U.S. Dep't of Hous. & Urban Dev., https://www.hud.gov/program_offices /enforcement/ecstrstf (last visited June 1, 2021).

33. 2 C.F.R. pts. 180 & 2424 (2021).

34. *Id.* § 180.605.

35. sam.gov, U.S. Dep't of Hous. & Urban Dev., https://sam.gov/content/home (last visited June 1, 2021).

36. *Debarments*, U U.S. Dep't of Hous. & Urban Dev., https://www.hud.gov/program_offices /enforcement/debarments (last visited June 1, 2021).

37. *Id.*

38. 2 C.F.R. pt. 2424, subpt. J (2021).

39. *Limited Denials of Participation Memo*, U.S. Dep't of Hous. & Urban Dev., https://www .hud.gov/program_offices/enforcement/theecmemo2 (last visited June 1, 2021).

As noted earlier, HUD may also assess financial remedies, such as CMPs and damages under PFCRA. CMPs may be assessed against participants who knowingly and willingly materially violate any one of a variety of HUD rules and regulations. HUD is required to send a pre-penalty notice to the participant before issuing a complaint and initiating a hearing. If a participant fails to respond to a CMP notice, it may inadvertently waive the right to respond later on, when HUD files a formal administrative complaint. In 2017, HUD published a final rule amending the CMP regulations to adjust for inflation and correct previous inaccuracies.[40] HUD may assess up to a certain amount for each violation. Different maximums are set for each program; for example, at the time of this writing in 2021, for HUD-insured multifamily project owners, each violation has a maximum penalty of $51,827,[41] while the maximum penalty for Section 8 owners is $40,282.[42]

Alternatively, the PFCRA provides an administrative remedy to address false, fictitious, or fraudulent claims and statements.[43] The PFCRA provides a cap for damages for each claim of $5,000, which is then adjusted upward for inflation.[44] The current maximum penalty assessed for a violation related to a HUD program in 2021 is $11,803.[45] Historically, HUD has been one of the few federal agencies to successfully impose penalties under the PFCRA on a consistent and repeated basis.[46]

Participants in rural affordable housing programs run by the Rural Housing Service (RHS), a department within the USDA, face similar suspension and debarment rules. RHS also has penalty authority.

B. HUD Civil and Criminal Enforcement Actions

Traditionally, federal government investigations took the form of prosecutions in formal, structured settings arising directly from investigations run by U.S. Attorneys' offices. Federal government investigations of businesses and their employees also can be initiated by regulatory officials. However, a significant recent trend in the federal government's investigative strategy has been the parallel and closely coordinated use of criminal and civil investigations.

Enforcement by agencies in the federal housing area begins with a typical, seemingly standard, audit or investigation. Investigators use the government's contractual and regulatory rights to inspect property and records to gain information before the target of an investigation realizes that they and their business enterprise may be the target of a criminal referral. Other collateral consequences include private civil actions for allegedly fraudulent claims made by a contractor to the government and brought through qui tam actions, also known as whistleblower actions.

---

40. Implementation of the Program Fraud Civil Remedies Act of 1986, 82 Fed. Reg. 102 (May 30, 2017).

41. 24 C.F.R. § 30.45 (2021).

42. *Id.* § 30.68.

43. 31 U.S.C. § 38.

44. *Id.* § 3802.

45. 24 C.F.R. § 28.10 (2021).

46. *Program Fraud Civil Remedies Act: Observations on Implementation*, U.S. Gen. Accounting Office, GAO-12-275r (2012).

One frequent area of investigation is criminal "equity skimming."[47] Criminal sanctions include fines and imprisonment for misuse of project funds for other than actual or necessary expenses. There is also a double damages penalty for unauthorized use of multifamily project assets and income in violation of the FHA Regulatory Agreement.[48]

C. Enforcement Where HUD Is Not Contract Administrator

1. Introduction

HUD also provides a substantial amount of funding through block grant programs that enable local municipalities to retain substantial control over how funding is used. Programs like the Community Development Block Grant (CDBG) and HOME Investment Partnerships (HOME) are structured to enable municipalities and states to focus funding where it is most needed on the local level. In providing such block grants, HUD also relinquishes many of the monitoring and enforcement responsibilities to the local administrators, as discussed later.

2. Grantee and Subgrantee Monitoring with the Community Development Block Grant Program

The CDBG program provides annual grants on a formula basis to states, cities, and counties to support community development activities such as infrastructure, economic development projects, public facilities installation, community centers, housing rehabilitation, and more.[49] For all CDBG programs, local jurisdictions make awards to subgrantees and are tasked with monitoring the subgrantees to ensure compliance with program requirements and enforcing program requirements if violations occur.[50] HUD, in turn, monitors the grantees.[51]

Grantees are required to maintain records to show how the grant funding is spent and confirm adherence to CDBG regulations, including eligibility, fair housing, displacement, and citizen participation requirements.[52] HUD completes annual reviews to determine whether the grantee is meeting the objectives of the CDBG program, meeting the goals of its Consolidated Plan (Consolidated Plan, as described later), and implementing the CDBG-funded activities in a timely manner.[53] Upon a finding that the grantee is not meeting the program goals and requirements, and after the grantee is afforded the opportunity for an administrative hearing,[54] HUD is authorized to reduce, withdraw, or adjust the grant.[55]

---

47. 12 U.S.C. § 1715z-19.
48. *Id.* § 1715z-4a.
49. *Community Development*, U.S. Dep't of Hous. & Urban Dev., https://www.hud.gov /program_offices/comm_planning/communitydevelopment (last visited June 1, 2021).
50. 24 C.F.R. § 570.501(b) (2021).
51. ICF, *Basically CDBG*, HUD, Office of Block Grant Assistance 13-21 (2007), https:// www.hud.gov/sites/documents/CDBGCHAPTER13.PDF.
52. 24 C.F.R. § 570.506 (2021).
53. *Id.* §§ 570.901–.903.
54. *Id.* § 570.913.
55. *Id.* § 570.911.

CDBG regulations require grantees to submit a Consolidated Annual Performance and Evaluation Report (CAPER) to HUD within 90 days of the close of the grantee's program year.[56] The CAPER provides HUD with the necessary information to assess the grantee's ability to carry out its programs in compliance with applicable regulations and requirements, and to report to Congress on the overall program, as well as describe its program achievements to the public.[57] The CAPER is based on the goals set by jurisdictions in their Consolidated Plans and carried out through their Annual Action Plan (Annual Action Plan). HUD provides the grantees with access to its electronic Integrated Disbursement and Information System (IDIS) to upload all required information.[58] Grantees are required to make the draft CAPER available to the public for 15 days before submission for review and comments.[59]

As part of the program administration, grantees are required to enter into agreements with subgrantees that include remedies for noncompliance and provisions on termination in accordance with 2 C.F.R. part 200, subpart D.[60] In training published by CDBG, it is recommended that the written agreements between grantees and subgrantees include three stages of intervention available to the grantee when noncompliance occurs.[61] The guidance suggests that the three stages of intervention begin with low-level intervention, such as developing a strategy with the subgrantee to correct problems and conducting more frequent monitoring reviews, and eventually rise to high-level intervention, such as temporarily suspending the subgrantee or terminating the subgrantee from the program.[62]

3. *Monitoring of Participating Jurisdictions in the HOME Investment Partnerships Program*

The HOME Program provides formula grants to states and localities, called Participating Jurisdictions (Participating Jurisdictions), to be used to fund a wide range of home-buying and building activities.[63] This program is the largest federal block grant designed exclusively with the goal of creating and maintaining affordable housing for low-income households.[64] Similar to the CDBG program, it is the Participating Jurisdictions that are responsible for the monitoring and enforcement of program requirements, which can vary widely because different localities use the grants for a diverse range of programs, including grants, direct loans, loan guarantees, and rental assistance.[65] Participating Jurisdictions are

---

56. *Supra* note 51 at 13-4.

57. 24 C.F.R. pt. 91 (2021).

58. *Integrated Disbursement and Information System*, HUD Exchange, https://www.hudexchange.info/programs/idis/#:~:text=IDIS%20is%20the%20draw%20down,for%20the%20CPD%20competitive%20grant (last visited June 1, 2021).

59. *Supra* note 51 at 13-6.

60. 24 C.F.R. § 570.503(b)(6) (2021).

61. *Supra* note 51.

62. *Id.*

63. *HOME Investment Partnerships Program*, U.S. Dep't of Hous. & Urban Dev. (Mar. 26, 2021) https://www.hud.gov/program_offices/comm_planning/home.

64. *Id.*

65. *Id.*

required to enter into agreements with the subrecipients that include HOME provisions, such as requirements related to disbursement of funds and recordkeeping.[66]

Participating Jurisdictions are required to review the use of HOME funds by subrecipients and contracts annually.[67] The stated goals of the monitoring are to ensure production and accountability, ensure compliance with HOME and other federal requirements, and evaluate organizational and project performance and project viability.[68]

HUD, in turn, is required to complete annual performance reviews of the Participating Jurisdictions.[69] HUD field office staff review the Participating Jurisdictions' records, with an emphasis on review of the Participating Jurisdictions' annual reviews of subrecipients.[70] When HUD identifies a deficiency, the Participating Jurisdiction may be required to submit a proposal to correct, mitigate, and prevent the deficiency.[71] HUD may also change the method of payment from an advance to a reimbursement basis or impose other special conditions or restrictions in the following year's allocation of funds.[72] HUD may reduce the funding to the Participating Jurisdiction, prevent further withdrawals of funds, restrict the activities funded in the Participating Jurisdiction, remove the Participating Jurisdiction from program participation, or require the Participating Jurisdiction to match contributions to the HOME fund accounts.[73]

III. MONITORING AND ENFORCEMENT OF LIHTC PROPERTIES

A. Introduction to Monitoring and Enforcement by the IRS

The IRS and the states that allocate federal LIHTCs share the responsibility for monitoring and enforcing regulatory agreements, known as Extended Use Agreements (EUAs), and other applicable requirements under Section 42 of the Internal Revenue Code that govern the LIHTC program.[74] The IRS also promulgates regulations and provides guidance to the states for administration of the LIHTC program. However, it is the state housing finance agency (and any designated local agencies) that adopts allocation plans, called Qualified Allocation Plans (QAPs), and enters into EUAs with the owners of the properties selected for participation in the LIHTC program to encumber the selected properties with low-income use and other restrictions required under the program.[75] The Internal Revenue Code requires that a states' QAP provides procedures for (1) noncompliance monitoring, (2) notifying the IRS of any noncompliance found, and (3) monitoring for habitability

---

66. 24 C.F.R. § 92.504 (2021).

67. *HOME Monitoring*, HUD EXCHANGE, https://www.hudexchange.info/programs/home/topics/monitoring/#policy-guidance (last visited June 1, 2021).

68. *Id.*

69. 24 C.F.R. § 92.550(a) (2021).

70. *Id.* § 92.550.

71. *Id.* § 92.551(c)(1).

72. *Id.* § 92.551(c)(2).

73. *Id.* § 92.552(a).

74. See Chapter 9 for a complete discussion of LIHTCs. See also Chapter 7 for a complete discussion of HERA, AARA, TCAP, and the Section 1602 Exchange programs to which these rules also apply.

75. See Chapters 9 and 10 for a full discussion of LIHTC regulations.

standard violations through regular site visits and physical inspections.[76] QAPs must meet these regulatory requirements or they will not be qualified by the IRS.[77] The EUAs run for the statutorily required initial compliance period of 15 years plus an additional extended use period of at least another 15 years.

After the end of the 14th anniversary of the start of the initial compliance period, an owner may seek a Qualified Contract (QC). The QC process starts with the owner applying to the housing finance agency that provided the LIHTCs to find a qualified buyer willing to purchase the property. If the agency does not find such a buyer after a one-year period, then the owner can terminate the EUA. However, the EUA would still have vitality for the statutory three-year transition period after such termination.

The EUA's main job is to implement rent and income use restrictions. The owner must agree to either the 20/50 or 40/60 set-aside test—that is, at least 20 percent of the units in the project are available for households at no more than 50 percent of area median income (the 20/50 test), or at least 40 percent of the units are available for households at no more than 60 percent of area median income (the 40/60 test). As noted above, this and other requirements under the EUA extend during the initial 15-year compliance period during which the LIHTCs are subject to recapture by the IRS for certain noncompliance matters, as well as the 15-plus-year extended use period thereafter. The initial 15-year compliance period and any extended use period taken together, are the Compliance Period (Compliance Period).[78] Per IRS regulations, the monitoring procedures contained in the regulatory agreement must include provisions regarding recordkeeping and retention of records; certification and review of tenant incomes and rent; physical inspections of the property; and notification to the IRS of noncompliance.[79]

B. State Agency Monitoring Function Required by the IRS

1. Recordkeeping

During the Compliance Period, the owner of a LIHTC property must provide evidence to the monitoring state allocation agency that it has abided by all recordkeeping requirements contained in the regulatory agreement. This process is often known as the 8823 Process, in reference to the IRS Form 8823 (Form 8823), used to acknowledge either compliance or lack of compliance. The 8823 Guide is also consulted.[80] Generally, the owner must keep annual records specifying the total number of residential rental units and the percentage of the units that are rented to low-income tenants; the rent for each unit; the number of occupants in each rent restricted unit, as it is applicable to calculate the rent; any vacancy amongst the restricted units; income certifications for each low-income tenant; the eligible and qualified bases for the building; and information about any nonresidential portion of the building.[81]

---

76. 26 U.S.C. § 42(m)(1)(B)(iii).

77. *See generally* 26 U.S.C.A. § 42(m)(1).

78. 26 U.S.C.A. § 42(m)(1) (2021); 26 C.F.R. § 1.42-5(c) (2021).

79. 26 C.F.R. § 1.42-5(1) and (2) (2021).

80. *Guide for Completing Form 8823, Low-Income Housing Credit Agencies Report of Noncompliance or Building Disposition*, Internal Revenue Service, https://www.irs.gov/pub/irs-utl/lihc-form8823guide.pdf (last visited June 1, 2021).

81. 26 C.F.R. § 1.42-5(b) (2021).

In addition to recordkeeping requirements, LIHTC regulatory agreements will often contain specific provisions for retention of records, including a six-year retention requirement for the records listed above. Additionally, records for the first year of the tax credit period must be kept for six years "beyond the due date (with extensions) for filing the federal income tax return for the last year of the initial 15-year compliance period of the building," which is generally at least 21 years.[82] It is critical for the owners of any LIHTC properties to engage a qualified management company experienced in managing under the LIHTC program and to have a detailed management agreement outlining the recordkeeping and retention responsibilities of the management agent.

2. Certification and Review

Owners of LIHTC properties must certify annually to the state allocation agency that their projects meet the LIHTC requirements in the regulatory agreement, including the following requirements: (1) owners must certify to the percentage of low-income units at the property and whether that percentage has changed (if the percentage did change, the owner must also provide an explanation of the change); and (2) owners must provide income certifications for low-income tenants with supporting documentation and certifications that each low-income unit was rent-restricted, per the regulatory agreement. Owner must also certify that (3) the project was open to the general public and there were no findings of discrimination under the Fair Housing Act; (4) the project is habitable under local and state codes; and (5) there was no change to eligible basis requirements,[83] or, if there was a change in eligible basis, the explanation for the change, as well as a certification that any common areas included in eligible basis were available to all tenants regardless of income on a comparable basis and free of charge. Finally, owner also must certify (6) regarding vacant units, increases in tenants' income, low-income housing commitments, and not using housing for transitional purposes.[84]

Upon receipt of an owner's certifications, the state allocation agency will review the certifications for compliance with LIHTC regulations. For projects new to the tax credit program, the state allocation agency must conduct on-site inspections of all buildings in the project by the end of the second calendar year following the year the last building in the project is placed in service and must inspect the units and review the low-income certifications, the documentation supporting the certifications, and the rent records for the tenants in the units.[85] After this initial review, the state allocation agency must inspect and review existing buildings every three years.[86] The state allocation agency must "conduct on-site inspections of all buildings in the project and inspect a certain percentage of the units as well as review the low-income certifications, the documentation supporting the certifications, and the rent records for the tenants in those units."[87]

---

82. *Id.* § 1.42-5(b).

83. "The eligible basis of a new building is its adjusted basis as of the close of the 1st taxable year of the credit period." 26 U.S.C.A. § 42(d) (2021). For more detailed analysis of eligible basis, please see Chapter 7.

84. 26 C.F.R. § 1.42-5(c)(1) (2021).

85. *Id.* § 42-5(c)(2)(ii)(A).

86. *Id.* § 1.42-5(c)(2)(B).

87. *Id.*

3. On-Site Inspections

As noted earlier, state allocation agencies are required to conduct on-site inspections of all buildings in a project every three years after the initial inspection. The state allocation agencies must inspect properties for compliance with habitability standards, as determined by the local health, safety, and building codes or the uniform standards for public housing promulgated by HUD. These on-site inspections can be conducted by the state allocation agency or an authorized delegate, as defined in the regulations.[88] The IRS in essence allows the states to choose which physical inspections standards and protocols to follow. The majority of states opt to follow the uniform housing qualify standards set by HUD.[89]

Previously, regulations required the state allocation agencies to inspect 20 percent of the units at the property; however, a rule issued by the IRS in 2019 now requires the state allocation agency to inspect a certain number of units based on a chart released by HUD's REAC.[90] For many properties, this increased the number of units inspected. The new rule also reduced the notice period for a physical inspection to 15 days.[91]

Owners must also keep all reports of building code violations until a building is re-inspected and the state allocation agency is satisfied that the owner corrected the violations. Owners must also report all violations in the annual report, which is due to the state allocation agency with a statement regarding compliance.[92]

4. Notification of Noncompliance

State allocation agencies are required to provide both owners and the IRS with notice of findings of noncompliance with the regulations. Specifically:

> The Agency must be required to provide prompt written notice to the owner of a low-income housing project if the Agency does not receive the certification described in paragraph (c)(1) of this section, or does not receive or is not permitted to inspect the tenant income certifications, supporting documentation, and rent records described in paragraph (c)(2)(ii) of this section, or discovers by inspection, review, or in some other manner, that the project is not in compliance with the provisions of section 42.
>
> The Agency must be required to file Form 8823, "Low-Income Housing Credit Agencies Report of Noncompliance," with the Service [IRS] no later than 45 days after the end of the correction period . . . and no earlier than the end of the correction period, whether or not the noncompliance or failure to certify is corrected. . . .[93]

Form 8823, submitted to the IRS by the state allocation agency, details noncompliance by the owner of a LIHTC property. The form lists each area of compliance and asks

88. 26 C.F.R. § 1.42-5(d) (2021).

89. Ellen Romano, *Navigating the Tax Credit Maze,* 66 J. PROP. MGMT. 3843 (Jan. 1, 2001), 2001 WL 14449749.

90. Amendments to the Low-Income Housing Credit Compliance-Monitoring Regulations, 84 Fed. Reg. 6076 (Feb. 26, 2019).

91. *Id.*

92. 26 C.F.R. § 1.42-5(c)(i)(B)(vi) (2021).

93. 26 C.F.R. § 1.42-5(e)(2) and (3)(i) (2021).

the state allocation agency to select "out of compliance" or "noncompliance corrected" for each applicable area. The form also offers a selection for filing when it is only being offered to show correction of a previously reported noncompliance problem.[94]

C. Implementation by the States

The state allocation agencies bear the primary responsibility for monitoring compliance with LIHTC regulations and, as a result, the same agencies are at the forefront of education efforts on compliance requirements.[95] Some states require owners and managers of LIHTC properties to document compliance training by their staff. Other states instituted online compliance reporting systems to allow owners to certify to compliance training.[96] Owners are encouraged by the state allocation agencies to (1) work with the agency to understand compliance and reporting requirements, (2) invest in technology that will assist in tax credit compliance efforts, (3) proactively engage auditors to review files, (4) develop strong forms and manuals to assist staff in compliance efforts, and (5) provide ongoing training to staff on compliance.[97] Resources are available to owners from a myriad of sources; for example, the National Council of State Housing Agencies releases a FAQ and Fact Sheet each year with details about the LIHTC program, compliance monitoring and requirements, and other issues related to LIHTC administration.[98]

D. Enforcement by the IRS

The IRS reviews Form 8823 and performs audits of LIHTC properties. Noncompliance findings by the IRS may lead to recapture or disallowance of tax credits against project partners, as well as penalties against unrelated parties who are responsible for reporting noncompliance.[99] The audit will review the documentation provided by the partnership and may also conduct an on-site review.[100]

In 2015, the Bipartisan Budget Act of 2015 overhauled the IRS procedures for auditing partnerships, including limited liability companies (LLCs) taxed as partnerships and

---

94. Internal Revenue Service, Form 8823 (Rev. 12-2019), https://www.irs.gov/pub/irs-access/f8823_accessible.pdf.

95. *State Allocating Agencies Require Mandatory Compliance Training for Tax Credit Owners* [Current Developments] Hous. & Dev. Rep. (Apr. 30, 2001), WL 28 No. CD-52 HDRCURDEV 16.

96. *State Agencies Adopt Online Systems for Tax Credit Applications, Compliance Monitoring Reports* [Current Developments] Hous. & Dev. Rep. (Jan. 19, 2004), WL 32 No. CD-2 HDRCURDEV 13.

97. Ruth L. Theobald, *Managing for Tax-Credit Compliance,* 61 J. PROP. MGMT. 30 (Mar. 13, 1996), 1996 WL 10063577.

98. *Fact Sheets and FAQs,* National Council of State Housing Agencies (updated May 26, 2021), https://www.ncsha.org/resource-center/fact-sheets/.

99. *I.R.S. Remains Vigilant for Misrepresentations, Culpable Parties in Tax Credit Projects* [Current Developments] Hous. & Dev. Rep. (Apr. 15, 2002). WL 29 No. CD-50 HDRCURDEV 14. ("Section 6701 authorizes penalties for any person who provides aid, assistance, or advice that [they] knows or [have] reason to believe would result in an understatement of someone else's tax liability. Individuals who are responsible for a misrepresentation or a mistake can be liable for up to $1,000 per occurrence, while corporations can be penalized $10,000 per occurrence.").

100. *I.R.S. Official Outlines Common Tax Credit Audit Strategies* [Current Developments] Hous. & Dev. Rep. (June 25, 2001). WL 29 No. CD-8 HDRCURDEV 14.

their partners.[101] The changes had a significant impact on LIHTC transactions. The new rule changed audit liability rules resulting in assessment of any liabilities at the partnership level, rather than the partner level.[102] Whereas in the past, partnerships would designate a tax matter partner, the new law requires partnerships to have a partnership representative who does not have to be a partner in the partnership.[103] The law also allows partnerships with fewer than 100 partners to opt out; however, partnerships with another partnership as a partner are generally excluded from opting out.[104] Additionally, under the new rules, audits may address previous tax years, in some cases prior to a transfer of ownership interests, in which cases partners no longer in the partnership may need to receive notice and participate in the audit.[105]

IV. CONCLUSION

HUD and the IRS monitor the nation's affordable housing stock with the help of many partners at the state and local levels. While this chapter gave a brief overview of the monitoring tools and enforcement mechanisms available to HUD, the IRS, and their partners, it is important for participants and practitioners to understand the regulations and requirements applicable to their projects in order to successfully navigate any inspections or audits. A proactive approach to monitoring can prevent serious enforcement problems in the future.

---

101. Bipartisan Budget Act of 2015, P.L. No. 114-74 (Nov. 2, 2015).
102. *Id.*
103. *Id.*
104. *Id.*
105. *Id.*

Preservation of Affordable Housing

15

Jessie Alfaro-Cassella[1]

I. INTRODUCTION

Hundreds of thousands of affordable housing units are lost every year, exacerbating a national housing affordability crisis. This chapter discusses the causes and impact of the loss of existing affordable housing units and highlights several key strategies for ensuring their long-term preservation and affordability.

A. The Importance of Affordable Housing Preservation

There are far more extremely low income households than affordable rental housing units in the United States. Current estimates indicate that on average, there are only 36 affordable rental housing units for every 100 extremely low income households.[2] Approximately 7 million additional affordable rental units are needed to fill this gap.[3] In addition, almost 11 million renters nationwide (or 40 percent of all renters) spend more than half of their income on housing and are considered severely rent-burdened.[4] The lack of affordable

---

1. Jessie Alfaro-Cassella is a Deputy City Attorney at the City and County of San Francisco. Any views or opinions expressed herein are hers alone and do not necessarily represent or reflect the views of the City and County of San Francisco.

2. *The Gap: A Shortage of Affordable Rental Homes*, NATIONAL LOW INCOME HOUSING COALITION, https://reports.nlihc.org/sites/default/files/gap/Gap-Report_2021 .pdf [https://perma.cc/Z68R-B3B6]. Extremely low-income households are defined as households whose incomes are at or below the poverty line or less than 30 percent of the area median income.

3. *Id.*

4. *America's Rental Housing 2020*, JOINT CENTER FOR HOUSING STUDIES OF HARVARD UNIVERSITY, https://www.jchs.harvard.edu/sites/default/files/Harvard_JCHS _Americas_Rental_Housing_2020.pdf [https://perma.cc/7YKP-KT6H].

housing units, and the rising number of severely rent-burdened households, has exacerbated a long-standing national housing affordability crisis.

This affordability crisis is the result of two main factors: the production of affordable housing units has not kept pace with the need, and currently affordable housing units are lost every year. Between 2011 and 2020, the number of affordable rental units shrunk by more than four million units.[5] In addition, in 2020, affordable rental units accounted for a shrinking share of the rental market; approximately 25 percent of rental units had contract rents under $600 per month, compared to 37 percent in 2000.[6] For every new affordable rental unit that is built, two units are lost because of their physical condition, financial condition, local housing market pressures, and other factors described in this chapter.[7] Therefore, without preserving and reinvesting in existing affordable housing, we take two steps back for every one step forward.[8]

In addition, preserving existing affordable housing is cheaper and more energy efficient than new construction,[9] and is essential to advancing racial and civil equality,[10]

---

5. *The State of the Nation's Housing 2019*, JOINT CENTER FOR HOUSING STUDIES OF HARVARD UNIVERSITY, https://www.jchs.harvard.edu/sites/default/files/Harvard_JCHS_State_of_the _Nations_Housing_2019.pdf [https://perma.cc/5L6S-FEGY].

6. *America's Rental Housing 2020*, *supra* note 4.

7. *What Is Preservation?* NATIONAL HOUSING TRUST, https://www.nationalhousingtrust.org /what-preservation [https://perma.cc/H8JU-QEZV].

8. *Id.*

9. *Id.*; Khalil Shahyd, *Why Affordable Housing Matters for Environmental Protection*, OPPORTUNITY STARTS AT HOME, https://www.opportunityhome.org/resources/why-affordable-housing -matters-for-environmental-protection/ [https://perma.cc/M2QH-GDAS] (last visited June 8, 2021); *Household Energy Insecurity 2015*, U.S. ENERGY INFORMATION ADMINISTRATION, https://www.eia .gov/consumption/residential/data/2015/hc/php/hc11.1.php [https://perma.cc/EZ7X-XUXG] (last revised May 2018); *Achieving Energy Efficiency for All Renters*, ENERGY EFFICIENCY FOR ALL, https://www.energyefficiencyforall.org/ [https://perma.cc/8KER-XNTM] (last visited June 8, 2021); Guillermo Ortiz, Heidi Schultheis, Valerie Novack & Aleah Holt, *A Perfect Storm, Extreme Weather as an Affordable Housing Crisis Multiplier*, CENTER FOR AMERICAN PROGRESS (Aug. 1, 2019, 9:01 AM), https://www.americanprogress.org/issues/green/reports/2019/08/01/473067/a-perfect-storm -2/ [https://perma.cc/K5TQ-MPZC].

10. *Ending Housing Discrimination Is the "Unfinished Business" of Civil Rights*, OPPORTUNITY STARTS AT HOME, https://www.opportunityhome.org/resources/housing-discrimination-unfinished -business-civil-rights/ [https://perma.cc/23S8-4NP9] (last visited June 8, 2021).

education,[11] economic mobility,[12] health,[13] and employment.[14] According to the Centers for Disease Control and Prevention, housing displacement exacerbates existing health inequities, disproportionately affecting low-income people, women, children, communities of color, and the elderly.[15] Research also suggests that households with residential instability suffer greater stress levels and poorer health outcomes.[16] As has been well-documented, where a child grows up has a profound impact on their opportunities and future earnings and can play a key role in reducing intergenerational poverty.[17]

Like any residential building, affordable housing needs regular reinvestment in its physical structure and operations to ensure that it remains available to serve current and future residents. Of the currently affordable properties with some form of publicly supported rental assistance, 81 percent were built before 1975 or have not received any new capital subsidy funds in the past 20 years.[18] Therefore, a critically important piece of addressing the national housing affordability crisis is to ensure that currently affordable

---

11. *See, e.g., Stable, Affordable Housing Drives Stronger Student Outcomes*, OPPORTUNITY STARTS AT HOME, https://www.opportunityhome.org/resources/stable-affordable-housing-drives-stronger-student-outcomes/ [https://perma.cc/VCJ9-EWKN] (last visited June 8, 2021); *A Place to Call Home: The Case for Increased Federal Investments in Affordable Housing*, CAMPAIGN FOR HOUSING AND COMMUNITY DEVELOPMENT FUNDING, http://nlihc.org/sites/default/files/A-Place-To-Call-Home.pdf [https://perma.cc/V756-SEYC] (last visited June 8, 2021); Raj Chetty, Nathaniel Hendren & Lawrence F. Katz, *The Effects of Exposure to Better Neighborhoods on Children: New Evidence from the Moving to Opportunity Experiment* (Nat'l Bureau of Econ. Research, Working Paper No. 21156, 2016), https://www.nber.org/papers/w21156 [https://perma.cc/WA7F-JH2R].

12. *See, e.g.*, Chetty, *supra* note 11; *Affordable Housing Enables Moving to Opportunity*, OPPORTUNITY STARTS AT HOME, https://www.opportunityhome.org/resources/affordable-housing-enables-moving-opportunity/ [https://perma.cc/DZR3-LRKR] (last visited June 8, 2021).

13. *See, e.g., Good Housing Is Good Health*, OPPORTUNITY STARTS AT HOME, https://www.opportunityhome.org/resources/good-housing-good-health/ [https://perma.cc/2GJK-BFH6] (last visited June 8, 2021); MEGAN SANDEL, ET AL., UNSTABLE HOUSING AND CAREGIVER AND CHILD HEALTH IN RENTER FAMILIES (2018), http://childrenshealthwatch.org/wp-content/uploads/Unstable-Housing-and-Caregiver-and-Child-Health-in-Renter-Families.pdf [https://perma.cc/24TN-LE2S]; Diana Cutts, et al., *Homelessness during Pregnancy: A Unique, Time-Dependent Risk Factor of Birth Outcomes*, MATERNAL & CHILD HEALTH J. (2015); Mary Glenn Fowler, Gloria A. Simpson & Kenneth C. Schoendorf, *Families on the Move and Children's Health Care*, 91 PEDIATRICS 934 (1993); Regina M. Bures, *Childhood Residential Stability and Health at Midlife*, 93 AM. J. OF PUB. HEALTH 1144 (2003).

14. *Preserving, Protecting, & Expanding Affordable Housing: A Policy Toolkit for Public Health*, CHANGELAB SOLUTIONS, https://www.changelabsolutions.org/product/preserving-protecting-expanding-affordable-housing [https://perma.cc/UQ3W-NBU4] (last visited June 8, 2021).

15. *Health Effects of Gentrification*, CENTERS FOR DISEASE CONTROL AND PREVENTION, www.cdc.gov/healthyplaces/healthtopics/gentrification.htm [https://perma.cc/EUA4-SB68] (last visited June 8, 2021).

16. CHANGELAB SOLUTIONS, *supra* note 14; JEFFREY LUBELL & MAYA BRENNAN, FRAMING THE ISSUES – THE POSITIVE IMPACTS OF AFFORDABLE HOUSING ON HEALTH, CENTER FOR HOUSING POLICY (July 2007). https://pdfs.semanticscholar.org/0dbf/ed563545d8b93877db82ee0634e68796ede7.pdf.

17. *See, e.g.*, Chetty, *supra* note 11.

18. *A Picture of Preservation Need*, National Housing Preservation Database, https://preservationdatabase.org/wp-content/uploads/2020/05/A-Picture-of-Preservation-Infographic-2020.pdf [https://perma.cc/WU2B-LBPZ] (last visited June 8, 2021).

housing units have the tools and resources, financial and otherwise, necessary for their long-term affordability and habitability.

B. Why Is Affordable Housing at Risk?

There are three key reasons why affordable housing properties are at risk of being lost: time-limited affordability restrictions, inadequate federal appropriations, and the effects of high cost local housing markets.

First, affordable housing programs involve public funding or benefits that require some degree of public regulatory oversight. In exchange for the benefit of a loan, grant, rental subsidy, or regulatory concession, affordable housing owners must agree to provide housing to a certain class of tenants for a specified term. This obligation is usually spelled out in applicable laws and contracts, such as regulatory or use agreements, deed restrictions, rental assistance contracts, zoning variances, or land disposition agreements. The duty to provide housing of a certain quality at a specific rental rate for a specific period is central to the arrangement. However, these affordability restrictions are usually time-limited.[19] According to the Joint Center for Housing Studies of Harvard University, affordability restrictions on nearly 1.2 million rental units are set to expire by 2029.[20] This includes 611,000 units assisted by the Low-Income Housing Tax Credit (LIHTC) program, 352,000 units of Section 8 project-based housing, and 221,000 units that are assisted through other federally supported affordable housing programs (i.e., the HOME Investment Partnerships Program, FHA-insured, Section 236, Section 202 Direct Loan, and the U.S. Department of Agriculture's Section 515 Rural Rental Housing programs).[21] When these affordability restrictions expire, affordable units can be converted to market-rate units that are no longer available to extremely low-income households.

Second, much of the federal government's affordable housing preservation policy is driven by policy or budget decisions made by Congress or the responsible agencies. Often, policy decisions are heavily influenced by their budgetary implications, or by larger budget decisions made with respect to taxation and spending for the entire federal government (i.e., not limited to the housing sphere). Preservation policies can be established through authorizing legislation, but then effectively repealed simply by a failure to provide adequate appropriations.[22] These pressures wax and wane with the overall fiscal picture of the federal government, as well as political conflicts between Congress and the prevailing

---

19. For example, the first temporary Emergency Low-Income Housing Preservation Act (ELIHPA) program in 1988 exchanged incentives for restrictions on an owner's right to prepay at the 20-year mark, thus effectively extending the use restrictions for the 40-year term of the mortgage. The successor Low-Income Housing Preservation and Homeownership Act of 1990 (LIHPRHA) program struck a harder bargain, trading incentives for use restrictions that stretched for the remaining useful life of the property. Section 236 Interest Reduction Payment (IRP) Decoupling requires an additional use restriction of five years, and the Mark Up to Market program similarly requires contract extensions of no less than five years.

20. *The State of the Nation's Housing 2019*, *supra* note 5.

21. *Id.*

22. Examples of strong preservation policies later starved by the appropriations process include the HUD property disposition program, 12 U.S.C. § 1701z-11 (as superseded by 12 U.S.C. § 1715z-11a(a)), and the Low-Income Housing Preservation and Resident Homeownership Act of 1990.

administration. For many years prior to the mid-1990s, federal housing appropriations were committed through long-term obligations and contracts. These long-term rental assistance contracts required substantial amounts of budget authority, which essentially covered estimated outlays for the entire contract term. Starting in the mid-1990s, all long-term contracts were converted to one-year terms upon renewal, or sometimes to longer terms, but always "subject to appropriations" in order to meet budget caps.

The absence of long-term, federally guaranteed funding commitments presents special challenges for preserving developments that need new private capital for acquisition or rehabilitation. Some lenders may be wary of making loans underwritten at market rents but which require annual appropriated rental assistance to support them. Public lenders or equity investors may have similar reservations, and for good reason. When rental subsidies are subject to annual congressional appropriations, funding levels often do not match the need. For example, public housing funding has been cut dramatically over the last decade,[23] which has forced public housing authorities to forego necessary capital improvements at their public housing properties. In addition, the expansion of rental assistance has slowed significantly since the mid-1990s,[24] which has only widened the gap between the number of affordable rental units and the number of extremely low-income households.

Third, the local housing market can create additional preservation risks. High-cost rental markets can put extra pressure on affordable rental housing properties with rents that are much lower than market rents because they create a strong financial incentive for the owner to not renew the rental assistance contract and to convert to market rate.[25] In a recent study, properties with rents below 80 percent of the fair-market rent were disproportionately more likely to not renew their rental assistance contract.[26] When the affordability restrictions at these properties expire, and without further protection for existing households, rents can be drastically increased to the market rate rents, resulting in the displacement of extremely low-income households. These high-cost housing markets are often located in metro areas, where the shortage of affordable rental housing is already acute.[27] For example, a 2018 study found that 60 percent of properties that had not renewed their subsidy contracts were located in an urban center.[28]

---

23. Douglas Rice, *Chart Book: Cuts in Federal Assistance Have Exacerbated Families' Struggles to Afford Housing*, Center on Budget and Policy Priorities (Apr. 12, 2016), https://www.cbpp.org/research/housing/chart-book-cuts-in-federal-assistance-have-exacerbated-families-struggles-to-afford [https://perma.cc/4MFD-J2P3].

24. *Id.*; *America's Rental Housing 2020*, *supra* note 4, at Figure 33.

25. For further discussion on gentrification and displacement, see JAPONICA BROWN-SARACINO, THE GENTRIFICATION DEBATES (2010).

26. Anne Ray, et al., *Opting In, Opting Out: A Decade Later*, 20 CITYSCAPE: A JOURNAL OF POLICY DEVELOPMENT AND RESEARCH 63 (2018), https://www.huduser.gov/portal/periodicals/cityscpe/vol20num1/ch3.pdf [https://perma.cc/ZX3Q-JF39].

27. In 2014, rural counties had 69 adequate and affordable units available for every 100 extremely low-income renters, compared with 42 units in metropolitan counties. *See* Liza Getsinger, Lily Posey, Graham MacDonald, Josh Leopold, & Katya Abazajian, *The Housing Affordability Gap for Extremely Low-Income Renters in 2014*, URBAN INST. (April 2017), https://www.urban.org/sites/default/files/publication/89921/2017.04.26_2016_gap_map_report_finalized.pdf [https://perma.cc/FY76-GLPT].

28. Ray et al., *supra* note 26.

Because of these risks, it is critical to identify properties whose affordability restrictions are approaching expiration, especially those properties in high-cost rental markets, so that they can be connected with potential tools for their long-term preservation. This identification requires the collection and organization of data into databases. Examples of such databases include the National Housing Preservation Database,[29] Chicago Rehab Network,[30] Florida Housing Data Clearinghouse,[31] and NY Subsidized Housing Information Project (SHIP) database.[32]

II. KEY PRESERVATION CHALLENGES AND TOOLS

A. Overview

The preservation of existing affordable housing is extremely challenging, and depends on a variety of factors, including the type of affordable housing assistance, local housing market, tenant rents, available financial resources, and the capacity of the owner and related parties. As discussed later, comprehensive preservation efforts focus on preserving the units themselves and the rental assistance associated with those units for current and future residents. If the existing units cannot be preserved, these efforts can shift to preserving rental assistance for current residents, in order to mitigate the effects of displacement. This section examines the main challenges and several key preservation tools that exist for several key affordable housing programs assisted by the U.S. Department of Housing and Urban Development (HUD). These challenges and available tools have fluctuated over time, with several tools developed in recent years in response to the aging condition of, and lack of new resources for, federally assisted properties.

B. Public Housing

Public housing is one of the oldest forms of federally assisted affordable housing. It is funded solely through annual congressional appropriations, in the form of operating funds and capital funds, which HUD then provides to local public housing authorities (PHAs) via an Annual Contributions Contract (ACC). PHAs are created under state law and are generally controlled by a local board of commissioners. The U.S. Housing Act of 1937 (the "Act")[33] allows federally appropriated public housing capital and operating funds to be provided to PHAs, and governs the use of those funds and activities pursued in connection with those funds. Local policies, including an annual plan, a five-year plan, and an admissions and continued occupancy policies, also govern the operation of public housing properties.

---

29. National Housing Preservation Database, https://preservationdatabase.org/ [https://perma.cc/BLR6-VBDZ] (last visited June 8, 2021).

30. Chicago Rehab Network, https://www.chicagorehab.org/crn/properties/index.aspx [https://perma.cc/VUW6-RFLE] (last visited June 8, 2021).

31. Florida Housing Data Clearinghouse, http://flhousingdata.shimberg.ufl.edu/ [https://perma.cc/8H9K-C2LK] (last visited June 8, 2021).

32. NY Subsidized Housing Information Project Database, https://furmancenter.org/coredata/userguide [https://perma.cc/JQV4-WA5V] (last visited June 8, 2021).

33. 42 U.S.C. §§ 1437 *et seq.*

Public housing was designed to be affordable in perpetuity, owned and operated by the government. However, congressional appropriations for public housing have fallen far behind the amounts needed to meet this goal.[34] As a result, public housing units nationwide have a capital needs backlog of approximately $50 billion, increasing by $3.5 billion every year. This shortfall creates significant habitability concerns and results in the loss of approximately 10,000 public housing units every year.[35] Because of this, HUD has recently focused on converting public housing to other types of federal housing subsidies (also known as "repositioning") to ensure its long-term preservation. In 2018, HUD sent a memo to each PHA executive director indicating its intent to focus on repositioning and outlining several key public housing repositioning tools.[36]

1. *Rental Assistance Demonstration Program*

One of the most recent public housing repositioning tools is the Rental Assistance Demonstration (RAD) Component 1 program, which converts public housing to project-based vouchers (PBV) or project-based rental assistance (PBRA).[37] Changing the type of housing subsidy from public housing to PBV or PBRA facilitates obtaining public and private financing to make repairs, ends the property's sole reliance on congressional appropriations for capital and operating expenses, and switches the public housing rental assistance to a subsidy that is more stably and adequately appropriated by Congress. As of September 2020, up to 455,000 public housing units nationwide are authorized to convert under the RAD Component 1 program.

The RAD Component 1 program is a budget-neutral program, which means that HUD does not provide any additional funding for RAD-converting properties. Therefore, the total subsidy amount for the property after the RAD conversion is largely the same as the subsidy amount for the property prior to the RAD conversion. However, switching from public housing subsidy to PBV or PBRA facilitates obtaining low-income housing tax credits (LIHTCs) as well as public and private construction and permanent loans, subject to certain conditions described later. These financing sources can then be used to pay for necessary repairs at the property and to ensure that the property is financially stable in the long term. In addition, PBV and PBRA subsidies have traditionally been more adequately appropriated by Congress, due to the public–private nature of those subsidies.

---

34. Rice, *supra* note 23.

35. Abt Associates, Inc., *Capital Needs in the Public Housing Program* (Nov. 24, 2010), https://www.hud.gov/sites/documents/PH_CAPITAL_NEEDS.PDF [https://perma.cc/6JXY-WHXC].

36. Letter from Dominique Blom, General Deputy Assistant Secretary for Public and Indian Housing to an Executive Director (Nov. 13, 2018), https://nlihc.org/sites/default/files/Repositioning_Public_Housing-PIH.pdf [https://perma.cc/7M8K-J4DZ].

37. *Rental Assistance Demonstration–Final Implementation, Revision 4*, U.S. Dep't of Hous. & Urban Dev., HUD Notice H 2019-09 (Sept. 5, 2019); *Rental Assistance Demonstration (RAD) Notice Regarding Fair Housing and Civil Rights Requirements and Relocation Requirements Applicable to RAD First Component—Public Housing Conversions*, U.S. Dep't of Hous. & Urban Dev., HUD Notice H 2016-17 (November 10, 2016). The main difference between PBV and PBRA is that the PHA is involved in administering PBVs to private owners, whereas PBRA assistance is administered directly by HUD (via Contract Administrators) to private owners. Amy McClain, Beginner's Guide to Public Housing Conversion under RAD (ABA Aug. 22, 2014).

In addition to ensuring that public housing properties to become more financial stable and leverage public and private financing, the RAD program includes a number of unique protections to protect the long-term affordability of these properties and to prevent displacement of existing public housing residents.

First, the RAD program requires the automatic renewal of the PBV or PBRA subsidy contract at the end of each term. The RAD PBV and PBRA Housing Assistance Payment contracts ("RAD HAP Contracts") specifically state:

> The Contract Administrator and the Owner acknowledge and agree that upon expiration of the initial term of the HAP Contract, and upon expiration of each renewal term of the HAP Contract, the Contract Administrator shall offer to renew the HAP Contract and the Owner shall accept each offer to renew the HAP Contract, subject to the terms and conditions applicable at the time of each offer, and further subject to the availability of appropriations for each year of each such renewal.[38]

This concept is unique to the RAD program; as discussed later in Section II.C, a non-RAD HAP Contract does not require renewal at the end of its term. This renewal requirement ensures that rental assistance will continue to be provided for residents at the property (subject to adequate federal appropriations).[39]

Second, the RAD program requires a RAD Use Agreement to be recorded in a senior position on the property.[40] The RAD Use Agreement runs concurrently with the term of the RAD HAP Contract, and automatically renews when the RAD HAP Contract renews. It also remains in effect for the remainder of the term of the RAD HAP Contract if the RAD HAP Contract is abated or terminated. If such abatement or termination of the RAD HAP Contract occurs, the RAD Use Agreement incorporates certain additional affordability requirements. Specifically, if the RAD HAP Contract is abated or terminated, the RAD Use Agreement requires that new residents have incomes at or below 80 percent of the area median income and that the portion of rent paid by these residents does not exceed 30 percent of 80 percent of the area median income. The RAD Use Agreement also requires HUD approval prior to any transfer, conveyance, or encumbrance of the property, and allows liens associated with public and private financing only if such liens are explicitly subordinate to the RAD Use Agreement. These requirements are intended to provide an additional layer of protection to ensure the long-term affordability of RAD properties.

---

38. *Part I Housing Assistance Payments Contract, Rental Assistance Demonstration (RAD) for the Conversion of Public Housing to Project-Based Section 8*, U.S. DEP'T OF HOUS. & URBAN DEV., HUD Form 52620; *Part II PBRA Housing Assistance Payments Contract Rental Assistance Demonstration (RAD) for the Conversion of Public Housing to Project-Based Section 8*, U.S. DEP'T OF HOUS. & URBAN DEV., HUD Form 52618; *Rental Assistance Demonstration (RAD) for the Conversion of Public Housing to the Section 8 Project-Based Voucher (PBV) Program PART 1 OF HAP CONTRACT*, U.S. DEP'T OF HOUS. & URBAN DEV., HUD Form 52621; *Rental Assistance Demonstration (RAD) for the Conversion of Public Housing to the Section 8 Project-Based Voucher (PBV) Program PART 2 OF HAP CONTRACT*, U.S. DEP'T OF HOUS. & URBAN DEV., HUD Form 52621.

39. Although this requirement is subject to congressional appropriations, congressional appropriations have been sufficient in recent years to renew all PBRA and PBV HAP Contracts.

40. *Rental Assistance Demonstration Use Agreement*, U.S. DEP'T OF HOUS. & URBAN DEV., HUD Form 52625.

Third, HUD requires some form of meaningful ownership and control by a public agency or nonprofit for all RAD properties. For properties that will be using LIHTCs, during the initial term and all renewal terms of the RAD HAP Contract, a public agency or nonprofit (directly or through an affiliate) must (1) hold a fee simple interest in the property site; (2) be the lessor under a ground lease with a new property owner; (3) have the direct or indirect legal authority (via contract, partnership share or agreement of an equity partnership, voting rights, or otherwise) to direct the financial and legal interests of the property's owner with respect to the RAD units; (4) own 51 percent or more of the general partner interests in a limited partnership or 51 percent or more of the managing member interests in a limited liability company with all powers of a general partner or managing member, as applicable; (5) own a lesser percentage of the general partner or managing member interests and hold certain control rights as approved by HUD; (6) own 51 percent or more of all ownership interests in a limited partnership or limited liability company and hold certain control rights as approved by HUD; or (7) demonstrate other ownership and control arrangements approved by HUD.[41] These requirements are intended to replicate, in some form, the public ownership of public housing properties that exist prior to the RAD conversion. In addition, many PHAs have created nonprofit affiliates and are considering one or more ways to be involved in the property after the RAD conversion.[42]

Fourth, the flexibility of the RAD program is intended to allow for repairs to be made at the property with the new public and private financing that is leveraged. The scope of repairs made at the time of the RAD conversion varies among properties and is largely dependent on the condition of the property and the amount of financing resources available. Some properties undergo minor rehab and others undergo substantial rehab; some properties pursue a demolition and rebuild on site; and others pursue a demolition of the current property and a rebuild offsite. Prior to the RAD conversion, HUD requires the PHA to submit a Capital Needs Assessment (CNA) in order to assess the property's condition and establish capital replacement reserve requirements, as well as a Scope of Work describing the proposed repairs to be made at the time of the RAD conversion. Regardless of the scope of repairs, HUD requires 1-for-1 unit replacement, with some limited exceptions.[43]

Finally, the RAD program includes certain unique and important resident rights.[44] Public housing residents living at the property prior to the RAD conversion cannot be permanently displaced and any resident that needs to be temporarily relocated to facilitate

---

41. HUD Notice H 2019-09, *supra* note 37, at Section 1.4(A)(11).
42. For further discussion about how PHAs are repositioning themselves, see Chapter 12.
43. HUD Notice H 2019-09, *supra* note 37; HUD Notice H 2016-17, *supra* note 37 ("Conversions may not result in a reduction of the number of assisted units, except by a de minimis amount. A de minimis reduction of units may include any of the following: a) The greater of five units or the number of units (rounded to the nearest whole number) corresponding to five percent of the number of ACC units in the Project (or RAD-converted portfolio, if both the portfolio and de minimis units are counted in the aggregate) immediately prior to conversion; b) Any unit that has been vacant for more than 24 months at the time of RAD Application; and c) Units that, if removed from assistance, will allow the PHA to more effectively or efficiently serve assisted households through: 1) reconfiguring apartments (e.g., converting efficiency units to one-bedroom units); or 2) facilitating social service delivery (e.g., converting a basement unit into community space), subject to HUD approval.").
44. HUD Notice H 2019-09, *supra* note 37; HUD Notice H 2016-17, *supra* note 37. *See also Rental Assistance Demonstration (RAD)*, NATIONAL HOUSING LAW PROJECT (Sept. 7, 2017), https://

rehabilitation or construction has the right to return to an assisted unit at the property once rehabilitation or construction is completed.[45] Current residents cannot be excluded from occupancy at the property after conversion based on any rescreening, income eligibility, or income targeting.[46] If, as a result of the RAD conversion, a current resident's rent would increase by the greater of 10 percent or $25, the rent increase must be phased in over three or five years.[47] Throughout the RAD application process, the PHA must provide affected residents with certain written notifications, conduct several meetings with residents to describe their rights and the conversion plans, and provide comprehensive written responses to any received comments.[48] Even after the RAD conversion, residents have the right to establish and operate a resident organization and are eligible to receive at least $25 per occupied unit per year for resident participation activities.[49] Owners must attach specific RAD house rules to residents' leases, which incorporate certain termination notifications, a grievance procedure, and resident mobility protections.[50] PHAs and owners must also comply with certain relocation rules for tenants who are temporarily relocated, and must have a written relocation plan if temporary relocation is anticipated to exceed 12 months.[51] In order to ensure that the RAD program achieves its objectives, it is critical that PHAs and owners pay close attention to these resident rights.

2. Section 18 Demolition/Disposition

The public housing ACC prohibits PHAs from demolishing or transferring an ownership interest in public housing properties without HUD approval. If public housing properties are in especially poor physical condition or if the location of the public housing properties has become unsuitable for residential use, PHAs can apply to HUD for demolition and/or disposition approval pursuant to Section 18 of the Act. Subject to HUD review and approval, Section 18 allows PHAs to remove public housing units from their public housing portfolio and to receive Tenant Protection Vouchers (TPVs), which the PHA can convert to PBVs at a subsidy level that more closely aligns with market-rate rents in the community.[52] This results in much higher levels of rental assistance than the RAD program, and can be used to leverage more public and private financing sources to preserve the property. Although Section 18 is not always used as a preservation tool, it can be an important resource for preserving rental assistance, especially when the PHA will be involved in the new ownership and management of the property after the Section 18 demolition or disposition, and when the PHA converts the TPVs to PBVs to be attached to the converted property.

---

www.nhlp.org/resources/rental-assistance-demonstration-rad/ [https://perma.cc/UNC3-9CYW] (last visited June 8, 2021).

45. HUD Notice H 2019-09, *supra* note 37, at Section 1.4(A)(5)(B).

46. *Id.* at Section 1.6(C)(1) and Section 1.7(B)(1).

47. *Id.* at Section 1.6(C)(3) and Section 1.7(B)(3).

48. *Id.* at Section 1.8.

49. *Id.* at Section 1.6(C)(5), Section 1.7(B)(5), and Attachment 1B.

50. *Id.* at Attachment 1E.

51. HUD Notice H 2016-17, *supra* note 37.

52. Section 18 of the U.S. Housing Act of 1937; 24 C.F.R. pt. 970; *Demolition and/or Disposition of Public Housing Property, Eligibility for Tenant Protection Vouchers and Associated Requirements*, U.S. Dep't of Hous. & Urban Dev., HUD Notice PIH 2021-07 (Jan. 19, 2021).

In order to pursue a Section 18 demolition or disposition, the PHA must submit an application to HUD and meet certain criteria.[53] In order to obtain HUD approval to demolish an existing public housing property, the public housing property must be "obsolete as to physical condition, location, or other factors, making it unsuitable for housing purposes, and no reasonable program of modifications is cost-effective to return the public housing project or portion of the project to useful life."[54] In reviewing an application's claim of physical obsolescence, HUD will consider whether there are structural deficiencies that cannot be corrected in a cost-effective manner (e.g., faulty structural design), or other design or site problems (e.g., severe erosion or flooding).[55] In reviewing an application's claim that the neighborhood is no longer suitable for residential use, HUD will consider whether there is physical deterioration of the neighborhood, change from residential to industrial or commercial development, or environmental conditions that jeopardize the suitability of the property for residential use.[56] In order to demonstrate that repairs will not be cost-effective, the PHA must show that the necessary repairs would exceed 57.14 percent of HUD's total development cost standards[57] (or 62.5 percent for elevator structures).[58]

In order to obtain HUD approval for a Section 18 disposition to transfer the property to a new owner, the PHA must certify that the retention of the property is not in the best interests of the residents or the PHA for at least one of the following reasons: (1) conditions in the area surrounding the property (density, or industrial or commercial development) adversely affect the health and safety of the tenants or the operation of the property by the PHA; (2) disposition would allow the acquisition, development, or rehabilitation of properties that will be more efficiently or effectively operated as low-income housing developments; or (3) the PHA has otherwise determined the disposition to be appropriate for reasons that are consistent with the goals of the PHA and the PHA Plan and that are otherwise consistent with the Act (i.e., the PHA only has 50 or fewer public housing units in its portfolio, the units are physically obsolete, or the units are scattered across multiple neighborhoods and inefficient to maintain).[59]

A Section 18 disposition requires the PHA to transfer the public housing property to a separate ownership entity. This new ownership entity can be an affiliate or instrumentality of the PHA, which enables the PHA to obtain more subsidy while retaining its control and ownership of the property. In addition, the PHA can retain fee title and transfer ownership of the property through a long-term ground lease. If a property will continue to serve as affordable housing after the Section 18 conversion, HUD will also require the PHA to ensure that the units are operated as affordable housing and reserved for residents at or below 80 percent of area median income for at least 30 years, and such affordability restriction must be senior to any other liens and must survive foreclosure.

---

53. *Id.*
54. 24 C.F.R. 970.15.
55. 24 C.F.R. 970.15(b)(1)(i).
56. 24 C.F.R. 970.15(b)(1)(ii).
57. *2019 Unit Total Development Cost (TDC) Limits*, U.S. Dep't of Hous. & Urban Dev., https://www.hud.gov/sites/dfiles/PIH/documents/TDCs_2019_Final.pdf [https://perma.cc/6GDU -HWKC] (last visited June 8, 2021).
58. 24 C.F.R. 970.15(b)(2).
59. 24 C.F.R. 970.17.

If the PHA's Section 18 demolition or disposition application is approved by HUD, the PHA can then apply to receive TPVs for the units at the property that have been occupied within the last 24 months prior to the application. These TPVs are valuable to PHAs because they are additional funds from HUD that are permanently added to a PHA's voucher pool, are renewed each year, and can be attached to certain properties as PBVs with subsidy levels that are often much higher than public housing operating and capital funds.[60] This means that PHAs do not have to use their existing resources to provide rental assistance for affected tenants, and can leverage a higher subsidy level to obtain public and private financing to rebuild or make repairs at these properties.

3. Section 22 Streamlined Voluntary Conversion

For PHAs with fewer than 250 public housing units remaining in their portfolios, another helpful public housing preservation tool can be the Streamlined Voluntary Conversion (SVC), pursuant to Section 22 of the Act.[61] Once approved by HUD, SVC enables PHAs to remove the public housing restrictions of the ACC and receive TPVs, which can be used to preserve the rental assistance through a different type of subsidy. In order to be eligible for the SVC, the PHA must have 250 or fewer public housing units remaining in its public housing portfolio and must use the SVC to convert the remainder of its public housing units and close out its public housing program.[62]

Similar to a Section 18 demolition or disposition, SVC enables the PHA to receive TPVs for affected residents, which can be used at the converting property or elsewhere in the private market. However, unlike a Section 18 demolition or disposition, the SVC TPVs are provided as tenant-based vouchers and the PHA must receive resident consent to attach the subsidy to a replacement property as PBVs.[63] If a resident does not give this consent, they must be allowed to use their TPV at the property as a regular tenant-based voucher. Similar to a Section 18 demolition or disposition, TPVs provide new and higher levels of rental assistance compared to public housing operating and capital subsidy, which enables the property to leverage public and private financing sources for repairs.

SVC can be an especially useful preservation tool if the PHA is retaining ownership of the property after conversion and is using SVC to obtain a higher level of subsidy, while simultaneously closing out its public housing portfolio.

4. Other Public Housing Preservation Tools

Although not discussed in detail in this chapter, there are several other HUD programs that can be used to preserve public housing. The Mixed Finance program was the predecessor to the RAD program and allows PHAs to provide public housing capital and operating funds to a private owner who commits to operate a certain number of units as public housing in

---

60. *Implementation of the Federal Fiscal Year (FFY) 2018 Funding Provisions for the Housing Choice Voucher Program*, U.S. Dep't of Hous. & Urban Dev., HUD Notice PIH 2018-09 (Dec. 31, 2018).

61. 42 U.S.C. § 1437t. *See also* 24 C.F.R. Part 972; *Streamlined Voluntary Conversions of Last Remaining Projects of Small Public Housing Agencies*, U.S. Dep't of Hous. & Urban Dev., HUD Notice PIH 2019-05 (Mar. 21, 2019).

62. HUD Notice PIH 2019-05, *supra* note 61.

63. *Id.*

accordance with all applicable public housing requirements.[64] The Choice Neighborhoods Initiative provides several planning and implementation grants each year, up to $30 million each, to comprehensively transform a selected neighborhood. These grants can be used to revitalize severely distressed public and/or federally assisted housing and to enable critical improvements to vacant properties, businesses, services, and schools.[65]

There is no one-size-fits all approach to preserving and revitalizing public housing, but these programs provide some tools to ensure housing stability, retain critical rental assistance, and leverage public and private debt and equity to pay for necessary repairs and improvements. Given the historic disinvestment in public housing funding that caused deterioration of the properties, the ability to obtain additional public or private funding is necessary to ensure the long-term preservation of public housing properties.

C. HUD Multifamily Housing

HUD also provides subsidized mortgages and project-based rental assistance contracts in other types of federally assisted properties. HUD's mortgage programs provide loans to private owners to build and operate affordable housing for a certain number of years and with certain rent restrictions. HUD's project-based rental assistance contracts provide rental assistance to supplement what low-income residents pay for rent (usually based on 30 percent of their adjusted income). Each type of assistance comes with certain risks for the long-term preservation of these properties.

Many of the preservation risks associated with HUD's mortgage programs are tied to the repayment of the mortgage, either as scheduled or earlier than expected. When a loan is fully repaid according to its original amortization schedule, the mortgage and accompanying affordable housing restrictions end. Mortgage maturity is when the owner fully repays the loan according to the original loan repayment schedule. Mortgage prepayment is when the owner fully repays the loan before it was originally scheduled to be paid off.

Many of the preservation risks associated with HUD's project-based rental assistance contracts are similarly tied to the term of the contract. When the project-based rental assistance contract ends, the rental subsidy ends. A contract "opt out" occurs when the owner decides not to renew the project-based rental assistance contract at the end of its term. Contract termination occurs when HUD terminates the rental assistance contract with the owner because the owner has violated the contract.

Responding to these risks depends on the type of federal assistance, the cause of the end of the assistance, local market pressures, and the capital needs of the property. Some of the tools to respond to these risks are described next.

1. Mortgage Maturity

As noted earlier, when the HUD-assisted mortgage matures, usually after 30 or 40 years, the affordability restrictions and accompanying regulatory agreement end with it. This

---

64. 24 C.F.R. Part 905. *See also Mixed Finance Public Housing*, U.S. DEP'T OF HOUS. & URBAN DEV., https://www.hud.gov/program_offices/public_indian_housing/programs/ph/hope6/mfph [https://perma.cc/B854-QTMT] (last visited June 8, 2021).

65. *Choice Neighborhoods*, U.S. DEP'T OF HOUS. & URBAN DEV., https://www.hud.gov/cn [https://perma.cc/2USX-GYPH] (last visited June 8, 2021).

leaves low-income tenants at risk of displacement, especially in high-cost markets where rents will be drastically increased to market rate rents. Until recently, there was no assistance for residents living at these properties.

Since 2011, Congress has annually appropriated rental assistance for residents at certain properties with maturing mortgages.[66] This rental assistance can be provided as TPVs or as "enhanced vouchers"[67] to at-risk tenants living in certain properties with maturing mortgages that are located in "low-vacancy areas."[68] The property owner is able to apply for this rental assistance on behalf of its residents if (1) the property is located in a "low-vacancy area," as defined by HUD;[69] (2) the mortgage maturity occurred within the last five years or will occur within 180 days of the owner's application to HUD; (3) the resident is living at the property at the time of the owner's application to HUD, is not currently assisted under any federal, state, or local rental assistance program, is eligible for voucher assistance, and, as a result of the mortgage maturity, either is paying or may have to pay more than 30 percent of their adjusted monthly income toward rent; and (4) there are no outstanding civil rights matters affecting the property.[70] Unfortunately, residents themselves are not able to apply directly to HUD for this rental assistance, and must rely on the owner to do so.

Although there are currently no federal notice requirements for residents residing at properties with maturing mortgages, there may be state or local notice or rent control laws that may add certain additional elements to preserving these properties. For a list of properties with maturing HUD-assisted mortgages in your community, please visit the National Housing Preservation Database.[71]

2. Mortgage Prepayment

Prepaying a HUD-assisted mortgage will also terminate the affordability restrictions and applicable regulatory agreement at the property, creating a similar risk of tenant displacement.

If the owner is prepaying a HUD-assisted mortgage prior to its original amortization schedule, there are certain notice requirements that the owner must comply with. Specifically, the owner must provide at least 150 days but not more than 270 days advance written notice of the proposed prepayment to tenants, HUD, and the local government. State laws

---

66. *See, e.g.*, Consolidated Appropriations Act of 2017, Pub. L. No. 115–31, div. K, tit. II, 131 Stat. 135, 760 (providing up to $5 million within $110 million set-aside for Section 8 tenant protection Vouchers); Consolidated Appropriations Act of 2018, Pub. L. No. 115–141, div. L, tit. II, 132 Stat. 348, 1009 (providing up to $5 million within $85 million set-aside for Section 8 tenant protection Vouchers).

67. Enhanced vouchers are similar to regular tenant-based vouchers, with two special elements: (1) enhanced vouchers can exceed the local housing authority's regular payment standard, which allows for a reasonable rental subsidy that is more comparable to market rents, and (2) enhanced vouchers provide the resident with a right to remain at the property, even after the mortgage matures and the property converts to a market rate property. If the resident decides to move from the property, the enhanced voucher will become a regular tenant-based voucher. 42 U.S.C. § 1437f(t).

68. *Funding Availability for Set-Aside Tenant-Protection Vouchers—Fiscal Year 2017 Funding*, HUD Notice PIH 2018–02 (Feb. 8, 2018).

69. "Low-vacancy area" was most recently defined by HUD Notice PIH 2018-02. *Id.*

70. *Id.*

71. National Housing Preservation Database, *supra* note 29.

may require additional notice to tenants and others in order to create some time to evaluate the risk for existing residents. In addition, some HUD-assisted mortgages require explicit HUD approval prior to prepayment, and HUD and owners must follow the standards and procedures required by Section 250 of the National Housing Act.[72]

In addition to these notice requirements, if the mortgage is prepaid, existing residents are also eligible for "enhanced vouchers." As described earlier, these enhanced vouchers provide existing residents with the right to continue living at the property, even after the prepayment of the HUD-assisted mortgage, and enable the local housing authority to provide rental assistance subsidy amounts that are more comparable with market rents to ensure that the resident has the rental assistance necessary to exercise their right to remain. There may also be state or local notice or rent control laws that may add certain additional elements to preserving these properties.

3. HAP Contract Renewal

Upon expiration of an existing HAP Contract, the owner has a choice whether to renew its participation in the program or to "opt out." If the owner decides to renew the HAP Contract, Congress and HUD have established rules and policies governing the rent level of the government's contract renewal offer that will be paid to the owner. For these properties, a project-based contract renewal under the Multifamily Assisted Housing Reform and Affordability Act of 1997 (MAHRAA) is the primary tool for providing necessary rental assistance to make preservation transactions financially feasible while preserving affordability for tenants. The rent levels obtainable under a Section 8 renewal contract are critical to determining the nature and scope of preservation efforts.

For properties that are in acceptable physical condition, there are four primary ways to renew the HAP Contract. The renewal options depend on a comparison of the Section 8 rent level under the expiring contract with the market rent level in the community. HUD describes these options in detail in its Section 8 Renewal Policy Guide, as summarized here:[73]

- *Renewal at current terms*: This most common option is used where the owner seeks to renew a HAP Contract and the pre-expiration contract rent is comparable to market rent. HUD and the owner simply extend the contract with essentially the same terms and rents as before. Owners with rents less than market value may also choose this option to bide their time for a year, before deciding to pursue one of the other contract renewal options below.
- *Mark-Up-to-Market or Mark-Up-to-Budget*: This option can be used if the contract rents are lower than the local market rents and the owner of an eligible property wants to increase project income via higher contract rents. Under a "mark up," the contract is renewed and HUD raises the contract rents to match the local market rents.[74] Participating owners must commit to remain in the Section 8 program

---

72. 12 U.S.C. § 1715z-15.

73. HUD, Office of Housing, Section 8 Renewal Policy Guide (issued Apr. 17, 2009), https://www.hud.gov/sites/documents/23815_S8RENEW.PDF [https://perma.cc/5FKD-LA37].

74. There are two options for renewing under Mark Up to Market—the Option One-A Entitlement Eligibility and the Option One-B Discretionary Authority Eligibility. Under the Entitlement

for at least five years, with only annual cost adjustments. The additional rental assistance available under this option can be used to finance some of the repair or acquisition costs or to increase distributions to the current owner. For properties already owned by nonprofits, HUD has created a "Mark Up to Budget" variant, which allows a nonprofit owner to increase rents to a new budget level that supports debt service on a new rehabilitation loan, under specific conditions, as long as the resulting new contract rent does not exceed the local market rents.

- *"Mark-to-Market" restructuring*: This approach is used where the contract rent is significantly higher than the local market rent. Usually, the owner cannot simply exit the Section 8 program without suffering financial hardship because project rental income would decrease too much, creating difficulties in maintaining debt payments and operating expenses. Under Mark-to-Market, the contract is almost always renewed, and HUD lowers the Section 8 rents for the property to market rents. The debt must be restructured (divided into two portions, one currently serviceable and the other not) or partially forgiven in order to maintain financial viability. Owners using Mark-to-Market restructuring must commit to a 30-year use agreement, and the term of the renewed HAP Contract is 20 years, subject to appropriations, and is renewable at expiration.[75]

- *Mark-to-Market "lite"*: This option can be used if the contract rent is only moderately higher than the market rent for the property, so that the owner can keep the property financially viable by renewing the rental assistance at the (lower) market rents. HUD and the owner renew the contract and reduce the rent to market rent without debt restructuring or partial forgiveness.

Regardless of the approach, the HAP Contract renewal process is complex. HUD and the owner may disagree on such key issues as the appropriate rent level and the physical condition of the property. In addition, residents have specific notice and participation rights, depending on the option chosen by the owner.[76]

Eligibility, the property must not have a Real Estate Assessment Center (REAC) physical inspection score below 60, the owner must be a profit-motivated or limited distribution entity, comparable rents must be at or above 100% of FMR, and the property must not have a low- or moderate-income use restriction on the property, such as a property subject to Section 250 prepayment approval. Under the Discretionary Authority, projects that are not automatically eligible under Option One-A or that seek rents in excess of 150 percent of FMR may still be approved by HUD if they meet one of three criteria: (1) tenants at the property are a "vulnerable population," as demonstrated by a majority of units rented to elderly, disabled, or large families (five or more persons); (2) the property is in a low-vacancy-rate area (less than 3%) and vouchers are difficult to use; or (3) the property is a high priority for the local community, as demonstrated by contribution of state and local funds.

75. SECTION 8 RENEWAL POLICY GUIDE, *supra* note 73. Note that a restructuring plan could include a conversion of some or all of the project-based assistance to vouchers, pursuant to a rental assistance assessment plan. Mark to Market also includes additional financial incentives for green rehabilitation, including energy efficiency and green building practices, under HUD's "Green Pilot." *M2M Green Initiative*, U.S. DEP'T OF HOUS. & URBAN DEV., https://www.hud.gov/program_offices /housing/mfh/presrv/presmfh/greenini [https://perma.cc/S9MX-PCZT]. The administration of Mark to Market has been the responsibility of HUD's Office of Affordable Housing Preservation.

76. SECTION 8 RENEWAL POLICY GUIDE, *supra* note 73.

If an owner instead decides not to renew its HAP Contract, it must provide at least 12 months' notice to existing residents and to HUD of its intent to opt out of the contract, or permit tenants to remain at the property while paying their current rent amounts until one year after proper notice is served. As of the date of the HAP Contract opt out, existing residents will be eligible to receive "enhanced vouchers," as described earlier. These enhanced vouchers will enable residents to exercise their right to remain at the property, even after the HAP Contract opt out, with rental assistance that supports their ability to exercise their right to remain.

4. RAD for PRAC

The HUD Section 202 program provides supportive housing for the elderly. Since the program was created in the 1950s, there have been several iterations of how HUD has financed these properties, initially with only direct loans (between 1959 and 1974), then with direct loans and Section 8 rental assistance contracts (between 1974 and 1990), and then most recently with capital advances and a rental subsidy called a Project Rental Assistance Contract (PRAC) (beginning in 1990 and continuing today).[77] Although each iteration of the Section 202 program brings its own set of preservation challenges, HUD has recently implemented a version of the RAD preservation program for Section 202 properties with PRAC assistance.[78]

Under the Section 202 PRAC program, HUD provides interest-free capital advances to nonprofit organizations to finance the construction, rehabilitation, or acquisition of properties that will serve as supportive housing for very low-income elderly residents, and provides rent subsidies via PRACs to help make those properties affordable to those elderly residents.[79] The PRAC subsidy level is designed to cover the difference between the HUD-approved operating costs for the property and the residents' contribution towards rent, which is generally 30 percent of their adjusted income. The owner goes through a budget-based rent increase process every year to set the PRAC subsidy levels and to renew the PRAC subsidy contracts. This annual renewal process makes it extremely challenging to access debt and equity to finance capital needs for these properties. This also means that the PRAC subsidy level can vary widely from property to property, depending on what is included and accepted in an owner's budget-based rent increase request. HUD has recently taken some steps to standardize the budget-based rent increase process across HUD field offices,[80] but current PRAC rent levels can range from less than 80 percent of

---

77. *FY 2020 HUD's Section 202 Supportive Housing for the Elderly Program (Section 202)*, U.S. Dep't of Hous. & Urban Dev. (May 26, 2021), https://www.hud.gov/sites/dfiles/SPM/documents/Section202SupportiveHousingfortheElderlyTechnicalCorrectionFR-6400-N-52.pdf [https://perma.cc/84YH-QAQM].

78. Section 237 of Title II, Division L, Transportation, Housing and Urban Development, and Related Agencies, of the Consolidated Appropriations Act of 201, Pub. L. 115-141; HUD Notice H 2019-09, *supra* note 37.

79. *Section 202 Supportive Housing for the Elderly*, U.S. Dep't of Hous. & Urban Dev., https://www.hud.gov/program_offices/housing/mfh/progdesc/eld202 [https://perma.cc/3L56-DB4V] (last visited June 8, 2021).

80. Juliana Bilowich, *HUD Issues Updated Rent Increase Guidance For PRAC Owners*, Leading Age (March 18, 2020) https://leadingage.org/regulation/hud-issues-updated-rent-increase-guidance-prac-owners [https://perma.cc/5TZ8-X2AG].

the fair-market rent in some areas to over 120 percent of the fair-market rent in other areas. This also means that replacement reserve amounts can vary widely by property, with some properties having no replacement reserves and other properties having significant reserve levels.

The RAD for PRAC program seeks to stabilize these Section 202 PRAC properties by converting them to PBV or PBRA, similar to the RAD Component 1 program described previously. At the time of the RAD for PRAC conversion, the Section 202 capital advance and PRAC documents are released and replaced with a new elderly housing use agreement (to be recorded in first position) and a 20-year HAP contract.[81] The initial contract rents are set at the lesser of the current PRAC rents or 120 percent of the fair-market rent, which will be subject to an annual operating cost adjustment factor for the term of the HAP Contract.[82] The RAD for PRAC conversion also allows more flexibility in the project ownership structure, in order to allow for the admission of low-income housing tax credit investors, as long as a nonprofit entity controls the owner or property. This enables the property to leverage equity from low-income housing tax credits, which can be used to make necessary repairs at the property. Finally, the RAD for PRAC conversion also allows properties to increase the budget line item for supportive services from $15 per unit per month to $27 per unit per month, which is especially important in elderly properties.[83] Although the RAD for PRAC program is new, the focus on preservation and financial stability for these properties will be especially critical to the long-term availability of housing dedicated to seniors.

D. Other Preservation Risks

While this chapter primarily addresses the preservation issues with respect to HUD-assisted properties, a variety of other programs raise many of the same types of expiring use issues.[84] For example, the LIHTC program, as discussed in Chapter 9, initially required limited rents for a 15-year "compliance period" only. Post-1989 LIHTC projects require limited rents for an "extended use period" of 30 years in total or such longer periods as determined by the credit allocating agency.[85] The first wave of expiring first-generation (pre-1990) tax credit properties has raised preservation issues closely akin to those of the HUD-subsidized mortgage stock, in which a deep subsidy such as project-based rental assistance may be unavailable as a preservation incentive. Even tax credit properties with extended use commitments may raise similar issues if owners exercise any "qualified contract" rights after their 14th year, or when they reach the end of their extended-use period.

In addition, the terms of the initial mortgages for many affordable housing properties subsidized by the U.S. Department of Agriculture will mature by 2028, with almost all mortgages maturing by 2050.[86] Similarly, a host of other state and locally distributed

---

81. HUD Notice H 2019-09, *supra* note 37.

82. *Id.*

83. *Id.*

84. One notable example is the Section 515 program, administered by the U. S. Department of Agriculture (USDA) through its Rural Development (RD) agency, which raises recapitalization challenges but still contains certain conversion restrictions.

85. 26 U.S.C. §§ 42(i)(1), (h)(6)(A)-(D).

86. An Advocate's Guide to Rural Housing Preservation: Prepayments, Mortgage Maturities, and Foreclosures, National Housing Law Project (2018), https://www

subsidy programs—such as the HOME Investments Partnership Program (HOME), Community Development Block Grant (CDBG) state and local affordable housing trust funds, and redevelopment tax-increment financing—all involve time-limited use restrictions. The tools available to preserve these properties look similar to those described earlier, and will need to similarly evolve to meet new challenges.

E. Key Financial Resources

Significant amounts of financing are often necessary to adequately preserve affordable housing properties for the long term. As described in Chapters 9 and 10, there are a variety of federal and state sources of financing for affordable housing properties. Often, preservation of existing affordable housing properties requires the use of multiple federal and state sources of financing, layered and intertwined together to ensure compliance with all applicable restrictions. Typical sources of financing used for preservation transactions include tax-exempt bonds, private equity generated from federal and state low-income housing tax credits, HUD FHA-insured financing, state and local housing trust fund programs, CDBG funds, and HOME funds.

F. State and Local Government Initiatives

As federal affordable housing preservation efforts have varied over the past decades, state and local governments have adopted a wide variety of preservation programs,[87] leveraging local funding, state-controlled resources, and/or state or local regulatory powers. Although budget constraints have restricted some state-funded efforts, many states and localities are nevertheless allocating housing trust funds, acquisition funds, and predevelopment loan funds to preservation efforts.[88] Many local governments also have redevelopment funds that can be used for affordable housing, including preservation of existing properties. Local property tax relief for preservation purposes or for nonprofit ownership is another important tool, providing an additional incentive for current owners to recommit to certain affordability restrictions.[89] In addition, many states now provide earmarks of 9 % LIHTCs or extra points in the tax credit allocation process to applications involving specific affordable housing preservation efforts. Some states and localities take a similar approach with allocating 4 % LIHTCs and bond financing.

.nhlp.org/wp-content/uploads/2018/05/Rural-Preservation-Handbook.pdf [https://perma.cc/86VJ -FG5M]; *Maturing USDA Section 515 Rural Rental Housing Loans*; ArcGIS, http://www.arcgis .com/home/webmap/viewer.html?webmap=362d12b9a06b41b1a7d76260ddd9fb00&extent =- 126.6724,22.4325,-61.7651,51.945 [https://perma.cc/2L4K-X27F] (last visited June 8, 2021).

87. *See generally*, *Components to a Successful Local Preservation Strategy*, National Housing Trust https://www.nationalhousingtrust.org/state-and-local-preservation-initiatives [https://perma .cc/JR2G-3DMW] for the state-by-state resources compiled by the NHT (last visited June 8, 2021).

88. *See Dedicated Funding for Preservation;* National Housing Trust, https://www.national housingtrust.org/dedicated-funding-for-preservation [https://perma.cc/NYP7-3NL6] (last visited June 8, 2021).

89. *See, e.g.*, Cook Co., Ill. Mun. Code Ch. 74, Art. II, Div. 2, http://library.municode.com /index.aspx?clientId=13805&stateId=13&stateName=Illinois [https://perma.cc/SR28-3G9D] (Class S property relief for certain project-based Section 8 contract renewals) (last visited June 8, 2021); Cal. Rev. & Tax. Code § 214 (2020).

State and local governments may also use their regulatory powers for preservation. These restrictions include notice and purchase opportunity laws, relocation protections, and generally applicable rent controls.[90] Such laws may also affect preservation efforts that involve refinancing. Localities may also utilize other programmatic initiatives, such as planning requirements, dedicated staffing, and data collection.[91]

III. CONCLUSION

The challenges and specific resources available to preserve existing affordable housing properties depends on the type of assistance currently provided at the property and the local housing market. But for every property, it takes a team of committed decision makers, significant amounts of financial resources, and preservation-focused programs to ensure the long-term availability and habitability of existing affordable housing properties.

---

90. *See generally State and Local Preservation Initiatives*, NATIONAL HOUSING LAW PROJECT (July 6, 2018) https://www.nhlp.org/our-initiatives/state-local-preservation-initiatives/ [https://perma.cc/N77G-8S53]. Such state and local laws may raise federal preemption issues, which have received inconsistent judicial treatment. *Compare, e.g.*, Forest Park II v. Hadley, 336 F.3d 724 (8th Cir. 2003) (federal law impliedly preempts local notice law), and Mother Zion Tenant Ass'n v. Donovan, 865 N.Y.S.2d 64 (N.Y. App. Div. 2008) (same, local purchase law) *with* Topa Equities v. City of Los Angeles, 342 F.3d 1065, 2003 WL 22072170 (9th Cir. Sept. 8, 2003) (no implied preemption of local rent-setting law after conversion) and Kenneth Arms Tenant Ass'n v. Martinez, 2001 U.S. Dist. LEXIS 11470, No. Civ. S-01-832 LKK/JFM (E.D. Cal. 2001) (no implied preemption of state notice law).

91. *See, e.g., Awards for State and Local Housing Preservation Leaders,* MACARTHUR FOUNDATION (Nov. 17, 2007), https://www.macfound.org/press/press-releases/awards-for-state-and-local-housing-preservation-leaders/ [https://perma.cc/TMY6-FQFK].

Federal Relocation and Replacement Housing Law

16

Karen Tiedemann

I. INTRODUCTION

This chapter describes federal relocation assistance and replacement housing requirements that may be triggered when an affordable housing developer acquires occupied property.[1] Affordable housing developers often acquire existing buildings with either an intent to rehabilitate the housing and make it available to low- and moderate-income households or to demolish the existing building and replace it with new affordable housing. Whenever a developer acquires a site with the intent to rehabilitate or demolish the existing housing or commercial structures, the developer needs to be aware of relocation and replacement housing requirements. If a public agency provides funding to the developer for new low and moderate income housing, any displacement of the existing tenants may result in relocation obligations. Additionally, certain programs impose an obligation on the developers to replace the housing units demolished. Developers need to distinguish between relocation requirements and replacement housing requirements. Relocation requirements generally provide benefits to the individuals residing in the housing to be demolished or rehabilitated and ensure that the individuals are compensated for their forced move. Replacement housing obligations ensure that publicly funded programs do not result in a decrease in the number of housing units available.

Use of federal funds, including HOME funds, Community Development Block Grant (CDBG), Housing Opportunities for Persons With AIDS (HOPWA), and other HUD funding programs will trigger relocation and may also trigger replacement housing obligations.[2] And, depending upon their requirements, funding from the particular state or local government may add

---

1. Certain relocation requirements are also discussed in Chapter 4 (condominium conversion) and Chapter 8.
2. See Chapter 7 for an overview of these federal funding programs.

additional or different relocation obligations.[3] Before asking any tenant to move or raising an existing tenant's rent, affordable housing developers should review the particular relocation and replacement obligations required by the applicable funding programs.

This chapter outlines the relocation and replacement housing requirements under federal law and some of the particular relocation obligations of certain federal funding programs. Section II has ten parts, and begins with an overview, Subsection A. Subsection B outlines the federal laws and regulations governing relocation. Subsection C covers relocation plans and surveys, and Subsection D discusses notice requirements. Subsections E and F discuss relocation benefits, including eligibility requirements and the types and manner of calculation of benefits for both commercial and residential relocatees. Subsection G covers last resort housing requirements. Subsection H describes grievance and appeal procedures. Subsection I discusses waiver of benefits. Section III discusses replacement housing obligations. Section IV discusses civil rights issues sometimes raised by relocation and replacement requirements.

In addition to federal law, many states have relocation laws that might also be applicable. This chapter makes occasional reference to California's relocation law. Developers attempting to determine their relocation obligations should review both the state and federal law to determine which laws are applicable.

Affordable housing developers should be aware of their relocation and replacement housing obligations before acquiring an occupied property. Although the relocation laws place the burden for relocation on the public agency that finances the development, in reality the public agencies typically transfer these obligations to the developer. Relocation and replacement housing obligations can add significant costs to the development budget and, if not considered early, can delay the project. A developer should understand these obligations (along with their financial and time implications) and plan early to meet them in order to avoid cost overruns and delays in any development involving acquisition of occupied buildings.

II. FEDERAL RELOCATION LAW

A. Overview

Massive federal urban renewal projects of the 1950s and 1960s and, in particular, federal highway projects of the same period, generated community pressure for relocation assistance to those displaced by the "federal bulldozer." A patchwork of benefit programs emerged as different federal agencies adopted procedures and policies in response to this political pressure. In 1970, after many years of consideration and argument, the 91st Congress passed the Uniform Relocation Assistance and Property Acquisition Act of 1970 (commonly known as the Uniform Relocation Act, or the URA). The URA created uniform policies and procedures applicable to all federal agencies involved in the acquisition of property. Where traditional condemnation law focused on the value of property taken from a property owner by the government, Congress enacted the URA to address the human cost of property acquisition by providing compensation for the displacement of people and businesses.

---

3. See Chapter 8 for an overview of state funding programs.

While Congress debated the URA, numerous states were considering state laws addressing displacement caused by state and local government. California adopted its first relocation law in 1969, which was applicable only to Los Angeles County. The state legislature amended it in 1971, making it applicable statewide and mirroring the Uniform Relocation Act.[4] Other states followed suit and adopted state relocation laws applicable to projects that received either state or local funds. Apart from a few references to California's relocation law, this chapter only discusses federal relocation law. It is likely that each state's relocation law varies either in minor or major ways from federal law, so it is important to check the state laws before beginning any relocation process.

B. Applicable Law

The federal Uniform Relocation Act and the Uniform Relocation Act Regulations located at 24 and 49 Code of Federal Regulations (C.F.R.) part 24, promulgated jointly by the U.S. Department of Housing and Urban Development (HUD) and the U.S. Department of Transportation (DOT), apply to projects receiving federal funds. These laws require that a developer provide certain relocation services and benefits to residents and businesses displaced as a result of publicly funded projects and programs. Both HUD and the DOT also publish relocation handbooks that further describe their regulatory requirements.[5] The DOT adopted significant amendments to the Uniform Relocation Act Regulations early in 2005 and is currently in the rulemaking process for adopting further significant amendments to the Uniform Relocation Act Regulation in part in response to the adoption of the Moving Ahead for Progress in the 21st Century Act (MAP-21) (Pub. L. 112-141, July 6, 2012). HUD has updated its handbook to conform to the changes to the URA enacted as part of MAP-21. Updated chapters of the HUD handbook are available at HUD's website. The DOT published an updated handbook in 2018.

Developers often utilize other federal programs such as the CDBG Program and the HOME Investment Partnership Program, to finance affordable housing. These programs include specialized relocation requirements that apply in addition to the Uniform Relocation Act requirements.[6] Additionally, Section 104(d) of the Housing and Community Development Act imposes a slightly different set of relocation requirements when a lower-income household is displaced from a lower-income unit that will be demolished or converted using certain federal funds (including Community Development Block Grant and HOME funds).[7]

Many affordable housing projects are funded with both state and federal funds. In this instance a developer may need to comply with both state and federal law depending upon

---

4. CAL. GOV'T. CODE §§ 7260 *et seq.* (2010).

5. *See* U.S. DEP'T OF HOUSING & URBAN DEV. HANDBOOK 1378: Tenant Assistance, Relocation and Real Property Acquisition [hereinafter *HUD Handbook*] (2007); *see, e.g.*, U. S. DEP'T OF TRANSPORTATION, FED. HIGHWAY ADMIN., REAL ESTATE ACQUISITION GUIDE FOR LOCAL PUBLIC AGENCIES (2009).

6. *See* Displacement, Relocation, Acquisition, and Replacement of Housing, 24 C.F.R. § 570.606 (2021) (CDBG relocation regulations); *see* Displacement, Relocation, and Acquisition, 24 C.F.R. § 92.353 (HOME relocation regulations) (2021).

7. 42 U.S.C. § 5304(d); Displacement, Relocation Assistance, and Real Property Acquisition for HUD And HUD-Assisted Programs, 24 C.F.R. § 42 (2021) (implementing Section 104(d)). See 24 C.F.R. § 42.305 for definitions of lower income persons and lower-income dwelling units.

that state's requirement. For example, in California if a developer receives both state and federal funds, the developer must comply with those provisions of each that provide the greatest benefit to the displaced household.[8]

C. Relocation Plans and Surveys

Under the federal Uniform Relocation Act Regulations, a formal relocation plan is not specifically required, but planning for relocation is required.[9] The regulations state that the level of planning for relocation must be tied to the complexity of the project.[10] Planning may include surveys or studies assessing occupants' needs and identifying available resources for the displaced businesses and residences. However, under the federal regulations, the surveys and studies do not have to be compiled into a single document or relocation plan and circulated publicly.

In contrast to federal law, some states may require the preparation of relocation plans prior to displacement. For example, in California these plans must include information on the needs of the households or businesses displaced and the resources available to them. The displacing entity must survey the existing tenants to determine their specific needs. In California, the relocation plan must also demonstrate that there are adequate housing resources available to meet the needs of the displacees and that the displacing agency has adequate funds to implement the relocation program. Finally, in California, relocation plans must be made available to the displaced persons or businesses and other interested parties prior to their adoption by the displacing entity.[11]

Prior to undertaking relocation where federal funds are involved, a developer should also consult the specific regulations for the applicable federal funding program, since some federal programs may require additional planning.

D. Notice Requirements

When a developer acquires a property with public funds, certain notices must be given to the occupants of that property. The notices are one component of the advisory assistance that must be given to occupants of an affected property (discussed in Section F, *infra*).

Occupants of the acquired property must receive (1) a general information notice, (2) an eligibility or non-displacement notice, and (3) a 90-day notice.[12] In addition, occupants may receive a notice of intent to acquire indicating that the agency intends to acquire the property. The notice of intent to acquire establishes an occupant's eligibility for relocation assistance prior to the initiation of negotiations or the provision of federal financial assistance.[13] Relocation notices should be given to all occupants of an affected property, whether the occupant is an owner or a tenant, whether the occupancy is residential or nonresidential, and whether or not the occupant is expected to be eligible for financial assistance.[14]

---

8. United Auto Workers v. Department of Transportation, 25 Cal. Rptr. 2d 290 (1993).

9. Relocation Planning, Advisory Services, and Coordination, General Relocation Requirements, 49 C.F.R. § 24.205(A) (2021).

10. *Id.*

11. CAL. GOV. CODE § 7261 (2021); 25 CAL. CODE REGS. tit. 25 § 6038 (2021).

12. Relocation Notices, 49 C.F.R. § 24.203 (2021).

13. *Id.* at § 24.203(d).

14. *HUD Handbook, supra* note 5, at Section 2-3.

The HUD Handbook provides specific guidance on the content of relocation notices under federal law, including suggested forms for some of the notices.[15] However, the forms usually require fact-based adaptation and should not be blindly copied. Since many state requirements are similar to federal requirements, the HUD Handbook forms may also be useful in situations where only state law applies.

1. General Information Notice

The first relocation notice is known as a general information notice, or GIN, and must give general information about the anticipated acquisition of the affected property and the potential relocation of occupants.[16] The contents of the general information notice depend on whether the occupant is expected to be relocated, but even occupants not expected to be relocated should receive a general information notice.[17] The 2005 revisions to the federal relocation regulations require that the general notice include a statement that displaced persons who are not lawfully present in the United States are ineligible for relocation benefits unless such ineligibility would result in exceptional and extremely unusual hardship to a spouse, parent, or child who is eligible for relocation benefits.[18]

Under federal law, the general information notice should be given "as soon as feasible," which will vary from project to project.[19]

2. Eligibility or Non-Displacement Notice

After the general information notice has been given, the developer must provide an eligibility notice, which provides more specific information about the relocation benefits and services available for an occupant of the property.[20] If no displacement is expected, then the eligibility notice is called a notice of non-displacement.[21]

The developer must give the notice of eligibility at the time that the displaced person or business becomes eligible for relocation benefits and services. Eligibility begins either on the date of a notice of intent to acquire, the initiation of negotiation, or actual acquisition of the property, whichever occurs first.[22] Unfortunately, the term "initiation of negotiations" has several possible definitions under federal relocation law, depending upon the facts of the project.[23] For most affordable housing developers, initiation of negotiations will be triggered either when notice is provided to the occupant that he or she will be displaced by the project or, if there is no notice, the actual move by the resident or business.[24] Timely

---

15. *Id.*
16. Relocation Notices, 49 C.F.R. § 24.203(a) (2021).
17. *HUD Handbook, supra* note 5, at Section 2-3.
18. 49 C.F.R. § 24.203(a)(4) (2021).
19. *Id.* at § 24.203(a).
20. Relocation Notices, 49 C.F.R. § 24.203 (b) (2021).
21. *HUD Handbook, supra* note 5, at Section 2-3(D).
22. 49 C.F.R. § 24.203(b) (2010); *HUD Handbook, supra* note 5, at Section 2-3(C).
23. Definitions and Acronyms, 49 C.F.R. § 24.2(a)(15)(ii) (2010) (defining initiation of negotiation as (i) the initial offer of just compensation if a public agency is acquiring property, (ii) notice to the person that he or she will be displaced if the relocation is the result of acquisition by a private party, or (iii) a formal announcement by the federal government when relocation is the result of a CERCLA order.).
24. *Id.*

delivery of an eligibility notice is particularly important for an occupant not expected to be a "displaced person" (as defined in Section E), because if such an occupant voluntarily moves after the "initiation of negotiations" without having received a notice of non-displacement, then state and federal law might automatically define the occupant as a "displaced person."[25]

If an occupant is not eligible for relocation assistance, such as a post-acquisition tenant, HUD policy requires that the occupant receive written notice of their ineligibility for relocation assistance, the reasons for such ineligibility, and information on the occupant's right to appeal the determination of ineligibility.[26] If an occupant moves after the initiation of negotiation and has not received a notice of non-displacement, it is HUD's view that the occupant is entitled to relocation benefits.[27]

3. Ninety-Day Notice

After the eligibility notice has given specific information about the relocation benefits and services available for an occupant of an affected property, a 90-day notice must give specific relocation date information to an occupant who will be relocated.[28] The 90-day notice should specify a date, at least 90 days away, on which the occupant is expected to be relocated.[29] Under federal relocation law, the 90-day period can be shortened if the displacing agency determines that 90 days is an impracticable period and that only lesser advance notice is practicable under the circumstances.[30] However, the displacing agency should make such a determination only in unusual circumstances, such as when continued occupancy poses a substantial danger to health or safety, and the public agency should not artificially create an urgent need.[31]

Unless the developer intends that the 90-day notice serve as a termination notice under landlord–tenant law, the 90-day notice should not specify the date on which the developer will relocate the occupant. Instead, it should state that a further notice (such as a 30-day or 60-day termination notice under the applicable state landlord–tenant law) will specify the precise date on which the occupant will actually be relocated. Since most states have specific landlord tenant laws with which the developer will need to comply in order to terminate tenancies, it is best to use the state law termination notices to specify the precise date on which the occupant will actually be relocated.

In certain situations, occupants need not receive a 90-day notice. Under federal law, no 90-day notice is needed where (1) there is no structure, growing stock, or personal property on the affected property; (2) the occupant makes an informed decision to relocate and vacates the affected property without prior notice; or (3) the occupant owns the affected property and enters into a negotiated agreement for delivering possession of the affected property (as in a purchase agreement).[32] A 90-day notice is also not required for

---

25. *See* Definitions and Acronyms, 49 C.F.R. § 24.2(a)(9) (2021) (defining displaced person).
26. *HUD Handbook, supra* note 5, at Section 2-3(D).
27. *Id.*
28. 49 C.F.R. § 24.203(c) (2021).
29. *Id.*
30. *Id.* § 24.203(c)(4) (2021); *HUD Handbook, supra* note 5, at Section 2-3(E).
31. *HUD Handbook, supra* note 5, at Section 2-3(E).
32. *Id.*

an occupant who will not qualify as a displaced person (as defined in Section E), such as a "post-acquisition tenant" (defined in Section E.2.b). However, it is prudent to give a 90-day notice to all persons being relocated, because it is not always clear 90 days before a scheduled relocation whether a particular person will qualify as a displaced person.

4. Post-Acquisition Tenant Notices

In addition to the notices required by federal or state relocation law, the prudent developer should ensure that a new tenant who moves into an affected property after the acquisition of the property by an agency is given a notice of non-eligibility for relocation benefits before the new tenant signs a rental agreement and before the new tenant moves into the affected property. Such a notice should cite to the relocation regulations that provide that post acquisition tenants are not eligible for relocation benefits[33] and have the new tenants acknowledge this notice in writing, confirming that they understand that they will not qualify as displaced persons eligible for monetary benefits. Such a notice is often called a post-acquisition tenant notice, and such tenants are referred to as post-acquisition tenants.[34]

5. Landlord–Tenant Law Termination Notices

Nothing in relocation law lessens a tenant's occupancy rights under a rental agreement or landlord–tenant law. Thus, a tenant's occupancy rights can be terminated only as set forth in the tenant's lease or rental agreement, if applicable, and as permitted by the applicable state landlord–tenant law. When the tenant's occupancy is on a month-to-month basis, the tenant usually must be given a 30-day termination notice specifying the date on which the tenancy will end. When the tenant's occupancy is for a fixed term, no special termination notice is usually required, but the tenancy will endure until the expiration of the fixed term.

E. Displaced Persons

The characterization of an occupant of a property as a displaced person is crucial to determining eligibility for certain types of relocation benefits, including moving expenses and long-term replacement housing payments for tenants and homeowners.

Federal law defines a displaced person as a person who moves him or herself or business from property as the result of acquisition of the property by a public agency, or by a private entity under contract with or on behalf of a public agency, or as a result of receipt of a notice of intention to acquire by a public agency.[35] "Displaced persons" also include people who move as a result of the rehabilitation, demolition, or other activity of an agency or private party acting under contract with or on behalf of an agency.[36] HUD generally presumes that a person is a displaced person if the occupant moves after the submittal of an application for assistance to HUD for the project.[37]

---

33. Definitions and Acronyms, 49 C.F.R. § 24.2(a)(9)(ii)(B) (2021).

34. *Id.*; *see also HUD Handbook, supra* note 5, at Section 1-4(J)(2); *see also infra* Section E.3.

35. 42 U.S.C. § 4601(6)(A)(i)(I) (2021); 49 C.F.R. 24.2(a)(9) (2021); *HUD Handbook, supra* note 5, at Section 1-4(I).

36. Definitions and Acronyms, 49 C.F.R. § 24.2(a)(9) (2021); *HUD Handbook, supra* note 5, at Section 1-4(I).

37. *HUD Handbook, supra* note 5, at Section 1-4(I).

An occupant can be classified as a displaced person even if he or she moves prior to property acquisition or rehabilitation by the federally funded developer.[38] Once negotiations for acquisition of the property are initiated for a federally funded project and an occupant moves, the occupant may be entitled to relocation benefits even though the developer has not yet formally taken title to the property if the occupant can show that the relocation was due to the imminent acquisition of the property.[39] If the developer elects not to acquire the property after the initiation of negotiations, occupants should promptly be given notices that the property will not be acquired and they will not be displaced, in order to establish that an occupant who then moves is not a displaced person.

1. Persons Displaced by the Actions of Private Entities

"Displaced persons" include people displaced by private entities acting under contract with or on behalf of public agencies.[40] This is a particularly important requirement for affordable housing developers who often acquire property with federal funds, or in anticipation of the receipt of federal funds, since the contract or allocation of federal funds will qualify the housing developer as a displacing agency under the relocation regulations.[41]

If a developer buys property and requires the occupants to move prior to obtaining federal assistance, the occupants may not be considered displaced persons, provided the tenancies were not terminated in anticipation of entering into a contract with the public agency.[42] Thus, if a private owner buys a property, terminates tenancies, and two years later begins negotiations for and enters into a loan agreement with the public agency involving federal funds, the tenants evicted two years earlier will not be considered displaced persons entitled to relocation benefits. However, if a developer evicts a tenant or fails to renew a lease in order to deliver a property as vacant for a HUD-assisted project, HUD will usually presume that the occupants were displaced for the project and require that the displaced tenants be found and provided appropriate relocation assistance.[43]

When a developer requires occupants to move after initiating negotiations with a public agency but before actually entering into an agreement with the agency, the occupants will be considered displaced persons because the forced move is generally in contemplation of the developer entering into an agreement with the public agency to perform an activity that will require relocation of occupants.[44]

Certain categories of people are specifically excluded from the definition of displaced person, as described here.

---

38. Definitions and Acronyms, 49 C.F.R. § 24.2(a) (9)(ii) (2021); *HUD Handbook, supra* note 5, at Section 1-4(I).

39. *HUD Handbook, supra* note 5, at Section 1-4(I).

40. 49 C.F.R. § 24.2(a)(9)(i) (2021).

41. *Id.* § 24.2(a)(1)(ii).

42. *See HUD Handbook, supra* note 5, at Section 1-4 (I)(1).

43. *See HUD Handbook, supra* note 5, at Section 1-4(I)(3).

44. Definitions and Acronyms, 49 C.F.R. § 24.2(a)(9)(i) (2021); 49 C.F.R. 24.2(a)(15) (2021); *HUD Handbook, supra* note 5, at Section 1-4 (I)(4).

2. *Exclusions from Displaced Persons Definition*

a. *Unlawful Occupants*

Unlawful occupants are not considered displaced persons.[45] A person is considered to be in unlawful occupancy if he or she occupies the property without right, title, or payment of rent or if the person has been legally evicted and has no right under state law to occupy the property.[46] The definition of unlawful occupant would include squatters.

b. *Post-Acquisition Tenants*

Persons who first occupy property after it is acquired by a public agency or by a private party receiving funds from a public entity, or who first occupy privately owned property after the owner enters into a contract for federal funds, are generally considered to be post-acquisition tenants who are not displaced persons eligible for monetary benefits.[47] The HUD handbook requires that post-acquisition tenants must be informed in writing of the pending displacement prior to their occupancy in order to prevent a post-acquisition tenant from being a displaced person under federal law.[48]

Because of the notice requirements, a developer should ensure that post-acquisition tenants do not sublet the property in a manner that allows subtenants to become eligible for relocation benefits. Thus, if the rental agreement allows subleasing or assignment, the rental agreement should specify that any sublease or assignment requires prior approval of the owner and that any sublease or assignment agreement must contain provisions that notify the subtenant or assignee that he or she is a post-acquisition tenant who is not entitled to relocation benefits. In addition, the rental agreement should contain a provision in which the tenant agrees to indemnify the owner for relocation benefits payable to the tenant's subtenants.

c. *Persons Not Required to Move*

A person who is not required to move as a result of a project and who was provided notice that he or she is not required to move but decides to move anyway will not qualify as a displaced person unless the project imposes an unreasonable change in the character or use of the property.[49]

Similarly, a tenant who occupies property pursuant to a lease may not be considered a displaced person if the developer can establish that the displacement resulted from a commercial disagreement over lease terms and not from the developer's intent to use the property for a publicly funded project.[50] However, if the developer is unwilling to agree to a new lease because it is implementing the federally funded development project, the tenant would be a displaced person entitled to monetary benefits.[51]

---

45. 49 C.F.R. § 24.2(a)(9)(ii)(K) (2021).
46. *Id.* § 24.2(a)(29).
47. Definitions and Acronyms, 49 C.F.R. § 24.2(a)(9)(ii)(B) (2021).
48. *Id.* § 24.2(a)(9)(ii)(B); *HUD Handbook, supra* note 5, at Section 1-4(J)(2).
49. 49 C.F.R. § 24.2(a)(9)(ii)(D) (2021); *HUD Handbook, supra* note 5, at Section 1-4(I)(7).
50. Peter Kiewit Sons' Co. v. Richmond Redevelopment Agency, 223 Cal. Rptr. 728 (1986).
51. *HUD Handbook, supra* note 5, at Section 1-4 (I)(7).

In most situations where a tenant occupies property pursuant to a short-term arrangement allowing termination of the tenancy by the landlord upon giving notice, it will be difficult to establish that the termination of the tenancy arises from a commercial disagreement over the terms of an extension of the tenancy. Therefore, a developer should expect to pay relocation expenses to most short-term tenants.

d. Owner-Occupants Who Voluntarily Sell

Under federal law, an owner-occupant who moves following a voluntary sale to a developer pursuant to a negotiated purchase agreement is not considered a displaced person, provided he or she has been informed in writing that if a negotiated agreement is not reached, the developer will not acquire the property.[52] In order to be considered a voluntary sale, the acquiring entity must inform the seller that if an amicable agreement is not reached between the parties the property will not be acquired.[53] The acquiring entity must also inform the seller what it believes to be the market value of the property.[54]

e. Code Enforcement

Persons who move as a result of routine housing or health code enforcement activities of a public agency are not displaced persons, unless the code enforcement is undertaken for the purpose of causing displacement for a particular program or project.[55]

f. Temporary Displacement

A person who is only temporarily displaced is entitled to specific temporary benefits but is not considered a displaced person under federal law, so long as certain conditions are satisfied.[56] However, if the conditions are not satisfied, then the temporary nature of the relocation will not prevent characterization of the person as a displaced person.

The 2005 changes to the federal relocation regulations provide that temporary relocation may not extend beyond 12 months.[57] Prior to the adoption of the amended regulations in 2005, the displacing agency could determine the duration of the temporary relocation. Under the current regulations, if a temporary relocation extends beyond one year, the displacing agency is required to offer a residential tenant who was temporarily displaced permanent relocation assistance. This permanent relocation assistance is in addition to any assistance already received during the temporary displacement.[58] The Uniform Relocation Act Regulations specify that a temporary displacee must be treated fairly and equitably. If the temporary displacee is a residential tenant, the developer must relocate the tenant to a decent, safe, and sanitary unit and must reimburse the tenant for all out-of-pocket costs,

---

52. Definitions and Acronyms, 49 C.F.R. § 24.2(a)(9)(ii)(H) (2021).
53. Applicability of Acquisition Requirements, 49 C.F.R. § 24.101(b)(1)–(2) (2021).
54. *Id.*
55. *HUD Handbook, supra* note 5, at Section 1-4(J)(3). *See* Price v. City of Stockton, 390 F.3d 1105 (9th Cir. 2004); *see* discussion *infra* in Part IV. For more on housing codes, see Chapter 5.
56. Definitions and Acronyms, 49 C.F.R. § 24.2(a)(9)(ii)(D) (2021); 49 C.F.R. 24 Appendix A (2021).
57. Uniform Relocation Assistance and Real Property Acquisition For Federal And Federally-Assisted Programs, 49 C.F.R. § 24 Appendix A (2021).
58. *Id.*

including moving costs and increased housing costs.[59] Temporary displacees also have the right to move back into a suitable, decent, safe, and sanitary unit in the same building or complex upon completion of the project, under reasonable terms and conditions. A temporary displacee must also receive a notice of non-displacement before moving out, assuring the tenant that he or she will be able to move back into the property.[60] Temporary displacees must also receive reasonable advance notice of the temporary relocation, typically at least 30 days.[61] If any of the temporary relocation requirements are not met (if, for example, the developer does not give the tenant a notice of non-displacement before the tenant moves or does not offer the tenant reimbursement for all out-of-pocket costs), HUD deems the relocatee to be permanently displaced and therefore eligible for full benefits for permanent displacement.[62] HUD's updated handbook contains extensive discussion about temporary displacement. HUD advises that whenever there is any possibility that a tenant will not be able to return to the project, particularly where a reduced number of units will be available after completion of the project, permanent relocation assistance should be provided.[63]

Many federal housing programs have additional temporary relocation requirements that apply to projects receiving funding under such programs. The requirements of these programs operate in addition to the requirements of the Uniform Relocation Act. For example, the program regulations for both the federal Community Development Block Grant (CDBG) program and the HOME Investment Partnership Program (HOME) include additional temporary relocation requirements.[64] Both programs specify that, after the temporary displacement, the tenant has the right to reoccupy the project at a rent (including utility allowance) that for at least 12 months does not exceed the *greater* of the monthly rent plus utility allowance before displacement or 30 percent of household income.[65]

g. Shelter Residents

The amendments to the Uniform Relocation Act regulations proposed by the Federal Highway Administration and currently pending include in the definition of persons who are not displaced occupants of temporary daily or emergency shelters, but provide that the displacing agency may determine that such persons are displaced due to factors that could include a reasonable expectation of a prolonged stay or other extenuating circumstances.[66]

3. Unqualified Aliens

Congress enacted amendments to the Uniform Relocation Act in 1997 that prohibit the payment of federal relocation benefits or the provision of relocation assistance to "an alien not lawfully present in the United States" except if the displacing agency finds that the denial of benefits will cause the alien to suffer "exceptional and extremely unusual hardship"

---

59. *Id.*
60. *HUD Handbook*, *supra* note 5, at Section 2-3.
61. *Id.*, Section 2-3(E)(3).
62. 49 C.F.R. § 24 Appendix A (2021); *HUD Handbook*, *supra* note 5, at Section 1-4(II).
63. *HUD Handbook, supra* note 5, see Section 2-7.
64. Displacement, Relocation, Acquisition, and Replacement of Housing, 24 C.F.R. § 570.606(2)(D)(1) (2021); Displacement, Relocation, and Acquisition, 24 C.F.R. § 92.353(b) (2021).
65. *Id.*
66. 84 Fed. Reg. 69,466 (2019).

and the alien is the parent, spouse, or child of a displaced person who is a citizen or lawful resident.[67] The Uniform Relocation Act Regulations, which were amended in 2005 to implement these statutory changes to the Act, include a provision that a person not lawfully in the United States is not considered a displaced person.[68]

F. Relocation Benefits

If it is established that a person is eligible for relocation benefits, then the particular benefits for which the person is eligible must be determined. The particular benefits will depend upon numerous factors, including (1) whether the displacement property is a business or a dwelling unit; (2) whether the person owns the dwelling unit or rents; (3) the length of time the person has occupied the property; (4) whether the person is a displaced person; (5) whether the applicable law is federal, state, or both; and (6) whether particular program-based rules (such as CDBG or HOME) apply. Despite all these variables, there are only three general kinds of relocation benefits.

The first general category of benefits is advisory assistance. Advisory assistance always includes the delivery of the information required by the applicable notices described in Section D *supra*. Advisory assistance may also include certain counseling and advisory services to assist a relocatee in locating and moving to a substitute location.[69]

The second general category of benefits is "moving assistance," and consists of paying for a relocatee's moving expenses.[70]

The third general category of benefits is "housing assistance" for residential occupants, and "reestablishment assistance" for business occupants. Housing assistance consists of providing for the relocated person's replacement housing to meet specified standards for a specified time period.[71] For business occupants, reestablishment assistance provides a payment in an amount sufficient for the relocatee to reestablish the relocated business.[72] As further described *infra*, some displaced businesses may choose an alternative to reestablishment assistance.

This section describes in greater detail the moving assistance, housing assistance, and reestablishment assistance requirements for both commercial occupants and residential occupants.

1. Business Relocatees

Businesses that are relocated as a result of federally funded activity are eligible for advisory assistance, moving expenses, and, if the business is a small business, as defined by the law, reestablishment expenses.[73] Moving expenses include transportation and storage,

---

67. 42 U.S.C. § 4605 (2021).

68. Definitions and Acronyms, 49 C.F.R. § 24.2(a)(9)(ii)(L) (2021).

69. *See* Relocation Notices, 49 C.F.R. § 24.203 (2010); Relocation Planning, Advisory Services, and Coordination, 49 C.F.R. § 24.205 (2021); *HUD Handbook, supra* note 5, at Section 2-4.

70. Payments for Moving and Related Expenses, 49 C.F.R. § 24.301–305 (2021); *HUD Handbook, supra* note 3, at Sections 3-2, 4-2.

71. Reestablishment Expenses—Nonresidential Moves, 49 C.F.R. § 24.304 (2021); Replacement Housing Payments, 49 C.F.R. § 24.401-403 (2010).

72. 49 C.F.R. § 24.304 (2021).

73. 49 C.F.R. § 24.301 (2021); 49 C.F.R. § 24.303–24.305 (2021); *HUD Handbook, supra* note 5, at Sections 4-1 through 4-8.

as well as the cost of disconnecting, dismantling, removing, and reinstalling machinery.[74] Moving costs also include searching for a new location (limited to $2,500[75]) and costs associated with re-lettering signs and replacing stationery.[76] There is no cap applicable to moving expenses.[77] Displacees may elect to move themselves, in which event they are entitled to reimbursement in an amount based on the low bid received for the cost of the move.[78]

In addition to moving expenses, the developer must provide small businesses with reestablishment expenses in an amount not to exceed $25,000.[79] A small business is defined as a business with not more than 500 employees.[80] Reestablishment expenses include the cost of necessary repairs or improvements to the replacement property, costs of exterior signage, advertisement of the replacement location, professional services in connection with the purchase or lease of the replacement property, and the estimated increased costs of operation during the first two years at the replacement site for items such as lease or rental charges, insurance, property taxes, and utility fees.[81]

Reestablishment expenses do not include the purchase of capital assets, manufacturing materials used in the normal course of business, aesthetic improvements to the replacement site, and interest on money borrowed to make the move or purchase the replacement property as reestablishment expenses.[82] Additionally, part-time businesses in the home that do not contribute materially to the household income are not entitled to reestablishment expenses.[83]

In lieu of receiving compensation for moving and reestablishment costs, a displaced business may elect to receive a fixed payment equal to the average annual net earnings of the business.[84] Annual net earnings are determined by calculating the net earnings before taxes for the business for the previous two years and dividing this amount in half.[85] Businesses claiming the alternative fixed payment must provide sufficient documentation to support the request, which may include providing income tax returns, certified financial statements, or other reasonable evidence as the displacing agency may deem sufficient.[86] This fixed payment may not be less than $1,000 nor more than $40,000.[87] The fixed payment may be paid only if the agency determines that the business cannot be relocated

---

74. 49 C.F.R. § 24.301(d) and (g) (2021).

75. The FHWA is proposing to increase this amount in the proposed amendments to the Uniform Relocation Act Regulations 84 Federal Register 69,466.

76. 49 C.F.R. § 24. 301(g)(13) and (g)(17) (2021); *HUD Handbook, supra* note 5, at Section 4-3.

77. 49 C.F.R. § 24.301(g) (2021); *HUD Handbook, supra* note 5, at Sections 4-1 and 4-4.

78. 49 C.F.R. § 24.301(d)(2) (2021).

79. 42 U.S.C. ch. 61 § 4622 HUD *Handbook, supra* note 5, at Section 4-6.

80. Definitions and Acronyms, 49 C.F.R. § 24.2(a)(24) (2021).

81. *Id.* § 24.304; *HUD Handbook, supra* note 5, at Section 4-6.

82. Reestablishment Expenses—Nonresidential Moves, 49 C.F.R. § 24.304 (b) (2021).

83. 49 C.F.R. § 24.304(b)(4) (2021).

84. *Id.* § 24.305; *HUD Handbook, supra* note 5, at Section 4-7.

85. Fixed Payment for Moving Expenses—Nonresidential Moves, 49 C.F.R. § 24.305(e) (2021); *HUD Handbook, supra* note 5, at Section 4-7.

86. 49 C.F.R. § 24.305(e) (2021); General Requirements—Claims for Relocation Payments, 49 C.F.R. § 24.207 (2021); 49 C.F.R. § 24 Appendix A (2021); *HUD Handbook, supra* note 5, at Section 4-7 and Appendix 17.

87. 42 U.S.C. ch. 61 § 4622; 49 C.F.R. § 24.305(a) (2021); *HUD Handbook, supra* note 5, at Section 4-7.

without a substantial loss of business and if the business is not part of a chain consisting of at least one other location.[88] For receipt of the fixed payment, the business must also own or rent personal property that has to be moved in connection with the displacement and for which an expense would be incurred to move the property.[89] A nonprofit business is entitled to the in-lieu payment only if the agency determines that the nonprofit cannot be relocated without a substantial loss of existing patronage and the organization is not part of an enterprise having more than three other establishments.[90] While for-profit businesses must provide sufficient documentation to demonstrate the need for the alternative fixed payment, a nonprofit organization is assumed to meet the requirements for the alternative fixed payment unless the displacing agency demonstrates otherwise.[91]

2. Residential Relocatees

This subsection describes some of the moving assistance and housing assistance requirements for residential occupants, including tenants and owner-occupants. Occupants of manufactured housing may have characteristics of both tenants and owner-occupants. Their relocation assistance is subject to special rules to accommodate the dual nature of their housing, as described in subsection c, *infra*.

a. Tenants

A residential tenant who the Act defines as a displaced person is eligible for either of the following two moving assistance payments, to be chosen by the displaced person:[92] (1) payment of the person's actual and reasonably incurred moving and related expenses, or (2) a fixed moving expense allowance based on a schedule issued by the federal Department of Transportation.[93]

When a displaced person chooses payment of actually incurred expenses, the regulations and the HUD handbook specify certain expenses that are always reimbursable and certain expenses that are never reimbursable.[94] In addition, a displacing agency may reimburse for expenses that the regulations and handbook do not specifically enumerate, so long as they are reasonable, necessary, and not specifically excluded from reimbursement.[95] The HUD handbook includes as an appendix a form that can (but need not) be used to document a displaced person's claim for moving assistance.[96]

---

88. 49 C.F.R. § 24.305(a) (2021).

89. *Id.* § 24.305(a)(1).

90. 49 C.F.R. § 24.305(d) (2021).

91. *Id.*

92. Pursuant to the HUD Handbook at Section 3-2, whenever public housing tenants are displaced from a public housing unit but are offered the opportunity to relocate to a comparable public housing unit, the Public Housing Authority has the option to choose the type of moving assistance. *HUD Handbook, supra* note 5 see Section 3-2(B).

93. Payment for Actual Reasonable Moving and Related Expenses, 49 C.F.R. § 24.301 (2021); *HUD Handbook, supra* note 5, at Sections 3-2.

94. *HUD Handbook, supra* note 5, at Sections 3-2.

95. *Id.*

96. *HUD Handbook, supra* note 5, at Section 3-2 and Appendix 11.

A residential tenant who is temporarily relocated but who the Act does not define as a displaced person is also eligible for moving assistance.[97] Such a relocatee must obtain, as moving assistance, reimbursement of all out-of-pocket expenses in moving from and then back into the original unit.[98] Without this moving assistance (and certain other specified assistance), such a temporary relocatee could be defined as a displaced person entitled to permanent relocation benefits.[99]

For a developer to meet his or her relocation obligations to a displaced person, at least one "comparable" replacement dwelling must be made available to the person. When possible, three or more comparable replacement dwellings must be made available.[100] This requirement can be waived by the federal agency whose funding triggers federal relocation law (usually HUD or the Department of Transportation) if the relocation results from a major disaster, national emergency, or other emergency in which continued occupancy constitutes a substantial danger to the health or safety of the occupants or the public.[101]

A replacement dwelling is comparable if it meets several criteria, including being decent, safe, and sanitary; functionally equivalent to the original dwelling; and adequate in size.[102] In addition, a comparable replacement dwelling must be within the financial means of the relocatee, although this criterion can be satisfied through the replacement housing payment described later in this section.[103] To make available a comparable replacement dwelling, a displacing agency should inform the relocatee of an actually available dwelling's location, and should ensure that the relocatee has sufficient time to negotiate a lease or purchase agreement and will receive the housing assistance described later in sufficient time to complete the transaction.[104]

A developer must also make replacement housing available to temporary relocatees who are not defined as displaced persons.[105] Under federal law, this temporary replacement housing need not meet the applicable definition of comparable, but it must still meet lesser standards.[106] As part of the lesser standards, the relocatee's cost for the temporary unit must not exceed the relocatee's cost for the original unit, but there is no requirement that the temporary unit's cost be affordable to the relocatee.[107]

A residential tenant who the Act defines as a displaced person and who has occupied the displacement property for 90 days prior to the initiation of negotiations is eligible for a

---

97. Additional Information, 49 C.F.R. § 24 Appendix A to pt. 24.2(a)(9)(ii)(D) (2021).

98. *Id.*; *HUD Handbook*, *supra* note 5, at Section 1-4(II) and Section 2-7.

99. *HUD Handbook*, *supra* note 5, at Section 1-4(II) and Section 2-7.

100. Availability of Comparable Replacement Dwelling Before Displacement, 49 C.F.R. § 24.204 (2021). It should be noted that comparable replacement dwellings for purposes of the relocation regulations may not be the same as the requirements to provide replacement housing, as discussed in Section III. Comparable replacement dwellings most often are existing housing units currently available on the market.

101. 49 C.F.R. § 24.204 (2021).

102. Definitions and Acronyms, 49 C.F.R. § 24.2(a)(6) (2021); *HUD Handbook*, *supra* note 5, at Section 1-4(F).

103. *Id.*

104. Availability of Comparable Replacement Dwelling Before Displacement, 49 C.F.R. § 24.204(a) (2021).

105. 49 C.F.R. § 24 Appendix A to 24.2(a)(9) (2021).

106. *Id.*

107. 49 C.F.R. § 24 Appendix A to 24.2(a)(9) (2021).

long-term replacement housing payment.[108] The formulas for calculating the replacement housing payment are designed to ensure affordability of the replacement housing for 42 months.[109] If the displaced person is considered low income as determined by the Section 8 regulations, the HUD regulations define affordability as paying no more than 30 percent of income for rent. If the displaced person is not considered low income, affordability is defined as the rent paid by the displaced person prior to displacement.[110] The amendments to the URA adopted in 2005 changed the basis for calculating benefits to limit the use of the 30 percent of income standard to displaced persons who qualify as low income. Prior to, the amendment benefits were determined by using the lower of prior rent at the displacement unit or 30 percent of income. The HUD regulations and handbook set forth the details regarding calculation of the amount payable, payment delivery, and conditions regarding the payment obligation.[111] The replacement housing payments described earlier are subject to a cap of $5,250.[112] However, the cap may be exceeded if necessary to satisfy "last resort housing" requirements, as discussed in Section G, *infra*.[113]

If a displaced person is not eligible for the replacement housing payment because the person did not live in the displacement dwelling for 90 days, the displaced person is still entitled to a replacement housing payment calculated in the same manner as for displaced persons who resided in the displacement dwelling for 90 days if the displaced person qualifies for last resort housing, as discussed in Section G, *infra*.[114]

When a developer uses funds provided through certain federal programs (including the Community Development Block Grant program and the HOME program), to demolish or convert a unit occupied by a low-income household at a rent that does not exceed the Section 8 fair-market rent, federal law extends the affordability period to 60 months in calculating the replacement housing payment payable to a residential tenant who is defined as a displaced person.[115] This requirement, imposed through Section 104(d) of the Housing and Community Development Act of 1974, is often called the 104(d) requirement. When Section 104(d) applies, the displaced person may choose to receive assistance under either 104(d) or the Uniform Relocation Act Regulations.[116] Under Section 104(d), a displaced person's benefits are determined by deducting the tenant's total tenant payment as determined for Section 8 purposes from the rent at the replacement dwelling unit.[117]

---

108. Replacement Housing Payment for 90-Day Occupants, 49 C.F.R. § 24.402.

109. 49 C.F.R. § 24.402(b) (2021).

110. *Id.*

111. *HUD Handbook, supra* note 5, at Section 3-4 (determining the amount of the payment in accordance with the following formula: 42* (X-Y), where X is the lesser of (1) the monthly housing cost for a comparable replacement home and (2) the monthly housing cost for the household's actual replacement home, and where Y is (3) the household's monthly housing cost in the original unit or (4) if the household qualifies as low income, 30% of the household's income if that is less than the household's monthly housing cost in the original unit).

112. 49 C.F.R. § 24. 402(a) (2021); *HUD Handbook, supra* note 5, at Section 3-4(b)(2).

113. Replacement Housing of Last Resort, 49 C.F.R. § 404(a) (2021); 49 C.F.R. § 24.404(c) (2005); *HUD Handbook, supra* note 5, at Section 3-8.

114. 49 C.F.R. § 24. 404 (c)(3) (2021); 49 C.F.R. 24.2(a)(6)(viii)(C) (2021); *HUD Handbook, supra* note 5, at Section 3-6.

115. 42 U.S.C. § 5304(d) (2021).

116. *Id.* § 5304(d); *HUD Handbook, supra* note 5, at Section 7-8.

117. 42 U.S.C. § 5304(d) (2021); *HUD Handbook, supra* note 5, at Section 7-10.

As an alternative to the replacement housing payment described earlier, a residential tenant who is defined as a displaced person may receive a replacement housing payment to assist the displaced person in buying a replacement home.[118]

b. Homeowners

As with residential tenants, homeowners who qualify as displaced persons are entitled to compensation for actual and reasonable moving costs.[119] Also as with residential tenants, the developer must offer to displaced homeowners comparable replacement housing that is decent, safe, and sanitary.[120] In addition to payment for moving costs, homeowners may receive a one-time replacement housing payment not to exceed a total of $31,000.[121] The actual amount of the payment is determined by the following factors: (1) the amount by which the purchase price of the displacee's replacement dwelling exceeds the amount paid by the developer acquiring the property for the original dwelling unit; (2) the amount necessary to compensate the owner for any increase in interest costs for the new dwelling that exceeds interest costs paid on the original dwelling unit; and (3) the amount of closing costs incurred by the displacee in acquiring a replacement dwelling.[122]

A homeowner is eligible for this one-time payment only if the homeowner purchases and occupies a replacement home within one year of the later of (1) the date the displaced person received payment for the dwelling unit acquired by the displacing entity, or (2) the date that the displacing entity fulfills its obligation to make available at least one replacement dwelling unit to the displacee.[123] In order to be eligible for this one-time payment, homeowners must have owned and occupied their homes for at least 90 days prior to the initiation of negotiations for acquisition.[124] A homeowner who has not occupied the home for at least 180 days, but who has occupied the home for less than 90 days, is entitled to the same benefits as a displaced tenant.[125]

c. Mobile Homes

Specialized rules apply to displaced mobile home occupants and owners.[126] The applicable relocation benefits depend in part on the form of occupancy or ownership interest that a displaced person holds in the mobile home. Mobile home occupancy frequently exhibits characteristics of both ownership and rental housing. The general categories of ownership/occupancy interest that may be held in a mobile home are as follows: (1) a displaced person may own both the mobile home and the space it occupies; (2) a displaced person may own

---

118. 49 C.F.R. § 24.402(c) (2021); *HUD Handbook*, *supra* note 5, at Sections 3-5(C) and 3-6(C)(2).

119. Payment for Actual Reasonable Moving and Related Expenses, 49 C.F.R. § 24.301 (2021).

120. Availability of Comparable Replacement Dwelling Before Displacement, 49 C.F.R. § 24.204.

121. 42 U.S.C. ch. 61 § 4623; Replacement Housing Payments, 49 C.F.R. § 24.401 (2021); *HUD Handbook*, *supra* note 5, at Section 3-9.

122. 49 C.F.R. § 24.401 (2021).

123. *Id.* § 24.401(a).

124. 42 U.S.C. ch. 61 § 4623; 49 C.F.R. § 24.401(a) (2021).

125. Replacement Housing Payments, 49 C.F.R. § 24.401–.402 (2021). *HUD Handbook*, *supra* note 5, at Section 3-6.

126. 49 C.F.R. § 24.501–.505 (2021); *HUD Handbook*, *supra* note 5, at Section 3-9. See Part I, Chapter 4 for more discussion of mobile homes and manufactured housing.

the mobile home and rent the space it occupies in the mobile home park; (3) a displaced person may rent both the mobile home and the space it occupies in the park; or (4) a person may own a mobile home and rent it to others, and own or rent the space in which the mobile home is located. The regulations generally treat the relocations of non-occupant owners as business relocations.[127]

All households displaced from mobile homes are eligible for moving assistance and replacement housing payments to the same extent and subject to the same requirements of persons moving from nonmanufactured housing.[128] Owner-occupants are entitled to payment for the cost of moving the mobile home, including utility hook-up charges; movement of porches, awnings, and similar improvements; economically feasible repairs or modifications necessary to move the unit or make it decent, safe ,and sanitary; and nonreturnable mobile home park entrance fees.[129] A household cannot receive moving assistance payments for moving the mobile home if the household receives a replacement housing payment, although it is entitled to assistance for moving personal property.[130] Under federal law, housing assistance payments are based on both the dwelling and the site.[131]

G. Last Resort Housing

If the displacing agency determines that it cannot relocate displacees to comparable housing, as defined in the federal regulations, without exceeding the maximum replacement housing payments set forth in the relocation regulations ($7,200 for tenants and $31,000 for owners), the displacing agency may provide additional assistance after determining that last resort housing assistance is justified.[132] The displacing agency should determine, on a case by case basis, if last resort housing assistance is necessary, after considering the availability of comparable replacement housing, the individual circumstances of the displaced persons, and the resources available to provide comparable replacement housing.[133] In addition, the regulations require that the displacing agency make a determination that the program or project cannot be implemented without last resort housing assistance and that the method for providing last resort housing assistance is cost effective.[134] The Uniform Relocation Regulations set forth a variety of methods for meeting last resort housing needs.[135] These methods include (1) replacement housing payments exceeding the caps of $7,200 or $31,000, as applicable; (2) rehabilitation or construction of replacement dwellings; (3) the provision of direct loans to the displacees; (4) the purchase of lands and/or replacement dwellings; (5) the removal of barriers to the disabled; and (6) the change in status of the displacee from tenant to homeowner.[136] State relocation laws may have additional methods for meeting last resort housing obligations. Most agencies elect to make replacement housing

---

127. Payment for Actual Reasonable Moving and Related Expenses, 49 C.F.R. § 24.301(2021); Applicability, 49 C.F.R. 24.501 (2021).
128. 49 C.F.R. § 24.301 (2021).
129. *Id.* § 24.301(c).
130. 49 C.F.R. § 24.301(a)(2) (2021).
131. Applicability, 49 C.F.R. § 24.501–.505.
132. Replacement Housing of Last Resort, 49 C.F.R. § 24.404(a) (2021).
133. *Id.*
134. *Id.*
135. 49 C.F.R. § 24.404(c) (2021).
136. *Id.*

payments in excess of the caps as this is generally the most cost-effective method of meeting last resort housing obligations.

Under federal law, tenants and homeowners who have not resided in their house or apartment for the time periods required to receive standard replacement housing relocation payments are still eligible to receive last resort housing payments.[137]

H. Grievances and Appeal Procedures

The federal Uniform Relocation Act sets forth a process for relocatees to appeal relocation determinations.[138] In the appeal process, the agency's executive director or his or her designee reviews the original determination of benefits, as well as any information submitted by the relocatee, and renders a written decision that must include an explanation of the basis for the decision.[139] If the determination of benefits on the appeal is not consistent with the relocatee's request, the decision must also indicate that the relocatee may pursue judicial review of the claim.[140]

I. Waiver of Benefits

The 2005 revisions to the regulations of the URA make it clear that a displacing agency cannot request that a displaced person waive his or her relocation benefits.[141] Appendix A to the regulation states that a displaced person, after being informed of the assistance and payments to which the person may be entitled, may provide the displacing agency with a written statement declining some of the assistance or benefits.[142]

III. REPLACEMENT HOUSING OBLIGATIONS

Under certain circumstances, public agencies or developers must replace housing removed as a result of the acquisition of the property. If the public agency or developer has received CDBG or HOME funds to acquire or develop the property and the rehabilitation or development of the property results in demolition of lower-income dwelling units, the units must be replaced on a one-for-one basis.[143] The replacement units must be sufficient to house the same number of occupants who could have been housed in the units that were demolished or converted to other uses.[144] They also must remain affordable to lower income households for a period of ten years.[145] Units constructed one year prior to the demolition or three years after the demolition can be counted toward the replacement obligation.[146] A public agency or developer may not be subject to a replacement housing obligation if the HUD

---

137. 49 C.F.R. § 24.404(c)(3) (2021).
138. Appeals, 49 C.F.R. § 24.10.
139. *Id.*
140. *Id.*; *HUD Handbook, supra* note 5, at Section 1-10.
141. General Requirements—Claims for Relocation Payments, 49 C.F.R. § 24.207(f) (2021).
142. 49 C.F.R. § Appendix A (2021).
143. One-For-One Replacement of Lower-Income Dwelling Units, 24 C.F.R. § 42.375 (2021).
144. *Id.* § 42.375(b)(2).
145. *Id.* § 42.375(b)(5).
146. *Id.* § 42.375(b)(4).

field office determines, based on objective data, that there is an adequate supply of vacant lower-income housing available in the area.[147]

In addition to the federal requirements for replacement housing, a developer may be subject to replacement housing obligations under state or local laws. For example, in California, if housing affordable to low- and moderate-income households is removed from a redevelopment project area, it must be replaced on a one-for-one basis within four years of its removal.[148] Such replacement housing must remain affordable for a minimum of 45 years if the housing is ownership housing and 55 years if the housing is rental.[149] The replacement units must be affordable at the same affordability levels as the household displaced as a result of the demolition.[150] California law governing the state's coastal zone regulates the conversion or demolition of low- and moderate-income housing in the state's coastal zone and also provides that replacement housing be constructed in some instances.[151]

IV. CIVIL RIGHTS ISSUES RAISED BY RELOCATION OBLIGATIONS AND REPLACEMENT HOUSING

Relocation obligations may also trigger a civil rights cause of action. A Ninth Circuit decision found that Section 104(d) and 104(k) of the Housing and Community Development Act may trigger enforceable civil rights under Section 1983. However, the court found that the obligations under Section 104(d) for public agencies to replace any housing demolished did not trigger individual rights that would give rise to a civil rights cause of action since these obligations are directed at governmental agencies without reference to individuals.[152]

---

147. *Id.* § 42.375(d)(1).

148. Cal. Health & Safety Code § 33413 (2021).

149. *Id.*

150. *Id.*

151. Cal. Gov. Code § 65590–65590.1 (2010). *See also* Cal. Pub. Res. Code § 30000 (2021) (requiring the inclusion of affordable housing in new developments in that area along with the availability of density bonuses, modifications of zoning and subdivision restrictions, expedited permit reviews and waivers of fees).

152. Price v. City of Stockton, 390 F.3d 1105 (9th Cir. 2004).

The Future of Affordable Housing and Community Reinvestment

17

George L. Weidenfeller

I. INTRODUCTION

The future of affordable housing is strong. That is similar to what every president says about the country generally, as he—or someday she—begins the annual State of the Union address to Congress. The future is strong for affordable housing demand, need, and interest in pursuing the lofty goals of addressing both the demand and the need. Also strong are the obstacles to meet the demand and needs. What is not as strong are the means to meet the needs and achieve the lofty goals. Funds for "community reinvestment" are often tied to housing development, with funds for community development largely dependent on state and local initiatives as well as the federal Community Development Block Grant (CDBG) program, which is constantly under attack. As discussed in this book, CDBG is an entitlement program, which provides states and localities with formula-based annual funds. CDBG is also increasingly the vehicle used to provide communities with disaster-assistance funding.

II. PANDEMIC

All of the foregoing reflects a world before the country faced the worst health crisis in a century. The pandemic that hit the world in 2020 changed life as everyone knew it—for more than a year—and the long-term impact is yet to be determined. Unlike the Great Recession of 2008, which most agree was man-made, caused by financing adventures relating particularly to the single-family housing market, the 2020 pandemic was not housing focused, but had a huge impact on housing. People were forced to stay home—wherever that was. People were fleeing from large metropolitan areas to avoid crowds, looking for more space, working from home, forced out of schools and every other aspect of normal everyday life. In addition to addressing the health crises, the government's immediate response was to assist those potentially facing eviction, caused by unemployment, by putting a moratorium on evictions and foreclosures and by providing subsidies to allow people to stay in their homes. Follow-up action further focused on rental assistance, with unpreceded funding proposals in the trillions. As the country seems to be pulling away from the pandemic, future funding proposals seek to do more of the same, while beginning to address systemic funding challenges. The success of such initiatives, which include funding that some argue exceeds a response to the pandemic, remains to be seen.

III. THE NEED

This is not the place to articulate the exact number of affordable housing units needed nationally. Those data are widely available and documented by states and at the national level, by academics, industry associations, think tanks, and all units of government. The problem was real before the pandemic, remains just as real, and is likely to grow as eviction moratoriums lapse. An overgeneralization would be that due to current, changing, and growing demographics, the need for affordable housing is huge and not likely to be fully satisfied through available channels. While the acute need in large metropolitan areas is best documented, with increasing pressures of technology, climate change, health and educational deficiencies, the need in rural areas is also as great as ever. As mentioned, recent events have resulted in somewhat of a shift from acceptance of smaller space requirements in metro areas to more generous space availability—for those who can afford it—in suburban, rural, and even previously viewed as only resort communities. During the pandemic, the rental housing market remained surprisingly stable—due primarily to continued payment of subsidies for affordable units and government support for rental assistance, in order to avoid both evictions and defaults. Given those government subsidies, the subsidized affordable housing market may come out of the pandemic in somewhat better shape than market-rate housing.

IV. THE OBSTACLES

It might go without saying, and too often it does, but perhaps the biggest obstacles to satisfying the demand for affordable housing are shrinking resources and lack of commitment. The federal government has all but abandoned the concept of funding affordable housing through appropriations—leaving it to tax credits for investors, as the primary source of capital for new development or preservation. While states and localities have attempted to fill the void, their efforts are limited by budget constraints and the will of government officials and individuals, faced with competing priorities. In addition to resources, increasing materials, land and labor costs, regulatory barriers, labor shortages, Not in My Back Yard (NIMBY) interests, and real concerns about management problems all get in the way. While interest rates have been historically low, ever since the end of the Great Recession, home prices have risen faster than incomes, and the supply of available single-family homes has shrunk, creating challenges for affordable homeownership. At the same time, the limited supply of rental housing keeps renters often in places considered to be less than "communities of opportunity." Affordable homeownership is further challenged by the movement out of metro area to single-family homes with more space outside the cities.

V. SOLUTIONS

To suggest that there are solutions would be perhaps overly optimistic. There is no magic proposal. It is somewhat encouraging that in 2020, there were presidential candidates who recognized the need for affordable housing, put it on the agenda, and developed proposals. Critiquing those proposals is another topic not appropriate for this endeavor. The one that suggested funding in the trillions was certainly an attention getter. While no doubt that amount would go a long way to address the supply deficit, the chances of it happening were extremely small. Then, during the height of the presidential campaign, along came the aforementioned pandemic and, with it, legislation to ease the pain.

A. American Recovery Act

Already oversubscribed efforts to address affordable housing were taxed beyond limits as people not only got sick, but many who did not lose jobs faced eviction or foreclosure, and housing became a significant part of the trillion-dollar American Recovery Act stimulus legislation. As mentioned, initial efforts to attack the problems were directed largely to address renter challenges to avoid evictions and foreclosures. Optimism suggests that the pandemic is staring to wind down as vaccinations wind up and now questions linger, as rental supplements, eviction moratoriums, and unemployment compensation end, about what will happen when back debts for rental housing, estimated to be in the range of $60 billion, and mortgage arrearages come due.

B. American Jobs Act/American Families Act

New proposals—initially labeled as efforts to address infrastructure deficiencies—are now focused on job creation, with the American Jobs Act, which as proposed includes approximately $200 billion to produce, preserve, and rehabilitate more than two million affordable housing units with targeted tax credits, formula funding grants, and project-based assistance. The housing proposals once again are, at this writing, targeted to renter protections—such as support for rent controls and renter tax credits. These suggestions certainly merit consideration and will enjoy broad support from low-income advocates. They will also endure either lukewarm support, criticism, or outright opposition from those who believe that such initiatives will not address and may impede efforts to address the inadequate supply of affordable housing.

C. HUD 2022 Budget

Another positive note for affordable housing, as of this writing, is the proposed HUD 2022 budget, which calls for a 15 percent increase to $68.7 billion, providing vouchers for 200,000 additional families and homeless assistance to more than 100,000 families, with $3.5 billion in grants, $3.2 billion for public housing modernization, $3.8 billion for CDBG—almost $300 million of which is targeted for infrastructure—$400 million to reduce lead-based paint, and $85 million for fair-housing enforcement.

All of the foregoing suggests positive action for returning the federal government to a meaningful role in funding affordable housing. At this writing, whether that support actually materializes remains to be seen. That being said, the federal financial involvement in affordable housing continues to be significant and impactful—especially in the area of preserving existing resources. Whether through existing long-term Section 8 contracts, direct debt financing insured by HUD through the Federal Housing Administration (FHA), or the Rental Assistance Demonstration (RAD) program relating to the conversion of public housing or the various tax credit programs, the financial contribution remains large—even if not yet apparent through direct appropriations.

D. Tax Credits

As indicated in this book, since enactment of the Tax Reform Act of 1986, the Low-Income Housing Tax Credit (LIHTC) has been the primary source of affordable housing development and it is anticipated that it will continue to be. At this writing, there is pending legislation to improve, expand, and make the LIHTC even more effective. In addition to the LIHTC legislation, the Historic Tax Credit, and New Market Tax Credit, and Energy Tax Credits will continue to be critical in the development of affordable housing and enhance community and economic development. As important as new legislative enhancements will be, critical to the continued success of the LIHTC will be what happens to LIHTC developments in year 15, when the LIHTC restrictions are removed, and these communities face the need for rehabilitation and refinancing. Underlying the concern about the future of the LIHTC projects is the tension between investors, seeking a return on their initial investment, and owners and residents, seeking to preserve the affordable housing resources at the lowest cost possible.

E. Regulatory Impact

Apart from funding, the federal government continues its statutory and regulatory impact on affordable housing, which—depending on one's perspective—is sometimes positive and sometimes negative. The enforcement of federal fair-housing laws and regulations is expected to continue to receive increased attention in a new administration. Regulations relating to affirmatively furthering fair housing and pursuit of cases involving disparate impact are expected to receive particular attention. Actions in recent years have demonstrated the impact of differences in interpretation and implementation of efforts to address racial inequities. Issues related to climate change are hotly debated. The practical application of existing environmental requirements often remain a challenge for affordable housing development. Efforts to ease the requirements, without subjecting properties to environmental hazards, such as new approaches to better defining "choice limiting activities" that cannot be undertaken before approval of environmental assessment, and release of funds, could allow certain essential predevelopment activities to proceed without delay, which could speed up delivery and reduce costs associated with delays. While any federal housing development requires compliance with Davis–Bacon statutory requirements, there have been considerable inconsistencies in the application of the law between the Department of Labor and HUD—especially with respect to the split wage determinations on the development of affordable housing. This is an administrative matter that could be resolved between the agencies, without Congress, and could make a big difference in the cost and efficient delivery of affordable housing.

F. Other Matters to Consider

There are numerous other matters that may be considered in the near future to address the demand and the increasing costs of affordable housing. They are described next.

1. Section 8 New Construction and Substantial Rehabilitation

Yes, the Section 8 New Construction and Substantial Rehabilitation programs were terminated in the 1980s primarily because of the cost associated with automatic annual rent adjustments, which were a program feature (until administratively fixed) and because they were considered a long-range drain on future appropriations. However, HUD practice is now to extend Project Based Rental Assistance (PBRA) contracts for extended periods, subject to annual appropriations, with rent increases no longer automatic but rather controlled by budgets or Operating Cost Adjustment Factors. Additionally, HUD has found a way to do new PBRA contracts under RAD. The time may be right for reinstatement of the new construction and substantial rehabilitation programs. They were effective tools in producing housing, with a minimum amount of HUD staffing resources, as many projects were developed through cooperative agreements with state housing finance agencies. The processing of Housing Assistance Payment Contracts was far more efficient and cost effective than the complexity involved in developing a LIHTC project with the need to compete for 9 percent credits, the need for bond authority within volume cap for 4 percent credit projects, and usually the need for multiple sources of financing to fill funding gaps. Section 8 projects required fewer participants and fewer sources of financing, and efficiently addressed the needs of low-, moderate- and very low-income households.

2. NOAH

Naturally Occurring Affordable Housing (NOAH) relates to existing housing that is considered to be Class B or C, which might mean that it does not have the fanciest amenities or is not as up to date as it could be but has rents that are somewhat below what the market could command, if fully updated. The trick is to keep it that way, while maintaining it as quality housing without the frills.

3. Modular Housing

Modular housing has come a long way since the days of "mobile homes." It is now used not only for attainable single-family housing, but it is also being used on multifamily housing and may lead to savings associated with materials and labor. To fully realize those cost savings achieved by transportation of the units to the site, installation and local code issues must be addressed.

4. Standardized Design

Standardized design is a concept that would apply similar plans and specifications to affordable projects being developed anywhere in the country. This is an interesting idea that could result in a big savings on design and approval costs. However, the concept does generate memories of the standardize design in place with early public housing developments, as well as early designs associated with FHA subsidized mortgage programs, which were readily identifiable on a windshield tour. The result was often disastrous for public housing and generally ugly with respect to the early FHA subsidized mortgage insurance programs. That said, while on the topic of design, the pandemic is also likely to have an impact on design going forward, with more thought being given to open spaces, wider stairways to encourage movement away from elevators, flexible work schedules leading to reconfigured homes to accommodate working arrangements, and other design changes learned through the Covid experience.

5. *Employer Housing*

Employer-supported housing could generate a significant number of units to support their expansion efforts to ensure that their employees have affordable housing opportunities—as long as the housing provided is marketed consistent with fair-housing requirements.

6. *Opportunity Zones*

Opportunity zones arrived with the Tax Cuts and Jobs Act of 2017 and provided for certain investments of capital gains taxes in lower-income areas. The benefit of the designation of an opportunity zone to the development of affordable housing remains questionable as to the actual impact on both affordable housing and community development and the benefit to lower-income residents.

7. *Interaction between Housing and Health Care*

Even before the pandemic, there was increased awareness of the link between suitable housing and health. A healthy home, free of pollutants, such as lead, radon, asbestos, or other environmental concerns, is essential to well-being, but the connection between housing and health goes beyond the often-addressed physical hazards. A suitable and safe environment is critical to the growth of young children, as is the need to address aging in place for the rapidly growing older population. Linking housing programs at HUD and health care programs at HHS, as well as those provided by the states, to providing supportive services in affordable housing can significantly improve the quality of life for young and old alike.

8. *Interaction between Housing and Infrastructure Enhancements*

Long before the Biden administration's ambitious infrastructure proposals, there was a recognized need to link housing with infrastructure development and improvements to support the housing being developed. More than concern for transportation-oriented development, infrastructure affects all aspects of acceptable communities, from playgrounds to sidewalks, streets, and water supplies. Coordinating community and economic development with affordable housing initiatives is essential to create resilient communities. The HUD CDBG program has been a major funding source for infrastructure development and improvement. There is constant pressure to reduce CDBG, as federal budget deficit hawks see it as a discretionary target. As a new administration moves forward with significant infrastructure proposals, CDBG is a likely and useful tool for the efficient deployment of funding. Much of the infrastructure funding will be channeled through the Department of Transportation (DOT) but cooperation between HUD and DOT is essential for the most effective use of available funding. Further, it is essential that the funds made available through CDBG are used for intended purposes—whether within the discretionary authority generally provided or more specifically targeted for disaster assistance.

9. *Funding for the National Housing Trust Fund*

The National Housing Trust Fund can be a game-changing resource to fill gaps that often exist in the financing available for LIHTC development. Continued funding with resources available from the Government Sponsored Enterprises (GSEs) will help to fill the void left by diminishing federal appropriations.

10. RAD—Funding for the HUD RAD Program, Including Elimination of the RAD Cap

The HUD RAD has strong bi-partisan support as the best vehicle to facilitate the much-needed capital improvements at the nation's 3,400 public housing authorities. While RAD has been successful in leveraging existing funding available to local PHAs, no additional funding is currently available. Most RAD development projects include LIHTC funding, and just as with many LIHTC projects, gaps often need to be filled. Funding specifically targeted for filling the gap for RAD developments would ease the pressure on non-RAD projects. Lifting the state ceilings on private equity bonds targeted for RAD projects could also generate more RAD transactions, while at the same time ease the demand on RAD transactions.

11. FHA Multifamily and Risk Sharing and the Federal Financing Bank

The HUD/FHA 221(d)(4) program is, and always has been, a very attractive product for new construction and substantial rehabilitation of moderate-income housing. The rents for these units are unregulated and the product allows for long-term, non-recourse, fixed interest rate financing for both construction and permanent loans under one processing mechanism. A major challenge to success through this program has been the extensive processing times, exacerbated by the limited resources at HUD. HUD continues to take steps to improve the processing times, and the increases in the HUD budget may help. The HUD/FHA Risk Sharing program (Section 524 of the U.S. Housing Act of 1934) provides FHA insurance without the delays often associated with the Section 221(d)(4) multifamily insurance program by allowing HUD/FHA to partner with qualified state housing finance agencies to assume part of the risk associated with loan insurance. While risk-sharing loans do not qualify for capitalization through Ginnie Mae, during the Great Recession following the 2008 crash of the housing market, the federal government implemented the Federal Financing Bank in the Department of Treasury. This authority was allowed to lapse under the last administration. Reinstatement of that authority would make the risk-sharing program a more viable option to facilitate the development of much needed moderate income/workforce housing.

12. Reducing State and Local Regulatory Barriers

While much of this look to the future is focused on the actions of the federal government, that is not to in any way diminish the role, responsibility, and importance of actions at the state and local levels. States and units of local government are often leading the way to take maximum advantage of using limited funding with creative solutions. As indicated, state housing finance agencies play a pivotal role in the allocation of LIHTCs and administration of private activity bonds, which support the 4 percent LIHTC program. Many states have also implemented their own tax credit and housing grant programs—especially used to fill the gaps in federal or conventional financing. Also, states are active in the aforementioned risk-sharing program and that trend is expected to continue. As we look to the future, localities are playing a greater and more important role in efforts to relieve regulatory barriers.

This is especially true with respect to zoning efforts—whether through inclusionary zoning initiatives or revising zoning codes to permit higher-density development—especially in urban areas and the near suburbs.

VI. CONCLUSION

This is by no means as exhaustive list of possible approaches to address the demand and the need for affordable housing and related community and economic development. Other approaches are more benign, for example, do not call it "affordable" or "low income" housing but call it something that does not generate negative reactions—something like "workforce" housing or "attainable" housing. The only sure thing about affordable housing development and community development is that, in good times and bad, the need will continue; support—political, financial, and emotional—will be critical; and there can never be enough creative solutions.

Appendix

Affordable Housing
Development Resource List

GENERAL RESOURCES

1. www.abanet.org/forums/affordable/home.html—ABA Forum on Affordable Housing and Community Development Law (hosts conferences and publishes the *Journal of Affordable Housing and Community Development Law* quarterly) (available on Westlaw and HeinOnline; future issues will be available on the Forum's website for Forum members only).

2. www.abanet.org/statelocal/home.html—ABA State and Local Government Law Section (serves as a collegial forum for its members, the profession, and the public to provide leadership and educational resources in urban, state, and local government law and policy)

3. www.hud.gov—U.S. Department of Housing and Urban Development (one of the primary federal agencies responsible for affordable housing development) (permalink: https://perma.cc/BF74-5NCB); www.huduser.org—HUD Policy Development and Research Information Service (providing housing information and research with over 800 publications and datasets) (permalink: https://perma.cc /G96T-AZN6)

4. www.fanniemae.com/—Fannie Mae (website includes information on Fannie Mae's initiatives to support affordable housing in the United States) (permalink: https://perma.cc/ZDP5-JJFA)

5. www.lisc.org—Local Initiatives Support Corporation (a national organization that helps resident-led, community-based development organizations transform distressed communities and neighborhoods into healthy ones by providing capital, technical expertise, training, and information; website includes an extensive resource library) (permalink: https://perma.cc/A6ZJ-P68E)

6. www.nlihc.org—National Low Income Housing Coalition (an organization dedicated solely to ending America's affordable housing crisis through public education, organizing, research, and policy advocacy) (permalink: https://perma.cc /F836-SM3Q)

7. www.nhlp.org—National Housing Law Project (a national housing law and advocacy center seeking to advance housing justice for people with the lowest incomes

by providing legal assistance, advocacy advice, and housing expertise to legal services and other attorneys, low-income housing advocacy groups, and others) (permalink: https://perma.cc/8GDS-UAA9)

8. www.communitychange.org—Center for Community Change (an organization dedicated to helping low-income people, especially people of color, build powerful, effective organizations through which they can change their communities and public policies for the better)

9. www.ruralhome.org—Housing Assistance Council (a nonprofit corporation helping local organizations build affordable homes in rural America since 1971) (permalink: https://perma.cc/9D3N-849Z)

10. www.taxcredithousing.com—Affordable Housing Resource Center/LIHTC (sponsored by Novogradac & Company LLP, this website offers news and information particularly concerning the LIHTC program) (permalink: https://perma.cc /Q3XA-WUFM)

11. Bipartisan Millennial Housing Commission, *Why Housing Matters*, FINAL REPORT 10-13 (2002), http://govinfo.library.unt.edu/mhc/ (permalink: https://perma.cc /BHL4-B8PZ)

12. ENCYCLOPEDIA OF HOUSING (William van Vliet ed., Sage Publications 1998) (the most comprehensive encyclopedia of housing available)

13. HOUSING FOR ALL UNDER LAW: NEW DIRECTIONS IN HOUSING, Land Use and Planning Law Report of the ABA Advisory Commission on Housing and Urban Growth (Richard P. Fishman ed., ABA 1978) (permalink: https://perma.cc /S759-FHYE)

14. Melanie Putnam, *The Internet Guide to Affordable Housing*, 7 INTERNET L. RESEARCHER 3 (2002) (available on Westlaw, subscription required)

15. www.prrac.org—Poverty & Race Research Action Council (civil rights law and policy organization promoting research-based advocacy strategies to address structural inequality and disrupt the systems that disadvantage low-income people of color)

16. nationalfairhousing.org—National Fair Housing Alliance (national civil rights organization dedicated solely to eliminating all forms of housing and lending discrimination and ensuring equal opportunities for all people)

17. www.nhc.org—National Housing Conference (a diverse continuum of affordable housing stakeholders that convene and collaborate through dialogue, advocacy, research, and education to develop equitable solutions that serve our common interest)

18. www.urban.org—Urban Institute (national research institute working on wide range of urban issues)

19. housingsolutionsummit.com—Housing Solution Summit (online workshops and resources providing practical strategies and inspirations for addressing housing affordability, evictions, and homelessness)

20. groundedsolutions.org—Grounded Solutions Network (national organization connecting local experts with the networks, knowledge, and support they need to promote housing solutions that will stay affordable for generations)

21. shelterforce.org—Shelterforce (independent, nonacademic publication covering the worlds of community development, affordable housing, and neighborhood stabilization)
22. www.housingfinance.com—Affordable Housing Finance magazine (provides the tools and best practices for financing, developing, and operating affordable rental housing)

TECHNICAL RESOURCES

1. 1000 Friends of Florida, *Creating Inclusive Communities in Florida* (2002), https://1000fof.org/wp-content/themes/Divi-child/formpop/form-pop.php?q =creating_inclusive_communities_in_florida (permalink: https://perma.cc/2TU4 -9U6F)
2. Growing Smart Legislative Guidebook: Model Statutes for Planning and the Management of Change (Stuart Meck gen. ed., American Planning Association 2002) (the guidebook and its accompanying user manual are an effort to draft the next generation of model planning and zoning legislation for the United States to help combat urban sprawl, protect farmland, promote affordable housing, and encourage redevelopment) (both the guidebook and handbook are available to download, permalink: https://perma.cc/4TUG-USWD)
3. Center for Community Change, Housing Trust Fund Progress Report 2007, http://housingtrustfundproject.org/wp-content/uploads/2011/10/2007-Housing -Trust-Fund-Progress-Report-2.pdf (permalink: https://perma.cc/9GKC-LLYC) (this report provides the only comprehensive description of the more than 275 existing housing trust funds in the United States)
4. Corporation for Supportive Housing, Between the Lines: A Question and Answer Guide on Legal Issues in Supportive Housing—National Edition (prepared by the Law Offices of Goldfarb and Lipman, 2010), https://www.csh .org/resources/between-the-lines-a-question-and-answer-guide-on-legal -issues-in-supportive-housing-national-edition/ (permalink: https://perma.cc/9B CR-E2TS)
5. Bennett L. Hecht, Developing Affordable Housing: A Practical Guide for Non Profit Organizations (3rd ed., John Wiley & Sons, Inc. 2006) (https:// www.worldcat.org/oclc/800329168)
6. Tim Iglesias, *Managing Local Opposition: A New Approach to NIMBY*, 12 J. Affordable Housing & Cmty. Devel. L. 78 (2002) (SSRN permalink: https:// papers.ssrn.com/sol3/papers.cfm?abstract_id=1018536)
7. Barry G. Jacobs, HDR Handbook of Housing and Development Law, 2020–2021 ed. (West 2020) (provides a concise description of federal housing, development, and mortgage finance programs, as well as important housing and development-related provisions of the Internal Revenue Code) (permalink: https:// perma.cc/4YQ8-Y7QB)
8. National Housing Law Project publications, especially on HUD Housing Programs (permalink: https://perma.cc/U5RS-VX7T)

9. SARA PRATT & MICHAEL ALLEN, ADDRESSING COMMUNITY OPPOSITION TO AFFORDABLE HOUSING DEVELOPMENT: A FAIR HOUSING TOOLKIT (Housing Alliance of Pennsylvania 2004) (provides practical tips and information on confronting common NIMBY concerns and launching a successful community campaign) (permalink: https://perma.cc/JT8W-KVPB)

10. Florence Wagman Roisman, *Housing, Poverty, and Racial Justice: How Civil Rights Laws Can Redress the Housing Problems of Poor People*, 36 CLEARINGHOUSE REV. (May-June 2002) (available through HeinOnline, requires a paid subscription; permalink: https://heinonline.org/HOL/P?h=hein.journals/clear36&i=21)

11. ROBERT G. SCHWEMM, HOUSING DISCRIMINATION: LAW AND LITIGATION (Thomson West 2021) (substantial coverage of fair housing issues, regularly updated) (permalink: https://perma.cc/4A4G-NS7A)

12. www.furmancenter.org—NYU Furman Center (NYU-based center that conducts academic and empirical research on legal and public policy issues involving land use, real estate, housing, and urban affairs in the United States)

13. www.ternercenter.berkeley.edu/research-and-policy—Terner Center for Housing Innovation (University of California at Berkeley–based center that identifies and reframes pressing issues in housing policy, research, and practice and produces empirical research–based policy recommendations)

14. www.urbandisplacement.org—Urban Displacement Project (a research and action initiative of UC Berkeley that conducts community-centered, data-driven, applied research toward more equitable and inclusive futures for cities)

COMPILATIONS AND EVALUATIONS OF AFFORDABLE HOUSING STRATEGIES

1. AM. PLANNING ASS'N, REGIONAL APPROACHES TO AFFORDABLE HOUSING (Stuart Meck, Rebecca Retzlaff & James Schwab eds., APA Planning Advisory Service Report/Number 513/514, 2003) (evaluates regional approaches to affordable housing including 23 specific programs across the nation, proposes a set of best and second-best practices, and provides extensive appendices) (permalink: https://perma.cc/YYZ6-3Y7L)

2. Lauren Breen, Louise Howells, Susan R. Jones & Deborah S. Kenn, *An Annotated Bibliography of Affordable Housing and Community Economic Development Law*, 13 J. AFFORDABLE HOUSING AND CMTY. ECON. DEVEL. L. 334 (Spring 2004) (available through HeinOnline, requires a paid subscription; permalink: https://heinonline.org/HOL/P?h=hein.journals/jrlaff7&i=354)

3. THE AFFORDABLE CITY: TOWARD A THIRD SECTOR HOUSING POLICY (John Emmeus Davis ed., Temple University Press 1994) (describing and promoting community-based nonmarket affordable housing strategies and programs)

4. Maria Foscarinis, Brad Paul, Bruce Porter & Andrew Scherer, *The Human Right to Housing: Making the Case in U.S. Advocacy*, CLEARINGHOUSE REV. (July-Aug. 2004) (https://papers.ssrn.com/sol3/papers.cfm?abstract_id=2483410)

5. A RIGHT TO HOUSING: FOUNDATION FOR A NEW SOCIAL AGENDA (Chester Hartman, Rachel Bratt & Michael Stone eds., Temple University Press 2006) (housing

policy reader) (available through JSTOR, requires a paid subscription; permalink: https://www.jstor.org/stable/j.ctt1bw1kqb)

6. Bruce Katz et al., *Rethinking Local Affordable Housing Strategies: Lessons from 70 Years of Policy and Practice*, BROOKINGS INST. CTR. ON URBAN & METRO. POL'Y & URBAN INST. (2003) (discussion paper) (https://www.brookings.edu /research/rethinking-local-affordable-housing-strategies-lessons-from-70-years -of-policy-and-practice/)

7. Bonnie L. Koneski-White, *Increasing Affordable Housing and Regional Housing Opportunity in New England: A Selected Bibliography*, 22 W. NEW ENG. L. REV. 431 (2001) (includes a section on affordable housing generally) (https://digital commons.law.wne.edu/lawreview/vol22/iss2/6)

8. ALAN MALLACH, A DECENT HOME: PLANNING, BUILDING, AND PRESERVING AFFORDABLE HOUSING (University of Chicago 2009) (a thorough analysis of planning issues regarding affordable housing)

9. MAYORS NATIONAL HOUSING FORUM, NATIONAL HOUSING AGENDA: A SPRING-BOARD FOR FAMILIES, FOR COMMUNITIES, FOR OUR NATION (2002) (offering 60 housing policy recommendations addressing a wide array of housing needs)

10. Peter W. Salsich, Jr., *Saving Our Cities: What Role Should the Federal Government Play?*, 36 URB. LAW. 475 (2004) (available through JSTOR, requires a paid subscription; permalink: https://www.jstor.org/stable/27895499?seq=1 &socuuid=c9c351c6-0a29-46cd-b41e-fc9882c2e205&socplat=email#metad ata_info_tab_contents)

11. Peter W. Salsich, Jr., *Will the "Free Market" Solve the Affordable Housing Crisis?*, CLEARINGHOUSE REV. (Jan.-Feb. 2002) (available through HeinOnline, requires a paid subscription; permalink: https://heinonline.org/HOL/P?h=hein.journals /clear35&i=573)

12. THE NATIONAL LEAGUE OF CITIES, AFFORDABLE HOUSING FINANCE RESOURCES: A PRIMER (resource guide to assist city and town officials in the identification of potential government and private funding resources for affordable housing programs) (permalink: https://perma.cc/QKM2-9DRX); STRENGTHENING PARTNER-SHIPS FOR HOUSING OPPORTUNITIES: PRACTICAL APPROACHES TO AFFORDABLE HOUSING CHALLENGES (guidebook for identifying, prioritizing, and implementing individualized action plans) (permalink: https://perma.cc/Q9XK-DKSG)

Index